CRIMINAL EVIDENCE

ASPEN COLLEGE SERIES

CRIMINAL EVIDENCE

From Crime Scene to Courtroom

■ Derek Regensburger

Wolters Kluwer
Law & Business

To contact Customer Service, e-mail customer.service@wolterskluwer.com, call 1-800-234-1660, fax 1-800-901-9075, or mail correspondence to:

> Wolters Kluwer Law & Business
> Attn: Order Department
> PO Box 990
> Frederick, MD 21705

Printed in the United States of America.

1 2 3 4 5 6 7 8 9 0

ISBN 978-0-7355-9474-6

Library of Congress Cataloging-in-Publication Data

Regensburger, Derek, 1970-
    Criminal evidence : from crime scene to courtroom / Derek Regensburger.
        p. cm. — (Aspen college series)
    Includes index.
    ISBN-13: 978-0-7355-9474-6
    ISBN-10: 0-7355-9474-0
    1. Evidence, Criminal—United States. I. Title.
    KF9660.R44 2011
    345.73′06—dc23
                        2011026641

SFI label applies to the text stock

About Wolters Kluwer Law & Business

Wolters Kluwer Law & Business is a leading global provider of intelligent information and digital solutions for legal and business professionals in key specialty areas and respected educational resources for professors and law students. Wolters Kluwer Law & Business connects legal and business professionals as well as those in the education market with timely, specialized authoritative content and information-enabled solutions to support success through productivity, accuracy, and mobility.

Serving customers worldwide, Wolters Kluwer Law & Business products include those under the Aspen Publishers, CCH, Kluwer Law International, Loislaw, Best Case, ftwilliam.com, and MediRegs family of products.

CCH products have been a trusted resource since 1913 and are highly regarded resources for legal, securities, antitrust and trade regulation, government contracting, banking, pension, payroll, employment and labor, and health-care reimbursement and compliance professionals.

Aspen Publishers products provide essential information to attorneys, business professionals, and law students. Written by preeminent authorities, the product line offers analytical and practical information in a range of specialty practice areas from securities law and intellectual property to mergers and acquisitions and pension/benefits. Aspen's trusted legal education resources provide professors and students with high-quality, up-to-date and effective resources for successful instruction and study in all areas of the law.

Kluwer Law International products provide the global business community with reliable international legal information in English. Legal practitioners, corporate counsel, and business executives around the world rely on Kluwer Law journals, looseleafs, books, and electronic products for comprehensive information in many areas of international legal practice.

Loislaw is a comprehensive online legal research product providing legal content to law firm practitioners of various specializations. Loislaw provides attorneys with the ability to quickly and efficiently find the necessary legal information they need, when and where they need it, by facilitating access to primary law as well as state-specific law, records, forms, and treatises.

Best Case Solutions is the leading bankruptcy software product to the bankruptcy industry. It provides software and workflow tools to flawlessly streamline petition preparation and the electronic filing process, while timely incorporating ever-changing court requirements.

ftwilliam.com offers employee benefits professionals the highest quality plan documents (retirement, welfare, and non-qualified) and government forms (5500/PBGC, 1099, and IRS) software at highly competitive prices.

MediRegs products provide integrated health-care compliance content and software solutions for professionals in health care, higher education, and life sciences, including professionals in accounting, law, and consulting.

Wolters Kluwer Law & Business, a division of Wolters Kluwer, is headquartered in New York. Wolters Kluwer is a market-leading global information services company focused on professionals.

Summary of Contents

Contents

PART I ■ THE COLLECTION AND PRESERVATION OF EVIDENCE

PART II ▪ PRETRIAL MATTERS

CHAPTER 5
THE CRIMINAL JUSTICE PROCESS   110

Chapter Topics   110
Objectives   111
Introduction   111

CHAPTER 6
PRETRIAL DISCOVERY   138

CHAPTER 7
THE EXCLUSIONARY RULE AND MOTIONS TO SUPPRESS EVIDENCE   164

PART III ■ ADMISSIBILITY OF EVIDENCE AT TRIAL

CHAPTER 8
BASIC EVIDENTIARY TERMS: RELEVANCE, BURDEN OF PROOF, AND CIRCUMSTANTIAL EVIDENCE   208

Chapter Topics   208
Objectives   209
Introduction   209

CHAPTER 9
WITNESSES PART I: EXPERT AND LAY WITNESSES   242

CHAPTER 10
WITNESSES PART II: COMPETENCY AND PRIVILEGE   278

CHAPTER 11
WITNESSES PART III: IMPEACHMENT AND CROSS-EXAMINATION   314

CHAPTER 12
CHARACTER EVIDENCE   336

CHAPTER 14
AUTHENTICATION OF EVIDENCE AND THE BEST EVIDENCE RULE 418

Preface

The idea for this book was borne out of my frustration with both my own legal education and the textbooks that were currently on the market when I began teaching evidence. Evidence is something that can only be learned by doing and seeing by example. In law school, evidence was taught in just the opposite fashion—through a series of cases and memorizing rules. As I began to practice criminal law, I soon realized that my legal education had prepared me little for the practical reality of the courtroom. Knowing the hearsay rule and understanding what types of situations it applied to were two totally different types of knowledge. Law school gave me the former; trial by fire in the district attorney's office gave me the latter. After years of practicing law and seeing different situations arise, I finally began to have a good handle on the law of evidence.

Years later when I began teaching criminal justice, I sensed that same frustration carrying over in my students. College textbooks on evidence seemed either too advanced for a beginning college student or stripped bare of any meaningful explanation of the law. Another criticism I had of other evidence textbooks is that many of them included several chapters on criminal procedure that I thought were better served for a specific course in that subject. The texts also focused on either the legal aspects of evidence law or the practical application for law enforcement. Most failed to combine the two.

The admissibility of evidence is a by-product of the two concepts, however. Evidence that is improperly handled, unlawfully seized, or not timely disclosed is often useless since it will likely be declared inadmissible by the court. Of course, students also need to understand the rules of evidence and what makes certain types of evidence admissible or inadmissible as well. Without a sufficient knowledge of the rules, a law enforcement officer would not know what kinds of evidence to collect or what types of questions to ask. Thus, students need to understand both the proper process for obtaining and handling evidence and the rules that govern its admissibility in court.

I have tried to correct these deficiencies in writing this textbook. First and foremost, I have tried to explain the rules and concepts relating to evidence law in a way that is understandable for most students who do not have a background in law. Yet, I have tried not to sacrifice content where possible. The book uses the Federal Rules of Evidence as the starting point of analysis for many evidentiary concepts. Students should keep in mind that each state also has its own set of evidence rules that may differ from the federal rules. I have tried to point out significant differences where possible, but instructors should still draw students' attention to their particular state's evidence code to be complete.

To help explain the concepts and rules, I have included practical examples of how evidentiary concepts discussed in the text are applied in the real world. These examples are found at the end of the topics discussed in each chapter. In addition, I have included Evidence in Action articles throughout the text that are exposés on famous cases or current events, illustrating some of the concepts discussed. I hope these will inform and entertain students as well as spark discussion in class.

The chapters are designed to include a listing of chapter topics and objectives to give students and instructors a roadmap of what is being taught in each chapter. At the end of the chapter, I have included review questions that review the basic terminology and concepts covered in each chapter. In addition, I have included application problems containing factual scenarios to test students' ability to apply the concepts that they have learned in the chapter.

I have tried to organize this textbook in as logical a manner as possible. To do so, I have arranged the topics into three sections: investigatory matters such as the collection of physical evidence and obtainment of confessions; pretrial matters such as discovery and the exclusionary rule; and the presentation of evidence at trial. I have found that this organizational structure has helped my classes stay engaged in the material from the outset since they are more familiar with evidence collection methods and less familiar with legal concepts and terms. Instructors are, of course, free to vary the presentation of material in this book as they see fit.

Chapter 1 introduces the topic of evidence by focusing on the definition of evidence, the sources of evidence law, and the development of the Federal Rules of Evidence. It also contains an overview of the state and federal court systems and introduces students to the players in the criminal justice system. Chapter 2 is devoted to the process of evidence identification and collection at the crime scene as well as maintenance of the chain of custody. Chapter 3 involves eyewitness identification of suspects, including a discussion of how false identifications may occur. The chapter concludes with a discussion of new protocols for how to improve identification procedures to reduce such errors. Chapter 4 deals with the process of obtaining statements from the defendant and what must be done in order to introduce them at trial. The chapter also discusses the issue of false confessions.

Chapter 5 discusses the various stages of the criminal justice process and how evidence is used during them. It also discusses how evidence is used at trial. Chapter 6 focuses on the pretrial discovery process.

Chapter 7 discusses the exclusionary rule as it applies to the Fourth, Fifth and Sixth Amendments. Although I believe topics in criminal procedure are best reserved for a separate course, I think some discussion of the topic is necessary, particularly as to how it may impact the admissibility of evidence in a case.

The last seven chapters focus on how evidence is handled at trial. Chapter 8 introduces many of the common terms that concern evidence and its admissibility such as relevancy and circumstantial evidence. Chapters 9, 10, and 11 deal with the law relating to witnesses. Chapter 9 focuses on the differences between lay and expert witnesses. Chapter 10 discusses the concepts of competency and privilege. Chapter 11 focuses on the impeachment of witnesses. Chapter 12 discusses character evidence and explains how the character of the defendant and/or the victim can be supported or attacked. Chapter 13 discusses the hearsay rule and reviews the many levels and exceptions to it. It also features an in-depth discussion of testimonial hearsay and how the Supreme Court has changed the landscape on this issue in recent years. Finally, Chapter 14 details the requirements for authentication of evidence as well as for introducing documentary and demonstrative evidence.

Acknowledgments

Many thank yous are in order for this book to have become a reality. I thank Everest College and my department chair, Geary Gorup, for encouraging me to pursue this project. I would also like to thank my research assistants, Amber Swan and Dana Northway, without whose help this project would have been infinitely harder. I would also like to thank the University of Denver for allowing me to use its mock courtroom to film the DVD which accompanies this text as well as Anna Bond, Armando C'DeBaca, Ron Miller, Vohn Regensburger, Mikala Astor, and Bob Poston for donating their time on the project.

I extend many thanks to David Herzig and Betsy Kenny at Aspen/ Wolters Kluwer Publishing for having faith in a first-time author. I would also like to thank the many editors of this text for their insightful and encouraging comments. In addition, I would like to thank the reviewers of the text:

Lisa Clayton, College of Southern Nevada
Nancy K. Dempsey, Cape Cod Community College
Jona Goldschmidt, Loyola University—Chicago
David Kotajarvi, Lakeshore Technical College
Christopher G. Kopacki, Virginia Commonwealth University
Jesse Weins, Dakota Wesleyan University
James Vardalis, Tarleton State University

Finally, I thank my father, Jack, for his tireless proofreading.

About the Author

Derek Regensburger is an Instructor III in the Legal Studies Department of the Thornton, Colorado campus of Everest College, where he has been teaching since 2005. Prior to that, he worked as a civil litigator in Denver and Boulder and as a deputy district attorney in Logan County, Colorado. He has been a member of the Colorado Bar since 1996. Since 2007, Derek has been a member of the Colorado Cold Case Task Force subcommittees on Best Practices and Curriculum Development. He was also a selected speaker at the 2010 annual conference of the Colorado Organization for Victim Assistance on the topic of testimonial hearsay. Derek published articles on computer searches and DNA databases in 2007 and 2008. He received his B.A. in chemistry and government from Wesleyan University in 1992 and his J.D. from George Washington University in 1996. He is an avid photographer and outdoorsman. He lives with his wife and two sons in Thornton, Colorado.

CRIMINAL EVIDENCE

CHAPTER 1

Introduction to Evidence and the Rules of Evidence

"Ours is an accusatorial and not an inquisitorial system—a system in which the state must establish guilt by evidence independently and freely secured and may not by coercion prove its charge against an accused out of his own mouth." —Felix Frankfurter

Chapter Topics

Objectives

After reading this chapter, students will be able to:

- Define the term *evidence* and distinguish between its various meanings

- Identify the various courts and distinguish between the federal and state court systems

- Understand the importance of the Federal Rules of Evidence and how they are organized

- Identify the four sources of evidence law

- Identify the various actors in the criminal justice process

I. DEFINITION OF EVIDENCE

When you hear the term *evidence*, the first things that probably come to mind are the items of physical evidence such as weapons, DNA, or drugs that are presented at trial. While physical evidence is certainly one type of evidence, evidence encompasses much more than that. Other tangible objects, such as photographs, documents, and demonstrative exhibits, may be admitted as evidence. The bulk of evidence, however, is admitted through the testimony of witnesses. Oral testimony not only gives context to the physical evidence that is admitted, but it also provides the story of the case from eyewitness accounts of the crime and summaries of the investigation performed by law enforcement.

Evidence
anything that can be used to prove or disprove a fact in a case. It can also refer to the collective mass of items admitted during the trial

In the context of a criminal case, the term **evidence** has many meanings. In a generic sense, evidence can be defined as anything that helps prove or disprove the existence of an alleged fact that is then used to prove a person's guilt or innocence. [1] It can also refer to the individual items of evidence presented at trial or the collective group of testimony and exhibits admitted to prove the defendant's guilt or innocence. While the most widely recognized use of evidence is to prove the guilt or innocence of the defendant at trial, the term is broader than that. Evidence can be used by law enforcement to determine if a crime has been committed and whether there is sufficient evidence to arrest a suspect. It can be used by the court to determine whether probable cause exists for the charges and at what amount to set bail. In short, evidence has many more uses than just helping prove a defendant innocent or guilty at trial.

Evidence comes in many forms. Evidence can be the physical objects found at a crime scene, such as weapons or drugs, or it can be presented through the testimony of witnesses. As you will see in later chapters, there are many types of witnesses, including eyewitnesses, character witnesses, and expert witnesses.

Admissible evidence

anything that can be lawfully admitted in court to prove the guilt or innocence of the defendant

If evidence is going to be used at trial, the evidence must be admissible. **Admissible evidence** is anything that can lawfully be admitted before the court and that the jury or judge can consider as proof of the defendant's guilt or innocence.[2] In order to be admissible, evidence must be relevant, reliable, and competent. These terms are discussed in more detail in Chapter 8. Essentially, evidence must relate to some topic of importance in the case and its source must be trustworthy enough to warrant the jury relying on it to decide some issue in the case.

Throughout this text, you will learn about the various uses of evidence during the stages of the criminal justice process and how it should be collected and preserved for later use. The goal of law enforcement is to collect admissible evidence. Obviously, it does little good to understand the procedures for admitting evidence at trial if you have no evidence to admit. Further, if proper procedures are not undertaken to document, identify, and preserve the evidence that is collected, its admissibility may be impaired. Thus, it is important to understand all of the requirements for both the collection and introduction of evidence.

II. THE COURT SYSTEM

A. Federal Courts

Before exploring the sources of evidence law, it is helpful to have a basic understanding of the layout of the court system. There are two separate court systems in the United States: the federal court system and state courts. **Federal courts** can only hear matters for which they have jurisdiction. Federal law provides that the federal courts can hear cases that involve federal statutes and other federal laws or that involve civil disputes about issues of state law between citizens of different states. With regard to criminal cases, federal courts can hear only cases that involve a violation of federal criminal laws.[3]

Federal courts

courts that can hear disputes involving federal laws or civil disputes between citizens of different states

Federal criminal laws are established by Congress and apply to all federal courts. For example, a person charged with counterfeiting must be tried in federal court since counterfeiting is a federal crime, and the elements of the crime would be the same regardless of which district he was charged in.

Federal courts have three levels: the district courts (trial courts), the circuit courts of appeal (intermediate appellate courts), and the United States Supreme Court. There are 94 **United States district courts** across the country. Each state has at least one district court, and many larger states have multiple district courts.[4] See Figure 1.1 for a diagram of the federal court system. The district courts are where pretrial matters are decided and cases are tried. For example, if a defendant wanted to file a motion to suppress evidence, he would file that motion in the federal district court in the district where he was charged.

United States district courts

the trial courts for the federal court system

Figure 1.1

Diagram of the Federal Court System

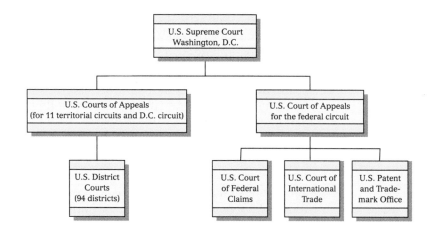

If a party is unhappy with the outcome of the case, he can file an appeal. In the federal system, the appellate court is called the **circuit court of appeals**. A circuit covers a given region and hears appeals from the various district courts within the circuit. There are 13 circuits across the United States. See Figure 1.2 for a breakdown of the circuits.

A circuit court hears the appeal and issues a ruling either granting or denying the appeal. On appeal, the court reviews the record of the proceedings in the trial court. It does not hear new evidence. Once the circuit court of appeals issues its decision, either side can petition the **United States Supreme Court** to hear the case. Nine justices, appointed by the president and confirmed by the Senate, sit on the Court. The Supreme Court has jurisdiction to hear appeals from all

Circuit court of appeals

a federal appellate court that hears appeals from the various district courts in its circuit or region

United States Supreme Court

the court of last resort in the federal system. It hears appeals from the circuit courts or from state high courts on constitutional issues.

Figure 1.2

A map of the United States showing the designation of the 13 circuits.

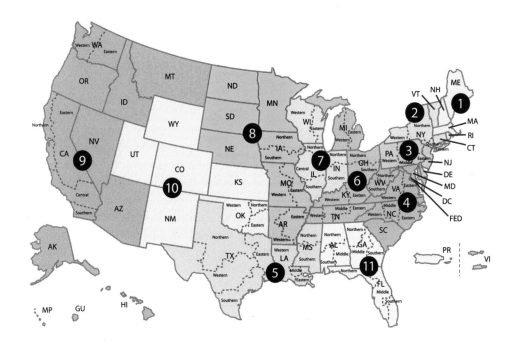

federal circuit courts. It can also review state cases involving issues of federal constitutional law. It cannot review state cases that were decided purely on state law grounds, however. Unlike circuit courts, the Supreme Court does not have to hear an appeal in most cases. It has discretion to decide which cases to hear. This means that the vast majority of decisions issued by the circuit courts are final and are not reviewed further.

Petition for certiorari
a Latin term meaning "to be more fully informed." It is a petition filed with the Supreme Court to determine whether the Court will accept review of the case

In order for an appeal to be accepted by the Supreme Court, a party has to file a **petition for certiorari**. *Certiorari* is a Latin term meaning "to be more fully informed."[5] The petition must set forth the legal issues being appealed plus the grounds for review of the case. The Supreme Court will generally grant certiorari only when:

(1) A federal court of appeals has rendered a judgment that conflicts with the decision of another federal court of appeals on the same question

(2) A federal court of appeals has decided a federal question in a manner that conflicts with a decision of the highest state court

(3) The highest court in a state has decided a federal question in a manner that conflicts with the decision of the highest court in another state or with a decision of a federal court of appeals

(4) A state court or a federal court of appeals has decided a federal question in a way that conflicts with a prior decision of the Supreme Court[6]

All the petitions for certiorari are screened and voted upon by the Court. It takes a "yes" vote by at least four of the nine justices on the Court for a petition to be granted. If the petition is granted, the Court will issue a writ of certiorari directing the lower court to deliver the record on appeal for review. The Supreme Court grants only about 1% of the petitions filed each year. For example, for the term ending in June 2009, 8,241 petitions were filed with the Court, but only 90 were granted.[7]

Practical Example

Jed is accused of defrauding investors using an Internet scheme that crossed state lines. He is charged in federal court. Jed is tried and convicted in the Central District of California. He appeals the decision to the Ninth Circuit Court of Appeals on the grounds that the trial judge improperly admitted evidence of Jed's three prior investment schemes that failed. The Ninth Circuit agrees with Jed. It reverses the conviction and remands the case back to the trial court for a new trial. The government appeals the decision to the Supreme Court. The Supreme Court refuses to grant certiorari in the case. The Ninth Circuit decision stands and Jed gets a new trial.

B. State Courts

Each state also has its own court system that is very similar to the federal court structure. **State courts** usually have a trial court and at least one appellate court. Each state has its own set of criminal laws that are developed by the state's legislature. States also have created rules of evidence and procedure for how business is to be conducted in court. While similar to the federal rules, each state's evidence rules are subtly different from one another, so students are encouraged to consult local statutes and rules where necessary.

Like the federal system, all cases originate in some sort of trial court. Each state has a different name for these courts. Some are called superior courts, while others are called district or circuit courts. Often each town or city also has a separate municipal court that handles city ordinance violations such as traffic infractions and noise complaints. In most states, cases are appealed to an intermediate appellate court, often known as the court of appeals. Eight states do not have this court, and appeals are instead made directly to the state's high court.[8] This court is often known as the state supreme court or the state court of appeals. See Figure 1.3 for a breakdown of state court systems. Just like the United States Supreme Court, these state high courts have discretion to hear appeals in most cases. The decision of the state high court is final in most instances unless the United States Supreme Court decides to review the case.

Figure 1.3

A Diagram of a Typical State Court System

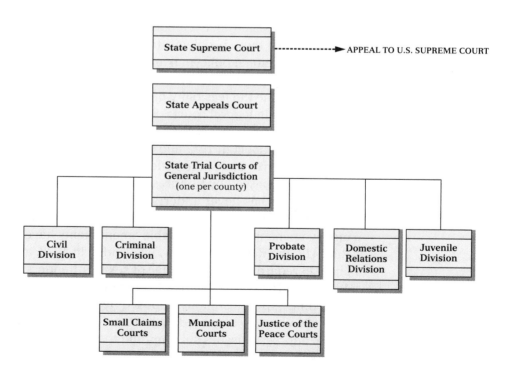

III. SOURCES OF EVIDENCE LAW

A. Federal Rules of Evidence

Most evidence law today is governed by evidence rules or codes. A code is a set of laws organized by topic. Codes are rules or statutes that are organized by topic. These codes compile evidentiary rules that were previously scattered throughout case law and statutes. Most of the state rules of evidence are based on the Federal Rules of Evidence. The Federal Rules only apply in federal proceedings, however, and do not apply to the states. Most of the references to the rules in this text will be to the Federal Rules.

Federal Rules of Evidence
a set of standardized rules that guide evidence practice in all federal courts. They were approved for use in 1975

Prior to the adoption of the **Federal Rules of Evidence**, evidentiary rulings made by federal judges were often inconsistent and varied from jurisdiction to jurisdiction. For example, until 1933, federal courts used the evidence laws of the state where the case was being heard instead of applying federal law. Later, the Federal Rules of Criminal Procedure provided that the admissibility of evidence should be guided by "principles of the common law as they may be interpreted by the courts of the United States in the light of reason and experience."[9] This meant that evidence law developed through the **common law**—a series of judicial rulings or precedents which build upon one another—rather than statutes or fixed rules. This vague standard left it to individual judges to determine the proper application of evidence law to the facts of a given case. As a result, evidence law had become a hodgepodge of court rulings, with little consistency existing between districts or circuits.

Common law
a series of judicial rulings or precedents that build upon one another to help the judge decide a ruling in the current case

To correct these problems, the Judicial Conference of the United States, the national policymaking body of the federal courts, established the Advisory Committee on the Rules of Evidence in 1961, whose mission was to examine the feasibility of creating a body of rules standardizing evidence law in federal courts. By 1969, the first preliminary draft of the rules was prepared. The final draft of the rules was approved by the Supreme Court in 1972 and submitted to Congress. After extensive hearings and revisions, the Federal Rules of Evidence were eventually adopted and passed by Congress in 1975.[10]

Congress has never undertaken a full-scale revision of the rules since their original passage. For the past 35 years, the rules have remained mostly unchanged. Some notable amendments have occurred, however. Rule 412, the Rape Shield Law, was added in 1978, and Rules 413, 414, and 415 regarding the character of sexual offenders were added in 1994. Rule 702 was substantially amended in 2000 to reflect the changes regarding expert testimony imposed by the Supreme Court in the 1990s. Rule 404 was also amended in 2000 and 2006. Rule 502 was added in 2008, which addressed issues surrounding the scope of the attorney/client privilege.

An effort to reword and restyle the Rules was begun in 2006 by the Judicial Conference of the United States Committee on Rules of Practice and Procedure. It released a final draft of its revisions in 2009. The comment phase ended in February 2010. The proposed amendments will take effect in December 2011 unless Congress acts to further amend the proposed revisions.[11] The intent of the Committee in making the changes was not to make any substantive revisions to the rules but simply to make them easier to read and understand.[12] Among the many proposed revisions, formatting changes were proposed to make subsections easier to read, and inconsistent or ambiguous word usage was eliminated where possible. See Table 1.1 on page 10 for a comparison of Current Rule 404 with Proposed Rule 404 for an example of the proposed revisions.

The Rules of Evidence are broken down into 11 articles or sections. This textbook will explore many of these articles in the coming chapters. Table 1.2 on page 11 lists the various articles contained in the rules.

Each state also has its own set of evidence rules or evidence code. While many states have modeled their rules after the federal rules, there are often numerous differences between the federal rules and a given state's rules. As a result, students should become familiar with the rules in their state as well. A comprehensive listing of links to most states' rules of evidence can be found at *Megalaw.com.*[14]

Practical Example

The prosecutor, an Assistant United States Attorney, is trying a first-degree murder and kidnapping case in Delaware federal court. He wants to know if the hearsay statement made by the victim to her neighbor about her husband's violent past will be admissible. He would examine Rules 801-807 of the Rules of Evidence to determine whether the statement is admissible. The outcome would be the same regardless of what federal district the case was brought in.

B. Common Law

The Rules of Evidence is not the only source of law that controls the admissibility of evidence. The common law still plays a large role in defining the scope and extent of the rules. To be effective, the Rules have to remain somewhat general and cannot cover every conceivable factual situation that may arise. As a result, judicial interpretation becomes necessary as the rules are applied to specific factual situations. For example, Rule 404(a) provides that the prior actions and character of a defendant are generally inadmissible to prove his guilt in the current case. Rule 404(b), however, creates an exception that permits those prior acts to be used in certain limited circumstances, such as to prove

TABLE 1.1 COMPARISON OF CURRENT RULE WITH PROPOSED REVISIONS

Current Version of Rule 404	Proposed Version of Rule 404
Rule 404. Character Evidence Not Admissible to Prove Conduct; Exceptions; Other Crimes	**Rule 404. Character Evidence; Crimes or Other Acts**
(a) **Character evidence generally.** Evidence of a person's character or a trait of character is not admissible for the purpose of proving action in conformity therewith on a particular occasion, except:	(a) **Character Evidence.** (1) **Prohibited Uses.** Evidence of a person's character or character trait is not admissible to prove that on a particular occasion the person acted in accordance with the character or trait.
(1) **Character of accused.** In a criminal case, evidence of a pertinent trait of character offered by an accused, or by the prosecution to rebut the same, or if evidence of a trait of character of the alleged victim of the crime is offered by an accused and admitted under Rule 404(a)(2), evidence of the same trait of character of the accused offered by the prosecution;	(2) **Exceptions in a Criminal Case.** The following exceptions apply in a criminal case: (A) a defendant may offer evidence of the defendant's pertinent trait, and if the evidence is admitted, the prosecutor may offer evidence to rebut it;

(2) **Character of alleged victim.** In a criminal case, and subject to the limitations imposed by Rule 412, evidence of a pertinent trait of character of the alleged victim of the crime offered by an accused, or by the prosecution to rebut the same, or evidence of a character trait of peacefulness of the alleged victim offered by the prosecution in a homicide case to rebut evidence that the alleged victim was the first aggressor;	(B) subject to the limitations in Rule 412, a defendant may offer evidence of an alleged crime victim's pertinent trait, and if the evidence is admitted, the prosecutor may:
	
	  (i) offer evidence to rebut it; and
	  (ii) offer evidence of the defendant's same trait; and
	
	(C) in a homicide case, the prosecutor may offer evidence of the alleged victim's trait of peacefulness to rebut evidence that the victim was the first aggressor.

(3) **Character of witness.** Evidence of the character of a witness, as provided in Rules 607, 608, and 609.	(3) **Exceptions for a Witness.** Evidence of a witness's character may be admitted under Rules 607, 608, and 609.[13]

Precedent
a prior case that forms the basis for determining the same or similar issue in future cases

motive or identity. A court may have to decide whether the prior acts of the defendant are admissible to prove one of those purposes under that exception. That decision then becomes precedent for other courts to follow in the future when interpreting Rule 404. A **precedent** is a previous case that forms the basis for determining the same or similar issues in future cases.[15] This judicial preference for following past

TABLE 1.2 ARTICLES OF THE RULES OF EVIDENCE

Article 1—General Provisions

Article 2—Judicial Notice

Article 3—Presumptions in a Civil Actions Proceedings

Article 4—Relevancy and Its Limits

Article 5—Privileges

Article 6—Witnesses

Article 7—Opinions and Expert Testimony

Article 8—Hearsay

Article 9—Authentication and Identification

Article 10—Contents of Writings, Recordings, and Photographs

Article 11—Miscellaneous Rules

Stare decisis
a Latin term meaning "to stand by things decided"; a judicial doctrine that obligates future courts to follow previous court rulings on similar issues

decisions is known as **stare decisis**, a Latin term meaning to stand by things decided.[16] As more and more cases are decided by interpreting various rules, a body of common law develops that future courts can rely on to guide them in determining the outcomes in their particular case.

Some states continue to rely almost exclusively on the common law to guide evidence practice in their courts. These states, such as New York, Connecticut, and Massachusetts, have resisted codifying evidence rules. Judicial decision making, as opposed to lawmaking, controls the law of evidence in these states. Fewer and fewer states are following this practice, however. Illinois, for example, recently adopted its own rules of evidence to codify the common law rules, which went into effect on January 1, 2011.[17]

Practical Example

Moe is charged with serving beer to a minor. Moe claims the act was a mistake. He claims he carded the 16-year old, but he provided a fake ID. The prosecutor wants to introduce evidence that Moe had been cited for doing the same thing on three prior occasions and did not card any of those individuals. The prosecutor alleges that the prior acts should be admissible under Rule 404(b) since they tend to show lack of mistake on Moe's part. The judge looks up a ruling on a similar case from three years ago in the same state. There, the judge admitted the prior acts and found that they did show lack of mistake on the defendant's part. Moe's judge then admits the prior acts and cites the previous case as precedent for his decision.

C. Constitutional Protections

The Constitution also contains several provisions that may impact the admissibility of evidence. The Constitution is the supreme law of the land, and the admission of evidence cannot violate one of its provisions. For example, under the Sixth Amendment to the Constitution, a defendant has a right to confront the witnesses against him and subpoena witnesses to testify on his behalf. This means that the prosecution cannot simply submit written police and laboratory reports as evidence without producing the witnesses who made the statements or performed the scientific analysis. A defendant also has a right to present evidence in his own defense. This means he can call witnesses to testify in his defense or even testify himself. A defendant cannot be prevented from testifying if he voluntarily chooses to do so.

A defendant also has a right to be protected from unreasonable searches and seizures under the Fourth Amendment. As you will learn later in this book, the remedy for a violation of this right is exclusion of the evidence from the prosecution's main case. He also has a right to remain silent and be free from compelled statements and confessions under the Fifth Amendment. Similarly, under the Sixth Amendment, a defendant has a right to an attorney and cannot be questioned about the case without the presence of his attorney once he has been charged with a crime. Evidence can also be excluded from trial if the police violate one of these constitutionally guaranteed rights. This text will explore the limits of the exclusionary rule and the many exceptions to it.

Practical Example

Jose is charged with possession of drugs with intent to distribute and drug smuggling. Ten pounds of cocaine are discovered in his trunk after his car is searched during a routine traffic stop. Jose moves to suppress the evidence found as a result of an illegal search. Jose claims the officer had no cause to search his trunk. The judge agrees and suppresses the evidence due to the illegal search. The prosecution cannot use the evidence at trial to prove Jose's guilt.

D. Statutory Law

The final source of evidence law is state or federal statutes. In addition to codifying the rules of evidence, many states and the federal government have passed separate statutes that impact the law of evidence. Such laws can govern the competency of witnesses, the admission of character evidence, or the preservation of evidence.

In particular, the law of privileges is one area where statutes often play a large role. Many states have chosen to pass separate laws governing privileges, rather than incorporating these requirements into their rules of evidence. Privileges are legal authorizations to withhold testimony based on a desire to preserve the confidential nature of the relationship. They will be discussed in further detail in Chapter 10.

IV. THE ACTORS IN THE CRIMINAL JUSTICE PROCESS

Before discussing how evidence is collected and used during each stage of the criminal justice process, it is helpful to understand who the players in the process are and what roles they play.

A. Investigative Personnel

Law enforcement agencies employ a number of investigative personnel to help solve major crimes. After patrol officers respond to the initial call for service, detectives are assigned to the case to conduct follow-up investigation. This includes interviewing witnesses, developing leads, and identifying evidence that may have been left at the scene. In larger agencies, detectives are often assigned to specific units, such as sex crimes or homicide. The FBI and other federal law enforcement agencies also use investigators, called **special agents**, for this purpose. These federal officers investigate violations of federal law, including mail fraud, cybercrime, and terrorist acts committed on United States soil.

Special agents
federal law enforcement officers who investigate violations of federal crimes

Specialized **crime scene investigators** (CSIs) are also used in many places to document the scene and collect physical evidence. CSIs are usually responsible for measuring and photographing the scene, searching the scene, and bagging and tagging any evidence that is found. Unlike on the television show *CSI*, however, CSIs rarely interview witnesses or suspects or perform other types of investigation. Their job is strictly to process the crime scene.

Crime scene investigators
law enforcement personnel who process the crime scene for evidence, including photographing and searching the scene, identifying evidence, and collecting evidence

B. Laboratory Personnel

Most larger law enforcement agencies also have their own crime laboratory. These labs provide a number of services, including fingerprint identification, firearms and toolmark identification, trace analysis, chemistry, and forensic biology. Some larger labs also conduct DNA analysis. States also operate crime labs to assist smaller agencies that do not have labs or cannot provide as broad a range of services as the labs in larger cities. The FBI operates the largest crime laboratory in the country in Quantico, Virginia.[18] It processes evidence not only for cases investigated by the FBI but also for cases submitted by local agencies.

The lab analysts are often called to testify as experts in criminal cases. Typically, the analyst who performed the examination and testing of the evidence will be called on to testify in court. For example, in a drug possession trial, the chemist who tested the suspected drugs and confirmed the presence of cocaine will be asked to testify.

C. Coroners and Medical Examiners

In cases involving suspicious or unattended deaths, coroners or medical examiners are called in to determine the cause and manner of death. **Coroners** are elected officials who are responsible for investigating suspicious deaths. They may or may not have the specialized training necessary to conduct autopsies. **Medical examiners**, on the other hand, are medical doctors who specialize in forensic pathology. Forensic pathologists are qualified to conduct autopsies and determine the cause and manner of death. Both coroners and medical examiners are called to testify in homicide cases. Their offices are responsible for taking possession of bodies and collecting all evidence associated with the body.

D. Attorneys

Each party in a criminal case is usually represented by an attorney. The **prosecutor** is the attorney who represents the governmental entity and the citizens of a particular jurisdiction (city, state, or federal government). Prosecutors do not represent the crime victim, although they do try to serve his or her interests. Prosecutors are responsible for deciding whether to file charges against a suspect, negotiating plea bargains, and trying that suspect. Prosecutors also handle most appeals for the government. Prosecutors are known by several different names. They are most commonly referred to as district attorneys but are sometimes known as state's attorneys or county attorneys. At the federal level, prosecutors are referred to as United States attorneys since they represent all citizens of the United States.

The defendant in a criminal case has a Sixth Amendment right to counsel. He can choose to hire counsel, or if he cannot afford an attorney, he can have one appointed to him by the state. All states and the federal system have public defenders for this purpose. The defendant can also choose to represent himself. This is known as appearing *pro se*. A **defense attorney** files motions on behalf of the client, cross-examines prosecution witnesses, and calls witnesses for the defense. His job is to protect the constitutional rights of the defendant and zealously represent his client.

The Evidence in Action article that follows highlights the importance of the proper collection of evidence and the reporting of evidentiary findings. It also shows the danger of relying heavily on expert testimony.

Coroner
an elected official who may or may not be qualified to conduct autopsies. He is responsible for investigation of suspicious or unattended deaths

Medical examiner
a medical doctor who is a trained forensic pathologist. He is responsible for investigation of suspicious or unattended deaths

Prosecutor
an attorney who represents the governmental entity and the citizens of a particular jurisdiction (city, state, or federal government). State prosecutors are often referred to as district attorneys or state's attorney while federal prosecutors are known as United States attorneys

Defense attorney
an attorney that represents the defendant. He files motions on behalf of the client, cross-examines prosecution witnesses, and calls witnesses for the defense

EVIDENCE IN ACTION

Gregory Taylor Declared Innocent by the North Carolina Actual Innocence Commission

On April 19, 1993, Gregory F. Taylor was convicted in Wake County, North Carolina for the first-degree murder of Jaquetta Thomas. Taylor was sentenced to life in prison. On July 23, 2007, 14 years after his conviction, Taylor's case was turned over to the North Carolina Innocence Inquiry Commission (NCIIC) for review. Taylor's case was accepted, and an evidentiary hearing was held before the Commission on September 3 and 4, 2009. At the hearing, it was revealed that another individual had confessed to the murder and several witnesses had changed their stories since Taylor's conviction.[19] On February 17, 2010, Taylor became the first convicted defendant to be exonerated by the NCIIC.[20]

One of the primary pieces of evidence against Taylor was a report prepared by a State Bureau of Investigations (SBI) agent, Duane Deaver, regarding the presence of blood found on or in Taylor's SUV after the murder. Deaver's report stated that a presumptive test for blood showed "positive indications" for the presence of blood. However, it was revealed during the NCIIC review process that Deaver's final report had omitted the negative results of a more sensitive follow-up test for blood.[21]

Taylor's exoneration prompted a sweeping investigation into the state lab's reporting process. In 2010, the North Carolina Attorney General commissioned an independent review of the activities and performance of the Forensic Biology Section of the North Carolina State Bureau of Investigation Crime Laboratory.[22] During the investigation, several deficiencies were found. For example, the SBI had no formal policy regarding the method of reporting laboratory test results prior to September 1997. The only guidance that

Figure 1.4   Gregory Taylor reacts as he hears the decision of the North Carolina Innocence Commission exonerating him of murder charges on February 17, 2010. His attorney, Christine Mumma, sits next to him as he is freed after serving 17 years in prison. © 2010 AP Photo/Shawn Rocco/Pool File.

was provided to analysts concerned the reporting of forensic test results in final lab reports. It was left to the analyst to apply his or her own judgment as to how to report the findings. No guidance was given on how to report a negative or inconclusive confirmatory test following a positive presumptive test. Even the certification agency for crime labs, the American Society of Crime Laboratory Directors, provided no specific report writing standards until 2004.

Continued on following page

Evidence in Action continued

A review of all 15,419 serology files processed in the lab from January 1987 to January 2003 revealed 230 instances where negative or inconclusive test results were omitted from a final lab report.[23] Of the total 269 individuals charged in such cases, 80 are still serving sentences (4 of which are on death row), 3 were executed, and 5 have died in prison.[24] Conversely, during the same time frame, all positive test results were included in the final reports.[25] Often, neither prosecutors nor defense counsel were made aware of the fact that more sensitive tests had been done. Factors that contributed to this issue were the absence of any written policies at the SBI lab prior to 1997; unclear and flawed policy guidance after 1997; minimal legal training; inadequate management overseeing the reporting; no internal legal review of lab reporting procedures, practices, or polices; and a mindset that report results should be tailored primarily for law enforcement's consumption.[26] The review committee found no evidence that any lab reports or files were concealed or that evidence was deliberately suppressed, however.

Several changes have been made since then that appear to have corrected the problem. In 2003, North Carolina established what is referred to as "open file discovery" in criminal proceedings. Under the new protocol, the complete files of all law enforcement and prosecutorial agencies are to be made available upon motion of the defendant, including "investigation officer's notes, results of test and examinations or any other matters of evidence obtained during the investigation."[27] On January 1, 2008, the SBI implemented an online electronic database that contains all laboratory files. By March 25, 2010 the SBI had successfully implemented online Web-based access to lab files for every district attorney's office in North Carolina.[28] In 2004, the American Society of Crime Lab Directors began phasing in a new program that established new report-writing standards. These new standards require that the results of "each test" be reported "accurately, clearly, unambiguously and objectively" and the appropriate language be included in all reports.

The Review Committee made several recommendations based on its findings, including:

- The SBI, in conjunction with each affected district attorney's office, should conduct a more detailed review of the cases identified in the report where the lab failed to report the existence of negative or inconclusive confirmatory tests for blood
- The SBI should ensure that current and future laboratory personnel are sufficiently trained in criminal discovery requirements
- The SBI laboratory should obtain the most current accreditations at the earliest possible date
- The SBI laboratory should ensure that the entire contents of all lab files relating to criminal prosecutions are routinely provided on a timely basis to prosecutors
- The SBI laboratory should post all non-privileged SBI laboratory policies and procedures on a public Website so that the operations of the lab are transparent and accessible to the public
- The SBI laboratory should conduct "spot audits" of the laboratory DNA testing programs to reassure the public of the efficacy of the current SBI laboratory test and procedures involving the testing of DNA[29]

CHAPTER SUMMARY

The term *evidence* has many different meanings in the criminal justice field. It can refer to anything that is used to prove the existence of a fact. It can also refer to only those items that are admitted at trial to prove the guilt or innocence of the defendant or even the collective whole of the evidence introduced. As a result, evidence can have many different uses during the different stages of the criminal justice system.

The court system in the United States is composed of two separate systems: the federal courts and the state courts. Federal courts hear disputes about federal law while state courts hear disputes concerning state law. The federal courts are broken down into three types: district courts (trial courts), circuit courts of appeal (intermediate level appellate courts), and the United States Supreme Court. State courts are arranged in a similar fashion. Each state has its own set of criminal laws, which, while similar, can have their own unique rules and definitions.

Evidence law has four main sources: constitutional law, the common law, the Rules of Evidence, and statutory law. Several constitutional provisions restrict the types of evidence that can be admitted. If the admission of a piece of evidence would violate one of these constitutional principles, then the court must exclude it. Prior court decisions known as *precedent* also help guide the court on how to rule on evidentiary issues in the current case. This body of judge-made law is known as the common law. Finally, the admission of evidence is governed by the Federal Rules of Evidence in federal court. This set of rules was created in 1975, and it establishes a uniform set of principles that sets the requirements for how certain types of evidence are to be admitted. Most states have a similar set of rules that govern the admissibility of evidence in state court. Finally, legislatures can pass statutory laws that impact the admission of evidence.

Law enforcement employs several types of investigative personnel, including detectives, crime scene investigators, and laboratory analysts. All may be potential witnesses at trial. Homicides are also investigated by the coroner's or medical examiner's office. A forensic pathologist will also perform an autopsy in all suspicious or unattended deaths. The coroner or medical examiner may also be called to testify as to the cause and manner of death. The attorneys for the parties in a criminal case are known as prosecutors and defense attorneys. Prosecutors represent the government while defense attorneys represent the accused.

KEY TERMS

- Admissible
- Circuit court of appeals
- Common law
- Coroner
- Crime scene investigators
- Defense attorney
- District courts

- Evidence
- Federal courts
- Federal Rules of Evidence
- Medical examiner
- Petition for certiorari
- Precedent
- Prosecutor

- Special agents
- *Stare decisis*
- State courts
- United States Supreme Court

REVIEW QUESTIONS

1. What is the definition of evidence? How is it broader than just evidence admitted during a trial?

2. Name three general categories or types of evidence.

3. Why is it important that evidence must be admissible in court? What three things dictate the admissibility of evidence?

4. What are the three levels of the federal court system? What types of cases can be heard in federal court?

5. What are circuit courts? How many are there in the federal system?

6. Does the United States Supreme Court have to hear all cases appealed to it? Explain. What is meant by the term *certiorari*?

7. How are state court systems organized?

8. How is evidence used differently during the investigation stage of a case than it is during the trial stage?

9. What are the Federal Rules of Evidence? Why were they created?

10. Do all states use the Federal Rules? If not, what do they use in their place?

11. How are the Rules of Evidence organized?

12. Name two sources of evidence law other than the Rules of Evidence.

13. What evidentiary errors led to the wrongful conviction discussed in the Evidence in Action box? Do you think that changes made subsequent to Taylor's conviction will prevent errors like this one from being made in the future? Explain.

APPLICATION PROBLEMS

1. Lisa is being investigated for fraud. The police have three witnesses who say she sold them worthless land. Investigators also uncover multiple copies of the same deed to the property that Lisa had allegedly sold to each victim. What evidence will the investigators rely on to arrest Lisa for fraud?

2. Sandra is on trial for abusing her grandmother. The prosecutor presents testimony from the grandmother that Sandra had bruised her and then caused her to fall and break her hip. He also has a physician testify as to the grandmother's injuries. Two additional witnesses, neighbors of Sandra, are called to testify that they often saw Sandra leave her grandmother locked inside of the house for hours and would hear her wailing. Finally, the prosecutor produces photographs of the grandmother's injuries.

Describe the various types of evidence introduced by the prosecutor.

3. Vinny Sprano is on trial for racketeering in a New Jersey federal court. His attorney objects to the introduction of prior uncharged acts of Vinny concerning prior incidents of bribes and loansharking. The U.S. Attorney argues that under federal Rule 404(b), the prior acts are admissible to prove a common plan or scheme. He also argues that the uncharged incidents are usable since he has proven them by a preponderance of the evidence, the federal standard. Vinny's attorney argues the prior incidents should be excluded under New Jersey law because prior uncharged incidents must be proven beyond a reasonable doubt. Which evidence law has to be followed? Explain.

4. Fat Tony is accused of murder. The prosecutor wants to introduce evidence from the grand jury of a witness who testified that Tony threatened to kill Little Eddie. The witness was not cross-examined during the grand jury. The testimony is hearsay because the witness cannot be found to serve a subpoena for trial. The statement does not fall under a listed exception to the hearsay rule but the prosecutor argues the testimony is reliable because it was made under oath. The Confrontation Clause of the Sixth Amendment states the defendant is entitled to confront the witnesses against him. Should the statement be admitted or excluded due to the fact that it violates the defendant's constitutional rights? Explain.

5. Wendy is accused of conspiring to rob banks in four different states with four other accomplices. The plot originates in Oregon. The purpose behind the robberies is to fund terrorist actions for environmental justice. Should Wendy and her accomplices be charged federally or with states crimes? Explain. Assuming the case goes to trial, what court should she be tried in?

Notes

1. *Black's Law Dictionary*, at 595 (8th ed. 2004).
2. *Black's Law Dictionary*, at 20 (3d pocket ed. 2006).
3. Uscourts.gov, *Understanding the Federal Courts*, http://www.uscourts.gov/FederalCourts/UnderstandingtheFederalCourts/Jurisdiction.aspx
4. Uscourts.gov, *The Difference between Federal and State Courts*, http://www.uscourts.gov/FederalCourts/UnderstandingtheFederalCourts/Jurisdiction/DifferencebetweenFederalAndStateCourts.aspx.
5. *Black's Law Dictionary*, at 93 (3d pocket ed. 2006).
6. Lawyers.com, *Appeal to the Supreme Court of the United States*, http://research.lawyers.com/Appeal-to-the-Supreme-Court-of-the-United-States.html.
7. Wikipedia, *Certiorari*, http://en.wikipedia.org/wiki/Certiorari.
8. Thefreedictionary.com, *Judicial Tribunals Established by Each of the Fifty States*, http://legal-dictionary.thefreedictionary.com/p/State%20Courts.
9. Josh Camson, History of the Federal Rules of Evidence, Trial Evidence, *ABA Litigation News*, http://www.abanet.org/litigation/litigationnews/trial_skills/061710-trial-evidence-federal-rules-of-evidence-history.html.
10. Camson, *supra* at note 3.
11. Federal Rules of Evidence – 2011 Pending Amendment to Restyle the Federal Rules of Evidence, available at http://federalevidence.com/node/304.
12. Id.
13. Federal Rules of Evidence – 2011 Pending Amendment to Restyle the Federal Rules of Evidencehttp://federalevidence.com/downloads/blog/2010/Current-Amendments/EV_Rules_101-415.pdf.
14. *See* Megalaw.com, *Evidence*, http://www.megalaw.com/top/evid.php.
15. *Black's Law Dictionary*, at 553 (3d pocket ed. 2006).
16. *Black's Law Dictionary*, at 672 (3d pocket ed. 2006).
17. Katerina Milenkovski, *Illinois Finally Codifies Rules of Evidence*, ABA, Litigation News, November 11, 2010, available at http://www.abanet.org/litigation/litigationnews/top_stories/111110-illinois-rules-evidence-supreme-court.html.
18. Yourdictionary.com, *Who Has the Largest Crime Laboratory in the World*, http://answers.yourdictionary.com/law/who-has-the-largest-crime-laboratory-in-the-world.html.
19. Chris Swecker & Michael Wolf, *An Independent Review of the SBI Forensic Laboratory*, at 5, available at http://www.ncaj.com/file_depot/0-10000000/0-10000/9208/folder/88864/Independent+Review+of+SBI+Forensic+LAB.pdf.
20. Id.
21. Id. at 3.
22. Id. at 3.
23. Id. at 3.
24. Id. at 9.
25. Id. at 25.
26. Id. at 28.
27. Id. at 8, *citing* N.C.G.S §15A-903(a)(1).
28. Id. at 28.
29. Id. at 29.

PART I

THE COLLECTION AND PRESERVATION OF EVIDENCE

CHAPTER 2

Physical Evidence

"Shows like CSI are teaching people that without forensic evidence you can't convict anybody." —Michael Asimow

Chapter Topics

Objectives

After completing this chapter, students will be able to:

- Understand the process for searching a crime scene and an automobile correctly

- Document a crime scene properly, including taking photographs of all aspects of the crime scene, taking accurate measurements of the scene, and creating diagrams and sketches of the scene

- Understand the proper collection methods for various types of physical evidence

- Understand the chain of custody

- Understand proper storage methods for evidence

Introduction

When people think of the term evidence, the first things that come to mind are probably the physical specimens collected at a crime scene, such as blood, hair, fibers, and weapons. The role that the crime scene investigator plays in solving crime through the collection of physical evidence at crime scenes has been popularized in shows such as *CSI*. This type of evidence can, after all, provide the key link between the suspect and the crime scene. But, as the opening quote points out, convictions do not and should not rest solely on the strength of forensic evidence.

Perhaps just as important as the collection of the evidence is the proper documentation and storage of evidence after it is collected. Investigators have to take detailed notes about how and in what order evidence is collected. The scene must be photographed and/or videotaped. Investigators also have to make sure that the evidence is properly accounted for and stored when it is brought back to the station. Although seemingly minor details, these steps are important in helping establish the foundation for admissibility of evidence. If law enforcement officers are unable to establish who handled the evidence or whether it was properly preserved after being collected, the court will rule that it is inadmissible.

This chapter will examine the process for collection and preservation of physical evidence, as well as the documentation of a crime scene. It will cover such topics as searching the crime scene, photography, note taking, and sketching. It will also review the steps necessary to establish the chain of custody. Finally, the chapter will examine issues surrounding the storage and retention of evidence.

I. CRIME SCENE SEARCHES

Scene assessment
a preliminary process conducted prior to searching the scene, which includes establishing a perimeter, identifying responsibilities for personnel at the scene, and conducting a scene walk through

Before evidence can be documented and collected, it must be located and identified as evidence. The search of the crime scene is thus one of the most important early stages of the investigation. Prior to conducting a thorough search of the crime scene, investigators should conduct a **scene assessment**. This includes establishing a scene perimeter, identifying specific responsibilities for the various personnel at the scene, and evaluating safety issues. As part of this process, the investigator in charge should conduct an initial scene walk through. During this process, he should choose the best path for entry and exit into and out of the crime scene, identify what evidence is present, and identify any special concerns, such as the collection of fragile evidence.[1]

Once it has been determined that a crime has been committed or that suspicious circumstances warrant further investigation, the scene should be searched. Use of a systematic search pattern is the best way to ensure that all evidence is located at the scene and not contaminated. There are several patterns an investigator can chose from to search the scene. The scene can be searched using a spiral pattern, or the area can be subdivided into zones or quadrants, a grid, or lanes. The precise layout of the scene and the location of evidence will often dictate which pattern is used by the investigator. The actual pattern chosen, however, is not as important as maintaining a systematic approach throughout the search.

Regardless of which pattern is selected, more than one officer should be involved in searching each area. The second officer should search the area that has just been searched in the opposite direction from the first officer to ensure that no evidence has been missed.

A. Inward or Outward Spiral Search

Spiral search
a search pattern that involves walking around the crime scene in increasingly bigger or smaller circles

A **spiral search** pattern involves using increasingly smaller circles to walk around the scene. For an inward spiral, the investigator would start at the perimeter of the scene and gradually work his way to the center of the scene, walking in progressively smaller circles. An outward spiral pattern would start at the center and work outward. This method works well when only one investigator or crime scene investigator is assigned to search the scene.[2] See Figure 2.1 for an example of a spiral search pattern.

B. Zone Search

Zone search
a search pattern that subdivides the area to be searched into separate zones or quadrants

In contrast to spiral patterns, the other search methods involve subdividing the scene into squares or rectangles. In a **zone search**, for example, the scene is subdivided into separate zones or quadrants. A house can be divided into zones simply by classifying each room in the house as a separate zone. A warehouse could be divided into four zones by drawing two intersecting lines through the middle of it. See Figure 2.2 for an example of a zone search.

Figure 2.1
Spiral Search Pattern

Figure 2.2
Zone Search Pattern

C. Grid Search

Grid search
a search pattern that
subdivides the search area
into small, square units
like a piece of graph paper

A **grid search** is similar to a zone search, but the search area is divided
into many smaller units. This type of search pattern is analogous to a piece
of graph paper. The search area is subdivided into small, square units
using many intersecting lines. This search pattern works best for outdoor
areas or very large, open interiors. See Figure 2.3 for an example of a grid
search.

Figure 2.3
Grid Search Pattern

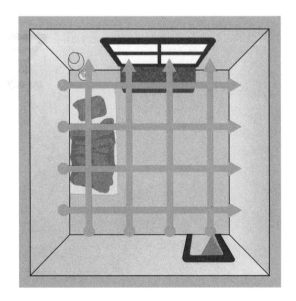

Figure 2.4
Parallel Search Pattern

D. Parallel or Lane Search

Parallel or lane search
a search conducted by dividing the search area into long lanes like a swimming pool

Finally, the **parallel or lane search** pattern is used to subdivide a large area by approximating the lanes of a swimming pool. The area is roped off into parallel lanes, and each is searched by a different investigator. Each searcher walks in a straight line from one end to the other end of the crime scene. Flags or ropes can be used to designate lanes. Like grid searches, parallel searches are often used for outdoor areas that have no set boundaries.[3] See Figure 2.4 for an example of a parallel search.

E. Searching in Stages

Three-stage search method
a method of searching a crime scene where only openly visible evidence is collected in the first stage, minimally intrusive methods such as opening windows and drawers are used in the second stage, and aggressive methods such as emptying drawers or searching files is reserved for the final stage

A crime scene should be searched in stages so evidence is not lost or destroyed. An effective **three-stage search method** has been devised by Greg Dagnan, an Assistant Professor at Missouri Southern State University. The first stage involves marking and collecting only the evidence that is open and obvious without disturbing anything in the scene. Doors and drawers should not be opened during this stage and furniture should not be moved. This is done to prevent contamination or destruction of evidence during the search process. Searchers should choose one of the above search patterns in executing this first level search. All the evidence is marked, measured, and photographed before it is collected at the end of this stage.

During the second stage, a minimal level of intrusiveness can be used to find additional evidence. Doors and drawers may be opened during this stage, but shifting of contents should be kept to a minimum. For example, the contents of desk or bureau drawers that have been opened should not be emptied at this point. Again, the idea is to not cover up or contaminate any evidence that is present. A similar type of search pattern used in the first stage is again used during the second stage. Once all evidence has been identified, the steps for marking, photographing, and collection of evidence should be repeated at the conclusion of this stage.

Finally, in the third stage, investigators may use more aggressive search methods. During this stage, drawers may be emptied and any destructive techniques such as cutting of carpet or removal of pieces of wall or floorboards may be used. This is also a good time to utilize development techniques such as dusting for fingerprints or swabbing for DNA. If the presence of biological fluids has not been obvious up to this point, chemicals such as Luminol may also be used to enhance the visibility of small traces or drops of blood. Unlike the first two stages, however, each item of evidence should be marked, photographed, and collected as it is found rather than waiting until the end of the stage. This is done to prevent loss of the evidence as the crime scene is literally turned upside down. It is not hard to imagine that small pieces of evidence could literally be buried as the contents of drawers are emptied on top of them.[4]

F. Alternate Light Sources

During a crime scene search, an officer or investigator should use more than one type of light source to locate evidence. A flashlight is a good starting tool for this purpose. It should be used at a low angle to help locate small objects in the scene. The long shadows produced with oblique lighting help make such items more noticeable. While it is hard to see such items by staring straight down on them, it is relatively easy to locate them by getting down on your hands and knees and shining a light across the floor.

Alternate light source
a light source that uses wavelengths other than white light, such as ultraviolet or infrared, to detect the presence of trace evidence

Officers should also use **alternate light sources** to detect trace evidence. An alternate light source is a tool capable of producing a wavelength of light other than white light (which is composed of all the wavelengths). Remember that light is composed of many different wavelengths, including those that are invisible to humans in the UV and IR range. See Figure 2.5 for the wavelengths contained in the light spectrum. Alternate light sources can be useful to detect the presence of biological fluids or other evidence that fluoresce under ultraviolet or infrared wavelengths. Blood, semen, urine, and even fingerprints will produce fluorescence under the right wavelength of light.

Several types of light sources are available for this purpose. The Multimaxx set pictured in Figure 2.6 contains several flashlights that emit different wavelengths of light. Other devices are capable of producing a range of wavelengths of light, such as the Crime Scope. It can produce

Figure 2.5

Visible light comprises just a small percentage of the light spectrum. Long-wave infrared and short wave ultraviolet light are used as alternate light sources to detect evidence at crime scenes. *Courtesy of Sirchie, Inc.*

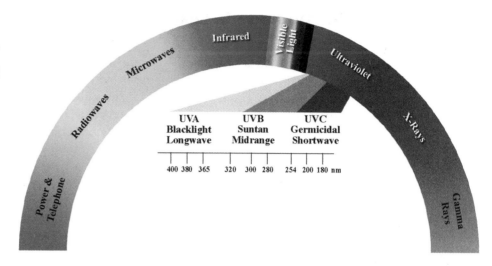

variable wavelengths of high-intensity light. This device is particularly convenient since the wavelengths can be adjusted simply by turning a dial. Investigators should remember to wear protective eyewear when using these devices since direct exposure to this type of light may damage a person's eyes.

Figure 2.6

The Megamaxx 100, made by Sirchie, is a series of seven flashlights, each with a separate wavelength of light. Colors range from red to ultraviolet. *Courtesy of Sirchie, Inc.*

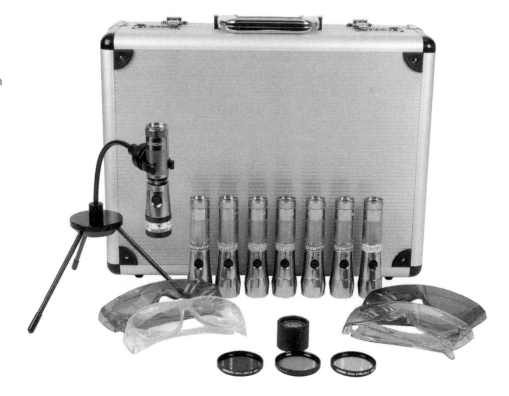

G. Automobile Searches

If the investigator is searching a motor vehicle, a systematic search should also be conducted. He should start with the exterior of the car and collect any fingerprints or other evidence present before proceeding to the interior. The trunk should be searched, including the spare tire. The investigator should then start on the driver's side, working his way across the front and then across the back seat in the opposite direction. If necessary, seats and door panels can be removed.

II. CRIME SCENE DOCUMENTATION

A. Crime Scene Notes

Investigators at the scene need to take detailed notes of the scene conditions, the items found at the scene, and the location and relationship of items in the scene. Notes can provide investigators with the foundation for a written report and aid in recalling the sequence of events at a later date. All sights, sounds, and smells present at the crime scene should be recorded.

General information regarding the crime scene should be noted first, including the date, place, and time as well as the address of the scene. Investigators should note both their dispatch time and arrival time on scene. If someone else responded to the scene first, investigators' notes should reflect who that was. Also, it should be noted who discovered the crime scene, including that person's contact information. A record should be kept of all persons present at the scene. This includes the names of all police officers and law enforcement personnel, ambulance and/or emergency personnel, family and relatives of the victim, and any witnesses who may be interviewed or detained by first responders. To establish a complete record of who is at the scene, a scene log should be generated with the names of all law enforcement personnel and civilians who are present.[5]

Upon their arrival, officers should record their initial observations of the crime scene, including the appearance and condition of the scene.[6] Notes should describe the crime scene in detail, including the weather and lighting conditions, the location of items in the crime scene, and the overall layout of the scene. If something catches the attention of an investigator at the crime scene, it should be recorded. Investigators should note whether light switches were on or off, if TV sets or radios were playing, the temperature of the room, whether blinds or drapes were open or closed, whether food was out, and other details of the crime scene.[7]

Notes should always be recorded in a notebook, not on loose pieces of paper. Each page should be numbered, dated, and marked with the case number. This will prevent accidental separation or loss of notes. When taking notes, officers should not record every word said but instead should summarize the important details. Officers should leave out insignificant details and words that do not add significant meaning, such as *a, an, and, but,* and *the.* Using standard abbreviations is recommended; investigators should not devise their own shorthand.

It is important to be objective when taking notes since they may later be discoverable by the defense. Investigators should be careful to record all relevant information obtained during the investigation, even if it does not support the main theory of the crime or a particular suspect's guilt. Investigators should not include their opinions about the evidence or the witnesses. They should simply record the facts as accurately as possible. Investigators should not include assumptions about the evidence, such as the presence of blood or drugs at the scene. Instead, investigators should simply note, for example, the presence of a "reddish brown material" or a "substance that appears to be cocaine."

A portable tape recorder can be used to record notes and any interviews of witnesses or suspects at the crime scene. Such recordings are useful since many can now be downloaded to a computer and transcribed using software. However, they should be used as a backup only, not as a replacement for notes. This is particularly true if wind or other background noise is prevalent at the scene.

Practical Example

Assume an investigator is conducting an undercover drug buy. A confidential informant (CI) is assigned to purchase drugs from a suspect. The CI is given $500 in marked bills prior to the buy. His person is thoroughly searched prior to the buy. Nothing is found. He is given a hidden "wire" to record the audio of the buy. He walks into a room occupied by three people. He allegedly buys crack from the woman leasing the apartment. After the CI conducts the buy, he is searched again by law enforcement. He is in possession of four rocks of crack and only $100.00 in cash. The investigator also searches the apartment where the drug buy is conducted and finds no drugs or money. He arrests the woman from whom the drugs were allegedly bought. He finds nothing. He also searches her car. He finds nothing.

In his notes, the investigator should describe the preparation of the CI as well as what was heard over the wire. He should note the results of all searches, including the fact that nothing was found on the suspect or in her car. Although this fact does not help prove her guilt, it is information that may be helpful to the defense and must be turned over to the defense prior to trial.

B. Crime Scene Photography

There's an old saying that one picture is worth a thousand words, and nothing could be truer in the context of a criminal trial. There are several purposes for taking **crime scene photographs**. First, photographs give the jury a picture of what the crime scene looked like when the investigators first found it. This helps give some context to the crime for the jury and allows the jury to visualize how the crime may have occurred. Second, photographs may help preserve evidence in the case, particularly if something in the photograph is lost or destroyed between the time it was photographed and the time of trial. Third, photographs may help trigger the memory of witnesses or investigators if they have forgotten the specific details of the crime scene by the time they testify at trial.

Crime scene photographs
photographs taken of anything in a crime scene. They may show scene layout or particular pieces of evidence found at a scene

The technology used for crime scene photography has evolved significantly over the last 50 years. In the past, investigators often would use large, bulky cameras on tripods to photograph crime scenes. Smaller, 35-mm cameras then became the main tool for this purpose. For many years, police agencies operated their own darkrooms to develop and print film. Today, digital cameras are the preferred tool for crime scene photography. Digital cameras allow the photographer to review the photograph in camera to ensure that it was taken properly. The digital process is also much less expensive since there is no need to maintain a darkroom.

When photographing a crime scene, officers should take care to be as complete as possible. Some tips for crime scene photography are listed in Table 2.1.

Three types of photographs should be taken of each piece of evidence: **wide angle**, **mid-range**, and **close-up**

For each piece of evidence found at the scene, a minimum of three photographs should be taken: a **wide angle** photograph showing the evidence's relation to the overall scene, a **mid-range** photograph, and a **close-up** of the item of evidence. Close-up photographs should first be taken without any identifying markers or scales in the photo, and then a second series should be taken with both a scale and a numbered or lettered

TABLE 2.1   TIPS FOR CRIME SCENE PHOTOGRAPHY

- Take photos showing an overview of the crime scene
- Photograph visible entry or exit routes
- Photograph the crowd of onlookers in case the perpetrator has remained behind
- Photograph identifying features in the scene, such as addresses, intersection signs, and building names
- Photograph the layout of the scene before taking close-ups of evidence
- Be careful not to contaminate or step on any evidence[8]

Figure 2.7
Image 1 shows a wide-angle photograph of a mock shooting scene in a parking lot. Image 2 is a mid-range shot of the same scene. Finally, image 3 displays a cartridge casing found at the scene. © 2010 Derek Regensburger

photo card. See Figure 2.7 for an example of wide, mid-range, and close-up photos of a crime scene. Each photograph should be noted in a photo log so that there is no question as to where and when the photo was taken.[9]

Practical Example

Assume an investigator is called to the scene of a possible homicide. A body is found with two bullet wounds, lying in a large pool of blood on the floor next to the couch. A gun is found next to the left hand of the victim. Two shell casings are found near the gun. The investigator should take a couple of photographs of the outside of the house, including the house number. Then an overview photograph of the scene should be taken inside the house. A series of shots should be taken of each piece of evidence, moving from wide to close. Close-ups should be taken with and without scales and photo markers. The investigator should then log all photos in his notes and, at the end of his shift, transfer the flash card to the evidence room.

1. Photography of Blood Stains and Pattern Evidence

Photographing blood spatter stains or other patterns requires some additional steps. When photographing blood spatter, the photographer should position the flash to the side of the camera so as to give more definition to the pattern. Blood stain patterns often contain complex mixtures of smaller patterns, so the photographer should pick out the separate patterns and photograph each one individually. Each different pattern should be labeled so the viewer is not lost in a maze of droplets. The stain patterns should first be photographed without any labels or scales. Then, since stains often cover a large area and are usually located on walls or ceilings, the photographer should apply large, adhesive scales to the perimeter of the stain. A wide view of the stain pattern should be taken, along with mid-range and close-ups.[10]

2. Photography of Shoe and Tire Impressions

Shoe and tire impressions are photographed in a similar manner. Such impressions can be left in dust, mud, or snow. Photographs should be taken before casts (filling the impression with a hardening paste like dental stone or plaster of Paris) are taken of the impressions. Like blood stains, these types of impressions should be photographed with the flash to the side of the camera, aimed at a low angle across the impression. This oblique lighting helps create better shadow detail than if the flash is pointed perpendicular to the impression. Figure 2.8 demonstrates the effect the use of direct versus oblique lighting has on the resulting image. Impressions should be photographed both with and without scales. A U-bracket scale is used to show the length of the impression as well as its width.

3. Panoramic Crime Scene Photographs

Many police departments are using new, sophisticated technology to take panoramic photographs of crime scenes in major cases. Using specialized cameras, an investigator can take overlapping, high-resolution shots of the entire crime scene in a matter of minutes. For example, panoramic cameras can render a 360-degree view of a crime scene by taking numerous shots as the camera rotates around a central point.[11] This can be useful particularly if one wants to show a three-dimensional crime scene view. Software has also been developed that can create "viewpoints" that simulate for the jury what the crime scene looked like from any particular point in the scene.[12]

C. Crime Scene Measurements

Before evidence can be collected, the scene must be measured. This includes recording the room or scene dimensions along with the precise location of evidence in relation to reference points within the scene. Measurements are taken so that the investigator can recreate the crime scene. In fact, investigators will create scale models of the crime scene to be shown to the jury in some cases. Measurements can be done in a

Figure 2.8
Image 1 shows the lack of shadow detail in a footwear impression taken with the flash positioned on top of the camera. Image 2 shows much greater shadow detail in the impression by placing the flash to the side of the camera. © 2010 Derek Regensburger

number of ways. The investigator can manually measure the scene using a tape measure or use more sophisticated measuring devices such as laser range finders (i.e., a surveying instrument known as a total station).

Rectangular coordinates
a method of measurement conducted by measuring the distance of an object to two points at right angles to one another

In indoor scenes, measurements are normally recorded as **rectangular coordinates**. In other words, the item's distance from two walls or fixed points perpendicular to each other is recorded. See Figure 2.9 for an example of rectangular coordinates. Measurements can also be taken to a **baseline** (an arbitrary straight line in the scene). The distance of the item to the baseline is recorded as well as its distance along the baseline. One tape measure should be laid along the baseline, and then measurements should be taken perpendicular to it by using a second tape measure. See Figure 2.10 for an example of measuring to a baseline.

Baseline
an arbitrary straight line placed in a scene that allows for the measurement of distances from an object to the line and along the line

In outdoor scenes, it is often necessary to triangulate measurements since straight lines are not present in the scene. **Triangulation** involves measuring an object to two fixed objects such as trees or light posts, much like a surveyor would do. See Figure 2.11 for an example of the triangulation method. The investigator can also record the GPS coordinates of the object. This ensures that the evidence's location can be determined at a later date, even if the fixed objects are later removed.

Triangulation
a method of measurement that involves taking measurements from the object to two fixed points such as trees or lampposts

Figure 2.9
Rectangular Coordinate Measurements

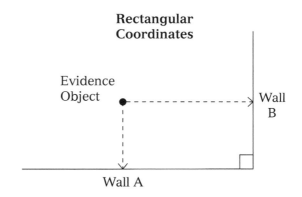

Figure 2.10
Baseline Measurements

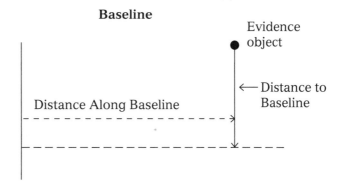

Figure 2.11
Triangulation to Two Fixed Objects in a Scene

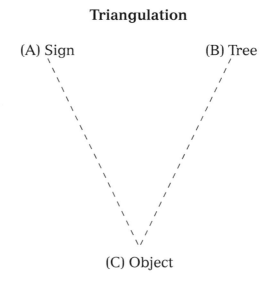

Triangulation

(A) Sign   (B) Tree

(C) Object

D. Crime Scene Sketches and Diagrams

Crime scene sketches and diagrams play an important role in the documentation of crimes scenes, including refreshing the memory of the investigators and witnesses and developing relationships between items in the crime scene. Investigators should draw a **rough sketch** of the crime scene at the time evidence is located and collected. A rough sketch is a hand-drawn representation of the crime scene as the investigator saw it during his initial examination of the scene. See Figure 2.12 for an example of a hand-drawn sketch. A more **formal diagram** is often prepared later and is usually drawn to scale. This diagram can either be done with an architect's rule or created on the computer using Computer-Aided Design (CAD) software.

When drawing a sketch, the investigator should show the position of the room or outdoor area where the crime occurred. He should also show the position of doors, windows, and other objects of significance, including furniture, evidence items, and the layout of the scene.[13] The sketch should also contain a legend. The purpose of the legend is to identify and explain any numbers and symbols on the sketch. If a scale is used in the diagram, the legend should also contain this information. Crime scene sketches should also contain the following information in the title block:

- The name and title of the investigator who drew the sketch
- The date and time the sketch was made
- The type of crime
- Identification of the victim, if any
- The case number
- The address of the crime scene
- A compass[14]

Rough sketch
a hand-drawn representation of the crime scene as the investigator saw it during his initial examination of the scene. It is not drawn to scale

Formal diagram
a scale drawing of the crime scene created using either an architect's rule or CAD software. It shows the precise relationship of items to one another in the crime scene

Figure 2.12
Hand-Drawn Sketch

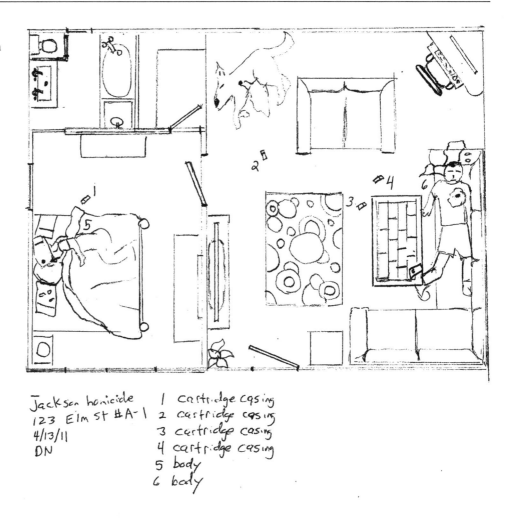

Jackson homicide   1 cartridge casing
123 Elm st #A-1   2 cartridge casing
4/13/11   3 cartridge casing
DN   4 cartridge casing
                                     5 body
                                     6 body

Even though the rough sketch is a freehand drawing, it should not be destroyed once the more formal diagram is constructed. The original sketch should be preserved just like the notes of the investigator; it is proof of what the scene looked like when the investigator observed it.

III. EVIDENCE COLLECTION

As discussed above, collection of physical evidence is an extremely important part of crime scene analysis. Investigators have to make sure that evidence is properly packaged and sealed so that it is protected from degradation and contamination. Investigators should remember to wear gloves and booties to prevent contamination. At the conclusion of the search, the gloves and booties should be bagged and tagged as evidence just in case any residual trace evidence has been transferred to them during the search.

As it is identified, evidence should be recorded in an evidence log, including a description of the evidence and its location in the scene. After each piece of evidence is packaged, the container should be labeled with the investigator's initials, the date the item was collected, a brief description of the evidence, the location where it was found, and the case number. It should also be sealed with red evidence tape, and the investigator should place his initials and date next to the seal. See Figure 2.13 for an example of a properly labeled and sealed evidence bag. This information will help identify the evidence at a later date so that the investigator can distinguish it from similar evidence collected at other crime scenes. The procedures for collecting some of the more common types of evidence are discussed in the following subsections.

A. Blood Stains and Other Biological Evidence

Blood stains and other biological fluids are important pieces of evidence because they often contain DNA that can be used to determine the identity of the source of the stain. Biological evidence should be collected using sterile swabs and air dried prior to storage. Plastic bags should never be used as storage containers since moisture may build up inside and cause bacterial growth. Instead, blood and other biological samples should be packaged in paper bags. Investigators must take care not to contaminate blood and other biological material with their own DNA. Gloves and masks should be worn at all times when collecting and handling this type of evidence.[15] See Table 2.2 for the proper procedures for collecting biological evidence.

Figure 2.13
Drew Darby, an investigator for the Hanover County Sheriff's Office, holds an item of evidence during the trial of John Allen Mohammed, the D.C. Sniper. Darby's testimony occurred on October 31, 2003 in Virginia Beach, Virginia. The evidence was collected from the Ponderosa Steakhouse shooting in Ashland, Virginia. *© 2003 Adrin Snider/Pool/CNP/Corbis*

TABLE 2.2   PROPER PROCEDURES FOR COLLECTING BIOLOGICAL EVIDENCE

- Sterile cotton swabs should be used to swab small stains and then placed back in original packaging to air dry
- Cotton swabs should be first moistened with distilled water before collecting dried samples
- For stains located on small, solid objects, entire item should be packaged and sent to lab for analysis
- For larger objects, stains should be scraped into paper bindles or cut out
- Biological stains should be fully air dried before storing[16]

Once biological samples have dried, the evidence must be refrigerated or frozen prior to analysis. This will help preserve DNA and other biological material. By way of example, the Houston crime lab was chastised for storing some of its biological samples on the top floor of its laboratory where no air conditioning or humidity control was present. Because of this, many samples were degraded and not suitable for analysis.[17]

information in week 2 lecture notes

B. Hair and Fiber Evidence

Hair and fibers are often transferred between the suspect and victim, particularly if there has been close physical contact during the commission of a crime. Thus, its collection and analysis plays an important step in many investigations. Investigators should try to recover all hair and fibers present in areas of interest, such as on clothing, bedding, and the interior of automobiles. Strands should be collected with tweezers or picked up with fingers. Hair and fibers should be placed in paper bindles and then sealed in larger envelopes. Each bindle should be placed in a different outside envelope so that if samples are disturbed during transit, they are not mixed together.[18]

C. Firearms Evidence

Firearms evidence comes in two basic forms: evidence from the weapon itself and bullets and spent cartridge casings fired or ejected from the weapon. Bullets or cartridge casings retrieved from a crime scene can be compared with test rounds fired from the suspect's weapon to determine if they match. This process relies on the fact that the barrels of most handguns and rifles are rifled; in other words, the barrel is bored out in a circular fashion so that the bullet spins after being fired to allow for a truer trajectory (shotgun barrels are not rifled and are therefore not useful for such comparisons). The rifling process leaves spiral rises in the

Lands and grooves
rises and depressions cut into the metal of gun barrels during the manufacturing process

metal known as **lands** and depressions in the metal known as **grooves**. Each manufacturer uses a slightly unique pattern to rifle their respective gun barrels. For example, one manufacturer may cut five lands and grooves with a left twist while another may cut six lands and grooves with a right twist. These help identify the make of the gun the bullet was fired from.

Other markings left on bullets and casings can be used to specifically identify the weapon they were fired from. The rifling process leaves unique, microscopic marks and scratches on the softer metal of the barrel known as **striations,** which are then imparted to the bullet during firing. A similar process leaves marks on the breech face of the cartridge casing (the bottom of the casing, which is struck by the firing pin of the gun).[19] These markings are then compared side by side under a microscope. See Figure 2.14 for a comparison of striation markings on a bullet.

Striations
unique, microscopic marks and scratches on the metal of the gun barrel that are imparted to the bullet during firing

Care must be taken in collecting firearms evidence. See Table 2.3 for the proper procedure for collection of firearms evidence.

D. Gunshot Residue

Gunshot residue (GSR) is composed of unburned powder that is ejected from a weapon during firing. It is comprised of three distinct elements: antimony, barium, and lead. The collection of gunshot residue occurs simply by swabbing the hands and face of a suspect with cotton swabs moistened with distilled water. A special applicator with a sticky substance can also be dabbed over the skin surface. If the suspect has

Figure 2.14
The striation markings on two bullets fired from the same weapon are compared side by side under a microscope. *Courtesy of Colorado Bureau of Investigation*

washed his hands after firing a weapon, it is unlikely that positive results will be obtained. Therefore, the investigator must prevent the suspect from washing his hands or trying to rub off the residue prior to its collection. Sometimes investigators will tape paper bags around the hands of the suspect to prevent loss of GSR evidence before such tests are conducted.

E. Drugs

Controlled substances come in three basic types: powders, pills, and plant material. A different container is used for the storage of each type. Powder forms should be placed in paper bindles and then placed in a larger envelope. They should not be placed in envelopes alone since the corners are not sealed and leakage can occur. Prescription pills or other pill forms can simply be kept in the original prescription bottles or placed in sterile pill bottles. Plant material should be air dried and stored in paper. It should not be stored in any type of plastic since the plants can rot, resulting in the destruction of evidence. Drug evidence should be weighed after it is dried.[22]

TABLE 2.3   PROCEDURES FOR COLLECTION OF FIREARMS EVIDENCE

Weapons

- Loaded weapons should be picked up with the thumb and forefinger on the textured part of the barrel or by the trigger guard where fingerprints are not likely to be found

- Before shipping or transporting a weapon, it should be unloaded

- The position of all chambered rounds should be noted in a diagram

- Weapons should be placed in a gun box for transportation and storage

- Ammunition and gun magazines should be stored and transported separately from the main weapon[20]

Bullets and Casings

- Bullets should never be marked; they should be wrapped in cotton wadding and placed in a pill box or envelope

- If a bullet has biological material on it (from entering and exiting a body), it should be air dried and wrapped in paper or cotton wadding

- Spent cartridge casings should be wrapped in cotton liner paper and placed in a pillbox or envelope

- If cartridge casings or shotgun shells are marked with case numbers and initials, care must be taken to mark such items only on smooth surfaces so as to not destroy the markings on the breech face[21]

F. Fingerprints

Fingerprints and other friction ridge impressions such as palmprints or footprints come in four basic types: **latent** (impressions that are not easily visible without development), **plastic** (impressions made in a malleable substance like soap or grease), **dust** (impressions left in dust), and **visible** (impressions that are visible due to being made while fingers were stained with a colored substance such as blood).[23] The method of collection and preservation used depends on the type of print present.

Latent fingerprints
impressions that are not easily visible without the aid of development

Plastic fingerprints
impressions made in a malleable substance like soap or grease

Dust fingerprints
impressions left in dust

Visible fingerprints
impressions that are visible due to being made while fingers were stained with a colored substance, such as blood

1. Development of Latent Prints Using Fingerprint Powder

The development of latent fingerprints using fingerprint powder is the development process most people are familiar with. Fingerprint powders are best used on smooth, nonporous surfaces such as windowsills, glass, and metal objects. Powders are not as useful on textured surfaces (such as some woods and metal) or porous surfaces (such as paper). Chemical development methods must be used instead.

Powders come in dark, light, and fluorescent colors. A contrasting powder should be used (i.e., dark powder should be used on a light-colored surface and light powder should be used on a dark-colored surface). Once the print is visible, it should be photographed with and without a scale. The investigator should then lift the print and place it on a backing card, again contrasting in color to the powder used. The print card should be marked on the opposite side of the taped side with the investigator's initials, the date, the case number, and the place where the print was taken from. The investigator should also draw an arrow on the card to indicate the direction of the print so an analyst does not mistakenly analyze it upside down.[24] See Figure 2.15 for an example of lifting a latent fingerprint.

Figure 2.15
A print is developed on a can of spray paint using black fingerprint powder. *Courtesy, Sirchie, Inc.*

2. Development of Latent Prints Using Chemical Developers

Chemical development of fingerprints relies on the reaction of the oils and proteins in fingerprints with certain chemicals. Iodine, cyanoacrylate (superglue), Ninhydrin, and 1.8 diazafluoren-9-one (DFO) are common chemicals used for fingerprint development.[25] A sample of a superglue-fuming chamber can be seen in Figure 2.16. Textured objects are developed in a fuming chamber, whereas Ninhydrin and DFO are used to develop prints on paper surfaces.

3. Collection of Visible and Plastic Prints

Visible prints should be photographed with and without a scale for preservation. Visible prints should be lifted where possible on fingerprint tape or other lifting device. Plastic prints should be photographed, and then the substance with the print impression in it should be collected to preserve the print where possible.

G. Shoe and Tiremark Impressions

Shoe impressions and tire impressions can be useful pieces of evidence since shoes and tires exhibit unique wear patterns that can be individualized back to a particular source. Once the impression has been photographed, a cast of it should be taken. Dental stone or plaster is used for this purpose. An analyst can then compare the cast of the impression

Figure 2.16
A SR600 fuming chamber is pictured with examples of objects that can be placed in the chamber for development of prints. *Courtesy, Sirchie, Inc.*

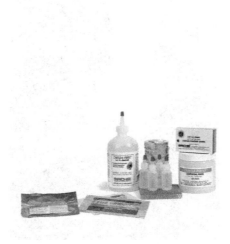

to a suspect's footwear. Figure 2.17 shows the process for casting an impression.

If the impression is left in dust or is on a two-dimensional surface, it can be lifted with fingerprint tape or an electrostatic dust lifter. This process is much like lifting a fingerprint. The dust sticks to the tape and can be placed on a piece of glossy photo paper as a backing. The bottom of the suspect's shoe is then inked and an impression is made for comparison purposes.

Practical Example

Assume an investigator discovers a gun, a cartridge casing, blood drops, and four green fibers at a crime scene. How should he collect the evidence? The gun should be checked for ammunition and its location in the weapon recorded. It should then be unloaded and placed in a gun box with tie downs for transport. Next, the shell casing should be placed in a small box or plastic bottle with cotton wadding to protect it during transport. The blood drops should be collected using a sterile cotton swab and placed in a paper bag after drying. Finally, the green fibers should be collected with tweezers and placed in a paper bindle and then into a larger outside envelope. All items should be sealed with evidence tape and marked with the investigator's initials, date, place of collection, description of the item, and the case number.

Figure 2.17
A footprint in the mud is being cast using a mixture of dental stone and water. *© 2010 Derek Regensburger*

IV. CHAIN OF CUSTODY

A. General Requirements

Chain of custody

the maintenance of control over an item of evidence such that it can be documented that the evidence has not been altered or tampered with since its collection, or if its condition has changed, an adequate explanation can be given for the change. Each person who handles an item of evidence after its collection is a link in the chain

Even if evidence is properly collected, the prosecution must still lay a sufficient foundation for its admission by establishing the chain of custody. The **chain of custody** is shown by proving that sufficient safeguards have been taken with respect to the possession and control of evidence such that it can be stated that the evidence is in substantially the same condition as when it was collected, or if it is not, an explanation can be provided as to how and why its condition has changed. The purpose of the chain of custody requirement is to establish that the evidence has not been altered or tampered with. The chain of custody is composed of links, with each link being anyone in the chain who has handled the evidence between its collection and its submission at trial.[26]

In order to prove the chain of custody, the prosecution must establish the following with regard to each link: 1) the receipt of the item; 2) the ultimate disposition of the item (i.e., transfer, destruction, or retention); and 3) the safeguarding and handling of the item between receipt and disposition.[27] It is not necessary for the prosecution to establish the chain of custody prior to when the evidence is discovered and collected by law enforcement. The clock begins ticking when the evidence is seized.[28] For example, the Supreme Court of Alabama held that the prosecution did not have to account for the whereabouts of a gun between the commission of the offense and its discovery by the police. Since there were no missing links in the chain once the gun was collected and an eyewitness positively identified it as the weapon used in the murder, the court found that the chain of custody had been sufficiently established.[29]

If there are significant gaps in the chain of custody, the evidence will likely be excluded. For example, an Illinois court held that the chain of custody had not been proven where there was no evidence presented as to whom a vial of drugs had been delivered to at the crime lab or what condition it was in when it was received.[30] To establish the chain of custody, however, the prosecution is not required to show that someone retained the evidence in his personal possession or kept it under constant watch.[31] Most states also do not require the prosecution to establish the chain perfectly; minor gaps are permitted. Courts do not require that every person involved in the chain must testify, nor do they require that the prosecution exclude all possibilities that the evidence was tampered with.[32] In other words, if one of the links is missing, a sufficient chain of custody is established as long as the testimony demonstrates that the condition of the evidence when it was delivered to the evidence room is the same as when it was subsequently examined or checked out for court.[33]

Another Illinois appellate court held that the prosecution had established an adequate chain of custody for a bag of cocaine seized from the defendant and delivered to the lab for analysis. Even though the prosecution did not present any testimony as to who took possession of the bag of cocaine once it was delivered to the crime lab, the court noted that the bag had been placed in a manila envelope and sealed and that the seal had not been broken until it was examined by a chemist at the lab. Since the seal had not been broken, the court found that there was no evidence that the cocaine had been tampered with, altered, or substituted; thus the chain of custody was intact.[34] It should be noted that some states like Alabama require that the prosecution establish all links in the chain of custody, and if one of the links is missing, the evidence is inadmissible.[35]

B. Establishing the Chain of Custody in Court

As discussed above, before physical evidence can be admitted in court, the prosecution must authenticate it and establish the chain of custody. If the item is uniquely identifiable (such as a scarf with monogrammed initials on it), then the person who collected it simply need testify that the item is in substantially the same condition as when it was collected. However, if the item is generic and is susceptible to change or alteration (such as a baggie of drugs), then a more complete chain has to be established.[36] To do this, the prosecutor may have to call several witnesses, particularly if the item was checked out for examination and testing. While not every link in the chain has to testify, the prosecutor should call, at a minimum, the person who collected the evidence and the person who examined or tested the evidence. The chain of custody log (showing all the places where the evidence was stored and who had possession of it) should also be introduced as an exhibit.

The prosecutor will ask a series of questions of each of the witnesses regarding chain of custody of the evidence. A series of sample questions is described below for admission of drugs found at a crime scene:

Q: Officer, I'm handing you what has previously been marked as People's Exhibit 3. Do you recognize what that is?

A: Yes, this is the hypodermic syringe filled with what appears to be heroin that I collected at the Harden murder scene.

Q: And how do you recognize it as such?

A: I marked the bag with my initials, the date, the case number, and a description of the object recovered.

Q: Where was the syringe found?

A: On a table near where her body was found.

Barry Bonds' Drug Sample and the Chain of Custody

Barry Bonds hit 762 career home runs as a member of the Pittsburgh Pirates and San Francisco Giants. Upon his retirement in 2007, he held both the single season and lifetime home run records. But it wasn't his prowess as a baseball player that attracted the attention of federal prosecutors.

Later that year, Bonds was indicted on 10 counts of perjury and 1 count of obstruction of justice stemming from his testimony before a federal grand jury on December 3, 2003. At that time, the grand jury was investigating the illegal distribution of steroids from the Bay Area Laboratory Cooperative (BALCO). Bonds was given immunity for his testimony, provided he gave truthful testimony regarding his involvement with BALCO and steroids. Bonds testified before the grand jury that he had never knowingly used steroids. Prosecutors contended Bonds lied on the witness stand about his use of steroids, alleging he had knowingly obtained steroids from BALCO.[37]

Some of the key pieces of evidence in the government's case were drug test results that allegedly showed the presence of steroids in Bonds' system. BALCO had kept lab test results for Bonds dating from 2000 and 2001. The government also wanted to introduce two urine samples of Bonds' that it had seized during the execution of a search warrant on an independent drug testing lab that had handled the exploratory round of steroid testing for Major League Baseball in 2003. The government alleged that tests of the samples had revealed the presence of a previously undetectable steroid—THG.

Bonds moved to suppress the test results from BALCO on the grounds that the chain of custody for the samples could not be established. Bonds'

Figure 2.18 Former San Francisco Giants left fielder, Barry Bonds, enters a federal courthouse for a hearing, ahead of his perjury trial in San Francisco, California on December 21, 2007. © 2007 *Robert Galbraith/Reuters/Corbis*

trainer, Greg Anderson, had allegedly delivered the samples to BALCO executive James Valente. Anderson, however, refused to testify that the samples belonged to Bonds. To make matters worse, BALCO did not follow strict chain of custody procedures. Apparently, another lab executive, Victor Conte, had decided to save money ($50 per sample) by agreeing to waive chain of custody protocols when he delivered the samples to Quest Diagnostics for testing. As a result, no records were kept as to who handled the samples prior to testing.[38]

The defense argued that the chain of custody could not be established for the samples.[39] The trial judge, Susan Illston, agreed with the defense. She excluded the test results, stating that without

Continued on following page

Evidence in Action continued

testimony from Anderson, the test results were classic hearsay. She ruled that "this is not a case in which the chain of custody has a few 'rusty' links; rather, crucial pieces of the chain are missing altogether."[40] She also excluded a doping calendar and other records seized from Anderson's home on Fourth Amendment grounds.

In April 2011, Bonds was tried on the three remaining perjury charges and one count of obstruction of justice. The jury deadlocked on the perjury counts but found Bonds guilty of obstruction of justice. Bonds' lawyers have moved to set aside the obstruction charge, but even if the verdict is upheld, it is unlikely that he will serve any prison time on the charge.[41]

Q: What did you do with the syringe once you collected it?

A: I sealed the bag with evidence tape, marked the bag near the seal with the date and my initials, placed it in a box in the back of patrol car, and transported it along with the other evidence in the case to the police department.

Q: What did you do with the syringe and other evidence once you returned to the station?

A: I gave it to our property room clerk, who logged in all the evidence on the chain of custody form on our computer system.

Q: Officer, is People's Exhibit 3 in substantially the same condition as when you collected it on January 5th of this year?

A: Yes, it is, except that a second seal has been placed on the bag by someone at the crime lab who apparently checked it out for analysis on April 15th of this year.

The prosecutor would then call the chemist who checked out and tested the heroin to complete the chain of custody.

V. EVIDENCE STORAGE

As part of maintaining the chain of custody, evidence must be properly stored and preserved once it has been collected. All police departments have some sort of evidence storage facility. They also all use some sort of system to catalog and identify evidence. Ideally, each department should have a system for logging and tracking evidence so that the location of a piece of evidence in any given case can be located within a few minutes. Unfortunately, the amount of space and quality of evidence identification and retrieval systems used vary greatly from department to department.

Prior to the twenty-first century, evidence storage often got short shrift in law enforcement agencies. Rooms were overstuffed with evidence; it was often thrown haphazardly into boxes with no assigned location. Evidence was logged in and tracked by hand. A variety of problems developed from using this type of system, including loss and destruction of evidence.

These reports highlight the need for the creation of national standards and controls on evidence storage and retention. Currently, there is little oversight by federal and state authorities to help guide individual departments on which evidence should be kept and which should be tossed. While it may seem obvious that biological evidence in rape and murder cases (which often have no statute of limitations) should never be destroyed until the suspect has been identified and prosecuted, few laws require its preservation.

States are slowly beginning to address these issues. For example, in 2009, the Colorado legislature passed a law that requires the retention and preservation of DNA evidence in many circumstances. If DNA evidence is collected during the investigation of a felony, it must be preserved for either the length of the statute of limitations period (if no suspect has been identified) or the life of the defendant (if the investigation results in a guilty plea or conviction).[53] The preservation requirement does not apply to other types of evidence, however.

Part of the problem is that many departments do not have well-defined evidence retention policies, or if they do, technicians are not always adequately trained on them. Photos of large items such as tires or car parts could be taken and submitted as evidence instead of keeping the physical items indefinitely. In other cases, only the portion of the item containing relevant evidence need be preserved. For example, if an item such as a mattress has a blood stain on it, the technician could cut out the area of the stain and throw away or give back the remainder of the mattress.

Another issue is that law enforcement departments are often under pressure to free up space in cramped and overcrowded evidence rooms. One survey of police departments nationwide estimated that 70 percent of departments face "highly critical" storage problems.[54] While increasing the amount of space allocated to evidence storage would help alleviate the problem, there is often a lack of funding to improve storage conditions. Even where money for extra space is provided, the collection of evidence quickly outpaces its destruction, and the cycle continues.

One way that many police departments are trying to alleviate the problem of lost evidence is the use of barcode technology. Computer software helps the department track evidence and print hard copies of electronic records for court. Each piece of evidence is assigned a barcode, given a location in the evidence room, and entered into a computer system when it is initially checked in. The barcode is scanned each time a piece of evidence is checked out. When evidence is checked out for court, a chain of custody sheet is generated by the computer that

Trashing the Truth

The importance of properly storing evidence in connection with maintaining the chain of custody cannot be overstated. If evidence is not properly stored or worse yet is destroyed, criminal cases can be crippled or dismissed altogether. In 2007, the *Denver Post* ran an investigative reporting series entitled *Trashing the Truth*, detailing the many errors and problems that plague police department evidence vaults across the country.

One of the problems uncovered by the expose is that evidence is often purged from evidence rooms without any guidelines. The authors examined evidence purges in 10 states and found that authorities had destroyed biological evidence in nearly 6,000 rape and murder cases over the past decade.[42] In 2004 and 2005, the Colorado Springs Police Department tossed more than 5,000 pieces of evidence from its evidence lockers. The purge was instituted to reduce the nearly half a million pieces of evidence in storage at the time. The department had given the task to interns with little guidance or standards for what to throw out. Unfortunately, the interns disposed of evidence in ongoing murder and sexual assault investigations as well as discarding old and unneeded evidence.[43]

Sometimes the evidence is destroyed before it even reaches law enforcement. In 2006, a New Mexico hospital threw out biological evidence from a rape kit (in violation of its own policy) before it could be turned over to investigators. Charges against the three suspects were dropped.[44] But no state laws were violated since preservation of biological evidence at the outset of an investigation is not required under New Mexico law. This example is not an isolated incident. The authors discovered 5,515 rape kits had been lost or destroyed across the United States in the past decade.[45]

Such mishaps can have drastic consequences. Prisoners who allege that they were wrongfully convicted often rely on DNA testing of biological evidence to prove their innocence. The *Denver Post* identified 141 such cases nationwide where biological evidence has been lost or destroyed, thus depriving prisoners of their best hope.[46] Lawyers for Floyd Brown, a mentally retarded man in North Carolina, had hoped biological evidence on a blood-stained stick would prove his innocence. He remains in a state mental hospital based solely on his questionable confession since the stick has disappeared from the evidence vault.

Another issue is that some evidence rooms are not weather sealed and/or use inadequate technology. When Hurricane Katrina ravaged the City of New Orleans, the evidence locker of the Orleans Parish Police Department (OPPD) was flooded. Prosecutors had to dismiss approximately half of the 6,000 pending cases because the flood waters destroyed and/or contaminated evidence in those cases.[47] Boxes of evidence had to be stored in the men's bathroom in the courthouse since the OPPD had run out of storage space for evidence. In Oklahoma City, the freezer in the evidence room malfunctioned in 2000, tainting biological specimens in nearly 1,100 cases.

In 2004, the Houston Police Department revealed that evidence from 8,000 cases had been improperly stored. As a result, evidence in at least 33 cases had been inadvertently destroyed. An independent audit of the Houston Crime Lab, which was concluded in 2007, also revealed that 19 guns were discovered missing from the property room, and two of those were later found in possession of arrestees.[48] Another issue identified by the auditors was the fact that retrieval of evidence was often made difficult due to the antiquated tracking system that was overreliant on the memory of the property clerk. The auditors made several recommendations for the proper storage and retrieval of evidence, including the following:

- Developing a new laboratory information management system for tracking the location and status of evidence
- Monitoring workflow in each section of the lab
- Updating the barcode tracking system used to catalogue evidence
- Requiring evidence be submitted to one central location[49]

Even after the running of this series, problems with evidence rooms have continued to come to light. In 2009, it was discovered that over $200,000 in cash went missing from the New Orleans evidence room after it was moved to a temporary trailer after Katrina. The money was stolen from the files of four or five cases where large amounts of cash were seized. Part of the problem was that too many keys were issued for the temporary building and little or no security was put in place.[50]

In San Francisco, an April 2010 report revealed that the evidence room was almost filled to capacity with 600 bicycles, numerous baseball bats, and thousands of other items. Evidence from cases as old as the 1940s still remained in the evidence room. One news report even uncovered feral cats running wild in the room. They were later trapped and removed.[51] These revelations came on the heels of a scandal involving San Francisco crime lab employee Deborah Madden, who admitted to taking samples of cocaine on several occasions from cases she had been working on.[52]

shows when the evidence was logged in or out, who checked the item in or out, and where it was stored. Thus, chain of custody can easily be verified.[55] While barcode-tracking systems have been around for a number of years, many departments still have not adopted them, often lacking the funds to do so.

VI. CONTAMINATION OF EVIDENCE

We often give an air of infallibility to the analysis of physical evidence found at crime scenes. People tend to think of science as neutral and unbiased and that it is not subject to the same human element as other types of evidence. Unfortunately, this is not always the case. Because humans are responsible for testing evidence and interpreting the results, mistakes can be made.

For example, in August 2008, the City of Baltimore discovered that its analysts were contaminating DNA samples with their own DNA. DNA of lab analysts was discovered in about a dozen samples. The problem came to light when a new DNA supervisor began comparing DNA profiles of lab workers with those from crime scene samples. Unlike most labs, the Baltimore lab had not previously kept DNA profiles of its own analysts on file, which prevented the problem from being detected sooner. Luckily, no suspects were falsely identified as a result of the contamination. The city fired its lab director due to the negative publicity surrounding the story, however.[56]

VII. *CSI* EFFECT

The role of the crime scene investigator and forensic science in solving criminal cases was relatively unknown prior to 2000, when CBS premiered the show *CSI* (Crime Scene Investigation). Seemingly overnight, the importance of physical evidence and forensic science became part of the public consciousness. Unfortunately, it may have helped raise awareness of these issues too much. A phenomenon dubbed the *CSI* effect began cropping up in courtrooms across the country. Jurors began expecting that physical evidence would be collected and tested in all kinds of cases, even where it would not ordinarily have been much use. And, in some cases, jurors were under the mistaken belief that science is infallible and always capable of getting its man.

For example, a jury in Phoenix noticed that a bloody coat entered into evidence had not been tested for DNA and alerted the judge to that fact. However, since the defendant admitted he was present at the murder scene, such tests were not necessary to prove that fact. In another case in Virginia, jurors asked whether a cigarette butt found at the scene could be tested for DNA. In fact, it was tested, but those test results had yet to be presented.[57]

These anecdotal reports led to further study of the problem. In 2008, a National Institute of Justice study surveyed over 1,000 prospective jurors prior to their participation in the trial process. It found that 46 percent of people questioned expected some sort of physical or scientific evidence to be presented in every criminal case. However, the study's authors found that jurors linked their expectations to certain types of evidence and crimes. For example, respondents expected DNA evidence to be presented in serious cases such as murder and rape but assumed fingerprint evidence would be presented in burglary cases. The study also found that while respondents did not demand to see scientific evidence as a prerequisite before convicting a defendant, *CSI* watchers were more likely to acquit a rape defendant without DNA evidence.[58]

Prosecutors and defense attorneys have begun fighting back. They routinely call experts to testify that DNA and other trace evidence are not found at every scene and to educate juries about how science works in the real world. Prospective jurors are also questioned about their television viewing habits and whether they watch shows such as *Law and Order* and *CSI*.[59] While jurors' increased interest in forensic science can be a good thing, both sides have to be aware of the potential pitfalls and educate the jurors accordingly.

CHAPTER SUMMARY

The detection, collection, and analysis of physical evidence play an important role in the criminal justice process. Proper procedures need to be followed at each step of the process, and if they are not, evidence could be compromised, lost, or even ruled inadmissible. First, investigators must properly document the crime scene. This is done through note taking, photography, measurements, and sketching. The next step is to locate physical evidence. The crime scene must be searched in a systematic fashion. Officers can use any number of search patterns to search a crime scene, including spiral, grid, zone, and lane searches. The scene should also be searched in stages to prevent destruction or loss of evidence. Once evidence is located, it must be collected and preserved in the proper manner. Investigators must be careful to place evidence in the proper type of container and to fully label and seal the container.

The chain of custody must also be established for evidence. This is done by tracking who had possession and control over the evidence at given points of the process and documenting that the evidence is in substantially the same condition as when it was collected. The purpose of establishing chain of custody is to show that evidence was not altered or tampered with since it was collected. While minor gaps or missing links are permitted in the chain of custody, there cannot be large gaps such that it is impossible to tell who received the evidence or where it was stored for long periods of time.

Evidence must be properly stored. Biological evidence should be refrigerated or frozen to prevent degradation. Evidence rooms should systematically catalog and track evidence so it can easily be found and monitored. Better procedures and standards need to be put in place for determining what evidence should be kept and when it can be destroyed or auctioned off. Currently, evidence rooms are overflowing and are at or near capacity.

Popular television shows such as *CSI* have spawned a phenomenon known as the *CSI* effect. Jurors may now have unrealistic expectations of the ability of forensic science to solve crime. Some jurors believe that physical evidence can be found at every crime scene and should be tested regardless of its importance. Prosecutors have to be careful to properly educate jurors about the role forensic science will or will not play in the case.

KEY TERMS

- Alternate light source
- Baseline
- Chain of custody
- Crime scene photographs
- *CSI* effect
- Formal diagram

- Grid search
- Latent fingerprint
- Parallel or lane search
- Plastic fingerprint
- Rectangular coordinates
- Rough sketch

- Scene assessment
- Searching in stages
- Spiral search pattern
- Triangulation
- Visible fingerprint
- Zone search

REVIEW QUESTIONS

1. What are four ways that a crime scene can be documented?

2. At a minimum, what are the three types of photographs that should be taken of each piece of evidence at a crime scene?

3. What are two reasons investigators should take notes at the crime scene?

4. What are the four types of search patterns that investigators can use to search a crime scene?

5. What does it mean to search a crime scene in stages? Describe how the three stages differ from one another when a crime scene is searched in stages.

6. In what type of packaging should biological evidence be placed? What happens if this type of evidence is placed in plastic?

7. How should a firearm be packaged for evidence preservation?

8. What are four things that should go on an evidence label?

9. What is the chain of custody? How is it established by the prosecutor?

10. What are the three types of fingerprints that can be found at a crime scene?

11. What are the differences between the three types of fingerprints?

12. What are two issues that face most departments in maintaining evidence or property rooms?

13. What are two suggestions you would make to help solve the issues facing departments regarding maintenance of their evidence property rooms?

14. What is the *CSI* effect? Do you think it has changed the way that jurors view criminal trials and the types of evidence that they expect to be presented?

APPLICATION PROBLEMS

1. Officer Krupke is called to a house with a bad odor coming from it. Inside, he finds a body on the floor. There is a blood pool next to the body and some drops leading away from it. The body has several apparent stab wounds. A bloody coat is found at the scene as well. Another officer finds a bloody knife in a bush a couple of blocks from the crime scene. Describe how the officers should collect each piece of evidence and how it should be labeled.

2. Detective Spade collects several pieces of evidence at the scene of a suspected sexual assault. He collects hairs and fibers from the bed sheets. A sexual assault kit is taken from the victim that contains vaginal swabs and hair samples. He takes it to the police department and gives the evidence to the property custodian. The custodian checks in the evidence. He puts the rape kit in a box with the other evidence and sits it on top of a bookshelf. It sits there for two months until the crime lab checks it out for analysis. The lab brings back the evidence four days later. The property room clerk forgets to sign for it. The prosecutor then tries to admit the evidence at trial. Will he be able to establish the chain of custody? Explain.

3. Detective McClain is called to the scene of a murder. A woman lies in her bed with a gunshot wound to the head. A man in found dead in the living room. He also has a gunshot wound. A .38 semiautomatic pistol lies beside him. Describe how Detective McClain should photograph this

crime scene and what sequence of photos he should take.

4. Detective Briscoe responds to a homicide scene. A body is found in a field. After conducting a walk through, Briscoe notes a couple of items of evidence. He notices some drag marks leading from the body to the road. He also sees some blood drops at the roadway. What type of search pattern should Briscoe use to search the scene? How should he take measurements of the scene and the evidence? Should he use a baseline or the triangulation method to take measurements?

5. Calleigh and Erik retrieve a gun from a lake where a body is found. The gun appears to have been in the water for about two weeks. They place the weapon in a bucket of lake water to prevent it from rusting. Back at the lab, the weapon is signed into evidence. The weapon is test fired. The firearms examiner compares the test bullet to one retrieved from the body. Due to the degradation the weapon suffered, the analyst can only state that the bullet probably came from the weapon retrieved from the water. The defense challenges the chain of custody on the ground that the condition of the weapon could not be accounted for while it was in the water for two weeks. Was the chain of custody properly preserved? Explain.

Notes

1. Vernon J. Geberth, *Practical Homicide Investigation*, Chapter 1 at 20-21 (4th ed., CRC Press 2006).
2. Julia Layton, *How Crime Scene Investigation Works, How Stuff Works* (December 2, 2005), available at http://science.howstuffworks.com/csi3.htm.
3. Id.
4. Greg Dagnan, *Searching in Stages to Prevent Destruction of Evidence at Crime Scenes* (March 17, 2007), available at http://www.crime-scene-investigator.net/SearchingStages.html.
5. Geberth, supra note 1, Chapter 5, at 108-109.
6. *Crime Scene Investigation: A Guide for Law Enforcement* at 17, United States Department of Justice (January 2000), available at http://www.ncjrs.gov/pdffiles1/nij/178280.pdf.
7. Id. at 18.
8. Royal Canadian Mounted Police Learning Center, *Crime Scene Photography* (August 7, 1997), available at http://www.rcmp-learning.org/docs/ecdd1004.htm.
9. Steven Staggs, *Crime Scene and Evidence Photography* (2d ed., Staggs Publishing 2005).
10. Daniel Winterich, *Documenting Bloodstain Patterns through Roadmapping*, Forensic Magazine (October/November 2009) at 19.
11. A video of panoramic crime scene photography can be seen at the Panoscan Web site, available at http://panoscan.com/DemoVideo.html.
12. Dough Schiff, *Who Says You Can't Do That? Crime Scene 3D Viewpoints Illustrating What Was Seen at the Scene*, Forensic Magazine (2007), available at http://www.forensicmag.com/articles.asp?pid=154.
13. Geberth, *supra* note 1, Chapter 7, at 160.
14. Id. at 165.
15. *Evidence Collection Guidelines*, adapted from the California Commission on Peace Officer Standards and Training's Workbook for the "Forensic Technology for Law Enforcement" Telecourse presented on May 13, 1993, available at http://www.crime-scene-investigator.net/collect.html.
16. Id.
17. Michael R. Bromwich, *Final Report of the Independent Investigator for the Houston P.D. Crime Lab. and Property Room*, at 25 (June 13, 2007), available at http://www.hpdlabinvestigation.org.
18. Crime Scene Investigator Network, *Evidence Collection Guidelines*, available at http://www.crime-scene-investigator.net/collect.html.
19. *Strengthening Forensic Science in the United States: A Path Forward*, A Report of the National Academy of Sciences, 2009 at 150-5, available at http://www.nap.edu/catalog/12589.html.
20. Id.
21. *Evidence Collection Guidelines, supra* note 15.
22. Id.
23. *Colorado Bureau of Investigation Forensic Laboratory Physical Evidence Handbook*, v. 5.1 at V-2 (August 2007).
24. *CBI Physical Evidence Handbook*, at V-6.
25. Id. at V-7-8.
26. Birge v. State, 973 So.2d 1085 (Ala. Crim. App. 2007).
27. Imwinklereid, *The Identification of Original, Real Evidence*, 61 Mil. L. Rev. 145, 159 (1973).
28. Ex Parte Jones, 592 So. 2d 210 (Ala. 1991).
29. Jones, 592 So.2d at 212.
30. People v. Resketo, 279 N.E.2d 432 (Ill. App. 1972).
31. State v. Burnett, 538 S.W.2d 950 (Mo. App. 1976).
32. People v. Irpino, 461 N.E. 2d 999 (Ill. App. 1984).
33. Irpino, 461 N.E.2d at 1005.
34. Id. at 1006.
35. Hale v. State, 848 So.2d 224, 229 (Ala. 2002), quoting Ex Parte Holton, 590 So. 2d 918, 920 (Ala. 1991).
36. Irpino, *supra* note 32 at 1003-04.

37. Mark Fainaru-Wada, Lester Munson, and T.J. Quinn, *Judge's Call on Bonds Document is Key*, ESPN.com (February 4, 2009), available at http://sports.espn.go.com/espn/print?id=3885121&type=story.

38. Lance Pugmire, *Victor Conte's long-ago decision to save money imperils case against Barry Bonds*, Los Angeles Times (February 27, 2009), available at http://articles.latimes.com/2009/feb/27/sports/sp-barry-bonds27.

39. A.J. Perez, *Excluding Drug Test Results Key to Bonds Legal Strategy*, USA Today (February 4, 2009), available at http://www.usatoday.com/sports/baseball/2009-02-04-Bondsside_N.htm.

40. Nathaniel Vinton, *Judge Throws Out Evidence of Barry Bonds' Positive Drug Tests*, New York Daily News (February 20, 2009), available at http://www.nydailynews.com/sports/baseball/2009/02/19/2009-02-19_judge_throws_out_evidence_of_barry_bonds.html.

41. Maura Doland & Jack Leonard, Barry Bonds Convicted of Obstruction of Justice in Steroid Scandal, *Denver Post* C-1, April 14, 2011, available at http://www.denverpost.com/sports/ci_17840605.

42. Miles Moffeit and Susan Greene, *Room for Error*, Denver Post (July 23, 2007), available at http://www.denverpost.com/evidence/ci_6439646.

43. Susan Greene, *Key Evidence Tossed in Colorado Springs*, Denver Post (July 24, 2007), available at http://www.denverpost.com/evidence/ci_6450576.

44. Miles Moffeit and Susan Greene, *Missing Rape Kits Foil Justice*, Denver Post (July 24, 2007), available at http://www.denverpost.com/evidence/ci_6446990.

45. Id.

46. Susan Greene and Miles Moffeit, *14 Years Later: Tell My Story*, Denver Post (July 25, 2007), available at http://www.denverpost.com/evidence/ci_6455487.

47. Moffeit and Greene, *Room for Error, supra* note 41.

48. Bromwich, *supra* note 17, at 25.

49. Id. at 26-27.

50. Laura Maggi, *$200,000 Missing from New Orleans Police Evidence Room*, New Orleans Times-Picayune (June 24, 2009), available at blog.nola.com/news_impact/print.html?entry=/2009/06/state_auditors_report_cites_pr.html.

51. Katie Worth, *Unclaimed Property Flooding SFPD Evidence Room*, San Francisco Examiner (April 10, 2010), available at www.printithis.clickability.com/pt/cpt?action=cpt&title=Unclaimed+property+flodding_SFPDevidence_room90330164.html

52. Katie Worth, *Interview With Lab Tech Details Alleged Drug Skimming* (April 13, 2010), available at www.printthis.clickability.com/pt/cpt?action=cpt&title=Interview+with+lab+tech+details_alleged_drug_skimming_90812694.html.

53. Colo. Rev. Stat. ß 18-1-1101, et seq.

54. Moffeit and Greene, *Room for Error, supra*.

55. *See* Barcodebook.com, available at http://www.barcodebook.com/solution.cfm?tbl=21&id=26.

56. Julie Bykowicz and Justin Fenton, *Director of City Police Crime Lab Fired*, Baltimore Sun (August 20, 2008), available at http://truthinjustice.org/baltimorepdlab.htm.

57. Richard Willing, CSI *Effect Has Juries Wanting More Evidence*, USA Today (August 5, 2004), available at http://www.usatoday.com/news/nation/2004-08-05-csi-effect_x.htm.

58. Donald E. Shelton, *Does the* CSI *Effect Really Exist?* 259 NIJ Journal (2008), available at http://www.ojp.usdoj.gov/nij/journals/259/csi-effect.htm.

59. Willing, *supra* note 56.

CHAPTER 3

Identification Evidence

"History is the study of lies, anyway, because no witness ever recalls events with total accuracy, not even eyewitnesses."—Nancy Pickard

Chapter Topics

Objectives

After completing this chapter, students will be able to:

- Distinguish between the various forms of pretrial identification procedures

- Understand what makes identification procedures suggestive and how to prevent bias from being introduced into the identification process

- Understand the factors the court will examine in determining the reliability of an identification

- List the factors that lead to misidentification of suspects

- Learn about the various reforms departments have undertaken to prevent suggestive lineups and misidentifications from occurring

Introduction

Eyewitness identification plays a significant role in the solving and prosecution of criminal cases. Juries rely on eyewitness identification perhaps more than any other factor in deciding the outcome of criminal cases. Witnesses are often asked in court to identify the defendant as the perpetrator of the crime, and testimony is frequently given about the witness's pretrial identification of the defendant in some form of lineup or other identification method. The presence of eyewitness identification evidence can have a dramatic impact on the outcome of a trial. One study showed that 72 percent of mock jurors would issue a guilty verdict with the admission of an eyewitness identification, as opposed to only 18 percent without one.[1] Other studies found that witnesses who were confident in their identification of a suspect swayed jurors to convict even where cross-examination pointed out significant flaws in the testimony.[2]

Memories of eyewitnesses are, unfortunately, not always accurate. Witnesses can give inaccurate descriptions or misidentify suspects in lineups. There are a number of reasons for this, including environmental factors, perception problems of the witness, and faults in human memory itself. These issues can be exacerbated by bias introduced into the identification process by police. Recent research indicates that the methods for conducting lineups and photo identifications used in many jurisdictions are inadequate to protect against eyewitness misidentifications. This chapter will discuss new recommendations for conducting lineups and photo identifications that departments should implement to protect against bias.

In this chapter, you will learn about the various types of lineup and identification procedures used by the police to identify suspects early on in a case. Officers must take care in conducting pretrial identification procedures because suggestive lineups can taint subsequent, in-court identifications. You will also learn the correct procedures for conducting these identification procedures. You will also learn the legal standards for admitting identification evidence at trial. This chapter will also discuss the new recommendations for performing identifications.

I. THE IDENTIFICATION PROCESS

A. Pretrial Identification Procedures

One of the key components of any case is establishing the identity of the perpetrator. To do so, the prosecutor often asks the witness or victim to identify the defendant in court as the person who committed the crime. The witness has also often made a pretrial identification of the suspect during a lineup or other identification procedure. If that pretrial lineup is tainted or suggestive, however, that may jeopardize the validity of the in-court identification.

There are three basic types of pretrial identifications: showups, photo arrays, and lineups. The **showup** is a brief one-on-one identification usually conducted at or near the crime scene. Typically, the witness or victim is briefly shown the person who matches the description of the suspect. The purpose is to quickly eliminate a person as a suspect and prevent a lengthy detention of an innocent person. This also prevents law enforcement from wasting time on questioning the wrong people while the trail is still fresh.[3]

A **photo array** involves a witness trying to pick out a suspect from a range of photographs of different individuals.[4] Traditionally, the witness was shown six to eight photographs on one card of persons matching the description of the suspect and asked if he or she recognized anyone. A witness might have even been asked to examine a mugshot book to see if he recognized anyone. Today, it is more common to show the witness individual photographs on a laptop or other device rather than a collection of shots simultaneously.

A **pretrial lineup** is what most people think of as a pretrial identification procedure. A lineup involves the witness trying to identify the suspect from five or six people either lined up in a row or shown sequentially to the witness.[5] Lineups should contain four to five **fillers**, other individuals who resemble the description of the suspect. In other words, the suspect should not "stick out like a sore thumb" in the lineup.

Showup
a one-on-one identification made at the crime scene or other location by the witness

Photo array
a series of photographs shown to a witness that are of persons similar in appearance to the described suspect

Pretrial lineup
a pretrial identification that involves showing the witness several individuals and asking if he or she recognizes anyone

Fillers
individuals used in a lineup who resemble the description of the suspect

B. Admissibility of Pretrial and In-Court Identifications

1. Suggestiveness of the Pretrial Lineup

Prior to the 1960s, pretrial identifications were not excluded from evidence even where law enforcement had clearly tipped off the witness as to which person to select from the lineup. Problems with identification procedures were dealt with strictly as credibility issues for the jury to determine. Starting with *Stovall v. Denno* in 1967, the Supreme Court held that the way pretrial lineup procedures were conducted could taint the witness's in-court identification and thus violate due process. In *Stovall*, the Court ruled that the witness's in-court identification of the defendant must be excluded from evidence where the pretrial procedure was "unnecessarily suggestive."[6] There, the Court found that the use of a showup identification in the victim's hospital room was necessary due to her critical condition at the time of the identification and the immediate need for action.[7] A year later in *Simmons v. United States*, the Court modified the standard somewhat, holding that an in-court identification was tainted by a pretrial identification if the pretrial procedure was "so impermissibly suggestive as to give rise to a very substantial likelihood of irreparable misidentification at trial."[8]

Impermissibly suggestive

a pretrial identification procedure violates due process if it is impermissibly suggestive. A suggestive procedure is one that indicates to the witness who the police have identified as the suspect

An identification procedure is **impermissibly suggestive** when the "police conduct it in such a way that the witness's attention is directed to a particular individual as the suspect upon whom the police have focused."[9] For example, a Washington, D.C. court found that it was suggestive to make a teenage boy stand on a box in a lineup with 13 other people who were all older and taller than he was. Such a procedure made the boy stand out since he was the only one in the lineup who approximated the witness's description of the suspect as a small, young male who looked 10 or 11 years old.[10] However, an identification from a lineup of a suspect who had a distinctive hairstyle is not necessarily suggestive.[11] The key is that lineup participants must not be so dissimilar in appearance or hairstyle as "to eliminate all participants except defendant."[12] In the same vein, the showing of mugshots of varying quality to a witness is not suggestive unless it is accompanied by verbal directions or markings that unfairly emphasize the suspect's photograph.[13] Similarly, a lineup identification is also not made suggestive simply due to the fact that the witness had identified the same suspect during a prior photographic lineup. In order to be suggestive, there must be some indication made to the witness that the same suspect he picked out of the photo array is in the current physical lineup.[14]

The only time the Supreme Court has found that an identification procedure violated due process, however, was in *Foster v. California*.[15] There, the witness was asked to identify the defendant in a showup at the police station, despite the fact he had failed to identify the suspect during a prior, suggestive lineup. After making only a tentative identification, the witness was again asked to identify the defendant in another lineup. The witness positively identified the defendant at the second lineup and again at trial. The court held that all of the identifications were inadmissible, concluding that they were "all but inevitable" under the circumstances.[16]

The Court applied a similar standard in assessing the suggestiveness of just the pretrial identification in *Neil v. Biggers*.[17] There, the defendant raped the victim at knifepoint after abducting her from her kitchen.

Over the next several months, the victim viewed between 30 and 40 photographs of suspects but identified no one as her rapist. Seven months later, the police called her to the police station to view a suspect who had been detained on another charge. Since he had an unusual physical description, they conducted a showup at the police station rather than a lineup. The Court held that the unfairness of a suggestive pretrial identification procedure depended on the likelihood of misidentification:

> It is, first of all, apparent that the primary evil to be avoided is "a very substantial likelihood of irreparable misidentification." While the phrase was coined as a standard for determining whether an in-court identification would be admissible in the wake of a suggestive out-of-court identification, with the deletion of "irreparable" it serves equally well as a standard for the admissibility of testimony concerning the out-of-court identification itself. It is the likelihood of misidentification which violates a defendant's right to due process, and it is this which was the basis of the exclusion of evidence in *Foster*. Suggestive confrontations are disapproved because they increase the likelihood of misidentification, and necessarily suggestive ones are condemned for the further reason that the increased chance of misidentification is gratuitous.[18]

The two tests set forth by the court can be summarized as follows: (1) an in-court identification may be excluded only if the pretrial identification procedure was so impermissibly suggestive that it created a very substantial likelihood of an irreparable misidentification at trial; and (2) a pretrial identification may be excluded only if the procedure was so impermissibly suggestive that it created a very substantial likelihood of misidentification.

Practical Example

Mary is suspected of being part of an extortion ring. One of the victims is willing to come forward to testify against the ring. She describes the female suspect as a short, fat blonde woman with a tattoo of a snake on her right arm. Mary is five feet one inch tall and weighs 200 pounds. She has blonde hair and has a tattoo of a dragon on her right forearm. She is placed in a lineup with five other women. All the women are five feet to five feet three inches tall. The largest woman is 160 pounds. No other woman has a tattoo. Mary is picked out of the lineup by the witness. The lineup is impermissibly suggestive. The fact that she is the only woman who weighs 200 pounds, coupled with the fact she is the only woman in the lineup with a tattoo, is impermissibly suggestive.

Eeny, Meeny, Miny Moe, Catch a Tiger by the Toe: The Suggestive Photo Array in the Duke Lacrosse Rape Case

The Duke lacrosse rape case grabbed national headlines in 2007 when the three indicted players were declared innocent of all charges and the District Attorney who had spearheaded the case against them, Mike Nifong, was disbarred. Besides violating basic discovery rules, Nifong also violated the North Carolina guidelines for the performance of eyewitness identifications when he helped design the key photo array in the case.

On March 30, 2006, Nifong was informed that DNA evidence from the rape kit performed on the alleged victim did not contain semen, saliva, or blood from any potential attacker. The following day, Nifong directed the police department to set up another photo identification procedure, despite the fact that the victim had failed to identify her attackers from two previous arrays. On March 16 and 21, 2006, the victim was shown photos of 36 of the 46 white lacrosse players in a series of arrays but only identified a handful of players who were at the party. She could not identify any of her attackers from the photos.[19]

Knowing that the victim's attackers had to be lacrosse players, Nifong instructed the Durham police to have the victim view photos of all 46 white lacrosse players (one player was black and was excluded). The photo lineup was conducted on April 4, 2006. This time the victim identified three players as her attackers. She stated that she was 100 percent sure that two of the players whose photos she recognized had participated in the rape and was 90 percent sure that David Evans was one of them, except that he had had a mustache at the time (in fact, he never had one).[20]

In 2003, the state adopted a set of best practices for the performance of eyewitness identifications. The Durham Police Department had adopted the guidelines just two months prior to conducting the photo array with the victim. In part, the state guidelines recommended that the arrays and lineups be conducted in a double-blind manner (the person conducting the array should not be aware of who the suspect is and the witness should be told that her attackers may or may not be in the lineup) and performed sequentially (the photos should be shown to the witness one at a time).[21]

Although North Carolina guidelines suggested lineups should be conducted by someone unfamiliar with the investigation, the lead investigator in the Duke case conducted the photo array. He instructed the victim that he wanted her to look at people "we had reason to believe attended the party." Filler photos of individuals who were not on the lacrosse team should have been included in the array but were not. Gary Wells, a member of the American Psychology and Law Society, commented, "There should have been people mixed in there who you knew clearly were not at the party, so that if the witness were to have picked one of then, you would know instantly that there's a credibility problem."[22] As a result, the victim could not help but select three lacrosse players as her attackers.

James Coleman, a University of North Carolina law professor who helped draft the state's eyewitness identification guidelines, commented that the design of this array did not comply with the guidelines and was fatally flawed:

> According to the police account of the identification, the police officer who presided over the proceedings told the alleged victim at the outset that he wanted her to look at people the police had reason to believe attended the party. Thus, the police not only failed to

Continued on following page

Evidence in Action continued

include people they knew were not suspects among the photographs shown the woman, they told the witness in effect that there would be no such fillers among the photographs she would see. This strongly suggests that the purpose of the identification process was to give the alleged victim an opportunity to pick three members of the lacrosse team who could be charged. Any three students would do; there could be no wrong choice.[23]

In other words, the photo array was clearly suggestive. As one commentator noted, "Telling most witnesses that the suspects are among the photos to be displayed would have the impact of encouraging identification and is therefore damaging to all those in the array. Giving this information to a questionable witness is a recipe for the disaster that occurred."[24] Thus, this commentator recommended that future courts allow the jury to hear expert testimony explaining the dangers of improper police procedures such as those employed in the Duke case.[25]

It should be noted that the mere failure to follow the state identification procedures would not have been fatal to the identification. At the time, failing to follow protocol was not a ground for suppressing the identification. Since then, North Carolina has amended the law to allow the court to consider noncompliance during a suppression hearing and allow the jury to consider it in determining the reliability of the identification.[26]

2. Reliability of the Identification

An impermissibly suggestive lineup or showup does not automatically make the identification inadmissible, however. The identification will be allowed if the prosecution can prove it was reliable despite the suggestive nature of the identification procedure.[27] In other words, once the defendant demonstrates that the pretrial identification was impermissibly suggestive, the burden shifts to the prosecution to demonstrate the identification was nonetheless reliable.[28] The Supreme Court developed five factors in **Biggers** for courts to examine in determining whether the suggestiveness of the identification procedure tainted the reliability of the witness's identification: (1) the opportunity of the witness to view the criminal at the time of the crime; (2) the witness's degree of attention at the time of the crime; (3) the accuracy of the witness's prior description of the criminal; (4) the level of certainty demonstrated at the time of the identification procedure; and (5) the lapse of time between the crime and the identification procedure.[29]

Biggers factors
factors developed by the Court to determine the reliability of an identification. They include: (1) the opportunity of the witness to view the criminal at the time of the crime; (2) the witness's degree of attention at the time of the crime; (3) the accuracy of the witness's prior description of the criminal; (4) the level of certainty demonstrated at the time of the identification procedure; and (5) the lapse of time between the crime and the identification procedure.

According to the Court, no one factor of the test is determinative. Courts should consider the "totality of the circumstances" in determining whether to admit the identification. For example, in *Biggers,* the Court upheld the admission of the pretrial identification despite its suggestive nature. The Court concluded that the showup at the police station was unnecessarily suggestive but found that the identification was reliable under the five-factor test described above. The victim testified that she had no doubt about her identification and stated that it had been light enough in the doorway to see her rapist's face the night of the rape.[30] The Court found it important that she had spent a considerable amount of time with the defendant, faced him directly, and provided a detailed and accurate description to police.[31]

The Supreme Court reiterated this balancing test in *Manson v. Brathwaite*.[32] In that case, an undercover officer identified the defendant as the person he had purchased heroin from by a single photo shown to him by a fellow officer. Although finding the identification procedure to be suggestive, the Court upheld its admission, concluding that "reliability is the linchpin in determining the admissibility of identification testimony."[33]

There is a growing body of research, however, that suggests a number of the *Biggers* factors for determining the reliability of an identification are not useful for this purpose.[34] Critics of these reliability factors point to the fact that three of the factors—view, attention, and certainty—are retrospective self-reports. In other words, these variables rely on the witness's interpretation of past events and are thus not very objective measures of the accuracy of the identification.[35] For example, studies show that witnesses grossly overestimate how long they had viewed the suspect and minimize the amount of time that their view was blocked.[36] In effect, these factors ask a witness to report on his or her own credibility. As Gary Wells noted, "it is a bit like assigning a student's grade based on his or her self-reports of how hard they studied."[37]

Another factor that can affect the accuracy of a witness's identification is the distance between the suspect and the witness. People with normal vision can perceive faces, with no loss of detail, up to 25 feet. Face perception diminishes past that point, and people cannot accurately identify human faces past 150 feet.[38] Research has also shown that the type of processing occurring while viewing a stimulus, such as a suspect's face, is much more important than the amount of time spent looking at it. Distractions such as the presence of a weapon can also reduce the ability to recognize a face later on. The weapon draws the attention of the person, pulling it away from the suspect's face.[39]

These researchers argue that the chief flaw in the Supreme Court's reasoning is that it assumes the witness retains a true memory of the event despite the suggestiveness of the procedure. According to the Court, this "true" memory may then be "independently sufficient" to reliably identify the proper suspect.[40] The unfortunate reality is that once a witness has mistakenly identified someone, that person "becomes the witness' memory," and that error will continue to repeat itself during subsequent identifications.[41] Moreover, suggestive lineup procedures can actually alter a witness's perception or memory of these facts. Simple comments such as "Good, you identified the suspect" can cause witnesses to develop a false level of certainty in their identification and overestimate how good a view they had of the suspect.[42] In one study, only 15 percent of witnesses who mistakenly identified the suspect in a lineup stated that they were "positive" or "nearly positive" about their identifications. However, if the witnesses received a confirmatory remark from the lineup administrator, that figure jumped to 50 percent.[43] Such results suggest that a court would need to know what was said to the witness during the identification procedure before ruling on the reliability of the identification. Because a witness can be influenced by the suggestive nature of the procedure itself, "a court cannot know exactly how reliable the identification would have been without the suggestiveness."[44] Thus, it would appear that the first and third *Biggers* factors (the opportunity of the witness to view the suspect and his level of certainty in the identification) are not independent of the suggestive identification procedure but are actually a byproduct of it.[45]

Furthermore, weighing the impact of the fourth *Biggers* factor, the accuracy of the witness's pre-lineup description, can be something of an exercise in circular logic. In order for the accuracy of the original description to be predictive of the reliability of the identification, one must assume that the original description was accurate and that the composition of the lineup was not influenced by that description. As one Alaska court pointed out, "one cannot know whether a witness' description of the perpetrator is 'accurate' unless one knows who the perpetrator is."[46]

As a result of such flaws, that court came to the realization that the *Biggers* factors may be "inadequate to the task of sorting reliable identifications from unreliable identifications."[47] Other state courts have come to similar conclusions. For example, New York, Massachusetts, and Wisconsin have abandoned the reliability test altogether and base the admissibility of a pretrial identification simply on its degree of suggestiveness.[48] Wisconsin will not admit a showup identification unless the prosecution can prove its use was necessary. A showup is not necessary unless the police lacked probable cause to make an arrest or could not have conducted a photo array or lineup due to exigent circumstances.[49]

Utah and Kansas have adopted a modified version of the *Biggers* test. These courts look at the following factors in determining the reliability of an eyewitness identification: 1) the opportunity of the witness to view the actor during the event; 2) the witness's degree of attention to the actor at the time of the event; 3) the witness's capacity to observe the event, including his or her physical and mental acuity; 4) whether the witness's identification was made spontaneously and remained consistent thereafter, or whether it was the product of suggestion; and 5) the nature of the event being observed and the likelihood that the witness would perceive, remember, and relate it correctly.[50]

Practical Example

Assume two men rob a bus driver at gunpoint. The robbery lasts a couple of minutes, during which time the driver is face to face with his assailants. The driver identifies one of the robbers from a mugshot. The driver then identifies the same man in a lineup. He is positive about his identification. The suspect has a scar on his forehead and a tooth that is filed down. No other participants in the lineup have these characteristics. Although the lineup is somewhat suggestive, the court will likely find the identification to be reliable since the witness had a good look at the suspect, identified the robber from his mugshot first, and was positive in his identification.

C. Right to Counsel

Prior to being charged with a crime, a suspect has no right to counsel being present at a lineup. Once the suspect is formally charged, however, the Sixth Amendment gives the suspect the right to have counsel present at all "critical stages" of the criminal justice process, including a post-indictment lineup.[51] Over the years, the Supreme Court has given various definitions of a **critical stage**, including those:

Critical stage
a segment of the criminal justice process in which significant adverse consequences can result, or where there is a reasonable likelihood of prejudice to the defendant from the absence of counsel.

(1) That present a moment when "[a]vailable defenses may be irretrievably lost, if not then and there asserted";

(2) "where rights are preserved or lost";

(3) that are "necessary to mount a meaningful defense";

(4) where "potential substantial prejudice" to the defendant's rights is inherent in the proceeding and where counsel has the ability to help the defendant avoid that prejudice; and

(5) that hold "significant consequences for the accused."[52]

The Sixth Circuit Court of Appeals consolidated these various tests into one workable definition: "In order to assess if a given portion of a criminal proceeding is a critical stage, we must ask how likely it is that significant consequences might have resulted from the absence of counsel at the stage of the criminal proceeding."[53] The defendant does not have to show that he suffered actual prejudice due to the absence of his counsel; it is sufficient that there is a "reasonable likelihood" that prejudice will result from counsel being absent from that stage of the proceeding.[54] The Supreme Court has held that most proceedings in the criminal justice process are critical stages. For example, it has held that arraignment hearings, preliminary hearings, and sentencing hearings are all critical stages.[55] Lower courts have found that plea negotiations and disposition hearings are also critical stages.[56] The Supreme Court has refused to extend critical stage designation, however, to pre-indictment lineups or post-indictment photo arrays.[57]

Practical Example

Hunter is a suspect in a robbery of a jewelry store. The store clerk describes the person who robbed the store as a tall, pudgy man in his forties or fifties. Hunter matches the description of the robbery suspect. He was recently paroled after serving time for committing a series of jewel heists. The police ask the clerk if she can identify anyone in the lineup as the robber. Hunter is included in the lineup. The clerk identifies Hunter as the robber and he is charged with robbery and theft. Did Hunter have a right to have his counsel present during the lineup? No. Since the lineup occurred before Hunter was charged with a crime, he did not have the right to counsel.

II. EYEWITNESS MISIDENTIFICATION

A. Factors That Contribute to Eyewitness Misidentification

Despite the fact that eyewitness identification is highly persuasive, mounting evidence suggests that it is also significantly flawed. Eyewitness misidentification of the defendant as the perpetrator is the number one reason given to explain wrongful convictions. In a 1987 study of 500 wrongful convictions, 60 percent were estimated to involve incidents of eyewitness misidentification.[58] Another study of DNA exonerations of wrongfully convicted persons estimated that eyewitness misidentification was a factor in 75 percent of those cases.[59]

Estimator variables
conditions affecting the witness's perception.

Memory variables
the witness's ability to recall and recognize faces.

Systemic variables
errors or biases injected into the process consciously or subconsciously by the police.

Research has shown that three basic types of errors lead to misidentifications—**estimator variables** (conditions affecting the witness's perception), **memory variables** (the witness's ability to recall and recognize faces), and **systemic variables** (errors or biases injected into the process consciously or subconsciously by the police). Estimator variables focus on the environmental conditions that can affect the quality of a person's perception of the suspect, such as lighting conditions, distance, and view of the suspect. The witness may also have physical limitations, such as poor eyesight, which can affect the accuracy of the description.

Second, human memories are often not permanent, and our brains are far from perfect recorders.[60] Memories are formed when neurons link together to form new connections in the brain. The area in our brains where memories are stored is constantly being altered and reordered. As a result, when a person recalls an event, he must reconstruct the memory, and each time he does so, the memory can be changed. As a result, one noted memory scholar commented: "Truth and reality, when seen through the filter of our memories, are not objective facts but subjective, interpretive realities."[61]

There are several explanations for this phenomenon. Memories are like low-resolution digital files compared to the original image. Remembered faces are not as clear as what people actually first observe. Memories also tend to fade over time. Second, people tend to reconstruct memories to fill in missing information, and that missing data can be supplied from faulty sources. Third, people's perceptions can distort reality (remembered colors can be brighter or darker or sizes can grow or shrink).[62]

Because law enforcement can do very little to affect the first two variables, it is important that officers limit errors produced by systemic variables and conduct identification procedures in as unbiased a manner as possible. Bias can be injected into the identification process in a number of ways. For example, the investigator can poorly choose fillers in lineups and arrays. The suspect should not stand out from the others, and each should have similar physical characteristics and dress. An Alaska case from the 1980s provides an example of a particularly biased lineup where the suspect, who was described as wearing a red baseball cap, was the only person in the lineup wearing a baseball cap.[63]

Poor communication between law enforcement personnel and the witness is another error that can occur. If the investigator fails to tell the witness that the suspect may not be in the lineup or array, the witness may feel compelled to pick someone even though the real suspect is not there. Where the witness is not told of this possibility, he is much more likely to make a false positive identification.[64] As Loftus and Ketcham point out:

> Although witnesses try hard to identify the true criminal, when they are uncertain—or when no one person in the lineup exactly matches their memory—they will often identify the person who best matches their recollection of the criminal. And often their choice is wrong.[65]

A third systemic error is caused by having an investigator who knows who the suspect is conduct the lineup or array. If he knows who the suspect is, the investigator may consciously or subconsciously tip off the witness as to the "correct" choice.[66] The investigator may also influence the witness's degree of confidence in the identification by confirming that the witness identified the suspect.[67]

Next, studies have shown that where photos of potential suspects are compared simultaneously (like in a six-person photo array), it is more likely for the witness to misidentify an innocent person as the suspect than if the photos are shown sequentially. Studies also show that if a photograph of the real perpetrator is not included with the photographs shown to the witness, he or she is much more likely to pick out an incorrect suspect when the photos are shown simultaneously than if they are shown separately from one another.[68]

Compounding the problems inherent in the identification process is the fact that cross-examination is not a very effective tool at detecting witnesses who are trying to be truthful but are genuinely mistaken.[69] Because the witness is not intentionally lying, he usually remains confident in his identification even though holes are being poked in his story during cross-examination.

B. The Use of Expert Testimony on Eyewitness Misidentification

As a result of the errors outlined above, defense attorneys may attempt to introduce expert testimony attacking the reliability of eyewitness identifications. Courts have examined this issue on a case-by-case basis but have largely rejected the admission of such testimony.[70] Expert testimony is more likely to be admitted, however, where the eyewitness testimony plays a particularly important role in the case (such as the where the prosecution's case is based solely on eyewitness testimony).[71]

Many courts have been reluctant to admit testimony from psychological experts, concluding that jurors can intelligently understand the limitations of eyewitness identification without it. As one court put it, "grasping and weighing the effects of lighting, lack of attention, and post-event information" are not the kinds of things jurors would be unqualified or unable to determine without the aid of expert testimony.[72] Of course, while this type of information is probably within the ready understanding of most people, this comment ignores the fact that errors associated with human memory or the lineup procedure itself are not. The Utah Supreme Court recognized the need for expert testimony in this regard:

> Although research has convincingly demonstrated the weakness inherent in eyewitness identification, jurors are, for the most part, unaware of these problems. People simply do not accurately understand the deleterious effects that certain variables can have on the accuracy of the memory processes of an honest eyewitness. Moreover, the common knowledge that people do possess often runs contrary to documented research findings.[73]

Publicity surrounding cases like Ronald Cotton's described below are making it abundantly clear that eyewitness testimony is susceptible to error. As more wrongful convictions are brought to light, judges' attitudes toward the need for expert testimony will hopefully change as well.

Picking Cotton: Jennifer Thompson's Misidentification Sends Ronald Cotton to Prison for a Rape He Didn't Commit

In 1984, Jennifer Thompson, a 22-year-old college student, and Ronald Cotton crossed paths in a way that they would never wish upon anyone. On July 28, 1984, a black man broke into Thompson's apartment, put a knife to her throat, and raped her. Despite the terrifying ordeal, Thompson kept her wits about her enough to study his face. She tricked her attacker into letting her make a drink for him, and she escaped out the back door. She vowed to track down her rapist.

Three days later, Cotton was identified as a suspect since he worked at a restaurant near Thompson's apartment and had a prior conviction for sexual assault. Thompson was asked to view a photo array at the police station. She picked Cotton's photo out of the array after studying the photos for about five minutes.[74] Thompson also picked Cotton out of a physical lineup and later identified him as her assailant at his 1985 trial. Thompson recalled, "I was absolutely, positively, without a doubt certain he was the man who raped me when I got on that witness stand and testified against him. And nobody was going to tell me any different."[75] When Cotton was sentenced to life in prison, Thompson celebrated her victory with champagne.

Her celebration was premature, however. Cotton was not the man who raped her. As it turned out, another man who looked like Cotton, Bobby Poole, had actually committed the rape. Coincidentally, Poole was imprisoned about a year later for committing a series of rapes. Both Poole and Cotton worked together in the prison kitchen, and Cotton couldn't help but notice the resemblance. Poole also

bragged to other prisoners that Cotton was doing some of his time for Thompson's rape. As a result of this newly discovered evidence, Cotton was awarded a new trial. The appeals court also ruled that evidence of another rape committed an hour later should have been presented at Cotton's trial. Unbelievably, however, Thompson still identified Cotton as her attacker, despite the fact that Poole was sitting in the courtroom during the second trial. The other rape victim also identified Cotton as her attacker. Cotton was convicted again.

What had gone so wrong? Human memory has several flaws, including the inaccuracy of cross-racial identifications. There were also numerous errors in the identification process that had tainted the process, leading to the misidentification of Cotton. First, Thompson was not informed when the photo array was conducted that her rapist's photo may not have been in the array. Second, after the lineup was conducted, Thompson was told she had picked the same man that she had previously selected out of the photographs.[76] Eventually, Thompson became so convinced Cotton was her attacker that she saw his face in her dreams about the attack. She couldn't help but pick Cotton out as her attacker in the courtroom.

But all hope was not lost. DNA would provide the evidence that would eventually free Cotton. Years later, Cotton successfully argued that his DNA should be compared to the physical evidence collected from both rape scenes. The test results confirmed what Cotton knew already—he was innocent and Poole was the rapist. Cotton was set free on June 30, 1995, after serving 10 years in prison for rapes he didn't commit.

Thompson was stunned when she heard the news. Later, she lamented, "Ronald Cotton and I are the same age, so I knew what he had missed during those 11 years. My life had gone on. I had

Continued on following page

Evidence in Action continued

gotten married. I had graduated from college. I worked. I was a parent. Ronald Cotton hadn't gotten to do any of that."[77] Determined to apologize for the mistake, Thompson eventually developed the courage to meet the man she had wrongfully imprisoned. When the two met, she said, "I'm sorry. If I spend every day for the rest of my life telling you how sorry I am, it wouldn't come close to what I feel." Cotton replied, "I'm not mad at you. I've never been mad at you. I just want you to have a good life." The pair talked for hours and came to the conclusion that they had both been the victims of Bobby Poole.

The story didn't end there. The pair became friends and worked together to reform the way identifications are conducted in the state of North Carolina. The two coauthored a book, *Picking Cotton*, to tell their story.[78] Thompson also helped Cotton lobby for more money for compensation of the wrongfully imprisoned. At the time, North Carolina only offered $500 per year to compensate the wrongfully imprisoned. Today, that amount has been raised to $20,000 per year.

III. PROTOCOLS FOR CONDUCTING UNBIASED PRETRIAL IDENTIFICATIONS

Based on his landmark research into eyewitness identification, Professor Gary Wells and others have recommended several rules for how lineups and photo identifications should be conducted. Care should be taken in all stages of the pretrial identification process to avoid contaminating any resulting identification. At the outset, the investigator should obtain as accurate a description of the suspect as possible. This is important so that the lineup or photo array contains filler subjects who closely resemble the actual perpetrator.

Next, the investigator should avoid any suggestive comments prior to the identification process. Investigators should never tell the witness that the person who committed the crime has been caught, that the victim's property was in the suspect's possession, that the suspect made admissions, or that the person in the lineup or photo array is a suspect. Instead, investigators should tell the witness that he should keep an open mind during the identification process and that the person who committed the crime may or may not be among those present in the lineup or array.[79] Also, no more than one witness should be allowed to participate in the procedure at the same time. Witnesses should not be allowed to discuss with each other the identification procedure or potential suspects prior to the identification.

Suggestiveness should also be avoided during the identification procedure. First, only one suspect should be included in each lineup or array. Second, the suspect should not stand out from the fillers used in the lineup or array. The lineup or photo array should be conducted using people of similar appearance. According to Wells, the other individuals in the lineup or photo spread should be chosen to match the description given by the eyewitness but not necessarily be selected so as to look like the suspect. When the eyewitness's description of the perpetrator does not fit the physical characteristics of the suspect, Wells recommends that such filler individuals be selected on the basis of both the description of the eyewitness and the physical characteristics of the suspect. For example, if the suspect is five feet seven inches tall, the lineup should not be filled with people who are all taller than six feet. Similarly, if the suspect has a distinguishing characteristic such as a scar or tattoo, all suspects should have such characteristics where possible.

Next, the person who conducts the lineup or photo array should not be aware of which person in the lineup or array is the suspect. In other words, the person conducting the identification procedure should not be the same person as the one conducting the investigation. This is known as double-blind testing. The witness should be told that the potential suspect may or may not be in the lineup or photo spread so that he does not feel compelled to make an identification. The witness should also be told that the person administering the lineup does not know which person is the suspect in the case.

Wells also recommends that a lineup or photo array should be performed sequentially rather than simultaneously. The investigator should also avoid making any comments or using body language during the identification procedure that would steer or guide the witness to identify the suspect.

Investigators should be careful not to contaminate any future identification by making comments after the identification procedure is concluded. For example, investigators should not tell the witness that he picked the right or wrong person out of the photo array or lineup. Finally, the person conducting the lineup or photo spread should immediately take a statement from the eyewitness as to his level of confidence in his identification that the person selected is the actual perpetrator.[80] However, investigators should not ask the witness to assign a percentage value or place it on a scale of 1 to 10.[81]

A list of suggestions compiled from various agencies across the United States for performing unbiased lineups and identification procedures is provided in Tables 3.1 through 3.4, on pages 74-76.

TABLE 3.1   SUGGESTIONS FOR OBTAINING AN ACCURATE SUSPECT DESCRIPTION

(1) Get a detailed description of the suspect, especially as to distinguishing characteristics such as scars, tattoos, moles, etc. Encourage the witness to tell you everything.

(2) Never lead the witness or say anything about the suspect.

(3) After establishing rapport with the witness and inquiring about the condition of the witness, try to get the witness to relax and to visualize the perpetrator's features.

(4) To get an accurate height estimate, ask the witness where her eyes would hit the suspect's body if she were looking straight ahead.

(5) Ask the witness to hold her hand up to approximate the height of the perpetrator.

(6) Ask the witness to estimate your height and weight.

(7) Ask to the witness to approximate the distance between her and the perpetrator by moving a similar distance away from the witness.

(8) Ask the witness to go slowly through the incident in her mind and have her try to determine how long she was looking at the suspect.

(9) Ask the witness whether she thought at the time of the crime about having to identify the suspect later.

(10) Go back over the witness's original statement to avoid any miscommunication. Tell the witness what you are going to put in your report and ask the witness if she wants to change or add anything.

(11) Encourage the witness to contact you with any additional information.[82]

TABLE 3.2   SUGGESTIONS FOR CONDUCTING A PHOTO ARRAY

(1) The witness should be shown at least six photographs, with only one being of the suspect.

(2) Filler photographs should match the physical characteristics of the description provided by the witness.

(3) Each photo should be numbered on the back.

(4) The suspect's photo should not be shown first since studies have shown that witnesses are reluctant to select the first photo.

(5) Two blank photo folders should be placed at the end of the array to prevent the witness from knowing when she is viewing the last photo.

(6) The witness should be shown each photo separately. The witness should not be able to view all six photographs at the same time.

(7) If the witness identifies a suspect prior to finishing the array, the witness should still be shown all the photographs in case she changes her mind.

(continued)

TABLE 3.2   *(CONTINUED)*

(8) The witness should be given something akin to the following instruction before conducting the photo array:

> I'm going to show you six photographs. Please look at all six photographs before making any comment. The person who committed the crime may or may not be among those shown in the photographs you're about to see. If you recognize any of the persons in the photographs as the person whom you believe committed the crime, go back and pick out the person you recognize. If you recognize any of the persons as the suspect, please do not ask me if your choice was "right" or "wrong," as I am prohibited by law from telling you.

(9) If the witness picks out a photo, it should be initialed by the investigator and the witness.

(10) The entire process should be videotaped.

(11) The array should be packaged, identified, and sealed as evidence.[83]

TABLE 3.3   SUGGESTIONS FOR CONDUCTING A LINEUP

(1) A lineup should include just one suspect and at least four (preferably five) non-suspect participants. The suspect should be randomly positioned in the lineup.

(2) The fillers in the lineup should be of the same race and sex as the suspect and have similar physical characteristics. If the witness reports any particular distinguishing characteristics, the fillers should also have those characteristics where possible. If that is not possible, then the distinctive feature should be concealed on the suspect.

(3) If the suspect wore distinctive clothing at the time of the incident, all participants should wear similar clothing.

(4) The lineup should begin with all participants out of view of the witness. The first person shown should always be a filler.

(5) The witness should be shown each participant in the lineup sequentially (one at a time).

(6) An instruction like the one for photo arrays should be given to the witness, i.e., that the suspect may or may not be present.

(7) The witness should be shown all participants in the lineup, even if the witness makes an identification prior to the end. If the identification of the suspect's voice is necessary, all participants in the lineup should say the same words.

(8) The names of all participants in the lineup and all persons present should be documented.

(9) Frontal and profile photographs should be taken of all persons in the lineup or the entire process should be videotaped to document how the lineup was conducted.

(10) Regardless of whether or not the witness picks the suspect, the choice should not be discussed with the witness.

(11) The witness should be instructed not to discuss the lineup with other witnesses.

(12) The person conducting the lineup should not be the investigator on the case.[84]

TABLE 3.4   SUGGESTIONS FOR CONDUCTING A SHOWUP

(1)   The witness's description of the suspect should be well documented.

(2)   The witness should be transported to the suspect's location, where possible, to limit the impact of seeing the suspect in custody.

(3)   The suspect should not be presented to the witness sitting in the back of the patrol car in handcuffs. If the suspect appears to be in custody, the witness should be told to keep an open mind and not let that fact sway her decision.

(4)   The witness should not be told that the offender has been apprehended and that the investigator just needs the witness to identify him. Instead, the witness should be instructed that the person may or may not be the perpetrator.

(5)   The showup should not be conducted in the presence of other witnesses or in a police station.

(6)   If the witness makes an identification, her level of certainty should be recorded.[85]

Many departments across the country have now adopted most or all of these recommendations. These include obtaining an accurate description of the suspect, conducting identification procedures in a blind, sequential fashion, and instructing the witness that the suspect may not be present.

The success of one county's efforts to adopt such procedures is described below.

EVIDENCE IN ACTION

Ramsey County, Minnesota Revolutionizes Lineup Procedures

The Ramsey County Attorney's Office located in St. Paul, Minnesota has recently instituted several reforms in the procedures its officers use in conducting photo arrays and lineups. In doing so, the county adopted many of the recommendations made by Professor Wells and others outlined above. It set up a pilot project in 2005 to test whether the implementation of blind sequential lineups was feasible and practical for law enforcement. The pilot proved to be successful,

and in April 2006, the protocol was adopted countywide for use in all county law enforcement agencies.

The new protocols instituted a number of changes, most notably the creation of blind, sequential lineups. Alternatively, an investigator familiar with the case could conduct the photo array or lineup procedure, but only if he does not know the order of people or photos presented to the witness.

The protocols suggest a number of different methods that could be used to conduct the array or lineup in a sequential fashion. The witness could be shown photographs of the potential suspects one at a time on a laptop computer. A box could also be constructed that would allow the witness to open a window to view each photograph but that would prevent viewing photographs simultaneously. A rather low-tech version can also be used by placing the photographs in six separate folders that are then shuffled randomly.[86]

Despite fears that this procedure would reduce the number of accurate, positive identifications from lineups, Ramsey County has reported no such issues four years into the program. More importantly, investigators feel that the confidence level of identifications that are secured has increased significantly. County prosecutors have also found that defense attacks on the reliability of identifications have declined considerably.

Other departments across the country have begun to develop similar protocols for conducting lineup identifications. Dallas, Denver, Boston, New Jersey, Wisconsin, and North Carolina have all adopted similar blind, sequential lineup procedures since 2001. For example, the state of Wisconsin adopted a Model Policy and Procedure for Eyewitness Identification in 2005. The policy features six recommendations:

- Utilize non-suspect fillers chosen to minimize any suggestiveness that might point toward the suspect;

- Utilize a double-blind procedure in which the administrator is not in a position to unintentionally influence the witness's selection;
- Give eyewitnesses an instruction that the real perpetrator may or may not be present and that the administrator does not know which person is a suspect;
- Present the suspect and the fillers sequentially (one at a time) rather than simultaneously (all at once). This discourages relative judgment and encourages absolute judgments of each person presented because eyewitnesses are unable to see the subjects all at once and are unable to know when they have seen the last subject;
- Assess eyewitness confidence immediately after identification; and
- Avoid multiple identification procedures in which the same witness views the same suspect more than once.[87]

The City of Dallas adopted a similar set of best practices for lineups in 2010 after a rash of DNA exonerations revealed flaws in its previous identification procedures. Twenty-one people have been exonerated by DNA tests in Dallas County since 2001. All but one case involved eyewitness misidentification.[88] Unfortunately, most other jurisdictions in the state have not adopted these best practices.

CHAPTER SUMMARY

There are three methods generally used by police to conduct identification of suspects prior to trial. A showup involves having the witness briefly look at a potential suspect face-to-face to confirm whether that person is in fact the correct suspect. A photo array involves showing a witness a number of photos matching the description of the perpetrator. A lineup involves using five to six individuals matching the description of the suspect.

Lineup identifications may be inadmissible if they were conducted in an impermissibly suggestive fashion. Suggestive lineups are those that tip off the witness as to who the suspect is. Even if lineups are found to be suggestive, however, the identification may still be found to be sufficiently reliable to be admitted into evidence. The judge must examine a range of factors to determine the reliability of the identification, including the accuracy of the initial description, the opportunity of the witness to view the suspect, and the length of time that has elapsed between the crime and the identification.

Eyewitness identification is a powerful piece of evidence, but it is subject to many errors. Environmental conditions may interfere with the witness's ability to clearly view the suspect during the commission of the crime. People's memories are also not perfect and are susceptible to change over time. Additionally, law enforcement officers themselves can inject error and bias into the process.

Officers need to perform lineups and other identification procedures in as unbiased a manner as possible. Care should be taken to select photos or individuals that closely resemble the physical description of the suspect. Witnesses should be told that the suspect may or may not be in the lineup or set of photos. Lineups should be conducted sequentially so that the witness cannot compare the people in the lineup to each other. Finally, someone other than the case investigator should perform the identification procedure where possible.

KEY TERMS

- *Biggers* factors
- Double-blind sequential lineup
- Estimator variables
- Fillers
- Impermissibly suggestive
- Lineup
- Memory variables
- Photo array
- Showup
- Systemic variables

REVIEW QUESTIONS

1. What are the three identification methods used by law enforcement prior to trial? Briefly describe each.

2. What causes a pretrial identification procedure to violate due process?

3. What makes a lineup or identification impermissibly suggestive?

4. If a lineup identification is impermissibly suggestive, can it still be admissible? Explain. What factors does the court consider in determining whether to admit the suggestive identification?

5. Name three reasons why eyewitness identifications are not always accurate.

6. When is expert testimony allowed on the subject of eyewitness identification?

7. What changes does Professor Wells think are necessary to make pretrial identifications more accurate and reliable?

8. What is meant by double-blind sequential lineups?

9. Some jurisdictions have changed their practices in recent years regarding lineups. Do you think this has improved the reliability of the identifications made by eyewitnesses? Explain.

APPLICATION PROBLEMS

1. Joan is raped at knifepoint. Her attacker holds a pillow over her head to prevent her from seeing his face. She gets a brief glimpse of him as he exits her apartment. Four weeks later, she is shown a photo array, including a possible suspect, with six photos shown all at once. Joan identifies one of the photos as "maybe" being the rapist. The officer says "good job." Later, at a lineup, she identifies the same man. The officer says, "Good. You identified the same suspect." What, if anything, did the officer do wrong in conducting the photo array and lineup?

2. Sam is mugged at gunpoint. He gets a brief look at his attacker as he flees the scene. The lighting conditions are dark but there is some light from one lamp in the alley. Sam picks his mugger out of a photo array two weeks later. He is certain that the photo he picked out is the mugger. His physical description was of a black man who was five feet eight inches tall and weighed 150 pounds, and the suspect is black man who is five feet eleven inches tall, weighs 180 pounds, and has a tattoo on his neck that Sam did not initially report. Do the *Biggers* factors favor a reliable identification or an unreliable one? Explain.

3. Susan is run over by a car while crossing the street. It is a hit-and-run accident. Susan provides a description of the driver as a white woman with dyed blonde hair wearing a red scarf. She says she was about 50 years old. Maddy is arrested two days later after investigators noted some damage to the front end of her car. She is put in a lineup with five other women. All of the women have dyed blonde hair. Maddy is the only one wearing a red scarf; the other women are wearing different colored scarves. The other women are also approximately 50 years in age. Is the lineup impermissibly suggestive? Explain.

4. Steve is arrested for a robbery. The witness's description is of a black man with short hair and a mustache. Steve is black and has a mustache. He is put in a lineup with five other men. The lineup is conducted with the witness observing all six men at once. The witness picks Steve out of the lineup. The officer asks no questions and says nothing at the conclusion of the lineup. The witness identifies Steve at trial but is very unsure of herself. What could have been done differently to secure a better identification?

Notes

1. Elizabeth F. Loftus & James M. Doyle, *Eyewitness Testimony: Civil and Criminal* (Michie Co. 1992).
2. Marc Green, *Errors in Eyewitness Identification Procedures*, available at http://www.visualexpert.com/Resources/mistakenid.html.
3. John Wasberg, *Lineups, Showups, and Photographic Spreads: Legal and Practical Aspects Regarding Identification Procedures and Testimony*, Washington Attorney General's Office, at 4 (last updated October 1, 2004).
4. Id. at 1.
5. Id.
6. 388 U.S. 293, 301-02 (1967).
7. 388 U.S. 293 (1967).
8. Simmons v. United States, 390 U.S. 377 (1968).
9. In re L.W., 390 A.2d 435, 438 (D.C. 1978).
10. Id.
11. Fields v. State, 333 N.E.2d 742 (Ind. 1975).
12. Little v. State, 475 N.E.2d 677, 682 (Ind. 1985).
13. Head v. State, 443 N.E.2d 44 (Ind. 1982).
14. Little, 475 N.E.2d at 682.
15. 394 U.S. 440 (1969).
16. Id. at 443.
17. Neil v. Biggers, 409 U.S. 188, 198 (1972).
18. Biggers, 409 U.S. at 198.
19. Robert P. Mosteller, *The Duke Lacrosse Case, Innocence, and False Identifications: A Fundamental Failure to "Do Justice,"* 76 Fordham L. Rev. 1337, 1397-98 (2007).
20. Id. at 1399.
21. North Carolina Actual Innocence Commission, *Recommendations for Eyewitness Identification*, available at http://www.innocenceproject.org/docs/NC_Innocence_Commission_Identification.html.
22. ABC News, *Video of Controversial Lineup in Duke Case Emerges*, December 15, 2006, available at http://abcnews.go.com/GMA/LegalCenter/story?id=2728563.
23. Robert K.C. Johnson, *North Carolina Norms*, Cliopatria a Blog Group, July 13, 2006, http://hnn.us/blogs/entries/28086.html.

24. Mosteller, *supra* note 19, at 1404.
25. Id. at 1410.
26. Id. at 1409.
27. Biggers, 409 U.S. at 199.
28. State v. Dubose, 699 N.W.2d 582, 591 (Wis. 2005).
29. Biggers, 409 U.S. at 199-200.
30. Id. at 193-94.
31. Id. at 200.
32. 432 U.S. 98 (1977).
33. Biggers, 409 U.S. at 214.
34. Gary L. Wells, et al, *Eyewitness Identification Procedures: Recommendations for Lineups and Photospreads,* 22 Law and Human Behavior 1, 6 (1998).
35. Gary L. Wells & Deah S. Quinlivan, *Suggestive Eyewitness Identification Procedures and the Supreme Court's Reliability Test in Light of Eyewitness Science: Thirty Years Later,* 33 Law and Human Behavior 1, 9 (2009).
36. Wells & Quinlivan, *supra* note 35, at 10.
37. Id.
38. Id.
39. Id. at 11.
40. Tegoseak, 221 P.3d at 355.
41. Id.
42. Id.
43. Wells & Quinlivan, *supra* note 35, at 12.
44. Dubose, 699 N.W.2d at 592.
45. Tegoseak, 221 P.3d at 356.
46. Id. at 357.
47. Id. at 354.
48. *See* People v. Adams, 423 N.E.2d 379 (N.Y. 1981); Commonwealth v. Johnson, 650 N.E.2d 1257 (Mass. 1995); Dubose, 699 N.W.2d at 594.
49. Dubose, 699 N.W.2d at 594.
50. *See* State v. Ramirez, 817 P.2d 774 (Utah 1991); State v. Hunt, 69 P.3d 571, 576 (Kan 2003).
51. United States v. Wade, 388 U.S. 218 (1967).
52. Van v. Jones, 475 F.3d 292, 312 (6th Cir. 2007) (citations omitted).
53. Van, 475 F.3d at 313.
54. Id.
55. *See* Hamilton v. Alabama, 368 U.S. 52 (1961); Coleman v. Alabama, 399 U.S. 1 (1970); Mempa v. Rhay, 389 U.S. 128 (1967).
56. King v. Bobby, 433 F.3d 483 (6th Cir. 2006).
57. *See* United States v. Ash, 413 U.S. 300 (1973).
58. C. Huff, *Wrongful Conviction: Societal Tolerance of Injustice,* 4 Research in Social Problems and Pub. Pol'y 99 (1987).
59. *See* The Innocence Project, *Facts on Post-Conviction DNA Exonerations,* available at www.theinnocence project.org/understand/eyewitness-misidentification.php.
60. *Frontline: How Can Eyewitness Identification Go Wrong?* Reprinted from Elizabeth Loftus & Katherine Ketcham, *Witness for the Defense: The Accused, the Eyewitness and the Expert Who Puts Memory on Trial* (St. Martin's Press 1991), available at www.pbs.org/wgbh/pages/frontline/shows/dna/photos/eye/text_06.html.
61. Id. at 2.
62. Green, *supra* note 2, at 2.
63. *Frontline, supra* note 60, at 4.
64. Green, *supra* note 2, at 2.
65. *Frontline, supra* note 60, at 4.
66. This is known as the Smart Hans effect. Smart Hans was a horse whose owner claimed it could count. When experts tested the horse with blinders on, however, they discovered that the horse was receiving subtle cues from its owner. With the blinders on, the horse could not see the owner and, of course, could not count.
67. Green, *supra* note 2, at 4.
68. Wells, supra note 34, at 31.
69. Id. at 6.
70. United States v. Brien, 59 F. 3d 274, 276 (1st Cir. 1995).
71. United States v. Rodriguez-Berrios, 455 F. Supp. 2d 190, 192 (D. Puerto Rico 2006).
72. Rodriguez-Berrios, 455 F. Supp. 2d at 192.
73. State v. Ramirez, 817 P.2d 774, 779-80 (Utah 1991).
74. Tegoseak v. State, 221 P.3d 345, 352 (Ak. 2009).
75. Mark Hansen, *Forensic Science: Scoping out Eyewitness Ids,* 87 A.B.A.J. 39 (2001).
76. Tegoseak, 221 P.3d at 353.
77. Jennifer Thompson, *I Was Certain, But I Was Wrong,* New York Times, op-ed, June 18, 2000, available at http://truthinjustice.org/positive_id.htm.
78. Jennifer Thompson-Cannino & Ronald Cotton, with Erin Torneo, *Picking Cotton: Our Memoir of Injustice and Redemption* (St. Martin's Press, 2009).
79. Wasberg, *supra* note 3, at 3.
80. Wells, *Eyewitness Identification Procedures, supra* note 34, at 21-27; Mosteller, *supra* note 19, at 1392.
81. Wasberg, *supra* note 3, at 8.
82. Id. at 2-3.
83. Id.; State of Wisconsin, Office of the Attorney General, *Model Policy and Procedure for Eyewitness Identification* (final draft April 1, 2010), at 8-12, available at www.doj.state.wi.us/dles/tns/EyewitnessPublic.pdf.
84. Wasberg, *supra* note 3, at 5-6; Wisconsin Model Policy and Procedure, *supra* note 83, at 18-22.
85. Wasberg, *supra* note 3, at 6; Wisconsin Model Policy and Procedure, *supra* note 83, at 23-26.
86. Susan Gaetner, *Successful Eyewitness Identification Reform: Ramsey County's Blind Sequential Lineup Protocol,* Police Chief Magazine, April 2009, http://www.policechiefmagazine.org/magazine/index.cfm?fuseaction=display_arch&article_id=1776&issue_id=42009.
87. Wisconsin Model Policy and Procedure, *supra* note 83.
88. Jennifer Emily, *Man Exonerated in '79 Dallas Rape Case Says, "It's a Joy to be Free Again,"* The Dallas Morning News, January 5, 2011.

CHAPTER 4

Confessions

"The introduction of a confession makes the other aspects of a trial in court superfluous, and the real trial, for all practical purposes, occurs when the confession is obtained."—C.T. McCormick

Chapter Topics

Objectives

After completing this chapter, students will be able to:

- Identify the requirements for admitting confessions into evidence

- Understand the goals of the interrogator and identify the various methods of interrogation

- Understand how confessions must be corroborated before being admitted

- Identify the reasons people give false confessions and how they can be prevented

- Distinguish the various situations where confessions of co-defendants can be admitted or must be excluded

- Describe the various types of immunity

Introduction

A critical component to most investigations is the interrogation of suspects. One of the best pieces of evidence to prove a defendant's guilt is the fact that he confessed to committing the crime. It is estimated that 80 percent of solved cases include confessions. Incriminating statements made by suspects can provide key pieces of evidence that link a suspect to a crime scene and, more importantly, provide insight into why or how he committed that crime. There is probably no more compelling piece of evidence than the suspect's admission that "I did it."

Confessions relieve doubt in the minds of jurors more than any other type of evidence.[1] Confessors are also more likely to be charged with a crime and to plead guilty or be found guilty at trial.[2] As a result, there is tremendous pressure on law enforcement to obtain a confession from a suspect. Of course, suspects may be reluctant to admit their guilt or involvement in a crime. Investigators may have to resort to persuasive tactics during the interrogation of suspects to obtain a confession from them. This chapter will explore some of those techniques and how effective they are at achieving the desired results. Chapter 7 will examine the constitutional concerns surrounding confessions, such as the *Miranda* requirements.

Before being admitted into evidence, confessions must also be corroborated. This is done by either proving the *corpus delicti*, the elements of the offense, or by corroborating the facts of the confession. Thus, a defendant cannot be convicted on the basis of his confession alone. Some evidence, independent of the confession, must be presented in order for the confession to be admissible. Because interrogation tactics can be so persuasive, there is a danger that an interrogator will extract a false confession from an innocent suspect. This chapter will examine the various reasons suspects may falsely confess to a crime and give suggestions for avoiding false confessions. As you will see, corroboration of a confession is an important step that helps to reduce the likelihood that people may be improperly convicted by providing a false confession to a crime.

This chapter will also discuss how confessions of co-defendants are admitted in cases involving multiple defendants. Confessions of co-defendants cannot be used against the other defendants in the same trial unless special precautions are taken. Of course, the prosecutor can try the defendants separately to avoid any issues.

I. OBTAINING CONFESSIONS

Interview
a nonconfrontational process designed to gain information from a witness or suspect

Interrogation
an accusatory process designed to get a suspect to confess

Confession
the admission by a suspect of guilt to all the necessary elements of a crime

Admission
a statement made by a suspect that connects him to the offense

Law enforcement officers obtain information about a case by questioning witnesses and suspects. While officers conduct both interviews and interrogations, this chapter focuses on the interrogation of suspects since the hearsay rule often precludes officers from testifying about statements obtained during witness interviews. Statements obtained from the defendant do not fall under those same restrictions, however. There is another distinct difference between the two forms of information gathering. The **interview** process is typically nonconfrontational, whereas an **interrogation** is accusatory in nature.[3] The goal of the interrogator is to make the suspect confess to the crime and, in the process, learn the truth about the suspect's involvement (or noninvolvement) in the crime. A **confession** is "the admission of guilt by the suspect to all the necessary elements of the crime of which he is charged, including the necessary acts and intent." In contrast, an **admission** "merely admits some fact which connects or tends to connect the suspect with the offense but not with all the elements of the crime."[4] Both are useful in the prosecution of a defendant.

A. Physical Torture

For much of the history of law enforcement, obtaining confessions meant one thing—physically or psychologically abusing the suspect until he talked. Third-degree tactics such as around-the-clock questioning and the whipping of suspects were commonplace. The Supreme Court outlawed these types of tactics starting in the late 1800s. Unfortunately, this did not prevent law enforcement from continuing to use some of these coercive methods of interrogation. Black suspects in the South, in particular, were subjected to beatings and other violent acts at the hands of the police. Thankfully, more subtle interrogation techniques have largely replaced physical violence today as the tools of the modern interrogator.

While interrogation tactics used by law enforcement became kindler and gentler in the last half of the twentieth century, the first decade of the twenty-first century saw a renewed interest in the use of more coercive interrogation methods in the fight against terrorism. On April 16, 2009, the Department of Justice released legal memos that detailed the use of **enhanced interrogation techniques** by military interrogators to extract information from terrorist suspects at the Guantanamo Bay detention facility. Enhanced interrogation techniques was the term used by the Bush administration to describe the physical interrogation methods used by military intelligence and the CIA to extract information from terrorist suspects. Some of the techniques used included facial slaps, wall standing (forcing a suspect to lean against a wall using only his fingers for support), sleep deprivation, and waterboarding (the suspect is strapped to an inclined board while water is poured over a cloth that is placed over the suspect's face).[5] Interestingly, the techniques were drawn from a survival training manual developed by the Air Force in the 1950s to combat false confessions produced by torture techniques used by the Chinese during the Korean War.[6]

The Bush administration's belief that such tactics would provide useful leads was based on a faulty premise—that suspects would release certain pieces of information from their long-term memories only after prolonged periods of coercive interrogation. Studies have shown that torturing suspects often has just the opposite effect. A 2006 report showed that soldiers who were subjected to food and sleep deprivation suffered impaired abilities to recall personal memories and information.[7] The stress caused by torture releases neurochemicals in the brain that impair or alter memory. As a result, tortured captives may simply regurgitate information fed to them by the interrogators rather than reveal new information.[8]

Another problem with torture or other coercive interrogation methods is that they prod the suspect to "talk at all costs."[9] Two distinctly different motivations are presented by the interrogator and the suspect. While the captor employs torture as a means of getting the captive to tell him the truth, the captive often talks simply to make the torture stop. The truth of the statements does not matter to the captive. Early CIA interrogation manuals recognized this fact and discouraged torture:

> Intense pain is quite likely to produce false confessions, concocted as a means of escaping from distress. A time-consuming delay results, while investigation is conducted and the admissions are proven untrue. During this respite the interrogatee can pull himself together. He may even use the time to think up new, more complex admissions to take still longer to disprove.[10]

The FBI was so adamant that these enhanced tactics would not produce accurate information that in 2008 it withdrew its participation from future CIA interrogations involving such tactics.[11]

Despite Bush administration claims to the contrary, many observers believe the Justice Department memos released in 2009 confirm the fact that little actionable intelligence was produced by the

Enhanced interrogation techniques
a term used to refer to the physical methods used to interrogate terrorist suspects after 9/11. Such methods included facial slaps, wall standing, and waterboarding

Television Show *24* Portrays Use of Torture to Prevent Ticking Time Bomb

In the years following the terrorist attacks of September 11, 2001, the Fox television show *24* popularized efforts to combat terrorism. The show was run in "real time" and based around efforts to stop terrorists from executing a plot to detonate a bomb or biological attack in the coming hours. It featured a day in the life of rogue operative Jack Bauer, employed by the mythical Counterterrorism Unit to battle terrorist attacks on U.S. soil. Bauer would attempt to obtain information from terror suspects at all costs. In one show, he fired two bullets at the head of a suspect to make her talk. In a different season, he fired a bullet into the knee of the suspect's husband to force her hand. In yet another, he cut off the thumb of a suspect to make him talk. A television watchdog group tallied 67 torture scenes in the first five seasons of *24*.[13] Invariably, Bauer got the information he was after and saved the United States from an imminent terror attack.

The premise of *24* revolves around the "ticking bomb" theory—a theory that torture is warranted where it is the only method that can be used to force a suspect to reveal the location of a bomb set imminently to go off. The only problem with the ticking bomb theory is that it is a myth. A retired CIA senior officer was quoted in a 2008 *Vanity Fair* article as saying, "Nobody in intelligence believes

in the ticking bomb. It's just a way of framing the debate for public consumption. That is not an intelligence reality." Joe Navarro, an FBI interrogator, also discounts the ticking bomb theory. He noted that torture is not an effective response with Islamic extremists: "These are very determined people, and they won't turn just because you pull a fingernail out. They almost welcome torture. They expect it. They want to be martyred.... They know if they can simply hold out several hours, all the more glory—the ticking time bomb will go off!"[14]

Although fictional, the show inspired a new generation of military officers to follow Bauer's creed: do "whatever it takes." Even Supreme Court Justice Antonin Scalia fell under the show's spell. At a 2007 Ottawa conference of international jurists, he told attendees that law enforcement officials should be given latitude when using some forms of torture in times of extreme crisis. He stated, "Jack Bauer saved Los Angeles.... He saved hundreds of thousands of lives. Are you going to convict Jack Bauer?"[15] The show's effect so concerned U.S. Army Brigadier General Patrick Finnegan, the dean of West Point, that he flew to California in 2006 to meet with the creative team behind *24*. He expressed his concern that the show was having a "toxic effect" on new cadets and was making it increasingly hard to convince them that they had to respect the rules of human rights and international law, even when terrorists did not.[16] Changes in the show's portrayal of torture did not occur, however.

enhanced interrogation methods. In fact, Jack Cloonan, a retired FBI counterterrorism agent, called the information obtained from al Qaeda operatives "pabulum."[12] It should be noted, however, that intelligence gathered at Guantanamo Bay about al Qaeda couriers was credited with helping locate Osama bin Laden, leading to his assassination in 2011. The question remains as to whether such information would have been obtained using traditional interrogation techniques.

Former Chicago Police Commander Convicted of Perjury for Lying About Use of Torture

On June 27, 2010, Jon Burge, a former commander with the Chicago Police Department, was convicted of perjury and obstruction of justice. The conviction came years after Burge and other officers in his unit were accused of torturing suspects to obtain confessions. Burge was fired from the department in 1993 after multiple allegations surfaced that he had abused suspects in his custody.

The perjury conviction stemmed from Burge's testimony during a 2003 civil suit in which Burge and other officers were alleged to have denied the civil rights of suspect Madison Hobley by beating and torturing him. Burge denied the abuse in his testimony during that civil case. Burge was sentenced to four and one half years in federal prison after he was convicted of all counts.[17]

Several other civil lawsuits were filed against Burge as well, detailing his torture of multiple suspects. In 2004, four former death row inmates, pardoned by Illinois Governor George Ryan in 2003, filed similar suits. They alleged that Burge and detectives under him had tortured them into confessing to murders they did not commit.[18] The case against Burge and other city officials was settled for $19.8 million in 2007. A separate suit was filed by another suspect against the Chicago police in 2010, alleging that he was beaten with a telephone book, smothered with a plastic bag, and nearly suffocated by having 7UP poured down his nose.[19]

Two special prosecutors investigated many of these torture allegations against Burge. They issued a report in 2006 that validated many of the claims. Of the 148 claims investigated, the report concluded that half were credible, including three that could have been proven beyond a reasonable doubt if tried.[20] The report found that officers had beaten, kicked, and shocked black suspects to get confessions. The report concluded that Burge and other officers could not be prosecuted, however, due to the expiration of the statute of limitations.[21] Due to the report's release, several more of the convictions Burge had obtained were overturned or reversed. Thus, while the torture of suspects got immediate results, they proved to be illusory.

The use of torture is not confined to the military. It unfortunately has continued to be employed by a small minority of law enforcement officers to obtain confessions. The dangers of such coercive techniques are explored in the next Evidence in Action articles above and on the preceding page.

B. The Reid Technique

Despite these egregious examples of officer misconduct, the beating and torturing of suspects has largely been replaced by more sophisticated interrogation techniques. Experienced counterterrorism operatives have found that rapport-building interrogation techniques such as the Reid

Technique discussed below are far more effective at producing information than torture.[22] For example, Jack Cloonan described his interrogation of an al Qaeda operative suspected in the 1998 U.S. Embassy bombings. After refusing to talk in the face of repeated torture, the suspect began talking after Cloonan offered to pay for his wife's medical treatment.[23]

Law enforcement officers are trained to interrogate suspects using a variety of techniques, ranging from playing on the suspect's fears to using trickery and deception. Currently, there are seven interrogation manuals available that give instruction on how to interrogate suspects. These manuals have disavowed third-degree tactics in favor of more subtle ones. Detectives are also taught to observe the body language and demeanor of the suspect to help detect whether the suspect is being truthful in his responses.

Although methods of interrogation used by law enforcement agencies differ subtly across the United States, the predominant method used is known as the Reid Technique.[24] The **Reid Technique** involves a nine-step interrogation process. The primary goal of the process is to break down the resistance of the suspect to confessing. Once this is achieved, the interrogator can then attempt to increase the suspect's desire to confess. It teaches that the primary purpose of interrogation is to learn the truth.[25] See Table 4.1 for a brief description of the nine Reid steps.

The Reid Technique primarily relies on subtle, psychological pressure to extract statements from suspects. It teaches that interrogation is a persuasive activity that attempts to alter the suspect's perception of the

Reid Technique
a nine-step process that is designed to establish a rapport with the suspect and then break down his resistance to confessing his guilt

TABLE 4.1   NINE STEPS OF THE REID TECHNIQUE

- Direct positive confrontation (confronting the suspect with the fact that he has definitely committed the offense)
- Theme development (suggesting themes such as a morally acceptable reason for the crime to minimize the implications of the crime or give the offender an excuse for the crime)
- Handling denials (interrupting denials, including use of "good cop/bad cop" routine)
- Overcoming objections (defeating objections or reasons the suspect may give for his innocence to gain a psychological advantage over the offender)
- Procurement and retention of the suspect's attention (invading the suspect's space by getting physically closer to the suspect)
- Handling the suspect's passive mood (focusing the suspect's attention on the central theme by attempting to appeal to the suspect's sense of decency)
- Presenting an alternative question (interrogator presents two possible alternatives for the commission of the crime and forces the suspect to choose between the two)
- Having the suspect orally relate various details of the offense (builds on an admission of involvement by getting the suspect to provide details of the circumstances of the crime)
- Converting an oral confession into a written confession (forcing the suspect to write down the details of the confession to prevent him from retracting an earlier oral confession)

situation and sell him on the idea that telling the truth is the best thing to do.[26] It is based on two broad premises: breaking down the denials and resistance of the suspect and increasing the suspect's desire to confess.[27] The Reid method relies on the interrogator first being able to develop a rapport or trust with the suspect to allow for an initial assessment of the suspect. This can help identify the suspect's general level of nervousness and set a behavioral baseline for the interrogation.[28] The interrogator can then proceed to make statements (as opposed to asking questions) that require the suspect to respond by either making admissions or denials.[29]

C. Success of Interrogation

In a 1996 study of police interrogations, Richard Leo found that interrogations were successful a majority of the time. Only 15 percent of the suspects who elected to talk to police made no incriminating statements as a result of their questioning.[30] Several factors led to interrogations being successful, including the length of the interrogation and the number of tactics used by the interrogator. Interestingly, Leo found that only 8 percent of interrogations lasted for more than 2 hours.

Other studies of interrogation practices show that interrogators use an average of between five and six different tactics during a given interrogation.[31] The most successful tactics used are appealing to the suspect's conscience, identifying contradictions in the suspect's story, using praise or flattery, and providing moral or psychological justifications for the suspect's actions.[32] Misrepresenting the nature of the offense and employing trickery are the most commonly used tactics. Such deceptive tactics include falsely claiming that a co-defendant has implicated the suspect, exaggerating the strength or nature of the evidence against the suspect, and falsely claiming the police possess forensic evidence that implicates the suspect.[33] As you will see in Chapter 7, courts usually do not have a problem with the use of deception as long as the tactics do not overbear the will of the suspect.

D. False Confessions

False confession
a statement made by an innocent person implicating that person in a crime that he did not commit

A **false confession** occurs where someone confesses to a crime that they did not commit. It may seem counterintuitive that a person would falsely confess, yet one can imagine a situation where a person might confess to take the blame for another person or confess to gain fame. False confessions are not just a hypothetical result of coercive or suggestive police interrogation techniques, however; they are a real problem. Studies have shown that false confessions are the second leading cause of wrongful convictions behind faulty eyewitness identifications.[34] It is estimated that somewhere between 8 and 13 percent of wrongful convictions of adults are the result of false confessions. That number is substantially higher for juveniles. A study of wrongful conviction of juveniles between 1989 and 2003 showed that 42 percent were convicted, in part, because of false confessions.[35] That being said, false confessions are a relatively rare occurrence. It is estimated that false confessions account for between only .001 and .04 percent of all convictions.[36]

1. Types of False Confessions

Research has shown that two types of errors are involved in confessions: false negatives, where guilty people fail to confess, and false positives, where innocent people confess to crimes they did not commit. The latter is a far more troubling issue for the criminal justice system. There are three types of false positive confessions. The first is a **coerced compliant confession,** which occurs where the suspect confesses to achieve some gain, such as ending a lengthy interrogation or avoiding physical injury. This is the most common type of false confession. Second, some people provide **voluntary false confessions** without prompting or interrogation by law enforcement. People seeking notoriety fall into this category. For example, over 200 people confessed to kidnapping Charles Lindbergh's baby in the 1930s. More than 30 people confessed to killing actress Elizabeth Short in the late 1940s, a case that became known as the "Black Dahlia" murder. In 2006, John Mark Karr confessed to Boulder, Colorado investigators that he killed Jon Benet Ramsey. DNA tests later ruled Karr out as a suspect.[37]

The third type of false confession is **coerced internalized confessions.** This occurs where an interrogator gets an innocent person to confess to a crime that he does not remember committing.[38] This is the least common form of false confession. Inbau and Reid (the authors of the Reid Technique) caution that investigators should never suggest to an innocent suspect that he committed the crime where he has no memory of committing it.[39] This type of confession is featured in the Evidence in Action article later in this section.

2. Causes of False Confessions

False confessions can be caused by a number of issues. Part of the problem is that the police can create an environment that is more favorable to producing false confessions. False confessions can result from overly aggressive interrogation tactics, including coercion and psychologically suggestive methods.[40] Dr. Richard Ofshe, a researcher and frequent critic of police interrogations, claims that psychologically coercive tactics are always present in interrogations that produce false confessions, even those obtained from seemingly normal suspects.[41] Another scholar described a police interrogator as "a salesman, a huckster as thieving and silver-tongued as any man who ever moved used cars or aluminum siding, more so, in fact, when you consider that he's selling

---

Coerced compliant confession

a confession made to achieve some gain

Voluntary confession

a confession made to gain notoriety

Coerced internalized confession

a confession made by a suspect who comes to believe he actually committed the crime long prison terms to customers who have no genuine need for the product."[42]

While this statement may be hyperbole, it points to the fact that the persuasive techniques used by the police to interrogate suspects can produce unintended results. These methods can be quite effective at eliciting confessions from hardened career criminals; when they are used against individuals who are easily manipulated, however, the results can be unpredictable. Suspects with low intelligence, low self-esteem, poor memories, lack of assertiveness, and anxiety tend to be more susceptible to giving false confessions.[43] If the interrogator is not careful under these circumstances, the suspect can provide a very believable but false confession.

According to Richard Conti, a noted criminal justice scholar, most false confessions have two things in common: (a) a vulnerable suspect (someone who has low intelligence or is very naive) and (b) the presentation of false evidence such as statements allegedly made by co-defendants or rigged forensic tests. Researchers have noted that susceptible subjects have trouble distinguishing false statements from true ones and fail to evaluate questions critically. This fact is compounded when such suspects are put under stress. As a result, investigators may mistake nervousness for guilt and suspects may give answers that are untrue but are plausible and consistent with the interrogator's questions.[44] Non-suggestible subjects, on the other hand, are capable of critically analyzing the situation that allows them to provide more accurate answers.

For instance, Gary Gauger was convicted of killing his parents in the 1990s, largely on the basis of his confession to authorities that it was possible he killed them in a drunken blackout. Gauger was a simple farmer with limited education. He spent three years on Illinois's death row before being freed. Two members of the Outlaws motorcycle gang confessed to the killings shortly thereafter.[45] In another case from the 1990s, Delbert Ward, a shy farmer with an IQ of 69, confessed to murdering his own brother. The confession was the product of several hours of intense questioning by five or six state patrol officers. However, there was no evidence linking Ward to his brother's death. In fact, the medical examiner had originally classified the death as resulting from natural causes. He changed his conclusion to homicide only after hearing of Ward's confession. The jury eventually acquitted Ward of murder.[46] The clinical psychologist who interviewed Ward for his defense concluded that, given his low IQ, Ward's focus would not have been on the questions he was being asked but on getting out of that unfamiliar, threatening environment.[47]

In particular, scholars have cautioned against the use of the seventh step of the Reid Technique, presenting the suspect with two alternative questions, with suspects who have below-average intelligence.[48] Such suspects may not be able to discern that there exists another possibility—namely, that neither choice is correct.

3. Prevention of False Confessions

Interrogators need to be aware of the factors that may lead to an increased risk of false confessions with certain types of suspects. Researchers suggest that the number of false confessions could be reduced significantly if a few simple steps were followed. First, investigators should receive training in dealing with suspects who have mental disabilities and how to interview such individuals. Second, investigators should focus more attention on obtaining the truth than a confession. To do so, it is recommended that interrogators take less of an adversarial role in the process. Another recommendation is that the length of interrogations be limited. The risk of false confessions dramatically increases with the length of interrogation.[49]

Perhaps the most important step in reducing false confessions is corroboration of the confession. Inbau and Reed suggest checking the authenticity of a confession by injecting fictitious aspects of the crime into the interrogation to test whether the suspect will accept them as actual facts.[50] Investigators should also compare the details of the confession to the facts of the crime. Dr. Ofshe describes the purpose for conducting this comparison:

> The reliability or truthfulness of a confession is measured by determining whether it includes information that accurately describes the crime that is not known to the general public and was not told to the suspect during the course of the interrogation. The unreliability or falsity of the confession is measured by determining whether it reveals gross errors of fact about the events of the crime that demonstrate the suspect lacks participant or eyewitness knowledge of what happened during the commission of the crime, and therefore is likely lying about his role in the crime and guessing when providing answers to police questions.[51]

Dependent corroboration
corroboration of a confession using the details of the crime that are purposefully withheld from the public

Independent corroboration
corroboration of a confession using details provided by the suspect

Rational corroboration
corroboration of a confession using logical motivations and accounts of the crime

There are three types of corroborative information. The first is known as **dependent corroboration,** which consists of details about the crime purposefully withheld from the public and the suspect. The only people who should know this information are the investigators and the guilty suspect. To effectively corroborate a confession, investigators must be careful not to contaminate the interrogation process by unwittingly disclosing such details to the suspect. The second type of corroboration is **independent corroboration**. This involves verifying facts about the crime that were not known until the suspect confessed. For example, the suspect may reveal that it took three minutes to strangle the victim and move her body into the living room. The third type of corroboration is **rational corroboration**. This is essentially a judgment of whether the suspect's alleged motives and account of the crime appear to be rational.[52] Obviously, this is the weakest form of corroboration since it relies on a subjective analysis of the suspect's behavior.

The final recommendation of scholars to improve the reliability of confessions is to video record the entire interrogation, not just the portion where the suspect confesses. Currently, only nine states require all interrogations to be video recorded, while two others require it in homicide cases only.[53] Many individual police agencies have successfully adopted mandatory video recording policies, however.

The benefits of video recording interrogations are that it (1) provides transparency to the interview process; (2) allows the interviewer to focus more on the suspect; (3) decreases cross-examination of the interviewer in court; (4) allows the jury to directly observe the suspect's demeanor; and (5) provides a good training resource.[54] Arguments against video recording full confessions are that it may be difficult to determine what procedures are legally required; some officers are reluctant to reveal investigative techniques to the public; and suspects may be less willing to cooperate if they know that they are on camera.

However, agencies that have adopted video recording policies enthusiastically support them.[55] One official from the Clackamas County Sheriff's Office in Oregon stated, "If a picture is worth a thousand words, it's been my experience that a video is worth ten thousand."[56] This is because the practice reduces the number of defense motions to suppress confessions since the video evidence generally does not support claims of coercion or other misconduct. Video recording also allows the investigator to concentrate on the interrogation without having to take detailed notes.[57]

Some scientific studies also support the use of video recording. They suggest that video recording will not impact a suspect's willingness to talk and may also have a significant effect on a confession's ability to sway the jury's conclusion about the case. In addition, a recent study showed that the use of full-length videos could reduce the impact of false confessions. The study's participants were much less likely to convict a person (who had confessed falsely) if they were shown the entire video of the suspect's interrogation than if they were shown only the portion where the suspect confessed.[58]

Some agencies have developed detailed protocols for the video recording of interrogations. The Denver Police Department, for example, has developed a Standard Operating Procedure and Training Bulletin for video recording interrogations. The policy provides for the complete recording of all interrogations using high-quality digital video cameras. All interrogation rooms are designed to contain a video camera mounted in the corner of the room along with a SMART board that allows officers to bring up computerized photos, drawings, and diagrams to show suspects as needed.[59]

Lieutenant Jon Priest of the Denver Police Department believes the recording policy ensures accuracy because "there's no question about what was said, there's no question about how it was said, and in the custodial situation, there's no argument about the circumstances of the interview. Was he properly advised of his rights? Did he waive his rights? Was there any coercion or threat involved?"[59a]

The Norfolk Four Are Granted Conditional Pardons After Falsely Confessing to a Rape and Murder That They Did Not Commit

Michelle Bosko was raped and murdered on July 8, 1997. She was found stabbed to death in the bedroom of her Norfolk, Virginia apartment by her husband, a Navy sailor returning from a ship tour. Daniel Williams, Joseph Dick, and Derek Tice, all veterans of the U.S. Navy, were convicted of raping and murdering Michelle Bosko. Omar Ballard, a friend of Bosko's, was also convicted of the rape and murder. All were sentenced to life in prison. Eric Wilson, a fourth Navy sailor, was acquitted of murder but convicted of rape and sentenced to eight and one half years in prison. Charges were dropped against three others.

The investigation quickly focused on Bosko's neighbor, Daniel Williams. Williams was reported to have been infatuated with Bosko, and he confessed to her murder on July 9, 1997 after a lengthy interrogation. In late December of that year, however, DNA testing conclusively eliminated Williams as the source of the semen found at the scene. The investigation then turned its focus to Williams's roommate, Joseph Dick. Dick originally denied any involvement in the crime, stating that he was on board his ship at the time of the murder. He, too, confessed after a lengthy interrogation. When confronted several months later with the fact that his DNA did not match that found at the scene, Dick implicated Wilson in the rape. Over time, Dick would provide four different statements, each time implicating additional individuals in the rape and murder. Eventually, seven Navy sailors would be charged with her rape and murder. Despite the fact that none of the sailors' DNA was found at the scene, four of the seven men would confess.[60]

In early 1999, Omar Ballard sent a female friend a letter confessing to Bosko's murder. On March 4,

Figure 4.1   Retired FBI agent Jay Cochran speaks at a news conference in Richmond, Virginia on November 10, 2008. Cochran and several other retired FBI agents asked the Virginia Governor to grant pardons for the four Navy sailors (pictured on the easel) known as the Norfolk Four, convicted of the 1997 murder and rape of Michelle Moore-Bosko. The governor granted conditional pardons for three of the four sailors almost a year later. © 2008 AP Photo/ Steve Helber

1999, DNA results confirmed that Ballard's DNA was a match to the DNA recovered from semen stains and skin under the victim's fingernails. It excluded all of the charged sailors as contributors of the DNA. On March 11, 1999, Ballard confessed to the rape and murder and stated that he had acted alone. Despite this confession, cases proceeded against four of the seven charged sailors. All either pled guilty or were found guilty at trial.[61]

One sailor, Derek Tice, was tried and convicted twice after his original conviction was overturned. Joseph Dick was the key witness against Tice, having received a plea bargain in exchange for his testimony. Dick testified that he and six other sailors had knocked on Bosko's door the day of the murder and were told to leave. Ballard then joined the group, and they forced their way into Bosko's apartment. He stated all eight carried Bosko into her bedroom, had forcible sex with her, and then took turns stabbing her.[62] However, the testimony of the medical examiner refuted much of this testimony. She stated that the three fatal stab wounds were consistent with having been inflicted by a single individual.[63] The crime scene evidence contradicted Dick's account as well. No signs of forced entry were found, and aside from the bedroom, the apartment appeared to be undisturbed.

The importance of the role that the sailors' confessions played in their convictions is highlighted by the lack of physical evidence and other credible evidence of their guilt. It is clear that Tice would not have been convicted without them. But if Tice and his three Navy co-defendants were truly innocent, why did they confess to crimes that they did not commit? Dr. Ofshe offered an explanation in his review of the case. He concluded that the cause of the false confessions was the psychologically coercive interrogation tactics, particularly the threat of severe punishment including the death penalty, used by Detective Robert Ford.[64] He noted that where objective evidence of a suspect's guilt is lacking, as was the case in this matter, accusatory interrogation techniques create the potential danger that an interrogation will produce a false confession.[65] Dr. Ofshe detailed multiple examples of where investigators misled the suspects. For instance, Williams was told by Detective Evans that a fictitious witness had seen him leaving Bosko's apartment after she was last seen alive. Evans also told Williams he had failed a polygraph and that DNA testing would prove he committed the crime. Detective Ford told Joseph Dick that an eyewitness placed him at the scene and that his alibi did not check out, despite the fact that he never attempted to confirm it.[66]

Dr. Ofshe was particularly critical of Detective Ford's threat that confessing to the murder was the only way to avoid the death penalty in the case. By the time Ford interrogated Derek Tice, all three "confessors" appeared to have been exonerated by DNA and inconsistencies in their stories. Yet, as Dr. Ofshe pointed out, Ford "appears to have developed a strategy—when DNA analysis failed to corroborate a suspect's confession, Ford would insist that Dick provide another name by repeating his prior death penalty threats."[67]

Inbau and Reid are also critical of using such threats. While they are careful to point out that the mere discussion of the consequences of a criminal act during an interrogation is proper, they caution that coercion can occur "when the investigator uses real consequences as leverage to induce a confession through the use of threats or promises." It is their position that "interrogation incentives that are apt to cause an innocent person to confess are improper."[68] They also caution that false statements or evidence should not be used in conjunction with promises of leniency. "Under these conditions it becomes much more plausible that an innocent person may decide to confess—not because fictitious evidence was presented against him, but because the evidence was used to augment an improper interrogation technique (the threat of inevitable consequences)."[69]

Dr. Ofshe was also critical of the fact that investigators appeared to have fed information to the suspects or forced them to change details in their stories. Williams initially claimed that he beat Bosko in the head with his shoe and that he did not choke her. Detective Evans persuaded Williams to change his story to reflect that the victim had been stabbed and strangled. Dick initially claimed that the rape and murder occurred in the living room, yet he changed his story when he was confronted with the fact that the room appeared to have been undisturbed. Tice was shown photos of the crime scene during his interrogation to ensure his confession was consistent with the facts.[70] Of course, this begs the question, if the evidence against the four sailors was so weak, apart from their confessions, how did the confessions make their way into the courtroom in the first place?

On August 6, 2009, three of the four men were granted conditional pardons by Virginia Governor Tim Kaine. Conditional pardons were granted since the sailors, according to the governor, had failed to conclusively prove that they were innocent. The fourth convicted sailor, Eric Wilson, was denied clemency since he had already been released from prison.[71] Detective Ford was convicted of extortion and lying to federal officials in an unrelated matter on October 27, 2010.

II. CORROBORATION OF CONFESSIONS

Historically, there has been reluctance on the part of courts to allow confessions to serve as the sole evidence of a defendant's guilt. Courts have universally held that the prosecution must corroborate the confession by either establishing the *corpus delicti* (the body or elements of the crime) or the reliability of the statements before a defendant can be convicted on the basis of his confession.[72]

A. *Corpus Delicti* Rule

Corpus delicti rule

a rule requiring the prosecution to prove that some harm or injury occurred that was caused by criminal activity before admitting a confession into evidence

Most states follow the *corpus delicti* rule to corroborate a confession. ***Corpus delicti*** means proof of the body or elements of the crime.[73] The *corpus delicti* rule requires the prosecution to establish the commission of the crime charged through facts independent of the defendant's confession. The rule developed in England after several famous cases where murder convictions were obtained largely on the basis of a confession, only to have the alleged victim reappear at a later date. To prove the *corpus delicti*, most courts require that the prosecution show that (a) an injury or harm constituting the crime charged occurred and (b) that the injury or harm was caused by the criminal activity. Most states do not require proof that the defendant committed the crime charged to establish the *corpus delicti*.[74] The North Carolina Supreme Court explained the rule as follows:

> Independent evidence of the *corpus delicti*, defined as it is in this jurisdiction to include proof of injury or loss and proof of criminal agency, does not equate with independent evidence as to each essential element of the offense charged. Applying the more traditional definition of *corpus delicti*, the requirement for corroborative evidence would be met if that evidence tended to establish the essential harm, and would not be fatal to the state's case if some elements of the crime were proved solely by the defendant's confession.[75]

For example, to prove the *corpus delicti* in a homicide case, the prosecution would have to establish the victim's death and that the death was a result of a criminal act. It does not have to prove other elements of the offense such as intent or identity, however. A Washington appellate court explained the limits of the rule:

> There is no requirement that the appropriate mental state (intent, recklessness, negligence), premeditation (in a first-degree murder charge), or identity of the killer, all of which would have to be established beyond a reasonable doubt to prove the case, be established in order to admit an incriminating statement. In essence, the gravamen in a homicide case is a dead body and a non-natural cause of death.... The evidentiary *corpus delicti* rule involves not a question of which crime was committed, but whether one

was committed. The rule is not designed as a method of distinguishing one crime from another. Rather, it is a safeguard to ensure that an incriminating statement relates to an actual offense.[76]

As the court pointed out, if this were not the rule, the prosecutor would have to charge the defendant with the crime he confessed to rather than the crime he actually committed.[77]

Practical Example

Assume Jim confesses to killing his sister. He says he drowned his sister in the river. The sister's body cannot be found. She is not at her home, nor is she at work. She has been missing for two weeks. Assume that six months passes before Jim's trial for murder. Under the corpus delicti *rule, the prosecution has to prove the fact of the sister's death and that she died as a result of criminal activity before it can admit Jim's confession against him. The fact that she has been missing for six months certainly suggests that the sister died. The prosecution can also show that the sister had no reason to disappear. Independent proof of criminal activity may be harder to come by, however. Without a body, this second element is harder to prove. The prosecution will have to show that the sister did not die of accidental causes. The fact that she allegedly drowned in the river makes this difficult. Thus, the court may conclude that the prosecution failed to prove the* corpus delicti.

B. Trustworthiness Rule

There has been growing dissatisfaction with the *corpus delicti* rule. While it does provide assurance that a person will not be convicted of a crime that did not occur, it does not protect against an innocent person being convicted "where a crime has been committed, but not by the accused."[78] Moreover, the rule's concerns that confessions could be the product of coercion have been largely alleviated by Supreme Court decisions such as *Miranda,* which significantly limit the opportunity for involuntary confessions to be admitted. One commentator believes that such developments "make it difficult to conceive what additional function the *corpus delicti* rule still serves in this context." [79] Of course, even with the protections of *Miranda,* it is still possible for an innocent person to voluntarily provide a false confession.[80]

Trustworthiness rule
a replacement for the *corpus delicti* rule and requires the prosecution to corroborate the essential details of a confession before its admission

As a result, the federal courts and a growing number of state courts have adopted a more flexible rule known as the **trustworthiness rule**, which focuses on the reliability or trustworthiness of the confession. The

Supreme Court abolished the *corpus delicti* rule for federal courts and instead announced the following rule in *Opper v. United States*:

> [W]e think the better rule to be that the corroborative evidence need not be sufficient, independent of the statements, to establish the *corpus delicti*. It is necessary, therefore, to require the Government to introduce substantial independent evidence which would tend to establish the trustworthiness of the statement. Thus, the independent evidence serves a dual function. It tends to make the admission reliable, thus corroborating it while also establishing independently the other necessary elements of the offense. It is sufficient if the corroboration supports the essential facts admitted sufficiently to justify a jury inference of their truth. Those facts plus the other evidence besides the admission must, of course, be sufficient to find guilt beyond a reasonable doubt.[81]

Independent evidence adequately corroborates a confession if it "supports the essential facts admitted sufficiently to justify a jury inference of their truth."[82] Under this rule, the adequacy of corroboration is "measured not by its tendency to establish the *corpus delicti* but by the extent to which it supports the trustworthiness" of the confession.[83] In other words, instead of requiring independent proof that a crime has been committed, this rule requires the prosecution to prove the truth of the essential facts of the confession.[84]

For example, in *Opper*, the defendant admitted to one element of the crime of bribing a federal official—payment of the money. The prosecution was able to corroborate that admission by showing the defendant had made phone calls to the Air Force employee who had allegedly been bribed and that employee had cashed a check written by the defendant.[85] Under the trustworthiness rule, the Court found the evidence was sufficient to corroborate the defendant's admission and allowed it into evidence.[86]

The Hawaii Supreme Court summed up the advantages of the trustworthiness rule as follows:

> Whatever the difference in the quantum and the quality of proof required under the particular rules adopted in the various jurisdictions, the basic purpose of each in requiring corroboration of the confession by independent evidence before it may be admitted or used is to meet the possibility that the confession may have been falsely given through misunderstanding, confusion, psychopathic aberration or other mistake. We are disposed to believe that the protection of the accused can be as well assured by the proper application of the flexible rule [that permits a confession to be relied on to prove the *corpus delicti* if the trustworthiness of the confession is established by corroborative evidence], as by the rigid rule which requires independent proof of all elements of the *corpus delicti* before the confession may be resorted to. With the additional safeguard requiring voluntariness of a confession to be shown, it appears to us that the possibility of misuse of the defendant's confession under the rule we favor is too remote to justify the additional restrictions of a more rigid rule.[87]

Under the trustworthiness rule, the government is not required to prove the truth of the entire contents of the confession.[88] While the prosecution must produce substantial evidence to corroborate the trustworthiness of the defendant's statement, it need not be sufficient, independent of the defendant's incriminatory statements, to establish the charged offense.[89] Although the prosecution must establish each element of an offense charged, it may do so "by independent evidence or corroborated admissions," and one "mode of corroboration is for the independent evidence to bolster the confession itself and thereby prove the offense through the statements of the accused."[90]

AUTHOR'S NOTE

One recent decision apparently disagrees with this flexible interpretation of the trustworthiness rule. In *State v. Dow*, the Washington Supreme Court ruled that the legislature's passage of RCW § 10.58.035, codifying the trustworthiness doctrine in Washington, did not replace the *corpus delicti* rule. The court held that the corroboration rule created in Opper simply creates an "alternative means" to prove the *corpus delicti*. It felt that the rule does not permit a defendant's confession to be the "sole evidence used to support a conviction," but instead every element of the crime charged has to be proven by evidence independent of the defendant's statement.[91] This is a misreading of Opper and the statute. Opper involved the introduction of only an admission, not a complete confession, so by necessity, other evidence had to be introduced to prove the defendant's guilt. The legislature's intent seemed to be clear that it was abandoning the *corpus delicti* doctrine. The Washington statute also plainly states that where "independent proof of the *corpus delicti* is absent," a defendant's confession or statement "shall be admissible into evidence if there is substantial independent evidence that would tend to establish the trustworthiness of the confession, admission, or other statement of the defendant."[92] A better reading of the rule is that expressed by the Fourth Circuit, which permits the confession to be the sole evidence of guilt as long as other evidence corroborates its trustworthiness.

Practical Example

Assume some wealthy homeowners have been cleaned out of their jewelry but they have not discovered it. Juan confesses to committing the series of jewelry thefts. He tells the police how he committed the crimes and the types of merchandise he stole. Under the trustworthiness standard, the prosecution has to corroborate the essential facts of the confession. Thus, it has to confirm that jewelry was stolen and some of the details of how the thefts may have been committed.

III. IMMUNITY

Immunity
a protection given to a witness in exchange for giving up his right to remain silent

Transactional immunity
a form of immunity protecting against prosecution for any crime disclosed in the immunized statements

Use immunity
a form of immunity protecting against use of the immunized statements

If a defendant refuses to talk to authorities or refuses to testify before a grand jury or trial, one tool available to the prosecution is to grant that witness immunity in exchange for his testimony. **Immunity** is the protection given to an individual from prosecution in return for giving up some conditional right, usually the right to remain silent. There are two types of immunity: transactional immunity and use immunity. **Transactional immunity** bars prosecution of the witness on any charge related to the subject matter of the witness's testimony or statement. **Use immunity**, meanwhile, is a more limited form of immunity. It only prohibits the prosecution from using the defendant's statements obtained from the immunity agreement or any information derived from those statements in any subsequent prosecution or investigation.[93] The defendant can still be prosecuted for the charged offense under a grant of use immunity as long as the information used in the prosecution is independent of the statements given to the prosecution by the defendant.

Most states and the federal courts do not require that transactional immunity be given; they only require use plus derivative use immunity. The Supreme Court has held that prosecution of a witness who has been given use immunity does not violate due process as long as the grant of immunity is co-extensive with the Fifth Amendment privilege against self-incrimination. Use plus derivative use immunity satisfies this requirement since it "provides a comprehensive safeguard, barring the use of compelled testimony as an investigatory lead, and also barring the use of any evidence obtained by focusing the investigation on a witness as a result of his compelled disclosures."[94]

Courts have held that use immunity precludes nonevidentiary uses as well as evidentiary use of the testimony at trial. Nonevidentiary uses are those that do not provide a link in the chain of evidence used to prove the defendant's guilt.[95] Such uses cover a broad range of activities, including:

- Focusing the investigation
- Deciding to initiate prosecution
- Refusing to plea bargain
- Interpreting evidence
- Planning trial strategy[96]

Some courts have held that tangential or incidental uses of immunized statements are not covered under immunity agreements, however. The focus should simply be on whether the prosecutor has actually used the witness's statements or whether he has a source, other than the immunized statements, for his course of conduct.[97] For example, a prosecutor could not reopen an investigation solely based on the immunized statements of a witness. This would violate the provisions of the immunity agreement since the prosecutor derivatively used the witness's statements as an investigatory lead. In contrast, if the prosecution reopened the case based on other leads such as tips, the mere fact that the prosecutor had gotten similar information from the immunized witness would not bar the prosecutor's actions.[98]

Despite the Supreme Court's acceptance of use plus derivative use immunity, some courts have clung to the more traditional rule that requires the witness be offered transactional immunity in exchange for his testimony or statements.[99] For example, Oregon courts have ruled that use immunity does not adequately protect the witness's right against self-incrimination under the Oregon constitution:

> A prosecutor who is aware of a witness' immunized statements is likely to allow that knowledge to affect discretionary decisions: whether to pursue the investigation, what direction to take in doing so, whether to prosecute the witness, whether to plea bargain and, if so, what to seek in the bargaining. It is hard to see how the most conscientious prosecutor could avoid letting the knowledge that the witness had admitted the crime while immunized affect these decisions. The immunized testimony might also be helpful in explaining other information in the prosecutor's hands, pointing out the significance of items previously ignored, aiding in the preparation of cross-examination and, more generally, in deciding trial strategy....A prosecutor may have used immunized testimony in any of these ways without introducing it or its fruits into evidence, but it is obvious that none of these actions would be possible if the witness had simply asserted the right to remain silent and had not testified.[100]

Another restriction on immunized testimony is that the information obtained by state law enforcement officials under a grant of immunity may not be turned over to federal prosecutors and used to prosecute the defendant for federal crimes. The Supreme Court established the following rule:

> We hold a constitutional rule to be that a state witness may not be compelled to give testimony which may be incriminating under federal law unless the compelled testimony and its fruits cannot be used in any manner by federal officials in connection with a criminal prosecution against him. We conclude, moreover, that in order to implement this constitutional rule and accommodate the interests of the state and federal governments in investigating and prosecuting crime, the Federal Government must be prohibited from making any such use of compelled testimony and its fruits.[101]

Practical Example

Assume Caesar, the defendant, is charged with murder. He is given transactional immunity. He tells the prosecutor that he was hired by Joseph to kill his wife. He also tells the prosecutor that he helped Joseph steal two million dollars from his real estate company. Caesar testifies against Joseph at his murder trial. Two months later, Caesar is charged with fraud and embezzlement in connection with the two million dollar theft. Is this charge valid? No. Since the prosecutor gave Caesar transactional immunity, he cannot charge Caesar with any crime related to the subject of his statement.

Now assume Caesar is given only use plus derivative use immunity. The prosecutor, who did not know about the two million dollar theft, now launches an investigation into the matter. He orders a search of the real estate business and uses the records showing the fraud to prosecute Caesar. Does this violate the immunity agreement? Although Caesar could be charged with the fraud crime, the prosecutor violated the immunity agreement by using the immunized testimony as an investigative lead. The prosecutor would not have obtained the information about the fraud without relying on the immunized statement.

IV. USE OF CONFESSIONS OF CO-DEFENDANTS THAT IMPLICATE THE DEFENDANT

Criminal acts often involve multiple participants or conspirators. Each participant in the crime may make statements to the police and may implicate the other participants or co-conspirators in the crime. These confessions can be damning admissions of guilt, and it is tempting to want to use these statements against all the defendants involved in a given case. This is a relatively easy process if the confessing co-defendant testifies against the other defendants. He can be cross-examined about his statements and motives to lie.

However, if the defendants are tried together, then the confessing co-defendant still retains the right to remain silent and may choose not to testify. To remedy this situation, the prosecution may have to offer immunity or a plea to the co-defendant to get him to testify. Alternatively, the prosecutor may have to try the defendants separately. Once the co-defendant's case is resolved, he no longer has a right to remain silent and can be forced to testify. Of course, at that point he no longer has any incentive to testify truthfully, either.

A. The *Bruton* Rule

In the past, prosecutors tried to get around this dilemma simply by introducing the statements of all defendants against each other in the same trial. The Supreme Court has held that a defendant's Confrontation Clause rights are violated when a non-testifying co-defendant's confession, naming the defendant as a participant in the crime, is introduced during a joint trial, even if the jury is instructed to consider the confession only against the co-defendant.[102] This is known as the

***Bruton* Rule**

a Supreme Court ruling barring the admission of a co-defendant's confession that implicates the defendant, absent the ability to cross-examine that co-defendant, where both parties are tried together

***Bruton* Rule**, after the Supreme Court case that announced it. The rule requires that the defendant be allowed an opportunity to cross-examine the co-defendant when the prosecution introduces that co-defendant's confession incriminating the defendant.[103] If, however, the confession does not incriminate the defendant on its face or does so only when linked with other evidence in the case, then its introduction does not violate the *Bruton* Rule.[104]

The court can protect the defendant's confrontation rights by (1) excluding the confession, (2) severing the trials of each co-defendant, or (3) redacting the confession to avoid mention or obvious implication of the non-confessing defendant.[105] Severance is the surest solution since *Bruton* issues can never arise if the defendants are tried separately.[106] Separate trials are more costly and create judicial inefficiency, however. Thus, the court must decide if the prejudice to the defendant from the introduction of a confession is so high that severance is the only fair solution.[107]

B. Redaction

Redaction is another solution if the defendants are tried together. The court must determine whether the confession can effectively be redacted by removing any incriminating references to the defendant. If references to the non-confessing defendant cannot be successfully redacted, then the defendants must be tried separately, or the confession must be excluded if they are tried jointly.

A confession can be redacted by the removal of any reference to the defendant's name or to his existence.[108] If the defendant's name is replaced with a generic pronoun or word such as "person" or "other individual," the confession may be admissible if it is not obvious that the redacted term refers to the defendant.[109] The Eighth Circuit concluded that a redacted confession, which replaced the defendant's name with a statement that "another individual" had been in on the planning and commission of the offense, was proper since the jury could have just as easily concluded it was the defendant's own words rather than a redaction.[110]

Not all redacted confessions can be used, however. The Supreme Court has rejected redactions that leave a blank space or notation such as "deleted" that obviously refer directly to a specific person.[111] The Fifth Circuit has also found that where "it is obvious from consideration of the confession as a whole that the redacted term was a reference to the defendant, an admission of the codefendant's confession that also inculcates the defendant does violate *Bruton*, regardless of whether the rejection was accomplished by use of the neutral pronoun or otherwise."[112] Another court refused to admit a redacted confession where the defendant's name was replaced with "other guy." The co-defendant's confession almost identically tracked the defendant's statement, and it would have been obvious as to whom the co-defendant was referring.[113] Courts have also rejected redaction as an option where it would be too cumbersome or confusing. For example, a federal court found redaction was not an effective option where the prosecution intended to introduce 150 pages of statements and it would have been confusing for the jury to determine which unnamed person the co-defendant was referring to.[114]

Practical Example

Suppose Louise and Thelma commit a string of crimes. They commit assaults, thefts, and even a murder. They are caught after a long car chase. They are tried together. Thelma confesses and admits that the two had a joint plan. She states that it was all Louise's idea to commit the crimes. Louise objects to the admission of Thelma's confession. The judge should grant her objection. The confession should only be used to show Thelma's guilt unless the confession can be redacted to remove any reference to Louise.

CHAPTER SUMMARY

Confessions are a powerful piece of evidence. Law enforcement officers are trained in obtaining confessions from suspects. Successful prosecutions often hinge on whether the suspect confessed. Police used to use physical coercion to extract confessions from suspects. Those methods have largely been replaced with more subtle, psychological methods of interrogation such as deception and persuasion. The main interrogation method that is taught today is known as the Reid Technique. This method emphasizes a nine-step process that breaks down the suspect's reluctance to confessing.

While these methods are largely successful, there is always a possibility that a suspect may offer a false confession. Pressuring or tricking suspects who have low IQs or low intelligence can increase the likelihood of obtaining a false confession. To prevent false confessions from occurring, investigators should take care to corroborate the details of confessions. They should also make sure that they do not contaminate the interrogation process by unwittingly providing details of the crime to the suspect.

The prosecution must also corroborate the confession before it can be admitted in evidence. In most states, this means that it must prove the *corpus delicti* or elements of the offense. This is done by showing that some injury or loss occurred and that it was due to criminal activity. Federal courts and some states use a slightly different rule that requires that the prosecution confirm the trustworthiness or the essential details of the confession.

Some witnesses refuse to waive their right against self-incrimination and will not testify. In such cases, immunity may be offered in exchange for their testimony. Use immunity prevents the prosecution from using the witness's statements against him at trial or to further the investigation. Transactional immunity, meanwhile, prevents the prosecution from charging the witness with any crime relating to the substance of his testimony.

If the case involves multiple defendants, the confessions of co-defendants may not be admissible. Where the confession implicates other defendants, it can be admitted against the other defendants only if each defendant is tried separately or that co-defendant testifies in the case. This is known as the *Bruton* rule. This means that where the defendants are tried together, a co-defendant's confession can usually be admitted only if references to the other defendants are redacted.

KEY TERMS

- Admission
- *Bruton* rule
- Coerced compliant confessions
- Coerced internalized confessions
- Confession
- *Corpus delicti*
- Dependent corroboration
- Enhanced interrogation techniques
- False confessions
- Immunity
- Independent corroboration
- Interrogation
- Interview
- Rational corroboration
- Reid Technique
- Transactional immunity
- Trustworthiness rule
- Use immunity
- Voluntary false confessions

REVIEW QUESTIONS

1. What is the difference between a confession and an admission?

2. What is the difference between an interview and an interrogation?

3. What are enhanced interrogation techniques? Where were they used?

4. Why is torture not effective in eliciting a true confession?

5. What is the Reid Technique?

6. Name two reasons a person would falsely confess.

7. Name three suggestions for decreasing the risk of false confessions.

8. Who were the Norfolk Four? Why did they confess to crimes they did not commit?

9. What must a court find about a confession before admitting it into evidence?

10. What is the *Bruton* rule? When can a co-defendant's confession be used against a defendant in the same trial?

11. What is the *corpus delicti*? Why does the prosecution have to prove it before admitting a confession in many states? How is it different from the trustworthiness standard?

12. What are the advantages of video recording confessions? What are the disadvantages? In your opinion, should the entire interrogation process be video recorded? Explain.

13. What is the difference between transactional and use immunity? Why do some courts still prefer to require transactional immunity?

APPLICATION PROBLEMS

1. Gomer, Otis, and Floyd are charged with robbery. Each of them is questioned by the Sheriff. Floyd can't stand the heat and fingers the other two in the robbery scheme. He says that both Otis and Gomer had guns and would stick up the customers as they left his barber shop. All three are tried together. The prosecutor redacts Floyd's confession and replaces Gomer's and Otis's name with "my accomplices." Can the prosecutor use Floyd's confession against the other two at trial? Explain.

2. Sue is a patient of a psychiatrist. She has schizophrenia. One day, she calls the police department and confesses to killing her daughter four years ago. What does the prosecutor have to show to admit her confession? Assume the state follows the *corpus delicti* rule. How would that change if the state follows the trustworthiness doctrine?

3. Jamie has an IQ of 85. She has been questioned about the disappearance of electronics from a store where she works as a stock shelver. The officers used the "good cop/bad cop" routine on her. The good cop sympathizes with her position and says that he'll understand if she had to take the merchandise to help pay the bills. She is interrogated for five hours. Finally Jamie confesses to taking the merchandise. The confession is false. How should the officers have approached the interrogation differently, knowing that Jamie had an IQ of 85?

Notes

1. Richard P. Conti, *The Psychology of False Confessions*, 2 J. Credibility Assessment & Witness Psy. 14 (1999).
2. J.P. Blair, *What Do We Know About Interrogation in the United States?* 20 J. Police & Crim. Psy. 44, 51 (2005).
3. Inbau, Reid, Buckley, & Jayne, *Criminal Interrogation and Confessions*, at 6 (4th ed. 2001).
4. E.H. Schopler, *Corroboration of Extrajudicial Confession or Admission*, 45 A.L.R. 2d 1316 §3 (1956), *quoting* State v. Masato Karmai, 126 P.2d 1047 (Utah 1942).
5. Shane O'Mara, *Torturing the Brain: On the Folk Psychology and Folk Neurobiology Motivating "Enhanced and Coercive Interrogation Techniques,"* 13 Trends in Cognitive Science: Science and Society 497 (2009).
6. Id.
7. *Newsweek*, The Tortured Brain, September 21, 2009, available at www.newsweek.com/2009/09/21/the-tortured-brain.print. html.
8. Id.
9. Id.
10. David Rose, Tortured Reasoning, *Vanity Fair*, December 16, 2008, available at www.vanityfair.com/magazine/2008/12/torture200812?printable=true.
11. Id.
12. Id.
13. Jane Mayer, *Whatever It Takes: The Politics of the Man Behind "24,"* New Yorker, February 19, 2007, available at www.newyorker.com/reporting/2007/02/19/070219fa_fact_mayer?printable=true.
14. Id.
15. *Wall Street Journal*, Law Blog, Justice Scalia Hearts Jack Bauer, June 20, 2007, available at http://blogs.wsj.com/law/2007/06/20/justice-scalia-hearts-jack-bauer/tab/print.
16. Mayer, supra note 15.
17. Wikipedia.com, Jon Burge, http://en.wikipedia.org/wiki/Jon_Burge.
18. Associated Press, *Cops Take 5th Amendment in Chicago Police Lawsuit Alleging Torture of Suspects*, November 17, 2004, available at http://www.policeone.com/investigations/articles/93672-Cops-Take-5th-Amendment-in-Chicago-Police-Lawsuit-Alleging-Torture-of-Suspects/.
19. Matthew Walberg, *Alleged Torture Victim Sues Daley, Burge*, Chicago Tribune, July 22, 2010, available at http://articles.chicagotribune.com/2010-07-22/news/ct-met-tillman-lawsuit-20100722_1_jon-burge-detective-john-yucaitis-chicago-police.
20. Wikipedia, Jon Burge, http://en.wikipedia.org/wiki/Jon_Burge.
21. Mike Robinson, *Chicago Police Again Mired in Scandal*, USA Today, September 30, 2007, available at http://www.usatoday.com/news/topstories/2007-09-30-359796777_x.htm.
22. Id.
23. Id.
24. Blair, *supra* note 2.
25. Inbau, et al., *supra* note 3 at 8.
26. Blair, *supra* note 2, at 45.
27. Gisli H. Gudjonsson, *The Psychology of Interrogations and Confessions: A Handbook*, at 11 (Wiley 2003).
28. Inbau, et al., *supra* note 3, at 93.
29. Gisli, *supra* note 27, at 8.

30. Id.
31. Blair, *supra* note 2, at 49.
32. Id. at 50.
33. Gudjonsson, *supra* note 27, at 8-9.
34. Conti, *supra* note 1, at 15.
35. Bill Moushey, *False Confessions: Coercion Often Leads to False Confessions*, Pittsburgh Post-Gazette, August 31, 2008, available at www.post-gazette.com/pg/062343/717790-84.stm.
36. Blair, *supra* note 2, at 52.
37. Conti, *supra* note 1, at 20.
38. Inbau, et al., *supra* note 3, at 413-14.
39. Id. at 427.
40. Id. at 22.
41. In re Dick, Petition for Absolute Pardon, Declaration of Dr. Richard Ofshe, at 11 (November 10, 2005), available at http://www.norfolkfour.com/images/uploads/pdf_files/Declaration_of_Dr._Richard_Ofshe.PDF.
42. Id. at 26, *quoting* D. Simon, *Homicide: A Year on the Killing Streets*, at 213 (Ivy Books 1991).
43. Id. at 24.
44. Id.
45. Moushey, *supra* note 35.
46. Norman Kunc and Emma Van der Klift, *False Confessions, Wrongful Convictions: Cases of Mentally Disabled Individuals Convicted on the Basis of False Confessions* (December 2008), available at http://www.normemma.com/artautboy.htm.
47. C. Wecht, *Cause of Death* at 255-56 (Onyx Books 1994).
48. Gudjonsson, *supra* note 27, at 19.
49. Conti, *supra* note 1, at 31.
50. Inbau et al., *supra* note 3, at 425.
51. Declaration of Dr. Richard Ofshe, *supra* note 41, at 2-3.
52. Inbau, et al., *supra* note 3, at 432-34.
53. *See* National Association of Criminal Defense Lawyers' Fact Sheet, *Departments That Currently Record a Majority of Custodial Interrogations*, available at http://www.nacdl.org/sl_docs.nsf/freeform/MERI_resources/$FILE/Deptsthatcurrentlyrecord(asof11210).pdf (last updated January 12, 2010).
54. James M. Cronin, et al., *Promoting Effective Homicide Investigations*, Chapter 5, Videotaped Interrogations, at 69 Police Executive Research Forum (August 2007), available at http://www.policeforum.org/upload/homicide_759980432_1282008145753.pdf.
55. Thomas P. Sullivan, *Police Experiences With Recording Custodial Interrogations, A Special Report of the Northwestern University School of Law Center on Wrongful Convictions*, (2004) available at http://www.law.northwestern.edu/wrongfulconvictions/issues/causesandremedies/falseconfessions/SullivanReport.pdf.
56. Id. at 7.
57. Id. at 10.
58. Ian Herbert, *The Psychology and Power of False Confessions*, 22 Observer (December 2009), available at www.psychologicalscience.org/observer/getArticle.cfm?id=2590.
59. Cronin, et al., *supra* note 54.
59a. Kevin Vaughan, Gun Case Against Colo. Firefighter Spotlights Interrogation Policy, Rocky Mountain News, March 27, 2006, available at http://www.firerescue1.com/print.asp?act=print&vid=84992.
60. Tice v. Johnson, 3:08-cv-00069-RLW, Memorandum Opinion on Habeas Corpus Petition, slip op. at 2-3 (September 14, 2009).
61. Slip op. at 4-5.
62. Id. at 6-7.
63. Id. at 14.
64. Declaration of Dr. Richard Ofshe, *supra* note 41.
65. Id. at 5.
66. Id. at 9-10.
67. Id. at 13.
68. Inbau, et al., *supra* note 3, at 418.
69. Id. at 428-29.
70. Declaration of Dr. Richard Ofshe, *supra* note 41.
71. Norfolkfour.com, Press Release, Four Innocent Navy Men Granted Conditional Pardons by Virginia Governor: After 11 Years Justice Still Eludes the Norfolk Four, (August 6, 2009), http://www.norfolkfour.com/images/uploads/pdf_files/N4_Clemency_Press_Release.pdf norfolkfour.com.
72. John W. Strong, et al., *McCormick on Evidence* §§ 146-47 (5th ed. 1999).
73. State v. Aten, 927 P.2d 210 (Wash. 1996).
74. State v. Parker, 337 S.E.2d 487, 492 (N.C. 1985).
75. Parker, 337 S.E.2d at 232.
76. State v. Angulo, 200 P.3d 752, 756 (Wash. App. 2009).
77. Id. at 758.
78. State v. Lucas, 152 A.2d 50, 60 (N.J. 1959).
79. J. Schwarz, Comment, *California's Corpus Delicti Rule: The Case for Review and Clarification*, 20 U.C.L.A. L. Rev. 1055, 1089 (1973).
80. *See* Smith v. United States, 348 U.S. 147, 153 (1954).
81. Opper v. United States, 348 U.S. 84, 93 (1954) (citations omitted).
82. Opper, 348 U.S. at 93.
83. United States v. Johnson, 589 F.2d 716, 718 (D.C. Cir. 1978).
84. Schopler, *supra* note 4, at § 7(c).
85. Opper, 348 U.S. at 94.
86. Id.
87. Parker, 235, *quoting* State v. Yoshida, 354 P.2d 986, 990 (Hi. 1960).
88. United States v. Dalhouse, 534 F.3d 803 (7th Cir. 2008).
89. United States v. Abu Ali, 528 F.3d 210 (4th Cir. 2008).
90. Abu Ali, 528 F.3d at 235, *quoting* Smith, 348 U.S. at 156. If the defendant did not confess to all elements of the crime, there must still be evidence of those elements, independent of the confession, to sustain a conviction, however. United States v. Irving, 432 F.3d 401 (2d Cir. 2005).
91. State v. Dow, 227 P.3d 1278, 1281 (Wash. 2010).
92. R.C.W. § 10.58.035(1).
93. State v. Delcambre, 710 So. 2d 846, 847-48 (La. App. 1998).
94. Kastigar v. United States, 406 U.S. 441, 490 (1972).
95. State v. Bryant, 983 P.2d 1181, 1186 n. 16 (Wash. App. 1999).
96. Bryant, 983 P.2d at 1186.
97. Id.
98. Id. at 1188.
99. *See e.g.*, State v. Miyasaki, 614 P.2d 915 (Hi. 1980).
100. State v. Soriano, 684 P.2d 1220, 1233 (Or. App. 1984).
101. Murphy v. Waterfront Comm. of N.Y. Harbor, 378 U.S. 52, 53-54 (1964).
102. Bruton v. United States, 391 U.S. 123 (1968).
103. United States v. Hill, 901 F.2d 880, 883 (10th Cir. 1990).
104. Richardson v. Marsh, 481 U.S. 200, 208 (1968).
105. Stanford v. Parker, 266 F.3d 442, 456 (6th Cir. 2001).
106. United States v. Lujan, 529 F. Supp. 2d 1315, 1322 (D.N.M. 2007).
107. Id.
108. Lujan, 529 F. Supp. 2d 1323.
109. Id., *citing* United States v. Vega Molina, 407 F.3d 511, 519-21 (1st Cir. 2005).
110. United States v. Logan, 210 F.3d 820, 822 (8th Cir. 2000).
111. Gray v. Maryland, 523 U.S. 185, 196 (1998).
112. United States v. Vejar-Urias, 165 F.3d 337 (5th Cir. 1999).
113. United States v. Williams, 936 F.2d 698 (2d Cir. 1991).
114. Lujan, 529 F. Supp. 2d at 1325.

PART II

PRETRIAL MATTERS

CHAPTER 5

The Criminal Justice Process

"Today the grand jury is the total captive of the prosecutor who, if he is candid, will concede that he can indict anybody, at any time, for almost anything, before any grand jury."—William J. Campbell

Chapter Topics

6. Closing Statements
7. Reading of the Jury Instructions
8. Objections
H. Appeal

II. **Trial Evidence**
A. Witnesses
B. Exhibits
C. Judicial Notice
D. Stipulated Facts
E. Things That Are Not Evidence

Objectives

After reading this chapter, students will be able to:

● Distinguish between the various stages of the criminal justice process and understand how evidence is used in each

● Identify the various types of evidence admitted during a trial

● Learn about the various components of a trial and how evidence is presented in each

● Identify what objections can be made during a trial to evidence

● Understand the appellate process

Introduction

In the previous section, you learned how evidence is collected and preserved during the investigative process. The investigation phase is just the beginning, however. The criminal justice process contains a number of steps or stages. A case can proceed through several stages and may eventually conclude in a trial. If one side is unhappy with the outcome of the case, an appeal may result. Evidence can affect the outcome of the case during most, if not all, of these stages.

Evidence is used differently during various stages of the criminal justice process. While evidence is located and collected by law enforcement during the course of an investigation, it must also be admissible in order for it to affect the outcome of a trial. Thus, the pool of usable evidence for trial is often smaller than that actually collected.

This is particularly true with respect to the amount of evidence needed at each stage to take some action. For example, while a police officer only needs enough evidence to establish probable cause for an arrest, a prosecutor must present a greater amount of evidence to prove a defendant's guilt beyond a reasonable doubt at trial. In this chapter, you will explore the various stages of the criminal justice process and see how evidence is used during each of these stages.

This chapter will also explore the types of evidence submitted at trial. Evidence can be introduced at trial in a number of ways, including the testimony of witnesses, exhibits, the judge taking judicial notice of a fact, or the parties stipulating to evidence.

I. THE STAGES OF THE CRIMINAL JUSTICE PROCESS

A. Case Investigation

In the early stages of a criminal investigation, an officer uses evidence to simply establish that a crime has been committed and who committed it. As the investigation progresses, officers may look for additional evidence linking a suspect to the crime, such as obtaining a search warrant or conducting surveillance. Once they have obtained sufficient evidence of a person's guilt to establish probable cause, officers will arrest that suspect or issue a warrant for his arrest if they cannot find him. Probable cause is a legal standard of proof that permits a reasonable person to conclude that a crime was probably committed and that a particular person probably committed it. Probable cause and other levels of proof are discussed more fully in Chapter 8.

At these early stages of the case, the job of the officers is to collect as much evidence as possible about the case. Much of the evidence may never be used. Some of it may simply show that a person who at one time may have been identified as a suspect did not actually commit the crime. Other pieces of evidence may prove to be inadmissible. Of course, the ultimate goal of the investigator is to collect as much admissible evidence as possible to prove the suspect guilty at trial.

Practical Example

Officer Jones gets a report that the tires of a professor's car have been slashed at the local college. The car has also been keyed. Jones talks to the professor, who reports that Stan Smith, one of his students, may be a suspect since he just failed him in a class. Jones fingerprints the car, but no prints other than the professor's are found. The officer talks to Smith, who states that he did not touch the professor's car. Does Officer Jones have probable cause to arrest Smith for the crime? No. At this point, all he has is conjecture and suspicion. There is no solid evidence linking Smith to the crime.

B. Charging Suspects

After law enforcement has conducted its investigation and identified a suspect, the case then shifts to the prosecutor to determine if there is sufficient evidence to charge the suspect and ultimately convict him of those charges at trial. A suspect can be charged either through a grand jury indictment or by filing a charging document called an information.

1. The Grand Jury Process

Grand jury
the purpose of which is to determine if there is probable cause to charge a suspect with a crime

In federal court, the defendant must be charged by **grand jury**. The Fifth Amendment requires federal prosecutors to empanel grand juries to charge suspects with felonies before trying them.[1] Many states also require that a grand jury be used to charge the defendant prior to trial. A grand jury is similar to a trial jury in that it is composed of ordinary citizens from the local community who are selected to serve on it. Grand jury service is typically much longer than trial jury service, however. Grand juries often hear a number of cases and can be empanelled for several months to over a year. Just like a trial jury, a pool of jurors is selected from the voter registration rolls to serve on a grand jury. Usually between 18 and 23 people are selected to serve on a grand jury panel.

The purpose of a grand jury is to determine whether there is probable cause to charge the suspect with a crime. Instead of hearing evidence in a trial and determining guilt or innocence, the grand jury determines if there is enough evidence to bring charges against the suspect. If the grand jury decides there is sufficient evidence to support the charges, it will issue

Figure 5.1
Activists from the Student Organization for Animal Rights (SOAR) demonstrate at the Minneapolis Federal Courthouse in 2000, denouncing the grand jury process. The protestors' message is, of course, ironic since the Fifth Amendment to the Constitution guarantees suspects the right to a grand jury.
© 2000 Layne Kennedy/ Corbis

Indictment

a charging document issued by the grand jury. It contains a list of the charges and a plain statement of the facts supporting the charges

a charging document called an **indictment**. The indictment contains a list of the charges and a plain statement of the facts supporting the charges. A grand jury can indict a person where there is sufficient evidence that a crime has been committed and that the suspect committed the offense.[2] Unlike a trial jury, a unanimous verdict is not required to obtain an indictment. Twelve votes are usually required to return an indictment against the defendant.

Evidence plays a big role in the grand jury process. The prosecutor may call witnesses and present physical evidence to establish probable cause. The grand jury itself has investigatory powers as well. It can subpoena witnesses to testify or require those witnesses to produce documents. The defendant often plays no role in the process. He is not present during testimony of other witnesses, cannot cross-examine those witnesses, and usually does not testify.

Since the grand jury is just a screening tool, the formal rules of evidence do not apply. The prosecution does not have to present all evidence of a defendant's guilt to the grand jury. The prosecution can also base its presentation of evidence to the grand jury solely based on hearsay (statements of someone other than witness testifying), although some courts discourage the practice.[3] It also is not obligated to present evidence that would be favorable to the accused or that would bear on the credibility of the witnesses. While a prosecutor does not have to present any evidence that suggests the defendant's innocence, he must present evidence that "clearly negates the target's guilt."[4] In other words, the prosecutor should not deliberately mislead the grand jury as to the suspect's guilt.

Practical Example

Roger is accused of lying to Congress. The United States attorney wants to charge Roger with several counts of perjury. Roger was asked to testify regarding athletes' use of performance-enhancing drugs. Roger testified that he had never knowingly used such drugs. His personal trainer contradicts this statement, however. The trainer states he personally injected Roger with such substances on multiple occasions and Roger had requested the drugs. If the prosecutor presents just the statement of the trainer before a grand jury, will that be enough to obtain an indictment? Yes. The testimony of the trainer establishes probable cause for the charges of perjury.

2. Informations and Preliminary Hearings

Due to concerns about the cost, efficiency, and effectiveness of grand juries, about half of the states have eliminated the requirement for grand juries. Those states permit prosecutors to directly charge suspects. If the

Information

a charging document prepared by the prosecutor that eliminates the need for a grand jury

Preliminary hearing

a pretrial hearing held to determine whether there is probable cause for the charges

prosecutor files charges without a grand jury, he must file what is known as an **information**. Like an indictment, an information is a charging document that provides notice of the charges against the defendant.

If a defendant is charged by information rather than grand jury indictment, he may also have a right to a **preliminary hearing**. Like a grand jury, the purpose of a preliminary hearing is to determine whether probable cause exists to support the charges that the accused committed a particular crime.[5] In effect, a preliminary hearing acts as a substitute for the grand jury—it is a determination of whether there is probable cause for the charges.[6] The Colorado Supreme Court summarized the purpose of a preliminary hearing as follows:

> [A] Preliminary hearing is a screening device and does not require that the prosecution lay out for inspection and for full examination all witnesses and evidence. The reasoning behind an early preliminary hearing is to afford the defendant an opportunity to challenge the sufficiency of the government's evidence to establish probable cause by forcing the government to present its evidence to an impartial judge for examination.[7]

Preliminary hearings are usually held where the suspect is unable to post bond while he awaits charges or trial. A preliminary hearing can also be used in conjunction with a grand jury where the suspect is in custody awaiting charges. Its purpose in that context is to determine whether there is sufficient evidence to merit transferring the case to a grand jury. Preliminary hearings are more like trials than grand juries since the defendant and the judge are present. As a result, the witnesses are subject to cross-examination, and the judge can exclude unreliable evidence.[8]

As in grand juries, the rules of evidence are not constitutionally required in preliminary hearings.[9] Thus, the prosecution can use hearsay evidence or illegally obtained evidence to make its case. Many states require at least some direct evidence of the suspect's guilt, however. A Colorado court explained this requirement:

> [T]he prosecution satisfies the minimum requirement for non-hearsay if it presents some competent non-hearsay addressing essential elements of the offense, and presents hearsay testimony through a witness who is connected to the offense for its investigation and is not merely reading from a report.[10]

Practical Example

Lisa is a teacher charged with sexually assaulting a student. At her preliminary hearing, the lead investigator is the only witness called. He testifies that the student's mother filed a police report after her son disclosed to her that the couple had had sex on several occasions. The student does not testify. The investigator has no independent proof of the assault other than the statement contained in his report. The judge will not bind over the charges since there is no direct evidence of Lisa's guilt.

C. Arraignment

Arraignment

the initial step in the court process. The defendant is advised of the charges against him and asked to enter a plea

Nolo contendere plea

a plea of no contest

Arraignment is the initial stage of the court process during which the court advises the defendant of the charges against him.[11] It is one of shortest and simplest hearings in the entire process. The defendant will also be asked to enter a plea. A defendant can enter three pleas: guilty, not guilty, or nolo contendere (no contest). A **nolo contendere plea** has the same effect as a guilty plea but has some advantages in civil court (a plea of guilty carries with it a presumption of liability that a plea of no contest does not). During the arraignment hearing, the court will also ask if the defendant wishes to have an attorney appointed for him if he cannot afford one.

D. Bail

Bail

the posting of some security in exchange for one's freedom pending trial

Personal recognizance bond

a type of bond that allows a defendant to be released in exchange for his promise to appear

If the defendant is incarcerated prior to trial, he can request **bail**. Bail is the provision of a security in exchange for one's freedom pending trial and the person's promise to appear at future court hearings.[12] A person can be released on a **personal recognizance bond** (PR bond) or a cash or surety bond. A PR bond allows the defendant to be released on his word that he will appear in court. It is usually reserved for misdemeanor offenses such as theft or minor assaults. Otherwise, if the defendant is released, he must post cash or have a surety (such as a bondsman) do so for him.

Prior to the 1960s, bail standards varied widely across the United States. In 1968, the American Bar Association drafted guidelines for determining pretrial release on bail. The guidelines show a preference for pretrial release.[13] A number of states have passed bail statutes that follow the guidelines. For example, Georgia's pretrial detention statute provides that a person may be released on bail if he:

(1) Poses no significant risk of fleeing from the jurisdiction of the court or failing to appear in court;
(2) Poses no significant threat or danger to any person, to the community, or to any property in the community;
(3) Poses no significant risk of committing any felony pending trial; and
(4) Poses no significant risk of intimidating witnesses.[14]

Similarly, Congress attempted to standardize the bail and pretrial detention process in federal courts by passage of the Bail Reform Act of 1984. The Act provides that the judge shall determine whether to detain a defendant prior to trial or whether to grant bail. The Act permits the judge to grant a PR bond, impose conditions of release including posting cash or surety, or order pretrial detention.[15] A defendant can be detained only if the judge determines that no combination of conditions will reasonably assure the appearance of the defendant or the safety of an individual or the community and where he is charged with committing a serious felony.[16] Congress specified a number of factors the court should consider in making this determination, including the nature and seriousness of the charges, the substantiality of the evidence against the defendant, the defendant's background and character, and the nature and seriousness of the danger posed by the defendant's release.[17] Prior to being detained, the defendant is entitled to a hearing, can request the presence of counsel at the hearing, can testify and present witnesses on his own behalf, and can cross-examine other witnesses appearing at the hearing.[18]

Initially, the defendant bears the burden of producing some evidence that he or she poses no significant risk of fleeing, committing a crime, or intimidating a witness.[19] This means that the defendant must produce some evidence of his ties to the community, employment status, and prior performance while out on bail.[20] Once the defendant has met this burden, the state may present evidence to rebut it. Depending on the quality of evidence presented by the defendant, the state may not need to present any evidence in this regard.[21] For example, if the defendant testifies that he has no job, has skipped out on bail before, and has no ties to the community, the government would not have to present any additional evidence that the defendant poses a threat to the community and should be denied bail.

Practical Example

Jose is charged with assaulting a federal agent and breaking her jaw. This qualifies as a crime of violence, permitting pretrial detention under the Bail Reform Act. Jose threatened to kill his girlfriend on a prior occasion and was convicted of drug charges three years ago. Jose also made comments prior to his arrest that he was planning to flee to Mexico. Is there enough evidence to warrant his detention prior to trial? Yes. The government would be able to show by clear and convincing evidence that no conditions of release would assure Jose's appearance in court and protect the community due to the nature of the charges and his prior history on bail.

Motion
a written or oral request asking the court to issue a particular ruling or order. Motions are commonly filed by parties to admit or exclude evidence

E. Motions Hearings

Either side may file various motions during the course of a case. A **motion** is a written or oral request to the court asking it to issue a particular ruling or order.[22] Motions can be filed to admit or exclude evidence or to resolve other legal issues in the case. A defendant, for example, might file a motion to suppress illegally seized evidence or to challenge an expert offered by the prosecution. The prosecution might file a motion to introduce prior bad acts or other negative character evidence about the defendant.

Motions are usually filed prior to trial so the issues can be resolved without delaying or interrupting trial. The parties will often submit written arguments called briefs in support of their position on the motion. This helps the judge become knowledgeable about the specific issues and facts that are contested prior to hearing arguments on the motion. The court will then schedule a hearing for the parties to present arguments and any testimony or other evidence in support of or in opposition to the motion. Finally, the court will normally enter an order deciding the motion, but the court may reserve ruling on the motion until trial. A court may decide to delay a ruling if it is unsure that the issue will actually be raised during trial.

Practical Example

Annie is tried for sexual assault on a minor. Her attorney moves to exclude one of the prosecution's expert witnesses—a psychologist who will testify that sexual predators prey on minors because they are easier to control. The expert also speculates that Annie may have some deep-seated issues with being abused as a child herself. The defense will file a motion along with a brief outlining the reasons why the expert's testimony should be excluded. The brief will discuss the applicable case law and statutes as well as the facts of the case. The prosecution will then file a response in opposition to the motion. The motion will be set for a hearing and the judge will hear arguments for and against the motion. He will then rule on whether the expert testimony will be admitted or not.

F. Evidence of Plea Negotiations

Rule 410. Inadmissibility of pleas, plea discussions, and related statements

Except as otherwise provided in this rule, evidence of the following is not, in any civil or criminal proceeding, admissible against the defendant who made the plea or was a participant in the plea discussions:

(1) A plea of guilty which was later withdrawn;

(2) A plea of nolo contendere;

(3) Any statement made in the course of any proceedings under Rule 11 of the Federal Rules of Procedure or comparable state procedure regarding either of the foregoing pleas; or (4) Any statement made in the course of plea discussions with an attorney for the prosecuting authority

which does not result in a plea deal or which results in a plea of guilty later withdrawn.

However, such a statement is admissible (i) in any proceeding wherein another statement made in the course of the same plea or plea discussions has been introduced and the statement ought in fairness be considered contemporaneously with it, or (ii) in a criminal proceeding for perjury or false statement if the statement was made by the defendant under oath, on the record, and in the presence of counsel.

Plea agreement

an agreement entered into between the defendant and the prosecution. It usually involves the defendant agreeing to plead guilty to a reduced charge or number of charges in exchange for a lesser sentence

During the next stage of the criminal justice process, the defendant may enter into a **plea agreement** with the prosecution. As part of a plea agreement, the defendant agrees to plead guilty to a reduced charge or a reduced number of charges, usually in exchange for some sentencing concession. For example, a person charged with armed robbery may plead guilty to a reduced charge of attempted armed robbery, which carries with it a lesser prison sentence.

In order to work out a plea, the prosecutor and defense attorney will communicate either in person or in writing. To do so effectively, both need to be able to communicate freely about the case. Obviously, if the defendant's statements made during plea negations could be used against him later at trial if no deal is reached, the defendant would have little incentive to speak freely and openly. Thus, Rule 410 provides that statements made by the defendant in connection with plea negotiations are inadmissible where the defendant later withdraws his plea and goes to trial. This situation often occurs where the judge rejects the plea or the defendant is unhappy with the recommended sentence. In such situations, the defendant is allowed to change his mind, withdraw his plea, and proceed to trial.

The rule covers all conversations and statements made during plea negotiations. Not every conversation with a law enforcement officer or attorney can reasonably be interpreted to be a plea discussion, however. Courts will look at the totality of the circumstances to determine whether the defendant "exhibited an actual subjective expectation to negotiate a plea at the time of the discussion and whether that expectation was reasonable."[23] The discussions between a prosecutor and the defendant leading up to the signing of a formalized plea agreement are usually covered by the rule. These preliminary discussions have to be covered because prosecutors have no incentive to plea without receiving information first, and defendants have no incentive to talk without some assurance that their statements will not be used against them. For example, the Tennessee Supreme Court found that the defendant's statement to officers that he was involved in the murder should be considered part of plea discussions since he was almost immediately given a reduced sentence in return for his agreement to testify against his co-defendant.[24]

Statements made to law enforcement officers but not in the presence of prosecutors can sometimes be covered under the rule as well. Where law enforcement officers act with the "express authorization" to accept the plea on behalf of the prosecuting attorney, statements made by the defendant to those officers are covered by the rule just as if they'd been made to a prosecutor for purposes of reaching a plea.[25] Without such an exception, prosecutors might be tempted to avoid the rules by authorizing law enforcement officers to conduct negotiations for them.

Courts have also held that statements made in connection with plea negotiations cannot be used for impeachment purposes, absent a waiver of those rights. For example, the New Mexico Supreme Court ruled that the prosecution could not impeach the defendant at trial with his statement made during plea negotiations that he recognized the undercover officer as the man to whom he sold heroin.[26] The court held that once the defendant withdraws his earlier plea or negotiations fail, the "slate is wiped clean" as if the plea discussions had never taken place.[27] Other state courts such as Vermont and Minnesota have issued similar rulings.[28] The federal rule requires that the prior statement be made on the record, under oath, and in the presence of counsel in order for the defendant to be impeached with it during a perjury proceeding.[29] The consistent theme of these decisions is that the state's interest in preventing perjury is outweighed by the interest in promoting free and open plea negotiations.

Mezzanatto agreement

an agreement signed by the defendant prior to plea negotiations that waives the protections of Rule 410

To avoid such issues, many prosecutors require the defendant to sign a form called a proffer agreement or **Mezzanatto agreement**, which waives the protections of Rule 410 in certain circumstances. These agreements usually permit the prosecution to introduce any statement made by the defendant during plea negotiations for impeachment purposes if the plea is later withdrawn or rejected. The United States Supreme Court approved the use of such agreements in *United States v. Mezzanatto*.[30] The Court found that agreements to waive evidentiary rules are generally enforceable and do not violate a defendant's constitutional rights as long as they are knowingly and voluntarily made.[31] The Court held that the rights contained in Rule 410 are not so fundamental to the reliability of the trial process that they cannot be waived since such agreements will enhance the truth-seeking functions of trials.[32]

To be enforceable, the prosecution must show that the defendant knowingly and voluntarily waived his rights when he signed the proffer agreement.[33] A waiver is made knowingly if the defendant has a "full awareness of both the nature of the right being abandoned and the consequences of the decision to abandon it," and it is voluntary if it is "the product of a free and deliberate choice rather than intimidation, coercion, or deception."[34] For instance, courts have found that a valid waiver exists where defendants have reviewed the terms of proffer agreements with their counsel prior to signing them.[35]

A waiver of the defendant's *Miranda* rights is insufficient to create a waiver of the protections of Rule 410. The Tennessee Supreme Court compared *Miranda* warnings and Rule 410 as follows:

> [A] Defendant's subjective knowledge of the contents of the right being waived is crucial, not irrelevant, for determining whether a waiver is knowing. We do not believe that *Miranda* warnings, which do not mention the rights provided by rules 410 and 11(e)(6), can make a defendant aware of the nature of those rights. Furthermore, the purposes and protections of *Miranda* are substantially different from the purposes and protections of rules 410 and 11(e)(6). The purpose of *Miranda* warnings is to secure the privilege against self-incrimination, ensuring that confessions are voluntary and intelligent. The purpose of the protections of rules 410 and 11(e)(6), on the other hand, is to foster frank and open discussions that lead to plea agreements.[36]

Practical Example

Lincoln is charged with the murder of his wife. The prosecutor and Lincoln's attorney engage in plea discussions. Lincoln and his attorney tell the prosecutor that Lincoln acted under extreme emotional stress when he killed his wife because he caught her having an affair with the plumber. The prosecutor offers a deal to Lincoln for 15 years if he pleads guilty to a reduced charge of manslaughter. Ultimately, Lincoln rejects the deal and goes to trial. At trial, Lincoln testifies that he did not kill his wife. The prosecutor attempts to introduce his statement made during plea discussions that Lincoln killed his wife. The evidence should not be admitted under Rule 410 unless Lincoln signed a proffer agreement.

G. Trial

Trial
the determination of the parties' legal issues by a fact finder based on a hearing of the evidence. A trial can either to be to the court or to a jury

If a plea cannot be reached, the case will go to **trial**. A trial is a hearing of the evidence of the case before some fact finder who then determines the outcome of the legal claims of the parties.[37] Most criminal trials are before a jury, but a case could be heard by a judge. The prosecutor has the burden of proof at trial. He must prove the defendant guilty beyond a reasonable doubt. Since the prosecution has the burden of proof, it goes first and presents its case of the defendant's guilt. The defendant will then have an opportunity to counter the allegations of the prosecution. The defendant may choose to testify, but he has the right to remain silent. The prosecution then has one final chance to rebut any evidence that the defense has introduced. The various stages of trial are discussed more fully below.

1. Jury Selection

Voir dire

the process of questioning jurors to determine their biases or conflicts prior to being seated on a jury

Although jurors are selected from a random pool of registered voters, both sides have some say on who ultimately will serve on the jury. Potential jurors are screened through a questioning process known as **voir dire**. Voir dire is a French term literally meaning "to see the speaking." Jurors are asked questions about their background and about potential biases they might have such as whether they know the parties, have some personal involvement in the case, or have some past personal experience that would prevent them from serving as an unbiased juror. Depending on the jurisdiction, either the judge or the attorneys can conduct the voir dire questioning.

At the start of the process, 12 potential jurors (12 jurors are used in felony cases, whereas 6 are usually used in misdemeanor cases), plus 1 or 2 alternates, are selected from the larger pool of candidates to sit on the jury. This panel is then questioned about its biases. Potential jurors can be stricken from the panel in one of two ways: the juror could be stricken for cause or stricken by a peremptory challenge. A **for-cause challenge** means that the juror is disqualified from sitting on the jury due to the fact that he or she cannot be a fair and impartial juror, usually due to some bias or prejudice.[38] For example, a juror should be stricken for cause when he or she is prejudiced against the racial minority group of the defendant or is related to one of the parties.

For-cause challenge

a challenge made to a potential juror on the ground that the juror should be disqualified from sitting on the jury due to the fact that he or she cannot be a fair and impartial juror, usually due to some bias or prejudice

Peremptory challenge

a challenge made by one of the parties against a potential juror that does not need to be supported by a reason

A **peremptory challenge**, on the other hand, is a challenge that does not need to be supported by a reason (unless there is an allegation of racial or sexual bias in making the strike). Each side gets a number of peremptory challenges equal to half the size of the final jury. For example, each side would get six challenges when a 12-person jury is being used. An attorney might choose to exercise a peremptory challenge on a potential juror for any number of reasons, such as a response a juror gave to a particular question, the occupation of the juror, or even a gut feeling. As jurors are stricken, other potential jurors are put in their place. Once the parties are out of peremptory challenges or they accept the panel as is, the jury is seated.

Practical Example

Julio is on trial for domestic violence assault. His attorney asks the potential jurors if any of them has been the victim of domestic violence. Three women raise their hands and state that they have been. When asked whether they could hear evidence and remain unbiased, two of the jurors state that they could not due to their feelings about domestic violence perpetrators. The third says that she could remain fair. These first two jurors should be stricken for cause since they stated that they could not remain fair and impartial. Julio's attorney must then use one of his peremptory challenges to strike the third juror if he so chooses.

2. Opening Statements

Opening statement
a summary of the evidence expected to be presented at trial

At the start of the trial, each side is given the opportunity to make an **opening statement**. An opening statement is a summary of the evidence that is expected to be presented during trial. The opening statement gives the jury a road map of each side's theory of the case and sets the tone for the trial. The defendant can make his opening statement at the start of trial or can reserve his opening until the start of the defendant's case. The opening statement is not evidence itself, however.

3. Prosecution's Case-in-Chief

Case-in-chief
the amount evidence presented by a party after the first witness is called until the party rests

The prosecution's **case-in-chief** is the opportunity for the prosecution to present evidence of the defendant's guilt. A case-in-chief is composed of the evidence presented between the time the first witness is presented and the party rests.[39] As you learned in the previous chapter, the prosecution must prove the defendant guilty beyond a reasonable doubt. It must present sufficient evidence as to each element of the crime in order to convict the defendant of the crime charged during its case-in-chief. During the case-in-chief, the prosecution will often present a wide range of witnesses and evidence, including eyewitnesses, expert witnesses, and physical evidence.

Practical Example

Assume the defendant is charged with domestic violence–related assault. The victim was allegedly punched and kicked in the fight and taken to the emergency room to treat her injuries. The prosecutor would call the victim, the emergency room doctor, the responding officer, and maybe one or two neighbors who may have heard or seen something when the fight took place. The prosecutor would also present photographs of the victim's injuries.

a. Direct Examination of the Witness

Direct examination
the process of putting on evidence for each side

Leading question
a question that implies the answer in the question

The process of putting on evidence for each side must be conducted through **direct examination**. Nonleading questions must be used during direct examination. **Leading questions** are questions that imply the answer in the question. An example of a nonleading question might be, "What color was the car?" An example of a leading question would be, "The car was red, correct?" Leading questions can be used on direct examination only when that party's witness is uncooperative or hostile. They are also sometimes used without objection to expedite the testimony about a person's background and education.

b. Cross-Examination of the Witness

Cross-examination
the process through which the opposing party questions a witness and attacks his credibility

Leading questions can be used during **cross-examination**, however. Cross-examination is the process through which the opposing party questions a witness. The intent of cross-examination is to attack the credibility of the other side's witnesses or challenge some flaw in the evidence. You will learn more about cross-examination in Chapter 11.

4. Defense's Case-in-Chief

Because the defendant has an absolute right to remain silent, he does not have to present a defense. The defense attorney could simply rest on the fact that the prosecution has failed to produce sufficient evidence of his guilt. This is a risky tactic, however. Even if the defendant chooses not to testify, most defense attorneys will at least call a few character witnesses to bolster the defendant's case.

5. Prosecution's Rebuttal

Rebuttal
the opportunity of the prosecution to present any evidence that counters evidence put on by the defense

Since the prosecution has the burden of proof, it has the opportunity to rebut any evidence the defense puts on. **Rebuttal** is the last phase of the trial where evidence can be presented. For example, if the defense had put on two alibi witnesses that testified the defendant was with them at the time of the murder, the prosecution could counter by producing two other witnesses who dispute the accounts of the alibi witnesses. The prosecution cannot introduce any new evidence that is outside the scope of the evidence presented during the defense's case, however. The purpose of rebuttal testimony is simply to refute or challenge the defendant's evidence.

6. Closing Statements

The closing statements or arguments allow the parties to argue about the meaning or significance of the evidence. Just like opening statements, they are not evidence. This gives the attorneys an opportunity to explain the meaning or significance of certain pieces of evidence. It also gives the attorneys another chance to lay out the theme of the case and allows them one final attempt to sway the jury. Who can forget Johnny Cochrane's famous line during the closing of the O.J. Simpson murder trial: "If it [the bloody glove] does not fit, you must acquit"?[40] Closing arguments very rarely win cases, however. Juries will ultimately decide guilt or innocence based on the presentation of evidence during the trial. It is likely most jurors have made up their minds long before closing arguments.

7. Reading of the Jury Instructions

Jury instructions
instructions read to the jury by the judge. They contain the law the jury must follow in deciding the guilt or innocence of the defendant

The last phase of a jury trial before the jury retires to deliberate is the reading of the **jury instructions**. Jury instructions contain the law that the jury must follow in deciding the guilt or innocence of the defendant. The instructions provide the jury with the elements of the crime that must be found to convict, such as the necessary mental state of the defendant. The instructions also contain definitions of several legal terms that may be necessary to determine the outcome, such as conspiracy or attempt. All states and the federal courts have form instructions that cover most common situations in criminal cases. This makes the reading of most instructions consistent between cases.

8. Objections

Objection

a statement opposing some action or question in court. The judge may either sustain or overrule the objection

Sometimes the attorneys for either side will object to a question asked of a witness. An **objection** is a statement by a party opposing an action or question in court that seeks an immediate ruling on the matter.[41] When an objection is made, the witness must wait for the judge to rule on the objection before answering. The judge can either sustain the objection or overrule it. If an objection is sustained, this means that the judge has granted the objection and the witness cannot answer the question. If the judge overrules the objection, this means the witness may answer the question.

Objections come in three basic forms: objections to the form of the question, objections to the substance of the testimony, and objections to the witness's answer. A form objection is made due to some defect in how the question is asked. For example, the question may be confusing or misstate the testimony of the witness. Another common form objection is that the attorney is asking a leading question of a witness on direct examination. When a form objection is made, the judge will usually ask the attorney to rephrase the question in a nonobjectionable way.

On the other hand, an objection to the substance of the testimony means that the questioner is attempting to introduce evidence that should not lawfully be admitted. If the objection is sustained, the attorney cannot simply rephrase the question. The contents of the answer, not the form of the question, is what is being objected to in this instance. For example, an objection can be made to a question that would provide irrelevant detail. A party may also attempt to introduce a piece of evidence without laying a proper foundation for its admission. In either case, the evidence cannot be admitted.

The final category of objection is that made to the answer given by the witness. Sometimes the witness will not give a proper answer to a question, such as providing hearsay (telling the jury what they heard someone else say). If the objection to a witness's answer is sustained, the judge will instruct the jury to disregard the answer of the witness.

Table 5.1 provides a list of common objections and gives examples of each.

TABLE 5.1   COMMON TRIAL OBJECTIONS

Objections to the substance of the testimony

(1) Relevance	Can you please tell us what the weather was like at the intersection the day before the accident?
(2) Hearsay	Can you tell us what Sam said about Melissa's finances the day before she died?
(3) Lack of Foundation	The people would offer photographs 1–5 into evidence (without any testimony about whether they accurately depict the scene).
(4) Beyond the scope of direct	The witness is asked about a stock deal she did with the defendant three years ago but on direct testifies about a car crash.

Objections to the form of the question

(1) Leading question	Isn't it true that the light was red?
(2) Calls for speculation	What was Lance Corporal Downey thinking when he stuffed the rag down the private's throat?
(3) Compound question	Tell us, what did you do when you got to the bar and how many people were at the bar and how long did you play pool for?
(4) Argumentative	Isn't it true that you would have not taken out a life insurance policy if you really loved your wife?
(5) Misstates facts in evidence	Isn't it true you testified that you were at the movies the night of the murder? (In fact the witness testified that she wanted to go to the movies that night.)
(6) Vague	At the time the fight occurred, what were the men doing?
(7) Assumes facts not in evidence	If the drugs had been present in the apartment before the sale took place, would your statement that Sally did not sell the drugs be any different? (There has been no testimony that drugs were in the apartment prior to the sale.)
(8) Cumulative	Can you please describe whether the Lieutenant was present when the Commander gave the order not to shoot? (Four other witnesses have testified to the same thing.)

Objections to the answer

(1) The answer is unresponsive to the question	The witness's answer speculates about the defendant's motive but the question asked was about the defendant's reputation for peacefulness.
(2) The answer is hearsay	The witness is asked about what she heard the defendant's wife say. The witness begins her answer by stating, "I overheard his wife say that he was not at home."

Practical Example

The following dialogue provides an example of how an objection is made during trial and ruled on by the judge:

DA: *At around what time did you see Ms. Spalding hit the man?*

Defense: *Objection, your honor. Leading.*

Judge: *Sustained. Please rephrase the question.*

DA: *Did you observe Ms. Spalding do anything unusual?*

Witness: *Yes. She hit the man on the corner with her purse.*

DA: *At about what time was that?*

Witness: *Approximately 5:30 in the afternoon.*

H. Appeal

Once the trial has concluded, the losing party may appeal. The party that files an appeal is known as the **appellant** or petitioner. The party that contests the appeal is known as the **appellee** or respondent. To start an appeal, the appellant must file a notice of appeal with the appellate court and must do so within a specified period after trial (usually 30 to 60 days after the judgment or verdict is rendered).

While the prosecutor can file an appeal of the defendant's acquittal, the decision of the appellate court will only affect future cases. In other words, the outcome of the particular case being appealed—the acquittal of the defendant—cannot change. Double jeopardy prevents the defendant from being retried once he has been acquitted. The prosecutor may still want to file an appeal, however, so that an incorrect ruling by the trial judge does not negatively impact future cases where that same issue may come up. Meanwhile, the defendant can overturn his conviction on appeal. Of course, even if he is successful, double jeopardy does not prevent a retrial. The defendant is simply granted a new trial.

The prosecutor can also file a special type of appeal called an **interlocutory appeal**. An interlocutory appeal is filed prior to the case becoming final (before a verdict or dismissal is entered). The one situation where this commonly occurs is where the judge has granted a motion to suppress evidence. Because all or a substantial part of the evidence may be excluded by the court, the prosecution is allowed the right to appeal this decision before a final order is entered in the case.

A defendant has one appeal of right. This means that the appellate court must hear the appeal. In most states and the federal courts, the defendant can appeal his case to the intermediate appellate court (eight states do not

Appellant
the party who files the appeal

Appellee
the party who responds to the appeal

Interlocutory appeal
an appeal filed by the prosecutor before the case has become final to challenge a ruling that excludes all or substantially all of the evidence

have an intermediate appellate court so the appeal is heard by the state's high court). On appeal, most cases are heard by three judge panels.

During an appeal, no new evidence is considered by the appellate court. Instead, it hears arguments about the disputed legal issues. The appellate court reviews the contested rulings made by the judge on any number of issues. For example, the trial judge may have decided to let an expert testify where the expert's opinion was based on unreliable scientific methodology and should have been excluded. The judge may have sustained or overruled an objection during trial that should have been ruled on in the opposite manner. The judge may have read an improper instruction to the jury. All of these are possible errors subject to appellate review. The factual determinations made by the jury are not reviewable, however. The jury must weigh the evidence to determine if the prosecution has met its burden of proof. To do so, it must assess the credibility of witnesses, make inferences based on the existence of certain other facts, and resolve factual disputes.

In order to determine if the judge made any legal errors that may have materially affected the outcome of the trial, the appellate court reviews the trial record. The record consists of the transcript of the trial, the exhibits admitted during trial, the jury instructions, and any pleadings and motions that were filed in the case. The appellate court will often also hear oral argument on the case by the attorneys representing each side. The appellate court will then issue its written ruling. The process can take months or even years in some cases.

II. TRIAL EVIDENCE

Since the ultimate goal of collecting evidence is to prove the guilt or innocence of a suspect, the remainder of this book will be devoted to learning the requirements for introducing evidence at trial. There are four general types of evidence that are presented at trial:

(1) Witness testimony
(2) Exhibits
(3) Judicially noticed facts
(4) Stipulations[42]

Witness
a person who provides testimony in a trial or hearing

Lay witnesses
witnesses who can testify as to what they personally observed

A. Witnesses

The largest amount of evidence is provided through the testimony of witnesses. A **witness** in a trial is anyone who provides sworn testimony in a hearing or trial about evidence in the case. Most exhibits are also introduced through the testimony of witnesses. Witnesses come in two basic types: lay witnesses and expert witnesses. **Lay witnesses** can testify

Expert witnesses
witnesses who can testify to their opinions about the evidence based on their training and experience

to what they personally observed or heard, while **expert witnesses** can issue opinions based upon their training and experience and examination of the evidence in the case.

B. Exhibits

Exhibit
any item of physical, tangible evidence such as a piece of paper or document that is admitted during a court trial or hearing to prove a fact

Exhibits are any items of physical, tangible evidence, such as papers or documents, that are produced and exhibited to a court during a trial or hearing and, on being accepted, are marked for identification and made a part of the court record.[43] There are three basic types of exhibits introduced in a criminal case: (1) photographs and other demonstrative aids such as video and animations; (2) documents such as emails, business records, or medical records; and (3) physical evidence such as bullets, DNA, or fibers. The jurors get to take the exhibits with them back to the jury room when deliberating a verdict. They can rely on exhibits just like any of the oral testimony in making their decision.

C. Judicial Notice

Judicial notice
a court practice that allows the judge to hold facts as being true without requiring proof of their existence by either party

A court can remove a party's burden of proving certain facts using a tool called **judicial notice**. Judicial notice means that facts are "taken as true without the necessity of offering evidence by the party who should have ordinarily done so."[44] It eliminates the need for the party wanting to introduce the item into evidence to prove the supporting facts and foundation for the evidence. The purpose of judicial notice is to speed up the trial by eliminating the need to prove well-known or obvious facts. Courts have routinely taken judicial notice of such items as a given location being within the city limits, the powers and duties of public officers, historical facts, and computation of time.[45]

Under the Federal Rules of Evidence, the court can take judicial notice of facts that are not subject to "reasonable dispute" and that are either (1) "generally known" or (2) capable of ready determination by "resort to sources whose accuracy cannot reasonably be questioned."[46] Generally known facts are those that most people know and take to be true. For example, a court could take judicial notice of the fact that the freezing point of water is 32 degrees. Authoritative sources, on the other hand, are those whose credibility and accuracy are taken for granted. Authoritative sources include things such as encyclopedias, maps, medical and historical treatises, almanacs, and public records. To determine whether something is an authoritative source, the Kentucky Supreme Court held that the judge should ask two questions: (1) does the source provide the precise fact to be noticed; and (2) is the source accurate?[47] For example, the court could take judicial notice of the fact that the defendant had two prior felony convictions by referencing its own court records.

The court cannot take judicial notice of a fact that is not an adjudicative fact—a fact that is at issue in the case. The comments to the Federal Rules of Evidence define an adjudicative fact as one that concerns the immediate parties to the case and that relates to "who did what, where, how, and with what motive or intent."[48] For example, the Kentucky Supreme court reversed a trial court's ruling that a defendant had a right to examine raw scientific data relied upon by a state lab. Since this was a matter of debatable law, not a fact at issue in the case, the Supreme Court ruled that the trial court could not take judicial notice of it.[49]

If a party wants the court to take judicial notice of some fact, it should bring it to the court's attention and offer into evidence the fact in question. When the court takes judicial notice of a fact, however, the jury is still free to disregard it and determine its truth like any other item of evidence; in other words, the judge's determination is not conclusive. Thus, in a criminal case, "judicial notice should only be used as a device to establish the prima facie existence of a particular fact which the finder of fact [the jury] is free to disregard despite the defendant's failure to introduce evidence to the contrary."[50]

Practical Example

Jill is on trial for child abuse. There is a question as to what date the abuse occurred on. The child testified that she was abused the day before her uncle's birthday and remembered that it was a Monday. The prosecution moves the court to take judicial notice of the fact that the uncle's birthday was June 22, and that the day of the abuse must have been June 21. The court cannot take judicial notice of the date because it is not easily verifiable as to what date the uncle was born on. The court could only take judicial notice of the day of the week that the date fell on since that information is easily verifiable from a calendar.

D. Stipulations

Stipulation
an agreement made between the parties as to the existence of some fact in evidence. A stipulation permits a piece of evidence to be introduced without proof of its existence or authenticity

Another way that evidence can be introduced is for the parties to stipulate to certain facts. A **stipulation** is an agreement between opposing parties "concerning some relevant point" in the case for the purpose of avoiding delay or expense.[51] The benefit of a stipulation is that the parties do not have to prove its existence and the trial process is speeded up as a result. Usually, the parties will stipulate to facts that neither seriously contests. The parties might stipulate, for example, to the authenticity of certain documents or the distance between two points. Another area where parties often agree on stipulations is the admission of lie detector results. The stipulation might set the parameters of how the lie detector test is to be administered and the extent the results can be admitted into evidence. A defendant may also enter into a stipulation to prevent even more damaging evidence from being admitted. For example, a defendant may try to stipulate to an expert's credentials rather than having the jury hear the witness's impressive resume. The prosecution, of course, is likely to object to this tactic because it wants the jury to hear the expert's qualifications.

E. Things That Are Not Evidence

Some things that are presented at trial or that one party had attempted but failed to introduce into evidence are excluded from the definition of evidence. Items that are not considered to be evidence include:

- Statements, arguments, and objections made by attorneys.
- Information obtained by the judge or jury outside the courtroom.
- Testimony that the judge strikes or excludes from evidence.
- Testimony or exhibits admitted for limited purposes. Such evidence can only be considered for the limited purpose for which it is admitted.
- Jury instructions given to the jury.[52]

The jury or judge can only consider things that have been admitted into evidence when determining the guilt or innocence of the defendant. For example, while the arguments of counsel can certainly persuade a juror to vote a certain way, a juror cannot rely on them as evidence of a person's guilt or innocence. If a witness answered a question in an objectionable fashion, then the jury cannot rely on that response in deciding the case. Of course, as the old saying goes, it is hard to unring the bell once it has already been rung. In other words, once the jury has heard a piece of information, it may be naive to think that all jurors will disregard it if the judge instructs them to disregard it.

EVIDENCE IN ACTION

Bruno Hauptmann Sentenced to Death for Murder of Lindbergh Baby

On March 1, 1932, the 20-month-old son of famed aviator Charles Lindbergh was kidnapped from his New Jersey home. The boy's nurse discovered him missing around 10 o'clock that evening. A search for the boy turned up a ransom note on the windowsill of the nursery. Outside in the yard, footprints were found as well as some impressions that indicated a ladder had been used to reach the window. A homemade, wooden ladder was found nearby. The bottom section of the ladder had been broken.[53]

The kidnapper soon sent a ransom demand of $70,000. The pajamas the toddler had been wearing the night of his adduction were delivered to show the baby was safe. On April 2, 1932, a box of marked bills was given to the alleged kidnapper. The ransom was paid in gold treasury notes that were taken out of circulation a year later. The baby was never produced in return, however. A huge search was launched for Charles, Jr., but nothing turned up. On May 12, 1932, a child's badly decomposed body was

Continued on following page

Evidence in Action continued

found four miles away from the Lindbergh residence. The body was identified as Charles Lindbergh, Jr., due to distinctive overlapping toes on his right foot. The cause of death was listed as a blow to the head.

The case went cold for months until Arthur Koehler, a University of Wisconsin professor, provided the key forensic analysis in the case. Koehler theorized that if he could identify the exact characteristics of the planer used to mill the rails for the ladder, he could match the source of the lumber. He was able to narrow down the list of possible sources to 25 mills in the area that dealt with North Carolina pine. Koehler determined that M.G. & J.J. Dorn Co. in South Carolina had milled the board. He was able to pinpoint a shipment date and determined which lumberyards in the local area had received recent shipments from Dorn. In November 1933, Koehler matched the ladder stock to the National Lumber and Millwork Company in the Bronx.

The next break came when some of the marked ransom notes began turning up in the Bronx in 1934. A suspect, Bruno Hauptman, was soon arrested after a suspicious gas station attendant reported receiving a gold note and wrote down his license number. A stash of $14,000 in gold treasury notes, the same as the ransom was paid with, was found in his garage.

The "trial of the century" as it was known took place in January and February 1935. It was swarmed by onlookers and media. One Sunday during the trial, more than 5,000 people came just to view the courthouse where the trial was taking place.[54] Huge crowds lined up outside the courthouse each day.

The prosecution produced a mountain of damning evidence against Hauptmann. Seven handwriting experts testified that Hauptmann's handwriting matched the ransom notes left at Lindbergh's home. Comparison of samples of Hauptman's handwriting revealed several similarities to the notes, including spelling and penmanship. Several witnesses testified that Hauptmann had passed some of the ransom notes. Evidence also showed that Hauptmann's finances had improved considerably just after delivery of the ransom.

Koehler also provided critical forensic testimony. He testified that a board cut from Hauptmann's floor matched one of the boards in the homemade ladder found at the Lindbergh home. Hauptmann was a carpenter and had worked at the lumberyard that Koehler had identified as the source of the wood. Hauptmann's chisel also had distinctive markings that were matched to the striations in the wood of the ladder.

Hauptmann's defense attorney, Edward Reilly, was ineffective. He claimed there was no such thing as a "wood expert." He tried to cast blame on the police for botching the investigation and suggested the real killers were Lindbergh's servants. The jury did not buy his arguments. It convicted Hauptmann and sentenced him to death. Hauptmann was executed on April 2, 1936.[55]

CHAPTER SUMMARY

Evidence is used during many stages of the criminal justice process. It is first used by investigators to determine whether a crime was committed and whether there is sufficient evidence to arrest a suspect. The prosecution then uses evidence to build a case and charge the suspect with a crime or crimes. Depending on the jurisdiction, prosecutors can either charge a suspect by obtaining a grand jury indictment or filing an information. Once the defendant is charged, he is then advised of the charges, and a hearing is set to determine if the suspect should be released on bail.

At this point, the defendant can enter into a plea with the prosecutor. Any statements made to the prosecutor during plea discussions are not usable to prove the guilt of the defendant at trial if the plea agreement is later withdrawn. The only exception to this is if the defendant had signed a proffer agreement prior to entering the plea.

If a plea is not reached, then the defendant is tried before a judge or jury. The prosecution puts on evidence first in its case-in-chief since it has the burden of proof. Witnesses must be asked direct questions during this process. Leading questions are reserved for cross-examination of the opposing witnesses. The defendant then has the opportunity to cross-examine the prosecution's witnesses. Once the prosecution rests, the defendant can then present evidence in his own defense, although he does not have to. The prosecution is allowed to present rebuttal evidence, challenging the defense's evidence.

Finally, the closing arguments are made by each side and the jury instructions are read to the jury before it deliberates on the verdict.

The parties sometimes object to the questions asked of witnesses or the responses that they give. Objections can be made to the form of the question, the substance of the question, or to the answer given. If an objection is made, the witness must wait for the judge to rule on an objection before answering.

Several types of evidence may be presented at trial. The testimony of witnesses is the most common form of evidence. Next, evidence may be introduced in the form of exhibits, which are any tangible, physical objects. Judicial notice allows the court to take certain facts as being proven without requiring the parties to actually produce evidence of the fact. Facts that are readily known or capable of being proven through authoritative sources such as almanacs or treatises can be taken judicial notice of. The parties can also agree to stipulate to the authenticity or existence of certain facts. The purpose of a stipulation is to speed up the trial process.

If either party is unhappy with the outcome of the case, it can file an appeal. No new evidence is heard on appeal. Instead, the appellate court will review the trial record and determine if any legal errors were made that affected the outcome of the trial. The appellate court can either reverse the decision of the lower court or uphold it. The defendant is awarded a new trial if he wins the appeal, but the ruling only affects future cases if the prosecution wins its appeal.

KEY TERMS

- Appellant
- Appellee
- Arraignment
- Bail
- Cross-examination
- Direct examination
- Exhibit
- Expert witness
- For-cause challenge
- Grand jury
- Indictment
- Information

- Interlocutory appeal
- Investigation witness
- Judicial notice
- Jury instructions
- Lay witness
- Leading questions
- *Mezzanatto* agreement
- Motion
- *Nolo contendere* plea
- Objection
- Opening statement
- Peremptory challenge
- Personal recognizance bond
- Plea agreement
- Preliminary hearing
- Rebuttal
- Stipulation
- Trial
- Voir dire
- Witness

REVIEW QUESTIONS

1. What is the purpose of a grand jury? What is an indictment, and what does it have to contain?

2. Is the defendant present during the grand jury? Do the rules of evidence apply to a grand jury? Explain.

3. What is an information? Who files it?

4. What is the purpose of a preliminary hearing? How is it different from a grand jury proceeding?

5. What is a plea bargain? Can the prosecution use the fact that the defendant originally agreed to a plea bargain but then withdrew it as evidence of his guilt? Explain. Can the prosecutor use the defendant's statements made in plea negotiations as evidence against the defendant? Explain.

6. What is voir dire?

7. What is a peremptory challenge? How is it different from a for-cause challenge?

8. What is the difference between direct and leading questions? When can leading questions be used?

9. What must be proven in the prosecution's case-in-chief?

10. What is the purpose of jury instructions?

11. What parties can appeal? If the prosecution wins its appeal, can the defendant be retried? Explain.

12. Is evidence reheard on appeal? If not, how is an appeal decided?

13. What is an objection? What are the three general types of objections? Give an example of each.

14. Name three types of evidence admitted during trial.

15. What is judicial notice? What types of facts can the court take judicial notice of?

16. What are stipulations? What might they be used for in criminal cases?

APPLICATION PROBLEMS

1. Dr. Bob Jackson is accused of Medicare fraud. He allegedly paid patients to claim illnesses they did not have and prescribed treatment that was never provided so he could collect Medicare payments. Bob is charged in federal court. Bob wants to cross-examine the witnesses during the grand jury. Will he be allowed to do so? What if he is charged in state court and is given a preliminary hearing? Can he cross-examine them now? Explain.

2. Steve is charged with possession of a controlled substance with intent to distribute and three counts of sale of a controlled substance. He is charged in Colorado state court. A preliminary hearing is held. The lead investigator testifies that a confidential informant bought an ounce of cocaine from Steve on three different occasions. He testifies that the confidential informant was searched prior to and after each buy and that he had no drugs on his person prior to the buys but did have cocaine on him after the buys. He testifies that he did the search and bagged the cocaine personally. Is there some direct evidence of Steve's guilt to warrant the judge concluding that there is probable cause for the charges? Explain.

3. John is accused of sexually molesting four young boys. The prosecutor offers him a deal to plead guilty to only one count in exchange for testimony against the leader of the child pornography ring also linked in the investigation. John states that he is thankful for the deal and feels he needs help. The prosecutor makes John sign a *Mezzanatto* agreement before signing the plea. At the trial of the child pornography leader, John refuses to testify. His deal is yanked. Can the prosecutor use John's statement about "needing help" in his trial? Explain.

4. The district attorney brings drug charges against a man who was transporting 200 pounds of marijuana in his car. Prior to trial, the defendant moves to suppress the evidence due to an illegal stop. The judge agrees and suppresses the evidence. The district attorney is furious and thinks the judge made an improper ruling. What type of appeal should the prosecutor immediately file prior to trial?

Notes

1. U.S. Const. Amend. V.
2. United States v. Motte, 251 F. Supp. 601 (S.D.N.Y. 1966); People v. Young, 620 N.Y.S.2d 223, 225-26 (S.Ct. 1994).
3. *See* United States v. Jett, 491 F.2d 1078 (1st Cir. 1974).
4. United States v. Prevor, 583 F. Supp. 259, 261 (D. Puerto Rico 1984).
5. People v. Quinn, 516 P.2d 420 (Colo. 1973).
6. Motte, 251 F. Supp. at 604, n. 3.
7. Quinn, 516 P.2d at 422.
8. 4 Wayne R. Lafave et al., *Criminal Procedure* sec. 14.4(b) & n. 12 (3d ed. 2007).
9. *See, e.g.,* People v. Huggins, 220 P.3d 977, 978-79 (Colo. App. 2009); Colo. R. Evid. 1101(d)(3).
10. Huggins, 220 P.3d at 979.
11. *Black's Law Dictionary*, at 44 (3d pocket ed. 2006).
12. *Black's Law Dictionary*, at 59 (3d pocket ed. 2006).
13. *See* ABA Pretrial Release Standards.
14. OCGA sec. 17-6-1(e).
15. 18 U.S.C. sec. 3142 (2008).
16. 18 U.S.C. sec. 3142(f).
17. United States v. Salerno, 481 U.S. 739, 742 (1987), citing 18 U.S.C. sec. 3142(g).
18. 18 U.S.C. sec. 3142(f).
19. Ayala v. State, 425 S.E.2d 282, 284 (Ga. 1993).
20. Id.
21. Ayala, 425 S.E.2d at 285.
22. *Black's Law Dictionary* at 467 (3d pocket ed. 2006).
23. State v. Hinton, 42 S.W.3d 113, 122 (Tenn. 2001).
24. Hinton, 42 S.W.2d at 121-22.
25. Id. at 123.
26. State v. Trujillo, 605 P.2d 232 (N.M. 1980).
27. Id. at 235.
28. *See* State v. Amidon, 967 A.2d 1126, 1134 (Vt. 2008); State v. Robledo-Kiney, 615 N.W.2d 25, 30 (Minn. 2000).
29. F.R.E. 410.
30. 513 U.S. 196 (1995).
31. Id. at 202.
32. Id. at 204.
33. United States v. Velez, 354 F.3d 190 (2d Cir. 2004).
34. Velez, 354 F.3d at 196, *quoting* Moran v. Burbine, 475 U.S. 412, 421 (1986).
35. *See e.g.*, United States v. Parra, 302 F. Supp. 2d 226 (S.D. N.Y. 2004).
36. Hinton, 42 S.W.3d at 126.
37. *Black's Law Dictionary*, at 733 (3d pocket ed. 2006).
38. *Black's Law Dictionary*, at 95 (3d pocket ed. 2006).
39. Id. at 89.
40. CNN.com, *Famed Attorney Johnnie Cochran Dead*, March 30, 2005, http://articles.cnn.com/2005-03-29/us/cochran.obit_1_johnnie-cochran-simpson-case-nicole-brown-simpson?_s=PM:US.
41. *Black's Law Dictionary*, at 500 (3d pocket ed. 2006).
42. Moneyinstructor.com, *What Is Evidence?* available at www.moneyinstructor.com/art/evidenceinfo.asp.
43. Freedictionary.com, http://legal-dictionary.thefreedictionary.com/exhibit.
44. Cordova v. State, 675 So. 2d 632, 635 (Fla. App. 3d Dist. 1996), citing Fla Stat. Ann. Sec. 90.206 (West 1979).
45. City of Hammond v. Doody, 553 N.E.2d 196 (Ind. App. 3d Dist. 1990).
46. F.R.E. 201(b); Doody, 553 N.E.2d at 198.
47. Clay v. Commonwealth, 291 S.W.3d 210, 217 (Ken. 2009).

48. F.R.E. 201, Advisory Committee's Note to Subdivision (a).

49. Clay, 291 S.W.3d at 217.

50. Cordova, 675 So. 2d at 635, citing United States v. Mentz, 840 F.2d 315, 322 (6th Cir. 1988).

51. *Black's Law Dictionary*, at 1455 (8th ed. 2004).

52. What is Evidence, *supra* at note 12.

53. Amanda T. Ross, *CSI Madison, Wisconsin: Wooden Witness*, March 31, 2009, available at http://www.fhsarchives.wordpress.com/2009/03/31/csi-madison-wisconsin-wooden-witness.

54. *The Trial of the Century*, http://www.nj.com/lindbergh/hunterdon/index.ssf?/lindbergh/stories/trial.html.

55. Id. at 2.

CHAPTER 6

Pretrial Discovery

"All truths are easy to understand once they are discovered; the point is to discover them."—Galileo

Chapter Topics

II. Defendant's Discovery Obligations
   A. Notice of Alibi
   B. Reciprocal Discovery

III. Sanctions for Violating Discovery Rules

Objectives

After completing this chapter, students will be able to:

- Understand the prosecution's duties to preserve and disclose exculpatory evidence

- Understand the prosecution's duty regarding disclosure and preservation of potentially exculpatory evidence

- Understand the requirements for preventing destruction of evidence during the testing process

- Understand the prosecution's and defendant's discovery obligations under Rule 16

- Understand the differences between the disclosure of investigators' notes, expert disclosures, witness statements, and witness lists

- Understand what materials are not subject to disclosure

- Define the defendant's obligations to provide discovery, notice of alibi, and reciprocal discovery

- Know what sanctions can be enforced for violating the discovery rules

Introduction

Discovery

the process through which each side discloses the relevant statements and other evidence it intends to produce at trial to prove its case

No matter how well evidence is collected and preserved, it still may face exclusion at trial if it is not disclosed to the prosecution or defense in a timely manner. The pretrial process of exchanging the statements of witnesses and evidence that may be presented at trial is known as **discovery**. Prior to discovery rules being adopted, trial by ambush was a common practice. Each side would attempt to spring surprise witnesses and evidence on the other side at the last minute. Such tactics are not always conducive to a fair trial. Without the current discovery requirements being in place, the prosecution could simply conceal evidence that would prove the innocence of the defendant.

Today, the process is much more open. The prosecution (and to a lesser extent the defense) has the responsibility to reveal what evidence each side intends to introduce at trial to avoid unnecessary surprise. The prosecution has a constitutional duty to provide exculpatory material that shows the innocence of the defendant within its possession or control. Such evidence must be disclosed even if it is within the possession of investigating agencies, not the prosecutor. Thus, law enforcement officers must be diligent in identifying and turning over evidence to the prosecutor so that discovery can be complete.

Both sides also have obligations to provide certain information under the applicable state or federal discovery rules. The prosecution, at a minimum, has to provide statements of the defendant to law enforcement as well as provide access to documents, photographs, and tangible objects it intends to use at trial to prove the defendant's guilt. The defense has similar obligations to provide the prosecution with discovery, although they are much less extensive than the prosecution's. Sanctions can be imposed by the court for failure to comply with discovery obligations.

I. THE PROSECUTION'S DUTY TO PROVIDE DISCOVERY

A. The Brady Rule: Duty to Preserve and Disclose Exculpatory Evidence

Due process
fundamental fairness; something essential to a fair trial

Exculpatory evidence
evidence that tends to show the innocence of the accused and is material to an issue of guilt or punishment

Brady rule
a Supreme Court ruling that due process is violated where the prosecution fails to disclose exculpatory evidence which can result in either suppression of the evidence or dismissal of the charges

The prosecutor has two basic obligations to provide discovery to the defense: a constitutional duty to provide exculpatory material and a separate duty to provide documents and statements requested under Rule 16 of the Federal Rules of Criminal Procedure. Under the United States Supreme Court's decision in *Brady v. Maryland*, the prosecution must disclose exculpatory material to the defense as part of the defendant's right to due process. **Due process** equates to fundamental fairness; in other words, something essential to a fair trial. **Exculpatory evidence** is that which is favorable to the accused (it tends to show his innocence) and is material to either guilt or punishment.[1] Evidence is material if there is a reasonable probability that the outcome of the trial would have been different if the evidence had been disclosed.[2]

The **Brady rule** can be violated in two ways: (1) suppression of exculpatory evidence or (2) bad faith destruction of potentially exculpatory evidence.[3] The first violation—failure to turn over exculpatory evidence—is a constitutional violation, regardless of whether the nondisclosure was done in good or bad faith.[4] Failure to disclose exculpatory evidence can result in suppression of the evidence and/or dismissal of the charges.

In order to establish a constitutional violation under *Brady*, the defense must show that:

(1) The evidence at issue must be favorable to the accused, either because it is exculpatory or because it may impeach other evidence or testimony;

(2) The evidence must have been suppressed by the prosecution, either willingly or inadvertently; and

(3) The defendant suffered prejudice.[5]

The key question is whether the defendant received a fair trial in the absence of disclosure of the evidence.

Practical Example

Assume a defendant is on trial for sexually assaulting a woman in her car. The prosecution has semen samples from the scene analyzed for DNA. The DNA test results do not match the profile obtained from the defendant. Does the prosecution have to disclose these results? The test results are exculpatory because they tend to show that the defendant did not commit the crime and are material since they relate to the identity of the perpetrator. If the prosecutor does not turn this information over to the defense, the case can be dismissed or the evidence excluded.

---

1. Timing of Disclosures

There is no constitutional right to receive *Brady* material prior to trial. It must be disclosed, however, in sufficient time for the defendant to make sufficient use of it at trial.[6] Implicit in the prosecution's duty to disclose exculpatory evidence is a duty to preserve such evidence for use by the defense.[7] Thus, it can be a due process violation to fail to collect or destroy obviously exculpatory evidence. The duty of the state to preserve such evidence is limited to "evidence that might be expected to play a significant role in the suspect's defense."[8]

EVIDENCE IN ACTION

District Attorney Disbarred for Failing to Turn Over Exculpatory Evidence in Duke Lacrosse Rape Case

On June 17, 2007, Durham, North Carolina District Attorney Mike Nifong was disbarred for ethical violations stemming from his prosecution of three Duke University Lacrosse players for the rape of a black woman that had allegedly occurred on March 13, 2006. The victim had alleged that three lacrosse players had raped her at an off-campus party where she had been hired to perform as a stripper. The allegations rocked the Duke campus, leading to several protests and the firing of the lacrosse coach. As was discussed in Chapter 3, three lacrosse players were picked out of a photo lineup. They were indicted and charged with the rape approximately a month after the allegations were made.

The prosecution's case quickly unraveled, however. The first round of genetic testing revealed no DNA present on the victim. Nifong then arranged for a private DNA lab, DNA Security, to test clothing and other material that the victim was wearing the night

Continued on following page

Evidence in Action continued

of the rape. The DNA laboratory report stated that one male DNA profile was present in a vaginal swab taken from the victim but that no lacrosse players were a match to the sample. The lab reported that the DNA profile belonged to the victim's boyfriend.[9] Nifong made statements on 11 separate occasions that he had turned over all evidence that was potentially helpful to the defense. He also stated that he knew of no additional exculpatory evidence, DNA test results, or information obtained from conversations with his DNA experts that would be helpful to the defense. It was not revealed until December 2006, however, that Nifong had concealed additional findings from the DNA tests.

It was disclosed during a pretrial hearing that DNA technicians had found the DNA profiles of several men on the victim's clothing, none of which matched the lacrosse players' profiles. This was potentially exculpatory evidence that should have been disclosed immediately to the defense. The director of DNA Security testified that he and Nifong had agreed to report only DNA matches with the player's profiles in the report, not other findings.[10] After this revelation surfaced along with strong alibi evidence in favor of two of the suspects, the rape charges were dismissed. Despite strong evidence showing the players' innocence as to all charges, however, Nifong continued to proceed with felony assault and kidnapping charges. Roy Cooper, the state's attorney general, was then appointed as a special prosecutor.

Figure 6.1   Durham County District Attorney Mike Nifong listens as rules violations are announced during his North Carolina State Bar trial in Raleigh, North Carolina on June 16, 2007. Nifong was disbarred for his conduct in handling the Duke Lacrosse rape case. © 2007 AP File Photo/Gerry Broome/Pool

After reviewing the evidence, he dismissed all remaining charges against the defendants on April 11, 2007 and declared their innocence.

The state attorney discipline committee then brought an ethics investigation against Nifong. In the face of mounting pressure, Nifong resigned as District Attorney on June 15, 2007. He was disbarred by the North Carolina Bar the following day due to his unethical conduct during the prosecution of the Duke case.[11]

2. Impeachment Material

Giglio material

material evidence that can impeach the credibility of one of the prosecution's witnesses. It must be disclosed under the *Brady* rule

Exculpatory evidence includes material that bears directly on the credibility of a witness.[12] Since the reliability of the testimony of a given witness can impact guilt or innocence, this type of evidence falls under the umbrella of the *Brady* rule.[13] Thus, the prosecution has a duty to turn over any material relating to the impeachment of its witnesses. Evidence relevant to impeachment is known as **Giglio material** after the United States Supreme Court case that mandated its disclosure.

Practical Example

Otto is on trial for bank robbery. The prosecution is going to call Wanda as a witness. The prosecution has evidence that Wanda has been previously

involved in conspiracy to commit theft and is actively working to double-cross Otto. Does this information have to be turned over to the defense in discovery? Yes. It is relevant to the impeachment of Wanda, so it must be turned over to the defense.

B. Potentially Exculpatory Evidence

1. Destruction of Evidence

Potentially exculpatory evidence
evidence whose exculpatory value is not clearly evident on its face

While the prosecution has a duty to preserve obviously exculpatory evidence, the rules are less clear with respect to **potentially exculpatory evidence**—evidence whose exculpatory value is not clearly evident on its face. Unlike evidence that is obviously exculpatory, the Supreme Court has held that the destruction of potentially exculpatory evidence violates due process only where the exculpatory value of the evidence was apparent to the government before it was destroyed and the defendant was unable to obtain comparable evidence through other means.[14] Where "no more can be said than that it [evidence] could have been subject to tests, the results of which might have exonerated the defendant," the defense must show the police failed to preserve or destroyed the evidence in bad faith.[15] Bad faith is more than mere negligence; instead, there must be a "calculated effort to circumvent the disclosure requirements" under *Brady*.[16] As a result, evidence that has not been examined or tested by government agents does not have "apparent exculpatory value" and thus cannot form the basis of a claim of **bad faith destruction of evidence**.[17]

Bad faith destruction of evidence
a calculated effort to circumvent the disclosure requirements of Brady by intentionally destroying evidence

The Iowa Supreme Court described the relationship of the *Brady* rule to potentially exculpatory evidence as follows:

> Where the lost evidence is only potentially exculpatory, where by its nature the lost evidence cannot be evaluated by a fact finder, a due process violation will not be found in the absence of a showing of bad faith. In other words, when potentially exculpatory evidence is at issue the third prong of the *Brady* test cannot, by definition, be satisfied and is replaced by a bad faith requirement. On the other hand, if the exculpatory value of the lost evidence is suitable for evaluation by a fact finder, a due process violation will be found upon a showing that the evidence was exculpatory and its destruction was deliberate.[18]

A balancing test is used to determine whether sanctions are appropriate for destruction of evidence.[19] In determining what sanction is appropriate, courts will examine the materiality of the evidence to the issue of guilt or punishment, the degree of prejudice suffered by the defendant due to its destruction, and whether the government was acting in good faith when it destroyed the evidence.[20] Mere negligence is usually insufficient to warrant the imposition of sanctions.[21] Even if sanctions are warranted, dismissal of the charges is a severe sanction and should be used only where intentional, bad-faith destruction of evidence has occurred.[22]

Mere speculation that the evidence may have some exculpatory value is not enough to warrant sanctions for its destruction.[23] For example, an Illinois court found that the destruction of drug evidence by a drug enforcement agent was not done in bad faith where the file contained evidence from a closed case and, unbeknownst to the agent, also contained evidence in an open investigation.[24] The Fourth Circuit also found that dismissal was not warranted where detectives had destroyed drug samples pursuant to departmental policy.[25] Since the drug samples were destroyed after the defendant had pled guilty on state charges, the court held the evidence had not been destroyed in bad faith since routine procedures were followed.[26]

Most courts have held that law enforcement does not owe a duty to the defendant to seek out and preserve potentially exculpatory evidence. For example, the Ninth Circuit held that the government is not required to take a rape kit sample on the ground that the result might exculpate the accused.[27] The Idaho Supreme Court concluded that law enforcement's failure to abide by department policies with respect to evidence collection and preservation does not automatically constitute bad faith:

> An inadvertent departure from normal practice, without more, does not rise to the level of bad faith. The district court's statement that the loss of the recording "although in good faith" was not "in accord with the normal practice of the police department" and therefore "cuts against" due process does not constitute the finding of bad faith required to substantiate a due process violation.[28]

Some state courts like Colorado have held, however, that "when evidence can be collected and preserved in the performance of routine procedures by state agents, the failure to do so is tantamount to suppression of the evidence."[29] Thus, in those states, law enforcement must develop regular procedures to preserve evidence where it is "reasonably foreseeable" that such evidence might be favorable to the accused.[30]

Practical Example

Assume that the police investigate an allegation of a rape complaint at a bar. They view the surveillance video that shows a woman somewhat distraught leaving the area where the rape allegedly took place. A few minutes later, the suspect is seen leaving the area. The tape is then placed into evidence. Before the tape can be turned over to the defense, the police accidentally write over the video during a training exercise. The defendant moves to have sanctions imposed for destruction of exculpatory evidence. Since the tape is not obviously exculpatory, the defense would have to show that the tape was destroyed in bad faith. This would be hard to do since the tape's destruction appeared to be accidental.

2. Preservation of Breath and Blood Alcohol Samples

The investigation of drunken driving offenses often involves the testing of a suspect's breath or blood alcohol content. The breath-testing process requires a suspect to blow into a machine that tests the alcohol content of his air sample. A **second sample** of air can be preserved for the defense to independently test. Similarly, two vacuum containers of blood can be taken from the defendant—one for the prosecution and one for the defense.

Second sample
a second sample of blood or breath taken by law enforcement at the time of sobriety testing. Most courts require the preservation of a second sample only where the defendant requests it at the time of sampling

In *California v. Trombetta*, the Supreme Court ruled that it is not a due process violation if law enforcement fails to preserve a second breath sample.[31] Since it is not obvious at the time the breath sample is taken that the results will be exculpatory (the assumption is that the results of the second sample will confirm the results of the first—namely that the defendant is intoxicated), the Court held that that there is no duty to preserve a second sample.[32] In order to show that a due process violation occurred for failure to preserve a second sample, most courts require the defendant to have requested the preservation of a second sample at the time the test was taken.[33]

3. Destruction of Evidence That Occurs During Testing

Most state and federal courts have ruled that the destruction of an evidentiary sample that occurs during scientific testing does not violate due process. In contrast to negligent or intentional destruction of evidence, courts have viewed the consumption of evidence during the testing process as simply part of the state's legitimate investigation of a criminal matter.[34] The California Supreme Court described the situation as follows:

> When a piece of evidence in the possession of the prosecution is destroyed because the prosecution finds it necessary to consume the evidence in order to test it, there is no due process violation. The prosecution must be allowed to investigate and prosecute crime, and due process does not require that it forego investigation in order to avoid destroying potentially exculpatory evidence.[35]

If the sample is destroyed during testing, the court will not suppress the testing results unless the defense can show deliberate destruction of the evidence or avoidance of the prosecution's discovery obligations.[36] For example, the Alaska Supreme Court held that the consumption during testing of the entire amount of heroin contained in a balloon did not constitute a discovery violation.[37] In another case, a Florida court held that where one vial of blood from the scene was consumed in testing and the other was inadvertently broken, no due process violation occurred.[38]

Some red flags may be raised where the defendant has requested the state to preserve samples of the evidence for independent testing but the samples are destroyed anyway.[39] To prevent this situation from occurring, the defendant should be notified beforehand that testing will destroy the sample. While most courts have held that failure to do so is not a due process violation, some states have stricter laws.[40] The Colorado Supreme Court found that where testing is likely to destroy the evidentiary sample, the prosecution must either take photographs of the testing results and/or notify the defendant of the testing to accommodate the presence of a defense expert.[41] Although noting that the court's power to preserve exculpatory evidence does not extend to dictating particular laboratory procedures or ordering the state to pay for defense experts, the trial court can prohibit testing procedures that do not permit independent evaluation of the evidence.[42] Under state law, Colorado law enforcement personnel must preserve evidence and/or notify the defendant where testing will destroy the sample.[43] The court cannot suppress the test results, however, if the testing was performed "in good faith and in accordance with procedures designed to preserve the evidence which might have been favorable to the defendant."[44]

Practical Example

Assume that the defense requests a copy of the videotape of the defendant's interrogation. The defendant confesses to the crime but the videotape will show that the police grilled the suspect, who was learning disabled, for several hours. Despite a court order to preserve the videotape, the prosecution cannot produce it. The tape was accidentally destroyed by the police department. While most states would find that the destruction of the tape does not amount to a due process violation, Colorado courts would likely find that the due process had been violated and would impose sanctions for the tape's destruction.

4. Videotaping of Evidentiary Tests

Due to concerns that the testing process can consume evidentiary samples, alternative procedures such as videotaping of the testing process have been proposed. The American Bar Association has developed a standard for the preservation of evidence in such circumstances, including the videotaping of testing procedures. ABA Standard 3.4(e) provides:

> If a motion objecting to consumptive testing is filed, the court should consider ordering procedures that would permit an independent evaluation of the analysis, including but not limited to the presence of an expert representing the moving party during evidence preparation and testing, videotaping or photographing the preparation and testing.[45]

Colorado recently became one of the first states to adopt the American Bar Association standards.[46]

AUTHOR'S NOTE

Videotaping of testing procedures is controversial. Colorado Bureau of Investigation protocols (as well as those of other public and private labs) prohibit the videotaping of the testing process itself (as opposed to just the results) since the evidence could be contaminated during the taping. The preferred method is to allow a defense expert to observe the testing process, subject to laboratory protocols.[47]

C. Discovery Obligations Under Rule 16

Rule 16
a rule of criminal procedure that requires the prosecution and defense to share certain information prior to trial through discovery, including statements the defendant made to law enforcement, expert witness reports, and any documents or other objects the prosecution intends to use at trial

In addition to its duty to provide exculpatory information, the prosecution also has several discovery obligations under **Rule 16** (or its state equivalent). Rule 16 governs the scope of pretrial discovery requests. These include providing copies of all statements the defendant made to law enforcement during interrogation, the defendant's prior criminal record, and providing access to any item that the prosecutor intends to use in its case-in-chief at trial. The prosecution must also provide a written summary of any expert testimony it intends to offer at trial.

Pursuant to Rule 16, the prosecution must disclose all items in its "possession, custody, or control." This includes information not within the physical possession of the prosecutor's office. Most jurisdictions follow the "prosecution team" model that requires, at a minimum, that the prosecution disclose information in possession of an agency that participated in the investigation or prosecution of the case.[48] Some courts such as the Ninth Circuit Court of Appeals have held that information should also be produced under Rule 16 if it is within the possession of any government agency where the prosecution has "knowledge and access to" the documents sought.[49]

1. Statements of the Defendant

One of the primary obligations of the prosecution under the rule is to provide statements made by the defendant that are in its possession or control. Rule 16(a)(1)(A) provides that the government must produce all oral statements made during police questioning that it intends to use at trial:

> Upon a defendant's request, the government must disclose to the defendant the substance of any relevant oral statements made by the defendant, before or after arrest, in response to interrogation by a person the defendant knew was a government agent if the government intends to use the statement at trial.[50]

The government must also disclose to the defense any relevant written or recorded statement by the defendant if it is within the government's possession, custody, or control and the government knows or should know that the statement exists. Finally, the government must produce any written report (or notes) of any oral statement by a defendant made in response to police interrogation.[51]

The prosecution's obligation includes producing more than just those statements made in response to police interrogation.[52] For example, if the defendant makes a statement to a witness and the witness reports that statement to the police, it is discoverable under the rule. However, statements by co-defendants or co-conspirators not made in furtherance of the conspiracy are not covered under the rule. As you shall see in Chapter 13, those statements are hearsay and are not admissible.[53]

Practical Example

John is charged with conspiracy to commit murder. John is questioned by the police. John states that he only asked the hit man about what price he might charge to kill his wife, but never intended for the hitman to kill her. The police note this statement in a report. The defendant requests pretrial discovery from the prosecution. The prosecution must produce a copy of the report containing the defendant's statement.

2. Documents, Photographs, and Tangible Objects

The prosecution also has the obligation to provide access to documents and physical objects that it intends to use at trial or that are material to preparing a defense. Section (a)(1)(E) of Rule 16 provides:

> Upon a defendant's request, the government must permit the defendant to inspect and to copy or photograph books, papers, documents, data, photographs, tangible objects, buildings or places, or copies or portions of any of these items, if the item is within the government's possession, custody or control and:
>
> **(1)** the item is material to preparing the defense;
> **(2)** the government intends to use the item in its case-in-chief at trial; or
> **(3)** the item was obtained from or belongs to the defendant.[54]

Under this portion of the Rule, the defense must make a specific request for a given item along with an explanation of how it will be helpful to the defense.[55] The request must be sufficiently clear to inform the prosecution what is being sought by the defense.[56] Vague or general descriptions of the material or documents sought are inadequate. As long as a defendant can show a connection between the item sought and his defense, he is entitled to any number of items, including laboratory test reports, copies of plea agreements that have been given in exchange for a witness's testimony, and copies of 911 tapes. This rule also covers the disclosure of electronically stored information (ESI) such as e-mails and medical records.

Practical Example

Assume the government has accounting statements that it intends to use to prove the defendant guilty of embezzlement. Although this evidence is not exculpatory, the government must turn those statements over to the defense if requested to do so prior to trial. Now assume that the prosecution's file contains evidence that drugs were seized from the defendant's home. This also must be produced under a Rule 16 request because the evidence was obtained from the defendant.

3. Investigator's Notes

Interview notes
investigator notes taken during witness interviews. The prosecution must provide copies of interview notes in discovery only where the contents of the notes have not been incorporated into a written report

A question often comes up about whether statements or other discoverable information contained in the **interview notes** of investigators are discoverable. Investigators often take notes of statements made during witness interviews. The general rule is that there is no duty to preserve rough interview notes where the contents of those notes are "accurately captured" in a typewritten report that has been disclosed to the defendant.[57] The comments to Rule 16 indicate that if all notes had to be produced, the prosecutor would have the almost impossible task of locating all oral statements contained in such notes.[58] In contrast, if the investigator's report does not contain all the statements of the defendant or witness, his notes must be provided in discovery.[59]

The fact that such notes were destroyed prior to trial is not enough to suggest that the report is inaccurate.[60] The defense must show that the notes were destroyed in bad faith. For example, the Rhode Island Supreme Court ruled that an officer's destruction of interview notes was not done in bad faith where he did not receive the message that the defense had requested them prior to their destruction.[61]

A related question is whether the notes of victim advocates are discoverable. Advocates are responsible for providing services and referrals (for counseling and other services) to crime victims. As part of their duties, they often meet with victims shortly after the crime has been reported. Victims may make statements to the advocate during their initial meetings that are inconsistent with the story told to law enforcement investigators. Although they are not investigators, they are usually employed by law enforcement agencies or prosecutors' offices. As a result, advocates are considered part of the prosecution team. Thus, most courts have held that notes of victim advocates must be turned over in discovery.[62] The prosecutor, therefore, has to determine whether the advocate is in possession of exculpatory material that must be turned over to the defense or any statements required to be produced under Rule 16.[63] To alleviate this problem, many advocates will simply encourage victims to make the same statements to the law enforcement officer on the scene so that they are included in the official police report.

Practical Example

Assume that the defendant is charged with sexual assault on a child. He requests the prosecution to preserve the investigator's notes of her interview with the child. Subsequently, the notes are destroyed by the investigator during a cleanup of her desk even though she knew of the court's order. Should the court sanction the prosecution for the notes' destruction? The court would probably sanction the prosecution since it had ordered the notes be preserved and the officer disregarded that order.

4. Expert Disclosures

Expert disclosures
written summaries of expert testimony that a party intends to offer at trial

Rule 16(a)(1)(G) requires that the government provide **expert disclosures** to the defense. Expert disclosures are written summaries of testimony of any expert witness that a party intends to offer at trial. Expert witnesses include both employees of the criminal justice system (i.e., crime laboratory employees and medical examiners) and paid experts who are retained by either party. Expert disclosures "must describe the witness's opinions, the bases and reasons for those opinions, and the witness's qualifications."[64] The purpose of this disclosure is to allow the defense an adequate opportunity to challenge the foundations and merits of the witness's testimony on cross-examination.[65] Typically, the prosecutor will produce a copy of the expert's report and his curriculum vitae.

5. Jencks Act

Jencks Act
a federal statute that requires the prosecution in a federal case to produce the statements of any witness after the witness is called to testify in court

Under federal law, the defendant is not entitled to pretrial discovery of statements of witnesses who are going to testify at trial.[66] Once trial has started, however, the prosecution does have an obligation to provide the statements of witnesses who have testified. The **Jencks Act** provides that the prosecution in a federal criminal case must produce the statements of any witness related to the subject matter of his testimony "after a witness called by the United States has testified on direct examination."[67]

Under the act, the prosecution must disclose witness statements in their custody or control. A statement covers the witness's own words; it does not include notes or summaries of the statements unless they were signed or ratified by the witness.[68] Although there is no right to pretrial discovery, statements must be turned over to the defense in time to permit effective cross-examination of the witness.[69] It should be noted, however, that many states require witness statements to be disclosed as part of pretrial discovery. For example, Colorado requires that the prosecution disclose "police, arrest and crime or offense reports, including statements of all witnesses" to the defense no later than 30 days prior to trial.[70]

6. Witness Lists

In federal court, neither side is required to provide a copy of its witness list prior to trial. The trial court can order that each side produce a witness list if the defendant shows some compelling reason to do so.[71] In contrast, most states require that the parties exchange witness lists prior to trial.[72] Even where witness lists are required to be exchanged, the failure to list a witness is not, in and of itself, a reason to exclude the testimony of that witness.[73] Instead, the court must determine whether the nondisclosure prejudiced the other party by preventing him from properly preparing for trial.[74]

In one case, the Ohio Supreme Court overturned the trial court's exclusion of all of the defense witnesses for failure to provide a witness list.[75] The court felt that the sanction was too severe since it had the effect of denying the defendant the right to present a defense. The court found that the opposing party must suffer prejudice if the undisclosed witness were permitted to testify in order for the witness to be excluded.[76]

7. Identity of Informant

Identity of a confidential informant
the name of a confidential informant can be withheld until the identity is relevant and helpful to the defense

The government is generally not required to disclose the **identity of a confidential informant** prior to trial. This is true despite the prosecution's obligation in most states to disclose the names of witnesses prior to trial. The purpose of withholding the informer's identity is twofold: it promotes effective law enforcement by allowing an informant to continue operating once charges have been filed, and it protects the safety of the informant.[77] The identity of a confidential informant must be revealed, however, if his identity is "relevant and helpful to the defense of an accused, or is essential to a fair determination of a cause."[78] Thus, the court must balance the defendant's need to learn the informant's identity versus the prosecution's need to keep it secret.

In balancing these interests, the court should consider the nature of the crime, the type of defense put forth, the available means of proving the charges and defenses, and the significance of the informant's role in the case.[79] The general rule is that the identity of the informant does not have to be revealed unless the informant will testify at trial. In that situation, the defense is entitled to learn the identity so it can prepare an adequate cross-examination of the informant or undercover operative.

Practical Example

Assume the defendant is charged with sale of a controlled substance. He is accused of selling an "eight ball" of methamphetamine to a confidential informant. The defense moves to have the identity of the confidential informant revealed at the preliminary hearing. The prosecutor objects, stating that ongoing investigations will be compromised if his identity is revealed. The court will likely rule that the identity of the informant does not have to be revealed until the defendant's case goes to trial. Then the informant's identity is relevant for impeachment purposes, such as to establish the informant's criminal history or his possible motives or biases.

8. Nondiscoverable Material

Work product

the documents and memoranda prepared by attorneys in connection with the investigation or preparation of a case. The attorney's work product, including memoranda and letters discussing trial strategy, is protected from disclosure during the discovery process

Rule 16 excludes certain types of documents from disclosure that are privileged or protected **work product**. This provision protects from disclosure any documents or memoranda that are prepared by a government attorney or other agent in connection with investigating or prosecuting the case.[80] Communications between prosecuting attorneys and law enforcement personnel are also protected under this provision. See Table 6.1 for a comparison of items that are discoverable and those that are protected from disclosure.

TABLE 6.1   EXAMPLES OF DISCOVERABLE AND NONDISCOVERABLE ITEMS

Discoverable Items	Nondiscoverable Items
• Statements of defendant	• Intraoffice memoranda regarding case or trial strategy
• Statements of testifying witnesses	
• Reports of testifying experts	• Communications between prosecuting attorneys and their investigators or law enforcement personnel
• Test results and analytical reports of the testing of physical evidence	
• Photographs and videotapes	• Expert reports not being used for trial testimony
• 911 call transcripts	
• Medical records	
• Documents such as death certificates	
• Investigators' notes	

Practical Example

The defendant is on trial for aggravated assault. He learns that the prosecutor interviewed the victim prior to trial and that the victim changed her story during this interview (the victim had told the defendant of this interview). The defendant now wants the prosecutor to turn over notes from that conversation. This information is not protected and must be disclosed pursuant to a defense request. Now assume the prosecutor wrote a memorandum of the conversation to his boss, detailing his findings. In that memo, he makes suggestions regarding trial strategy based on the interview. This memo is not discoverable since it discusses the prosecutor's trial strategy.

D. Relationship Between the Prosecution's Duty to Disclose Exculpatory Material and Its Obligations Under Rule 16

The obligation to produce exculpatory material under the *Brady* Rule is self-executing; in other words, the prosecutor must disclose the information without waiting for a motion from the defense seeking its disclosure.[81] The prosecutor, therefore, has an "affirmative duty" to seek out exculpatory information that is in the government's possession and disclose it. This obligation is not excused by inconvenience, expense,

TABLE 6.2 SUMMARY OF PROSECUTION'S DISCOVERY OBLIGATIONS

Obligations Required by Brady	Disclosures Required by Rule 16

• Disclosure of exculpatory evidence
• Disclosure of evidence relevant to impeachment of prosecution witnesses
• Prevention of bad-faith destruction of potentially exculpatory evidence
	• Statements of the defendant made pursuant to police interrogation
	• Documents, photographs, and tangible objects that:
	  ○ Prosecution intends to use at trial;
	  ○ Are material to preparation of a defense; or
	  ○ Were obtained from or belong to the defendant
	• Disclosure of expert testimony
	• Disclosure of witness lists and statements where defendant has made a showing of necessity
	• Disclosure of informant's identity where defendant has made a showing of necessity

or delay.[82] Unlike *Brady* material, the government's duty to produce information covered under Rule 16 is not self-executing; the defendant must first request it. The prosecution's discovery obligations under these two rules work together as follows: if the defense is aware that the prosecution possesses exculpatory evidence, it should request such evidence under Rule 16, but even if no request is made, the government must still provide it under the *Brady* rule.[83] See Table 6.2 for a summary of the prosecution's discovery obligations.

II. DEFENDANT'S DISCOVERY OBLIGATIONS

Although they are not as extensive as the prosecution's, the defense also has obligations to provide discovery to the prosecution under Rule 16.

A. Notice of Alibi

Notice of alibi

a requirement that the defendant must provide the basis of his alibi defense along with the names and addresses of all alibi witnesses (except in Nebraska) to the prosecution prior to trial

If the defendant intends to offer an alibi defense at trial, he must provide notice to the prosecution. This is known as a **notice of alibi**. Most states and the federal government require that the defendant provide both the location of where he allegedly was at the time of the incident and the names of any supporting witnesses. For example, the Georgia Notice of Alibi statute provides:

> Upon written demand by the prosecuting attorney within 10 days after arraignment, or at such time as the Court permits, stating the time, date, and place at which the alleged offense was committed, the defendant shall serve within 10 days of the demand of the prosecuting attorney or 10 days prior to trial, whichever is later, or is otherwise ordered by the court, upon the prosecuting attorney a written notice of the defendant's intention to offer a defense of alibi. Such notice by the defendant shall state the specific place or places at which the defendant claims to have been at the time of the alleged offense and the names, addresses, dates of birth, and telephone numbers of the witnesses, if known to the defendant, upon whom the defendant intends to rely to establish such alibi unless previously supplied.[84]

While the above statute is commonplace, one state, Nebraska, only requires that the defendant disclose his intent to rely upon an alibi but does not require disclosure of the names and addresses of his alibi witnesses.[85]

If the defendant fails to notify the prosecution in a timely fashion of his alibi defense, sanctions can be imposed by the court, including loss of the defense. The exclusion of an alibi witness is a drastic remedy since the defendant has a right to prove his defense. However, if the defense fails to comply with the disclosure rules and gives no "reasonable justification" for its failure to disclose an alibi, then exclusion is proper.[86] This is so even if the defendant is the only alibi witness.[87] For instance, the Rhode Island Supreme Court held that exclusion of the defendant's alibi witness was proper where he failed to notify the prosecution of his alibi until the day of trial.[88]

Practical Example

The defendant is charged with sexually assaulting a woman. He claims that he was in Kansas City on business the day of the rape. At the start of trial, four days before he puts on his defense, the defendant discloses his alibi to the prosecution and provides the names of two witnesses who will verify his whereabouts in Kansas City. The prosecution moves to strike the alibi defense as untimely. The court will deny the motion to strike on the ground that the prosecution did not suffer prejudice. It still has time to prepare a cross-examination of those witnesses and investigate the alibi.

B. Reciprocal Discovery

The defendant also has the obligation to produce certain information when requested by the prosecution. If a defendant requests documents for inspection or copying from the prosecution, then the defense has an obligation to permit the prosecution to do the same. The defense has to disclose any information in its possession and control that the defendant intends to produce at trial during its case-in-chief.[89] The defense also has to provide information regarding expert testimony, including the expert's report and list of his qualifications if the defendant intends to call that expert at trial.[90]

III. SANCTIONS FOR VIOLATING DISCOVERY RULES

Motion to compel discovery
a motion requesting that the court compel the opposing party to comply with a given discovery request. The court can sanction a party for failing to comply with a discovery violation or court order

If a party fails to comply with a discovery request, the opposing party can file a **motion to compel discovery**. This is a motion requesting that the court compel the opposing party to comply with a given discovery request. The court can also impose sanctions for violating a discovery obligation, even in the absence of such a motion.[91] If either side violates a discovery rule or order, the court can exclude the evidence, grant a continuance, or even dismiss the case. In determining what sanction to impose, the court should consider a range of factors, including the reason for the nondisclosure, the importance and materiality of the information not disclosed, the degree of negligence involved, the level of effort made by the party to comply with the order, the extent of prejudice to the other party, and the feasibility of granting a continuance.[92] The mere fact that the disclosure is late does not amount to prejudice.[93] The standard for determining prejudice is whether the government or defense conduct would have had at least some impact on the verdict.[94]

The court should impose the least severe sanction that will adequately remedy the violation. Continuances are the preferred remedy for discovery violations in the absence of bad faith. Dismissal is a severe sanction that should be imposed only where no other sanction will restore a level playing field. It is usually reserved for situations involving only willful misconduct.[95] Willful misconduct has been found even where the government recklessly disregarded its obligation to turn over exculpatory information.[96]

For example, in a Colorado case, the prosecution provided the defense with information that its chief witness was a heavy drug user and may have been under the influence on the date in question. The disclosure was late under Colorado law. Just before trial, the prosecution provided additional evidence about the witness's cocaine use. The trial court excluded the witness's testimony as a discovery sanction. The Colorado Supreme Court overturned the ruling, finding that a continuance would have cured any prejudice the defendants might have suffered as a result of the late disclosure.[97] Similarly, an Ohio court criticized the trial court for failing to consider all of the relevant factors before imposing a dismissal sanction.[98]

Practical Example

Lil' Will is on trial for cocaine distribution. Two days before trial, the prosecution wishes to endorse a witness who will testify that she saw Lil' Will sling some dope to a kid on the date in question. The witness is Lil' Will's ex-girlfriend. What sanction, if any, should the judge impose? The judge could grant a continuance to the defense, or he could do nothing. The defense personally knows the witness and should not be prejudiced by the late disclosure.

Failure to Disclose Exculpatory Evidence Results in Tim Masters' Release from Prison

Tim Masters was released from prison in 2008 after serving almost 10 years in prison for a murder he did not commit. He was convicted in 1999 largely on the basis of questionable expert testimony and weak circumstantial evidence. In 1987, the body of Peggy Hettrick was found in a vacant lot in Fort Collins, Colorado across from where the then 15-year-old Masters lived. He discovered the body while walking to school the next morning but did not report it to authorities because he thought it was a mannequin. While at school, he drew graphic drawings of the murder scene and Hettrick's body. He also owned a hunting knife collection. There was no physical evidence tying Masters to the murder, nor was there any motive established for the murder. Although questioned extensively about the murder, Masters never admitted his guilt and continued to maintain his innocence. He was tried for the murder 12 years later and was convicted largely on circumstantial evidence, along with the testimony of a psychologist who portrayed his drawings as an indication of a guilty conscience.

Masters spent nearly 10 years in prison until his defense team filed motions for a new trial based on the fact that the prosecution had destroyed or concealed exculpatory evidence. After Masters' conviction, it was discovered that a doctor living near the murder scene had kept sexually explicit videotapes of his patients. Investigators seized hundreds of videos that the doctor had taken over the years. The defense requested the videos, theorizing that Hettrick may have been one of the doctor's patients and that she was on the videos. However, the police destroyed all the tapes after the doctor committed suicide. Thus, Masters' defense

Figure 6.2   Dutch DNA scientist Selma Eikelenboom hugs Tim Masters during a party on January 22, 2008 to celebrate his release from prison. Masters spent almost 10 years in prison after being convicted of the murder of Peggy Hettrick in 1999. He was released after DNA tests pointed to a different suspect and it was revealed that the prosecution had failed to turn over exculpatory evidence during his trial. © 2008 Steve Dykes/Reuters/Corbis

argued that it was denied an opportunity to view the tapes for potentially exculpatory evidence.[99]

The big break for Masters came when it was revealed that the police had failed to turn over hundreds of pieces of evidence during his original trial. An entire box of documents and physical evidence was disclosed during the hearing for a new trial.[100] Some of the material was exculpatory, including FBI profiler memos criticizing the psychological theory that Masters' artwork had revealed a fantasy motive to kill Hettrick. The special prosecutor appointed to oversee the case concluded that discovery rules were violated during Masters' initial trial as a result of the nondisclosure.[101] In fact,

Continued on following page

Evidence in Action continued

one of the experts who had testified at Masters' trial changed his original assessment of the physical evidence based on this newly revealed information. He determined that it was now impossible for a 15-year-old boy to have dragged the body of Peggy Hettrick into the field by himself. The expert concluded that the evidence indicated that at least two individuals had instead moved her body.

The final blow to the prosecution's case came when Dutch scientists tested several of the garments retrieved from Hettrick's body. They used a new, sophisticated, more sensitive DNA test known as LCN, or low copy number. These tests revealed the presence of a male's DNA on her clothing but not Masters' DNA.[102]

As a result of this newly discovered information and the fact that evidence had been withheld and/or destroyed, Masters' motion for a new trial was granted and he was set free.[103] Larimer County and the City of Fort Collins then settled Masters' wrongful imprisonment lawsuit for a reported $10 million.

CHAPTER SUMMARY

The pretrial exchange of information about each party's case, such as the physical evidence and witnesses each side intends to call, is known as discovery. The prosecution has two basic discovery obligations. It must provide all exculpatory evidence to the defense prior to trial and must also provide any information requested by the defense relevant to its case. As part of its obligation to provide exculpatory evidence, the prosecution has a duty to preserve such evidence. If the evidence is destroyed and is not obviously exculpatory, sanctions can only be imposed for its intentional, bad faith destruction.

Rule 16 also imposes duties on each side to produce discovery pursuant to a request by the opposing party. Items such as statements of the defendant, notice of certain defenses, physical evidence, documents, photographs, and reports of expert witnesses have to be produced. In most states, each side also has to provide a copy of the list of witnesses it intends to call at trial.

If either side fails to comply with a discovery request, the court can impose sanctions. Before imposing sanctions, the court should consider the reason for the violation and if the other party suffered prejudice as a result. The general rule is that the least restrictive sanction will be imposed to remedy the violation.

KEY TERMS

- Bad faith destruction of evidence
- *Brady* Rule
- Discovery
- Due process
- Exculpatory evidence
- Expert disclosures
- *Giglio* material
- Interview notes
- Jencks Act
- Motion to compel discovery
- Notice of alibi
- Potentially exculpatory evidence
- Rule 16
- Second sample
- Work product

REVIEW QUESTIONS

1. What is the discovery process?

2. What is exculpatory evidence? Under what two circumstances does the prosecution have a duty to preserve and turn over such evidence?

3. What three things does a defendant have to show to establish a *Brady* violation?

4. Give two examples of exculpatory evidence.

5. What is potentially exculpatory evidence? Give an example of bad faith destruction of such evidence.

6. Does the prosecution have to preserve evidence if the testing process will destroy it? If not, what should the prosecution do to ensure the testing process is fair to the defendant?

7. Name three items that the prosecution has to turn over under Federal Rule of Criminal Procedure 16.

8. What two things does a defendant have to disclose when he claims an alibi defense?

9. What is the Jencks Act, and what type of evidence must be disclosed under it?

10. Under the federal rules, do the parties have to exchange witness lists prior to trial?

11. Does the prosecution always have to disclose the identity of a confidential informant? If not, under what circumstances does it have to disclose the identity?

12. Is dismissal or mistrial a typical remedy for a discovery violation? If not, when is it warranted?

APPLICATION PROBLEMS

1. Calleigh, a crime scene technician, discovers several pieces of evidence at a crime scene. Among the items, she finds blood, a revolver, and cartridge casings. Back at the lab, she develops a latent print on the weapon. When she runs the print through the American Fingerprint Identification System (AFIS), she does not get a match. One week later, Horatio identifies Cuzz, the ex-boyfriend of the victim, as a suspect. He asks Calleigh to compare his print with the prints on the gun. She determines Cuzz's print to be a match. However, she also determines that there is another print on the gun that is not a match to Cuzz. She does not report this in her findings. Two weeks before trial, Cuzz's fingerprint expert discovers the second print on the gun when he examines the evidence. Did the prosecution violate *Brady* by failing to notify the defense of the existence of the nonmatching print?

2. Gil, a crime scene technician, responds to a crime scene. He collects evidence belonging to the victim. He finds a pool of blood at the scene. He takes a swab of the blood. En route to the police station, Gil stops for a burger. He spills ketchup on the blood, contaminating the sample. He notes this in his report. Heather is later identified as a suspect. She challenges the contamination of the evidence as a *Brady* violation, arguing that exculpatory evidence was destroyed. Should the prosecution be sanctioned under *Brady*? Explain.

3. Mack, a homicide investigator, finds a very small blood stain at a crime scene. It is a small drop near the scene. He is barely able to swab enough to put it on one cotton swab. The laboratory runs a DNA test that consumes the sample. A DNA profile is obtained. The profile

is entered into a database and searched against the profile of known offenders. The search hits to the profile of a man who was imprisoned for rape three years ago. The man challenges the evidence that the testing consumed the entire sample and thus that his right to examine exculpatory evidence was violated. Is he right? Explain.

4. Jack is a prosecutor. He is prosecuting a murder case in federal court. The defense files a motion for discovery. The defendant wants copies of all police reports, witness statements, photographs, and any other documents the prosecutor intends to use at trial. He also requests the prosecutor's witness list and all memoranda in his file relating to the case investigation. What does Jack have to produce under the discovery request?

5. Bonnie and Clyde are wanted on robbery and kidnapping charges. They are arrested and charged with the crimes. At trial, Bonnie and Clyde provide the prosecutor with notice of their alibi. They were allegedly at the movies at the time of the crimes. The prosecutor objects on the ground that the notice is not timely. Is she right? Explain.

6. George is charged with the murder of Rex. The prosecution has a statement from one witness, Sue, an employee at the pharmacy where George works, that George was at work at the time of the murder. All of the other witnesses interviewed at the pharmacy state that George was not there. Sue's statement is not produced to the DA's office and thus is not turned over to the defense during discovery. George's attorney interviews Sue and finds out about her statement. He then moves to dismiss the charges for failure to disclose exculpatory material. Should the motion be granted? Explain.

7. Detective Cross investigates a murder. He obtains a warrant to search the suspect's house. During the search, Cross finds the murder weapon in the house. He takes photographs of the scene and interviews the neighbors. He records the statements in his notes. He also interrogates the suspect where the weapon was found. He then writes a report and incorporates all statements in his notes into the report. The defense requests Cross's notes and all statements of the defendant made to Cross. Cross complies by producing the report. However, he cannot produce his notes because he destroyed them prior to the request being made. The defense attorney moves for sanctions on the ground Cross destroyed his notes. Should the motion be granted? Explain.

8. Detective King investigates a drug case. He conducts an undercover drug buy. He sets up an undercover operative with a concealed recording device (a "wire") and gives him $500 in marked bills. He then searches the operative and finds no drugs. The undercover operative buys drugs from one of four individuals inside an apartment. He tells King that he bought the drugs from a woman identified as Tizzy. Tizzy's apartment is subsequently searched, but no drugs are found. King searches her vehicle and again finds no drugs. Tizzy is arrested for sale of a controlled substance and her person is searched. Again, no drugs are found. King does not take note of these facts and does not put them in his report. Tizzy's counsel requests discovery of all potentially exculpatory information. King does not tell the DA about not finding any drugs during the various searches. Tizzy's counsel files a motion for sanctions as a result of King's failure to turn over his notes and to preserve and record exculpatory information. Should sanctions be imposed? Explain.

Notes

1. Brady v. Maryland, 373 U.S. 83 (1963).
2. United State v. Bagley, 473 U.S. 667 (1985).
3. State v. Craig, 490 N.W.2d 795 (Iowa 1992).
4. *See e.g.,* Brady, 373 U.S. 83; People v. Sams, 685 P.2d 157, 161 (Colo. 1984).
5. Strickler v. Greene, 527 U.S. 263, 281-82 (1999).
6. United States v. Frank, 11 F. Supp. 2d 322 (S.D. N.Y. 1998).
7. State v. Lewis, 156 P.3d 565 (Id. 2007).
8. Trombetta, 467 U.S. at 488-89.
9. Chris Cuomo, Gerry Wagschal, Chris Francescani, and Lara Setrakian, *Duke Lacrosse DNA: Mystery Man Revealed Accuser's Boyfriend is "Single Source" of DNA on Vaginal Swab,* ABC News, May 13, 2006, available at rehttp://abcnews.go.com/US/LegalCenter/story?id=1958031&page=1.
10. *Former Duke Lacrosse Rape Prosecutor Charged With Withholding Evidence, Misleading Court,* Fox News, January 24, 2007, available at foxnews.com/story/0,2933,246281,00.html.
11. *Mike Nifong disbarred Over Ethics Violations in Duke Lacrosse Case,* Associated Press, (June 17, 2007), available at foxnews.com/story/0,2933,283282,00.html.
12. People v. District Court of Colorado's Seventeenth Judicial District, 793 P.2d 163 (Colo. 1990).
13. Giglio v. United States, 405 U.S. 150 (1972).
14. California v. Trombetta, 467 U.S. 479 (1984).
15. Arizona v. Youngblood, 488 U.S. 51, 57-58 (1988).
16. Trombetta, 467 U.S. at 488.
17. Youngblood, 488 U.S. at 57.
18. Craig, 490 N.W.2d at 797.
19. United States v. Ungar, 648 F. Supp. 1329, 1335 (E.D.N.Y. 1986)
20. United States v. Cooper, 662 F. Supp. 913, 918 (D.R.I. 1987).
21. Ungar, 648 F. Supp. at 1336.
22. Cooper, 662 F. Supp. at 918.
23. State v. Alfonso, 486 A.2d 1136 (Conn. App. 1985).
24. People v. Tsombanidis, 601 N.E.2d 1124 (Ill. App. 1992).
25. United States v. Smith, 451 F.3d 209 (4th Cir. 2006).
26. Smith, 451 F.3d at 220-21.
27. Hilliard v. Spalding, 719 F.2d 1443 (9th Cir. 1983).
28. State v. Lewis, 156 P.3d 565, 568 (Id. 2007).
29. People v. Greathouse, 742 P.2d 334, 336 (Colo. 1987).
30. Id.
31. 467 U.S. 479 (1984).
32. Trombetta, 467 U.S. at 489; *see also* State v. Cornelius, 452 A.2d 464 (N.H. 1982); State v. Young, 614 P.2d 441 (Kan. 1980).
33. State v. Dulaney, 493 N.W.2d 787 (Iowa 1992).
34. State v. Herrera, 365 So. 2d 399 (Fla. App. 3d Dist. 1978).
35. People v. Griffin, 761 P.2d 103 (Cal. 1988).
36. Lee v. State 511 P.2d 1076 (Ak. 1973).
37. Id.
38. State v. Erwin, 686 So. 2d 688 (Fla. App. 5th Dist. 1996).
39. People v. Newberry, 638 N.E.2d 1196 (Ill. App. 1994).
40. *See e.g.,* Griffin, 761 P.2d at 108; State v. Kersting, 623 P.2d 1095 (Or. App. 1981).
41. People v. Gomez, 96 P.2d 1192, 1197 (Colo. 1979).
42. People v. Wartena, 156 P.3d 469, 473 (Colo. 2007).
43. Colo. Rev. Stat ß16-3-309.
44. Colo. Rev. Stat. ß 16-3-309(1).
45. A.B.A. Criminal Justice Section Standards on DNA Evidence, Standard 3.4(e) (2006).
46. People v. Wartena, 156 P.3d 469 (Colo. 2007).
47. Wartena, 156 P.3d at 474 (Coats, J., concurring).
48. United States v. W.R. Grace, 401 F. Supp. 2d 1069, 1075 (D. Mont. 2005).
49. W.R. Grace, 401 F. Supp. 2d at 1078; *see* United States v. Santiago, 46 F.3d 885, 893-94 (9th Cir. 1995).
50. F.R.Crim.P. 16(a)(1)(A).
51. F.R.Crim.P. 16(a)(1(B).
52. United States v. Williams, 792 F. Supp. 1120, 1125 (S.D. Ind. 1992).
53. Williams, 792 F. Supp. at 1126 n. 3.
54. F.R.Crim.P. 16(a)(1)(E).
55. United States v. Jordan, 316 F.3d 1215, 1250 (11th Cir. 2003).
56. W.R. Grace, 401 F. Supp. 2d at 1074.
57. Jordan, 316 F.3d at 1227.
58. United States v. Van Nguyen, (N.D. Ga. 2006).
59. United States v. Walker, 272 F.3d 407, 417 (7th Cir. 2001).
60. In re Gary G., 115 Cal. App. 3d 629, 641 (Cal. App. 1981).
61. State v. Garcia, 643 A.2d 180 (R.I. 1994).
62. *See* Commonwealth v. Liang, 747 N.E.2d 112 (Mass. 2001).
63. Liang, 747 N.E.2d at 116.
64. F.R.Crim.P. 16 (a)(1)(G).
65. United States v. Vasquez, 258 F.R.D. 68 (E.D. N.Y. 2009).
66. Williams, 792 F. Supp. at 1131.
67. 18 U.S.C. ß 3500(a).
68. Jordan, 316 F.3d at 1252.
69. Id. at 1253.
70. Colo. R. Crim. P. 16(a)(1)(I).
71. United States v. Harris, 542 F.2d 1283, 1291 (7th Cir. 1976).
72. *See e.g.,* Colo. R. Crim. P. 16(a)(1)(VI).
73. Patterson v. State, 419 So. 2d 1120 Fla. App. 4th Dist. 1982).
74. Patterson, 419 So. 2d at 1123.
75. City of Lakewood v. Papadelis, 511 N.E.2d 1138, 1141 (Ohio 1987).
76. Id.
77. Smith v. City of Detroit, 212 F.R.D. 507, 509 (E.D. Mich. 2003).
78. Id., *quoting* Roviaro v. United States, 353 U.S. 53, 59 (1957).
79. United States v. Carino-Torres, 549 F. Supp. 2d 151 (D. Puerto Rico 2007).
80. F.R.Crim.P. 16(a)(2).
81. United States v. Aichele, 941 F.2d 761, 764 (9th Cir. 1991).
82. W.R Grace, 401 F. Supp. 2d at 1077.
83. Id.
84. O.C.G.A. ß 17-16-5(a).
85. Neb. Rev. Stat. ß 29-1927; State v. Woods, 577 N.W.2d 564 (Neb. App. 1998).
86. State v. Hopper, 315 S.W.3d 361 (Mo. App. 2010).
87. *See* State v. Charboneau, 635 S.E.2d 759 (Ga. 2006).
88. State v. Engram, 479 A.2d 716 (R.I. 1984).
89. F.R.Crim.P. 16(b)(1)(A).
90. F.R.Crim.P. 16(b)(1(C).
91. City of Lakewood v. Papadelis, 511 N.E.2d 1138 (Ohio 1987).
92. People v. Daley, 97 P.3d 295, 298 (Colo. App. 2004); State v. Hill, 454 S.E.2d 427, 434 (W.Va. 1994).
93. Hopper, 315 S.W.3d at 366-67.
94. United States v. Fitzgerald, 615 F. Supp. 2d 1156 (S.D. Cal. 2009).

95. Daley, 97 P.3d at 298.

96. Fitzgerald, 615 F. Supp. 2d at 1159.

97. District Court, 793 P.2d at 168.

98. State v. Engle, 850 N.E.2d 123 (Ohio App. 2006).

99. Miles Moffeit, *Attorney: Larimer Withheld Suspect,* Denver Post, September 26, 2007, available at http://www.denverpost.com/ci_6998461.

100. Miles Moffeit, *Police Files Surface, Bring Call for Conference in Masters Case,* Denver Post, November 30, 2007, available at http://www.denverpost.com/ci_7595222.

101. Miles Moffeit, *Innocence Bid Gets Boost,* Denver Post, January 3, 2008, available at http://www.denverpost.com/ci_7866888;

102. Howard Pankratz, *Masters Released from Jail,* Denver Post, January 22, 2008, available at http://www.denverpost.com/ci_8045113.

103. Miles Moffeit, *DA Urges Masters' Release,* Denver Post, January 19, 2008, available at http://www.denverpost.com/ci_8015651.

CHAPTER 7

CROSS **POLICE LINE DO NOT CROSS** POLICE LINE

The Exclusionary Rule and Motions to Suppress Evidence

"The criminal is to go free because the constable has blundered."[1]—*Judge Cardozo*

Chapter Topics

Objectives

After completing this chapter, students will be able to:

- Understand the purpose behind the exclusionary rule and how it protects people's rights under the Fourth Amendment

- Identify all the exceptions to the exclusionary rule

- Learn how certain illegally seized evidence can still be used for impeachment purposes

- Understand the *Miranda* requirement for advising a suspect of his rights

- Identify the exceptions to the *Miranda* rule

- Understand the right to counsel and the stages at which it applies

- Understand the application of the exclusionary rule to the Fifth and Sixth Amendments

- Understand the process for filing a motion to suppress

Introduction

In previous chapters, you learned about the importance of obtaining physical evidence and confessions and the rules for their admission. In this chapter, you will learn how confessions and physical evidence may be excluded if they are illegally seized or obtained in violation of the defendant's Fourth, Fifth, or Sixth Amendment rights. This ban on the use of illegally seized evidence is known as the exclusionary rule.

Exclusionary rule
a Supreme Court rule that bars illegally seized physical evidence and statements from being admitted as evidence in a defendant's trial. It is designed to deter the police from violating suspects' constitutional rights

The **exclusionary rule** was developed by courts to "deter police from violations of constitutional and statutory protections."[2] As the opening quotation from Judge Cardozo points out, the criminal may sometimes go free due to the exclusionary rule since the prosecution will be left with little or no evidence to proceed to trial.

The Supreme Court has developed slightly different rules for excluding evidence under each of the three amendments mentioned above. The Fourth Amendment exclusionary rule bars physical evidence obtained during an illegal search or seizure from being introduced in the prosecution's case-in-chief. The rule covers both illegally seized evidence and any derivative evidence (evidence that would not have been discovered but for the illegal search or seizure). The exclusionary rule is not absolute, however. Illegally seized evidence is excluded only where the police intentionally, or with deliberate indifference, violate the suspect's constitutional rights. The Court has also created four exceptions to the rule: independent source, inevitable discovery, attenuation, and good faith. If one of these exceptions applies, the prosecutor may use the evidence at trial despite its having been unlawfully seized.

The Court has also created exclusionary rules to protect the defendant's Fifth and Sixth Amendment rights to remain silent and to have an attorney. To ensure that statements obtained while a suspect is in custody are made voluntarily, the police must advise the suspect of his *Miranda* rights (that he has a right to remain silent and to have counsel present) prior to questioning. The suspect must then voluntarily waive those rights. If he does not, the statements will be excluded. Even if a suspect does waive his rights and agree to talk to police, his statements will not be admissible if they were coerced. The defendant also has a Sixth Amendment right to have counsel present during all "critical stages" of the criminal justice process. This means that once a suspect is charged with a crime, he cannot be questioned by police without the presence of his attorney unless he waives that right.

Finally, this chapter will examine how the exclusionary rule is enforced. To do so, a defendant will typically file a pretrial motion to suppress the evidence. After hearing arguments on both sides, the court will determine whether the evidence was illegally seized, and if so, whether it should be excluded from trial. Regardless of its admissibility, illegally seized evidence can still be used for impeachment or other collateral purposes.

I. THE FOURTH AMENDMENT

Fourth Amendment
an amendment to the Constitution that protects against unreasonable searches and seizures. It also provides that no warrant shall issue without probable cause

The **Fourth Amendment** has two parts: it provides that no warrant shall issue without probable cause, and it protects against unreasonable searches and seizures.[3] The Supreme Court has interpreted these clauses as being independent from one another. In other words, some searches may be reasonable even though they are conducted without warrants. The mere fact that the police obtained a warrant prior to searching, however, does not immunize the evidence from exclusion. Defendants can still challenge the warrant as being defective.

A. The Warrant Requirement

Search warrant
a judicial authorization to search a given premises for contraband or evidence of a crime. It must be supported by probable cause and specify the place to be searched and the items to be seized

A **search warrant** is a judicial authorization to search a given premises for contraband or evidence of a crime. In order to obtain a search warrant, officers have to apply to a magistrate or judge, alleging facts to support the need for a warrant. A warrant must be supported by probable cause that the person or place to be searched contains contraband or evidence of a crime. Second, the warrant must also specify the place to be searched and the items to be seized.[4] General warrants that allow the police to search anywhere, for evidence of any type of crime, are not permitted. A magistrate or judge must review the warrant application and sign the warrant. Even after it has been reviewed by a magistrate and executed by police, a warrant can still be held invalid as lacking probable cause, being overboard, or lacking particularity.

As stated above, search warrants are not required for every search. The Supreme Court has held that police are required to obtain a warrant only when they search a person's home or business office. The circumstances may even justify a warrantless entry into a home or office. Table 7.1

TABLE 7.1 EXCEPTIONS TO THE WARRANT REQUIREMENT

- **Exigent circumstances** (threat of danger to persons inside residence or office justify police entry into the home without a warrant)
- **Hot pursuit** (police may follow a fleeing suspect into a home or office without a warrant)
- **Imminent destruction of evidence** (reasonable belief that evidence will be destroyed if immediate, warrantless entry is not made into the home or office)
- **Plain view** (evidence not covered by a warrant may be seized if it is in plain sight and it is clearly identifiable as contraband)
- **Open fields** (an open field away from the primary residence can be searched and evidence seized without a warrant because there is no expectation of privacy)
- **Automobiles** (the mobile nature of cars and other vehicle justifies the search of a car and any containers within the car without a warrant)
- **Search incident to arrest** (area within the lunge, grasp, or control of a suspect may be searched pursuant to a valid arrest)
- **Abandoned property** (garbage or other property that owner has abandoned may be searched without a warrant because there is no expectation of privacy)
- **Areas open to the public** (areas exposed or open to public view where owner has no legitimate expectation of privacy require no warrant to search)
- **Consent** (the person in possession of the place to be searched agrees to a warrantless search of the premises)

provides a list of exceptions to the warrant requirement that the Court has recognized.

B. The Reasonableness Requirement

Even where a warrant is not required to search a given area, the search must still be reasonable. This means that probable cause or some other level of suspicion is usually required in order for the police to conduct a search. For example, the police must have probable cause that a vehicle contains evidence of a crime before they can search it (assuming the driver does not consent to the search). Similarly, the police need reasonable suspicion that a person is involved in criminal activity before they can stop and frisk him for weapons.[5] Since the Fourth Amendment only prohibits unreasonable searches and seizures, the Court has held that even suspicionless searches may be conducted under certain circumstances. Table 7.2 provides a list of exceptions to the probable cause requirement.

Defendants may challenge warrantless and/or suspicionless searches on the ground that the police lacked the necessary level of suspicion to conduct the search or that an exception justifying such searches did not apply to the circumstances of their case. For example, a defendant may argue that a roadblock to search for drivers transporting drugs does not address public safety concerns that a roadblock for intoxicated drivers does.

TABLE 7.2 EXCEPTIONS TO THE PROBABLE CAUSE REQUIREMENT

- **Pat-down searches** (reasonable suspicion is required to stop a person and search his person for weapons using a pat down)
- **Traffic stops** (reasonable suspicion that someone has committed a traffic violation is required to pull over a vehicle)
- **Border searches** (no suspicion is required to pull over and search vehicles or persons at the international border)
- **Automobile roadblocks** (no suspicion is required to set up a roadblock to conduct an immigration check or DUI check)
- **Administrative searches** (reduced level of probable cause is required to search homes or businesses for administrative purposes, such as code inspections)
- **Special needs** (reduced level of suspicion is required to conduct a search where government has special needs beyond the ordinary need for law enforcement, such as administration of a school)
- **Persons with reduced expectations of privacy** (a lower level of suspicion or no suspicion is required to search people with reduced expectations of privacy, such as prisoners, parolees, and probationers)
- **Public safety** (suspicion is not required to conduct certain searches where public safety is at risk, such as drug testing of airplane pilots)

C. The Exclusionary Rule

In order to protect these rights guaranteed under the Fourth Amendment, the Supreme Court developed the exclusionary rule to bar the use of illegally seized evidence. It is a judge-made rule; no statute or constitutional provision requires it. In 1914, the Supreme Court announced the rule for federal courts in *Weeks v. United States*.[6] There, federal law enforcement officers conducted a warrantless search of Weeks' home for evidence of illegal gambling. The Court reversed his conviction, holding that the Fourth Amendment barred the use of illegally seized evidence (as stated above, a home cannot be searched without a warrant).

The rule initially only applied to the federal courts. States were still free to admit illegally seized evidence if their courts had not adopted the exclusionary rule under state law (most states had not done so at that point in time). In 1949 in *Wolf v. Colorado*, the Supreme Court refused to make the rule applicable to all states.[7] It applied the exclusionary rule in state cases only where the police conduct violated due process or "shocked the conscience." For instance, in *Rochin v. California*, the Court excluded drug evidence that had been obtained by the forcible administration of an emetic to help a suspect pass narcotic capsules he had swallowed.[8] Such cases were the exception rather than the rule, however.

Slowly, the tide began to turn in favor of widespread adoption of the rule. By 1960, 22 states had adopted the exclusionary rule. In 1961, the Supreme Court finally applied the exclusionary rule to all states in *Mapp v. Ohio*.[9] In that case, a woman who ran a boarding house was prosecuted for possession of obscene material and sentenced to seven years in prison. The police had demanded entry into her home to question a boarder about a recent bombing. The woman refused entry without a warrant. The police then forced their way into her home using a fake warrant. They searched her home and found the obscene materials in the basement. The Court overturned her conviction and ruled that the exclusionary rule should apply to all states under the due process clause of the Fourteenth Amendment.[10]

1. Fruit of the Poisonous Tree

The exclusionary rule covers not just the evidence seized as a result of the police misconduct but also any evidence derived from the unlawful invasion of a person's Fourth Amendment rights.[11] This is known as the **fruit of the poisonous tree** doctrine. For example, any statements or evidence obtained subsequent to an unlawful arrest would be considered to be fruits of the illegal arrest and would be suppressed.

Suppression of the derivative evidence is not justified, however, unless "the challenged evidence is in some sense the product of the illegal governmental activity."[12] In other words, the unlawful action of the police must be the "but for" cause of the discovery of the derivative evidence.

Fruit of the poisonous tree
all derivative evidence related to the illegal seizure must be excluded from evidence as well as the original, illegally seized evidence

The Supreme Court summed up the test of whether evidence should be suppressed as fruit of the poisonous tree as follows:

> We need not hold that all evidence is "fruit of the poisonous tree" simply because it would not have come to light but for the illegal actions of the police. Rather, the more apt question in such a case is whether, granting establishment of the primary illegality, the evidence to which instant objection is made has been come at by exploitation of the illegality or instead by means sufficiently distinguishable to be purged of the primary taint.[13]

Practical Example

Assume that the police search Juan's house without a warrant for evidence of drug dealing. During that search, they seize some cocaine. They also learn that Juan is expecting a shipment of drugs from Carlos on Tuesday. The police then seize a much larger amount of cocaine on Tuesday when Carlos delivers it to the house. Both seizures of cocaine should be suppressed under the exclusionary rule. The first seizure occurred as a result of the illegal search. The second seizure is also invalid because the police would not have known about the delivery but for their illegal search. Thus, both pieces of evidence must be excluded.

2. Exceptions to the Exclusionary Rule

Evidence that is illegally seized is not always suppressed. The court must balance society's interest in deterring illegal police conduct against its interest in having juries receive all relevant evidence of a crime "by putting the police in the same, not a worse, position than they would have been in if no police error or misconduct had occurred."[14] The Supreme Court has created several exceptions to the exclusionary rule that are dependent on the circumstances surrounding the illegal conduct. The four main exceptions to the exclusionary rule are discussed below.

a. Independent Source

Independent source
an exception to the exclusionary rule. Evidence that is lawfully discovered through a source independent from the illegal seizure is admissible

The first exception to the exclusionary rule is the **independent source** exception. This exception permits the prosecution to admit evidence that is discovered "wholly independent" of any constitutional violation of a defendant's rights. In other words, if officers discover facts x and y through illegal means but discover fact z through separate, lawful methods, fact z is admissible because it is derived from an independent source.[15] The Court explained that this exception is necessary to prevent penalizing the police too much for illegal conduct: "When the challenged evidence has an independent source, exclusion of such evidence would put the police in a worse position than they would have been in absent any error or violation."[16] Thus, evidence collected properly can be admitted under this exception despite the fact that an illegal search or seizure has occurred at some point during the investigation.[17]

For example, in *Segura v. United States*, the Court held that the subsequent seizure of drug evidence under a warrant was not tainted by the initial, illegal entry into the premises.[18] Agents had entered the defendants' apartment without a warrant to secure the scene and prevent destruction of evidence since a warrant could not be obtained until the next day. Although drug evidence was observed during the first entry, it was not disturbed until agents executed the search warrant the following day. Because none of the information gathered by the agents during the initial, illegal entry was used to obtain the warrant, the Court found that there was an independent source for the drug evidence seized during the subsequent execution of the warrant.[19]

Similarly, in *People v. Castillo*, a trial court held that the discovery of a woman's body should not be suppressed as the fruit of the defendant's illegal arrest and interrogation since the officers had an independent source for the information—they had received an anonymous tip about a strong odor coming from the residence.[20] Subsequent to his arrest, the police located the woman's body and charged the defendant with her murder. Although the defendant was interrogated about the disappearance of the woman, he did not provide any additional information to the police that they did not already have. The court could therefore infer that the officers would have discovered the body even if the illegal arrest and questioning had not occurred.

Practical Example

Assume officers search the residence of Sam, a person of interest in a homicide investigation, without a warrant. They find a photo of the victim in the suspect's desk. They also find a .38 handgun, the same caliber as used to kill the victim. They then arrest the suspect on suspicion of murder. At this point, the arrest is invalid since the officers did not have a warrant or consent to search Sam's house. Sam then tells the officers where the victim's body is buried. Both the evidence seized from Sam's house and the statement of where the body was buried should be suppressed as the product of an illegal search.

Now assume that before the illegal entry, officers had developed a solid case against Sam but they could not find her body. They then get a tip that Sam has an old cabin in the woods and had been seen with the victim shortly before her death. While the evidence obtained from the illegal search should still be suppressed, the discovery of the woman's body should not be suppressed. The location and discovery of the woman's body now has a source independent of the illegal search.

b. Inevitable Discovery

Inevitable discovery
an exception to the
exclusionary rule. Evidence
that is illegally seized but
would have been inevitably
discovered through lawful
means is admissible

The next exception to the exclusionary rule is the **inevitable discovery** exception. Under this exception, illegally obtained evidence can still be admitted against the defendant if the prosecution can establish by a preponderance of the evidence that the information ultimately or inevitably would have been discovered by lawful means.[21] In order to establish the inevitable discovery of evidence, the prosecution must prove:

- a reasonable probability that the evidence in question would have been discovered by lawful means but for the police misconduct;
- that the police possessed the leads making the discovery inevitable at the time of the misconduct; and
- that the police were actively pursuing an alternative line of investigation prior to the misconduct.[22]

This means that the prosecutor must prove that law enforcement would have discovered the tainted evidence lawfully by following "routine procedures."[23] Many courts have held that this exception applies even where the suspect has been coerced into disclosing the location of the evidence. For instance, an Ohio federal court held that government agents would have inevitably discovered cocaine during their execution of a search warrant of the defendant's house, despite compelling his disclosure of the cocaine's location.[24] Since the police had already developed leads and the search was already underway at the time of the police misconduct, the court found that the police would have discovered the cocaine legally.[25]

Practical Example

Assume Glenn is accused of murdering his wife. The police cannot locate the body. They beat Glenn and learn that he buried her body in the local landfill. Her body is discovered one day later. This coerced statement is of course involuntary and thus inadmissible. Since the discovery of the body derives from the illegal interrogation, it must also be suppressed.

Now assume that prior to the beating, the police have begun to search the landfill on their own. Using garbage dump records, they have located the area that is likely to contain her body. It is almost certain that within 48 hours, the police would have discovered the wife's body, even without Glenn's statement. With his statement and precise time and date, they are able to locate the body within two hours. The evidence of the discovery of the wife's body would now be admissible since it would have inevitably been discovered.

c. Attenuation

Attenuation

an exception to the exclusionary rule. Discovery of evidence that is far removed or attenuated from an earlier illegal seizure of evidence is admissible

The third exception is **attenuation.** Attenuate means to reduce in force, value, or amount. Thus, the discovery of evidence that is sufficiently attenuated or far-removed from the illegal police action to break the causal connection between the illegal activity and its discovery is admissible.[26] For example, a federal district court also concluded in *Castillo* that the statements obtained from the defendant as a product of his illegal arrest were sufficiently attenuated to "destroy any possible causal connection from the unlawful events."[27] The court found that the information obtained from the prior interrogation and the subsequent discovery of the woman's body should not be suppressed because it did not put the police in a better position than they would have been without the evidence.

Practical Example

Assume that William is suspected of committing a string of sexual assaults. The police question William about the incidents. He claims the sex was consensual in all three cases. The victims claimed they were choked during the incidents. One of the officers then chokes William and asks him if he thinks that was consensual. William then says that "those women got what they deserve." Simultaneously, other officers obtain a warrant to search William's home. They find a cord that tests positive for the DNA of two of the victims. While William's statement that the women got what they deserve should be suppressed, the cord should not be suppressed because it is attenuated from the illegal confession.

d. Good Faith Exception

Good faith exception

an exception to the exclusionary rule. Where an officer reasonably relies in good faith on a search warrant, the evidence will be admissible even if the warrant is later declared invalid

The final exception to the exclusionary rule (and perhaps the most controversial one) is the **good faith exception**. Under the good faith exception, evidence seized under a warrant that is later declared invalid can still be admitted as long as the agents had a good faith basis for relying on the warrant in the first place. In other words, the officer's reliance on the defective search warrant must be reasonable.[28] Essentially, the rule recognizes that a search conducted pursuant to a mistaken belief that a warrant was valid is less of a threat to constitutional rights than a search that is conducted deliberately and intentionally in violation of those rights.[29]

The Supreme Court explained this distinction in terms of the rule's deterrence function in *United States v. Leon*:

> The deterrent purpose of the exclusionary rule necessarily assumes that the police have engaged in willful, or at the very least, negligent conduct which has deprived the defendant of some right. By refusing to admit evidence gained as a result of such conduct, the courts hope to instill in those particular investigating officers,

or in their future counterparts, a greater degree of care towards the rights of the accused. Where the official action was pursued in complete good faith, however, the deterrence rationale loses much of its force.[30]

The Court believed that extending the exclusionary rule to cover judicial mistakes would not effectively deter magistrates and judges from approving defective warrant applications in the future.[31]

Conversely, the good faith exception does not apply where officers are "dishonest or reckless" in preparation of their affidavits or could not have had an "objectively reasonable belief" that the warrant was supported by probable cause.[32] The key factor is whether a reasonably well-trained officer should have known the warrant was illegal, despite the magistrate's authorization of it. More than a "bare bones" affidavit is needed to support a warrant. An affidavit must contain facts "sufficient to justify a conclusion that evidence or contraband will probably be found at the premises to be searched." It must also contain information to conclude that a "fair probability existed that seizable evidence would be found in the place sought to be searched."[33]

The situations where the good faith exception does not apply (and the evidence is thus inadmissible) can be summarized as follows:

- Where "the magistrate or judge issuing a warrant was misled by information in an affidavit that the affiant knew was false or would have known was false except for his reckless disregard of the truth";
- Where the issuing magistrate wholly abandons his judicial role;
- Where the affidavit supporting the warrant is "so lacking in indicia of probable cause as to render official belief in its existence entirely unreasonable"; or
- Where, depending upon the circumstances of a particular case, a warrant is "so facially deficient—i.e., in failing to particularize the place to be searched or the things to be seized—that executing officers cannot reasonably presume it to be valid."[34]

The *Leon* decision started a trend under which the Supreme Court has increasingly restricted the situations to which the exclusionary rule applies. Over the years, its focus has slowly shifted from penalizing all police misconduct to only those situations where the police are "flagrantly abusive" of a person's constitutional rights.[35] This process has accelerated in recent years.

In 2006 in *Hudson v. Michigan*, the Court declared that the exclusionary rule did not apply to the unauthorized execution of a no-knock warrant. The police must ordinarily knock and announce their presence when executing a warrant, unless they have obtained a no-knock warrant. In *Hudson*, officers discovered evidence pursuant to a valid search warrant but failed to comply with the knock-and-announce rule before entering the residence. The Court concluded that the sanctions of the exclusionary rule are unnecessary where "the interest protected by the constitutional guarantee that has been violated would not be served by suppression of new evidence obtained."[36] The Court also noted that the deterrent effect resulting from penalizing knock-and-announce violations would be minimal.[37]

The Court continued its transformation of the exclusionary rule in *Herring v. United States* in 2009. There, the police seized drugs after searching the defendant's person incident to his arrest. The defendant's arrest was ruled unlawful, however, since the police failed to remove the arrest warrant from the system after the court had recalled it months earlier.[38] The Court applied the good faith exception despite the fact that the mistake was attributable to the police. The crucial fact in the Court's mind was that the mistake was unintentional. It held that the applicability of the exclusionary rule turned on the "culpability of the police and the potential of exclusion to deter wrongful police misconduct."[39] The Court summed up the circumstances requiring exclusion as follows:

> To trigger the exclusionary rule, police conduct must be sufficiently deliberate that exclusion can meaningfully deter it, and sufficiently culpable that such deterrence is worth the price paid by the justice system. As laid out in our cases, the exclusionary rule serves to deter deliberate, reckless, or grossly negligent conduct, or in some circumstances recurring or systemic negligence.[40]

Because the failure to withdraw the warrant from the system in this case was an isolated incident, the error did not merit exclusion of evidence.[41]

Prior to this ruling, most courts and commentators had interpreted the good faith exception as applying only to judicial misconduct, not police misconduct. Justice Breyer acknowledged as much in his dissent.[42] For example, in *Arizona v. Evans,* the Court ruled that the exclusionary rule was inapplicable where a court clerk had failed to delete the warrant from the system once it had been canceled. It held that the exclusionary rule "was historically designed as a means of deterring police misconduct, not errors by court employees."[43] The *Herring* Court rejected this distinction between court and law enforcement personnel, holding that the degree of culpability, not the title of the actor, was the determinative factor in deciding whether the exclusionary rule should apply.[44]

Interestingly, Canada's Supreme Court also recently handed down a ruling similar to the one in *Herring*. In a quartet of cases in 2009, the Court ruled that exclusion of evidence is not the proper remedy for a police violation of *Canada's Charter of Rights and Freedoms* (the Canadian equivalent of the Bill of Rights) unless the violation is committed in blatant disregard of those freedoms.[45] The Canadian Supreme Court concluded that "[t]he more severe or deliberate the state conduct that led to the Charter violation, the greater the need for the courts to disassociate themselves from that conduct, by excluding evidence linked to that conduct, in order to preserve public confidence in and ensure state adherence to the rule of law." However, where the police conduct is a "brazen and flagrant" disregard for a suspect's rights, the Court upheld exclusion as a sanction.[46]

Practical Example

Assume officers are investigating what appears to be a racially motivated series of beatings occurring on subway platforms. Black gang members are beating up white subway riders. The officers get an anonymous tip that Charles "Tookie" Jackson has a video of the incidents in his home. They obtain a search warrant based on the tip. The officers find the video in Tookie's home. In court, the judge rules that the officers did not have probable cause to obtain the warrant because they did not corroborate details of the tip. The judge would not exclude the video evidence, however, on the ground that the officers acted in good-faith reliance on the warrant.

Now assume that one of the officers exaggerated the extent of the injuries and the hate crime motivation to obtain the search warrant. He also made up a story that Tookie had been victimized by several white teenagers and had masterminded the assaults as revenge for this act. The judge would now likely suppress the evidence since the officers did not obtain the warrant in good faith.

Practical Example

Suppose an officer pulls over Samantha Samuels for speeding. A check of her identification reveals an outstanding warrant for a DUI. The officer arrests Samantha and searches the passenger compartment of her car incident to arrest. She finds a baggie of cocaine under the passenger seat. As it turns out, the court had withdrawn the warrant last month but the warrant clerk in the sheriff's office mistakenly forgot to clear the warrant. Samantha moves to suppress the evidence. The court should deny her motion since the error was merely negligent on the part of the warrant clerk.

Now suppose the police department has had several recent instances where a person was either mistakenly arrested or arrested under a warrant that had been withdrawn. The court would now likely grant Samantha's motion since the officer could not have reasonably relied on the warrant system as being accurate. Due to systemic errors, a situation has been created where it was just a matter of time before the next person was arrested under an improper warrant. The mistake now rises to the level of being reckless and can hardly be called negligent.

3. Private Parties and Third Parties

The exclusionary rule does not apply to evidence illegally obtained by private parties as long as they are not acting at the direction of the police. Since the Fourth Amendment protects only against invasions by government actors, evidence unlawfully obtained by private citizens is not excluded.[47] For example, if a private detective breaks into a person's home and searches the residence without a warrant, the prosecutor could use any evidence he turned over to police as a result of his illegal search.

Similarly, illegally seized evidence taken from a third party can be used to prosecute the defendant. A person's Fourth Amendment rights are personal to the individual. According to the Supreme Court, a "court may not exclude evidence under the Fourth Amendment unless it finds that an unlawful search or seizure violates the defendant's own constitutional rights."[48] In other words, a defendant must have standing to challenge the violation.

Standing

the capacity to file a lawsuit. To challenge a Fourth Amendment violation, the defendant must argue that his own rights were violated by the police's unlawful conduct, not those of some third party

Standing is a legal requirement that the court litigant (the defendant) have the capacity to initiate a lawsuit. To establish standing in a criminal case, a person must prove that he has suffered an actual injury and that he is asserting his own legal rights, not those of third parties. For example, in *Rakas v. Illinois*, the passenger of a car was prosecuted for unlawful possession of a weapon after a gun and ammunition were found during a search of the car.[49] The passenger attempted to claim that the evidence was obtained as a result of an unlawful search of the car. The Court found that he did not have standing to challenge the search since he neither owned nor leased the vehicle. Thus, a defendant does not usually have standing to suppress the evidence if a third party's rights are violated, not his own.

Practical Example

Assume Carmen had asked a friend, Slim, to hold some cocaine for her. Slim put it in his backpack. Slam's backpack is then searched by a police officer without his consent after he pulls him over for a broken taillight. Slim tells the officer the coke is Carmen's and Carmen is charged with drug possession. Carmen would not have standing to suppress the cocaine since the car is not hers. Thus, it would still be usable against Carmen even though it was illegally seized.

4. Grand Jury Proceedings and Parole Revocation Hearings

The exclusionary rule applies only to trials; it does not apply to grand jury proceedings and other pre- or post-trial hearings. For example, the Supreme Court held that exclusion of evidence from grand jury investigations would not further the deterrence goal since only police who had seized evidence solely for use in a grand jury (a very small percentage) would be potentially deterred.[50] Thus, illegally seized evidence can be admitted as part of the evidence presented to the grand jury.

The rule also does not apply to parole revocation hearings. The Supreme Court again held that exclusion of evidence in such proceedings would provide only minimal levels of deterrence.[51] The Court also noted that the cost of excluding evidence from parole hearings is particularly high since the state has an "overwhelming interest" in ensuring that parolees comply with the requirements of parole.[52]

5. Has the Exclusionary Rule Outlived Its Usefulness?

The exclusionary rule is a twentieth-century creation. Prior to the Supreme Court decisions that established it, it was assumed that civil suit or internal police discipline would be sufficient to protect citizens' rights under the Fourth Amendment. Exclusion was not even thought of as a possible remedy for such constitutional violations. Dean John Henry Wigmore, one of the pioneers of evidence law, expressed the view that constitutional violations did not impact the admissibility of evidence:

> It has long been established that the admissibility of evidence is not affected by the illegality of the means through which the party has been enabled to obtain the evidence. The illegality is by no means condoned; it is merely ignored.[53]

One legal scholar noted that "supporters of the exclusionary rule cannot point to a single major statement from the Founding Fathers —or even the antebellum Reconstruction eras—supporting Fourth Amendment exclusion of evidence in a criminal trial.... Both before and after the Revolution, the civil trespass action tried to a jury flourished as the obvious remedy against haughty customs officers, tax collectors, constables, marshals and the like."[54]

At the time *Weeks* and *Mapp* were decided, however, those alternate procedures were woefully inadequate. Police routinely violated the law, often oblivious to legal requirements. In adopting the exclusionary rule under state law, the California Supreme Court commented in 1955 that "other remedies have completely failed to secure compliance with the constitutional provisions on the part of police officers with the attendant result that the courts under the old rule [favoring admissibility] have been constantly required to participate in, and in effect condone, the lawless activities of law enforcement officers."[55] In deciding *Mapp*, the Court cited California's failed experience without the exclusionary rule, noting that other remedies had been "worthless and futile" in protecting Fourth Amendment rights.[56]

Perhaps the most damning evidence of the ineffectiveness of alternative remedies to exclusion was the actions and reactions of law enforcement officers prior to and subsequent to the *Mapp* decision. Yale Kamisar, a noted scholar on the exclusionary rule, speculated that prior to *Mapp*, alternate forms of protection were so ineffective that police officers were ignorant of the requirements of the Fourth Amendment or simply assumed that its terms did not apply to them.[57] As evidence of this lack of concern for the law of search and seizure, the Cincinnati Police Department applied for all of three search warrants in the two years preceding the *Mapp* decision.[58] After the *Mapp* decision was handed down, Michael Murphy, the then–New York police commissioner, admitted that the case created "tidal waves and earthquakes" that required the department to rebuild its institutions by holding retraining sessions from the top down.[59] A New York prosecutor also recalled that "it was as though we had made a belated discovery that the fourth amendment applied in the state of New York."[60]

A Canadian Commission made similar findings prior to the passage of the *Canadian Charter on Rights and Freedoms* in 1982:

> The files of the [Royal Canadian Mounted Police (RCMP)] disclose that there is a significantly general attitude that, since the courts of Canada have held that illegally obtained evidence is admissible, this means that the judges do not condemn unlawful investigative conduct, and this in turn is taken as implied authorization of unlawful investigative conduct if the result is the obtaining of evidence relevant to an issue before the Court.[61]

Critics of the exclusionary rule have also pointed to the fact that clearly guilty criminals can go free as a result of its all-or-nothing approach. Professor Kamisar notes that recent Supreme Court decisions in the area of search and seizure law have lessened the impact of the exclusionary rule to such an extent that such fears are no longer founded:

> Judge Cardozo's oft-quoted criticism of the exclusionary rule—"[t]he criminal is to go free because the constable has blundered" —is out of date. The court has taken a grudging view of what amounts to a "search" or "seizure" within the meaning of the Fourth Amendment and has taken a relaxed view of what constitutes consent to an otherwise illegal search or seizure; it has so softened the "probable cause" requirement, so increased the occasions on which the police may act on the basis of "reasonable suspicion" or in the absence of any reasonable suspicion, and so narrowed the thrust of the exclusionary rule that nowadays the criminal only "goes free" if and when the constable has blundered badly.[62]

Former Supreme Court Justice Potter Stewart has speculated that the real complaint of critics is not with the exclusionary rule, but with the Fourth Amendment itself:

> Much of the criticism leveled at the exclusionary rule is misdirected; it is more properly directed at the fourth amendment itself. It is true that, as many observers have charged, the effect of the rule is to deprive the courts of extremely relevant, often direct evidence of the guilt of the defendant. But these same critics sometimes fail to acknowledge that, in many instances, the same extremely relevant evidence would not have been obtained had the police officer complied

with the commands of the fourth amendment in the first place....The inevitable result of the Constitution's prohibition against unreasonable searches and seizures and its requirement that no warrant shall issue but upon probable cause is that the police officers who obey its strictures will catch fewer criminals. That is not a political outcome impressed upon an unwilling citizenry by unbeknighted judges. It is the price the framers anticipated and were willing to pay to ensure the sanctity of the person, the home, and property against unrestrained governmental power.[63]

Perhaps the best argument against the exclusionary rule, at least in its original form, is that it turns a blind eye to the circumstances of the case and motivations of the officer. If evidence is suppressed, regardless of the fault of the officer, then officers who tried to respect suspects' rights would be frustrated when seemingly innocent conduct was punished by the courts. In this context, it can also be argued that the exclusionary rule is a uniquely American tradition. The United States had been the only country that applied a blanket rule of suppression regardless of the fault of the police or the strength of the evidence. Other countries rejected this approach in favor of a balancing test that weighs the degree of police misconduct, the strength of evidence against the defendant, and the seriousness of the offense.[64] Although criticized for gutting the exclusionary rule, the *Leon* line of decisions can be seen in this light as simply bringing American law in line with the rest of the western world.

Many scholars and even judges have argued that times have changed to such an extent that the exclusionary is no longer needed. Because of increased police professionalism and availability of civil rights lawsuits, they contend that alternate remedies are sufficient to protect defendants' rights.[65] Even assuming that this would be the case, the existence of these alternatives is still something of a hollow remedy. The defendant may not have much incentive to sue if the illegally seized evidence has been used to convict him of the crime and he is sentenced to prison. Also, the jury may not feel much sympathy toward a defendant who claims his rights were violated when his drugs or other contraband were taken in violation of his rights. Finally, if the exclusionary rule disappears, police professionalism may also disappear with it. There is legitimate concern that the police will revert to their prior behavior of ignoring the Fourth Amendment if there is no longer an incentive for them to follow the rules.

II. THE EXCLUSIONARY RULE FOR THE FIFTH AND SIXTH AMENDMENTS

While the Fourth Amendment exclusionary rule is the most well known and commonly thought of in connection with the term, the Supreme Court has also adopted exclusionary rules to protect a defendant's Fifth and Sixth Amendment rights to remain silent and his right to counsel. As you learned in Chapter 4, confessions play an important role in solving cases and can provide key evidence of a suspect's guilt. If certain rules are not followed by the police in obtaining confessions, however, that evidence can be excluded.

A. The Right to Remain Silent and *Miranda*

The Fifth Amendment to the Constitution provides in part that no person "shall be compelled in any criminal case to be a witness against himself."[66] Thus, before admitting a defendant's statements given to law enforcement, a trial court must determine whether the suspect knowingly and intelligently waived his **Fifth Amendment right to remain silent**.[67] The Supreme Court recognized in *Miranda v. Arizona* that where a suspect is interrogated while in custody, such interrogations can generate "compelling pressures which work to undermine the individual's will to resist and to compel him to speak where he would not otherwise do so freely."[68] The Court expressed concern that existing judicial safeguards were insufficient to protect against involuntary or coerced confessions.[69] The Court concluded that a suspect cannot voluntarily waive his right to remain silent unless he is first advised of that right. Because the defendant was not advised of his rights before being questioned in custody, the Court excluded his confession.

Thus, before a suspect can be interrogated, he must be advised as follows: (1) he has the right to remain silent, (2) anything he says can and will be used against him in a court of law, (3) he has the right to an attorney, and (4) if he cannot afford one, one will be appointed for him.[70] These are known as the **Miranda rights**. Once the suspect invokes either his right to remain silent or his right to an attorney, all questioning must stop.[71]

The *Miranda* decision was quite controversial at the time it was handed down in 1966. In reaction to it, the Chief of Police of Garland, Texas remarked, "It's the damnedest thing I ever heard—we may as well close up shop."[72] That doomsday prophecy proved to be inaccurate, however. While the *Miranda* rights have become universally known, that fact has not stopped law enforcement's ability to talk to suspects or to obtain confessions. A majority of suspects still waive their rights, and almost all juvenile suspects continue to do so.[73] Consequently, *Miranda* has effectively balanced the need for obtaining confessions as a law enforcement tool against the risk that the police will cross the line between "legitimate efforts to elicit admissions and constitutionally impermissible compulsion."[74]

1. Scope of Custody and Interrogation

The requirement to advise a suspect of his *Miranda* rights only applies to custodial interrogations. A person is in **custody** if he is placed under arrest or his freedom is limited in any "significant way."[75] *Miranda* does not apply to questioning that occurs before the suspect is placed in custody. A person who is questioned by police pursuant to a traffic stop or who is questioned inside of his own home and is not under arrest, for example, would not have to be Mirandized.

Fifth Amendment right to remain silent
a provision in the Fifth Amendment that provides that no person "shall be compelled in any criminal case to be a witness against himself"

Miranda **rights**
the rights suspects must be advised of prior to being interrogated while in custody. Those rights are: (1) you have the right to remain silent, (2) anything you say can and will be used against you in a court of law, (3) you have the right to an attorney, and (4) if you cannot afford one, one will be appointed for you

Custody
a level of detention where a person is placed under formal arrest or his freedom is limited in a significant manner and he does not feel free to leave

Interrogation
any questions or conduct of the interrogator designed to elicit an incriminating response

Interrogation includes express questioning and words or conduct designed to "elicit an incriminating response from a suspect."[76] An incriminating response includes any response of the suspect that the prosecution may seek to introduce at trial.[77] For example, the Court held that a conversation between two officers about the potential of a missing shotgun to injure children, while the suspect was riding in the back of the patrol car, was not interrogation.[78] The Court felt it was not reasonably likely that the suspect would feel compelled to make an incriminating statement based on a few offhand remarks by the officers.

Practical Example

Sammy is pulled over for speeding. Sammy flees the scene. Sammy is then forced to pull over. He is ordered out of the car by several officers with their weapons drawn. The officers then question Sammy about why he ran. Sammy states he was involved with a bank robbery 20 minutes ago and thought that was why he was being pulled over. Should Sammy have been Mirandized under the circumstances? Yes. Sammy was under arrest because the officers stopped his car with their weapons drawn, and at that point, it was clear he was not free to leave.

Practical Example

The state patrol pulls over a car driven by Tina. Sarah is a passenger in the car. The patrolman discovers that the pair is wanted for several crimes. He radios for backup. The pair is placed under arrest. They are not given Miranda warnings. Sarah is driven back to the station by the other officer who has arrived on scene. As they are driving back, the officer says that he bets Tina is telling the other officer that the crimes were all Sarah's idea. Sarah then tells the officer that she just went along for the ride and that Tina threatened to kill her if she ever said anything. Are the officer's comments interrogation? Yes. His comments were designed to make Sarah make an incriminating response.

2. Waiver of *Miranda* Rights Must Be Voluntary

The prosecution must prove that the suspect "voluntarily, knowingly and intelligently" waived his *Miranda* rights before making a statement to police.[79] First, the court must determine that the suspect's statements were the product of a "free and deliberate choice rather than intimidation, coercion, or deception."[80] **Coercion** includes not just physical violence but other interrogation methods as well that are calculated to "break the suspect's will."[81] In determining whether police action is coercive,

Coercion
interrogation methods that are calculated to "break the suspect's will"

courts have examined such factors as the duration and conditions of the detention, the attitude of the police toward the suspect, the suspect's physical and mental state, and other methods that may sap the suspect's "powers of resistance and self-control."[82]

The Court has held, for example, that certain misrepresentations amount to coercion, such as telling the suspect that her friend would lose her job or that her welfare benefits would be terminated if she failed to cooperate.[83] Law enforcement officers can use a certain degree of deception and trickery, however, to convince suspects to waive their rights. For example, the police do not have to inform the suspect of the complete subject matter of the interrogation before advising him of his rights.[84]

Second, the court must determine whether the defendant fully understood his rights and the consequences of waiving them.[85] "Once it is determined that a suspect's decision not to rely on his rights was uncoerced, that he at all times knew he could stand mute and request a lawyer, and that he was aware of the State's intention to use his statements to secure conviction, the analysis is complete and the waiver is valid as a matter of law."[86] It is not necessary that the police recite the *Miranda* warnings perfectly verbatim. In *Florida v. Powell*, the Court held that a warning that, in part, informed a suspect that he had a right "to talk to a lawyer before answering any of our questions" was sufficient even though it did not expressly state that the right continued throughout the interrogation.[87] The Court noted that the inquiry is simply whether "the warnings reasonably convey to a suspect his rights as required by *Miranda*."[88] The Court also found it significant that the warning in question did not omit any information that was required under *Miranda*.[89]

Perhaps the best predictor of whether a court will find the waiver was voluntary, however, is simply whether the suspect was properly advised of his *Miranda* rights at the outset of the interrogation. Generally, when the officer properly advises the defendant of his rights, courts have found statements made thereafter to be voluntary. If he is not so advised, courts have generally reached the opposite conclusion. In *Missouri v. Seibert*, the Supreme Court summarized this trend:

> *Miranda* conditioned the admissibility at trial of any custodial confession on warning a suspect of his rights: failure to give the prescribed warnings and obtain a waiver of rights before custodial questioning generally requires exclusion of any statements obtained. Conversely, giving the warnings and getting a waiver has generally produced a virtual ticket of admissibility; maintaining that a statement is involuntary even though given after warnings and voluntary waiver of rights requires unusual stamina, and litigation over voluntariness tends to end with the finding of a valid waiver.[90]

In order to invoke his right to remain silent, a suspect must do so unambiguously. The suspect must state that he wants to remain silent or does not want to talk to the police.[91] The prosecution does not have to show that the waiver was express—in other words, there is no requirement that the defendant state, "I waive my rights and want to talk." A refusal to sign an advisement form does not automatically mean the suspect has invoked his right to remain silent, either.[92] There is also no requirement that the suspect's waiver be in writing.[93] It is enough that the defendant understood his rights yet engaged in conduct that was inconsistent with invoking his right to remain silent. The Supreme Court has held that "[w]here the prosecution shows that a *Miranda* warning was given and that it was understood by the accused, an accuser's uncoerced statement establishes an implied waiver of the right to remain silent."[94] In other words, the *Miranda* rule is satisfied "if the suspect receives adequate *Miranda* warnings, understands them, and has an opportunity to invoke the rights before giving any answers or admissions."[95]

For example, in *Berghuis v. Thompkins*, the Court found that the suspect had waived his rights where he largely remained silent during three hours of questioning, answering only a few select questions. The suspect was advised of his rights but refused to sign the written advisement and waiver form. At no point during questioning did the suspect state that he wanted to remain silent. Near the end of the interrogation, the suspect was asked whether he prayed to God to "forgive you for shooting down that boy."[96] The suspect answered "Yes" and then looked away. Since the defendant had given sporadic answers to a few other questions during the interrogation, the Court concluded his conduct was consistent with waiver.[97]

Practical Example

Stewie is interrogated by police on suspicion of attempted murder of his mother. He is advised of his rights. The police ask Stewie to sign the waiver form. He tells the officer he cannot write but states that he will talk. Officers ask him several questions about his conduct concerning his mother. He admits to drawing a kitchen knife and attempting to stab his mother but says it was in self-defense. The officers then ask if he had been plotting to kill his mother. Stewie says he does not want to talk any further. The officers then tell Stewie that if he does not talk, they cannot help him. Stewie then admits that he had been plotting to kill his mother but then decided he could not go through with it. He is charged with attempted murder. Stewie moves to suppress his last statement, claiming he had invoked his right to remain silent. The court would likely find Stewie's last statement was involuntary since he had made a clear request that interrogation stop before officers asked the last question.

3. After-the-Fact *Miranda* Advisements

Officers sometimes use a **two-step interrogation** process where they first obtain un-Mirandized statements from a suspect in custody, subsequently advise him of his *Miranda* rights, and then complete the interrogation. Any statements made prior to the warnings being given are per se inadmissible under *Miranda* since the suspect was not properly advised of his rights before making the statements. The legality of the statements obtained subsequent to the warnings, however, depends on the reasons for the officer's failure to Mirandize the suspect at the outset of the interrogation. If the officer intentionally withheld warnings in an attempt to obtain an un-Mirandized confession, then the court will likely exclude the resulting Mirandized statements. On the other hand, if the officer's failure to advise the suspect was a good-faith mistake, then the statements will likely be admissible.

In *Missouri v. Seibert*, the Court held in a plurality opinion (five justices agreed to overturn the defendant's conviction but could not agree on the proper test for evaluating the legality of such procedures) that a two-step process violates *Miranda* where the officers deliberately withhold warnings until after they have obtained a confession, unless they take curative measures to mitigate the impact of the prior, unwarned statements.[98] Thus, lower courts must conduct a two-part analysis—first, they must determine whether the interrogators deliberately withheld *Miranda* warnings, and if so, they must then determine whether the delayed warnings were effective in apprising the suspect of his right to remain silent.[99]

Seibert involved the use of a police protocol that instructed officers to withhold warnings until after a suspect confessed. The officer was then instructed to give *Miranda* warnings and obtain a second confession. That policy was promoted by not only the local police department but by a national training organization.[100] The Court struck down the policy, holding that it created an intentional end-run around the *Miranda* requirements.

Even where officers are not operating under explicit policies to withhold warnings, courts have found their conduct to be intentional. For instance, in *Thompson v. Runnel*, the Ninth Circuit Court of Appeals instructed lower courts to consider both direct and circumstantial evidence of the officer's intent in initially withholding the warning:

> In determining whether the interrogator deliberately withheld the *Miranda* warning, courts should consider whether objective evidence and any available subjective evidence, such as an officer's testimony, support an inference that the two-step interrogation procedure was used to undermine the *Miranda* warning.... Once a law enforcement officer has detained a suspect and subjects him to interrogation...there is rarely, if ever, a legitimate reason to delay giving a *Miranda* warning until after the suspect has confessed. Instead, the most plausible reason for the delay is an illegitimate one, which is the interrogator's desire to weaken the warnings' effectiveness. [101]

There, the suspect was interviewed at the police station for two hours about the death of his girlfriend. He was confronted by officers with a fictional eyewitness account and falsely informed that physical evidence tied him to the scene. Only after the suspect admitted his involvement in the stabbing was he given *Miranda* warnings. Although no formal policy existed, the court concluded that the only "reasonable inference" was that the officers deliberately withheld *Miranda* warnings until after obtaining a confession.[102]

In contrast, in *Oregon v. Elstad*, the Supreme Court permitted the two-step procedure where the officer failed to Mirandize a suspect he had arrested inside his home but later advised at the police station.[103] The Court found that the officer's failure to administer *Miranda* warnings inside the house was not intentional but was rather due to the officer's mistaken belief that warnings were not required.

As to the second part of the test, the effectiveness of the subsequent warning, the Court has instructed lower courts to focus on whether the post-questioning warning "could function as effectively as *Miranda* requires."[104] The Court reasoned that if the answer to that question is yes, then the court should consider the question of whether the suspect voluntarily waived his rights and confessed. If the answer is no, then "the subsequent statement is inadmissible for want of adequate *Miranda* warnings, because the earlier and later statements are realistically seen as parts of a single, unwarned sequence of questioning."[105]

The Court laid out several factors that courts should examine when determining the answer to the above question:

- the completeness and detail of the questions and answers in the first round of interrogation;
- the overlapping content of the two statements;
- the timing and setting of the first and the second interrogation;
- the continuity of police personnel; and
- the degree to which the interrogator's questions treated the second round as continuous with the first.[106]

Unless the subsequent warnings let the suspect make an informed choice about whether he can stop talking at that point and minimize the damage from his earlier comments, the Court concluded that "the sensible underlying assumption is that with one confession in hand before the warnings, the interrogator can count on getting its duplicate, with trifling additional trouble."[107] Similarly, in *Thompson*, the Ninth Circuit concluded that the after-the-fact warnings were ineffective since the second interrogation was simply a rehashing of the first one. The Court noted that all the *Seibert* factors favored exclusion of the confession:

> The pre-warning interrogation was highly confrontational and detailed; the two sessions took place in the same small interrogation room, back-to-back, with no

break at all; the police personnel were exactly the same, and, as described above, the officers' questioning treated the two sessions as continuous and drew, in one instance, on Thompson's pre-*Miranda* statement during the second session to ensure that the earlier exculpatory material was reiterated after the requisite warnings were given.[108]

In summary, two-step interrogations are likely to be found to violate *Miranda* where the officer's failure to initially advise the suspect of his rights was intentional. In such a situation, the second set of statements will be admitted only if the initial interrogation was brief, did not occur in the same place as the second, and did not cover the same ground (i.e., it was a mere prelude to the subsequent interrogation). If the second interrogation is instead a mere carbon copy of the first, occurring shortly after the first, then the subsequent statements will be inadmissible.

Practical Example

Julie makes a 911 call that her husband has been shot. When police show up to her door, they discover her husband's dead body. After a brief investigation, officers conclude that Julie probably shot her husband. They inform Julie of their suspicions and ask if there is a gun in the home. She replies that her husband has a revolver. The officers seize the gun and note it has been recently fired. They then handcuff Julie. On the way to the station, an officer asks Julie why she did it. Julie replies that her husband had been having an affair and she couldn't let him do that to her. Later at the station, Julie is Mirandized. She waives her rights and gives a full confession. She then moves to suppress her confessions. Since she was not Mirandized prior to her questioning in the police car, Julie's first statement should be suppressed. The second set of statements would be admissible, however. While the officer's conduct in not advising her of her rights appears to have been intentional, the second interrogation was distinct from the first. It was conducted at the station and was much more comprehensive than the one question asked of Julie inside the squad car.

4. Right to Counsel Under *Miranda*

Fifth Amendment right to counsel
a suspect must be advised of his right to counsel and voluntarily waive that right before being interrogated while in custody under *Miranda*

Under *Miranda*, a suspect must also be advised of his **Fifth Amendment right to counsel**. This is done as an additional safeguard to protect his Fifth Amendment right to remain silent. Just like the right to remain silent, the defendant must knowingly and voluntarily waive his right to an attorney before talking to police. A suspect must clearly invoke his right to an attorney; an ambiguous or equivocal reference to an attorney (such as "do I need an attorney?") is not sufficient.[109] Once the suspect invokes his right to counsel, all questioning must cease until an attorney is present, or the suspect voluntarily reinitiates the conversation.[110] For example, the Ninth Circuit Court of Appeals held that it was improper for officers to inform the suspect that it "might be worse" for him to talk to an attorney, and that it was in his best interest to talk to them without one, after he had requested a lawyer.[111]

The Supreme Court recently held that the police can reinterview a suspect who invokes his right to counsel, but only after a sufficient break in custody has occurred. In *Maryland v. Shatzer*, the suspect was serving prison time on an unrelated offense at the time of his interrogation about the sexual abuse of his son.[112] He refused to talk and requested counsel. Two and a half years later, he was reinterviewed about the allegations while still in prison. This time, he elected to talk to investigators. The Court found that where a "suspect has been released from his pretrial custody and has returned to his normal life for some time before the later attempted interrogation, there is little reason to think that his change of heart regarding interrogation without counsel has been coerced."[113] The Court held that, at a minimum, a 14-day break in custody is sufficient to remove any "residual coercive effects" from a suspect's prior custody.[114] The Court explained that "confessions obtained after a two-week break in custody and a waiver of *Miranda* rights are most unlikely to be compelled, and hence are unreasonably excluded."[115] The Court also distinguished interrogative custody (holding a suspect on suspicion of the charges he is being questioned about) from incarceration (a sentence of imprisonment on an unrelated offense). Only the former creates the coercive pressure to waive a suspect's *Miranda* rights, thus triggering the need for a 14-day break in custody.[116]

Practical Example

Assume Mark is arrested for drug possession. Officers Mirandize Mark, and he signs a waiver of rights form. When officers ask about Mark's suppliers, he asks for an attorney. Thirty minutes later, but before Mark's attorney can make it to the station, an officer then tells Mark he can get a better deal if he tells him who his dealer is. Mark then says he got the "coke" from Peanut Head Williams. Mark is charged with possession. He moves to suppress his statement about the dealer. The court should suppress this statement because Mark did not reinitiate the conversation once he had asked for an attorney and there was not a sufficient break in custody between the two interrogations.

Practical Example

Jackson is questioned about a sexual assault that occurred two days ago. He invokes his right to an attorney. The officers stop questioning Jackson. Eighteen days later, Jackson is arrested on an unrelated charge of burglary. The officers

Mirandize Jackson and question him about the burglary case. He does not invoke his right to counsel. They also question him about the sexual assault. Jackson confesses to both charges. He then moves to suppress the confessions on the ground that he had previously asked for an attorney. The court will not suppress the confessions. Since more than 14 days had elapsed between the time Jackson invoked his right to counsel on the first offense, he could be questioned about it again without initiating the conversation. Jackson never invoked his right to counsel with regard to the burglary case, so the court will not suppress his confession to the burglary, either.

5. Public Safety Exception

Normally, the police must advise the suspect of his *Miranda* rights before questioning him in custody. However, the Supreme Court has created an exception where public safety is at risk. In *New York v. Quarles*, the Court held that a suspect could be questioned about matters implicating public safety before being advised of his *Miranda* rights.[117] The exception applies where there is an objective belief that the police or public safety was threatened by an "immediate danger," such as the presence of a weapon.[118]

In *Quarles*, a rape suspect was fleeing police and ran into a supermarket. He hid the gun he was carrying in the store before being arrested by police. Before being given *Miranda* warnings, the officers asked the suspect where the gun was. He nodded and told officers the gun was "over there."[119] Once the gun was located, the suspect was advised of his rights and questioned further about the rape. The Court held the officer's conduct was proper, noting that the officer had limited his questioning to ending the threat to the public:

> Officer Kraft asked only the question necessary to locate the missing gun before advising respondent of his rights. It was only after securing the loaded revolver and giving the warnings that he continued with investigatory questions about the ownership and place of purchase of the gun. The exception which we recognize today, far from complicating the thought processes and the on-the-scene judgments of police officers, will simply free them to follow their legitimate instincts when confronting situations presenting a danger to public safety.[120]

In upholding the admission of the statement concerning the location of the weapon, the Court found that the concerns that ordinarily justify the need for *Miranda* warnings were outweighed by public safety concerns in this instance:

> Here, had *Miranda* warnings deterred Quarles from responding to Officer Kraft's question about the whereabouts of the gun, the cost would have been something more than merely the failure to obtain evidence useful in convicting Quarles.

Officer Kraft needed an answer to his question not simply to make his case against Quarles but to insure that further danger to the public did not result from the concealment of the gun in a public area.[121]

Public safety exception

an exception to the *Miranda* requirement that allows officers to question a suspect, without advising him of his rights, about the presence of a weapon or other item that presents an immediate danger to officer safety or public safety

Courts are split as to whether the **public safety exception** allows unwarned questioning about a weapon that is located inside a private home. Some courts have held that the exception only extends to those situations where the public has general access to the weapons or dangerous items.[122] For example, one federal court held that the exception does not apply where officers questioned a suspect about a weapon located inside a home in the presence of young children.[123]

Other courts have held that the exception does apply behind closed doors, as long as the officers have an objectively reasonable concern for their safety and the questioning is related only to the location of that weapon.[124] The Michigan Supreme Court held the public safety exception applied where officers arrested a suspect in his home who had threatened his wife with a gun. After the officers allowed the suspect to get dressed, he began rummaging through his drawers. Fearing for their safety, the officers asked the suspect where his gun was. He told them he gave it to his brother. The court found that the questioning about the weapon was covered under the public safety exception since the officers knew the suspect had been armed and they were legitimately concerned for their safety.[125]

Practical Example

Assume the police are chasing a suspect in connection with a string of jewelry store heists. The suspect used a weapon in two of the robberies. The police observe the suspect dart into an apartment building. The police catch up to the suspect inside of his second-floor apartment. The police handcuff and arrest the suspect. Without giving him a Miranda advisement, the officers question the suspect about where the weapon is located. He points to a box in the hall closet. The officers take the gun and then interrogate the suspect about the robberies after he is transported to the station and advised of his rights. The suspect moves to suppress his statements about the gun as having been obtained in violation of Miranda. The officers argue the public safety exception. They testify that they feared for their safety when they asked about the gun since they knew he had been armed. The court would likely rule that the questioning was not covered under the public safety exception. The weapon was located inside the suspect's home and did not pose a threat to the public. The officers also had the suspect in handcuffs at the time of questioning and could have legitimately searched the area within the lunge, grasp, and control of the suspect pursuant to the search incident to arrest doctrine. As a result, the officers could not have reasonably been in fear for their safety or others at the time of questioning.

6. Booking Questions Exception

The Supreme Court has recognized another exception to *Miranda* for routine booking questions.[126] Under this exception, a *Miranda* advisement is not necessary where the police merely ask identification questions for administrative purposes, such as those seeking a person's name, address, and date of birth. Not all questions asked during the booking process, however, are covered under the exception. Questions that go beyond mere administrative needs, but are instead intended to elicit an incriminating response, are still covered by *Miranda*.[127] For example, a Colorado court held that neither the **booking exception** nor the public safety exception applied to the questioning of a new inmate about whether he was carrying contraband before being searched and admitted into the jail. The court held that *Miranda* warnings must be given in that instance because the questions went beyond a request for basic identifying information.[128]

Booking exception
an exception to the *Miranda* requirement that allows detention officers to ask basic identifying information of the suspect when booking him into jail without giving him a *Miranda* advisement

Practical Example

Suzie is arrested on suspicion of murdering her husband. She is booked into jail. When asked where she lives, Suzie breaks down and admits she "did not mean to kill him." Suzie later moves to suppress that statement since she had not been advised of her Miranda rights. The court should deny this request. Although her response was incriminating, it came in response to a routine question for her address. Thus, the booking exception applies.

B. Due Process Concerns

Even if a court finds that the suspect voluntarily waived his *Miranda* rights and agreed to talk to police, it can still exclude his statements on due process grounds. The Fifth and Fourteenth Amendments to the Constitution provide that a person cannot be deprived of life, liberty, or property without due process of law.[129] **Due process** can be equated to fundamental fairness.[130] Thus, courts have held that some interrogation techniques are "so offensive to a civilized system of justice" that their use violates due process.[131] A defendant is protected against coercive police conduct, regardless of whether he is in custody and whether he had waived his *Miranda* rights.[132]

Due process
a fundamental fairness requirement of the Constitution. It requires that the police not use interrogation techniques that are so offensive to a civilized system of justice that their use is considered to be unfair

Many of the same factors are used for determining whether a suspect's statements are voluntary as are used for determining whether a person voluntarily waived his *Miranda* rights. A voluntary statement is one that is the product of the suspect's free will and not the result of undue pressure

Voluntariness
a statement that is the product of a suspect's free will. Factors such as the length of the interrogation, the suspect's age and maturity, and the interrogation tactics used are examined by the court to determine voluntariness

by police. **Voluntariness** is determined by examining a number of factors, including:

- whether the interrogation involved an element of police coercion or punishment;
- the defendant's susceptibility to coercion;
- the length of the interrogation;
- the location of the interrogation;
- the defendant's age, maturity, and education; and
- the defendant's mental health.[133]

Before finding that a confession is involuntary, a court must find that the police used coercive conduct to obtain the confession and that those coercive tactics were responsible for producing the confession.[134] Coercion can be the result of both psychological and physical "overreaching" by the police.[135] Thus, a statement may be involuntary if it results from physical violence, torture, threats of violence, or unkept promises.[136]

1. Physical Violence or Torture

Courts have held that the use of physical violence or threats to obtain a confession automatically violates due process unless the prosecution can establish that those threats or acts of violence did not induce the confession.[137] One of the more notorious examples of torture used to compel confessions occurred in the case of *Brown v. Mississippi*.[138] There, three black men were arrested for the murder of a white shopkeeper. The men were denied access to attorneys and brutally beaten by police. The tactics included driving one suspect over the state line, whipping him, and threatening to leave him in Alabama if he did not confess. Another man was lynched, and he still had the rope mark around his neck when he appeared in court. The men eventually signed written confessions.[139] The Supreme Court noted that the account of the torture read "more like pages torn from some medieval account than a record made within the confines of a modern civilization which aspires to an enlightened constitutional government."[140]

2. Deception and Other Psychological Interrogation Methods

In contrast, courts have held that the use of deception or other psychological methods of interrogation are not "inherently coercive."[141] Short of an "overbearing inducement," trickery and deceit are viewed as a "valid weapon" in the fight against crime.[142] In other words, as long as the deceptive tactics are not "reasonably likely to procure an untrue statement," their use has been upheld.[143] Courts have upheld the use of such deceptive tactics as misrepresenting the fact that a co-defendant has implicated the suspect in the crime[144] or lying about the state of the physical evidence against the suspect.[145] For example, the Maryland Court of Appeals held that a confession was voluntary despite the fact that the police misinformed the suspect that he had failed a polygraph, that his fingerprints were found at the crime scene, and that his cousin could identify him as the killer.[146] Informing the suspect of his options or the consequences of his actions (such as telling him he can be arrested or get the death penalty) is also not considered to be coercive conduct.[147] Neither is giving the suspect advice or urging him to tell the truth.[148] In contrast, the Colorado Supreme Court held that persistent questioning of a suspect after she suffered an emotional breakdown subsequent to being told of the death of the victim was coercive and violated due process.[149]

On the lighter side (or heavier as the case may be) is the story of Bruce Tuck. Tuck was accused of having committed a number of rapes in Tennessee in 2009. Due to his morbid obesity, Tuck was placed on a lettuce-only diet at the jail. He claimed that investigators coerced his confession to the rapes by offering him a bag of chips and a cold drink in exchange for his statement. His arguments were rejected by the court. He ultimately pled guilty to three assaults in one county and had 21 pending felony counts in another.[150]

3. Manufacturing False Evidence

Courts are split as to whether manufacturing false evidence (as opposed to oral misrepresentations about the evidence) crosses the line. Police sometimes may present a fake DNA test result or polygraph result to a suspect in an attempt to gain a confession. Some state courts have concluded that this practice does violate due process. For example, a Florida appellate court drew an "intrinsic distinction" between verbal deception and manufactured documentation of those untruths.[151] It noted that "unlike oral misrepresentations, manufactured documents have the potential of indefinite life and the facial appearance of authenticity."[152] The court held that the use of two fabricated reports showing that the semen recovered from the crime scene matched the defendant violated due process. Similarly, a New Jersey court held that a fabricated audiotape that appeared to contain an eyewitness identification of the defendant was a per se violation of due process.[153]

Other courts have upheld the use of manufactured evidence. The Nevada Supreme Court concluded that manufactured evidence should be evaluated under the totality of the circumstances test just like other deceptive techniques.[154] The court held that the appropriate test is "whether the deception, whatever its nature, would have induced the confession under the circumstances."[155] A Maryland appellate court also rejected a bright line rule barring the use of manufactured evidence, noting that "it is a simplistic generality that a written false assertion by the police, regardless of its substance, always will have a greater impact on a suspect's thinking than an oral assertion, and that every written assertion by the police will have precisely the same coercive effect as all other false written assertions by the police."[156]

AUTHOR'S NOTE

Regardless of the legality of the practice, the use of manufactured documents to obtain a confession is risky business. If investigators have to go to the extreme of manufacturing false evidence to obtain a confession, the jury may sympathize with the defendant. This is particularly true in light of the growing number of agencies that videotape the entire interrogation process. Seeing the suspect being confronted with fake evidence on video may not play well with the jury.

Practical Example

Assume a suspect is being questioned about his involvement in the murder of his eight-year-old son. He is Mirandized and agrees to talk to police. The officers question the man for three hours. Finally, one officer says he can understand how hard it must be to raise a child who is unruly and does not obey the rules. He urges the man to "come clean" and make it easier on himself. The suspect then says he was just angry at his son because he wouldn't clean up his room. He states he didn't mean to hurt him, but he ended up suffocating his son. Before trial, the man claims his statement was coerced. The court will find that this statement was not coerced since the police did not overbear the father's will or make promises that they could not keep.

Now assume the father is interrogated for 18 hours. He has an IQ of 85 and has never been interrogated before. The police tell the man he will spend the rest of his life in prison and he will go to hell for killing his son. The man then confesses to the killing. The court is much more likely to find this statement was coerced due to the length of the interrogation, the man's low IQ, and his unfamiliarity with the process.

Practical Example

Mai is accused of stealing from her employer. While questioning her, the police tell Mai that her fingerprints were found on the family's jewelry box, an item she is not supposed to touch as part of her job. This fact is untrue. Mai then confesses to the crime. She then claims her statement was coerced due to the police deception. The judge would likely rule that this was appropriate use of police trickery and not a due process violation.

Now assume that the police concoct a fake fingerprint match that purports to show that Mai's print matches the one found at the crime scene. Depending on the jurisdiction, this may be a due process violation. Some states treat written, falsified evidence more stringently than oral misrepresentations.

4. Exclusion of Compelled Statements

The Fifth Amendment provides that a person cannot be "compelled in any criminal case to be a witness against himself."[157] Thus, in order to give full meaning to that right, the constitution requires that unlawfully compelled evidence be excluded. The Court originally established this exclusionary rule in *Boyd v. United States* in 1886.[158] There, the defendant's business was illegally searched without a warrant, and he was forced to turn over invoices that incriminated him in importing fraud. The Court equated the compelling of the production of papers with being compelled to be a witness against oneself. It held that the evidence had to therefore be excluded from trial.[159] The Court extended the rule to cover involuntary confessions in *Bram v. United States*.[160]

C. Sixth Amendment Right to Counsel

Sixth Amendment right to counsel
right to counsel that applies to any critical stage of the criminal justice process

***Massiah* doctrine**
a Supreme Court doctrine that requires police to refrain from questioning a suspect outside the presence of his attorney once he has been charged with a crime

As discussed in Chapter 3, criminal defendants also have a **Sixth Amendment right to counsel** that applies to any critical stage of the criminal justice process. This right applies to the post-indictment interrogation of suspects. Thus, after charges have been filed, a defendant cannot be questioned in the absence of his attorney unless he expressly waives that right. This is known as the ***Massiah* doctrine**. The *Massiah* doctrine applies once the criminal case has been started. A criminal case starts once the prosecution has committed itself to prosecuting a defendant, whether through formal charge, indictment, preliminary hearing, or arraignment.[161]

In *Massiah v. United States*, the defendant and his co-conspirator were charged with importing and selling cocaine.[162] The pair was indicted and charged but released on bail. The co-defendant then agreed to cooperate with authorities and have a transmitter installed in his automobile. Agents then listened to conversations between the defendant and the conspirator and used those statements against the defendant at trial. While this technique is a perfectly legal investigative technique prior to a suspect being charged, the Supreme Court held that it violates the defendant's right to counsel once charges have been filed.[163]

In *Brewer v. Williams*, the Court again rejected officers' attempts to question a suspect without the presence of counsel once he had been charged.[164] There, the officers arrested and the defendant and charged him with abducting a 10-year-old girl. He was then transported 160 miles back to where the crime had been committed. Despite an agreement between his attorneys and the police that Williams was not to be questioned during transport, one of the officers persuaded the defendant to tell him where he had buried the girl's body. The Court held that the statement was inadmissible, stating that the "clear rule of *Massiah* is that once adversary proceedings have commenced against an individual, he has a right to legal representation when the government interrogates him."[165] The Court also ruled that it is the prosecution's burden to prove the defendant had expressly waived his right to an attorney.[166] Although the defendant had not asked for counsel during his transport, the Court found he had clearly indicated his intent to invoke his rights by securing counsel on either end of his trip and there was no evidence that the officer had made any efforts to determine if Williams wished to waive that right.[167]

In summary, prior to the commencement of a criminal case but where police seek to interrogate a suspect in custody, that suspect must be informed of his rights to remain silent and to counsel. He can choose either to waive those rights and speak to police or remain silent. The police can still clandestinely attempt to monitor a suspect's conversations at this point. Once formal charges have been filed, however, the defendant cannot be questioned or monitored without the presence of counsel, unless he expressly waives that right.

III. USE OF ILLEGALLY OBTAINED EVIDENCE FOR IMPEACHMENT

While the exclusionary rules generally prevent illegally seized evidence from being used to prove the guilt of the accused directly, such evidence can be used for impeachment—the process of attacking the credibility of a witness. For example, in *Walder v. United States*, the defendant testified that he had never possessed or sold narcotics.[168] The prosecutor impeached the defendant with the fact that government agents had seized heroin, albeit illegally, two years prior to the current narcotics offense. The Supreme Court stated the illegal search could not shield the defendant from perjury:

> It is one thing to say that the government cannot make an affirmative use of evidence unlawfully obtained. It is quite another to say that the defendant can turn the illegal method by which evidence in the government's possession was obtained to his own advantage, and provide himself with a shield against contradiction of his untruths.[169]

In *James v. Illinois*, the Court refused to extend the impeachment exception to all defense witnesses, however. It found that broadening the impeachment exception would not serve the truth-seeking function but instead would "significantly undermine" the deterrent effect of the exclusionary rule.[170] The Court cautioned that if this expansion were permitted, it would dramatically increase the number of instances where illegally seized evidence could be used. It also noted that while defendants can easily avoid making statements that directly contradict the illegally seized evidence, witnesses generally are more unpredictable and do not have the same incentives. Thus, defendants might be deterred from calling certain witnesses on their behalf for fear that the illegally seized evidence would be used to impeach them. Thus, the Court concluded that:

> Our prior cases make clear that defendants ought not be able to "pervert" the exclusion of illegally obtained evidence into a shield for perjury, but it seems no more appropriate for the state to brandish such evidence as a sword with which to dissuade defendants from presenting a meaningful defense through other witnesses. Given the potential chill created by expanding the impeachment exception, the conceded gains to the truth-seeking process from discouraging or disclosing perjured testimony would be offset to some extent by the concomitant loss of probative witness testimony. Thus, the truth-seeking rationale supporting the impeachment of defendants in *Walder* and its progeny does not apply to other witnesses with equal force.[171]

Similarly, voluntary statements obtained without a proper *Miranda* advisement or in violation of a defendant's Sixth Amendment right to counsel can be used to impeach the defendant.[172] Similar to the Fourth Amendment exclusionary rule, the *Miranda* rule is not constitutionally mandated.[173] Thus, the Court permitted statements obtained in violation of *Miranda* to be used for impeachment purposes to prevent the defendant from using such statements as a shield against perjury.[174] It concluded that the exclusion of such evidence would be too high a price to pay for vindication of those rights.[175]

Coerced statements, however, cannot be used for impeachment because such statements are inherently unreliable and are not trustworthy.[176]

Practical Example

Assume that Wayne is arrested for distribution of marijuana. Officers search his apartment and find several plastic baggies full of marijuana packaged for distribution. The evidence is seized without a warrant. The police plant an informant in his jail cell after he is charged. Wayne makes a statement that his drug dealer is going to be mad at him that the cops took the drugs. Wayne successfully suppresses both the drugs and the statement from evidence. Wayne then testifies at trial that the drugs were someone else's and that he did not know they were in the house. The prosecutor tries to impeach Wayne with the illegally seized evidence. The judge should allow the impeachment since the statement was voluntary and the evidence is being used to impeach the defendant's perjured statement.

IV. MOTIONS TO SUPPRESS

Motion to suppress
a request filed by the defendant, alleging that certain evidence was illegally seized or obtained

If a defendant believes his rights have been violated, he can enforce the exclusionary rule by filing a **motion to suppress** the illegally seized evidence. A motion to suppress is simply a request made to the judge to exclude certain items of evidence on the ground that it was illegally seized. A defendant must file this motion prior to trial.[177] In this motion, the defendant alleges the facts and legal arguments that support his belief that the evidence was illegally obtained. The prosecution is then allowed to file a response to the motion, arguing the facts and legal arguments as to why the evidence should be admitted. A hearing is then held on the motion.

Since the burden is on the prosecution to prove that the evidence was lawfully obtained, it has to call witnesses, usually police officers involved in the investigation, to testify about how the evidence was obtained. The defense can cross-examine those witnesses and call witnesses of its own. The judge then rules on the merits of the motion.

Colorado Rule of Criminal Procedure 41 provides a good example of the procedures for filing such a motion:

> **Motion for Return of Property and to Suppress Evidence.** A person aggrieved by an unlawful search and seizure may move the district court for the county where the property was seized for the return of the property and to suppress for use as evidence anything so obtained on the ground that:
>
> **(1)** The property was illegally seized without warrant; or
> **(2)** The warrant is insufficient on its face; or
> **(3)** The property seized is not that described in the warrant; or
> **(4)** There was not probable cause for believing the existence of the grounds on which the warrant was issued; or
> **(5)** The warrant was illegally executed.
>
> The judge shall receive evidence on any issue of fact necessary to the decision of the motion. If the motion is granted the property shall be restored unless otherwise subject to lawful detention and it shall not be admissible in evidence at any hearing or trial.... The motion shall be made and heard before trial unless opportunity therefor did not exist or the defendant was not aware of the grounds for the motion, but the court, in its discretion, may entertain the motion at the trial.[178]

Practical Example

Suppose Sheri is pulled over for speeding. She is giggling and had bloodshot eyes. The officer asks her to perform roadside maneuvers. She refuses, stating she is not drunk. The officer then arrests her for DUI. Sheri elects a breath test back at the station and blows a .09, just over the legal limit of .08. A few weeks before trial, Sheri would file a motion to suppress the evidence on the grounds that the officer did not have probable cause to arrest her for DUI since the performance of roadside maneuvers is voluntary. She would allege that the officer did not have probable cause for the arrest since bloodshot eyes and the act of speeding are not enough to suggest she was drunk. A hearing would be scheduled to determine the motion. The prosecutor would then call the arresting officer, and he would testify as to why he arrested Sheri. If the judge is not convinced there was probable cause for the arrest, he will suppress the arrest and the breath test. At that point, the case would be dismissed by the prosecutor for lack of evidence.

CHAPTER SUMMARY

Confessions and physical evidence can be excluded if the constitutional rights of the defendant were violated in obtaining the evidence. The Court has created so-called exclusionary rules to protect a person's rights under the Fourth, Fifth, and Sixth Amendments. The purpose of these exclusionary rules is to deter unlawful police misconduct.

The Fourth Amendment protects against unreasonable searches and seizures and requires that warrants be supported by probable cause. The Court has created many exceptions to the warrant and probable cause requirements to accommodate the various needs of law enforcement. In fact, warrants are required only where the police search a person's home or business office.

The Court erected the exclusionary rule to deter violations of the Fourth Amendment. Today, that rule applies to police actions that are conducted in willful or reckless disregard for the defendant's rights. It does not apply to good-faith mistakes. The exclusionary rule applies to both the illegally seized evidence and anything that is tainted by the original illegality. This is known as the fruit of the poisonous tree doctrine. Under the exclusionary rule, illegally seized evidence cannot be used in the prosecution's case-in-chief. The evidence can still be used to impeach the

defendant or for other collateral purposes. The exclusionary rule only applies to trials. It does not apply to pretrial hearings such as grand juries or post-trial hearings such as parole revocation hearings. A defendant must have standing to challenge an illegal search or seizure. He cannot assert the rights of third parties whose rights were violated.

There are four main exceptions to the exclusionary rule. If the police had an independent source, apart from the illegally obtained information, for the evidence in question, then the exclusionary rule does not bar its admission. Likewise, if the police would have inevitably discovered the evidence without the illegally obtained information, then the evidence is admissible. The same applies if the newly discovered evidence is attenuated or removed from the taint of the illegally seized evidence. Finally, the good faith exception applies if the officers reasonably rely on a judge's authorization of a warrant only to have it invalidated at a later date.

Exclusionary rules have also been created to protect a suspect's rights to remain silent and to an attorney guaranteed under the Fifth and Sixth Amendments. First, if statements are obtained while a suspect is in custody, the suspect must be advised of his *Miranda* rights. The suspect must then freely agree to waive those rights before being questioned. He can do so expressly by signing a waiver form or through his conduct such as agreeing to answer questions. If a suspect asserts either his right to remain silent or his right to an attorney, all questioning must cease. He cannot be requestioned unless he initiates the conversation or a sufficient break in questioning has occurred. If the court finds that police conduct did violate *Miranda,* then any statements obtained in violation of *Miranda* will be suppressed. The Court has created exceptions to the *Miranda* rule for public safety and for routine booking questions.

Where police obtain statements in a two-stage process, the admissibility of the statements obtained after the giving of *Miranda* warnings depends on whether the officer deliberately failed to Mirandize the suspect in an attempt to obtain an unwarned confession. If both sets of statements are similar in content and the place of interrogation and the interrogators are the same, then the statements will likely be suppressed.

If the suspect properly waived his *Miranda* rights, the court must next determine whether the confession was voluntarily made. Confessions are voluntarily given if they are the product of free will and not the product of physical or psychological force or threats. The police can, however, use most forms of deception and trickery to obtain a confession as long as those methods did not overwhelm the will of the suspect. Involuntary confessions or evidence that is otherwise compelled from the defendant in violation of his right to remain silent cannot be used at trial or for impeachment.

Once they are charged with a crime, defendants also have a right to counsel at all critical stages. Thus, defendants cannot be questioned by police without counsel being present unless they waive that right. This is known as the *Massiah* doctrine.

Finally, if a defendant believes any of his rights have been violated, he must file a motion to suppress the evidence. The prosecution has an opportunity to respond to the motion in writing. A hearing is then held to determine whether the defendant's rights were violated.

KEY TERMS

- Attenuation
- Booking exception
- Coercion
- Custody
- Due process
- Exclusionary rule
- Fifth Amendment right to counsel
- Fifth Amendment right to remain silent
- Fourth Amendment
- Fruit of the poisonous tree
- Good faith exception
- Independent source
- Inevitable discovery
- Interrogation
- *Massiah* doctrine
- *Miranda* rights
- Motion to suppress
- Public safety exception
- Search warrant
- Sixth Amendment right to counsel
- Standing
- Two-step interrogation
- Voluntariness

REVIEW QUESTIONS

1. What is the exclusionary rule? What is its purpose?

2. How are the exclusionary rules different for the Fourth and Fifth Amendments?

3. What is the fruit of the poisonous tree doctrine?

4. What are the four exceptions to the exclusionary rule? Give an example of each.

5. What factors will a court look at in determining the voluntariness of a confession?

6. What is coercion? Give an example of both a physical and psychological use of coercion to obtain a confession.

7. What are the four *Miranda* rights? When are they required to be read?

8. What is interrogation? Does it include more than questions?

9. What must the prosecution prove with respect to whether a suspect waived his *Miranda* rights before talking to police?

10. What is the public safety exception? When is it used?

11. When does a suspect have a right to an attorney? What must happen when a suspect requests an attorney?

12. Does the exclusionary rule apply to impeachment questions? Why not?

13. What is standing? Who has standing to challenge a Fourth Amendment violation?

14. Can an involuntary confession be used for impeachment? Why?

15. Does the exclusionary rule apply to grand jury proceedings? Explain.

16. What standard did the Supreme Court apply in *Herring* to police conduct to determine whether the illegally seized evidence should be suppressed?

17. What is a motion to suppress? Who is it filed by and when is it filed?

APPLICATION PROBLEMS

1. Bart and Walker concoct a plan to set up smoke bombs in the school. The principal gets wind of the plot and orders that the pair be searched. No smoke bombs are found on their persons. The case is referred to the police department and they request a warrant from the judge. The warrant is based on a tip they got from one of the other students, Martin. The details of the tip are not corroborated. The judge signs the warrant. When officers execute the search warrant, they find several smoke bombs at Bart's home. Bart moves to suppress the search on the ground that the warrant was not supported by probable cause. The judge agrees, finding that the tip was not sufficiently corroborated. Should the judge throw out the evidence or admit it at trial? Explain.

2. Dr. Yes, Number Three, and Mini You concoct a plot to steal artwork. They steal several famous pieces from a local museum. Officers get a tip

that the trio might be involved in the thefts. Just before one investigative team gets a warrant, two other officers knock down Number Three's door and have a look around. They find two pieces from the museum. They then interrogate Three and he tells the officers where the other art is. All three are arrested and charged with the thefts. The trio moves to have the evidence suppressed on the ground that Three's home was searched without a warrant and the other evidence is tainted by the illegal search. Is the trio correct? Explain.

3. Juanita is stopped for speeding. When doing a records check, the officer notices Juanita has an outstanding warrant for failure to appear on her last speeding ticket. He arrests her. He searches her car incident to arrest. He discovers a loaded gun underneath her seat and some marijuana. Juanita says the stuff must be her boyfriend's. As it turns out, Juanita's warrant

should have been cleared from the system. The deputy whose job it was to enter and clear warrants went on maternity leave and no one noticed until six weeks later. Juanita is charged with illegal possession of a weapon. She moves to suppress the gun and drugs on the ground that the initial arrest was invalid. Is she correct? Explain.

4. Terrence is 32. He is questioned by the police about his involvement in a series of robberies. Although not advised of his rights, he willingly talks to police. No pressure is put on him to talk. He confesses to committing the robberies and thanks the police for finally catching him since the robberies were weighing on his conscience. He was desperate for money for food. Terrence is charged with robbery. His attorney moves to suppress the confession. Will he succeed on the motion? Explain.

5. Roger is inside his home. Two officers show up at his door to question him about illegal steroids. They do not advise him of his rights. The officers want to know if Roger is associated with a doctor who has been linked to writing false prescriptions for HGH and steroids. Roger denies any involvement. The officers then question Roger for the next hour. Roger finally admits to going to the doctor for a knee injury and that he was given steroids by the doctor. The officers arrest Roger. Roger then moves to suppress his statement on the ground that it was taken in violation of *Miranda*. Is he correct? Explain.

6. Sally is questioned about the disappearance of her 8-month-old daughter. She is questioned at the police station. Officers advise her of her rights. She does not sign the waiver form but does not refuse to talk. Two hours into the interrogation, Sally responds to a question about whether her daughter is dead and whether she should get a proper burial. Sally says she never meant to hurt her and hopes her daughter does not go to hell because of it. That is all she says. Sally is arrested on murder

charges two weeks later after her daughter's body is found. Sally moves to suppress her statement on the ground she invoked her right to remain silent and did not expressly agree to waive it. Is she correct?

7. Homer is suspected of stealing sugar from an overturned tanker truck. Homer appears to be a good suspect since there are a large number of bees around his backyard and his home appears to be infested by ants. The chief of police brings Homer down to the station and questions him. He is given a *Miranda* advisement and Homer decides to talk. Interrogation takes about half an hour. The chief finally asks Homer if he stole all that sugar. Homer responds by saying, "Do you have Lionel's number? I want an attorney." The chief gets his number but then asks him one final question. He asks Homer whether it was worth all the trouble to take the sugar. Homer responds by saying it was worth every last ant. Homer is charged with stealing the sugar. He then moves to suppress his statement about the ants since he had requested an attorney. Is he right? Explain.

8. Sam is accused of theft from his employer. Officers interrogate Sam at his office. They arrest him and ask him some questions in the squad car on the way back to the police station. Sam makes several statements on the ride back, implicating him in the theft. The officers then Mirandize Sam at the station. Sam makes a full confession after waiving his rights. Can the prosecutor use the statements Sam made either prior to the *Miranda* advisement or afterwards at the police station? Explain.

9. Stan is arrested on suspicion of being connected to a fraudulent investment scheme. He refused to talk but the officers beat a confession out of him. He admits to knowing about the scheme and assisting his boss. Stan testifies at trial that he knows nothing about the scheme. The prosecutor moves to impeach Stan with his confession. While the confession is thrown out of evidence by the judge, should the court allow it to be used for impeachment?

10. An officer applies for a search warrant to search Glenn's home for evidence of a stolen auto parts operation. He does not knock and announce his presence; instead, he kicks in Glenn's door. While at the residence, the officer makes what he believes to be an honest mistake—he searches for evidence of the auto parts in Glenn's wife's diary. A rookie officer should know that the warrant does not give Glenn the authority to search the diary because it exceeds the scope of the search warrant. Will the court suppress the evidence or rule it admissible under the good faith exception? Explain.

Notes

1. People v. Defore, 150 N.E. 585, 587 (N.Y. 1926).
2. Nix v. Williams, 467 U.S. 431, 442 (1984).
3. U.S. Const. Amend. IV.
4. Maryland v. Garrison, 480 U.S. 79, 84 (1987).
5. Terry v. Ohio, 392 U.S. 1 (1968).
6. 232 U.S. 383 (1914).
7. Wolf v. Colorado.
8. 342 U.S. 165 (1952).
9. 367 U.S. 643 (1961).
10. Mapp, 367 U.S. at 655-56.
11. Wong Sun v. United States, 371 U.S. 471, 484-88 (1963).
12. Segura v. United States, 468 U.S. 796, 815 (1984).
13. Wong Sun, 371 U.S. at 487-88 (1963).
14. Murray v. United States, 487 U.S. 533, 537 (1988).
15. Murray, 487 U.S. at 538.
16. Id. at 537.
17. United States v. Baldwin, 114 Fed. Appx. 675, 681 (6th Cir. 2004) (unpublished decision), quoting United States v. Dice, 200 F.3d 978, 984 (6th Cir. 2000).
18. 468 U.S. 796 (1984).
19. Segura, 468 U.S. at 814.
20. People v. Castillo, 2008 WL 640451, slip. op. at 18 (V.I. 2008) (unpublished opinion).
21. Nix v. Williams, 467 U.S. 431 (1984).
22. United States v. Buchanan, 904 F.2d 349, 356 (6th Cir. 1990).
23. United States v. Kennedy, 61 F.3d 494, 499 (6th Cir. 1995).
24. United States v. Alexander, 2007 WL 2815205 (N.D. Ohio) (unpublished decision).
25. Alexander, slip op. at 4.
26. Brown v. Illinois, 422 U.S. 590 (1975).
27. Castillo, 2008 WL 640451, slip. op. at 17.
28. United States v. Martin, 297 F.3d 1308 (11th Cir. 2002).
29. United States v. Leon, 468 U.S. 897, 909 (1984).
30. Leon, 468 U.S. at 919, quoting Michigan v. Tucker, 417 U.S. 433, 447 (1974).
31. Id.
32. Id. at 926.
33. Martin, 297 F.3d at 1314.
34. Leon, 468 U.S. at 923.
35. Herring v. United States, 129 S.Ct. 695, 702 (2009), quoting Brown v. Illinois, 422 U.S. 590, 610-11 (1975) (Powell, J., concurring in part).
36. Hudson v. Michigan, 547 U.S. 586, 593 (2006).
37. Id. at 596.
38. Herring, 129 S.Ct. at 698.
39. Id.
40. Id. at 702.
41. Id. at 703-04.
42. Id. at 710, (Breyer, J., dissenting) (prior cases holding that clerical errors were insufficient to trigger the exclusionary rule were entirely "premised on a distinction between judicial errors and police errors").
43. 514 U.S. 1, 14 (1995).
44. Herring, 129 S.Ct. at 701, n. 3.
45. CBC News, *Supreme Court Quashes Drug Conviction over Illegal Search*, July 17, 2009, available at http://www.cbc.ca/canada/story/2009/07/17/court-search-charges017.html.
46. Id.
47. Burdeau v. McDowell, 256 U.S. 465 (1921).
48. United States v. Payner, 447 U.S. 727, 731 (1980).
49. Rakas v. Illinois, 439 U.S. 128, 139 (1978).
50. United States v. Calandra, 414 U.S. 338 (1974).
51. Penn. Bd. of Probation and Parole v. Scott, 524 U.S. 357 (1998).
52. Scott, 524 U.S. at 365.
53. John Henry Wigmore, IV, *A Treatise on the System of Evidence in Trials at Common Law*, § 2183 at 2954 (1st ed. 1905).
54. Adam Liptak, *U.S. Is Alone in Rejecting All Evidence if Police Err*, New York Times (July 19, 2008), available at http://www.nytimes.com/2008/07/19/us/19exclude.html, *quoting* Akhil Reed Amar.
55. Yale Kamisar, *In Defense of the Search and Seizure Exclusionary Rule*, 26 Harv. L. J. & Pub. Pol'y 119, 121, *quoting* People v. Cahan, 282 P.2d 905, 911-12 (Cal. 1955).
56. Mapp, 367 U.S. at 30.
57. Kamisar, *supra* at 124-25.
58. Timothy Lynch, *In Defense of the Exclusionary Rule*, Harv. J. L. & Pub. Pol'y (2000), available at www.thefreelibrary.com/_/print/PrintArticle.aspx?id=65278849.
59. Kamisar, *supra* note 55, at 123-24.
60. Id. at 124.
61. Eileen Skinnider, *Improperly or Illegally Obtained Evidence: The Exclusionary Rule in Canada*, International Centre for Criminal Law Reform and Criminal Justice Policy, December 2005, available at http://www.icclr.law.ubc.ca/Publications/Reports/ES%20paper%20-%20exclusionary%20evidence%20rule.pdf.
62. Kamisar, *supra* note 55, at 133.
63. Potter Stewart, *The Road to* Mapp v. Ohio *and Beyond: The Origins, Development and Future of the Exclusionary Rule in Search and Seizure Cases*, 83 Colum. L. Rev. 1365, 1392-93 (1983).
64. Liptak, *supra* note 54.
65. *See* Hudson v. Michigan, 547 U.S. 586 (2006).
66. U.S. Const. Amend. V.

67. State v. Scott, 584 N.W.2d 412 (Minn. 1998).
68. 384 U.S. 436, 467 (1966).
69. Miranda, 384 U.S. at 467.
70. Id. at 479.
71. Id. at 473-74.
72. *The Supreme Court: New Rules for Police Rooms*, Time Magazine (June 24, 1966), available at http://www.time.com/time/magazine/article/0,9171,835800-1,00.html.
73. Ian Herbert, *The Psychology and Power of False Confessions*, 22 Assoc. for Psy. Sci. Observer at 1 (December 2009), available at www.psychologicalscience.org/observer/getArticle.cfm?id=2590.
74. New York v. Quarles, 467 U.S. 649, 656 (1984).
75. Miranda, 384 U.S. at 444.
76. Rhode Island v. Innis, 446 U.S. 291, 300-01 (1980).
77. Innis, 446 U.S. at 302 n. 5.
78. Id. at 303.
79. Miranda, 384 U.S. at 444.
80. Moran v. Burbine, 475 U.S. 412, 421 (1986).
81. Id.
82. Culombe v. Connecticut, 367 U.S. 568, 602 (1961).
83. *See* Spano v. New York, 360 U.S. 315 (1959); Lynumn v. Illinois, 372 U.S. 528 (1963).
84. Colorado v. Spring, 479 U.S. 564 (1987).
85. Burbine, 475 U.S. at 421.
86. Burbine, 475 U.S. at 422.
87. 130 S.Ct. 1195 (2010).
88. Powell, 130 S.Ct. at 1204.
89. Id.
90. Missouri v. Seibert, 542 U.S. 600, 608-609 (2004).
91. Berghuis v. Thompkins, 130 S.Ct. 2250, 2260 (2010).
92. State v. Derrico, 434 A.2d 356 (Conn. 1980).
93. United States v. Murdock, 491 F.3d 694 (7th Cir. 2007).
94. Thompkins, 130 S.Ct. at 2262.
95. Id. at 2263.
96. Id. at 2257.
97. Id. at 2263.
98. 542 U.S. 600 (2004). Lower courts have struggled with what standard to apply from Seibert. Some courts have relied on the plurality opinion, some on Justice Kennedy's concurring opinion, and still others simply analyze the situation under *Miranda*. *See* State v. O'Neill, 936 A.2d 438, 453 (N.J. 2007). Justice Kennedy's concurring opinion is considered the law of the case in federal habeas proceedings since it is the narrower of the two tests set out by the plurality. *See* Thompson v. Runnel, 621 F.3d 1007, 1016 n. 8 (9th Cir. 2010).
99. Thompson, 621 F.3d at 1016-19.
100. Missouri v. Seibert, 542 U.S. 600, 609 (2004).
101. Thompson, at 1016-17, *quoting* United States v. Williams, 435 F.3d 1148, 1158-59 (9th Cir. 2006).
102. Thompson, 621 F.3d at 1018.
103. 470 U.S. 298 (1985).
104. Seibert, 542 U.S. at 611-12.
105. Id. at 612.
106. Id. at 615.
107. Id. at 613.
108. Thompson, 621 F.3d at 1019.
109. Davis v. United States, 512 U.S. 452, 459 (1994).
110. Davis, 512 U.S. at 458.
111. Collazo v. Estelle, 940 F.2d 411 (9th Cir. 1991).
112. 130 S.Ct. 1213 (2010).
113. Shatzer, 130 S.Ct. at 1221.
114. Id. at 1223.
115. Id.
116. Id. at 1224-25.
117. 467 U.S. 649 (1984).
118. Quarles, 467 U.S. at 659.
119. Id. at 652.
120. Id. at 658.
121. Id. at 657.
122. United States v. Baxter, 830 F. Supp. 28, 38 n. 6 (D. Mass. 1993).
123. Baxter, 830 F. Supp. at 38.
124. People v. Attebury, 624 N.W.2d 912, 917-18 (Mich. 2001).
125. Id. at 918.
126. Pennsylvania v. Muniz, 496 U.S. 582 (1990).
127. Muniz, 496 U.S. at 602, n. 14.
128. People v. Allen, 199 P.3d 33, 35-36 (Colo. App. 2007).
129. U.S. Const. Amend. V.
130. Miller v. Fenton, 474 U.S. 104 (1985).
131. Brown v. Mississippi, 297 U.S. 278 (1936).
132. Dickerson v. United States, 530 U.S. 428 (2000).
133. United States v. Abu Ali, 528 F.3d 210, 232 (4th Cir. 2008).
134. People v. Humphrey, 132 P.3d 352 (Colo. 2006), *citing* Colorado v. Connelly, 479 U.S. 157, 167 (1986).
135. Colorado v. Connelly, 479 U.S. 157, 163 (1986).
136. People v. Clark, 857 P.2d 1099 (Cal. 1993).
137. Williams v. State, 825 A.2d 1078 (Md. 2003); State v. Cayward, 552 So.2d 971, 973 (Fla. App. 1989).
138. 297 U.S. 278 (1936).
139. Brown, 297 U.S. at 282-83.
140. Id. at 282.
141. State v. Galloway, 628 A.2d 735 (N.J. 1993).
142. Ball v. State, 699 A.2d 1170 (Md. 1997).
143. Sheriff, Washoe County v. Bessey, 914 P.2d 618, 620 (Nev. 1996).
144. State v. Simmons, 944 S.W.2d 165, 176 (Mo. 1997); Hopkins v. State, 311 A.2d 483 (Md. App. 1973).
145. Finke v. State, 468 A.2d 353 (Md. App. 1983).
146. Finke, 468 A.2d at 490.
147. United States v. Miller, 450 F.3d 270, 272 (7th Cir. 2006).
148. People v. Musselwhite, 954 P.2d 475 (Cal. 1998).
149. Humphrey, 132 P.3d at 361.
150. Lawrence Buser, *Heavyset Confessed Rapist Claims Police Use Heavy-Handed Diet Tactics*, The Commercial Appeal (June 19, 2010), available at www.commercialappeal.com/news/2010/jun/19/confessed-rapist-cites-coercion/?print.
151. State v. Cayward, 552 So.2d at 973-74.
152. Id. at 974.
153. State v. Patton, 826 A.2d 783 (N.J. App. 2003).
154. Bessey, 914 P.2d at 620.
155. Id. at 621.
156. Lincoln v. State, 882 A.2d 944, 956-57 (Md. App. 2005).
157. U.S. Const. Amend. V.
158. 116 U.S. 616 (1886).
159. Id. at 633-34.
160. 168 U.S. 532, 542-43 (1897).
161. Rothgery v. Gillespie County, 554 U.S. 191 (2008).
162. 377 U.S. 201 (1964).
163. Id. at 205-06.
164. 430 U.S. 387 (1977).

165. Brewer, 430 U.S. at 401.
166. Id. at 405.
167. Id.
168. Walder v. United States, 347 U.S. 62 (1954).
169. Walder, 347 U.S. at 65.
170. James, 493 U.S. 307, 313 (1990).
171. James, 493 U.S. at 317.
172. Harris v. New York, 401 U.S. 222 (1971).
173. Kansas v. Ventris, 129 S.Ct. 1841, 1845 (2009).
174. Harris, 401 U.S. at 224.
175. Ventris, 129 S.Ct. at 1846.
176. New Jersey v. Potash, 440 U.S. 450, 458-59 (1979).
177. F.R. Crim. P. 12 and 41.
178. Colo. R. Crim. P. 41(e).

PART III

ADMISSIBILITY OF EVIDENCE AT TRIAL

Basic Evidentiary Terms: Relevance, Burden of Proof, and Circumstantial Evidence

"Even the clearest and most perfect circumstantial evidence is likely to be at fault, after all, and therefore ought to be received with great caution."—**Mark Twain**

Chapter Topics

Objectives

After reading this chapter, students will be able to:

- Understand the three requirements for admissibility of evidence

- Understand the difference between direct and circumstantial evidence

- Distinguish between the various burdens of proof

- Learn the various defenses that can be raised, such as self-defense or insanity

- Become familiar with various terms used throughout the study of evidence

Introduction

There are many evidentiary terms that are used throughout the trial process, regardless of the topic being discussed. Terms such as *relevance, prejudicial effect,* and *circumstantial evidence* are applied to all aspects of evidence. The purpose of this chapter is to familiarize yourself with this basic terminology before exploring more specific evidentiary concepts in later chapters.

The first part of this chapter will detail the basic requirements for admitting evidence. Evidence must meet three requirements before being admitted. It must be relevant, reliable, and competent. If the evidence satisfies all three requirements, it is admissible if its prejudicial effect does not substantially outweigh its relevance.

The next section discusses the burden of proof. This is the duty of one party to produce both a sufficient amount of evidence and persuade the jury of its truth by some standard of certainty. The chapter will describe the various levels of persuasion that a judge or jury must be convinced of before making certain legal determinations. The prosecution always has the burden of persuasion in a criminal case and that burden is to prove the defendant guilty beyond a reasonable doubt. The section will also focus on presumptions. Presumptions are inferences that the jury is entitled to make if a basic set of facts is proved first. The presumption of innocence is the most well-known presumption.

While the defendant maintains a presumption of innocence and does not have to present a defense, he is certainly entitled to do so. The defendant can assert several defenses that can relieve him of responsibility for criminal acts such as an alibi or self-defense. This chapter will also explore the various forms of the insanity defense. Depending on the type of defense offered, the defendant may also have the burden of proof to establish that defense.

The third major concept discussed in this chapter is the difference between direct and circumstantial evidence. Although many people think of circumstantial evidence as being a weaker form of evidence, most courts do not treat it any differently than the direct testimony of witnesses. You will learn that entire cases can be founded on circumstantial evidence, including murder prosecutions.

I. ADMISSIBILITY OF EVIDENCE

A. Relevancy

Rule 401. Definition of Relevant Evidence

"Relevant evidence" means evidence having any tendency to make the existence of any fact that is of consequence to the determination of the action more probable or less probable that it would be without the evidence.

Rule 402. Relevant Evidence Generally Admissible; Irrelevant Evidence Inadmissible

All relevant evidence is admissible, except as otherwise provided by the Constitution of the United States, by Act of Congress, by these

rules, or by other rules prescribed by the Supreme Court pursuant to statutory authority. Evidence which is not relevant is not admissible.

Prior to the development of the Rules of Evidence, many states applied strict guidelines for the admissibility of evidence. In the past, witnesses could be disqualified from testifying because of certain conditions, such as being a felon or atheist. Evidence that appeared to be relevant was excluded for being too prejudicial or irrelevant. The meaning of relevance has changed dramatically over the years. Today, the Federal Rules favor a more liberal admission policy. Under Rule 402, evidence that is relevant and not otherwise excluded under some statute or rule is admissible. There are situations where relevant evidence is inadmissible, however. For example, evidence of a sexual assault victim's character, which might have otherwise been admissible, can be excluded under Rule 412, the rape shield law. Similarly, relevant evidence that is seized in violation of a person's constitutional rights can be excluded.

Relevance
the tendency of evidence to make the existence of facts more or less probable than they would be without the evidence. Relevant evidence is both material and probative

Rule 401 defines relevant evidence as evidence that has "any tendency to make the existence of any fact that is of consequence to the determination of the action more probable or less probable than it would be without the evidence."[1] **Relevance** has two components—materiality and probative value. **Materiality** means that the evidence has some logical connection to a fact that is important to the outcome of the case. For example, in a drunken driving case, the person's degree of sobriety is material to the outcome. Thus, evidence concerning how much the driver had had to drink, where he had been drinking, and his blood alcohol content would all be relevant to the ultimate issue of whether he drove under the influence. However, evidence concerning the fact that the defendant owned and operated a rare bird store would not be material to the outcome.

Materiality
the logical connection evidence has to a fact that is important to the outcome of the case

Probative value
the evidence's ability to prove or disprove a fact

Probative value, on the other hand, simply refers to the evidence's ability to prove or disprove a fact. It is the ability of the evidence to persuade people of the probability or possibility of the existence of that fact.[2] If evidence is highly probative, then it increases the likelihood that the fact the evidence is offered to prove is true. For instance, the Utah Court of Appeals found that testimony concerning an earlier search of the defendant's residence for drugs (just hours before her arrest for introducing contraband into the jail) was highly probative of her intent to possess drugs. The defendant had denied any knowledge of the fact that there were drugs in the pocket of her borrowed jeans when she was searched entering the jail. The court found the state's need to present the evidence of the prior search was substantial since there was no direct evidence of her knowledge or intent.[3]

Where the defendant has denied committing the crime, evidence of the identity of the alleged criminal is always relevant. For example, courts have found that evidence of possession of a weapon allegedly used in the commission of an offense is probative of identity. An Idaho court even held that the prosecutor could present evidence of the fact that the defendant was in possession of a shotgun when he was arrested though no weapon was seen during the commission of the bank robbery. The court held that the weapon evidence had slight relevance to prove identity since the defendant had at least threatened use of a gun during the commission of the robbery.[4]

In contrast, courts have excluded evidence that lacks sufficient probative value. Such examples include the exclusion of evidence that the defendant owned a rifle in a case involving the shooting of a stolen cow where there was no proof that the defendant's rifle was used to shoot the cow.[5] In another case, the court ruled that the defendant's casual marijuana use was not probative of the issue of whether he conspired to smuggle marijuana in the current case.[6] Another court found that evidence proffered by the defendant about his mother's rape was not probative of his self-defense claim in his murder trial. The defendant tried to argue the evidence was relevant since he thought the victim had been trying to rape him prior to his death and he flashed back to his mother's ordeal. The court rejected the evidence, however, on the ground that the defendant's thoughts of his mother's rape did nothing to mitigate his use of excessive force in the present case and, therefore, it was not relevant.[7]

Practical Example

Taking our DUI example from above, evidence that the driver's blood-alcohol content was .175 at the time of his arrest is highly probative that the driver was drunk since that is nearly twice the legal limit. Conversely, evidence that the driver was an alcoholic is not probative since there is no way for a jury to conclude how much the person had had to drink prior to driving or what his level of intoxication was at the time of the accident.

B. Reliability

Reliability
the degree of accuracy or authenticity of the evidence

Reliability is the second requirement for the admissibility of evidence. It is defined as something that is dependable or trustworthy or which is capable of producing the same results from different experiments or trials. Reliability can be thought of as the amount of confidence that a person has in the accuracy or authenticity of the evidence. To ensure that evidence is reliable, the party offering it must establish a sufficient foundation for its admissibility. A **foundation** is the evidence or testimony that establishes the admissibility of some other piece of evidence.[8] The foundation is laid by either having a witness who has personal knowledge about the evidence testify that it is what it appears to be or by establishing the chain of custody.

Foundation
the evidence or testimony that establishes the admissibility of some other piece of evidence

In order to be admissible, evidence must have at least some minimal amount of reliability. As long as the evidence has sufficient reliability for a reasonable person to consider it, then flaws in the evidence go to the weight the jury can give the evidence, not its admissibility. The weight of the evidence is the persuasiveness of a given piece of evidence in comparison with other evidence.[9] Thus, the judge should not exclude evidence as unreliable unless the evidence is so untrustworthy that no reasonable juror could rely on it as proof of guilt or innocence.

For example, questions about the accuracy of test results supporting an expert opinion go to the weight given to the evidence, not its admissibility.[10] Similarly, bare allegations that physical evidence was tampered with go to its weight, not its admissibility.[11] In contrast, if a vital link in the chain of custody is missing, then the evidence is inadmissible.[12] Other examples of wholly unreliable evidence include some forms of hearsay, scientific evidence that is based on faulty logic or improper scientific technique, or physical evidence that has been contaminated or degraded.

Practical Example

John is charged with conspiracy to commit murder. The prosecution wants to introduce evidence that John was overheard telling a friend that he wanted the victim dead by whatever means necessary. The prosecutor wants to call Jim, who heard it from Bob, who heard John actually make the statement. Although the evidence is relevant since it goes to John's motive for murder, the evidence will be excluded on reliability grounds due to the fact that it is third-hand information.

C. Competency of Evidence

Competent
evidence is competent if it is not subject to some statutory or other restriction on its admissibility

The third requirement for evidence to be admissible is that it must be **competent**. Evidence is competent if it is not subject to any statutory or other legal restrictions that prevent its admission at trial. Evidence that is otherwise relevant and reliable may still be ruled inadmissible because of some other policy concern such as preserving the defendant's constitutional rights. Examples of things that make evidence incompetent are that it is subject to some privilege like the attorney/client privilege or that it was seized in violation of the defendant's Fourth Amendment rights.

Practical Example

Jerry is accused of harassing Tom. The prosecution wants to introduce evidence that Jerry told his attorney that he enjoyed repeatedly taunting Tom and that he would do it again. Although the evidence is relevant and Jerry's statement to his attorney is reliable, it is incompetent and must be excluded. Admission of the statement would violate the attorney/client privilege.

D. Exclusion of Evidence Due to Its Prejudicial Effect

Rule 403. Exclusions of Relevant Evidence on Grounds of Prejudice, Confusion, or Waste of Time

Although relevant, evidence may be excluded if its probative value is substantially outweighed by the danger of unfair prejudice, confusion of the issues, or misleading the jury, or by considerations of undue delay, waste of time, or needless presentation of cumulative evidence.

Prejudicial evidence
evidence that has a tendency to sway a jury to decide an issue on some improper basis such as bias, sympathy, or hatred

Under Rule 403, relevant evidence can be excluded on the ground that its probative value is strongly outweighed by its prejudicial effect. Courts have defined **prejudicial evidence** as evidence that has a strong tendency to sway decisions on an improper basis such as "bias, sympathy, hatred, contempt, retribution, or horror."[13] The court should exclude evidence only where its prejudicial effect (its potential to mislead or confuse the jury) clearly outweighs its probative value. The Utah Supreme Court described the balancing process as follows:

> The critical question is whether certain testimony is so prejudicial that the jury will be unable to fairly weigh the evidence.... Absent a substantial, not potential or minor, prejudicial effect, the... evidence is admissible for the jury's consideration in reviewing all other facts. Moreover, relevant evidence is presumed to be admissible if it does not have an unusual propensity to unfairly prejudice, inflame, or mislead the jury. And even if the evidence has the potential for prejudicing a defendant, it will be admitted if it has unusual probative value. On the other hand, even minimally probative evidence need not... be excluded unless it is substantially outweighed by the danger of unfair prejudice.[14]

Thus, the greater the probative value of the evidence, the less likely it is that it will be excluded as prejudicial. In order to be prejudicial, the evidence must be more than simply unfavorable to the accused, however. The Tenth Circuit described this distinction as follows:

> [T]he unfair prejudice aspect of Rule 403 cannot be equated with testimony which is simply unfavorable to a party, and here, evidence of the value of the drugs directly addresses an element of the offense—[the defendant]'s knowledge. If that evidence is interpreted by the jury to connect [the defendant] to a drug ring or to bad people who smuggle drugs, that cannot be considered "unfair" prejudice since that is at the core of the criminal charges against him.[15]

Several types of evidence have been considered by courts to be highly prejudicial, including gruesome photos and a rape victim's past sexual activities with someone other than the accused. When considering the prejudicial effect of photographs, courts should assess the number, size, detail, and gruesomeness of the photographs.[16] The key factor is whether a given photograph or set of photographs will encourage the jury to decide an issue on an "inappropriate emotional basis."[17] The prejudicial effect of the photos must be balanced against the value of the photographs to clarify observations and conclusions about the victim's injuries or manner of death.[18] For example, the Utah Supreme Court ruled that close-up video of the victim's stab wounds and her slit throat were so gruesome that they should have been excluded under Rule 403.[19]

Practical Example

Anne is accused of smuggling drugs into the country illegally. The prosecution wants to introduce evidence that Anne is an undocumented alien and has been deported twice before. The judge would exclude this fact from evidence because it has little probative value of her drug dealing but could unnecessarily inflame the passions of the jury.

II. BURDEN OF PROOF

Burden of proof
the duty of one party to prove a disputed charge or assertion

Burden of persuasion
a party's duty to convince the fact-finder of the strength of evidence in favor of that party

You have probably heard of the term "innocent until proven guilty." This means that the defendant has no obligation to present evidence in his defense and the prosecution has the burden of proof in a criminal case. The **burden of proof** is the duty of one party to "prove a disputed assertion or charge."[20] It is also referred to as the **burden of persuasion**. The burden of persuasion can be thought of as the degree of confidence or level of certainty that a person must have in the evidence before taking some action. The Supreme Court has characterized the burden of persuasion as a party's duty to "convince the fact-finder to view the facts in a way that favors that party." It should properly be thought of as the "duty of a person alleging the case to prove it" rather than the "duty of the one party or the other to introduce evidence."[21]

A. Burden of Persuasion

The prosecution always maintains the burden of persuasion. It never shifts to the defendant; he is cloaked with the presumption of innocence. There are several degrees or levels of persuasion that a judge or jury can be asked to use before it finds the existence of facts. It is best to think of these levels as lying on a spectrum. On one end of the spectrum is zero confidence. On the other end is absolute certainty or confidence. The various burdens of proof used in the criminal justice system lie somewhere in between, with reasonable suspicion requiring the least amount of confidence and beyond a reasonable doubt requiring the most. See Figure 8.1 for the spectrum of suspicion. In criminal cases, the prosecution's burden of persuasion is to prove the guilt of the accused beyond a reasonable doubt.

1. Reasonable Suspicion

The first burden of proof standard used is reasonable suspicion. Reasonable suspicion exists where facts and inferences suggest that criminal activity is taking place. This level of proof is necessary to justify brief detentions such as traffic stops and pat-down searches. You can think of it as the point where you are somewhat convinced that a person has committed a crime.

Practical Example

Officer Ned sees a juvenile male wearing a red bandana and flashing gang signs outside of a movie theater. He stops the youth and pats him down. He discovers a 9-mm handgun and some drugs in his pocket. Does he have reasonable suspicion for the stop? No. The officer does not have reasonable suspicion that the youth is committing or about to commit criminal activity. He knows that he is only a possible gang member.

2. Probable Cause

The next standard used is probable cause. Probable cause means that a person has an objective, reasonable belief that a person has or is committing a crime or that a place contains specific evidence connected with a crime.[22] Probable cause is most commonly used in the context of searches and seizures. Officers need probable cause to obtain warrants, conduct many types of warrantless searches, and arrest suspects.

Practical Example

Detective Stabler suspects that Juan has sexually assaulted a 16-year-old girl. He wants to search Juan's apartment. The girl tells the detective that Juan raped her and took her panties as a trophy. Can Stabler get a warrant to search Juan's apartment? Yes. He has probable cause to believe Juan committed the rape. The victim's statement and identification of the rapist is enough to obtain a warrant.

Figure 8.1

This figure represents the continuum of levels of suspicion. On the left is zero or no suspicion. On the far right is 100 percent suspicion or absolute certainty of guilt. The five levels of suspicion used in the criminal justice system are found on the continuum somewhere in between the two extremes.

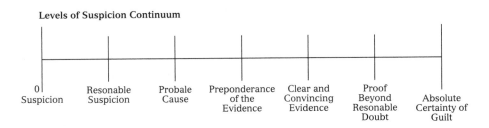

Levels of Suspicion Continuum

| 0 Suspicion | Resonable Suspicion | Probale Cause | Preponderance of the Evidence | Clear and Convincing Evidence | Proof Beyond Resonable Doubt | Absolute Certainty of Guilt |

3. Preponderance of the Evidence

Preponderance of the evidence is the standard that lies in the middle of the spectrum. It is the burden of proof used in civil cases. This means that the jury has to be convinced that just slightly more evidence exists in favor of an item of evidence than against it. It can be thought of as a scale, and the burden is satisfied at the point where the scale tips just in favor of one party or the other. If we were to attach a number to this standard, it would be 51 percent.

Practical Example

Mel is arrested for assault. He is accused of punching a man at a bar and breaking his jaw. Mel argues that he had to use self-defense. He calls three witnesses who testify that Mel was jumped by the victim first and Mel only threw a punch after he told the man to stop or he would get hurt. Has Mel proved his self-defense claim by a preponderance of the evidence? Yes. Although the jury could still believe the victim, Mel's story is supported by substantial evidence that the victim was the first aggressor and the use of force was justified.

4. Clear and Convincing Evidence

The next standard that is used is clear and convincing evidence. This standard is used to make special findings in civil cases and sometimes in criminal cases. For example, a state could require that a party seeking custody of minor children has to rebut by clear and convincing evidence the presumption that it is not in the best interests of the child to give primary custody of the child to a parent with a history of domestic violence.[23]

Practical Example

Jason wants to overturn his conviction for sexual assault. He alleges another man was responsible for perpetrating the assault. He first alleges that he was at home with his girlfriend the night of the assault. He also obtains a court order to perform DNA tests on the evidence found on the victim's clothing. The DNA test shows that the semen on the victim's clothing is not Jason's. Has he proven by clear and convincing evidence that he did not commit the rape and that he should be granted a new trial? Yes. The DNA sample and his alibi create strong proof that his conviction was in error.

5. Beyond a Reasonable Doubt

The final standard that is used in the criminal justice system is proof beyond a reasonable doubt. This is the burden of persuasion that is used in criminal cases to convict the defendant. Beyond a reasonable doubt does not mean that the prosecution has to prove the case beyond any doubt or beyond a shadow of a doubt, however. A reasonable doubt is defined as:

> [A]n actual doubt, not an imaginary doubt. It is a doubt that a reasonable person, acting in a matter of this importance, would be likely to entertain because of the evidence that was presented or because of the lack of convincing evidence. Proof of guilt beyond a reasonable doubt is proof that leaves you so firmly convinced of the defendant's guilt that you have no reasonable doubt of the existence of any element of the crime or of the defendant's identity as the person who committed the crime.[24]

The reasonable doubt standard is constitutionally mandated. The Supreme Court has held that due process is violated unless the prosecution can prove "every fact necessary to constitute the crime with which he [the defendant] is charged" beyond a reasonable doubt.[25] The standard is set high, as Justice Harlan once observed, because "it is far worse to convict an innocent man than to let a guilty man go free."[26] The Supreme Court has stated that the standard provides "concrete substance over the presumption of innocence."[27]

The key point to remember about the burden of proof is that no one piece of evidence has to prove the defendant's guilt beyond a reasonable doubt by itself, unless it is the only evidence proving one of the essential elements of the offense. Each piece of evidence introduced by the prosecution must simply make the defendant's guilt more probable than without the evidence. It is the sum total of the evidence taken together that must convince the jury of the defendant's guilt beyond a reasonable doubt.

Practical Example

Wendy is charged with murdering her ex-husband. The prosecution presents evidence that the couple had been having marital problems and that Wendy had threatened to kill her ex at a wedding party two weeks ago. The husband died from a gunshot wound. The prosecution presents evidence that Wendy owned a gun of the same caliber that was used to kill the husband. Has the prosecution proven the case beyond a reasonable doubt? No. There are too many holes in the case. Although there is certainly probable cause for the wife's arrest in the case, the evidence falls short of proof beyond a reasonable doubt.

B. Burden of Production

Burden of production
the party's duty to produce some evidence of a fact's existence such that the jury can decide the issue rather the court

The second component to the burden of proof is the **burden of production** or, as it is sometimes called, the burden of going forward with the evidence. The burden of production is a "party's duty to introduce enough evidence on an issue to have the issue decided by the fact-finder, rather than decided against the party in a peremptory ruling," such as a directed verdict.[28] Under this burden, a party must produce sufficient evidence of a claim or defense so that the jury can reasonably consider the issue. For example, the prosecution must present sufficient evidence of a defendant's guilt such that the jury could reasonably convict the defendant of the charges. The test for sufficiency of the evidence is "whether, after viewing the evidence in the light most favorable to the prosecution, any rational trier of fact could have found the essential elements of the crime, beyond a reasonable doubt."[29]

Thus, as one legal scholar noted:

> The burden of production is said to prevent verdicts based on conjecture by excluding from the jury's consideration legal issues that are not sufficiently supported by the evidence. The burden serves as a mechanism for legal assessment of the sufficiency of the evidence. The party bearing the burden of production for a defense must adduce sufficient evidence to either support or negate, as the case may be, its existence.[30]

prima facie case
a Latin term meaning on the face of it. The prosecution establishes a prima facie case if it presents a sufficient amount of evidence to convict the defendant as to each and every element of the offense

Initially, the prosecution bears the burden to produce sufficient evidence on each and every element of the offense. This is known as establishing the **prima facie case** (on the face of it). If the prosecution fails to meet this burden with respect to at least one element of the crime, then the judge must direct a verdict in favor of the defendant.

Once the prosecution establishes a prima facie case of the defendant's guilt, the defendant has the opportunity to rebut that evidence. The jury will then be asked to determine whether the prosecution has met its burden of persuasion—i.e., have the elements of the offense been proven beyond a reasonable doubt? A federal court explained how the various evidentiary burdens work in a criminal case:

> At the outset of a criminal trial, the state has both burdens upon it. If during the presentation of its case the State presents sufficient evidence to rebut the accuser's presumption of innocence beyond a reasonable doubt, then the burden of going forward with the evidence shifts to the accused; otherwise, he would stand convicted. The accused is under no duty to present evidence or to establish it by any quantum of proof. He is merely in the interest of justice given an opportunity to rebut the State's evidence. If the accused fails to rebut the State's evidence, he will be convicted. If his rebuttal is successful, he will be acquitted. At no time during the criminal trial does the burden of proof shift to the accused.[31]

Practical Example

Assume that the prosecution has charged Mel with drunken driving, running a red light, and careless driving. The prosecution presents evidence that Mel had a BAC of .150 at the time of his arrest. Witnesses saw him driving the vehicle and testify that he got out of the driver's side just after the accident. The witnesses testify that the light was red in Mel's direction at the time of the accident. However, no one testifies as to what color the light was at the time Mel's car entered the intersection. Since this is an essential element of the offense of running a red light, the judge would direct a verdict in favor of Mel on that charge before submitting the remainder of the charges to the jury.

C. Defenses

1. Right to Present Evidence in Your Own Defense

A defendant has a constitutional right to present evidence in his own defense. That right is not absolute, however. The Supreme Court has recognized that courts may exclude evidence under "well-established rules of evidence" such as the balancing test outlined in Rule 403.[32] A state cannot create evidence rules, however, which "infringe upon a weighty interest of the accused" or are "arbitrary and disproportionate to the purposes they are intended to serve."[33] A rule of evidence violates due process if it "offends some principle of justice so rooted in the traditions and conscience of our people as to be ranked as fundamental."[34]

For example, the Court declared unconstitutional a statute that barred witnesses from testifying in defense of another alleged participant in the crime unless the witness himself had been acquitted of the charges.[35] The Court found the rule to be arbitrary since there was no logical argument to be made that such persons were more likely to commit perjury. Similarly, the Court struck down a rule that barred the admission of

II. Burden of Proof   **221**

hypnotically refreshed testimony of the defendant. The Court held that the rule was unconstitutional because the wholesale exclusion of a defendant's testimony was an "arbitrary restriction on the right to testify in the absence of clear evidence by the State repudiating the validity of all post-hypnosis recollections."[36]

In *Holmes v. South Carolina*, the Court examined South Carolina's rule that excluded evidence from being offered on the guilt of a third party if there was strong evidence of the defendant's guilt.[37] The Supreme Court noted that South Carolina's trial courts were asked to make the wrong inquiry under this rule:

> The trial judge does not focus on the probative value or the potential adverse effects of admitting the defense evidence of third-party guilt. Instead, the critical inquiry concerns the strength the prosecution's case: if the prosecution's case is strong enough, the evidence of third-party guilt is excluded even if that evidence, if viewed independently, would have great probative value and even if it would not pose an undue risk of harassment, prejudice, or confusion of the issues.[38]

Unlike the South Carolina rule, some states permit the introduction of third-party perpetrators as long as the evidence "directly connected" the third party with the substance of the crime and clearly pointed to the guilt of someone other than the accused.[39] Other states like Tennessee have rejected this approach and simply weigh the probative value of the evidence against its prejudicial effect. In light of the *Holmes* decision, this would seem the better test for determining relevancy of third-party culpability.

2. Types of Defenses

Defense
an allegation made by the defendant as to a set of circumstances or conditions that existed, relieving him of responsibility for the criminal offense

A **defense** is any set of "identifiable conditions or circumstances" that a defendant can present to avoid conviction of a criminal offense.[40] A defendant can raise any number of defenses, such as insanity, mistake, or self-defense. One noted legal scholar, Paul Robinson, has broken down defenses into five general categories: failure of proof defenses, offense modification defenses, justifications, excuses, and nonexculpatory public policy defenses.[41] For purposes of allocating the burden of proof, courts have lumped defenses into two broad categories—negating defenses and affirmative defenses.

a. Negating Defenses

Negating defense
a defense that attempts to negate or modify one or more elements of the offense. An alibi and consent are examples of negating defenses

Negating defenses attempt to negate or modify one or more elements of the charged offense. Failure of proof and offense modification defenses fall into this category. A failure of proof defense simply negates one or more of the elements of the crime. Alibis, consent, impossibility, and mistake of fact are examples of failure of proof defenses. For example, consent is a complete defense to rape because it negates one of the essential

TABLE 8.1 NEGATING DEFENSES

- **Alibi** alleges that the defendant could not have been the perpetrator because he was not at the crime scene at the time the crime was committed. It negates the element of identity.

- **Consent** negates the intent element of the crime. The defense alleges that the victim consented to the alleged criminal conduct such as sexual conduct.

- **Impossibility** alleges that although the defendant acted with criminal intent, the crime could not be accomplished due to some factual or legal impossibility. It negates the element of criminal conduct.

- **Mistake of fact** negates the element of intent. It alleges that the defendant thought he was innocently acting or doing one thing when in reality he was doing another.

- **Extreme emotional distress** mitigates the element of intent. It alleges that the defendant was acting under extreme distress during the commission of the offense.

elements of the crime—that the victim was forced to have sexual relations against his or her will. Offense modification defenses are similar because they reduce the defendant's culpability by modifying the elements of a particular offense. For example, a defendant could argue that he was acting under extreme emotional distress when he committed the crime of murder and thus should instead be convicted of the lesser-included offense of manslaughter. See Table 8.1 for a list of negating defenses.

b. Affirmative Defenses

Affirmative defense
a defense that seeks to justify, excuse, or mitigate the commission of an offense. Insanity and self-defense are examples of affirmative defenses

The burden of proof can be shifted to the defendant, however, when he asserts one of the latter three categories of defenses. These are considered affirmative defenses. An **affirmative defense** seeks to justify, excuse, or mitigate the commission of the offense even if all the elements of the charged offense have been proven.[42] In other words, these defenses do not attempt to modify or negate an element but instead attempt to relieve the defendant of culpability due to some public policy or extenuating circumstance. See Table 8.2 for a list of common affirmative defenses.

i. Justification Defenses

A justification defense relieves a person of criminal liability due to the fact that the harm caused by the crime is outweighed by the defendant's need to avoid an even greater harm.[43] In order to prove a justification defense, the defendant must show that some condition existed that triggered or entitled him to break the law.[44] The defendant must then show that the

TABLE 8.2   LIST OF AFFIRMATIVE DEFENSES

- **Duress** alleges that a defendant participated in the charged crime under force or pressure from another individual, usually through threat of physical harm.

- **Entrapment** asserts that a government official, usually a law enforcement officer, persuaded a defendant to commit a crime where that defendant had no prior intention or predisposition to committing such crime.

- **Involuntary intoxication** alleges that a defendant involuntarily ingested alcohol or drugs and was unable to appreciate the nature of his actions at the time of the alleged offense. Voluntary intoxication is usually not a defense to a crime.

- **Mental disease or defect (insanity)** states that at the time of an alleged crime, a defendant could not tell the difference between right and wrong and/or could not appreciate the nature of his actions and is therefore not criminally responsible for his actions.

- **Necessity** states that an actor's criminal conduct is justified to prevent some greater harm from occurring, such as trespassing to escape a hurricane.

- **Self-defense** is the use of force to protect one's self or others from what the actor responsibly believes to be the use or imminent use of unlawful physical force.

- **Collateral estoppel** or "issue preclusion" prevents a legal issue from being reheard by another court after one court has already ruled on the matter.

- **Double jeopardy** protects a defendant from being tried or punished multiple times for the same crime, arising out of the same set of facts or circumstances.

- **Statute of limitations** means that the prosecution failed to charge the defendant within the statutorily defined time period for charging a person with a given type of crime. Murder and rape often have no statute of limitations period.

conduct was "necessary to protect or further the interest at stake" and that the amount of harm he caused was "proportional, or reasonable in relation to the harm threatened or the interest to be furthered."[45]

Self-defense is the classic example of a justification defense. Even though a person assaults another individual, he may be justified in doing so to protect himself or others from physical harm. A defendant can claim self-defense in order to "defend himself or a third person from what he reasonably believes to be the use or imminent use of unlawful physical force by another person."[46] In exercising self-defense, a person may use the degree of force that he "reasonably believes to be necessary" to defend himself or others.[47] A person is not justified in using physical force, however, if he provokes the use of unlawful physical force by the other person or he is the initial aggressor in the confrontation.

Practical Example

Susan is walking on a bike path. Suddenly, a man on a bicycle corners her and attempts to sexually assault her. Susan sprays the man with Mace and kicks him. Susan has committed the crime of assault but her conduct is justified because she was acting in self-defense. She used a reasonable amount of force to avoid serious bodily harm.

ii. Excuse Defenses

An excuse, meanwhile, is designed to relieve the actor of liability due to some disability such as insanity or involuntary intoxication. Recognized disabilities include involuntary conduct (the defendant has a seizure before running over a person), inability to perceive the nature of the consequences (the defendant was under an insane delusion), inability to understand that the conduct or its results are wrong, or inability to adequately control or conform conduct.[48]

The insanity defense is the most well-known form of this type of defense. The insanity defense is used in only about .9 percent of felony cases. The defense is only successful in about one in four of those cases.[49] Of course, even if the accused does succeed on his defense, he must be confined to a mental institution until such time as he has been rehabilitated.

There are several different standards used to prove the insanity defense. The most common form is the M'Naghten Rule.

M'Naghten Rule
a standard for proving the insanity defense. It requires the defendant to prove insanity either by showing that he failed to understand the nature of his actions or that he could not distinguish the difference between right and wrong

The **M'Naghten Rule** comes from an 1843 English case. M'Naghten assassinated the private secretary to Prime Minister Robert Peel, mistaking him for Peel. M'Naghten suffered from an insane delusion that Peel intended to kill him.[50] The court stated that in order for insanity to be shown, "it must be clearly proved that, at the time of committing the act, the party accused was laboring under such a defect of reason, from disease of the mind, as not to know the nature and quality of the act that he was doing, or if he did know it, that he did not know he was doing what was wrong."[51]

Many states have adopted all or part of the M'Naghten Rule. It has two basic components. The first half of the M'Naghten Rule is known as the cognitive incapacity test. It asks whether the defendant understood what he was doing at the time of the commission of the offense. For example, did the defendant believe that he was cutting up paper rather than stabbing someone with scissors? Defendants rarely suffer from such a lack of knowledge, so the second prong of the test—whether the defendant knew that what he was doing was wrong—is used more frequently.[52] Ten states have adopted just this part of the M'Naghten Rule (known as the moral incapacity test), while six states follow the full version, allowing a defendant to allege either prong of the test.

Some states developed a different insanity rule known as the **irresistible impulse test**. Under this test, the defendant must show that a mental defect or disease kept him from controlling his conduct, even though he knew what he was doing and knew that it was wrong.[53] The Model Penal Code version of the test states that "a person is not responsible for criminal conduct if at the time of such conduct as a result of mental disease or defect he lacks substantial capacity either to appreciate the criminality [wrongfulness] of his conduct or to conform his conduct to the requirements of law."[54]

Dissatisfaction with the irresistible impulse test came about after John Hinckley, Jr. successfully claimed insanity under that test after he tried to assassinate President Reagan in 1981. Hinckley claimed that he had acted out of an insane delusion that actress Jodie Foster would fall in love with him if he shot the President. Federal law was amended in 1984 such that a defendant must now prove that he was unable to appreciate the nature and quality of the wrongfulness of his acts as a result of severe mental disease or defect. [55]

The Supreme Court has never held that the availability of an insanity defense is constitutionally required.[56] Four states, Idaho, Kansas, Montana, and Utah, have abolished the insanity defense altogether but do allow the defendant to present evidence of mental illness to negate the intent component of the crime.[57]

Irresistible impulse test

a version of the insanity defense that requires the defendant to prove that he lacked the substantial capacity to appreciate the wrongfulness of his acts or conform his conduct to law

Practical Example

Jeffrey is under an insane delusion that Martians are living in his next-door neighbor's house. He does know the difference between right and wrong and realizes that killing people is wrong, however. He believes he is killing a Martian who is out to abduct him when he kills his neighbor. He raises the insanity defense at trial. Under the M'Naghten Rule and the Cognitive Incapacity Test, Jeffrey will succeed on his insanity defense. He can show that he did not appreciate the nature of his conduct—that he was killing another human being, not a Martian. However, under the other rules he will not succeed because he knew killing a person was wrong.

iii. Public Policy Defenses

The third category of affirmative defense is public policy defenses. Public policy defenses do not excuse the defendant's conduct but rather absolve him of responsibility due to some overriding public interest. Examples of this type of defense include expiration of the statute of limitations, collateral estoppel, double jeopardy, diplomatic immunity, and testimonial immunity.

3. The Burden of Proof for a Defense

It violates due process to shift the burden of proof to the defendant to prove a negating defense. This is so because the defendant cannot be forced to disprove one of the elements of the offense since the prosecution always has the burden of proof in this regard. The defendant merely has the burden of producing sufficient evidence of the defense's existence so that the jury may consider it. For instance, the Delaware Supreme Court held that a defendant is entitled to have the jury consider an alibi defense if he presents "some credible evidence" of his alibi.[58] If, however, the defendant fails to present sufficiently credible evidence of the existence of the alibi, then the judge can prevent the jury from considering it.

Unlike negating defenses, the Supreme Court has held that it does not violate due process to shift the burden of proof to the defendant to prove an affirmative defense. For example, in *Leland v. Oregon*, the Court held that it does not violate due process to require a defendant to prove his defense of insanity beyond a reasonable doubt.[59] Similarly, in *Patterson v. New York*, the Court held that due process is not violated by requiring a defendant to prove the affirmative defense of extreme emotional disturbance by a preponderance of evidence.[60] The Court has also upheld the common-law rule that the defendant must prove he acted in self-defense.[61] According to the Court, the distinction between negating defenses and affirmative defenses is that proof of an affirmative defense does not "serve to negative any facts of the crime which the State is [required] to prove in order to convict."[62] Instead, an affirmative defense is a separate issue that seeks to relieve the defendant of culpability and that the burden of proof is more properly placed on the defendant.

Despite these rulings, many states still place the burden on the prosecutor to disprove affirmative defenses. For example, in Colorado, the prosecution always bears the burden of proof, regardless of the type of defense alleged.[63] Once an affirmative defense is raised, the prosecution must establish the guilt of the defendant on that issue as well as all elements of the offense.[64] In effect, proof of absence of the affirmative defense becomes one of the elements of the crime the prosecutor must prove. Most states follow this rule with respect to self-defense.[65] Only Ohio and South Carolina still require the defendant to carry the burden of persuasion with respect to self-defense.[66] Likewise, at the time the *Patterson* case was decided in 1977, 28 states required the prosecution to disprove insanity (where raised).[67]

> **AUTHOR'S NOTE**
>
> The preceding rule, which places the burden on the prosecutor to disprove an affirmative defense, is somewhat strange. Ordinarily, the burden of proof to prove an affirmative defense is placed on the party claiming it because he is in the best position to produce evidence in support of the defense. By way of comparison, the defendant in a civil case does have the burden of proof to establish affirmative defenses (i.e., the comparative fault of the plaintiff). Since self-defense and insanity are absolute justifications for murder and other crimes, one would think the defendant should have a high, not low, burden to establish the defense. If states wish to keep the burden of proof on the prosecution to prove absence of self-defense or insanity, then the term "affirmative defense" should be done away with altogether.

D. Presumptions

Presumption
a given conclusion which can be inferred by the jury once a set of other facts has been proven

Permissive inference
a presumption that allows, but does not require, the jury to reach a certain conclusion

Mandatory presumption
a presumption that requires the jury to reach a certain conclusion

Conclusive presumption
an irrebuttable presumption that relieves a party of the burden of proof on that issue once it has been established

Rebuttable presumption
a presumption that allows the other party an opportunity to produce facts that refute the permitted conclusion

A **presumption** allows the jury to infer a given conclusion or fact once a set of other facts has been proven. In other words, if a party proves A (some fact or commission of an act), then the jury may infer B (the existence of some other fact or conclusion). Presumptions can either be permissive or mandatory. A **permissive inference** or presumption "allows but does not require the fact finder to find an element of the crime (elemental fact) upon proof by the prosecution of another fact (basic fact), and it places no burden of any kind on the defendant."[68] In contrast, a **mandatory presumption** is one that informs the jury that it "must infer the presumed fact" if the prosecution proves certain basic facts.[69]

There are two types of mandatory presumptions, conclusive (irrebuttable) and rebuttable. A **conclusive presumption** relieves a party of the burden of proof on that issue once a party proves certain facts giving rise to the presumption. An instruction that informs the jury that "every person is conclusively presumed to intend the natural and necessary consequences of his act" is an example of an irrebuttable presumption. A **rebuttable presumption** allows the other party an opportunity to produce facts to disprove or rebut the presumption. The jury must find the elemental fact has been proven unless the defendant offers evidence to the contrary.[70] An example of a rebuttable mandatory presumption is one that provides that the jury must infer the reasonableness of the charges once evidence of the amount of plaintiff's medical expenses has been introduced.

The due process clause prohibits the prosecution from using evidentiary presumptions in a jury instruction "that have the effect of relieving the State of its burden of persuasion beyond a reasonable doubt of every essential element of the crime."[71] The Supreme Court has held that both types of mandatory presumptions violate due process since both shift the burden of proof to the defendant:

> First, a reasonable jury could well have interpreted the presumption as "conclusive," that is, not technically as a presumption at all, but rather as an irrebuttable direction by the court to find intent once convinced of the facts triggering the presumption. Alternatively, the jury may have interpreted the instruction as a direction to find intent upon proof of the defendant's voluntary actions (and their "ordinary" consequences), unless the defendant proved the contrary by some quantum of proof which may well have been considerably greater than "some" evidence—thus effectively shifting the burden of persuasion on the element of intent.[72]

For example, the Supreme Court held that a presumption that instructed the jury that the acts of a person of sound mind and discretion are presumed to be the product of the person's will and that a person "is presumed to intend the natural and probable consequences of his acts" violates due process. Since an essential element of the offense was proof of intent to kill, the Court found the instruction violated due process.[73]

Permissive inferences, on the other hand, do not violate due process unless the suggested conclusion is not one that "reason and common sense" would justify.[74] The defendant must be allowed an opportunity to present evidence to disprove the presumption once the prosecution has established it, and the jury must be allowed a choice of whether to infer such a conclusion from the evidence. Thus, an instruction that informs the jury that it can infer intent from the natural and probable consequences of the defendant's actions as long as there are "no circumstances to the contrary" is permissible since it does not shift the burden of proof.[75]

Sometimes it may be difficult to determine whether a given instruction creates a mandatory or permissive presumption. Although the word "presumption" is used quite often in jury instructions, its use, by itself, does not determine whether an instruction creates a conclusive presumption or permissive inference. The key is whether the jury could have read the challenged instruction as removing the burden of proof on that element.[76] See the discussion below about the presumption of intoxication for an example of such an instruction.

1. Presumption of Innocence

Presumption of innocence
a presumption that the defendant is not guilty, and it must be overcome by the prosecution's presentation of evidence of his guilt beyond a reasonable doubt.

Under our system of justice, the defendant has the **presumption of innocence** until proven guilty. The Supreme Court has held that "the principle that there is a presumption of innocence in favor of the accused is the undoubted law, axiomatic and elementary, and its enforcement lies at the foundation of the administration of our criminal law."[77] One court long ago characterized how the presumption should operate during jury deliberations:

A defendant's friends may forsake him, but the presumption of innocence, never. It is present throughout the entire trial; and, when the jury goes to their room to deliberate, the "presumption of innocence" goes in with them, protesting against the defendant's guilt. And it is only after the jury has given all of the evidence in the case a full, fair, and impartial consideration, and has been able to find beyond a reasonable doubt that the defendant is guilty as charged, that the presumption of innocence leaves him.[78]

Although the concepts of burden of proof and the presumption of innocence are closely related, the Supreme Court has rejected the argument that the giving of an instruction on one or the other would be sufficient. The Court explained how the two concepts relate to one another but remain separate and distinct:

While the legal scholar may understand that the presumption of innocence and the prosecution's burden of proof are logically similar, the ordinary citizen may well draw significant additional guidance from an instruction on the presumption of innocence.... "[T]he rule about burden of proof requires the prosecution by evidence to convince the jury of the accused's guilt, while the presumption of innocence, too, requires this, but conveys for the jury a special and additional caution... to consider, in the material for their belief, nothing but the evidence... This caution is indeed particularly needed in criminal cases." This Court has declared that one accused of a crime is entitled to have his guilt or innocence determined solely on the basis of the evidence introduced at trial, and not on grounds of official suspicion, indictment, continued custody, or other circumstances not adduced as proof at trial.... [I]t has long been recognized that an instruction on the presumption is one way of impressing upon the jury the importance of that right.[79]

Although the Supreme Court stopped short of requiring that the jury be advised of the presumption of innocence via a jury instruction, many states have imposed such a requirement.[80] An Oklahoma court explained that an instruction on the presumption of innocence, in addition to one on the burden of proof, is necessary because it "fixes the burden of proof and designates that the duty rests upon the State to produce evidence and to effect persuasion beyond a reasonable doubt before the jury is authorized to convict."[81] Courts have rejected instructions that advise the jury that the defendant is not guilty rather than he is innocent until proven guilty. One court noted that the correct starting point should be that there is an absence of guilt, not the absence of sufficient proof of guilt.[82]

2. Presumption of Intoxication

In a drunken driving case, many states instruct the jury that it can infer the person is intoxicated if his blood or breath alcohol is above a certain concentration. Such presumptions do not shift the burden of proof. The Supreme Court of Georgia held that such an instruction was permissible because (1) the prosecution is still required to prove beyond a reasonable doubt that the defendant committed the act of driving while having a blood alcohol level of .10 or higher, and (2) the defendant can challenge the evidence that he had such a blood-alcohol level or that he was driving.[83] Although the instruction was worded in terms of a presumption, the court found that it simply created a permissive inference that a person was intoxicated. The court noted that the defendant could still present evidence that the blood-alcohol test was inaccurate or that she did not commit the offense.[84]

III. DIRECT AND CIRCUMSTANTIAL EVIDENCE

A. Direct Evidence

Direct evidence
evidence that does not require any assumptions or inferences to prove the existence of facts. It comes directly from the witness's personal observations and knowledge.

Direct evidence is evidence that is "based on personal knowledge or observation and that, if true, proves a fact without inference or presumption."[85] It helps prove or disprove some fact at issue in the case without the jury having to make any assumptions or draw conclusions about the meaning of the evidence. Direct evidence is sometimes referred to as testimonial evidence since it is based on the personal observations or direct knowledge of the witness. Eyewitness testimony is the classic example of direct evidence. Videotape footage of the defendant committing the crime and incriminating statements made by the defendant are also examples of direct evidence.

Practical Example

Jesus testifies in Jorge's trial that he saw Jorge steal three televisions from K-Mart. The evidence is direct evidence of Jorge's guilt since Jesus has personal knowledge of the events and saw Jorge commit the crime.

B. Circumstantial Evidence

1. Definition

Circumstantial evidence
evidence that allows proof of one fact by drawing inferences or conclusions from the proof of another set of facts

Circumstantial evidence is defined as "evidence based on inference and not on personal knowledge or observation."[86] It involves proving collateral facts and circumstances from which a jury can infer the existence of the main fact according to its "reason and experience."[87] An inference is a conclusion that can be reached by considering other facts and "deducing a logical consequence" that must result from them.[88] Circumstantial evidence differs from direct evidence because there is no eyewitness or firsthand account of the evidence. Examples of circumstantial evidence include most physical evidence (finding someone's DNA or fingerprints at a crime scene) and evidence of motive or opportunity. See Table 8.3 for a comparison of direct and circumstantial evidence.

Circumstantial evidence has been compared to a set of links in a chain or a series of strands that make up a cable since the jury must connect a series of facts to draw inferences about the guilt or innocence of the defendant. As one court explained, the cable analogy is perhaps more appropriate:

> [The strength of the cable] does not depend upon one strand, but is made up of the union and combination of the strength of all of its strands. No one wire in the cable that supports the suspension bridge across Niagara Falls could stand much weight, but when these different strands are all combined together, they support a structure which is capable of sustaining the weight of the heaviest engines and trains. We therefore think it is erroneous to speak of circumstantial evidence as depending on links, for the truth is that in cases of circumstantial evidence each fact relied upon is simply considered as one of the strands and all of the facts relied upon should be treated as a cable.[89]

Certain types of facts can be inferred from the existence of circumstantial evidence. Knowledge of contraband or weapons can be inferred, for example, from the fact of a person's possession of the items. In this way, the driver of a vehicle can be said to have knowledge of its contents because the owner and/or driver of a vehicle is viewed as having heightened control over the contents as opposed to the passengers.[90] A Georgia court found that there was sufficient evidence to convict the driver of cocaine possession (as opposed to the passenger) where the drugs were found in the trunk of the car. The court concluded that the inference of knowledge of the contents of the trunk was permissible since there was no evidence that anyone other than the driver had access to the keys to open the trunk.[91]

TABLE 8.3 EXAMPLES OF DIRECT AND CIRCUMSTANTIAL EVIDENCE

Examples of Direct Evidence	Examples of Circumstantial Evidence
• Testimony of an eyewitness that the defendant committed the crime	• Fingerprints of the defendant found at the crime scene
• Surveillance video of the defendant robbing the store	• A receipt for the gun that the defendant used to commit the crime
• Drugs in the possession of the defendant	• Testimony that the defendant owed a large debt to the victim and thus had a motive to kill him
• Audio tape of the defendant selling drugs to an undercover informant	• Testimony that the defendant was the last person to see the victim alive
• Incriminating statements of the defendant	

Practical Example

Lois is found dead with a stab wound to the heart. Stewie's fingerprints are found on the murder weapon. There is also testimony that Stewie was seen in Lois's bedroom just a few minutes before her body was found. Stewie's brother testifies that Stewie had told him how much he hated his mother. All of this is circumstantial evidence. One piece of it in isolation is not sufficient to convict Stewie of murder, but when all the evidence is compiled together, Stewie certainly appears to have had the motive, opportunity, and intent to kill his mother.

2. Sufficiency of Circumstantial Evidence

Given that the strength of circumstantial evidence is based on inferences, not direct evidence, the key question is whether the amount of it offered is sufficient to establish the defendant's guilt. Circumstantial evidence is sufficient to convict a person if "the evidence and reasonable inferences that may be drawn from the evidence establish the defendant's guilt beyond a reasonable doubt."[92] In other words, just because there are rational, alternative conclusions to be drawn from the facts, the jury "is not lawfully barred against discarding one possible inference when it concludes such inference unreasonable under the circumstances."[93] Thus, under the modern rule, the jury may solely consider circumstantial evidence as proof of guilt unless the court rules there is an insufficient amount of evidence to convict.

The Rhode Island Supreme Court explained the process as follows:

> The pivotal question in determining whether circumstantial evidence is sufficient to prove guilt beyond a reasonable doubt is whether the evidence in its entirety constitutes proof beyond a reasonable doubt or is of such a nature that it merely raises the suspicion or conjecture of guilt. Under this test it is possible for the state to prove guilt by a process of logical deduction, reasoning from established circumstantial facts through a series of inferences to the ultimate conclusion of guilt. The pyramiding of inferences during this process of deduction becomes speculative, however, and thus insufficient to prove guilt beyond a reasonable doubt when the initial inference in the pyramid rests upon an ambiguous fact that is equally capable of supporting other reasonable inferences clearly inconsistent with guilt.[94]

For example, the Nebraska Supreme Court found that circumstantial evidence was sufficient to uphold an arson conviction where, among other things, the defendant was seen near the warehouse shortly before the fire started and traces of accelerant were found at the fire scene.[95]

i. Reasonable Hypothesis of Innocence Test

Years ago, most courts assumed that circumstantial evidence was "inherently suspicious and less trustworthy" than direct evidence.[96]

Reasonable hypothesis of innocence rule

a rule that requires the prosecution to prove not only that circumstantial evidence establishes the guilt of the accused but that it also is inconsistent with a theory of innocence

Therefore, courts developed the **reasonable hypothesis of innocence rule** that imposed an additional burden of proof on the prosecution where the defendant's guilt rested solely on circumstantial evidence. In that instance, the jury is instructed not only that it had to find the evidence is "consistent with guilt" but also that it is "inconsistent with innocence."[97] Consequently, under this rule, courts held that where facts were capable of two different interpretations, equally consistent with guilt or innocence, the jury could not "arbitrarily adopt that interpretation which incriminates the accused."[98] For example, a New York court held that the rule was not satisfied where the only proof of the defendant's alleged theft of gemstones from a jewelry store was the fact that he had an opportunity to commit the crime. No one saw him steal the gems and they were not recovered.[99]

Some states still adhere to the rule and require that the jury must be specially instructed on the law of circumstantial evidence. For example, Georgia gives the reasonable hypothesis of innocence instruction where the prosecution's case is "wholly circumstantial."[100] California gives the instruction if circumstantial evidence is "substantially" relied upon by the prosecution; conversely, it does not do so if the circumstantial evidence is merely "incidental to and corroborative of the direct evidence" in the case.[101]

ii. The Modern Rule

While some states still use the reasonable hypothesis of innocence rule, it has been heavily criticized. The distrust of circumstantial evidence is based on a faulty premise—that it is weaker or less trustworthy than direct evidence. The Supreme Court has held that "direct evidence of a fact is not required. Circumstantial evidence is not only sufficient, but may also be more certain, satisfying and persuasive than direct evidence."[102] In some cases, direct evidence may be quite suspect (such as a faulty eyewitness identification) while the circumstantial evidence might be quite strong (such as fingerprint evidence).[103]

The reasonable hypothesis test has also been criticized for being too confusing because it deflects the jury's attention from its real task—determination of reasonable doubt.[104] As a result, the Supreme Court rejected the reasonable hypothesis of innocence test for use in federal courts in 1954:

> Admittedly, circumstantial evidence may in some cases point to a wholly incorrect result. Yet this is equally true of testimonial evidence. In both instances, a jury is asked to weigh the chances that the evidence correctly points to guilt against the possibility of inaccuracy or ambiguous inference. In both, the jury must use its experience with people and events in weighing the probabilities. If the jury is convinced beyond a reasonable doubt, we can require no more.[105]

Today, most courts are of the view that circumstantial evidence is not less probative than direct evidence, and the jury is instructed in these states that there is no difference between direct and circumstantial evidence.[106]

Thus, the prosecution can establish proof of guilt by "circumstantial evidence as well as by real evidence and direct or testimonial evidence, or any combination of these three classes of evidence."[107]

The reasonable hypothesis of innocence test is still useful in one situation—where the prosecution's proof of an element of the crime consists of a single strand of circumstantial evidence and, thus, may be legally insufficient to sustain a conviction. Maryland has limited the use of the reasonable hypothesis of innocence test to this situation:

> [W]here the defendant posits that the State's evidence consists of a single strand of circumstantial evidence that is not inconsistent with a reasonable hypothesis of innocence, he is effectively charging that the evidence is legally insufficient. If that claim is made timely and properly, it is incumbent upon the judge to rule upon it as a matter of law, in the context of a motion for judgment of acquittal. If the motion is granted, of course, the count(s) to which it applies may not be submitted to the jury. If the motion is denied, the court must instruct on reasonable doubt, but should not supplement that instruction with any special focus on hypotheses arising from circumstantial evidence.[108]

The court went on to explain why this is the case:

> It is not necessary that the circumstantial evidence exclude every possibility of the defendant's innocence, or produce an absolute certainty in the minds of the jurors. The rule does not require that the jury be satisfied beyond a reasonable doubt of each link in the chain of circumstances relied upon to establish the defendant's guilt. While it must afford the basis for an inference of guilt beyond a reasonable doubt, it is not necessary that each circumstance, standing alone, be sufficient to establish guilt, but the circumstances are to be considered collectively.[109]

AUTHOR'S NOTE

This interpretation of the rule is more logical since the only time that the prosecution need refute all reasonable hypotheses of innocence is where a single strand of evidence is the only evidence of guilt as to one or more elements of the offense. Remember, where there are multiple strands of circumstantial evidence (or direct facts for that matter) offered to prove an element of the crime, no one strand need be sufficient, in and of itself, to prove that element beyond a reasonable doubt.

---

iii. Use of Circumstantial Evidence in Murder Cases

Courts have also refused to apply different rules for the introduction of circumstantial evidence in murder prosecutions. For example, the Ohio Supreme Court rejected the argument that evidence of murder should be treated differently than other crimes:

[W]e know of no reason that the crime of murder should be treated any differently from other crimes when considering the use of circumstantial evidence to establish their commission. Given the extensive precedent in Ohio on the use of circumstantial evidence to prove the commission of a crime and the abundant case law in other jurisdictions on the use of such evidence in homicide prosecutions, we hold that in the absence of a human body, a confession, or other direct evidence of death, circumstantial evidence alone may be sufficient to support a conviction for murder.[110]

Corpus delicti

a Latin term meaning the body or substance of the crime. The prosecution must establish all elements of the crime in order to sustain a conviction

To sustain a murder conviction, the prosecution must establish the ***corpus delicti*** (the body or substance of the crime) by proving the fact of death and a criminal act as the cause of death.[111] The *corpus delicti* can be established through either direct or circumstantial evidence.[112] Where circumstantial evidence alone is used to prove the *corpus delicti*, however, some states have applied the reasonable hypothesis of innocence test.[113] In one case, the Washington Supreme Court ruled that the *corpus delicti* could not be proven where the medical examiner could not determine whether the death of the defendant's infant daughter resulted from suffocation or sudden infant death syndrome (SIDS). Even though one logical inference from the facts is that the child died as a result of a criminal act, the court concluded that the *corpus delicti* could not be proven where the evidence supported inferences of both criminal and noncriminal cause.[114]

AUTHOR'S NOTE

As discussed earlier, the reasonable hypothesis of innocence test is based on a largely outdated view of circumstantial evidence—namely, that it is a weaker form of evidence. Thus, many courts have held that it would be "inconsistent to require more from circumstantial evidence to establish the *corpus delicti* than is required to establish guilt beyond a reasonable doubt."[115] Oddly, the Washington Supreme Court had repudiated the use of the reasonable hypothesis of innocence test for evaluating circumstantial evidence generally nine years before its decision regarding proof of the *corpus delicti*.[116] Thus, the court's ruling appears to be based on a rickety foundation. The better view is to admit circumstantial evidence to prove the *corpus delicti* as long as the evidence is probative of the murder.

It is not necessary to produce the body of the victim in order to prove the death of the murder victim.[117] For example, the Washington Supreme Court held that to require "direct proof of the killing or the production of the body of the alleged victim in all cases of homicide would be manifestly unreasonable and would lead to absurdity and injustice."[118] In a California case, the prosecution was able to establish the murder of the victim through circumstantial evidence even though no body or sign of violence was found at time of the victim's disappearance.[119] The court found that there was abundant other circumstantial evidence of her death and murder:

> (1) the victim was in good physical and mental health prior to her disappearance; (2) the victim would not have left home without her eyeglasses and her dentures which had been found behind the couple's home; (3) if the victim intended to leave home, she would've taken money, baggage and a wardrobe; (4) it would have been impossible for the victim to conceal herself for several years and live without withdrawing money from her bank account; (5) the defendant had a strong motive for killing his wife—to give himself the opportunity to steal her money through forging her checks; (6) the defendant had previously persuaded his wife to convert her securities into cash which made it easier for him to obtain her property through forgery; and (7) the defendant had told conflicting stories to explain her disappearance, and how he had obtained large sums of her money.[120]

Thus, the court concluded that the "circumstantial evidence of the fact of death by criminal means was as strong and convincing as a confession would have been and much stronger than a confession of questionable validity."[121]

EVIDENCE IN ACTION

Michael Blagg Convicted of Murdering His Wife After Her Body Was Discovered in a Landfill

On November 12, 2001, Michael Blagg reported to Grand Junction, Colorado police that his wife, Jennifer, was missing when he returned home from work around 4:00 p.m. that day. Jennifer was a stay-at-home mom and was supposed to be at home with the couple's six-year-old daughter. When Michael had come home, he found signs of a struggle and a large pool of blood on the couple's bed. Only after the 911 dispatcher told Michael to check the garage for his wife's minivan did Michael think to check his daughter's room. That's when he discovered her missing too. At least that's what he said. A huge search involving 200 volunteers was launched over a period of 11 days to look for the missing pair, but no sign of them turned up.

Two months after reporting their disappearance, Michael reported to police that he discovered some of his wife's jewelry was missing as well. The police became suspicious of Michael as the facts did not add up to robbery. After he was placed under surveillance by police, Michael was observed apparently stealing over $500 worth of office materials from his employer in January of 2002. He was questioned about the incident in February of 2002 and attempted to commit suicide the following day.

Law enforcement officials began to suspect Michael in the disappearance of his wife and daughter. They found small drops of Jennifer's blood in the rear of the couple's minivan and believed it was used to transport the bodies from the residence. Officers theorized the Michael had shot his wife, suffocated his daughter, wrapped their bodies, and dumped them in a trash dumpster at his workplace. Using global positioning technology and landfill logs, the officers searched the Mesa County landfill for 16 days.

On June 5, 2002, authorities received the big break in the case they were looking for. Jennifer's body was discovered in the landfill as it fell out of the backhoe. Examination of Jennifer's body showed that she was killed from a gunshot to her left eye. Authorities believe she was killed while she slept. Abby's body was never found.

Blagg was tried for first-degree murder, largely on the basis of circumstantial evidence. The prosecution argued that the fatal weekend began with a fight on Friday night over Michael's addiction to Internet pornography. It argued that Jennifer wanted a divorce, but instead Michael shot her in the face. The prosecution played up Michael's lack of emotion about the disappearance of his wife and daughter during his initial interviews with police. The other pieces of evidence that the prosecution relied on were the blood in the couple's minivan and the

Figure 8.2   Michael Blagg looks at the jury after closing arguments during his murder trial on April 14, 2004. He was charged with the murder of his wife after he reported her and his daughter missing on November 12, 2001. He was convicted of first-degree murder. *© 2004 AP Photo/Pool/ Gretel Daugherty*

fact that the evidence did not add up to a burglary and kidnapping as Michael had argued. Blagg was convicted of first-degree murder and sentenced to life in prison.[122]

CHAPTER SUMMARY

First, in order to be admissible, evidence must be relevant, reliable, and competent. Relevance is made up of two components—materiality and probative value. The evidence must have a logical connection (materiality) to the case, and it must prove or disprove some fact (probative value). Evidence that lacks either of these two elements is not relevant and, thus, is inadmissible. Evidence must also be reliable. The reliability of the evidence depends on the quality or source

of the evidence. Evidence is not reliable if the witness lacks personal knowledge of the subject he is testifying about, the source of the evidence is highly questionable, or there is no scientific basis for the expert opinion he provides. Some forms of hearsay evidence are excluded on this basis as well as expert testimony based on "junk" science. Competency is the final requirement for the admission of evidence. In order to be competent, evidence must not be subject to some legal restriction. Otherwise relevant evidence can be excluded from trial because the protection of other rights is considered to be more important. Evidence that is protected by a privilege such as the attorney-client privilege is protected from disclosure in this manner. Evidence that is otherwise admissible can also be excluded under Rule 403 if its prejudicial effect greatly outweighs its probative value. Gory photos or inflammatory information about a witness's background are examples of potentially prejudicial evidence.

Once a party establishes the admissibility of evidence, it also has to meet any applicable burden of proof. The burden of proof is broken down into two elements: the burden of persuasion and the burden of production. The burden of production is the burden placed on the party introducing a claim or defense to set forth at least some evidence of each element of the claim or defense. For example, the prosecution must prove the prima facie case of the defendant's guilt by producing some evidence of each element of the crime. The burden of persuasion, meanwhile, is the party's burden to convince the jury of the strength of the evidence. The prosecution always has the burden to prove the defendant guilty beyond a reasonable doubt. It never shifts to the defendant to prove his innocence.

Presumptions may remove the burden of proof on a party. They permit the jury to make certain inferences once another set of facts has been proven. The presumption of innocence is one example of a presumption. Presumptions can be divided into mandatory and permissive types. Mandatory presumptions, those that require the jury to make certain inferences, violate due process.

The defendant can allege a number of defenses. They are divided in two categories— negating defenses and affirmative defenses. Negating defenses remove or mitigate an element of an offense, whereas affirmative defenses attempt to excuse or justify the defendant's actions. The prosecution always must disprove the existence of defenses that negate an element of the offense, such as consent or an alibi. However, the defendant can be required to prove certain affirmative defenses, such as insanity or self-defense.

There are two basic types of evidence introduced in trials—direct and circumstantial evidence. Direct evidence relies on eyewitness testimony to establish material facts in the case, whereas circumstantial evidence requires the jury to infer certain facts or conclusions from the existence of other facts. In most states, there is no difference between the two forms of evidence. Some states, however, require the prosecution to show that the evidence does not have a reasonable inference of innocence before admitting circumstantial evidence.

KEY TERMS

- Affirmative defense
- Burden of persuasion
- Burden of production
- Burden of proof
- Circumstantial evidence
- Competent
- Conclusive presumption
- *Corpus delicti*
- Defense

- Direct evidence
- Foundation
- M'Naghten Rule
- Mandatory presumption
- Materiality
- Negating defense
- Permissive inference
- Prejudicial evidence
- Presumption

- Presumption of innocence
- Prima facie case
- Probative value
- Reasonable hypothesis of innocence rule
- Rebuttable presumption
- Relevance
- Reliability

REVIEW QUESTIONS

1. What are the three things that evidence must possess in order to be admissible?

2. What is relevance? What are the two main components of relevance?

3. What is meant by the reliability of evidence? Give an example of unreliable evidence.

4. What is meant by the competency of evidence? Give an example of evidence that is otherwise reliable and relevant but that is not competent.

5. What is the standard for barring evidence that is too prejudicial? Give an example of evidence that is often ruled as being too prejudicial.

6. What is meant by the term *burden of proof*? What is the burden of proof in a criminal case, and who has it? Why do you think the burden of proof in a criminal case is so much higher than in a civil case?

7. How is the burden of persuasion different from the burden of production of evidence?

8. What level of suspicion or proof is needed to obtain a search warrant or arrest a suspect?

9. What is a presumption? What kinds of presumptions are not allowed under the Constitution?

10. Why is the defendant presumed innocent until proven guilty?

11. What is an affirmative defense? Name two common affirmative defenses.

12. Who has the burden of proof to prove an affirmative defense? Can states lawfully shift the burden to prove an affirmative defense onto the defendant? Explain.

13. What is the M'Naghten Rule? How is the federal rule different?

14. What is circumstantial evidence? How is it different from direct evidence? Give an example of each type of evidence.

15. When is the reasonable hypothesis of innocence test used?

APPLICATION PROBLEMS

1. John is charged with stealing money from his employer. The prosecution wants to introduce evidence that John has a gambling problem and needed money to pay off the debt. Is the evidence relevant to his theft and embezzlement charges? Explain.

2. Jennifer is charged with DUI. She wants to call an expert witness to testify that she was not intoxicated at the time of driving even though she had a blood alcohol level of .16, twice the legal limit. The expert bases his conclusion on the fact that she ate food before drinking six margaritas and two beers. There is no scientific basis for the expert's opinion. Is the evidence admissible since it is clearly relevant to the charge? Explain.

3. Pedro is chasing immortality. He is about to win his fifth Super Bowl title as a quarterback. A federal agent suspects Pedro is using performance-enhancing drugs. He attempts to obtain a urine sample to confirm his suspicions. A judge will not sign a warrant, so he raids the testing laboratory for the NFL. He identifies Pedro's drug test sample and test results and seizes them. The test results show Pedro used HGH and female hormones to lower his

testosterone levels. Is the evidence admissible since it is clearly relevant to the case? Explain.

4. George is charged with assault with a deadly weapon. The prosecution wants to introduce 86 photographs of the assault, including several close-ups of the victim's bloodied head and fractured skull. Should the close-up photos be admissible since they are clearly relevant to the case, or should they be excluded as prejudicial? Explain.

5. Jackson is arrested for sale of a controlled substance. An undercover informant claims she bought the drugs from Jackson. She was wearing a wire but it was not working for much of the time. You can hear Jackson's voice on the tape and can hear a conversation discussing drugs. The actual transaction is not on the tape, however. There are three other individuals in the apartment at the time. The confidential informant is searched after the alleged buy and drugs are found on her person. Some of the money she was given to buy drugs is missing. When the police raid the apartment, they discover three marked one hundred dollar bills on the coffee table. Is there enough evidence to arrest Jackson for sale of a controlled substance? Is there enough evidence to convict Jackson beyond a reasonable doubt? Explain.

6. Gary is involved in a bar fight. He hit a man over the head with a bar stool. He claims the incident was self-defense. He will testify in his own defense, and one witness in the bar will state the other man started the incident. Two other witnesses will testify that it was Gary's fault. Assuming the case is not in Ohio or South Carolina, what will the prosecution have to prove to win the case?

7. Cathy the Crazy Cat Lady is charged with assault with a deadly weapon. She injured a man when she hurled several cats and unfortunately a frying pan at him. She thought he was a foreign spy who was trying to kill her. Cathy suffers from schizophrenia and is under a delusion that foreign spies are out to get her. She can distinguish right from wrong and knew at the time of the offense that she could hurt the man by hurling cats and a frying pan at him. Is she legally insane under either the M'Naghten Rule or the federal rule? Explain.

8. Juanita Cruz is accused of murdering her husband. His body is never found. The prosecution introduces evidence that Juanita had been abused during the marriage and had contacted a person about contracting a hit on her husband. Can the prosecution sustain a murder conviction even though there is no direct evidence of the husband's death? Explain.

Notes

1. F.R.E. 401.
2. *Black's Law Dictionary*, at 1316 (8th ed. 2004).
3. State v. Downs, 190 P.3d 17 (Utah App. 2008).
4. State v. Wadle, 873 P.2d 171, (Idaho App. 1994).
5. United States v. Bad Cob, 560 F.2d 877 (8th Cir. 1977).
6. United States v. Masters, 450 F.2d 866 (9th Cir.).
7. Johnson v. United States, 960 A.2d 281 (D.C. 2008).
8. *Black's Law Dictionary*, at 682 (8th ed. 2004).
9. *Black's Law Dictionary*, at 775 (3d Pocket ed. 2006).
10. United States v. Bonds, 12 F.3d 540, 561-63 (6th Cir. 1993).
11. United States v. Smith, 308 F.3d 726, 739 (7th Cir. 2002).
12. State v. Thibodeau, 353 A.2d 595, 603 (Me. 1976).
13. Downs, 190 P.3d at 21.
14. Id., *quoting* State v. Johnson, 784 P.2d 1135, 1141 (Utah 1989).
15. Downs, 190 P.3d at 20, *quoting* United States v. Rodriguez, 192 F.3d 946, 950-51 (10th Cir. 1999).
16. *See* Long v. State, 823 S.W.2d 259, 270 (Tex. Crim. App. 1991).
17. Fuller v. State, 829 S.W.2d 191, 206 (Tex. Crim. App. 1992).
18. Juhasz v. State, 827 S.W.2d 397, 402 (Tex. Crim. App. 1992).
19. State v. Dibello, 780 P.2d 1221, 1230 (Utah 1989).
20. *Black's Law Dictionary*, at 209 (8th ed. 2004).
21. Director v. Greenwich Collieries, 512 U.S. 267, 274 (1994).
22. *Black's Law Dictionary*, at 1239 (8th ed. 2004).
23. *See e.g.,* N.D. Cent. Code § 14-09-06.2(j) (If the court finds credible evidence that domestic violence has occurred, and there exists one incident of domestic violence which resulted in serious bodily injury or involved the use of a dangerous weapon or there exists a pattern of domestic violence within a reasonable time proximate to the proceeding, this combination creates a rebuttable presumption that a parent who has perpetrated domestic violence may not be awarded residential responsibility for the child).

24. New York Criminal Jury Instructions, available at http://www.nycourts.gov/cji/1-General/CJI2d.Presumption.Burden.Reasonable_Doubt.pdf.
25. In re Winship, 397 U.S. 358, 364 (1970).
26. Winship, 397 U.S. at 372 (Harlan, J., concurring).
27. Id., quoting Coffin v. United States, 156 U.S. 432, 453 (1895).
28. Black's Law Dictionary, at 209 (8th ed. 2004).
29. Jensen v. State, 732 A.2d 319, 326 (Md. App. 1999).
30. Paul H. Robinson, Criminal Law Defenses: A Systematic Analysis, 82 Colum. L. Rev. 199, 250 (1982).
31. Smith v. Whitlock, 321 F. Supp. 482, 489 (N.D. Ga. 1970).
32. Holmes v. South Carolina, 547 U.S. 319, 327 (2006).
33. Holmes, 547 U.S. at 324, quoting United States v. Scheffer, 523 U.S. 303, 308 (1998).
34. Montana v. Egelhoff, 518 U.S. 37, 43 (1996).
35. Washington v. Texas, 38 U.S. 14 (1967).
36. Rock v. Arkansas, 483 U.S. 44, 61 (1987).
37. Holmes, 547 U.S. at 329.
38. Id.
39. See David McCord, But Perry Mason Made It Look So Easy! The Admissibility of Evidence Offered by a Criminal Defendant to Suggest That Someone Else Is Guilty, 63 Tenn. L. Rev. 917 (1996).
40. Robinson, supra note 38, at 203.
41. Id.
42. People v. Mullins, 209 P.3d 1147 (Colo. App. 2009).
43. Robinson, supra note 38, at 213.
44. Id. at 216.
45. Id. at 217.
46. Colo. Rev. Stat. § 18-1-704.
47. Robinson, supra note 38, at 217.
48. Id. at 222.
49. Matthew T. Huss, Forensic Psychology, at 166 (Wiley-Blackwell 2009).
50. See United States v. Freeman, 357 F.2d 606 (2nd Cir. 1966).
51. Clark v. Arizona, 548 U.S. 735, 747 (2006), quoting M'Naghten's Case, 10 Cl. & Fin. 200, 8 Eng. Rep. 718 (1843).
52. Clark, 548 U.S. at 747.
53. Id. at 749.
54. Id. at 752, n. 15, citing Model Penal Code sec. 4.01(1).
55. 18 U.S.C. § 17.
56. Id.
57. Clark, 548 U.S. at 752, n. 20.
58. Brown v. State, 958 A.2d 833, 838 (Del. 2008).
59. See Leland v. Oregon, 343 U.S. 790 (1952).
60. 432 U.S. 197 (1977).
61. Martin v. Ohio, 480 U.S. 228 (1987).
62. Patterson, 432 U.S. at 207.
63. People v. Lara, 224 P.3d 388 (Colo. App. 2009).
64. Id. at 393.
65. See e.g., Berrier v. Egeler, 583 F.2d 515, 521 (6th Cir. 1977).
66. See Martin, 480 U.S. at 236.
67. Patterson, 432 U.S. at 208, n. 10.
68. Muller v. State, 289 N.W.2d 570, 582 (Wis. 1980).
69. Francis, 471 U.S. at 314.
70. Muller v. State, 289 N.W.2d at 583.
71. Francis v. Franklin, 471 U.S. 307, 313 (1985).
72. Sandstrom v. Montana, 442 U.S. 510, 517 (1979).
73. Francis, 471 U.S. at 316.
74. Francis, 471 U.S. at 314-15.
75. Muller, 289 N.W.2d at 584.
76. State v. Johnson, 440 A.2d 858, 863 (Conn. 1981).
77. Coffin v. United States, 156 U.S. 432, 453 (1895).
78. Flores v. State, 896 P.2d 558 (Ok. Crim. App. 1995), quoting Miller v. State, 106 P. 538 (Ok. Crim. App. 1910).
79. Taylor v. Kentucky, 436 U.S. 478, 484-85 (1978).
80. See Flores, 896 P.2d at 561.
81. Id.
82. Id. at 562.
83. Lattarulo v. State, 401 S.E.2d 516, 518 (Ga. 1991).
84. Id.
85. Black's Law Dictionary, at 596 (8th ed. 2004).
86. Id. at 595.
87. State v. Anderson, 842 So. 2d 1222 (La. App. 2d Cir. 2003).
88. Black's Law Dictionary, at 356 (3d Pocket Ed. 2006).
89. Hebron v. State, 627 A.2d 1029, 1033 (Md. 1993), quoting Ex Parte Hayes, 118 P. 609, 614 (Ok. Crim. App. 1911).
90. State v. Smith, 823 A.2d 664, 678 (Md. App. 2003).
91. Lombardo v. State, 370 S.E.2d 503 (Ga. App. 1988).
92. State v. Ellis, 393 N.W.2d 719, 722 (Neb. 1986).
93. State v. Benivienga, 974 P.2d 832, 834 (Wash. 1999).
94. State v. Caruolo, 524 A.2d 575, 581-82 (R.I. 1987).
95. Id.
96. State v. Gosby, 539 P.2d 680, 685 (Wash. 1975).
97. Betancourt v. Commonwealth, 494 S.E.2d 873, 878 (Vir. App. 1998).
98. Betancourt, 494 S.E.2d at 879.
99. People v. Aleo, 233 N.Y.S.2d 47 (App. Div. 4th Dept. 1962).
100. Harris v. State, 479 S.E.2d 717, 718-19 (Ga. 1997).
101. People v. Williams, 162 Cal. App. 3d 869 (Cal. App. 5th Dist. 1984).
102. Michalic v. Cleveland Tankers, Inc., 364 U.S. 325, 330 (1960).
103. State v. Jenks, 574 N.E.2d 492 (Ohio 1991).
104. Jenks, 574 N.E.2d at 502.
105. Holland v. United States, 348 U.S. 121, 137-38 (1954).
106. See e.g., Colo. CJI 4:01.
107. State v. Nicely, 529 N.E.2d 1236, 1240 (Ohio 1988), quoting 1A Wigmore, Evidence 944, sec. 24 et seq. (Tillers Rev. 1983).
108. Hebron v. State, 627 A.2d 1029, 1031 (Md. 1993), quoting Wilson, supra at 519-20.
109. Id.
110. Nicely, 529 N.E.2d at 1242-43.
111. Id. at 1240.
112. State v. Smith, 570 P.2d 409 (Or. App. 1977).
113. State v. Aten, 927 P.2d 210 (Wash. 1996); State v. Walker, 1994 WL 617262 (Tenn. Crim. App. 1995) (unpublished decision).
114. Aten, 927 P.2d at 220.
115. Smith, 570 P.2d at 411.
116. See State v. Gosby, 539 P.2d 680 (Wash. 1975).
117. Id.
118. State v. Lung, 423 P.2d 72, 76 (Wash. 1967).
119. People v. Scott, 176 Cal. App. 2d 458 (Cal. App. 1959).
120. Scott, 176 Cal. App. 2d at 496.
121. Id.
122. Rebecca Leung, Dark Side of the Mesa, CBS News, June 14, 2004, available at www.cbsnews.com/stories/2004/10/05/48hours/main647548.shtml.

CHAPTER 9

Witnesses Part I: Expert and Lay Witnesses

"Every witness is an editor: he tells you not everything he saw and heard, for that would be impossible, but what he saw and heard and found significant, and what he finds significant depends on his preconceptions."[1]—*Patrick Devlin*

Chapter Topics

Objectives

After reading this chapter, students will be able to:

- Identify the various kinds of witnesses who testify in criminal trials

- Distinguish between lay and expert witnesses

- Understand the judge's role in screening expert testimony

- Distinguish between the *Frye* and *Daubert* standards for admitting expert testimony

- Identify some of the more common types of expert testimony in criminal cases

- Understand the issues surrounding forensic analysis and testimony in criminal cases

- Understand how subpoenas are issued

Introduction

Almost all evidence is introduced by way of a witness. Under the American system of law, the criminal defendant is entitled to be confronted with the witnesses against him. Without this requirement, the prosecutor could simply introduce the evidence in a case through submitting a series of exhibits, such as written witness statements, photographs, and physical evidence. Our Founding Fathers decided that this method invited too much risk of rumor, innuendo, and false accusation being used as a substitute for actual proof. Instead, they wanted to give the jury the opportunity to assess the credibility of a witness testifying live, in person—something it could not get by simply reading the same statement on a piece of paper.

The use of live testimony provides another benefit. It gives the party offering the evidence a chance to give some meaning to the evidence by having the witness explain the context of the statement or physical evidence. We are all familiar with situations where something that is said is subject to two different interpretations, depending on the circumstances under which it was said. Imagine a situation where a spouse says, "Oh, I could kill him for what he did." In most cases, this is nothing more than an expression of frustration, not to be taken literally. However, in some cases the speaker could actually be expressing the intent to kill the other spouse. Without knowing the context of the statement, the jury would not be able to figure out which of these two different interpretations was intended by the speaker. The use of live testimony also makes for a more interesting presentation of evidence. It obviously makes a much more powerful statement to the jury to have the grieving parent testify about how her murdered child died in her arms rather than just having the jury read about it in a report.

In this chapter, you will learn about the various types of witnesses, including several kinds of experts who routinely testify in criminal cases. Different rules govern the testimony of lay and expert witnesses. Experts are subjected to much closer scrutiny and stricter rules governing their testimony than are lay witnesses. Because an expert is deemed to have more knowledge of a particular subject by virtue of his training and experience, there is a very real danger that the jury could be improperly swayed or influenced by an expert's testimony. To prevent this, the judge is given the task of filtering out speculative or substandard expert testimony.

I. TYPES OF WITNESSES

Witness
someone who has personal knowledge about some fact in the case based on his observations of an incident or relationship with the people involved in that incident

A **witness** is someone who has personal knowledge about some fact in the case based on his observations of an incident or relationship with the people involved in that incident. In other words, a witness is a person who "sees, knows, or vouches for something."[2] A person who witnesses an incident may not necessarily be called to testify about it in court. For example, 15 people may have witnessed a bar fight, but the prosecutor may decide to call only 3 of them as witnesses at trial. Witnesses ordinarily testify during the case-in-chief for each side that calls them. However, a special type of witness can be called by the prosecution, known as a **rebuttal witness**. A rebuttal witness provides testimony that is designed to contradict evidence put on by the defense during its case. His testimony is limited to the scope of the evidence introduced by the defendant. For example, a defendant may call an alibi witness to state the defendant was somewhere else at the time of the crime. The prosecution can then call a rebuttal witness to challenge the testimony of the alibi witness.

Rebuttal witness
a witness called by the prosecution to rebut or challenge some evidence put on by the defense during its case-in-chief

A. Lay Witnesses

Rule 701. Opinion Testimony by Lay Witnesses

If the witness is not testifying as an expert, the witness' testimony in the form of opinions or inferences is limited to those opinions or inferences which are (a) rationally based on the perception of the witness, and (b) helpful to a clear understanding of the witness' testimony or the determination of a fact in issue, and not based on scientific, technical, or other specialized knowledge within the scope of rule 702.

Lay witness
a witness who offers testimony based on his own personal observations or perceptions of an event and who needs no specialized training or experience to offer such testimony

Remember that witnesses are divided into two basic types: lay witnesses and expert witnesses. A **lay witness** is anyone who can provide testimony on the details and facts of the case based on his or her own personal knowledge of them. The witness needs no specialized training or experience to be able to offer such testimony. A lay witness can be anyone: a driver who witnesses a car accident, a bar patron who witnesses a fight, or a healthcare worker who can describe the nature of the victim's injuries. In some cases, a lay witness can also offer evidence of the accused's or victim's character. In other words, a lay witness provides testimony based on his ordinary perceptions and observations without having to rely on any sort of expertise to do so.

Eyewitnesses
witnesses who have personal knowledge about the case

Alibi witness
a witness who provides testimony about a defendant's alibi

Investigation witnesses
witnesses connected in some fashion to the law enforcement investigation of the case

Character witnesses
witnesses who provide background information about the defendant or other witnesses in the case

Lay witnesses can be further divided into three types: eyewitnesses, investigation witnesses, and character witnesses. **Eyewitnesses** include anyone who has personal knowledge about the commission of the crime or the circumstances surrounding the crime. An eyewitness might observe, for example, the occurrence of an accident, a robbery, or a domestic violence incident. A special type of eyewitness is an **alibi witness**. While this witness does not observe the crime, he can allegedly place the defendant at some place other than the crime scene at the time of the crime. **Investigation witnesses** include law enforcement officers who respond to the scene, as well as detectives who perform follow-up investigation. Crime scene technicians who search for and collect physical evidence are also included in this group of witnesses. **Character witnesses** are usually not connected to the criminal incident and have no personal knowledge of the incident itself. Instead, they help provide background information about the case as well as giving the jury a picture of the defendant or victim. Friends and family members are the most common types of character witnesses. The various types of witnesses are listed in Table 9.1.

Admissibility of lay witness testimony is governed by Federal Rules 602 and 701. Under Rule 602, a witness must have personal knowledge of the events or facts that he is testifying to. This simply means that the witness must have observed the events or heard the statements that he testifies about. For example, a person could not testify about an auto accident if he did not actually witness it but only heard about it on the news.

TABLE 9.1   TYPES OF WITNESSES

- **Lay witness:** a person whose testimony does not depend on specialized training, education, or experience
  - ○ **Eyewitness:** someone who personally observes a criminal act or the events leading up to it
  - ○ **Alibi witness:** a person who attests to the fact that the defendant was in a different location at the time the crime was alleged to have occurred
  - ○ **Character witness:** a person who testifies about another's character traits or reputation
  - ○ **Investigation witness:** a witness who testifies about the law enforcement investigation or independent investigation of the case

- **Expert witness:** a witness qualified by training, education, or experience to provide a scientific, technical, or other specialized opinion about the facts or evidence

- **Rebuttal witness:** a witness who attempts to contradict testimony presented by a previous witness

Unlike experts, lay witnesses may give opinions only under certain circumstances. Under Rule 701, opinions of lay witnesses are limited to those that are "rationally based on the perception of a witness."[3] Perception is not limited to just what is actually observed by the witness but includes information obtained from all five senses.[4] Perception is "an observation, awareness or realization, usually based on physical sensation or experience."[5] The Third Circuit offered the following explanation of lay witness opinion testimony:

> The prototypical example of the type of evidence contemplated by the adoption of Rule 701 relates to the appearance of persons or things, identity, the manner of conduct, competency of a person, degrees of light or darkness, sound, size, weight, distance, and an endless number of items that cannot be described factually in words apart from inferences.... Other examples of this type of quintessential Rule 701 testimony include description of an individual, the speed of a vehicle, the mental state or responsibility of another, whether another was healthy, the value of one's property and other situations in which the difference between fact and opinion blur....[6]

Even though a lay witness may not have previously experienced or observed the type of situation he is testifying about, he is allowed to give opinions and inferences that a "normal person would form on the basis of the facts he observed and on what he heard."[7] For example, a witness can offer a conclusion that the defendant ran over the victim's body even though he had not previously witnessed such an occurrence.

Practical Example

Assume that the defendant is on trial for driving while under the influence of alcohol. The defendant allegedly ran off the road and crashed into a fence several hundred feet from the road. Assume a homeowner in the area observed the defendant to be belligerent, slurring his words, and stumbling about when he got out of the vehicle. Can this homeowner offer an opinion as to the defendant's state of intoxication at the time of the accident? Yes. This witness can offer an opinion as to the defendant's state of intoxication, since this opinion is based on the witness's observation of the defendant and everyday perceptions. In other words, it would not take any specialized training or experience to offer an opinion as to whether the defendant was intoxicated.

Now assume in the above example that the defendant claims that his vehicle was malfunctioning at the time of the accident and that is what caused him to run off the road. The defendant attempts to call a friend of his who is a mechanic as a witness. He wants the mechanic to testify that in his opinion the motor vehicle was experiencing a brake problem at the time of the accident. Can the auto mechanic testify to his opinion as a lay witness? No. Unless he is endorsed as an expert witness, the witness would not be allowed to offer an opinion as a lay witness because it requires specialized training and experience to determine whether a car was in fact experiencing a brake problem at the time of the accident. Therefore, the mechanic would only be allowed to testify as to his examination of the car but not give an opinion as to his findings or conclusions.

B. Expert Witnesses

Rule 702. Testimony by Experts

If scientific, technical, or other specialized knowledge will assist the trier of fact to understand the evidence or to determine a fact in issue, the witness qualified as an expert by knowledge, skill, experience, training, or education, may testify thereto in the form of an opinion or otherwise, if (1) the testimony is based upon sufficient facts or data, (2) the testimony is the product of reliable principles and methods, and (3) the witness has applied the principles and methods reliably to the facts of the case.

Expert witness
a witness who is qualified to give an opinion based on specialized training and experience that is outside the realm of most ordinary people

Expert witnesses are witnesses whose testimony is based on some specialized training or experience that is necessary to forming a given opinion or conclusion. As a result, expert witnesses possess knowledge about a given subject that ordinary lay people do not have. For example, a lay person could not testify that blunt force trauma to the head was the cause of death in a murder case. The witness would need training as a

Figure 9.1
Dr. Kevin Beir holds up a CAT scan, detailing the injuries of sniper victim Caroline Seawell, while testifying as an expert in a Virginia Beach courtroom on October 28, 2003. John Allen Muhammed, the D.C. sniper, was convicted. © 2003 Adrin Snider/Pool/CNP/ Corbis

medical doctor and a forensic pathologist before being able to make that determination and offer a useful opinion to the jury. See Figure 9.1 for an example of an expert testifying.

1. Types of Experts

Forensic evidence is playing an increasingly large role in criminal cases, and much of this evidence is admitted in the form of expert testimony. Expert testimony in criminal cases can be broken down into two basic categories: that based in hard sciences, such as medicine, biology, and chemistry, and that based more on the experience of the examiner, such as firearms and fingerprint identification. Experts are commonly used in criminal cases to establish an element of the crime. A few of the more common types of experts are detailed in Table 9.2.

2. Preliminary Screening of the Admissibility of Expert Testimony

a. The Trial Judge's Gatekeeping Function

Because expert testimony can be so persuasive to a jury, the trial judge has an obligation to screen out testimony that does not meet minimum standards of admissibility. For example, a witness may be unqualified to testify as an expert on a given topic. In other instances, an expert could have used "junk science" in arriving at his conclusions or used a theory or technique that is so new that there has not been sufficient time to adequately test the reliability of it. In either case, the conclusions reached by the expert may be too speculative to admit into evidence. To prevent such testimony from improperly influencing a jury, the trial judge must screen it prior to trial and determine whether the jury will be able to hear it. Before admitting expert testimony at trial, therefore, the trial judge acts as a **"gatekeeper"** and must find that the proffered expert testimony is competent, relevant, and reliable.[8]

Gatekeeper
the role of a trial judge to screen out expert testimony that does not meet minimum standards of relevancy or reliability

TABLE 9.2   TYPES OF EXPERTS UTILIZED IN CRIMINAL CASES

Scientific Experts

- Biologists who testify about DNA analysis or identification of other biological fluids, such as blood, semen, and saliva
- Chemists who conduct tests to identify drugs and other unknown substances
- Entomologists who identify the link between insect activity found on the body and the stage of decay
- Toxicologists who measure alcohol, drug, and poison levels in the human body
- Anthropologists who identify and reconstruct human remains

Medical Experts

- Doctors and nurses who testify about injuries sustained by victims and their causes
- Forensic pathologists (medical examiners or coroners) who testify about the cause and manner of death of the victim and any findings from an autopsy

Psychological Experts

- Psychiatrists or psychologists who provide testimony as to the mental condition of a defendant or victim

Social Work Experts

- Social workers and victim advocates who testify about general reactions of rape, domestic violence, and child abuse victims
- Child forensic interviewers (specially trained police officers and social workers) who interview child victims of abuse and sexual assault.

Comparison Experts

- Handwriting analysts who compare handwriting samples of suspects to forensic items such as ransom notes
- Hair and fiber analysts who compare hair and fiber samples found at the crime scene to standard samples taken from suspects
- Forensic odontologists who identify remains through dental records or compare bitemarks found on the victim to the suspect's teeth

Reconstruction Experts

- Crime scene reconstructionists who recreate crime scenes and prepare computerized crime scene diagrams
- Accident reconstructionists who recreate automobile accidents using crash data and prepare computerized models

At this stage of the proceeding, the judge should not determine whether the expert's conclusions are correct (this is the job of the jury) but merely determine whether his findings and conclusions rest upon good scientific grounds. Disputes as to the strength of an expert's credentials, faults in the way a particular methodology was carried out, or a lack of authority for an opinion go to the weight, not the admissibility, of an expert's testimony. The gatekeeping function of a trial court is thus confined to "keeping out unreliable [or irrelevant] expert testimony, not to assessing the weight of the testimony."[9] Simply because there is a dispute amongst the experts as to which methodology should be used or what conclusions can be drawn from the evidence, the judge should not settle the dispute for the jury by excluding the less-convincing expert. As a result, if the expert is competent, his opinions are relevant, and his methodology is reliable, the jury should be permitted to hear an expert's testimony.

i. The Expert Must Be Competent

In exercising this gatekeeping function, the judge must first determine whether the expert is competent—i.e., that he is qualified to render an opinion on the subject matter of his testimony. Even if the expert has impressive credentials and education, the witness's expertise must relate to the subject of his testimony. For example, if the expert is a medical doctor, he may not necessarily be qualified to give an opinion about whether a defendant suffers from a rare heart condition.

Practical Example

John is on trial for murder. He hires an expert to review the findings of the prosecution's DNA evidence. He will offer an opinion that the DNA lab did not use proper safeguards to prevent contamination and therefore claims the results are not reliable. The expert is trained in laboratory procedures and contamination practices generally. He is not a molecular biologist and has no experience with actually extracting DNA profiles. The prosecution challenges the expert as incompetent to testify on the issue of the reliability of the profiles. The judge should grant the motion at least in part. While the expert may be allowed to testify about laboratory practices and quality control in general, he should not be allowed to make any conclusions about the specific results achieved in this case.

ii. The Testimony Must Be Relevant

Second, the judge must determine whether the expert's testimony is relevant—in other words, whether it would actually assist the judge or the jury. There must be a connection or "fit" between the scientific or technical research being presented and a disputed factual issue in the case.[10] Thus, the judge should assess "whether the reasoning or methodology underlying the testimony is scientifically valid and whether that reasoning or methodology properly can be applied to the facts at issue."[11] For example, if an expert is going to conduct an experiment to replicate the occurrence of an event in the case, then the experiment must have a "substantial similarity" to the circumstances of the incident in question.[12]

The court should also exclude testimony as irrelevant if it is unnecessary. A witness should not be endorsed as an expert if his opinion is based on information within the common understanding of most lay people. The Seventh Circuit noted that if this were not the case, "the expert at best is offering a gratuitous opinion, and at worst is exerting undue influence on the jury."[13] For example, it is not necessary to have an expert testify that a small woman would not deliver as much force by striking blows with her fists as would a man weighing 400 pounds. This fact is within the common understanding of most people. Thus, if the expert testimony merely duplicates knowledge within the grasp of everyday laymen or is simply a conclusory statement, the judge should exclude it. However, if the judge determines that the expert testimony would be helpful and relevant with respect to an issue in the case, the court should not exclude the testimony just because it may cover matters that are within the average person's comprehension.[14]

Practical Example

Suzy is being tried for driving under the influence of drugs. She hires an expert to testify that Suzy could not have been under the influence of a drug, given the low levels found in her system after arrest. He will also testify that given the time of night and her tired condition, sleep deprivation would mimic some of the effects of being under the influence. Is the testimony relevant? Although an expert is not needed to tell the jury that sleep deprivation could mimic signs of intoxication, the remainder of the testimony is helpful and necessary and should not be stricken. Thus, the court should admit the entire opinion of the expert.

3. The Testimony Must Be Based on Reliable Methodology

Finally, the judge must determine if the expert has used reliable methodology as a basis for reaching his conclusions. Expert testimony is considered to be reliable if: (1) "the expert testimony is based upon sufficient facts or data; (2) the testimony is the product of reliable principles and methods; and (3) the expert applied the principles and methods reliably to the facts of the case."[15] Thus, the trial court should "undertake a rigorous examination of the facts on which the expert relies, the method by which the expert draws an opinion from those facts, and how the expert applies the facts and methods to the case at hand."[16]

Evaluating the reliability of the technique or method used by the expert is particularly important where the expert has used a new or novel technique in his analysis. New or novel techniques can be unreliable, particularly if they have not been subject to rigorous review or replication testing. Two tests are primarily relied upon by courts in making this determination.

a. *Frye* Test

Frye test

a test for the admission of new or novel scientific evidence that requires the expert to have used a scientific technique that is generally accepted in the scientific community

Prior to the adoption of the Rules of Evidence, admission of expert testimony relating to novel scientific evidence was governed by the **Frye test**. The test originated in a 1923 court case, *Frye v. United States*,[17] which held that expert testimony about novel scientific evidence was admissible only if the proponent could show that the theory and methods used by the expert to form his opinions were generally accepted within the relevant scientific community.[18] The court rejected the admission of polygraph evidence since polygraphs had not gained general acceptance at that point.

The adoption of Rule 702 in 1975 called into question the continued viability of the *Frye* test, however. Rule 702 provides that if "scientific, technical, or other specialized knowledge will assist the trier of fact to understand the evidence or to determine a fact in issue, a witness qualified as an expert by knowledge, skill, experience, training, or education, may testify thereto in the form of an opinion or otherwise."[19] There is no mention of the technique needing to be generally accepted in order for it to be admissible under the Rule.

b. *Daubert* Test

Daubert test

a test for the admission of expert testimony that requires the judge to evaluate the reliability of a scientific theory or technique relied upon by an expert, using various factors, not just whether it is generally accepted

In 1993, the Supreme Court held in *Daubert v. Merrell Dow Pharmaceuticals, Inc.* that Rule 702 had, in fact, superseded the *Frye* standard. There, the Supreme Court held that the trial judge needed to make a preliminary determination of whether the reasoning or methodology of the expert was scientifically valid and set out a range of factors that needed to be considered in determining the admissibility of expert testimony.[20] These **Daubert** factors include (1) whether the theory or technique in question has been or can be tested; (2) whether it has been subjected to peer review and publication; (3) its potential error rate; (4) the existence and maintenance of standards controlling the technique's operation; and (5) whether the theory or method has been generally accepted by the scientific community.[21] The Court also held that an expert's opinion will not be permitted if there is "too great an analytical gap" between the experimental data and the opinion of the expert.[22]

The Supreme Court's interpretation of Rule 702 is both more liberal and more conservative than the *Frye* test. It is more liberal because the trial judge may now admit expert testimony that is based on reliable scientific methods that are on the cutting edge of scientific theory, not just those that are already established and, thus, generally accepted. However, it can also be more restrictive in the sense that the trial judge must now determine whether the expert's conclusions are based on reliable methodology and whether that testimony is relevant to the case at hand.

Practical Example

Assume that the defendant is charged with killing his wife. The defendant offers a defense that he was suffering from a mental illness at the time of the killing. He endorses an expert witness to testify that he is suffering from an illness known as chronic life stress. The expert is a psychiatrist and has authored two papers on the subject of this new illness. This new theory has not been subject to peer review, nor has it been generally accepted by the psychiatric community. The theory essentially relies on the fact that patients exhibit symptoms similar to posttraumatic stress disorder yet have not experienced any traumatic event in their life. The two papers have been published in the publication of the clinic where the doctor works. The doctor offers testimony exclusively for defendants and has not been hired by the prosecution. Should the court admit this novel psychiatric theory, or should it exclude it? The court should exclude the theory under either test. It should be excluded under the Frye test because it has not been generally accepted by other psychologists. It should also be excluded under Daubert because the method relied on by the expert is unreliable. His theory has not been subject to peer review, it was published in trade journal of his own clinic, and the doctor appears to be a hired gun. Thus, this testimony is missing key components of reliability that the court must look for in exercising its gatekeeping function.

4. *Daubert* Hearing

Daubert hearing
a pretrial hearing to assess the qualifications of an expert witness and whether that expert used reliable methodology in reaching his conclusions

If the qualifications or the reliability of the expert's methodology are challenged, then the court must decide whether to hold a hearing (often referred to as a ***Daubert* hearing**) to determine these issues prior to trial. Any number of questions can arise about forensic testimony in a criminal case, including the expert's qualifications, the adequacy of the sample tested, the procedures used to collect and preserve it, and the reliability of the technique used to analyze the evidence.[23] This hearing can be quite lengthy since the court has to hear testimony about the particular technique in question and how the expert applied it in that case.

The general rule is that a *Daubert* hearing will be held where the courts in that jurisdiction have not previously ruled on the reliability of the technique in question. Once the reliability of a technique is well-established, the court can take judicial notice of it, rather than holding a hearing.[24] For example, the use of radar guns by police to measure vehicle speed has become so commonplace that trial courts simply take judicial notice of the science behind their effectiveness. Testimony about radar is routinely admitted in speeding cases as long as the officer can show that his radar gun was properly tuned and calibrated and that he was qualified to operate the device.

Practical Example

Assume that the defendant is a firefighter, that he is accused of starting fires, and that he is being tried in federal court. The defendant gives notice of an insanity defense and plans to introduce expert testimony on the question of whether he was able to appreciate the nature and quality of the wrongfulness of his acts (the elements of the insanity defense). The defendant hires a psychologist who diagnoses him with Klinefelter's syndrome, a psychological disorder that diminishes frontal lobe function and decision-making capability. Since this syndrome has not been admitted in this jurisdiction before, the court would have to conduct a hearing as to the admissibility of this testimony if the prosecution objects to its reliability. The psychologist administered a battery of standardized tests to measure the defendant's cognitive functions and intelligence and relied on one study that shows a link between Klinefelter's and fire setting. The study and techniques relied upon by the expert have not been subject to peer review, and this theory is not generally accepted by most psychologists. The expert also failed to account for the obvious alternative explanation that the defendant started fires in order to get a promotion or because of the fact that he was paid more when fighting fires. The fact that the psychologist administered a battery of standardized tests to measure the defendant's cognitive functions and intelligence suggests that the expert's theory can be tested. However, given that there is only one study that shows a link between Klinefelter's syndrome with insanity and fire setting, this information is not enough to conclude that it is statistically likely that such patients will set fires or even that they do not appreciate the wrongfulness of their acts. The fact that this theory has not been subject to peer review also weighs against the admissibility of the evidence. The expert's failure to account for alternative explanations also weighs against admitting his testimony. On balance, the court would likely rule that the proposed testimony is inadmissible.

5. Other Technical Expertise

The court's gatekeeping function does not apply to just scientific evidence, however. The Supreme Court ruled in *Kumho Tire v. Carmichael* that expert testimony that is based on specialized experience and training (such as the testimony by a handwriting examiner that two signatures match) should not be treated more permissively by the court simply because it is outside the realm of hard science.[25] Rather, nonscientific expert testimony should receive the same degree of scrutiny from the judge and is admissible (just as scientific evidence is) as long as it is based on reliable principles and methods.[26] The Court concluded that the key question is whether the expert has used "the same level of intellectual rigor that characterizes the practice of an expert in the relevant field."[27]

Practical Example

The prosecution attempts to introduce expert testimony based on bitemark identification. The procedure does not rely on scientific principles but instead relies on the experience of the forensic odontologist in making the comparison and interpreting the results. The odontologist has testified in several prior cases and has made hundreds of identifications in the past. The trial court should not simply admit the evidence on the basis that the examiner is qualified. It must determine whether the technique rests on reliable principles and whether the dentist accurately performed the identification in this case. Unless the court is convinced about the reliability of the identification, it should not admit the evidence.

6. How Widespread Is the Use of the *Daubert* Test?

The *Daubert* test applies to the admissibility of expert testimony in all federal courts and some state courts. However, some states still use the *Frye* test. Currently, 28 states have adopted the *Daubert* test or a similar approach to assessing the reliability of expert testimony.[28] Twelve states still apply the *Frye* test in some manner. Six others have not completely rejected the *Frye* test but apply the *Daubert* factors in making a determination of whether to admit expert testimony. Four states do not use either the *Daubert* or *Frye* test but instead have developed their own unique tests. For example, Utah admits expert testimony if it is "inherently reliable."[29] See Figure 9.2 for a breakdown of states that have adopted the *Daubert* standard and that still use the *Frye* test.

Figure 9.2

States that have adopted either the Frye or Daubert test. States shaded in blue have adopted the Daubert test, while states shaded in red still use the Frye test. States shaded in green apply some of the Daubert factors. Finally, states shaded in yellow use their own unique test.

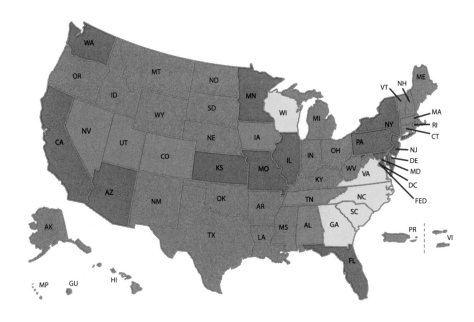

National Academy of Sciences report on forensic science

a national report which was critical of many aspects of the state of forensic science across the United States. The report made several recommendations to improve the scientific underpinning of several forensic disciplines

7. Applicability of *Daubert* to Particular Types of Expert Testimony

The importance of the judge's gatekeeper role under *Daubert* is highlighted by the **National Academy of Sciences report on forensic science**. The report identified several issues that currently confront the forensic science community, including wide disparities and inconsistencies in the operation of laboratories at various law enforcement levels, a lack of mandatory certification and accreditation standards, and issues relating to interpretation of evidence.[30]

EVIDENCE IN ACTION

National Academy of Sciences Report on Forensic Science

In 2005, Congress authorized the National Academy of Sciences (NAS) to create a forensic science committee to study issues relevant to that community. Among other things, the committee was instructed to assess the future resource needs in forensic science, identify potential scientific advances for assisting law enforcement, and disseminate best practices for the collection and analysis of forensic evidence.[31] After extensive research and testimony, the committee released a report in 2009 entitled *Strengthening Forensic Science in the United States: A Path Forward.*[32]

The committee concluded that "the law's greatest dilemma in its heavy reliance on forensic evidence, however, concerns the question of whether—and to what extent—there is *science* in any given forensic science discipline."[33] It identified two questions that should be the court's focus in determining whether to admit expert testimony: (1) the extent to which a particular forensic discipline is founded on a reliable scientific methodology that gives it the capacity to accurately analyze evidence and report findings and (2) the extent to which practitioners in a particular forensic discipline rely on human interpretation that could be tainted by error, the threat of bias, or the absence of sound operational procedures and robust performance standards.[34]

The report was particularly critical of both the forensic community and the courts for failing to develop an adequate set of standards to assess the reliability of an expert's conclusions.[35] Although noting that some problems still exist with respect to standardization, independence, and training in the hard sciences, the committee concluded that analytically based disciplines such as DNA testing hold a "notable edge" over those fields that are based on the experience and interpretation of the examiner.[36] Unlike DNA testing, the authors noted that many other forensic disciplines lack the necessary scientific research to establish adequate standards of reliability.[37] The committee criticized the routine admission of comparison evidence such as fingerprint and toolmark identification despite "any meaningful scientific validation, determination of error rates, or reliability testing to explain the limits of the discipline."[38]

The committee found that one explanation for this problem is that courts have been reluctant to exercise their review powers under *Daubert* in criminal cases. Where challenges to expert testimony are taken seriously, courts have mainly relied on past precedent, rather than on a stringent analysis of the expert's methods, to determine admissibility. The NAS report noted that "many [forensic science] techniques have been relied on for so long that courts might be reluctant to rethink their role in the trial process."[39] For example, while expressing his belief that toolmark identification

evidence "ought not to be considered admissible under *Daubert*," a district court judge described his dilemma:

> I reluctantly [admit the evidence] because of my confidence that any other decision will be rejected by appellate courts... The more courts admit this type of toolmark evidence without requiring documentation, proficiency testing, or evidence of reliability, the more sloppy practices will endure; we should require more.[40]

Defendants also often lack the resources to adequately challenge forensic evidence. The NAS report noted that the results of *Daubert* challenges almost always favor the prosecution. In a 2000 study of federal appellate decisions, the prosecution defeated a defense challenge to one of its experts in 61 of 67 cases. Conversely, defendants lost 44 of the 54 challenges prosecutors made to their proffered experts.[41] One commentator explained the situation this way:

> Unlike the extremely well-litigated civil challenges, a criminal defendant's challenge is usually perfunctory. Even when the most vulnerable forensic sciences—hair microscopy, bite marks, and handwriting—are attacked, the courts routinely affirm admissibility citing earlier decisions rather than facts established at the hearing. Defense lawyers generally fail to build a challenge with appropriate witnesses and new data. Thus, even if inclined to mount a *Daubert* challenge, they lack the requisite knowledge and skills, as well as the funds, to succeed.[42]

These shortfalls are highlighted in another recent study by Brandon Garrett and Peter Neufeld, which examined the effects of invalid forensic testimony in cases of wrongful convictions. The authors looked at cases where defendants had been exonerated by DNA evidence after their conviction at trial, usually for sexual assault offenses. They reported that in 60 percent of wrongful convictions, one or more forensic analysts called by the prosecution provided invalid testimony at trial in some form—that is, testimony that misstated data or was wholly unsupported by the data.[43] Prosecutors often magnified errors of the analysts, exaggerating the evidence's probative value beyond levels that even the analysts themselves had claimed.[44]

Continued on following page

Evidence in Action continued

The study also examined how courts monitored the expert's interpretation and reporting of his findings. Courts rarely reviewed the actual testimony of an expert once he had been permitted to take the witness stand,[45] yet errant testimony was provided by serologists and hair analysts 57 and 38 percent of the time, respectively.[46] One notable example given by the authors was the testimony of a forensic serologist in a rape case. He testified that the defendant and the rapist possessed the same B blood type, a type shared by only 11 percent of white males. What the analyst did not tell the jury was that the victim was also type B and that her fluids were mixed in the sample. Therefore, her blood type markers could have overwhelmed or masked those from the rapist. As a result, the testimony was misleading because no percentage of the population could have been eliminated as a suspect, given the mixture of blood types.[47]

Both studies concluded that these problems can be corrected only by national regulation and oversight of the forensic science community. As one jaundiced commentator noted, "clinical laboratories must meet higher standards to be allowed to diagnose strep throat than forensic labs must meet to put a defendant on death row."[48] The NAS Committee made 13 recommendations to improve the forensic science community that are briefly summarized below:

(1) The creation of the National Institute of Forensic Science to establish and enforce best practices for forensic science professionals and laboratories.

(2) The establishment of standard terminology to be used in reporting on and testifying about the results of forensic science investigations.

(3) The funding of peer-reviewed research to establish and demonstrate the validity of forensic methods, the development and establishment of quantifiable measures of reliability and accuracy of forensic analysis,

and the development of quantifiable measures of uncertainty in the conclusions of forensic analyses.

(4) The removal of all public forensic laboratories and facilities from the administrative control of law enforcement agencies or prosecutors' offices.

(5) To increase research on bias and error in forensic examinations.

(6) The establishment of protocols for forensic examinations, methods, and practices.

(7) The accreditation of forensic laboratories and certification of individual forensic science professionals should become mandatory.

(8) The establishment of routine quality assurance and quality control procedures to ensure the accuracy of forensic analyses in the work of forensic practitioners.

(9) The establishment of a national code of ethics for all forensic science disciplines.

(10) The development of graduate education programs in forensic science disciplines.

(11) The replacement of existing coroner systems with medical examiner systems as well as the development of national standards for forensic pathology and death investigation.

(12) The development of standards for fingerprint comparison and the facilitation of sharing of fingerprint data among law enforcement agencies at all levels.

(13) To provide funding for the managing and analysis of evidence from events that affect homeland security.[49]

The American Society of Crime Laboratory Directors (ASCLD) reacted positively to the report and echoed the recommendations for better standardization and resources for local crime labs. It encouraged lab personnel to embrace the changes and to prepare for the inevitable focus on the science behind many forensic disciplines.[50]

Courts have applied varying degrees of scrutiny to forensic evidence since the *Daubert* decision was announced. For the most part (with some notable exceptions), courts have typically admitted expert testimony in criminal cases. Let's look at how courts have handled the admission of various types of forensic testimony to date.

a. DNA Evidence

DNA evidence has now become one of the major tools for identifying criminal suspects. It has been used since the late 1980s in criminal cases to link suspects to crime scenes.

DNA profiling occurs in four stages. First, DNA is extracted or isolated from a biological sample. It is then amplified during a process known as **polymerase chain reaction** (PCR). A DNA profile or sequence is then developed and compared to a profile from a known suspect. If the suspect's profile matches the crime scene profile, the examiner must calculate the probability of a different individual having the same DNA profile.[51] Scientists are able to take advantage of the fact that human DNA contains variable, short, repeating sequences (short tandem repeats [STRs]) that occur at the same location in everyone's DNA.[52] The variations at those locations allow scientists to develop DNA profiles that can then be compared to one another and exclude or include a person as the source of a crime scene sample. See Figure 9.3 for an example of how DNA profiles of suspects can be compared to a DNA profile retrieved from a crime scene.

According to the NAS report, DNA analysis is scientifically sound for a number of reasons: there are biological reasons for individual differences; the chances of two people having a matching profile at all locations is extremely small; the probabilities of false-positive identifications has been quantified; the laboratory procedures are well specified and subject to validation and proficiency testing; and there are clear and repeatable standards for analysis, interpretation, and reporting.[53] DNA analysis has also been subjected to more scrutiny and testing than other forensic science disciplines.

Ironically, DNA profiling is the one forensic science technique that has been subject to the most rigorous review by courts. It survived numerous *Daubert* challenges in the 1990s, and courts have universally concluded that DNA profiling satisfies the reliability requirements under rule 702.[54] By way of example, one federal court concluded that DNA identification evidence was admissible because the process was capable of verification, it had been subject to peer review, the error rate was insignificant, and the FBI laboratory maintained high standards.[55] State courts that still adhere to the *Frye* standard have also found that DNA testing satisfies the *Frye*

DNA profiling

a scientific process by which the DNA sequence at given locations in a forensic DNA profile is compared to the same locations in a known suspect's DNA profile

Polymerase chain reaction

a method of DNA amplification commonly used in preparing forensic DNA profiles

Figure 9.3

Partial DNA profiles of two suspects are compared to the DNA profile obtained from a crime scene. The figure compares the profiles at three STR locations on the DNA known as loci (a full profile would contain 13 loci). Each locus contains two peaks since chromosomes come in pairs. In the figure, Suspect #1 has been excluded as the source and Suspect #2 has been included. *Figure courtesy of Colorado Bureau of Investigation.*

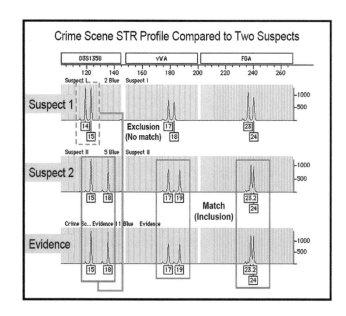

test since methods such as PCR analysis have been generally accepted by the scientific community.[56] As a result, courts today for the most part do not conduct *Daubert* hearings on the reliability of DNA testing itself but instead simply take judicial notice of it.[57]

However, this does not mean that DNA evidence should be automatically admitted. New techniques are constantly being developed. The reliability of such new techniques may not be as well established as traditional extraction and amplification techniques. The court must also determine whether the individual examiner is qualified to give an opinion as well as whether he properly performed the analysis.[58] Therefore, a *Daubert* hearing may need to be conducted to resolve one or more of these issues.

b. Friction Ridge Analysis and Fingerprint Identification

Friction ridge analysis is the technique used to identify fingerprints, palm prints, and sole prints. It shares similarities with other experience-based methods of pattern recognition, such as footwear and tire impressions, toolmarks, and handwriting analysis. The field of **friction ridge identification** rests on two basic premises: that each person's fingerprints are unique and that the pattern of a person's prints does not change over time.[59]

The technique used to examine prints is known as ACE-V, which stands for analysis, comparison, evaluation, and verification. The process begins with an analysis of the unknown (crime scene) print. If the print does not have sufficient detail to permit either an identification

Friction ridge identification

the process of comparing details in the friction ridge patterns of a forensic sample to those found in an impression obtained from a known suspect or an exclusion, the examiner does not complete the remainder of the process. If there is sufficient detail in the latent print, the examiner begins the rest of the process. The comparison phase consists of examining the details between the comparable areas of the known print and unknown print. The overall shape of the print, ridge flows and numbers, and the location of minutiae (ridge endings, bifurcations, etc.) are examined during this process. The examiner then performs an evaluation by determining the agreement of the friction ridge formations between the two prints and the sufficiency of the detail present to establish an identification. If there are details that do not agree between the two prints, the print is excluded as being a match. If a sufficient number of friction ridge details are found to agree between the known print and the unknown print, the examiner can conclude that the prints are a match. Finally, verification occurs when another qualified examiner confirms the conclusions of the first.[60] See Figure 9.4 for examples of ridge details identified in a fingerprint.

Other than this general framework, there is no set protocol for conducting friction ridge analysis. There are no specific measurement criteria, and each examiner selects the particular features to be compared. There is also no agreement on the specific number of details that must be in agreement before the examiner can declare a match.[61] Since statistical probabilities for how frequently certain friction ridge details appear in the population have not been developed, definitive estimates of the probability that two prints match cannot be given.[62] In its report, the NAS cautioned that "uniqueness does not guarantee that prints from two different people are always sufficiently different that they cannot be confused, or that two impressions made by the same finger will also be sufficiently similar to be discerned as coming from the same source."[63] It also urged fingerprint examiners to document in more detail their findings and methodology in making fingerprint comparisons.[64]

Figure 9.4
Several ridge details are identified in an inked fingerprint, including a bifurcation, an ending ridge, and a dot. *Photo courtesy of Colorado Bureau of Investigation.*

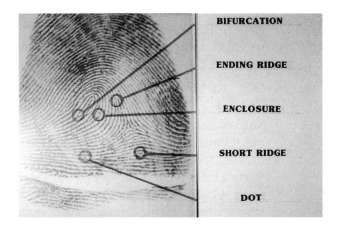

BIFURCATION

ENDING RIDGE

ENCLOSURE

SHORT RIDGE

DOT

Despite the need for more research into the reliability of fingerprint analysis, examiners often testify that the error rate in making fingerprint comparisons is essentially zero and express their conclusions in terms of absolute certainty.[65] This led one commentator to conclude such claims are unjustified:

> Given the general lack of validity testing for fingerprinting; the relative dearth of difficult proficiency tests; the lack of a statistically valid model of fingerprinting; and the lack of validated standards for declaring a match, such claims of absolute, certain confidence and identification are unjustified.... Claims of "absolute" and "positive" identification should be replaced by more modest claims about the meaning and significance of a "match."[66]

Defendants face an uphill battle, however, if they challenge the reliability of identifications offered by fingerprint examiners. Identification evidence based on fingerprint comparison was first admitted in 1911 and has been universally accepted since. Courts have been reluctant to buck that trend, even in the face of growing concern that fingerprint identification testimony may lack sufficient scientific reliability.[67]

A couple of cases decided since the release of the NAS report are illustrative of this point. While recognizing some of the weaknesses inherent in fingerprint examination, a federal district court in Maryland admitted fingerprint identification testimony without a *Daubert* hearing.[68] The court concluded that the ACE-V methodology is sufficiently reliable since it is generally accepted in the relevant scientific community and has a very low incidence of misidentification.[69] Similarly, the Tenth Circuit upheld the admission of fingerprint identification testimony in *United States v. Baines*.[70] Although noting that the reliability of fingerprint identification has not been tested as rigorously as it might have been, the court found that it has been sufficiently tested in real-world situations to be proven accurate. It found that while the error rate and chance of misidentification were likely higher than that testified to by the FBI examiner (as zero or almost zero), the actual rate was still "impressively low."[71] While recognizing that better research as to the reliability of fingerprinting would be "all to the good," the court refused to postpone use of fingerprinting until such research is developed because it would be to "make the best the enemy of the good."[72]

c. Firearms Identification

Firearms identification
the matching of bullets and cartridge casings to particular firearms based on the idea that the machining and wear of firearm barrels and other parts is unique

The discipline of **firearms identification** is one of the oldest forensic disciplines and most commonly performed analyses by forensic labs. As detailed in Chapter 2, the matching of bullets and cartridge casings to particular firearms is based on the idea that the machining and wear of firearm barrels and other parts is unique. The examiner can compare the microscopic striations on the bullet or cartridge casing recovered from the crime scene with those found on test-fired rounds. If a sufficient amount of marks correspond between the unknown round and the test round, the examiner can then declare a match.

While testimony by firearms examiners has been routinely admitted by courts, the NAS report found that the examination of firearms and other toolmarks remains a "subjective decision based on unarticulated standards and no statistical foundation for estimation of error rates."[73] For example, the Association of Firearm and Tool Mark Examiners issued a theory of identification that states that an examiner may offer an opinion that two sets of toolmarks have a common origin when "sufficient agreement" exists between the patterns of surface contours. Sufficient agreement is said to exist between the two toolmarks when "the agreement is of a quantity and quality that the likelihood another tool could have made the mark is so remote as to be considered a practical impossibility."[74] The accuracy of the match is thus highly dependent on the training and experience of the individual examiner. To be fair, the rate of misidentifications appears to be quite low based on the published results of several proficiency studies.[75] Some examiners also use a more rigorous set of matching criteria that requires that a minimum number of consecutive matching striae must be present before declaring a match.[76]

As a result of these variations, the NAS found that a specific protocol needs to be developed to guide examiners through the identification process and that a significant amount of research is needed to scientifically determine "the degree to which firearms-related toolmarks are unique."[77] In response to those concerns outlined in the NAS report, the Scientific Working Group for Firearms and Toolmarks (SWGGUN) recently issued a set of requirements and recommendations for the performance of firearms identification. It blamed past errors on unethical examiners or those who had received inadequate training, noting that the conclusions of examiners are "accurate when appropriate methods are followed by a competent examiner."[78] To ensure consistent findings and conclusions are made by examiners in the future, SWGGUN recommended that labs institute a comprehensive training program for all examiners, in conjunction with the development of a comprehensive quality-assurance program. The cornerstone of this program is the development of standardized procedures for the examination, documentation, and reporting of firearm and toolmark evidence.[79]

Subsequent to the NAS report, a number of appeals were filed, challenging the reliability of firearms examination. Courts largely rejected these challenges, finding that the AFTE theory of identification satisfied the *Daubert* reliability criteria.[80] However, courts have limited the scope of examiners' testimony in some instances. For example, a California federal court held that examiners could testify to the fact that their identification was held to a "reasonable degree of certainty in the ballistics field," but could not testify that a match was identified to the exclusion of all other firearms.[81] Similarly, a Massachusetts federal court found that the testimony of each individual examiner needs to be closely monitored.[82] The court noted that firearms identification is something of a blend between science and experience and found it significant that there is no set of quantitative standards for determining whether two cartridge cases were fired from the same gun.[83] Thus, the court held that before a qualified examiner is allowed to testify about firearms identification, he has to show that he has documented his results and had a second qualified examiner verify his results.[84]

d. Handwriting Analysis

Handwriting analysis
the comparison of forensic handwriting samples to handwriting samples of a known suspect based on similarities in style and grammar

Handwriting analysis is performed by comparing a known sample of handwriting to the document in question to determine if the two documents were written by the same person. To do so, an analyst will collect several contemporary samples written by the suspect as well as have him or her write several dictated exemplars. The examiner will then compare the structure and spacing of the known samples and the writer's grammar and spelling to those in the questioned document. The examiner can then testify to the likelihood that the same individual wrote both documents. This analysis is based on the premise that two individuals' handwriting is rarely identical.[85]

Expert testimony on handwriting analysis is routinely admitted by courts. In 2005, the Ninth Circuit upheld the admission of such testimony by a Secret Service expert, noting that the bulk of published research in the field indicated that handwriting was individualistic and had been subjected to peer review. Studies showed handwriting analysis to be very accurate with a low error rate.[86] The court also found it important that the Secret Service required each analyst's conclusion to be confirmed by a second examiner.

Criticisms of the reliability of handwriting examination have recently surfaced, however. A federal district court noted that the reliability of the technique is suspect since there is no set specific number of characteristics that an examiner has to find before declaring that a positive match has been made. The court also noted that the examiner in that case was not subject to blind proficiency testing. As a result, it concluded that handwriting analysis testimony lacked the validity and reliability of other forensic disciplines and excluded testimony that the samples matched.[87] Many of these same criticisms were noted by the NAS report on forensic science.[88] While recognizing that the discipline "has some value," the committee recommended that the scientific basis for handwriting comparisons be strengthened.[89]

e. Polygraph Evidence

Polygraph
a machine that detects physiological responses to questions such as respiration rate, blood pressure, and pulse rate

A lie detector or **polygraph** is a machine that detects physiological responses to questions such as respiration rate, blood pressure, and pulse rate.[90] The examiner asks a series of control questions to establish a base rate. The examiner will typically ask a control question that the subject is instructed to lie to or is intended to elicit a probable lie.[91] The examiner then asks questions about the alleged incident and measures any changes in the subject's baseline rates.

Prior to the 1980s, most courts categorically excluded polygraph evidence to show that a person is being truthful or untruthful because it was not based on a generally accepted scientific theory under the *Frye* test.[92] However, as courts have reconsidered the admissibility of polygraph evidence after *Daubert*, some have adopted a more flexible approach.[93] All but two circuits now permit polygraph evidence on a case-by-case basis, admitting it pursuant to a stipulation or under special circumstances such as to impeach or corroborate the testimony of a witness.[94] Even so, it is only admissible for limited purposes such as to corroborate a defendant's testimony. Polygraph evidence is still not admissible to prove the truth of the test result. Thus, the defendant is not allowed to testify about the specific questions posed or his responses. Instead, only the results of the polygraph can be offered.

Despite *Daubert*'s more flexible approach, courts are still reluctant to admit polygraph evidence without restrictions. The United States Supreme Court, for example, has ruled that there is no constitutional right to have polygraph evidence admitted in one's defense since there is no scientific consensus that it is reliable.[95] Many lower courts have also concluded that polygraph evidence is still unreliable. For example, the Tenth Circuit noted that "nothing in *Daubert* would disturb the settled precedent that polygraph evidence is neither reliable nor admissible to show that one is truthful."[96] Even where courts have conceded that polygraph evidence could be admissible under Rule 702, they have often still excluded it under Rule 403, however.[97] For example, courts have rejected polygraph tests as prejudicial where the opposing party did not have an opportunity to participate in the administration of the exam or due to its potential to unduly influence the jury.[98]

Practical Example

A defendant is charged with possession of a controlled substance. He is accused of selling it to a confidential informant. The defendant claims that he did not sell the drugs to the confidential informant and states that he has never met the informant. The defendant takes a polygraph exam. The examiner is certified and asks several control questions. His conclusion is that the defendant is telling the truth when he states that he does not know the confidential informant and did not sell drugs. In addition to the examiner's conclusion, the defendant wants to introduce evidence that he correctly answered the questions as to whether he had ever abused drugs or sold drugs in the past. There is no stipulation as to the admission of polygraph evidence in the case. The prosecutor objects to the admission of polygraph evidence as unreliable. How should the trial court rule?

In jurisdictions that have an absolute bar to polygraph evidence, the evidence will be excluded. In other jurisdictions that analyze polygraph evidence on a case-by-case basis, the evidence might be admissible. The court would have to find that polygraph evidence satisfies the reliability prong of the Daubert test. Assuming the court does admit the evidence, the defendant will be allowed to introduce evidence of the polygraph exam and the examiner's conclusion that the defendant passed it. However, he would not be allowed to introduce evidence of his answers to the specific questions.

EVIDENCE IN ACTION

Improper Forensic Analysis in Several Cities' Crime Labs Leads to Wrongful Convictions

The importance of the judge's gatekeeper role under *Daubert* can be seen in a couple of recent exposès on the inadequacy of forensic testing. An independent audit of the Houston Crime Lab conducted from 2002 to 2007 revealed several deficiencies in its testing procedures. In Chapter 2, we examined the issues surrounding the storage and preservation of evidence at the Houston Crime Lab. Unfortunately, the mistakes did not end there. The lab also suffered from an array of problems with respect to the performance of scientific analysis of evidence. In particular, the report noted the lab's serology and DNA analysis was "extremely troubling."[99]

The report identified major flaws in 32% of the lab's DNA analysis from 1992 to 2002. The report criticized the lab's practices, including the absence of a quality assurance program, inadequately trained analysts, incorrect interpretations of data, and poor analytical technique.[100] Such errors in DNA analysis directly led to the wrongful conviction of Josiah

Sutton and presented major issues in four other capital cases. Mr. Sutton served over four years in prison for a rape he did not commit. He was released from prison after it was discovered that the DNA testing results that linked him to the rape were misinterpreted by the analyst.[101]

The lab's performance of serological or blood-typing tests was equally disturbing. The report found major flaws in 180 of the 850 tests it performed from 1980 to 1992. The report also documented four instances of "drylabbing"—analysts claiming that drug testing had been done when, in actuality, it had never been conducted. The report recommended sweeping changes be made in the lab's practices, including instituting training and certification programs for lab analysts. Unfortunately, even after numerous reforms were instituted, the Houston Crime Lab was again in the news in 2009 after an audit revealed numerous problems in its fingerprint comparison unit.[102]

Regrettably, these findings are not an isolated incident. In 2001, Joyce Gilchrist was fired from the Oklahoma City crime lab after it was discovered that her flawed and often erroneous DNA, hair, and fiber analyses had led to several wrongful convictions. The wrongful conviction of Greg Taylor, based in part on the erroneous testimony of a North Carolina state crime lab analyst, was discussed in Chapter 1. As you may remember, that case involved the failure of a serologist to report negative confirmatory test results. While some of these cases involved older, less-discriminating forensic techniques, these stories show that a lack of proper training and oversight can still lead to problems involving DNA analysis.

The good news is that many crime labs are now being operated in a scientifically rigorous manner and follow proper training and certification procedures. The American Society of Crime Laboratory Directors/ Laboratory Accreditation Board (ASCLD/LAB) is a nonprofit whose mission is to develop testing standards for crime labs and review applications for those labs seeking accreditation.[103] Currently, 178 state-run labs have been accredited by ASCLD/LAB.

In order to obtain accreditation, labs must conduct a self-evaluation prior to applying. The lab must then take corrective action to fix any nonconformity prior to applying for accreditation. Once the lab applies, an assessment team is sent to visit the lab to review records and inspect the lab. Each analyst in the lab is required to pass a proficiency test in his given discipline prior to performing casework. Thus, the process is designed to create standards of operation and provide an independent and impartial review of the work performed by the lab.[104]

Some cities have also announced plans to build new state-of-the-art facilities to update technology and combat backlogs. Denver voters approved a new $36 million lab that should be completed in 2012. There is also a strong push to create a national forensic science agency that would oversee standards and accreditation for labs nationwide.[105]

8. The Degree of Certainty to Which Experts Have to Hold Their Opinions

Many courts require that in order for experts to testify, they must hold their opinions to a reasonable degree of medical or scientific certainty. This standard is a reflection of the fact that the prosecution must prove the defendant guilty beyond a reasonable doubt. In 2007, the Colorado Supreme Court held, however, that experts do not have to hold their opinions to such high levels of certainty in order to testify.[106] There, a pediatric nurse examined a young victim of sexual assault and reported her findings as "suspicious."[107] She was permitted to testify as an expert even though she could not state to a reasonable degree of medical certainty that her findings were definitive of abuse. The court rejected the argument that such testimony is speculative because an expert's opinion is stated with less than certainty. Instead, the court held that speculative testimony is that which has "no analytically sound basis."[108] The court distinguished opinions that are held to varying degrees of certainty from those that are based on unreliable methodology:

> Testimony is not speculative simply because an expert's testimony is in the form of an opinion or stated with less than certainty, i.e., "I think" or "it is possible." If such were the case, most expert testimony would not be admissible, as rarely can anything be stated with absolute certainty, even within the realm of scientific

evidence. Instead, speculative testimony that would be unreliable and therefore inadmissible under C.R.E. 702 is opinion testimony that has no analytically sound basis. Admissible expert testimony must be grounded in the "methods and procedures of science rather than subject to belief or unsupported speculation."[109]

Thus, the court held that the proper standard under Rule 702 should measure levels of relevance and reliability, not certainty. Of course, many prosecutors will still prefer experts to state their opinions to a reasonable degree of scientific certainty since this demonstrates to the jury that the witness has a high level of confidence in his conclusions.

AUTHOR'S NOTE

This Colorado decision is a reflection of the fact that evidence in criminal trials is like a puzzle. Each piece of evidence helps assemble the overall picture of the defendant's guilt; it does not have to be capable, in and of itself, of proving the defendant's guilt. While most states still unfortunately require experts to hold their opinions to artificially high levels of certainty, such as reasonable medical certainty, Colorado may have started a trend in the right direction.

C. Lay Opinions Versus Expert Opinions

Sometimes, the line between expert testimony and lay witness testimony is blurred. When a witness who is capable of being qualified as an expert testifies to events he personally perceived, the evidence could fall under either Rule 701 or 702. This situation occurs commonly with police officers and medical doctors. Either could be asked to testify as a lay witness by relaying the facts of his observations, such as the size or nature of a victim's wounds or the description of a motor vehicle accident. Thus, even though the witness has specialized training and experience, he may be allowed to testify under Rule 701 to events he personally observed.[110] For example, a police officer who is a narcotics expert does not need to be qualified as one to give an opinion that a room smelled like marijuana smoke. That conclusion can be drawn by anyone who has personally experienced the smell.[111]

Conversely, if a witness is only endorsed as a lay witness, despite his qualifications to be an expert, should he be permitted to testify to opinions based on that training and experience? Courts are split on this issue. The more liberal view allows a lay witness to testify to opinions that are based on his specialized knowledge or training so long as the testimony is rationally based on the witness's personal perceptions.[112] The Fifth and Seventh Circuits follow this approach. For example, a mechanic was permitted to testify as a lay witness to his opinion that a particular design feature had caused a series of accidents, the aftermath of which he had personally observed.[113]

Most courts, however, view the issue much more narrowly, ruling that lay witnesses may not express an opinion on matters that are beyond the realm of common experience or that require special skill and knowledge of an expert witness.[114] Thus, the witness must be qualified and received as an expert before being allowed to give such testimony. The Fourth, Eighth, Ninth, Tenth, and Eleventh Circuits use this approach. This view closely mirrors the 2000 Amendments to Rule 701, which prohibit lay witnesses from offering testimony that is "based on scientific, technical or other specialized knowledge within the scope of Rule 702."[115] The rule was amended to reduce the risk that the reliability and relevancy requirements of Rule 702 would be avoided simply by dressing up expert testimony in lay witness's clothing.[116]

This issue often comes up with regard to the testimony of police officers who are rarely endorsed as experts yet are asked to render opinions upon their training and experience as police officers. For example, a Colorado court held that a police officer who was trained in accident reconstruction could not issue an opinion as to its cause without first being qualified as an expert.[117] Similarly, a Maryland court held that investigators had to be qualified as experts before testifying that activities they had witnessed were evidence of a drug transaction based on their extensive training as narcotics officers.[118] Essentially, the court held that the observations made by the investigators would not have been indicative of drug dealing to the average lay person and thus expert testimony was required.

Practical Example

Assume that a police officer had observed a substance on the table during a search warrant and believed it to be methamphetamine. The basis for this opinion is the officer's experience as a drug task force officer. Under the more liberal view, the police officer would be allowed to testify without being endorsed as an expert witness because his opinion is rationally based on his personal observation of the drugs at the scene. Under the latter view, however, the evidence would be excluded unless the officer was endorsed as an expert witness.

Now assume that the police officer is asked to give an opinion about whether a defendant is intoxicated based on his performance of the horizontal gaze nystagmus (HGN) test. Since the HGN test is based on scientific theory and requires special training to administer, the officer's opinion could not be considered to be that of a lay witness under either test. As a result, the testimony would only be admissible under Rule 702, and the officer must be endorsed as an expert.

II.   SUBPOENAS

A. General Requirements

Regardless of the type of witnesses called to testify, witnesses usually do not just appear at trial out of the goodness of their hearts. The Sixth Amendment to the Constitution provides that a criminal defendant has a right to "compulsory process for obtaining witnesses in his favor."[119] To accomplish this, the parties issue subpoenas to witnesses. A **subpoena** is a court order commanding a person to appear in court or other tribunal.[120] The party is personally served with a copy of the subpoena or must agree to sign a waiver of personal service.

Subpoena
a court order commanding a person to appear in court or other tribunal

Thus, the court can impose sanctions on a witness for failing to appear or refusing to testify, including ordering a jail sentence. For example, in the 2010 murder trial of Willie Clark, who was accused of shooting and killing former Denver Broncos cornerback Darrent Williams, two witnesses refused to testify out of fear of retaliation by the Tre Tre Crips street gang. The witnesses were in the SUV with Clark at the time he allegedly shot at the limousine Williams was riding in. The witnesses and the defendant were all suspected members of the gang. Since both witnesses were under subpoena, the judge ordered the pair to spend time in jail for contempt of court.[121]

In contrast, if a party fails to subpoena a witness, the court cannot impose any sanctions or grant other relief such as allowing a continuance of the trial or hearing. In some situations, a witness may agree to voluntarily appear in court. Even if the party calling a given witness is confident the person will appear at trial, however, the best practice is to still issue a subpoena to the witness.

B. Out-of-State Subpoenas

Subpoenas issued for appearance in federal court are valid anywhere as long as they are served in the United States. However, if the subpoena is issued for appearance in a state or municipal court, extra steps have to be taken to ensure the validity of the subpoena. Subpoenas are valid only in the state in which they are issued. A court in the jurisdiction where the witness lives must therefore approve an out-of-state subpoena. Each state has adopted the Uniform Act to Secure the Attendance of Witnesses From Without a State in Criminal Cases to streamline this process.

The Act provides that a court in the jurisdiction where the out-of-state witness resides must approve the subpoena. To get the ball rolling, the party wishing to call the witness has to draft an application and a certificate for the out-of-state court's review. The certificate must state that the witness's presence is material and necessary in a pending case and note for how many days that witness's presence is required. After being presented with the certificate, the court must hold a hearing to determine whether the witness is "material and necessary" to the out-of-state proceeding and that the witness's appearance in that proceeding will not cause an undue hardship on the witness. If the court determines the witness's presence is necessary, it will issue a subpoena commanding the witness's presence in the out-of-state proceeding.[122] The courts are split, however, as to whether the party calling the witness must pay for reasonable travel or mileage fees for that witness.[123]

Practical Example

Suppose Sid is on trial for harassing Manny. The trial takes place in Alaska. Sid wants to call Diego as a witness. Diego lives in California. An Alaska subpoena will be invalid unless it is approved by a California court first. Sid's attorney will have to send a copy of the subpoena he wants issued to the district court in California where Diego resides. Diego will have to appear in that court for a hearing. The judge then will determine if Diego is a material witness. If the answer is yes, then the California court must issue an order for Diego to appear in the Alaska court.

CHAPTER SUMMARY

In this chapter, you have learned that there are two basic types of witnesses: lay witnesses and expert witnesses. Lay witnesses are fact or character witnesses who can testify to factual observations. However, the opinions they can give are limited to those that are based on their ordinary perceptions and knowledge. On the other hand, experts can testify not only to factual observations but also to opinions they have formed as a result of their training and experience in a particular field.

Because of the sway expert testimony can have with a jury, experts must meet preliminary standards before being allowed to testify. The trial judge must find that the expert's testimony is competent, his methods and analysis are reliable, and his testimony is relevant. The expert is competent if he has the necessary training and experience in the field he is testifying about. His testimony is relevant if it relates to a material

fact in the case and it is necessary to address the issue.

Two different tests are used to determine the reliability of the expert's testimony. Under the *Frye* test, the expert's methods are reliable if they are generally accepted in the scientific community. In contrast, under the *Daubert* test, general acceptance is only one of several factors that the judge can use to assess the reliability of the expert's methods. Other factors include whether the method can be duplicated or tested, its potential error rate, whether it has been subject to peer review, and whether it can be used in other contexts outside of court. Federal courts and about half the states apply the *Daubert* standard. Twelve states still apply the *Frye* test. A few others apply their own unique test to evaluate expert testimony.

Special concerns have recently been raised about the adequacy of forensic science and its use in criminal trials. The National Academy of Sciences issued a report in 2009 that recommended that several changes be made to the current system, including better oversight and standardization of many of the disciplines. The report also called for courts to pay closer attention to the admission of forensic experts in court.

Depending on the circumstances, witnesses can be either lay or expert witnesses. For example, police officers often testify as lay witnesses since they are providing just their observations about a particular incident. However, if that same officer is asked his opinion based on specialized training and experience, he becomes an expert witness. In most states, that officer must now be endorsed as an expert and must satisfy the preliminary qualifications before he can testify.

In order to compel the attendance of witnesses, the parties can subpoena them to appear in court. If witnesses fail to appear or refuse to testify, the court can find them in contempt of court. Parties who want to call out-of-state witnesses must take extra steps to ensure that the subpoena satisfies those states' requirements.

KEY TERMS

- Alibi witness
- Character witness
- *Daubert* test
- *Daubert* hearing
- DNA profiling
- Expert witnesses
- Eyewitness

- Friction ridge identification
- Firearms identification
- *Frye* test
- Gatekeeper
- Handwriting analysis
- Investigation witness
- Lay witnesses

- National Academy of Sciences report on forensic science
- Polygraph
- Polymerase chain reaction
- Rebuttal witness
- Subpoena
- Witness

REVIEW QUESTIONS

1. What is a lay witness? How is a lay witness different from an expert witness?

2. What types of opinions may a lay witness give?

3. What three things must the court find in order to admit the testimony of an expert?

4. What is the *Frye* test? What is the key component of the *Frye* test for determining whether an expert opinion is admissible and reliable?

5. How has the analysis of novel scientific or technical evidence changed since the adoption of Federal Rule 702?

6. What is the significance of the *Daubert* decision?

7. What are the five factors that a court must consider when determining the reliability of scientific evidence under *Daubert*?

8. Do all states now apply the *Daubert* test? Explain.

9. How many states still use the *Frye* test?

10. What did the National Academy of Sciences report on forensic science conclude about the state of forensic science today? What were some of the criticisms it made about the introduction of forensic science testimony in court?

11. Why is DNA testing considered the gold standard of forensic evidence as it applies to the reliability of the technique?

12. Name two flaws with respect to the reliability of fingerprint identification testimony.

13. Courts have generally ignored the flaws concerning fingerprint identification on the ground that fingerprint identification has been universally accepted for a century. Do you agree with this approach, or should the court require more before admitting such evidence? Explain.

14. What are two criticisms of firearms evidence? What is the Scientific Working Group (SWGGUN) doing to improve the quality of firearms examination?

15. What are the three different approaches courts use with respect to the admissibility of polygraph evidence?

16. What was the Colorado Supreme Court's conclusion about whether an expert has to testify to a certain confidence level (reasonable degree of medical or scientific probability or certainty)? Do you agree with this conclusion? Explain.

17. What is the majority view on whether lay witnesses can issue opinions based on specialized training or experience without being qualified as an expert?

18. What two professions are often endorsed as lay witnesses in criminal cases but could testify to their opinions based on their training and experience?

APPLICATION PROBLEMS

1. Sally is on trial for murdering her husband. She killed him while he was asleep. Her defense is that she was suffering from battered women's syndrome. Is expert testimony on this syndrome admissible to show that she lacked the necessary intent to murder her husband? Explain.

2. Ward is a chemist. He has a bachelor's degree in chemistry and has worked in the lab for three years. He is endorsed as an expert in toxicology. He is asked to provide an opinion as to whether the alcohol levels in the defendant's system made her so intoxicated that she couldn't understand the nature of her actions. Ward has analyzed biological samples and poisons previously but has no experience or training in physiological response of alcohol on the body. Is he qualified to render an expert opinion in this case? Explain.

3. Sue is a PhD biologist. She has training in the area of DNA profiling. Sue uses an experimental technique to obtain trace amounts of DNA from a pair of underwear found at the crime scene. Her report states that the defendant's DNA was not found on the underwear but an unidentified male's

DNA was found. The technique she used has not been tested and has not received peer review, and the results have not been replicated. Should Sue's expert opinion be admitted into evidence? Explain.

4. Homer is on trial for shooting Monty. A witness is set to testify that she saw Homer take out a gun and pull the trigger. Homer claims it was only a cellphone and someone else shot Monty. He wants to call an expert to testify that eyewitness testimony suffers from several flaws. Should the judge admit Homer's expert? Explain.

5. Evelynn Forest is accused of beating up her husband with a golf club. She denies the charge. The prosecution wants to introduce expert testimony on impressions. The expert will testify that she matched the impression left on Mr. Forest's chin with the toolmarks on the four iron used by Evelynn. The expert has been a toolmark examiner for 20 years. She did the match by enhancing the marks on the chin using a black light. There is no set number of marks or lines that must corroborate between the two before a match can be declared. Should the expert be allowed to testify? Explain.

6. Doug is a police officer. He has training in accident reconstruction. He is asked to testify to what he observed when he responded to a three-car accident at the corner of Elm and Main. The prosecutor then wants him to offer an opinion as to the cause and whether a failure in the defendant's brake system could have caused the accident. Doug has only been endorsed as a lay witness. Should he be allowed to give an opinion as to the cause of the accident or the impact of the defendant's brake failure? Explain.

7. Charlie is on trial for menacing and domestic violence. He is accused of holding a knife to his wife's throat. He claims he only restrained his wife, who was being verbally abusive and was intoxicated. He agrees to take a polygraph. He passes it. The examiner was certified and asked control questions. If his case is in the Tenth Circuit, should the judge admit or deny the results of the polygraph examination? Explain.

Notes

1. Patrick Devlin, *The Criminal Prosecution in England,* at 66 (1960).
2. *Black's Law Dictionary,* at 1633 (8th ed. 2004).
3. F.R.E. 701.
4. *See* Mark v. State, 289 S.W.3d 923 (Ark. 2008).
5. *Black's Law Dictionary,* at 1172 (8th ed. 2004).
6. Asplundh Mfg. Div. v. Benton Harbor Eng'g, 57 F.3d 1190, 1196-98 (3d Cir. 1995).
7. Mark, 289 S.W.3d at 926-27.
8. Perkins v. Origin Medsystems, Inc., 299 F. Supp. 2d 45 (D. Conn. 2004).
9. Commonwealth v. Martin, 290 S.W.3d 59 (Ky. App. 2008).
10. United States v. Pollard, 128 F. Supp. 2d 1104, 1119 (E.D. Tenn. 2001).
11. Daubert v. Merrell Dow Pharmaceuticals, Inc., 509 U.S. 579, 592-93 (1993).
12. Hoganson v. Menard, 567 F. Supp. 2d 985, 990 (W.D. Mich. 2008).
13. United States v. Hall, 99 F.3d 1337 (7th Cir. 1996).
14. Id.
15. F.R.E. 702.
16. United States v. Monteiro, 407 F. Supp. 2d 351, 358 (D. Mass. 2006), *quoting* Amorgianos, 303 F.3d at 267.
17. Frye v. United States, 293 F. 1013 (D.C. App. 1923).
18. Frye, 293 F. at 1014.
19. F.R.E. 702.
20. Daubert, 509 U.S. at 592-93.
21. Id. at 593-94.
22. General Electric Co. v. Joiner, 522 U.S. 136, 146 (1997).
23. *Strengthening Forensic Science in the United States: A Path Forward,* A Report of the National Academy of Sciences, at 92 (2009), available at http://www.nap.edu/catalog/12589.html.
24. Johnson v. Commonwealth, 12 S.W.3d 258, 262 (Ky. 1999).
25. 526 U.S. 137, 148 (1999).
26. F.R.E. 702 Advisory Comm. Note (2000 Amendments).
27. Kumho Tire, 526 U.S. at 156.
28. Alice B. Lustre, *Post*-Daubert *Standards for Admissibility of Scientific and Other Expert Evidence in State Courts,* 90 A.L.R. 453 (2001).
29. State v. Butterfield, 27 P.3d 1133 (Utah 2001).
30. Strengthening Forensic Science, *supra* note 23, at 5-6.
31. Id. at 2.
32. Id. at 4.
33. Id. at 87.
34. Id.
35. Id. at 107.
36. Id. at 87.
37. Id. at 101.
38. Id. at 108.
39. Id. at 110.
40. Id. at 108, *quoting* United States v. Green, 405 F. Supp. 2d 104, 107-08 (D. Mass. 2005).
41. P.J. Neufeld, *The Irrelevance of* Daubert *to Criminal Justice: Some Suggestions for Reform,* 95 Am. J. Pub. Health 107, 110 (2005).
42. Neufeld, *supra* note 41, at 109-110.
43. Brandon L. Garrett and Peter J. Neufeld, *Invalid Forensic Science Testimony and Wrongful Convictions,* 95 Vir. L. Rev. 1, 2 (2009).
44. Id. at 85.
45. Id. at 11.
46. Id. at 15.
47. Id. at 4-5.
48. Id. at 93, quoting Eric S. Lander, *DNA Fingerprinting on Trial,* 339 Nature 501, 505 (1989).
49. *Strengthening Forensic Science, supra* note 23, at 19-33.
50. ASCLD.org, ASCLD's Comments on the Release of the NAS Report on Forensic Science (February 19, 2009), http://ascld.org/news/nas-report-asclds-comments.
51. Since everyone's DNA profile is not on file, scientists cannot conclusively state whether the DNA collected from the crime scene positively matches the suspect's profile. What the DNA scientist can do is state the probability that a different individual, other than the suspect, left the same profile at the crime scene. To do this, the examiner compares the suspect's profile to profiles contained in a population database (the FBI maintains a database of profiles taken from random individuals made of different races and ethnic backgrounds). The odds calculated of two people having the same DNA profile are usually so low that one could conclude that the suspect has been positively identified.

52. For example, one person at a given location on chromosome one might have five repeats of the sequence A-T-C-G (short for the bases adenine, thymine, cytosine, and guanine). A second individual might have seven repeats at this location. Of course, two people could have the same number of repeats at a given location. But, if you measure enough locations along the DNA, the odds of two people have the exact number of repeats at all locations you test for is astronomically low. Derek Regensburger, *DNA Databases and the Fourth Amendment: The Time Has Come to Reexamine the Special Needs Exception to the Warrant Requirement and the Primary Purpose Test,* Albany L.J. Sci. & Tech. (2009).
53. *Strengthening Forensic Science, supra* note 23 at 133.
54. Thomas M. Fleming, *Admissibility of DNA Identification Evidence,* 84 A.L.R. 4th 313 (1991).
55. United States v. Ewell, 252 F. Supp. 2d 104 (D.N.J. 2003).
56. *See* Zack v. State, 911 So. 2d 1190 (Fla. 2005).
57. *See* United States v. Beasley, 102 F.3d 1440, 1445 (8th Cir. 1996).
58. United States v. Coleman, 202 F. Supp. 2d 962, 968 (E.D. Mo. 2002).
59. United States v. Baines, 573 F.3d 979, 982 (10th Cir. 2009).
60. *Strengthening Forensic Science, supra* note 23, at 137-138.
61. Id. at 139.
62. Id.
63. Id. at 144.
64. Id. at 143.
65. *See, e.g.,* Baines 573 F.3d at 983 (the examiner testified that the FBI error rate was one in every 11 million examinations).
66. *Strengthening Forensic Science, supra* note 23, at 142, *quoting* Jennifer Mnookin, *The Validity of Fingerprint Identification: Confessions of a Fingerprinting Moderate,* 7 Law, Probability & Risk 127 (2008).
67. *See* United States v. Spotted Elk, 548 F.3d 641 (8th Cir. 2008); United States v. Vargas, 471 F.3d 255 (1st Cir. 2006); and United States v. Mitchell, 365 F.3d 215 (3d Cir. 2004).
68. United States v. Rose, 672 F. Supp. 2d 723 (D. Md. 2009).
69. Rose, 672 F. Supp. 2d at 726.
70. 573 F.3d 979 (10th Cir. 2009).
71. Id. at 991.
72. Id. at 992, quoting United States v. Llera Plaza, 188 F. Supp. 2d 549, 572 (E.D.Pa. 2002).
73. *Strengthening Forensic Science, supra* note 23, at 153-54.
74. Ronald Nichols, *The Scientific Foundations of Firearms and Toolmark Identification—A Response to Recent Challenges,* citing AFTE Criteria for Identification Committee, "Theory of Identification, Range of Striae Comparison Reports and Modified Glossary Definitions—an AFTE Criteria of Identification Committee Report," 24 AFTE J. 336 (1992), available at http://firearmsid.com/Feature%20Articles/nichols060915/AS%20Response%20110805.pdf.
75. Nichols, *supra* note 74, at 12, n. 64.
76. Richard Grzybowski, et al., *Firearm/Toolmark Identification: Passing the Reliability Test under Federal and State Evidentiary Standards,* available at http://www.swggun.org/resources/admissibility/Firearm%20and%20Toolmark%20Identification%20Reliability%20Article_14.pdf; Ronald Nichols, *The Scientific Foundations of Firearms and Toolmark Identification—A Response to Recent Challenges,* available at http://firearmsid.com/Feature%20Articles/nichols060915/AS%20Response%20110805.pdf.
77. Id. at 154-55, *quoting* National Research Council, Ballistic Imaging at 3 (National Academies Press 2008).
78. SWGGUN Systemic Requirements/Recommendations for the Forensic Firearm and Toolmark Laboratory, available at http://www.swggun.org/swg/index.php?view=article&catid=13%3Ageneral&id=3%3Aswggun-systemic-report&tmpl=component&print=1&layout=default&page=&option=com_content&Itemid=10.
79. Id.
80. *See e.g.,* United States v. Cerna, No. CR 08-0730 WHA, Order Denying Motions to Exclude Firearms-Related Expert Testimony and Latent Fingerprint ID Expert Testimony Without Prejudice to Further Proceedings (N.D. Cal. September 1, 2010).
81. Cerna, slip op. at 6.
82. United States v. Monteiro, 407 F. Supp. 2d 351, 355 (D. Mass. 2006).
83. Id. at 363.
84. Id. at 372.
85. United States v. Prime, 431 F.3d 1147, 1153 (9th Cir. 2005).
86. Id.
87. United States v. Rutherford, 104 F. Supp. 2d 1190 (D. Neb. 2000).
88. *Strengthening Forensic Science, supra* note 23, at 166.
89. Id. at 165.
90. James R. Wygant, *Uses, Techniques, and Reliability of Polygraph Testing,* 42 Am. Jur. Trials 313 (1991).
91. United States v. Gilliard, 133 F.3d 809 (11th Cir. 1998).
92. *See e.g.,* Brown v. Darcy, 783 F.2d 1389, 1396 n. 13 (9th Cir.1986).
93. *See* U.S. v. Cordoba, 104 F.3d 225 (9th Cir. 1997).
94. *See e.g.,* United States v. Piccinonna, 885 F.2d 1529 (11th Cir. 1989).
95. United States v. Scheffer, 523 U.S. 303 (1998).
96. Call v. United States, 129 F.3d 1402, 1405 (10th Cir. 1997).
97. *See* United States v. Benavidez-Benavidez, 217 F.3d 720, 725 (9th Cir. 2000).
98. United States v. Thomas, 167 F.3d 299 (6th Cir. 1999); Benavidez-Benavidez, 217 F.3d at 725.
99. Michael R. Bromwich, *Final Report of the Independent Investigator for the Houston Police Dept. Crime Lab and Property Room,* at 4 (June 13, 2007), http://www.hpdlabinvestigation.org.
100. Id. at 5.
101. Id. at 14.
102. Moises Mendoza and James Pinkerton, *HPD Says Print Unit Fix Won't Be Cheap,* Houston Chronicle (December 4, 2009).
103. Ascld-lab.org, programs of accreditation, http://www.ascld-lab.org/programs/programs_of_accreditation_index.html.
104. Association of Crime Laboratory Directors/Lab Accreditation Board, Accreditation Program Overview, Approved March 5, 2007, available at http://www.ascld-lab.org/documents/alpd3013.pdf.
105. Just-science.org, Quality Assurance, Accreditation and Certification, http://www.just-science.org/reform.html
106. People v. Ramirez, 155 P.3d 371 (Colo. 2007).
107. Id. at 373.
108. Id. at 381.
109. Id. at 378 n.2.

110. Osbourn v. State, 92 S.W.3d 531 (Tex. App. Crim. 2002).

111. Chess v. State, 357 S.W.2d 386, 387-88 (Tex. Crim. App. 1962).

112. United States v. Riddle, 103 F.3d 423, 428-29 (5th Cir. 1997).

113. United States v. Sweeney, 688 F.2d 1131, 1145 (7th Cir. 1982).

114. Certain Underwriters at Lloyd's, London v. Sinkovich, 232 F.3d 200, 203 (4th Cir. 2000).

115. F.R.E. 701.

116. F.R.E. 701, Advisory Committee Comm.

117. People v. Stewart, 55 P.3d 107 (Colo. 2002).

118. Ragland v. State, 870 A.2d 609 (Md. App. 2004).

119. U.S. Const. Amend. VI.

120. *Black's Law Dictionary*, at 1467 (8th ed. 2004).

121. Tom McGhee, *Day 2: Testimony in Williams' Death Continues*, Denver Post (February 24, 2010), available at www.denverpost.com/ci_14461314?IADID.

122. Robert G. Scofield, *The Basic Idea Behind the Out-of-State Subpoena* (2008), available at http://www.legalargument.net/outsubpoenas.html.

123. *See, e.g.,* State v. Harris, 615 P.2d 363 (Or. App. 1980) (state must pay reasonable travel expenses); cf State v. Fouquette, 221 P.2d 404 (Nev. 1950) (state may not be forced to pay reasonable travel expenses).

CHAPTER 10

Witnesses Part II: Competency and Privilege

"With the privilege, we and our clients are secure in the knowledge that we cannot be subpoenaed or otherwise forced to divulge what they tell us. Only with the protection of attorney-client privilege can our clients tell us the whole story and only then can we provide effective counsel or advocacy. Any undermining of the privilege is a cause of great concern to the profession."—Michael Williams

Chapter Topics

B. Specific Privileges
    1. Privilege Against Self-Incrimination
    2. Attorney/Client
        a. The Existence of an Attorney/Client Relationship
        b. The Provision of Legal Advice
        c. Waiver of the Privilege
        d. Inadvertent Disclosure
        e. Death of the Client
    3. Clergy/Communicant
    4. Family Relationships
        a. Spousal Privilege
        b. Parental/Child Privilege
        c. Sibling Privilege
    5. Physician/Patient
    6. Psychotherapist/Patient
    7. Counselor or Advocate/Crime Victim
    8. Reporter/Source

Objectives

After reading this chapter, students will be able to:

- Understand the general requirements for determining competency of witnesses

- Learn the various types of witness incapacity

- Understand the purpose of having the witness swear an oath or affirmation

- Understand the purpose of privileges and how they are invoked and waived

- Distinguish between the various types of privileges

Introduction

In the previous chapter, you learned about the various types of witnesses who can testify in a criminal case. You will learn in this chapter about some of the reasons a witness could be disqualified from testifying. There are two preliminary requirements that a witness must meet before he will be permitted to testify: the witness (1) must be competent and (2) must swear an oath or affirmation that he will tell the truth. A witness is competent to testify if he is capable of understanding his obligation to tell the truth and effectively communicating to the jury in an understandable fashion.

For the most part, witnesses are presumed to be competent and are rarely found to be incompetent. In many states, the judge must first determine the competency of a young child before allowing the child to testify, however.

The second part of this chapter deals with the concept of privileges. A privilege is created by the court or the legislature to prevent an otherwise competent witness from testifying about confidential communications. Privileges are designed to protect the confidential nature of certain relationships such as those between an attorney and a client or a psychotherapist and a patient. This chapter will discuss what privileges exist, how they are created, and how they are applied in a given situation. It will also discuss how the holder of a privilege may waive his ability to assert it, such as by revealing confidential information to third parties.

I. COMPETENCY OF WITNESSES

A. General Requirements

Rule 601. General Rule of Competency

Every person is competent to be a witness except as otherwise provided in these rules. However, in civil actions and proceedings, with respect to an element of a claim or defense as to which State law supplies the rule of decision, the competency of a witness shall be determined in accordance with State law.

Competent
a witness is competent to testify if he has personal knowledge of the events he is testifying to; capable of understanding the oath to testify truthfully; and capable of testifying coherently

In order to testify in court, a witness must be **competent** to testify. In the most basic sense, this simply means that the witness must be capable of testifying coherently and understanding the obligation to tell the truth. Historically, entire classes of witnesses were often excluded from testifying because they were unwilling to profess a belief in God, were under a certain age (typically seven or younger), were a party to a suit, or were convicted of a crime. For example, the Arkansas Constitution still contains a provision that prohibits any person who "denies the being of a God" from holding elected office or testifying as a witness.[1] Although it is no longer enforceable (such provisions have been found to violate the First Amendment), this provision provides an insight into the historical beliefs surrounding witness competency.[2] Today, the rules are much more liberal. Federal Rule of Evidence 601 provides that every witness is presumed to be competent unless otherwise provided in the rules.[3] In other words, a witness cannot be excluded from testifying simply because he has a mental infirmity (i.e., schizophrenia) or is a young child. Most states have also adopted a competency provision similar to the federal rule.

Despite the rule's presumption of competency, a witness must still meet some basic requirements. In order to be competent, the witness must be able to (1) give a coherent statement on the subject of testimony; (2) have the ability to recall events surrounding his testimony; (3) have the capacity to observe facts and give a correct account of those facts to the trier of fact; and (4) understand the obligation of an oath to testify truthfully.[4] For example, a one-year-old probably does not have a sufficient vocabulary to communicate in a meaningful way to the jury and would likely be found incompetent to testify by the judge. Similarly, an elderly person may lack the ability to recall events or communicate coherently due to the onset of Alzheimer's or other mental disease and could likewise be found incompetent.

The issues of witness competency and credibility often blur together. The determination of a witness's competency (capacity to testify) is a question of law that is left exclusively to the judge to decide.[5] The determination of a witness's credibility (his or her believability) is a question of fact left to the jury. If a witness is found to be incompetent, this means that the witness's ability to recall, relate, or be truthful does not meet minimum standards. Therefore, the witness is considered to be entirely untrustworthy, and the judge will find him incompetent and not permit him to testify. On the other hand, even if a witness is considered to be competent, he can still have his credibility called into question on these issues. Thus, the question of whether some testimonial impairment renders a person incompetent or merely impeaches his credibility "is one of degree."[6]

Practical Example

Susie has early stages of Alzheimer's. She witnessed a robbery and is asked to testify. When she is on her medication, she is lucid. She has a slight speech impediment but is still understandable. She tells the judge that she often forgets things but remembers the robbery. She understands what court is and what it means to tell the truth. Should Susie be allowed to testify? Yes. She understands the nature of the proceedings, is able to communicate, and understands the obligation to tell the truth.

B. Determining Incapacity

Courts have disagreed as to what impact the adoption of Rule 601 has had on the judge's ability to determine a witness's competency. The majority of federal courts have concluded that a judge still has the authority to rule on the issue of competency. These courts have concluded that Rule 601 only establishes a presumption that witnesses are competent, which can then be overcome by substantial evidence to the contrary. This means that the judge should allow a witness to testify unless some legitimate challenge is made to his or her capacity to do so. If a challenge to the witness's competency is made in these jurisdictions, the judge must then decide whether to conduct a competency hearing.[7]

A judge can elect to conduct a formal competency hearing, including the questioning of the witness by both sides and appointment of an independent expert, or he can simply ask the witness some questions out of the presence of the jury.[8] The judge is not required to order an investigation or hearing into the witness's competency unless he feels that he has "some doubt" about competency after observing the witness.[9] If the witness cannot demonstrate the ability to perceive and understand the events, remember the facts about the subject of his testimony, or narrate his testimony in an understandable manner, the judge should find the witness incompetent and not permit him to testify.

A minority of circuit courts, however, have interpreted Rule 601 as eliminating the need for competency hearings altogether.[10] This view stems from the fact that the Advisory Committee Notes to the Rule suggest that a witness who is "wholly without capacity" to testify is "difficult to imagine" and that the question is one "particularly suited to the jury as one of weight and credibility."[11] In jurisdictions that adhere to this strict interpretation of the Rule, the issue of witness competency is left solely to the jury to decide as an issue of credibility. Thus, some scholars have concluded that the better approach is for the judge to focus on the relevance and prejudicial effect of the witness's testimony under Rules 401 and 403 rather than on the witness's competency under Rule 601.[12]

AUTHOR'S NOTE

The majority rule is the more logical position. Rule 601 was intended to prohibit blanket exclusions of certain classes of witnesses, not strip the trial judge of his authority to rule on competency altogether. Thus, the Rule should be viewed as creating a rebuttable presumption of competency. If a witness truly is unable to effectively communicate or incapable of telling the truth (a situation not as hard to imagine as the Advisory Committee would like to think), then the judge should step in and prevent the witness from testifying.

C. Types of Incapacity

1. Physical or Mental Infirmity

As discussed above, the judge should not exclude witnesses solely on the ground that they suffer from some mental disease or defect such as being mentally retarded. Even if a person has been found to be incompetent to stand trial, this does not mean he is automatically excluded from testifying as a witness in another matter.[13] Typically, sanity is not a test for competency and is only considered to the degree it affects credibility.[14] For example, an Ohio appellate court found that the trial judge did not err by allowing a witness to testify who was an inmate in an insane asylum at the time of his testimony.[15] Similarly, the Pennsylvania Supreme Court held that "mere mental derangement," which is unconnected to the subject of the trial and does not affect the testimonial ability of the witness, was not to be considered by the jury in determining the credibility of the witness.[16]

However, in a small number of states, including Missouri and Washington, mental incapacitation creates a rebuttable presumption that the witness is incompetent to testify and can only be overcome by a showing that the witness has the necessary capacity.[17] In order to be presumed incompetent, however, it must be shown that the person is confined to a mental institution or has been adjudicated as mentally ill. Mere treatment in a mental hospital is insufficient to raise such a presumption.[18]

Courts have also considered the issue of whether a temporary mental or physical impairment can render a witness incompetent. For instance, the Second Circuit upheld the conviction of a man where a government witness, who had ingested opium on the stand, was permitted to continue testifying. Although the appeals court cautioned that the better practice would have been to immediately halt the witness's testimony once the judge observed his actions and question him out of the presence of the jury, the court found the judge's actions to be harmless error since the witness remained coherent and the jury could still understand him.[19]

Practical Example

Assume that you are a detective assigned to the crimes against seniors division of the police department. You investigate a complaint against the local nursing home. A resident of the nursing home claims to have been sexually assaulted by one of the staff. The woman's daughter reports the incident to police. The daughter had the mother adjudicated incompetent due to her schizophrenia and placed in the nursing home. When you take the woman's statement, you learn that she has trouble remembering events. She also does not see very well. The woman suffers from schizophrenia. She also reports to having paranoid delusions when she does not take her medication. The woman is fairly coherent and can communicate her story to you. She is sure that the certified nursing assistant known as Stan was the one who assaulted her. Should the woman be allowed to testify? In most states, the woman will be allowed to testify. Although she has a diagnosed mental disorder, she can communicate effectively enough for the jury to understand her. Her delusions and visions are issues that the defense can attack on cross-examination. If the state had a statute like Washington's, however, which creates a presumption of incompetence for mentally incapacitated persons, the outcome would be different. Since the mother has been committed, the burden would be on the prosecutor to prove that the mother is competent to testify and an independent evaluation would likely be ordered.

2. Child Witnesses

The question of witness competency is raised more often when young children are offered as witnesses. Children can be witnesses to crimes, victims of crimes, or even perpetrators of crimes. Under English common law, children under the age of 14 were not competent to testify as witnesses and were absolutely barred from testifying.[20] The harshness of that rule was lessened in the 1700s when young children were permitted to testify upon a showing that they possessed "sufficient knowledge of the nature and consequences of an oath."[21] In 1895, the United States Supreme Court adopted this rule in American federal courts.[22] States have also gradually lessened the restrictions on child witnesses since the early 1900s.

Today, states have varying requirements for the admission of child testimony. Despite the widespread adoption of Rule 601, many states do not apply the Rule's presumption of competency to young children. Although children are no longer barred from testifying in these states exclusively due to their age, the judge must still determine the **competency of a child** if the child is under a certain age. For example, some states require a competency determination for children under the age of 10, while other states require it for children under the age of 12 (New York recently lowered their cutoff to children under 9). The child's competency at the time of trial, not at the time of the incident, is what is relevant.[23] For example, if the witness was 7 years old at the time of the incident but now is 13 years old at the time of trial, no competency determination would be required.

These types of laws create a rebuttable presumption of incompetency for young children that can only be overcome by a showing that a child younger than the cutoff is competent to testify. The intent of this type of rule is to "mitigate the danger" that untrustworthy testimony will be presented to the jury because the witness "has not yet obtained the mental capacity necessary to understand and accurately recall and narrate an occurrence."[24] The court must determine that a child witness is capable of observing and recollecting facts, narrating them to a jury, and understanding the obligation to tell the truth.[25] Thus, a young child must appear to "have the capacity both to receive just impressions and to relate them truthfully."[26] Some states even require the judge order an independent evaluation of the child's competence by a forensic psychologist.[27]

In order to determine competency, children are often asked their names, where they go to school, how old they are, if they know what a

Competency of a child

children are presumed to be competent to testify in many states only if they are older than a certain age, usually 10 or 12. The judge must determine the competency of a child witness under that age lie is, and what happens when one tells a lie.[28] A child need not be able to define an oath, only understand that upon taking an oath, the child has promised to tell the truth.[29] The fact that the child has made inconsistent or contradictory statements does not usually require a finding of incompetence.[30] The judge retains the authority to determine competency of a child witness throughout the trial. Thus, even if he has initially determined that a child is competent, the judge can reconsider that ruling after listening to the child's testimony.[31]

Some commentators have criticized child competency statutes like these as being too restrictive, suggesting that the better practice is to simply allow the testimony of all child witnesses and let the jury weigh the credibility of the testimony.[32] In response, some states have relaxed the rules regarding child witnesses, requiring the judge to make a competency determination of the child only if a "substantial question" as to the witness's competency is raised by the party opposing the witness.[33] "Substantial" has been defined as "consisting or relating to substance, not imaginary or illusory."[34] Mere allegations that a child has made inconsistent statements or blanket statements that young children may lack the ability to distinguish fact from fiction are insufficient to create a substantial question as to competency.

Despite the presumption of competency that this type of rule would seem to create, the trial judge is still required to determine the competency of all child witnesses in six of those states (Alabama, Georgia, Hawaii, Indiana, New Mexico, and Texas) that have adopted it.[35]

Many states have also lessened the requirements for determining competency of young children in cases where the child is a victim of sexual or physical abuse. For example, one state statute provides that a child victim of sexual abuse under the age of 10 "shall be considered a competent witness and shall be allowed to testify without any prior qualification."[36] Under such a statute, the judge is not allowed to make a detailed inquiry into the child's competence.

Table 10.1 summarizes the differences between states for determining child competency.

TABLE 10.1 STANDARDS FOR DETERMINING CHILD COMPETENCY

- Presumption of incompetency if child is under a certain age (usually 10 or 12). May only be overcome by evidence showing child is competent to testify.

- Both children and adults are presumed to be competent. However, if "substantial question" is raised as to child's competency, then the judge must make a competency determination.

- Both children and adults are presumed to be competent, but the judge is still required to determine competency of all child witnesses in six states.

- Child is presumed to be competent to testify if he or she is the victim of a sexual assault.

Practical Example

An officer investigates an accusation of incest. The incest occurred against Mary, age nine. The child's sister, Alice, is four years old and was a witness to the assault. Prior to trial, the judge asks Alice whether she understands where she is and whether she knows what a lie is. Alice replies, "This is about what my dad did to my sister." She states that a lie is bad. She says, "You're supposed to tell the truth." Assume the state has a statute that creates a presumption of incompetency for witnesses under the age of 10. Is Alice competent to testify? Because Alice has demonstrated at least some ability to recount events and recollect what has happened and can also distinguish between a lie and the truth, she should be permitted to testify.

D. Personal Knowledge

Rule 602. Lack of Personal Knowledge

A witness may not testify to a matter unless evidence is introduced sufficient to support a finding that the witness has personal knowledge of the matter. Evidence to prove personal knowledge may, but need not, consist of the witness' own testimony. This Rule is subject to the provisions of Rule 703, relating to opinion testimony by expert witnesses.

In addition to requiring that a witness have the necessary mental or physical capacity to testify, the Federal Rules of Evidence impose two additional requirements on witnesses: the witness (1) must have personal knowledge of the matter he is testifying about and (2) must take an oath or affirmation to tell the truth. First, Rule 602 provides that a witness may not testify about a matter unless "evidence is introduced sufficient to support a finding that the witness has personal knowledge of the matter."[37] Such evidence "may, but need not, consist of the witness' own testimony."[38] The **personal knowledge** requirement ensures that the witness's testimony is based on events perceived by the witness through one of the five senses. In order to establish personal knowledge, the witness need not demonstrate "absolute certainty" in either her observations or recollection of the facts.[39] A broad, general recollection of events is sufficient.

The party offering the witness must establish his personal knowledge. The judge should exclude a witness's testimony on this ground only if "no reasonable juror could conclude the witness possessed personal knowledge as to the substance of his or her testimony."[40] Thus, the judge should permit the testimony as long as it is possible that the witness could have witnessed or perceived the events he or she is

Personal knowledge
a requirement that a witness's testimony must be based on events perceived through one of the five senses

testifying about. Witnesses can also testify about information they have obtained second-hand through performance of job duties.[41]

Practical Example

Assume that a witness is scheduled to testify about the occurrence of a car accident. The prosecutor asks her to describe what happened. She replies that she doesn't remember clearly what happened but believes the white car ran the red light and crashed into the light pole because she heard a loud bang after she saw the light turn red. The defense objects on the ground that the witness does not have personal knowledge. The judge should overrule the objection since the witness witnessed part of the events and heard the collision occur. This is enough to establish personal knowledge.

E. Oaths and Affirmations

Rule 603. Oath or Affirmation

Before testifying, every witness shall be required to declare that the witness will testify truthfully, by oath or affirmation administered in a form calculated to awaken the witness' conscience and impress the witness' mind with the duty to do so.

Oath or affirmation
a declaration by a witness that he will testify truthfully

The second requirement imposed by the Rules is that the witness must take an **oath or affirmation** to tell the truth. Originally, the oath had to be sworn to God.[42] This was done as an attempt to compel the witness to tell the truth based upon a belief of divine retribution for false swearing. Today, that requirement has been dropped. The Supreme Court has held that a State may not "constitutionally force a person to 'profess a belief or disbelief in any religion.'"[43] As a result, several courts have held that a person cannot be made to swear an oath to God before being permitted to testify. A witness need only declare that he will testify truthfully, by oath or affirmation, in a "form calculated to awaken his conscience and impress the witness' mind with the duty to do so."[44]

Rule 603 is intended to give flexibility in dealing with atheists, conscientious objectors, the mentally ill, and children.[45] If a witness is unwilling to swear an oath under God, the judge must then inquire as to what form of an oath or affirmation would not offend the witness's religious beliefs but would still impart a duty to tell the truth. The witness must declare that he will "testify truthfully by oath or affirmation," which is administered in a form intended to "awaken the witness's conscience" and impress upon him a duty to do so.[46] The exact words of the oath are immaterial; all that is required is that the witness recognize them as binding under his own set of beliefs.[47]

Practical Example

Assume a witness is about to take the stand to testify. The witness, who is an atheist, is asked to swear that she will tell the truth. The witness refuses to do so. The judge should not make her swear an oath to God but should instead have her declare or affirm her obligation to tell the truth and make sure that she understands it.

F. Judges and Jurors

Rule 605. Competency of Judge as Witness

The judge presiding at the trial may not testify in that trial as a witness. No objection need be made in order to preserve the point.

Rule 606. Competency of Juror as Witness

(a) At the trial.—A member of the jury may not testify as a witness before that jury in the trial of the case in which the juror is sitting. If the juror is called so to testify, the opposing party shall be afforded an opportunity to object out of the presence of the jury.

Under Federal Rule of Evidence 605, the trial judge presiding over the trial may not testify as a witness in that case.[48] A similar prohibition applies to jurors hearing the case.[49] Under Rule 606, if a juror is called to testify, the opposing party can object. As an additional precaution, the judge will ask all prospective jurors during voir dire (jury selection) if they know anything about the facts of the case or the participants involved. The judge will strike any prospective jurors for cause if they do have personal knowledge of the facts to prevent personal bias from tainting the verdict. Rule 606 also prevents jurors from being questioned about the jury deliberation process. The only things that may be properly inquired into by the court are whether "extraneous prejudicial information" was brought to the jury's attention or "outside influence" was used to sway a juror's decision.

II. PRIVILEGES

A. General Requirements

Privilege
a legal right that prevents a witness from being compelled to disclose confidential information

Even though a witness may be competent to testify, the judge may still exclude the testimony on the ground that it is privileged. A **privilege** is a legal right to withhold information or testimony without fear of reprisal (being held in contempt of court). Privileges were developed to prevent witnesses from revealing the contents of certain confidential communications in open court. Typically, these privileges developed around the desire to protect the confidential nature of certain relationships such as that between attorney and client or the clergy and communicant. They can be created through legislative or judicial action.

1. Creation

The legal system looks to produce evidence of guilt or innocence by compelling testimony from witnesses. Because a privilege attempts to restrict evidence by preventing a witness from revealing confidential communications, it conflicts with the truth-seeking function of trials and other court proceedings. Privileges are thus strictly construed since their effect is to restrict or prohibit testimony.

In federal court, privileges can be provided for in the Constitution, in Congressional statute, or through the common law (court decision). Federal Rule of Evidence 501 does not list the specific privileges that are recognized by the federal courts; instead, it generally provides that the law of privilege should be governed by the principles of common law as they may be interpreted in light of "reason and experience."[50] Thus, the Rule does not freeze the law of privilege at any one particular point in time but instead allows for the law to be fluid, adding or subtracting new privileges as societal attitudes change over time.[51] The Supreme Court has held that privileges will be recognized in federal court only (1) where they serve important private and public interests; (2) where the evidentiary cost of recognizing the privilege is likely to be minimal; and (3) where similar privileges or protections are recognized by the states, either through legislation or court decision.[52] Currently, the federal courts recognize the defendant's privilege against self-incrimination along with the attorney/client, psychotherapist/patient, clergy/communicant, and spousal privileges.

The states have also adopted privileges for use in state courts. All fifty states have created at least some of their privileges through statutory enactment, while others are recognized through the development of the common law. Some states, like Oregon and Nevada, recognize a significant number of privileges. Others, like Wyoming, recognize only a few. Table 10.2 contains a list of the 26 privileges that have been recognized by one or more states.

All states and the federal government recognize the five privileges listed in Table 10.3.

2. Assertion and Waiver of the Privilege

The client or party whom the privilege is intended to protect typically holds the privilege. This means that the client (or his guardian or personal representative if he is incapacitated or deceased) has the power to assert the privilege and/or waive it. The professional (attorney, clergy, and physician) can only assert the privilege on behalf of the client.[53] For

TABLE 10.2   LIST OF PRIVILEGES

(1) Accident report	**(14)** Physician/patient
(2) Accountant/client	**(15)** Political vote
(3) Attorney/client	**(16)** Psychotherapist/patient
(4) Clergy/penitent	**(17)** Public office
(5) Counselor/patient	**(18)** Reporter/source
(6) Domestic violence advocate/victim	**(19)** School employee/student
(7) Husband/wife	**(20)** Self-incrimination
(8) Identity of informer	**(21)** Sex assault counselor/victim
(9) Marital counselor	**(22)** Speech therapist
(10) Non-English speaking interpreter	**(23)** State secrets
(11) Optometrist/patient	**(24)** Telecommunications
(12) Parent/child	**(25)** Trade secrets
(13) Peer law enforcement counselor	**(26)** Union representative

example, an attorney may assert the attorney/client privilege, but only to protect the interests of the client, not his own. Thus, an attorney can refuse to answer questions or instruct a client not to answer on the ground that it would violate the attorney/client privilege but not to hide his own malpractice.

It is more difficult to predict who holds the privilege with respect to the spousal privilege. The power to invoke it varies from jurisdiction to jurisdiction. In some states, the defendant spouse has the power to invoke the privilege, regardless of the wishes of the witness spouse. Nevada's spousal privilege statute is typical of this type, which provides in part: "A husband cannot be examined as a witness for or against his wife without his consent, nor a wife for or against her husband without her consent."[54] In other states, the witness spouse retains the sole right to invoke the privilege. For example, in a criminal proceeding under Pennsylvania law, a

TABLE 10.3   UNIVERSALLY RECOGNIZED PRIVILEGES

- Attorney/client
- Clergy/penitent
- Husband/wife
- Psychotherapist/patient
- Self-incrimination

spouse "shall have the privilege, which he or she may waive, not to testify against his or her then spouse."[55]

Waiver
the relinquishment of the privilege holder's right to invoke the protections of the privilege.

Express waiver
a waiver of a privilege that occurs where the holder consents to disclosure of the contents of the communication to outside parties

Implied waiver
a waiver of a privilege that occurs by engaging in conduct that is inconsistent with maintaining the confidentiality of the communication

Waiver of a privilege occurs when the holder relinquishes his right to invoke the protections of the privilege. An **express waiver** results from an authorization to disclosure of the contents of the communication to outside parties (either through a written waiver or verbal agreement). An **implied waiver** occurs by engaging in conduct that is inconsistent with maintaining the confidentiality of the communication (revealing the content to third parties).[56] Many state laws provide that a privilege is waived if the person "voluntarily discloses or consents to disclosure of any significant part of the matter or communication."[57] The extent of the waiver is often limited to the subject matter of the disclosure and does not cover all confidential communications.[58] Only the holder of the privilege has the power to waive it. Thus, an attorney or other professional representative cannot waive the privilege for the client without explicit authority to do so.

Practical Example

Assume a client tells her attorney in confidence that she killed her husband and got the old man's money. She then tells her best friend, "I made sure I inherited my husband's fortune, if you now what I mean." Has the client waived the attorney client privilege? Yes. By making the statement to a third party, the client has engaged in conduct that is inconsistent with keeping her disclosure to her attorney confidential. Therefore, the privilege has been waived and the best friend or the attorney can testify to the statement.

---

3. Comments at Trial

The opposing party may not comment upon the witness's decision to invoke a privilege.[59] Although the preference is to raise the issue of privileges outside the presence of the jury, the jury can also be instructed that it cannot draw any inferences from the fact that a witness has invoked a privilege.[60]

B. Specific Privileges

1. Privilege Against Self-Incrimination

Privilege against self-incrimination
a person's right to choose not to testify or otherwise provide information to the police that would tend to incriminate himself

The Fifth Amendment provides that no one shall be compelled to be a witness against himself. This is known as the **privilege against self-incrimination.** This right applies to questioning by both the police and the prosecutor. It also applies to all judicial proceedings, not just trials. For example, in 2005 when several baseball players were called to testify in front of Congress on their use of steroids, the players could have elected to invoke their privilege against self-incrimination because their testimony was being given under oath. Mark McGwire, in effect, did invoke the privilege when he refused to "talk about the past."

Because the defendant's right to remain silent is so important, the judge must first advise the defendant outside the presence of the jury of his rights. This advisement must inform the defendant that he has an absolute right to remain silent and does not have to testify if he chooses not to. Once the defendant chooses to testify, however, he cannot selectively answer questions. He must answer all questions asked of him, and he is subject to being impeached with his criminal history.

If the defendant chooses to remain silent, that decision cannot be commented upon by the prosecutor because it would violate the defendant's constitutional right to remain silent.[61] This prohibition applies equally to a refusal to testify as well as a refusal to talk to the police during questioning.[62] In determining whether a prosecutor has impermissibly commented on the defendant's right to remain silent, the federal courts look at whether the language used by the prosecutor was "manifestly intended to be a comment on the failure of the accused to testify, or whether the language was of such a character that the jury would naturally and necessarily take it to be such a comment."[63] Some states use a more restrictive test, however, which makes the comments impermissible if they are "susceptible of the inference" that the jury is to use the defendant's silence as evidence of his guilt.[64] If the comments are found to be impermissible, the usual remedy is granting a mistrial (or a new trial on appeal).[65]

Practical Example

The defendant in a rape case elected not to talk to the police about the incident at the time of the investigation. At the time of trial, he decides to testify and claims that the sex was consensual. The prosecutor then argues during his closing that the defendant's defense is not a believable one or otherwise he would have told this story to the police at the outset of the investigation. The defense then objects to the comment and moves for a mistrial. The court must grant the motion for a mistrial since the prosecutor cannot comment on the defendant's exercise of his Fifth Amendment right, no matter how illogical it may seem.

Attorney/client privilege
a privilege that protects the disclosure of confidential information to an attorney for the purpose of seeking legal advice

2. Attorney/Client

The **attorney/client privilege** is one of the oldest recognized privileges. It originated from the oath of secrecy that attorneys and barristers swore to in England, similar to that of the vow of silence priests take with regard to the contents of the confessional.[66] It is designed to promote the full and frank communication between attorneys and their clients. The privilege is a recognition that sound legal advice depends upon the lawyer being fully informed about the facts of the client's situation without fear of those details becoming public.[67]

All states and the federal courts recognize the attorney/client privilege.[68] It protects unwanted disclosure of confidential communications between the attorney and client but does not protect against disclosure of the underlying facts.[69] It protects both oral statements and written documents. The privilege protects corporate as well as individual clients. Thus, attorneys who represent the interests of a company rather than an individual may not be forced to reveal confidential communications made for the benefit of the corporation. For example, if the board of directors of Pharmco Drug tells his corporate counsel in confidence that the company is establishing a fund to cover the costs of potential litigation over a potentially dangerous new arthritis drug, then that information is protected by privilege. In the wake of many corporate accounting scandals in the early part of the twenty-first century, however, the attorney client privilege must now give way in cases of fraud.

In order for a person to assert a claim of attorney/client privilege, he must prove the following facts: (1) the asserted holder of the privilege is or sought to become a client; (2) the person to whom the communication was made is an attorney or his subordinate and was acting as a lawyer in connection with the communication; (3) the communication relates to a fact that the attorney was informed of by his client without the presence of strangers for the purpose of securing a legal opinion, legal services, or assistance in some legal proceeding; (4) the communication was not for the purpose of committing a crime or tort; and (5) the privilege is claimed and has not been waived by the client.

a. The Existence of an Attorney/Client Relationship

An attorney/client relationship can be established even though no formal relationship was established between the client and the attorney and no fee agreement was signed. The key is that the client must have provided confidential information to the attorney in seeking legal advice from the attorney. The privilege may even apply if the person the client sought advice from was not a licensed attorney. It is sufficient that the client reasonably believed the person was an attorney and could give legal advice.

b. The Provision of Legal Advice

An attorney provides legal advice where he applies the facts of a client's case to the law. In order to establish that a sufficient relationship existed between the client and the attorney, the client must prove that he provided confidential information to the attorney in an attempt to seek an answer to a question involving his legal rights. In other words, the disclosure of confidential information has to relate to a legal matter, not a purely personal matter. For example, the attorney/client privilege would not apply if the attorney's client revealed at a cocktail party that his wife was having an affair with someone at the client's accounting firm.

The attorney/client privilege applies only to disclosures regarding past criminal conduct; it does not apply to communications by the client regarding ongoing or future criminal conduct. Thus, the attorney/client privilege does not apply if the client seeks advice from the attorney on how to commit a crime or solicits his cooperation in a conspiracy. In fact, the attorney has an ethical obligation to report such solicitations.

Practical Example

Assume Bob comes into Larry's law office and reveals that he is being investigated for murder. He tells Larry that he in fact did kill Mel. He says he hit Mel on top of his head. Larry declines to take Bob's case and refers him to Ned. Is Bob's disclosure covered by the attorney/client privilege? Even though Larry rejected Bob's case, Larry cannot reveal the contents of the communication because Bob came to him seeking legal advice. The communication involved a past crime that is covered by the privilege.

Now assume that Bob reveals to Larry his grand plot to kill Bart. He tells him that he will kidnap the boy and detonate a bomb, killing him. Does Larry have the right to reveal Bob's plot? Larry can now reveal the contents of Bob's communication because it relates to a future crime, and he has a duty to protect the safety of individuals.

c. Waiver of the Privilege

The client holds the privilege and is the only one who can decide to waive it or claim it. Waiver occurs where a disclosure of the information is "inconsistent with maintaining the confidential nature of the attorney-client relationship."[70] As discussed above, waiver can be either express or implied. The client impliedly waives the privilege by making the content of the communications an issue in the case (by suing the attorney for legal malpractice) or disclosing the information to a third party.[71] For example, if the client permits his attorney to testify about a privileged communication, the privilege is deemed to have been waived.[72] The waiver extends only to the subject matter of the waiver, not all confidential communications, however.[73]

d. Inadvertent Disclosure

Rule 502. Attorney-Client Privilege and Work Product; Limitations on Waiver

The following provisions apply, in the circumstances set out, to disclosure of a communication or information covered by the attorney-client privilege or work-product protection.

(a) Disclosure made in a Federal proceeding or to a Federal office or agency; scope of a waiver.—When the disclosure is made in a Federal proceeding or to a Federal office or agency and waives the attorney-client privilege or work-product protection, the waiver extends to an undisclosed communication or information in a Federal or State proceeding only if:
(1) the waiver is intentional;
(2) the disclosed and undisclosed communications or information concern the same subject matter; and
(3) they ought in fairness to be considered together.
(b) Inadvertent disclosure.—When made in a Federal proceeding or to a Federal office or agency, the disclosure does not operate as a waiver in a Federal or State proceeding if:
(1) the disclosure is inadvertent;
(2) the holder of the privilege or protection took reasonable steps to prevent disclosure; and
(3) the holder promptly took reasonable steps to rectify the error, including (if applicable) following Federal Rule of Civil Procedure 26(b)(5)(B).

Sometimes confidential information is inadvertently disclosed, such as when a legal secretary faxes or emails a document to the opposing party by mistake. Under Rule 502, an inadvertent disclosure does not waive the privilege as long as the holder of the privilege took reasonable steps to prevent disclosure and took prompt steps to rectify the error. Many states have also adopted rules that require the attorney receiving the inadvertent disclosure to alert the other party to the mistake and return or destroy the information without reading it.

Practical Example

Assume Al hires Johnny to be his attorney. Johnny's law firm has a policy in place that requires staff to double-check all faxes and emails of client documents. Johnny's secretary inadvertently faxes a copy of Al's letter to the prosecutor. The disclosure would not waive the privilege unless the strict accountability approach was used. Since the disclosure was inadvertent and the firm had a policy to double-check client documents, the privilege would not be waived under the other two approaches.

---

e. Death of the Client

The attorney/client privilege survives the termination of the attorney/client relationship or, in many states and the federal courts, the death of the client.[74] It does not apply, however, to statements made to the attorney after the relationship has ended. In *Swidler and Berlin v. United States*, the Supreme Court held that the privilege survives the death of the client because it will encourage clients to "communicate fully and frankly with counsel" knowing that communications will remain confidential even after death.[75] Justice O'Connor dissented, noting that the state's interest in protecting an innocent defendant outweighs the interest a deceased client has in preserving the confidences of the attorney/client relationship.[76]

In addition to the privilege, attorneys are also bound by an ethical duty to preserve the confidences of their clients. This ethical duty is broader than the privilege and extends to matters not covered by the privilege, such as representation of joint clients. In other words, even if the matter is not privileged, the attorney may still not reveal the confidential communication if it is covered by his ethical duty.

Practical Example

James is accused of murder and rape. Matthew is his alleged accomplice. James tells his lawyer before trial that he committed the murder alone and no one assisted him. Can James' attorney reveal this information to Matthew's attorney? No. The admission is protected by attorney/client privilege. Matthew is convicted of the rape and murder, as is James. Matthew and James are sentenced to life. James dies in prison two weeks later. Can James' attorney now reveal the admission after James' death? In most states, the answer is no. The attorney/client privilege survives the death of the client. See the Evidence in Action Box on the next page for how some states are now relaxing the privilege if the client's interests would not be negatively impacted by disclosure, however.

Attorneys' Secrets Could Have Freed Innocent Men

For 26 years, two attorneys kept a secret that could have freed Alton Logan, who was convicted of killing a security guard at a Chicago McDonald's in 1982. Despite the fact his family testified that he was at home, asleep at the time of the murder, Logan was convicted and sent to prison. Defense lawyers Dale Coventry and Jamie Kunz knew Logan was innocent, too. Their client, Andrew Wilson, had confessed to killing the security guard during their representation of him on unrelated murder charges. Because of attorney/client privilege, the attorneys could not reveal their client's confession. Wilson made an agreement with his attorneys that, upon his death, this information could be given to Logan. So when Wilson died in 2007, the attorneys could finally reveal their secret. Shortly thereafter, Logan's conviction was thrown out and he was freed.[77]

Within months, another attorney in North Carolina revealed that he had a similar story to tell. In 2007, North Carolina Appellate Public Defender Staples Hughes had to defend an ethics complaint after he disclosed confidential information of one of his former clients, Jerry Cashwell, who died in 2003. Hughes had defended Cashwell in 1985 against murder and conspiracy charges in the deaths of a couple murdered in Fayetteville, North Carolina in 1984. Cashwell was charged along with two other defendants, Lee Wayne Hunt and Kenneth West. Cashwell and Hunt were both convicted of murder charges while West accepted a plea to reduced charges in exchange for his testimony against the other two if either filed posttrial motions or were retried. Another person involved in the alleged conspiracy, Gene Williford, was given immunity in exchange for his testimony against Hunt and Cashwell in their original trials.[78]

During a conference with Cashwell early on in his representation, Hughes was informed by his client that he had committed the murders but had acted alone. He also told Hughes that Hunt was not involved in any way with the murders. Because of attorney/client privilege, however, Hughes could not reveal this information to Hunt's lawyer. Cashwell was convicted of both murders and sentenced to life in prison. Hunt was tried shortly thereafter for his involvement in the murders and was convicted of double murder and given two consecutive life sentences. Hughes had advised Cashwell against testifying in Hunt's trial and accepting sole responsibility for the murders for fear it would eliminate any chance he would have had for parole.

Hughes kept Cashwell's secret, even after Cashwell committed suicide in prison in 2002. Then, the rules surrounding the privilege began to change. In 2003, the North Carolina Bar amended the Rules of Professional Conduct to permit an attorney to reveal client confidential communications if he reasonably believes it would prevent "reasonably certain death or bodily harm" to another individual. In 2004, the North Carolina Supreme Court ruled that the attorney/client privilege was not absolute after death. According to the court, the privilege is no longer viable after death if the court determines that disclosure would have "no negative impact" on the client's interests such that it would not subject the client's estate to liability or harm his reputation.[79]

Apparently empowered by these changes of events, Hughes revealed Cashwell's admission in 2007. He informed Hunt's attorney and drafted an affidavit revealing the details of his conversations with Cashwell as to Hunt's innocence. The trial judge refused to admit the affidavit on the ground that the information violated attorney/client privilege and denied Hunt's motion for a new trial. The North Carolina Supreme Court also denied Hunt's request

Continued on following page

Evidence in Action continued

for a new trial. His fate now rests in the hands of the North Carolina Innocence Inquiry Commission, a panel designed to review claims of innocence, the first of its kind in the country.

For his efforts to free an innocent man, Hughes was referred to the state Bar Grievance Committee by the trial judge for revealing the confidential communications of a client without his permission.[80]

On January 25, 2008, the North Carolina Bar Grievance Committee determined that there was not probable cause to believe that Hughes had violated the ethical rules under a new provision of the North Carolina Rules of Professional Conduct, which permits an attorney to disclose confidential communications where he believes a failure to do so would result in "serious bodily harm."[81]

3. Clergy/Communicant

Clergy/communicant privilege
a privilege that applies to confidential communications made to ordained priests and ministers for the purpose of seeking religious salvation

Another privilege that developed early in our history is the **clergy/ communicant privilege**. It is designed to protect the confidential communications between a member of the clergy and members of the church. It was recognized as the legal equivalent of the Seal of Confession, which bound Catholic priests to a vow of silence for anything revealed during confession.[82] It prevents any member of the clergy from having to testify about confidential communications revealed to him. Like the attorney/client privilege, it is universally recognized in American courts.

The privilege covers communications made to ordained ministers only. Typically, communications made to mere spiritual and religious advisers are not covered by the privilege. For example, Kansas restricts the privilege to "duly ordained ministers of religion," such as rabbis, priests, and ministers.[83] The privilege also applies to the communications made by leaders of the church to each other. For example, in the sexual abuse scandal that rocked the Roman Catholic Church in the 1990s, bishops and other church officials could not be compelled to testify about admissions of abuse that priests had confided to them.

Practical Example

Tony has "offed" a rival gangster. He is feeling some guilt about this hit since the gangster had several children. He confesses his feelings to Vinny, a spiritual advisor to the mob family, known as the "Priest." Is Tony's admission protected by the clergy/communicant privilege? No. Vinny is not a duly ordained priest so Tony's confession is not covered.

4. Family Relationships

Spousal privilege
a privilege that protects against the disclosure of confidential communications that occur during the marriage

a. Spousal Privilege

Most states and the federal government recognize the **spousal privilege** in some form in criminal cases. While almost all states protect confidential communications that occur during the marriage, some states also bar one spouse from testifying without the other's consent. The marital privilege originated in its early form as a complete spousal disqualification. A spouse was thus not competent to testify as a witness against the other spouse under the doctrine of marital unity (the husband and wife being one).[84] Spousal disqualification came into disfavor in the twentieth century, however. The rule was amended to require that the defendant spouse must object to the other spouse's testimony. In other words, while the adverse spouse was now considered competent to testify, he or she could not be compelled to do so against the wishes of the other spouse. A separate privilege, which protected confidential marital communications, was recognized soon after.[85]

Thus, two separate forms of spousal privilege developed and now exist today in the United States. One, known as the **testimonial privilege**, retains the testimonial bar, precluding one spouse from testifying without the other's consent. Alaska law, which provides that "a husband shall not be examined for or against his wife, without his consent, nor a wife for or against her husband, without her consent," is an example of this type of privilege.[86] The second, known as the **marital communications privilege**, is a more limited form of spousal privilege that prevents one spouse from testifying about communications that occurred between the spouses during the marriage. The Arkansas Rules of Evidence, which provides that an "accused in a criminal proceeding has a privilege to prevent his spouse from testifying as to any confidential communication between the accused and the spouse," is an example of this latter type of privilege.[87] Typically, under the communications privilege, the witness can testify to events that the spouse witnessed but not to what was said. For example, the Eighth Circuit held that the ex-wife of the defendant could testify to the fact that she saw her husband place a package of heroin in her underwear since it was not a communication.[88]

All states but Arizona recognize some form of the spousal privilege in criminal cases.[89] Half of the states recognize just the confidential communications privilege. Seven states recognize the testimonial privilege alone, while 18 states and the federal courts recognize both forms of the privilege in limited form. See Figure 10.1 for a breakdown of the states' marital privilege laws.

In some of the states that recognize the full testimonial privilege, the defendant spouse holds the privilege and can prevent the witness spouse from testifying against him, regardless of the wishes of the witness spouse.[90] Originally, the federal courts also recognized this broader form of the testimonial privilege, but the United States Supreme Court modified the privilege in 1980.[91] Under this revised version, the witness spouse now holds the privilege and can elect whether to testify or not. If the witness spouse elects to testify, however, the disclosure of confidential communications is still not permitted. The rationale behind the court's

Testimonial privilege
a form of the marital privilege that prevents one spouse from testifying against the other spouse without the consent of that spouse

Marital communications privilege
a form of the marital privilege that protects against the disclosure of confidential communications that occurred between the spouses during the marriage but does not prevent the other spouse from testifying about matters he or she observed during the marriage

Figure 10.1

States shaded in blue recognize the confidential communications privilege alone, while states shaded in red recognize the testimonial privilege. States shaded in green recognize both forms of the privilege. States shaded in yellow do not recognize the privilege.

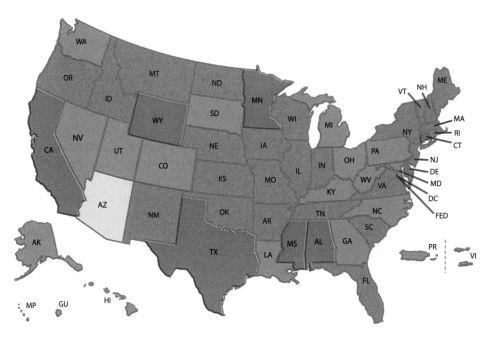

decision was that allowing an accused spouse the power to prevent adverse spousal testimony was more likely to "frustrate justice" than to "foster family peace."[92]

Despite rulings like this one, the testimonial privilege is still broader than other types of privileges. Usually, privileges are designed to prevent the disclosure of confidential communications, such as preventing a lawyer from disclosing statements his client made to him. The testimonial privilege, on the other hand, can completely bar the testimony of the spouse. The testimonial privilege is also broader in the sense that it applies to actions that occurred prior to the marriage, not just those made during the marriage.[93]

In recognition of this fact, states have riddled the testimonial privilege with several exceptions in criminal cases. First, there must be a valid marriage in existence at the time the spouse asserts the privilege. In other words, unlike the communications privilege, it does not survive the termination of the marriage due to death or divorce.[94] Some states have also placed limits on the testimonial privilege, depending on the severity of the crime. For instance, Colorado, which recognizes both forms of the spousal privilege, limits the use of the testimonial privilege to less severe crimes. In more serious cases, the spouse only retains a communications privilege.[95] For example, if the husband is charged with murder, then the wife would be permitted to testify as to things she observed the husband do related to the crime but not the statements he made to her about the murder.

Many states also exempt either form of the spousal privilege from cases involving crimes committed by one spouse against the other or in cases of child abuse.[96] The spousal privilege is also inapplicable to cases where both spouses are co-conspirators. Courts have reasoned that such communications are not marital communications because they concern the commission of a crime rather the privacy of the marriage itself.[97]

Ten states currently recognize common-law marriage. In those states, being a common-law spouse is sufficient to assert the privilege, but simply being boyfriend and girlfriend is not. The privilege also applies to same-sex couples in those states that have recognized same-sex marriages or registered domestic partnerships.[98] Most states, however, do not currently extend the privilege to same-sex couples. For example, in New York, which does not recognize same-sex marriage, a gay man unsuccessfully tried to invoke the privilege to prevent his partner from testifying against him in an embezzlement case.[99] Another interesting question is whether the privilege applies in federal cases filed in states that recognize the privilege for gay and lesbian couples. The Defense of Marriage Act (DOMA), a federal law that defines marriage as only between a man and a woman, would appear to prevent same-sex couples from invoking the privilege in federal cases. The issue was raised in 2009 when a lesbian unsuccessfully attempted to invoke Iowa's marital privilege to prevent answering questions in a federal deposition about her wife's embezzlement case.[100]

Practical Example

A police officer investigates a string of burglaries. He interviews the suspect's wife, who says she saw her husband stash a bunch of electronics boxes in the garage. She also states that her husband told her that he had scored a bunch of loot and not to tell anyone. Can the wife testify to any of the statements she made to the police? If the state recognizes only the confidential communications privilege, the wife can testify as to what she saw but not to what her husband told her. The same would be true if the state recognizes the testimonial privilege but allows the witness spouse to hold the privilege. However, if this is one of the states where the defendant spouse holds the privilege, then the wife would not be able to testify at all, assuming her husband objects.

Now assume that the officer is investigating an incident of domestic violence. The husband gives a statement that his wife hit him over the head with a golf club and smashed out the windows of his SUV. He also states that his wife told him that's what he gets for having an affair. In most states, the privilege does not apply to crimes committed by one spouse against the other. Thus, the husband would be able to testify to everything, including the statements his wife made to him regarding the assault.

b. Parental/Child Privilege

Since protecting the sanctity of marriage is at the heart of spousal privilege, it would seem only natural that communications between a parent and child should be protected as well. Supporters of such a privilege argue that fostering the confidential relationship between a parent and child is necessary to promote the child's development of moral values. For example, what would happen to a child's trust in his parents if statements made to the parents in confidence about issues concerning his physical or mental health or criminal involvement were revealed to authorities? A New York appellate court laid out the dilemma for parents that would be created without such a privilege:

> It would be difficult to think of a situation which more strikingly embodies the intimate and confidential relationship which exists among family members than that in which a troubled young person, perhaps beset with remorse and guilt, turns for counsel and guidance to his mother and father…Shall it be said to those parents, "Listen to your son at the risk of being compelled to testify about his confidences?"[101]

Parent/child privilege
a privilege protecting against disclosure of confidential communications made between parents and their children. Only five states recognize a parent/ child privilege. As a result, parents and children can be compelled to testify against one another in the vast majority of states

Despite the logic of this argument, only a handful of states have recognized a **parent/child privilege**: Connecticut, Idaho, Massachusetts, Minnesota, and New York.[102] Many courts have resisted recognizing a familial privilege on the ground that it conflicts with the state's interest in the fair and efficient administration of justice.[103] In essence, these courts have found that the state's need to fully develop evidence in a case outweighs the need to maintain family secrecy.[104] For instance, in *State v. Maxon*, the Washington Supreme Court held that it was not necessary to recognize a parent/child privilege because its creation was not essential to the development of a successful parental-child relationship. The court found that children are more likely to discuss intimate details of their lives with friends rather than parents, and creation of such a privilege was not likely to increase communication between parents and children.[105]

Even where the privilege has been recognized, it is strictly limited. Communications made in the presence of third parties, even siblings, are not covered by the privilege.[106] Courts have also refused to recognize the privilege where the communication is not made for the purpose of obtaining parental guidance and support. For example, a New York court allowed a mother to testify to statements her son had made to her during a telephone conversation where the son had merely asked if the police were looking for him.[107] Confidential communications between extended family members are also not typically covered under the parental privilege.[108] Finally, the privilege does not survive into the child's adulthood.[109]

c. Sibling Privilege

There is no privilege for confidential communications made between siblings. For example, the Maine Supreme Court held that a murder defendant's sister was properly held in contempt of court for refusing to testify against her brother. The court rejected the argument that such a privilege should be recognized under the constitutional right to privacy. It held that such privileges must be expressly provided for in the constitution.[110] It noted that the value of privacy would not be substantially impaired by failing to recognize such a privilege.

5. Physician/Patient

Physician/patient privilege
a privilege that covers confidential statements made to a physician that are necessary for the patient's diagnosis or treatment, and covers medical records as well as the statements made between the physician and the patient. Forty states, but not the federal courts, recognize it

Most states have recognized a **physician/patient privilege**. Currently, 40 states have such laws. No physician/patient privilege exists in federal criminal cases, however, since it did not exist at common law and no federal statute has created it.[111] The privilege covers confidential statements made to a physician that are necessary for the patient's diagnosis or treatment. It covers the medical records as well as the statements made between the physician and the patient. It includes statements made in the presence of other medical professionals who are not doctors but who are participating in the diagnosis or treatment of the patient. The privilege is held by the patient but may be asserted by the patient's attorney or legal guardian. The patient's physician is also often allowed to claim the privilege on behalf of the patient.[112]

The Illinois Code of Civil Procedure contains a typical example of the physician/patient privilege:

> No physician or surgeon shall be permitted to disclose any information he or she may have acquired in attending any patient in a professional character, necessary to enable him or her professionally to serve the patient, except only (1) in trials for homicide when the disclosure relates directly to the fact or immediate circumstances of the homicide...(6) in any criminal action where the charge is either first degree murder by abortion, abortion, or attempted abortion, (7) in actions, civil or criminal, arising from the filing of a report in compliance with the Abused and Neglected Child Reporting Act...and (9) in prosecutions where written results of blood alcohol tests are admissible.[113]

Even where a state has recognized such a privilege, however, it is easily waived in criminal cases. One such instance is where the person's physical condition is an element of the crime or defense. For example, if the victim has put his or her medical condition at issue in the case (such as in an assault case), then the victim's medical records as to that condition must be produced.[114] The privilege is also waived if the patient seeks to have the physician aid in the commission or cover-up of a crime. In fact, physicians are under a duty to report many types of injuries to authorities, including stabbings, gunshot wounds, and child abuse. Thus, a defendant cannot assert the physician/patient privilege with respect to those types of injuries. Similarly, a defendant waives the privilege with respect to his mental health history where he claims an insanity defense. Due to the numerous exceptions, some states, such as California, have eliminated the privilege altogether in criminal cases.[115]

Practical Example

Assume Mack is shot in a robbery attempt. He seeks treatment at a local health clinic. Mack tells the doctor at the clinic that his gun accidentally went off. The doctor must report the gunshot wound to authorities under state law. After he does so, Mack is charged in the robbery. The district attorney calls Mack's physician to the stand. Mack objects on the ground of physician/patient privilege. The judge would overrule his objection and let the physician testify because the privilege is waived under the circumstances.

6. Psychotherapist/Patient

Psychotherapist/ patient privilege
a privilege that protects confidential communications made between licensed psychologists and psychiatrists. All courts recognize the psychotherapist/patient privilege, and some states even protect statements made to counselors and social workers

The **psychotherapist privilege** is universally recognized in American courts. While many states limit it to disclosures made to licensed psychiatrists and psychologists, other states apply the privilege to confidential communications made to all mental health professionals in the course of treatment, including counselors and social workers.[116] The privilege is based on the need for trust and confidence in the relationship between the patient and the therapist. Courts have been more receptive to recognizing a psychotherapist privilege than a physician privilege because the need for confidentiality is arguably greater in the case of the psychotherapist. As the Supreme Court pointed out in *Jaffee v. Redmond*, a physician can often accomplish a diagnosis with a simple physical exam, whereas a psychotherapist has to delve into the intimate details of people's lives in order to effectively treat the patient.[117] The latter obviously depends upon an "atmosphere of trust and confidence" between the therapist and patient that may be absent during a physical exam.

Some exceptions do exist to the privilege. In 1976, California became the first state to impose a duty to warn on the part of the psychotherapist where the patient makes a credible threat of violence against a "readily identifiable" third party. In *Tarasoff v. Regents of the University of California*, the California Supreme Court held that a therapist could be subject to civil liability if he failed to warn the victim of such a threat.[118] The court concluded that the rationale behind the privilege, protecting the privacy of patients, must yield to "the extent to which disclosure is essential to avert danger to others."[119] Thus, if the therapist learns that the patient has made violent threats toward others, he must reveal those threats to the victim or to authorities.

Most states now impose some kind of *Tarasoff* duty to warn. About half the states impose a mandatory duty to warn.[120] Montana's statute is an example of a mandatory duty to warn:

A mental health professional has a duty to warn of or take reasonable precautions to provide protection from violent behavior only if the patient has communicated to the mental health professional an actual threat of physical violence by specific means against a clearly identified or reasonably identifiable victim.[121]

Some of those states require the therapist to alert both law enforcement and the victim, while others require that the therapist only alert either one. Nine states plus the District of Columbia allow the therapist to decide whether a warning should be given. For example, Illinois law provides that confidential communications may be disclosed at the "sole discretion" of the therapist.[122] Thirteen states and the federal courts have not yet considered the issue. One state, Virginia, has rejected the *Tarasoff* ruling outright and imposes no duty on therapists.

Practical Example

Jean Claude is an action movie star. Kelsey is a big fan. She admits to her therapist that she is in love with him. She writes Jean Claude but is rejected. Kelsey then plots to kill Jean Claude. She tells her therapist that if she cannot have Jean Claude, no one can. Does the therapist have to report this statement to the authorities and Jean Claude? Yes, if the therapist believes Kelsey's statement is a credible threat against Jean Claude's life or safety.

7. Counselor or Advocate/Crime Victim

While confidential communications between psychotherapists and their patients are universally protected, communications between unlicensed counselors or advocates and their clients may not be protected. This distinction has significant consequences for crime victims, many of whom cannot afford to pay for counseling with licensed psychologists or psychiatrists. Domestic violence and rape victims are more likely to seek counseling from centers specifically established to help victims of those crimes since they often cannot afford more traditional mental health services.[123] Unfortunately, if the state does not protect the disclosure of such communications, counselors or advocates could be called to testify about deeply personal revelations of the victim.

Victim advocate privilege
a privilege that covers confidential communications made to rape crisis or domestic violence abuse counselors. It is recognized by about one third of states. It does not cover statements made to victim advocates working for law enforcement agencies

In response to this inequitable situation, eighteen states have adopted statutes recognizing a separate **victim advocate privilege** for domestic violence and/or rape crisis counselors. Such statutes usually define counselors as those who provide services to victims of sexual abuse or domestic violence for a program organized for the purpose of providing assistance, counseling, or support services.[124] The privilege can be characterized as absolute, semi-absolute, or qualified. Some states (Colorado, Florida, New Jersey, and Pennsylvania) have adopted absolute privileges that prevent disclosure of confidential records or communications under any circumstances without the victim's consent. Courts in these states have held that these types of statutes do not violate the Confrontation Clause.[125] Other states, such as Alaska and Hawaii, allow limited disclosure of the confidential communications if it is in the public interest. The remaining states, such as Arizona, California, and Indiana, permit disclosure if the court finds the value of the disclosure to the defendant outweighs the victim's need to keep the communication confidential.[126] Obviously, this last type of statute is the least protective of confidential communications because the counselor can never assure the victim that such communications will be protected from disclosure. See Table 10.4 for a breakdown of the various kinds of advocate privileges.

Courts that use the balancing approach have concluded that the privilege must give way where the defendant's constitutional rights may be restricted by the privilege. An Indiana court recently pointed out that if this were not the case, a victim, for example, could inform an advocate that she fabricated the whole story, and the truth would never be revealed.[127] Of course, this is the case with other privileges. In his dissent in *Commonwealth v. Wilson*, Justice Zappala of the Pennsylvania Supreme Court framed the issue as follows:

> The hallowed principle that one remains innocent until proven guilty is hollow indeed if one's constitutional rights must always bend to a statutory privilege. When a defendant has shown a legitimate need for access to communications, the testimonial privilege ... must yield to the constitutional rights of a criminal defendant to due process and to confront his accuser.[128]

Regardless of what form of the privilege is recognized, the privilege extends only to advocates who are employed by non–law enforcement organizations; it does not extend to victim advocates employed by law enforcement agencies. For example, the Supreme Judicial Court of Massachusetts held that confidential communications made to victim advocates who work for the district attorney's office are not privileged.[129] Since advocates are included under the state's definition of prosecutor and

TABLE 10.4   TYPES OF VICTIM ADVOCATE PRIVILEGE

- **Absolute privilege** prevents disclosure of confidential communications under any circumstances without the victim's consent.
- **Semi-absolute privilege** permits disclosure of confidential communications if it is in the public interest.
- **Qualified privilege** balances privacy of the victim versus the defendant's need for disclosure of information.

are generally employees of the prosecutor's office, the court held that the notes of victim's advocates are subject to the same discovery rules as the notes of prosecutors. However, the court noted that advocates should also be considered as part of the prosecutor's "legal staff," which means that their work product is protected from disclosure. The court found that unless the advocate's notes contain exculpatory evidence or statements of witnesses, the advocate's notes are protected from disclosure as "work product."[130]

Practical Example

Monica is sexually assaulted. She contacts a local rape awareness hotline in her town to seek counseling. During one of the sessions, she tells the counselor that she had consensual sex with her attacker two weeks ago. Does the counselor have to turn over this information to the prosecutor or defense attorney if requested, or is it privileged? In most states, this statement is not protected and would be subject to disclosure. In those states that do recognize a privilege, disclosure may also be required. In absolute privilege states, the statement could not be disclosed. In those states that use a balancing approach, however, the statement would likely have to be disclosed because the statement is potentially exculpatory since it shows the victim and defendant had consensual sex two weeks prior to the alleged attack.

8. Reporter/Source

Reporter/source privilege
a privilege that protects a journalist from having to reveal the identity of his source. If the state does not have such a privilege, the reporter could be found in contempt of court and face jail time for failing to reveal his source

Journalists often promise confidentiality to their sources in order to get information for stories. You may have heard of "Deep Throat," Woodward and Bernstein's FBI source, who was critical to the pair's exposing of the Watergate scandal in the 1970s. His identity was not revealed until 2005, when he willingly came forward to reveal the truth. But what happens if the journalist is called into court and ordered to reveal the identity of his source? Some states have recognized a **reporter/source privilege**, which protects the journalist from having to reveal the identity of his source. While many courts have been reluctant to recognize a common-law reporter/source privilege, a number of states have passed laws creating one.

In *Branzburg v. Hayes,* the United States Supreme Court refused to find that a reporter/source privilege is guaranteed by the First Amendment. The Court determined that the First Amendment does not grant reporters a testimonial privilege that would protect them from having to identify their sources in front of grand juries or trial courts. It noted that just as a reporter is not immune under the First Amendment from facing criminal prosecution for stealing documents or conducting illegal wiretaps to gain information, neither is he immune from testifying against a source.[131] The Court held that the interest in pursuing and prosecuting crime reported to the press by confidential informants takes precedence over the public's need to be informed about crimes from such undisclosed, unverified sources.[132]

In jurisdictions that do not recognize a reporter/source privilege, the journalist often faces a Hobson's choice—either reveal the identity of the source and risk putting his credibility in jeopardy or be prepared to go to jail after being found in contempt of court by failing to reveal the source's identity. This is not an idle threat, as the Evidence in Action Box discusses below.

Reporters Avoid Jail Time in Grand Jury Leak Involving Balco Investigation

In a rather infamous case in 2006, two San Francisco Chronicle reporters, Lance Williams and Mark Fainaru-Wada, were almost sent to federal prison when they refused to reveal the identify of their source for leaked grand jury testimony. The pair wrote several articles and a book entitled *Game of Shadows*, detailing the involvement of several professional athletes (most notably San Francisco slugger Barry Bonds) with steroids produced by the Bay Area Laboratory Cooperative (Balco). A major source for the stories was a leaked transcript of Bonds' testimony before a grand jury investigating the matter.

A federal grand jury had been empaneled to investigate the Balco lab for illegal steroid distribution. The investigation included the testimony from several athletes who were linked to steroids from the lab, including Bonds. The reporters relied on leaked testimony from that investigation for much of the information in the articles. The pair was subpoenaed by the government, which required them to appear before a grand jury to disclose the source of the leak.[133] The reporters refused to reveal the identity of their source. The judge found the

Figure 10.2   San Francisco Chronicle editor Phil Bronstein (left) and reporters Lance Williams and Mark Fainaru-Wada exit the federal courthouse in San Francisco on August 4, 2006. Lawyers for the reporters unsuccessfully argued that the First Amendment protected the reporters from revealing their sources for leaked grand jury testimony of athletes involved in the Balco steroids probe. © *2006 AP Photo/Benjamin Sklar*

reporters in contempt and sentenced them to prison. The reporters avoided jail time for failing to reveal the source of the leak only after their source, Troy Ellerman, a defense attorney for two of the Balco defendants, revealed his identity. He admitted in a plea agreement with prosecutors that he had allowed the reporters to view the grand jury transcripts of several of the athletes who had testified. Ellerman pled guilty to four felony counts of obstruction of justice and disobeying court orders and had to pay a $250,000 fine and serve up to two years in prison.[134]

CHAPTER SUMMARY

Today, most witnesses are presumed competent to testify in court. This presumption can be overcome only by a showing that the witness cannot provide testimony in an intelligible or truthful manner such that no juror could reasonably rely on it. If the opposing party does challenge the competency of a witness, the judge in most states must review the witness's qualifications to testify. At a minimum, the witness must be able to (1) give a coherent statement on the subject of testimony; (2) have the ability to recall events surrounding his testimony; (3) have the capacity to observe facts and give a correct account of those facts to the trier of fact; and (4) understand the obligation of an oath to testify truthfully. Thus, witnesses should not be excluded from testifying simply because they have a mental infirmity or disease.

The only exception to this rule is that many states require the court to assess the competency of young juveniles before permitting them to testify. Even in these situations, the rules are often relaxed to permit juveniles to testify where they have been the victim of a crime. If the child witness's competency is challenged, the child is usually questioned about his or her understanding of the circumstances and whether he or she understands the obligation to tell the truth.

Privileges, on the other hand, prevent otherwise competent witnesses from testifying. They are designed to protect confidential communications between professionals and a client. Some privileges, such as the attorney/client, psychotherapist/patient, and clergy/communicant, are universally recognized. Some states have chosen to recognize a number of other privileges as well. Typically, a privilege is created where the nature of the relationship relies on the free flow of communication between the parties.

A privilege can be waived only by the holder of the privilege; this is usually the client. Waiver occurs either by express authorization, such as the signing of a written release, or by conduct that is inconsistent with keeping the communications confidential. Where the privilege has been waived, the confidential communications can be testified to in court.

KEY TERMS

- Attorney/client privilege
- Child witnesses
- Clergy/communicant privilege
- Competent
- Competency of child witnesses
- Express waiver
- Implied waiver
- Marital communications privilege
- Oath or affirmation
- Parent/child privilege
- Personal knowledge
- Physician/patient privilege
- Privilege
- Privilege against self-incrimination
- Psychotherapist privilege
- Reporter/source privilege
- Spousal privilege
- Testimonial privilege
- Victim advocate privilege
- Waiver

REVIEW QUESTIONS

1. What makes a witness competent to testify?

2. Who is competent to testify in courts?

3. Is an atheist or other person who refuses to swear an oath to God competent to testify in a trial?

4. Is a six-year-old child automatically barred from testifying in a trial where she witnessed a gunman rob her parents? If not, what must be shown before she can testify?

5. Why do you think some states have maintained the requirement that the judge rule on a young child's competency even though the Rules state all witnesses are presumed to be competent?

6. Define the term *witness privilege*.

7. Is the law of privileges frozen in time; in other words, can additional privileges be recognized as time passes? If not, what factors will the federal court examine in determining whether to recognize a new privilege?

8. What types of communications does the attorney/client privilege cover?

9. When does the attorney/client privilege attach?

10. Does an attorney have to report statements by his client that report his involvement in a crime that has already occurred? What about a crime that the client is planning to commit in the future?

11. Does an attorney have the ability to waive the privilege for the client?

12. How can the privilege be waived?

13. What is the difference between the spousal incapacity privilege and the marital communications privilege?

14. How many states recognize a parent/child privilege?

15. What is the reporter/source privilege? Do the federal courts recognize such a privilege?

16. Do federal courts distinguish between a physician/patient and psychotherapist privilege? If so, which one is recognized by federal courts?

17. Does a domestic violence counselor or victim advocate privilege cover advocates employed by law enforcement agencies? If not, who does it cover?

APPLICATION PROBLEMS

1. John is called to testify in his uncle's murder trial. John is a member of the Natural Alliance, a church group that believes in Mother Nature as the omnipotent being. They do not believe in God per se. When called to the witness stand, the judge asks John if he promises to tell the truth, so help him God. John refuses to answer due to his religious beliefs. The judge then refuses to permit John to testify on the ground that he will not swear an oath. John's attorney objects. Is John's attorney right? If so, what should the judge have done differently?

2. Lisa is eight years old. She witnesses her father drive drunk while she is in the car. She is subpoenaed to testify against her father. She lives in a state that has a presumption that children under ten are incompetent. The judge asks her some questions before she testifies. She says she is here to talk about her dad's driving. She states that she knows lies are bad but some are okay,

like when you get a gift you don't like. Is Lisa competent to testify?

3. Suzanne is a victim in a child sexual assault case. She is five years old. The judge asks her what she thinks court is. She says, "To tell what my stepdad did to me and touched me in a bad place." The judge then asks her if she knows what a lie is. She responds, "That's when you say something that isn't true." The judge asks her if she can tell the truth. Suzanne says that it is bad to tell lies. Should Suzanne be allowed to testify? Explain your reasoning.

4. Maggie is two and a half. She is the victim of a child sexual assault. She can state that the bad man touched her under her diaper. She does not really understand the concept of lies or the truth yet. She does have a vocabulary sufficient to communicate to the jury. Do you have enough information to determination whether Maggie is competent to testify? If not, what additional information do you need before making this determination?

5. Mary walks into the offices of Dewey, Cheatham, and Howe, seeking legal counsel. She meets with Thomas Dewey about her pending divorce. During the meeting, Mary reveals several intimate details about her marriage to Mr. Dewey. At the end of the meeting, Mary ultimately decides not to hire Dewey due to the high cost of his fees. Several months later, Thomas Dewey is subpoenaed to testify in Mary's divorce trial. Mary asserts attorney/client privilege. Can she properly do so? Explain your reasoning.

6. Assume the following trial is occurring in the state of Colorado. Colorado has a spousal privilege law that prevents one spouse from testifying against the other in criminal matters unless the charged crime is committed by one spouse against the other or the charged crime is a class 1, 2, or 3 felony and no confidential communications that occurred during the marriage are part of the testimony. Juan is on trial for selling a controlled substance, a fourth-

degree felony. The prosecutor calls his wife, Marisol, to testify against him. Juan asserts the spousal testimonial privilege. Is Marisol barred from testifying, or can she testify? Explain your reasoning.

7. Now assume Juan is charged with domestic violence–related assault, a first-degree misdemeanor. He is accused of punching his wife in the stomach. Can Marisol now testify under Colorado law?

8. During the investigation into baseball slugger Barry Bonds and Balco, the San Francisco Chronicle ran a news story that contained leaked transcripts of federal grand jury testimony of several individuals, including Barry Bonds. The two reporters, Lance Williams and Mark Fainaru-Wada, were issued subpoenas regarding the source of the grand jury leak. The two reporters moved to quash the subpoenas, asserting the reporter/source privilege. The case was being heard in federal court. Did the reporters correctly assert the privilege? Explain your reasoning.

9. Jason is being prosecuted for illegal possession of a weapon. He is a player in the NFL. He is injured when the gun he has illegally concealed in his sweatpants falls out and goes off. He is treated at the hospital for his injuries. He tells the doctor what happened. The doctor reports the gunshot wound to authorities and the prosecutor calls him to testify about the incident at Jason's trial. Jason asserts the physician/patient privilege. Is he correct, or can the doctor testify? Explain your reasoning.

10. Heather goes to consult James, a noted criminal defense attorney in Boston. Heather explains that she has been charged with fraud and aggravated assault involving Mitch. She tells James that she frequents bars and picks up men, drugs them, and then steals their money. Heather brags to a friend two days later that she got Mitch good and robbed him blind. Can the prosecutor introduce the statements she made to James in confidence? Explain your reasoning.

Notes

1. Ark. Const. Art 19, § 1.
2. *See* Torcaso, *infra* at note 45.
3. F.R.E. 601.
4. *See* Pittsburgh & W. Ry. Co. v. Thompson, 82 F. 720, 726-27 (6th Cir. 1897); Kentucky v. Stincer, 482 U.S. 730, 741 (1987).
5. United States v. Gerry, 515 F.2d 130 (2d Cir. 1975), *cert. denied* 423 U.S. 832 (1975).
6. McMaster v. State, 512 P.2d 879, 881, n.4 (Ak. 1973).
7. United States v. Gutman, 725 F.2d 417 (7th Cir. 1984), *cert. denied* 469 U.S. 880 (1984) (a trial court has a duty to conduct a competency hearing as to sanity in certain situations).
8. United States v. Gerry, 515 F.2d at 137.
9. Commonwealth v. Anderson, 552 A.2d 1064 (Pa. Super. 1989).
10. United States v. McRary, 616 F.2d 181 (5th Cir. 1980), *cert. denied*, 456 U.S. 1011 (1982).
11. Advisory Comm. Note to F.R.E. 601.
12. State v. Stacy, 371 S.E.2d 614, 617 (W.V. 1988), quoting F. Cleckey, *Handbook on Evidence for West Virginia Lawyers*, 2.2(B) at 28 (1986).
13. United States v. Lightly, 677 F.2d 1027 (4th Cir. 1982).
14. Clark v. Otis Elev. Co., 653 N.E.2d 771, 773 (Ill. App. 1995).
15. State v. Braden, 9 N.E.2d 999 (Ohio App. 1936).
16. Commonwealth v. Kosh, 157 A. 479 (Pa. 1931).
17. State v. Beine, 730 S.W.2d 304, 307 (Mo. App. 1987), *citing* § 491.060(1), R.S.Mo. (1986).
18. Id.
19. United States v. Meerbeke, 548 F.2d 415 (2d Cir. 1977).
20. State v. Schossow, 703 P.2d 448, 449 (Ariz. 1985), *citing* 81 A.L.R. 2d 386, 389-90 (1962).
21. Id., *quoting* Rex v. Brasier, 168 Eng. Rptr. 202 (1779).
22. Wheeler v. United States, 159 U.S. 523 (1895).
23. State v. Clark, 644 N.E.2d 331, 335 (Ohio 1994).
24. Schossow, 703 P.2d at 451.
25. Kentucky v. Stincer, 428 U.S. 730, 741 (1987).
26. Beine, 730 S.W. 2d at 306-07.
27. Stacy, 371 S.E. 2d at 617.
28. Id., *citing* Comment, *The Competency Requirement for the Child Victim of Sexual Abuse: Must We Abandon It?*, 40 U. Miami L. Rev. 245, 263 n. 78 (1985).
29. Perry, 848 A.2d at 637-38.
30. *Id.*
31. Stincer, 428 U.S. at 743.
32. *See* McCormick, *Handbook of the Law of Evidence*, § 62 at 156 (3d ed., E. Cleary 1984).
33. Perry v. State, 848 A.2d 631, 639 (Md. App. 2004) (under Rule 601, a child witness can be challenged for competency only where a substantial question is shown as to the witness's competency).
34. Id., quoting *Merriam-Webster's Collegiate Dictionary* at 1170 (10th ed. 2001).
35. Nora A. Uhlein, 60 A.L.R. 4th 369, *Witnesses: Child Competency Statutes*, (1988); *see e.g.*, Newsome v. Indiana, 686 N.E.2d 868 (Ind. App. 1997) (held that the repeal of the statute which removed presumption of competency for children under 10 did not affect prior case law, which held that a judge must make a competency determination of child witnesses).
36. *See e.g.*, V.A.M.S. § 491.060(2); § 76-5-410, Utah Code Ann. (1986). It should be noted that this provision of the Utah

Code was adopted in 1985 but shortly thereafter was superseded by Utah Rule 601 when the Rules of Evidence were adopted.
37. F.R.E. 602.
38. Id.
39. United States v. Armstrong World Indus., Inc., 923 F. Supp. 1442, 1445 (D.N.M. 1996).
40. United States v. Hickey, 917 F.2d 901, 904 (6th Cir. 1990); United States v. Owens, 699 F. Supp. 815, 817 (C.D.Cal. 1988).
41. Los Angeles Times Comm., LLC v. Department of the Army, 442 F. Supp. 2d 880, 886 (C.D. Cal. 2006).
42. *See* United States v. Looper, 419 F.2d 1405, 1406 n. 2 (4th Cir. 1969).
43. Torcaso v. Watkins, 367 U.S. 488, 495 (1961).
44. F.R.E. 603.
45. Looper, 49 F.2d at 140, n. 3.
46. United States v. Saget, 991 F.2d 702, 710 (11th Cir. 1993).
47. United States v. Ward, 989 F.2d 1015, 1019 (9th Cir. 1993).
48. F.R.E. 605.
49. F.R.E. 606.
50. Jaffee v. Redmond, 518 U.S. 1, 8 (1996).
51. Jaffee, 518 U.S. at 9.
52. In re Grand Jury Subpoenas, 438 F. Supp. 2d 1111, 1118 (N.D. Cal. 2006), *citing* Jaffee, 518 U.S. at 10-15.
53. *See, e.g.*, Ak. R.E. 503(c).
54. N.R.S. § 49.295(1)(a).
55. 42 Pa. C.S.A. § 5913.
56. In re Commercial Financial Serv., Inc., 247 B.R. 828, 846 n. 20 (N.D. Okla. 2000).
57. *See, e.g.*, Ak. R. E. 510.
58. Interfaith Housing Del., Inc., 841 F. Supp. 1393, 1398 (D. Del. 1994).
59. *See, e.g.*, Ak. R.E. 512(a).
60. *See, e.g.*, N.M.R.E. 11-513.
61. Griffin v. California, 380 U.S. 609 (1965).
62. Commonwealth v. Beavers, 424 A.2d 1313 (Pa. 1981), *citing* Gillison v. United States, 399 F.2d 586, 587 (D.C. Cir. 1968).
63. Allen v. State, 787 A.2d 152, 161 (Md. App. 2001) (concurring op).
64. Id. at 155, (majority op).
65. Id. at 159.
66. Electronic Privacy Information Center, *Privileges*, http://epic.org/privacy/privileges (last viewed May 1, 2009).
67. X Corp. v. Doe, 805 F. Supp. 1298 (E.D. Va. 1992), *citing* Upjohn Co. v. United States, 449 U.S. 383, 389 (1981).
68. Thirty-nine states have codified the attorney/client privilege by statute. The other 11 states and the federal courts have created one through the common law.
69. Upjohn, 449 U.S. at 395.
70. X Corp., 805 F. Supp. at 1306.
71. In re Commercial Financial Serv., Inc., 247 B.R. 828 (N.D. Ok. 2000).
72. B.H. v. Gold Fields Mining Corp., 239 F.R.D. 652, 656 (N.D. Ok. 2005).
73. Interfaith Housing Del., Inc. v. Town of Georgetown, 841 F. Supp. 1393 (D. Del. 1994).
74. United States v. Tomero, 471 F. Supp. 2d 448 (S.D.N.Y. 2007).
75. 524 U.S. 399, 406 (1998).
76. Id. at 411 (O'Connor, J., dissenting).

77. CBS News, *60 Minutes, 26-Year Secret Kept Innocent Man in Prison*, March 9, 2008 (updated May 23, 2008), available at http://www.cbsnews.com/stories/2008/03/06/60minutes/main3914719.shtml.

78. Robert P. Mosteller, *The Special Threat of Informants to the Innocent Who Are Not Innocents: Producing "First Drafts," Recording Incentives, and Taking a Fresh Look at the Evidence*, 6 O.S.U.J.Crim. L. 519 (2009).

79. In Re Miller, 595 S.E.2d 120 (N.C. 2004).

80. Mosteller, *supra* note 81, at 521.

81. N.C.R. Prof. Conduct sec. 1.6(b)(3).

82. EPIC, *supra* note 69, at 4.

83. Kan. Stat. Ann. § 60-429(a).

84. Pamela A. Haun, *The Marital Privilege in the Twenty-First Century*, 32 U. Memphis L. Rev. (2001).

85. Wolfle v. United States (1934).

86. Ak. R. E. 505(a)(1).

87. Ar. R. E. 504(b).

88. United States v. Smith, 533 F.2d 1077 (8th Cir. 1976).

89. Ariz. Rev. Stat. § 12-2232.

90. *See* State v. Adamson, 72 Ohio St. 3d 431, 433-434 (Ohio App. 1995).

91. Trammel v. United States, 445 U.S. 40 (1980).

92. Id. at 52.

93. Bruce I. McDaniel, *Marital Privilege under Rule 501 of the Federal Rules of Evidence*, 46 A.L.R. 735 at § 2(a) (1980).

94. Robert Kardell, *Spousal Privileges in the Federal Law*, 72 FBI Law Enforcement Bulletin (2003).

95. Colo. Rev. Stat. § 13-90-107(1)(a)(II).

96. *See e.g.*, Fla. Stat. § 90.504(3) (2008) (no spousal privilege exists in a proceeding brought by one spouse against the other, in a criminal proceeding in which one spouse is charged with a crime against the person or property of the other spouse, or the person or property of a child of either).

97. United States v. Mendoza, 574 F.2d 1373 (5th Cir. 1975).

98. Oregon's domestic partnership law confers the benefits of marriage on registered domestic partnerships, including the spousal privilege. http://www.osbar.org/public/legalinfo/1191_LGBTLegalRelationships.htm (last viewed May 15, 2009).

99. Karla Schuster & Eden Laikin, *Gay Partner Seeks Spousal Privilege in New York Case*, Los Angeles Times, November 25, 2005, available at http://articles.latimes.com/2005/nov/25/nation/na-partner25.

100. Tom Witosky, *"Stevens' Partner Asserts Spousal Privilege,"* Des Moines Register (October 29, 2009), http://www.desmoinesregister.com/fdcp/?1285016369823.

101. People v. Doe, 403 N.Y.S.2d 375, 378 (N.Y. App. Div. 1978).

102. Kelly Korell, *Testimonial Privilege for Confidential Communications between Relatives other than Husband and Wife—State Cases*, 62 A.L.R. 5th 629 at § 3 (1998).

103. *See e.g.*, State v. Willoughby, 532 A.2d 1020 (Me. 1987); State v. Maxon, 756 P.2d 1297 (Wash. 1988).

104. *See e.g.*, United States v. Davies, 768 F.2d 893 (7th Cir. 1985).

105. Maxon, 756 P.2d at 1301-02.

106. *See* People v. Johnson, 644 N.E.2d 1378 (N.Y. 1994) (presence of defendant's brother during confession to mother violated confidentiality).

107. People v. Tesh, 508 N.Y.S.2d 560 (2d Dep't 1986).

108. State v. Good, 417 S.E.2d 643 (S.C. App. 1992) (testimony of defendant's uncle should have been admitted since it was not subject to parental privilege).

109. People v. Hilligas, 670 N.Y.S.2d 744 (Sup. Ct. 1998).

110. State v. Willoughby, 532 A.2d 1020 (Me. 1987).

111. In re Grand Jury Subpoena John Doe No. A01-209, 197 F. Supp. 2d 512 (E.D. Va. 2002).

112. *See e.g.*, Idaho R. Evid. 503(c).

113. Ill. L.C.S. 5/8-802.

114. Benton v. Superior Court, 897 P.2d 1352 (Ariz. App. 1994).

115. *See* California Evidence Code § 998.

116. Auster v. Smith, 517 F.3d 312 (5th Cir. 2008), *citing* Jaffee v. Redmond, 518 U.S. 1 (1996). Compare Colo. Rev. Stat. Ann. § 13-90-107(g) (privilege covers "licensed psychologist, professional counselor, marriage and family therapist, social worker, unlicensed psychotherapist, or licensed addiction counselor") with Haw. R. Evid. 504 (privilege extends only to licensed physicians and psychotherapists).

117. Jaffee v. Redmond, 518 U.S. 1, 10 (1996).

118. 551 P.2d 334 (Cal. 1976).

119. Id. at 347.

120. Paul B. Herbert & Kathryn A. Young, *Tarasoff at Twenty-Five*, 30 J. Am. Acad. Psychiatry L. 275 (2002).

121. Mont. Code Ann. Sec. 27-1-1102.

122. Ill. Comp. Stat. Ann. Ch. 740, sec. 110/11 (viii).

123. Office of Victims of Crime Archive, *Privacy of Victims' Counseling Communications*, Legal Series Bulletin #8 (November 2002), http://www.ncjrs.gov/ovc_archives/bulletins/legalseries/bulletin8/3.html.

124. *See e.g.*, Vt. Stat. Ann. § 12-61-1614(a)(1)(A).

125. *See* V.B.T. v. Family Serv. Of Western Penn., 705 A.2d 1325 (Sup. Ct. Pa. 1998); In Re: People v. Turner, 109 P.3d 639 (Colo. 2005).

126. Id.

127. State v. Fromme, 930 N.E.2d 1169, 1188 (Ind. App. 2010).

128. Commonwealth v. Wilson, 602 A.2d 1290, 1299 (Pa. 1992) (Zappala, J., dissenting).

129. Commonwealth v. Liang, 747 N.E.2d 112 (Mass. 2001).

130. Id. at 119.

131. Branzburg v. Hayes, 408 U.S. 665, 691 (1972).

132. Id. at 695.

133. In Re Grand Jury Subpoenas, 438 F. Supp. 2d 1111 (N.D. Cal. 2006).

134. A.P., *Lawyer's Plea Agreement Will Keep Reporters Out of Jail* (February 14, 2007), http://www.espn.go.com.espn/news/story?id=2766011.

CHAPTER 11

Witnesses Part III: Impeachment and Cross-Examination

Lawyer: Doctor, before you performed the autopsy, did you check for a pulse?

Witness: No.

Lawyer: Did you check for blood pressure?

Witness: No.

Lawyer: Did you check for breathing?

Witness: No.

Lawyer: So, then it is possible that the patient was alive when you began the autopsy?

Witness: No.

Lawyer: How can you be so sure, Doctor?

Witness: Because his brain was sitting on my desk in a jar.

Lawyer: But could the patient have still been alive nevertheless?

Witness: Yes, it is possible that he could have been alive and practicing law somewhere.[1]

Chapter Topics

Objectives

After reading this chapter, students will be able to:

- Identify the six types of impeachment

- Understand how impeachment is conducted and what types of evidence may be used for impeachment

- Understand the process for cross-examining witnesses

Introduction

As you have learned by now, the vast majority of evidence is admitted through the testimony of witnesses. Witnesses testify about what they saw and heard, help lay the foundation for the admission of photographs and other demonstrative evidence, give opinions on a variety of topics, and introduce physical evidence found at the scene. But if the jury just had the witness's version to go by, it would often only get one side of the story. In some cases, witnesses may truly believe what they saw or heard but do not provide accurate testimony because they did not have the necessary vantage point or lacked the ability to perceive it clearly. A witness's view may have been partially obstructed. He may have forgotten his eyeglasses and not been able to see clearly. His mind may even have played tricks on him.

People also have inherent biases or prejudices. A witness may give testimony to try and protect another person, such as a boyfriend or girlfriend, from going to jail. A person may testify out of self-interest in return for a better deal. Some people may be afraid of the consequences and fear retaliation if they give an accurate version of events. Others are racially prejudiced. In addition, many witnesses in criminal cases are criminals themselves and may not be trustworthy.

Pointing out the flaws or weaknesses of the witness's testimony is done through a process known as impeaching the witness. In this chapter, you will learn the various methods of impeachment, including showing the bias of a witness, demonstrating his incapacity to properly observe events, or pointing out contradictions and inconsistencies in his statement. Impeachment is usually carried out during cross-examination. The hope is that by allowing both parties to question a witness, a truer, more accurate version of events will be presented to the jury. Unlike on television or in the movies, however, witnesses very rarely recant their stories when confronted by the cross-examiner. It is left to the jury to fill in the gaps and decide what the truth is.

I. IMPEACHMENT

Credibility
the believability of a witness's testimony as determined from his ability to perceive events and provide unbiased testimony

Impeachment
the process of challenging a witness's credibility such as pointing out inconsistencies in his story or attacking his character

The degree of believability of a witness's testimony is known as **credibility**. A witness's credibility is assessed from a number of factors, including his ability to provide unbiased testimony, his prior character, and his ability to relate events fully and accurately. The process through which the parties discredit or challenge various aspects of the witness's credibility is called **impeachment**. Rule 607 permits any party to impeach a witness, including the party calling the witness.[2] In other words, a party can impeach his own witness. Witnesses can be impeached in a variety of ways, including challenging their ability to perceive or relate events, questioning their motives to lie or shade the truth, and confronting them with prior inconsistent statements they have made concerning the topic of their testimony.

Prior to the adoption of the Rules of Evidence, there were six methods used to impeach witnesses: (a) impeachment by demonstration of some bias, prejudice, interest in the litigation, or motive to testify in a particular fashion; (b) impeachment by demonstration of incapacity to perceive, remember, or relate; (c) impeachment by contradiction; (d) impeachment by conviction of a crime; (e) impeachment by prior inconsistent statement; and (f) impeachment by demonstration of a person's untruthful character.[3] The Rules of Evidence have incorporated the last three methods of impeachment: reputation and character for truthfulness or prior acts that show the same (Rule 608); a felony conviction or other qualifying crime

(Rule 609); and inconsistent statements (Rule 613). Despite the fact that the Rules recognize only the last three types, all six methods of impeachment are still used.

One method of impeachment that is no longer used, however, is impeachment by attacking a person's religious beliefs. Witnesses who were atheists or nonbelievers often had their character for truthfulness impugned. Today, Rule 610 expressly prohibits impeaching a witness's credibility through questions about his religious beliefs.[4] A brief discussion of each type of impeachment follows. Examples of each type of impeachment are also provided.

A. Bias or Motive to Lie

Impeachment by bias or motive
a method of impeachment that attacks the credibility of the witness by showing that he has some reason to lie due to some relationship to a party

Impeachment by bias or motive rests on two assumptions: (1) that certain relationships or circumstances may impair the impartiality of the witness; and (2) that a witness who is not impartial may, consciously or otherwise, shade his or her testimony in favor of or against a party.[5] Examples of relationships or circumstances that would create such a bias include being related to a party, being involved in an intimate relationship with a party, having a financial interest in the outcome of the case, being paid by a party to testify as an expert witness, or having been granted immunity or a reduced sentence in exchange for testimony. If a witness is testifying in exchange for a reduced sentence, the defense attorney will question the witness about that fact and what the terms of that agreement are. Often, the prosecution will introduce this issue first, asking the witness about it on direct examination to avoid the appearance that the prosecution is hiding something from the jury.

Biases of witnesses may not be readily apparent. It is therefore important for an investigator to determine what biases or motives a witness may have near the outset of a case. If they are not discovered, the prosecutor or defense attorney may not realize that a witness could be fabricating his testimony. A brief background investigation should be done to determine if the witness is related to the defendant, has a bias or prejudice against a certain racial or ethnic group, or is biased against the defendant. This process can be done during the initial investigation or after charges have been filed.

Extrinsic evidence
evidence independent of the testimony of the witness being impeached

In order to establish a bias or motive on the part of the witness, the opposing party may inquire into the nature of the relationship between the witness and the party during cross-examination. If the witness denies the relationship or bias, the opposing party may prove it by introduction of **extrinsic evidence** (evidence independent of the testimony of the witness being impeached).

Practical Example

Assume that the defendant has called his girlfriend to testify about his alibi on the night of the alleged incident. The jury has a right to know that the witness testifying on behalf of the defendant is in fact his girlfriend and thus may have a strong bias or self-interest to lie on his behalf. On cross-examination, the prosecutor may question the girlfriend about her relationship to the defendant and ask if she would do anything to prevent him from going to jail.

B. Lack of Capacity to Perceive or Recall

Impeachment by incapacity
a method of impeachment that involves questioning a witness about his or her ability to accurately perceive events such as whether the witness could have gotten a good look at the suspect

Impeachment by incapacity to perceive or recall events is the second type of impeachment. This involves challenging the witness' ability to accurately observe certain events or her memory of them. In this case, the witness usually does not have a conscious motive to lie but may still provide inaccurate testimony due to flaws in her observations or memory. This method is commonly used to challenge the accuracy of eyewitness testimony or identifications. Although the witness may have been present at the scene, she may not have gotten a good look at the suspect because she was not wearing her glasses at the time or had her view partially blocked. For example, the witness can be asked whether she was wearing glasses at the time of the incident and whether she needed them to accurately observe events. If she was not wearing glasses, then her testimony would be seriously called into question. Similarly, the witness may have trouble accurately recalling details of the events, even if she had initially perceived them correctly. Either way, a good cross-examiner can do serious damage to the credibility of a witness using this method of impeachment.

Practical Example

Assume that a defendant is on trial for robbing someone at gunpoint. The defense could challenge the witness's identification of the defendant as the robber by impeaching his ability to perceive the robber's face in the first place. He could point out that the witness was robbed from behind, the alley was dark, the witness was focused on the gun, and that the witness only caught a glimpse of the robber as he ran away.

Impeachment by contradiction
a method of impeachment that attacks the witness's credibility by getting the witness to admit to flaws or errors in his testimony or by calling a separate witness to do the same

C. Contradiction

The third common law method of impeachment is **impeachment by contradiction**. This involves showing that the witness's testimony is incorrect or false, either by introducing separate evidence showing the

EVIDENCE IN ACTION

The Scottsboro Boys Rape Trial

A classic example of impeachment by lack of capacity was used by Samuel Leibowitz in the notorious Scottsboro Boys rape trial. There, nine young black men were accused of raping two white women on a train in Alabama in the 1930s. The case attracted national attention because it appeared from the outset that the women had fabricated the rape story.

The case produced four trials, and guilty verdicts were twice overturned by the Supreme Court. The first trial was nothing more than a sham. The boys' alleged defense attorney only met with them for 20 minutes prior to trial and barely contested the prosecution's evidence. Not surprisingly, the boys were convicted and sentenced to death. When the guilty verdicts were overturned on due-process grounds, the Communist Party took over the case and named Samuel Leibowitz, a noted criminal defense attorney from New York, to represent the boys in future trials.

During the second trial, Ory Dobbins, a man from a nearby farm, claimed to have seen the incident and testified that he saw "one of the Negroes grab one of the women and throw her down." Knowing that the witness could not have clearly seen the incident as the train rushed by, Leibowitz asked the man what type of clothes the women were wearing at the time of their alleged rape. Dobbins responded by stating that the pair had been wearing dresses. Leibowitz then produced newspaper photos from the date of the incident that showed the pair dressed in overalls. Dobbins clung to his story, even in the face of prodding from the judge as to whether he really meant the pair was

Figure 11.1 Famed defense attorney Samuel Leibowitz cross-examines Ory Dobbins during the second trial in the Scottsboro Boys rape case in Decatur, Alabama on April 5, 1933. Dobbins admitted his testimony was different than that given during the first trial but could not explain the discrepancies. © *Corbis*

dressed in overalls.[6] The inescapable conclusion was that the man had lied about witnessing the incident to bolster the prosecution's case. Despite this and other damning evidence of the boys' innocence, four of the defendants were convicted a second time and sentenced to death. This time, the judge threw out the verdict and granted new trials.

After two more rounds of trials, some of the boys were again convicted but were sentenced to life in prison. Plea deals were then reached. Five of the defendants were released without conducting trials, and the remaining convicted defendants were eventually all released from prison.

contradiction or by getting the witness to contradict his own testimony on cross-examination.[7] For example, the prosecutor might ask the defendant whether he believes all the witnesses who testified to one version of events must be lying if we are to believe the defendant's contrary version of events. The opposing party can also contradict the testimony of a witness by calling another witness in rebuttal such as to contradict an alibi witness.

Practical Example

Assume the defendant is on trial for sexual assault. He calls his friend to testify to his alibi. The friend testifies that the defendant was with him at the restaurant eating dinner at the time of the alleged rape. The prosecutor's impeachment might sound like this:

DA: *You know the friends of the defendant, correct?*

Witness: *Yeah.*

DA: *Johnny the Lip is a good friend of the defendant's, correct?*

Witness: *Yeah. He and Johnny are good buddies.*

DA: *And Johnny would have no reason to lie or to hurt the defendant, right?*

Witness: *Yeah. They're tight.*

DA: *So if Johnny testified that the defendant left the restaurant around 7:30, there'd be no reason to doubt his testimony, would there?*

Witness: *No.*

DA: *So is it possible that the defendant left the restaurant earlier than you testified to?*

Witness: *I guess that's possible.*

D. Impeachment by Character and Conduct

1. Attacking Character by Reputation or Opinion

Rule 608. Evidence of Character and Conduct of Witness

(a) Opinion and reputation evidence of character.—The credibility of a witness may be attacked or supported by evidence in the form of opinion or reputation, but subject to these limitations: (1) the evidence may refer only to character for truthfulness or untruthfulness, and (2) evidence of truthful character is admissible only after the character of the witness for truthfulness has been attacked by opinion or reputation evidence or otherwise.

EVIDENCE IN ACTION

The Perjury Trial of Alger Hiss

Alger Hiss, a State Department official, was tried and convicted of perjury in 1950 for lying about being a Soviet spy and his involvement with Whittaker Chambers, a former Communist. The trial contained a classic example of impeachment by contradiction. In 1948, Hiss had been called to testify before the House Committee on Un-American Activities led by then Congressman Richard Nixon. While under oath, Hiss had claimed he was neither a Communist nor a spy.

Subsequently, Chambers claimed Hiss was a member of an underground organization of the Communist Party and had provided him copies of State Department documents. Chambers produced photos of the documents, the film of which he had hidden in a hollowed out pumpkin. Chambers' evidence was dubbed the "Pumpkin Papers" by the press.

Hiss was then tried for perjury based on this evidence. During his second trial, Hiss called Dr. Carl A. Binger, a psychiatrist, in his defense. The expert testified that Whittaker Chambers exhibited signs of being a psychopath and a pathological liar. He based these conclusions on his observations of Chambers during the trial and his writings. He noted that Chambers' tendency to look up at the ceiling during his testimony was an indication of his psychopathic personality. He also stated that his lack of concern for his appearance and his untidiness were also signs. Dr. Binger found it significant that Chambers had hidden the evidence in a pumpkin (as we learned in the previous chapter, such testimony would today

Figure 11.2 Alger Hiss, a former State Department employee, is seen here on December 15, 1948, issuing a statement that his testimony before a federal grand jury had been "entirely truthful." Hiss was indicted by the grand jury on charges of giving false testimony before the House Committee on Un-American Activities. © *Bettmann/Corbis*

be labeled as junk science under *Daubert* and likely not allowed).

The prosecution attacked Dr. Binger's credibility on cross-examination through impeachment by contradiction. He asked Dr. Binger what should be made of the fact that Dr. Binger himself had looked up at the ceiling 50 times during his own testimony. He also asked Dr. Binger if Albert Einstein, Thomas Edison, and Bing Crosby were all psychopaths since they were well known for their untidiness as well. He also pointed to several famous instances of hidings and asked whether those were also indicative of a serious personality disorder.

His credibility in tatters, Dr. Binger proved to do more harm than good for Hiss's defense. Hiss was subsequently convicted and sentenced to five years in prison.[8]

Impeachment by character

a method of impeachment that involves demonstrating that the witness has a poor character for truthfulness. This is usually demonstrated through reputation or opinion evidence by calling a second witness to testify to the first's character

The fourth method for challenging a witness's credibility is **impeachment by character**. It is governed by Rule 608. Under Rule 608(a), the witness's credibility can be attacked or supported through either opinion or reputation evidence subject to a couple of restrictions. Such evidence can only refer to the witness's character for truthfulness or untruthfulness, and evidence of a witness's truthful character can only be presented once his character has been attacked.[9] This method of impeachment usually involves calling a separate witness to rebut the character of the first. That witness would either have to have knowledge of the first witness's reputation in the community for truthfulness or have personal knowledge of the witness's character. The person calling the character witness would thus have to establish a foundation that the character witness has sufficient knowledge of those items.

Practical Example

Assume the defendant is on trial for aggravated assault. The defense calls a witness to testify that he saw the alleged incident and that he believes the victim started the whole thing and was acting in self-defense. The prosecutor can call a rebuttal witness to testify that the first witness has a very poor reputation for truthfulness in the community. The defense could then attempt to rehabilitate the character of that witness by introducing evidence of that person's good character.

2. Attacking Character by Prior Conduct of Witness

Rule 608. Evidence of Character and Conduct of Witness

(b) Specific instances of conduct.—Specific instances of the conduct of a witness, for the purpose of attacking or supporting the witness' character for truthfulness, other than conviction of crime as provided in rule 609, may not be proved by extrinsic evidence. They may, however, in the discretion of the court, if probative of truthfulness or untruthfulness, be inquired into on cross-examination of the witness (1) concerning the witness' character for truthfulness or untruthfulness, or (2) concerning the character for truthfulness or untruthfulness of another witness as to which character the witness being cross-examined has testified. The giving of testimony, whether by an accused or by any other witness, does not operate as a waiver of the accused's or the witness' privilege against self-incrimination when examined with respect to matters that relate only to character for truthfulness.

The second method for impeaching the character of a witness under Rule 608 involves attacking that witness's character by questioning him

Impeachment by prior conduct
a method of impeachment that involves asking the witness about prior instances of misconduct that relate to untruthfulness but that did not result in a conviction

about his prior conduct. Rule 608(b) permits a party to impeach a witness by asking about prior bad acts. These prior acts must be probative of truthfulness but must have not resulted in a conviction that would be admissible under Rule 609.[10] Thus, **impeachment by prior conduct** involves asking a witness about charged or uncharged misconduct that did not result in a criminal conviction. For example, the prosecutor might ask a character witness for the defendant if he recalls making false statements on a job application, such as listing he had a Master's degree when he only had a Bachelor's.

However, if the witness denies the prior bad conduct, the rule prohibits the introduction of extrinsic evidence to prove that such acts occurred. Extrinsic evidence is that which is not contained in the witness's testimony but which is available from outside sources such as documents or testimony from other witnesses.[11] Ironically, impeachment using this method often works best when the witness is honest enough to admit the prior acts of untruthfulness.

3. Attacking the Defendant's Character

The process of attacking the credibility of the accused occurs in the reverse order than that of attacking the credibility of a witness. In this case, the prosecution cannot attack the character of the accused unless he testifies in his own defense or opens the door by presenting evidence of his good character. We will explore the topic of attacking the character of the accused more in depth in the next chapter. Under Rule 608, however, the prosecution can challenge the defendant's good character once a witness testifies on behalf of the defendant as a character witness.

If a witness testifies that he believes the defendant has a good reputation for truthfulness, the prosecutor can ask the witness if he is familiar with specific instances of misconduct committed by the defendant that show he has been untruthful in the past. For example, suppose the witness testifies that the defendant is an honest individual. The prosecutor then asks the witness on cross-examination whether he is familiar with any acts of dishonesty on the part of the defendant. The witness then testifies that he saw the defendant dilute drugs he sold to customers on several occasions. The prosecutor can also call a witness to rebut the character witness's testimony. In the above example, the prosecutor could call a witness to testify that the defendant's reputation for truthfulness in the community was not a very good one. The decision of whether to use one or both methods of impeachment is left up to the prosecutor.

In addition, if the defendant elects to testify, the prosecutor can impeach him just like any other witness, including questioning him about prior convictions. Remember that although the prosecution cannot use evidence seized in violation of the Fourth Amendment in its case-in-chief to prove the defendant's guilt, it can use such evidence to impeach his testimony. For example, while the prosecutor cannot introduce evidence that six kilos of cocaine were seized from the defendant's home because they were taken without a warrant, the prosecutor could impeach the defendant with this evidence if he testifies he has never been around drugs. Similarly, the prosecutor can impeach the defendant with statements that were obtained in violation of *Miranda*.

Practice Example

Assume the defendant is being tried for possession of a weapon and a controlled substance. Although nearly 100 pounds of marijuana were found in the defendant's apartment, the evidence is suppressed because the court finds neither probable cause nor consent existed for the search. However, the gun and some crack cocaine found on his person during an earlier pat-down search are allowed in evidence. If the defendant elects to testify, the prosecutor can now impeach his testimony with the 100 pounds of marijuana seized from his house.

E. Impeachment by Conviction

Rule 609. Impeachment by Evidence of Conviction of Crime

(a) General rule.—For the purpose of attacking the character for truthfulness of a witness,

(1) evidence that a witness other than an accused has been convicted of a crime shall be admitted, subject to Rule 403, if the crime was punishable by death or imprisonment in excess of one year under the law under which the witness was convicted, and evidence that an accused has been convicted of such a crime shall be admitted if the court determines that the probative value of admitting this evidence outweighs its prejudicial effect to the accused; and

(2) evidence that any witness has been convicted of a crime shall be admitted regardless of the punishment, if it readily can be determined that establishing the elements of the crime required proof or admission of an act of dishonesty or false statement by the witness.

Impeachment by conviction
a method of impeachment that involves questioning a witness about his prior felony convictions or any misdemeanor that relates to dishonesty or false statements

The fifth method for impeaching a witness is **impeachment by conviction** by pointing out that the witness has been previously convicted of a felony or other qualifying offense. Under Rule 609, a witness can be asked about any felony conviction that is probative of truthfulness or any felony or misdemeanor offense that involves dishonesty or false statement. An example of this latter type of offense would be a conviction for fraud, perjury, or providing false information to a police officer.

The Federal Rule prohibits impeaching a witness with convictions older than ten years unless the court finds that it is in the interests of justice to do so.[12] Some states, such as South Carolina, also use a balancing test for admitting remote convictions.[13] In assessing the probative value of a remote prior conviction, the South Carolina courts will look at such factors as the impeachment value of the evidence, the similarity of the past crime to the charged offense, and the centrality of the credibility issue.[14] Note, however, that some states such as Colorado do not use a balancing test, and a defendant can be impeached with any felony, regardless of its remoteness.[15]

1. Acts That Are Probative of Truthfulness

One question that must be answered is what constitutes a crime or act that is probative of truthfulness. Unlike offenses relating to dishonesty that are automatically admissible under 609(a)(2), Rule 609(a)(1) requires that the probative value of the conviction must outweigh its prejudicial effect. Rule 609 presumes that all felonies, regardless of their nature, are probative, to at least some degree, of a witness's credibility.[16] Courts have generally weighed the balance of interests in favor of admissibility since crimes that do not bear directly on dishonesty may still be "highly probative" of a witness's credibility.[17]

A rule of thumb that some courts have used to balance these interests is that "convictions which rest on dishonest conduct relate to credibility whereas those of violent or assaultive crimes generally do not."[18] However, if a violent crime involves planning or premeditation (as opposed to impulsive violence alone), courts have often allowed a witness to be impeached by it since such planning is indicative of a witness's willingness to break the law when it favors his interests.[19]

For example, courts have held that violations of narcotics laws, prostitution, firearms offenses, and violent offenses are not probative of truthfulness.[20] In contrast, courts have held acts of escape, sexual abuse of a child by a person in a position of trust, and crimes involving dishonesty (i.e., forgery, providing false information to police officers, and misrepresentation) to be probative.[21] Courts have split, however, as to whether acts of theft such as shoplifting relate to truthfulness. Most federal courts and some state courts have concluded that acts of theft do not reflect on a person's truthfulness. These courts require an act that is probative of truthfulness to contain an element of deception or false statement.[22] Many state courts, however, have taken a more expansive view, concluding that conduct that seeks to take personal advantage by taking from others is probative of a witness's credibility. This seems to be the more common sense approach to the issue. The Colorado Supreme Court noted that "common experience informs us that a person who takes the property of another for her own benefit is acting in an untruthful or dishonest way."[23]

Practical Example

Assume that a witness is testifying for the defense. The prosecutor wants to impeach the witness with the fact that he was convicted of felony drug possession seven years ago. The prosecutor would not be able to introduce such evidence in federal court or in many state courts since a drug conviction is not very probative of credibility.

Now assume that the prosecutor wants to introduce evidence that the witness was convicted of stealing from her company three years ago. The evidence would now be admissible since it is probative of the witness's credibility.

Next, assume that the conviction in the above example is 15 years old. The prosecutor would not be able to question the witness about it unless the court found that its probative value substantially outweighed its prejudicial effect. However, the conviction would be automatically admissible in a state like Colorado, which has no such time limit.

---

2. Elements of the Underlying Conviction

When impeaching a witness, the party cross-examining the witness is usually limited to asking the witness about the name of the offense, the date of conviction, and the nature of the offense.[24] The witness cannot be questioned about specific details of the offense. Unlike Rule 608, if the witness denies that he has been convicted of a felony, the opposing party can present extrinsic evidence of the conviction, usually by introducing a certified copy of it.

Practical Example

Assume a witness is testifying as a character witness on behalf of the defendant. The district attorney can cross-examine the witness about the nature of his prior felonies but not the specific acts underlying them.

DA: *You were convicted of armed robbery in 2007, correct?*

Witness: *Yes.*

DA: *And you were convicted of that crime in Illinois?*

Witness: Yes.

DA: And under Illinois law, that crime is a felony, correct?

Witness: Yeah, I guess so.

The prosecutor cannot ask the witness about the specifics of the underlying crime, however.

DA: You pointed a gun at a nun and demanded her purse in that incident, isn't that right?

Defense: Objection, your honor. The prosecutor can't inquire into the specifics of the incident.

Judge: The objection is sustained.

---

3. Juvenile Adjudications

A question that often comes up is whether a witness can be impeached with offenses committed while he was a juvenile. Juveniles under 18 are ordinarily tried in juvenile court, and rather than being convicted of a crime, they are adjudicated as juvenile delinquents. In federal court, **juvenile adjudications** are not ordinarily usable to impeach a witness unless the offense is one that would be admissible to attack the credibility of an adult and the evidence is "necessary for a fair determination of guilt or innocence."[25] In other words, the impeaching party has to show more than that the juvenile offense bears on the witness's credibility. In order to determine whether an adjudication is necessary for a determination of guilt, courts look at several factors, including whether there is other evidence that the witness can be impeached with and whether it is probative of dishonesty.[26]

> **Juvenile adjudication**
> a judicial finding that a juvenile has committed the equivalent of a criminal offense. It is usable to impeach a witness with only if the party makes a showing that the witness cannot be impeached with other evidence and it is probative of dishonesty

States have varying rules about whether juvenile offenses are usable for impeachment. Some states follow the federal rule and allow the use of juvenile adjudications for impeachment where it bears directly on guilt or innocence of the defendant.[27] In some states, the use of juvenile adjudications is barred outright for impeachment purposes.[28] The idea behind this philosophy is that juveniles should be protected from the embarrassment and permanent stigma that attaches to adults who are convicted of crimes. Even where the cross-examiner cannot use the fact of the adjudication to impeach, he can bring out the underlying acts in some states like New York.[29] Finally, some states like California do not distinguish between juvenile adjudications and criminal convictions for purposes of impeachment.[30] As long as the conviction concerns "moral turpitude," the impeaching party can use it regardless of whether it is a juvenile conviction or not.

Practical Example

Assume the defendant is on trial for robbery. There is a witness who will testify that she was with the defendant in a coffee shop at the time of the robbery. The witness has a juvenile adjudication for fraud and forgery but no other convictions in the past five years. The court would likely allow the use of the adjudication to impeach the witness because there are no other convictions and her testimony is highly relevant to guilt or innocence.

F. Prior Inconsistent Statements

Rule 613. Prior Statements of Witnesses

(a) Examining witness concerning prior statement.—In examining a witness concerning a prior statement made by the witness, whether written or not, the statement need not be shown nor its contents disclosed to the witness at that time, but on request the same shall be shown or disclosed to opposing counsel.

(b) Extrinsic evidence of prior inconsistent statement of witness.—Extrinsic evidence of a prior inconsistent statement by a witness is not admissible unless the witness is afforded an opportunity to explain or deny the same and the opposite party is afforded an opportunity to interrogate the witness thereon, or the interests of justice otherwise require. This provision does not apply to admissions of a party-opponent as defined in rule 801(d)(2).

Impeachment by prior inconsistent statement
a method of impeachment that occurs by comparing a statement made during a witness's testimony with one made by the witness at an earlier date. If the witness admits making the earlier statement, the impeachment is complete. If the witness denies it, then the other party can introduce evidence of the earlier statement

The final method of impeachment is conducted through questioning the witness about his **prior inconsistent statements**. This is the most frequently used method of impeachment.[31] The witness is impeached by showing that his prior declarations, statements, or testimony contradict, or are inconsistent with, the witness's trial testimony. Rule 613 allows the impeaching attorney to immediately confront the witness with the statement without first drawing the witness's attention to it.[32] While the rule does not require that the impeaching party has to show the prior statement to the witness (such as a copy of a grand jury transcript), he should still direct the witness's attention to the time, place, and circumstances under which it was made for the sake of clarity. If the witness admits making the contradictory statement, then the impeachment is complete.[33]

On the other hand, if the witness denies making the prior statement or cannot remember making it, then the impeaching party is allowed to admit extrinsic proof of the statement. This could involve either admitting a copy of the statement, such as a copy of a grand jury transcript, or by calling the witness to whom the statement was made. It should be noted that inconsistent statements are generally used only to impeach the credibility of the witness and cannot be admitted as substantive evidence of guilt.

Cross-Examination of Mark Fuhrman and Introduction of the "Fuhrman Tapes"

The O.J. Simpson murder trial produced one of the historic examples of impeachment by inconsistent statements. Detective Mark Fuhrman was credited with finding the infamous "bloody glove" at the Simpson compound in Brentwood. In order to discredit his testimony and his character, the defense learned during its pretrial investigation that Detective Fuhrman had espoused racist views. Given the racial makeup of the jury and the fact that O.J. Simpson was African American, this revelation would be the death knell to the prosecution's case.

During cross-examination of Detective Fuhrman on March 15, 1995, F. Lee Bailey elicited the following testimony about his use of the word "nigger":

> **Mr. Bailey:** Do you use the word "nigger" in describing people?
>
> **Fuhrman:** No, sir.
>
> **Mr. Bailey:** Have you ever used that word in the past 10 years?
>
> **Fuhrman:** Not that I recall, no.
>
> **Mr. Bailey:** I want you to assume that perhaps at some time since 1985 or 1985, you addressed a member of the African-American race as a nigger. Is it possible that you have forgotten that act on your part?
>
> **Fuhrman:** No, it is not possible.
>
> **Mr. Bailey:** Are you therefore saying that you have not used that word in the past 10 years, Detective Fuhrman?
>
> **Fuhrman:** Yes, that is what I'm saying.

Figure 11.3 O.J. Simpson defense attorney F. Lee Bailey cross-examines Mark Fuhrman on March 15, 1995 during Simpson's murder trial. © *Ted Soqui/Sygma/Corbis*

> **Mr. Bailey:** And you say under oath that you have not addressed any black person as a nigger or spoken about black people as niggers in the past 10 years, Detective Fuhrman?
>
> **Fuhrman:** That's what I'm saying, sir.
>
> **Mr. Bailey:** So that anyone who comes to this court and quotes you as using that word in dealing with African Americans would be a liar, would they not, Detective Fuhrman?
>
> **Fuhrman:** Yes, they would.
>
> **Mr. Bailey:** All of them, correct?
>
> **Fuhrman:** All of them.

The defense then introduced the so-called "Fuhrman Tapes" in its case-in-chief. Mark Fuhrman had been interviewed by a freelance writer, Laura Hart McKinny, 10 years earlier about life as a police officer for use in her screenplay. She had preserved most of the tapes. The tapes contained 40 uses of the term "nigger" in referring to black persons in a racially disparaging context. The tapes were played to the jury with devastating effect. In fact, Detective Fuhrman pled the Fifth when recalled by the defense in an effort to question him about his earlier statements to the contrary.[34]

Practical Example

Assume the defendant is on trial for assault involving a bar fight. The defense counsel might impeach the victim in the following manner:

DA: *Do you remember testifying at the preliminary hearing in this case on December 7 of last year?*

Witness: *Yes.*

DA: *And do you recall testifying that the defendant punched you in the face outside the bar on the night of March 1 of last year?*

Witness: *Yes.*

DA: *But your testimony today is that the defendant only tripped and fell into you, is that correct?*

Witness: *Yes, that's correct.*

DA: *Is it fair to say you had a clearer recollection of what happened at the bar when you testified this past December than you do now?*

Witness: *Yes.*

The impeachment is thus complete. But if the witness denies making the prior statement or refuses to explain the inconsistency, the impeaching party may introduce extrinsic evidence of the statement.

DA: *Do you recall testifying that the defendant punched you in the face outside the bar on the night of March 1 of last year?*

Witness: *No, I didn't say that. I said only that I thought the defendant was being belligerent.*

DA: *So you're denying you stated he hit you?*

Witness: *Correct.*

DA: *Let the record reflect I am showing the witness Exhibit 13, a copy of his preliminary hearing testimony. Can you read lines 7 and 8 out loud to the jury?*

Witness: *The defendant was arguing with me about his girlfriend. He then pushed me into the table and took two swings at me.*

DA: *Your honor, I'd like to admit Exhibit 13 into evidence.*

II. CROSS-EXAMINATION OF WITNESSES

Rule 611. Mode and Order of Interrogation and Presentation

(a) Control by court.—The court shall exercise reasonable control over the mode and order of interrogating witnesses and presenting evidence so as to (1) make the interrogation and presentation effective for the ascertainment of the truth, (2) avoid needless consumption of time, and (3) protect witnesses from harassment or undue embarrassment.

(b) Scope of cross-examination.—Cross-examination should be limited to the subject matter of the direct examination and matters affecting the credibility of the witness. The court may, in the exercise of discretion, permit inquiry into additional matters as if on direct examination.

(c) Leading questions.—Leading questions should not be used on the direct examination of a witness except as may be necessary to develop the witness' testimony. Ordinarily leading questions should be permitted on cross-examination. When a party calls a hostile witness, an adverse party, or a witness identified with an adverse party, interrogation may be by leading questions.

Cross-examination
the process by which one party questions the opposing party's witness, usually to attack the credibility of that witness

Cross-examination is one of the hallmarks of the trial process. It is the process of questioning the other party's witnesses. There are several purposes for cross-examination, including clarifying the testimony of a witness, pointing out inconsistencies in the testimony, or attacking the character of the witness.

Rule 611 outlines the process for cross-examination. The scope is limited to subjects discussed during direct examination of the witness or matters affecting the witness's credibility. If an attorney asks a question of the witness outside of those guidelines, it will usually be objected to. While judges will often grant attorneys leeway to explore issues of credibility, parties will usually not be able to ask questions concerning completely unrelated events.

For example, suppose a witness testifies about what he observed during a bar fight. His testimony is limited to what he observed that night at the bar. The opposing attorney cannot ask about unrelated events such as whether the witness had smoked marijuana with the defendant a week before the incident. Such a question does not concern the bar fight and bears little on the witness's credibility. However, if the attorney instead asks whether the witness had smoked marijuana two hours before going to the bar, this question is now relevant because it directly relates to whether the witness was under the influence at the time he observed the fight.

Leading questions
questions that imply the answer in the question itself

Rule 611 permits cross-examination to be conducted using leading questions. **Leading questions** are questions that imply the answer in the question itself. For example, a direct question would ask, "What was the color of the light?" In contrast, a leading question would ask, "The light was red, wasn't it?" Remember from Chapter 3 that direct examination of witnesses is usually limited to nonleading (direct) questions.

The process of cross-examination involves asking a series of questions that forces the witness to admit the answer to the question or at least qualify previous answers. The ultimate goal is to poke holes in the witness's testimony by having the witness admit to a series of facts that leads to the conclusion that his original testimony was incomplete or inaccurate. It essentially allows the jury to make conclusions based on logic: if a, b, and c are true, then the jury can infer that d must be true as well.

Unlike portrayals of trials on television, most cross-examiners stop short of accusing a witness of lying or shading the truth. Most people are not going to admit that they are lying, even in the face of overwhelming evidence to the contrary. As a result, good cross-examiners let the jury come to the inescapable conclusion that the witness is lying without having the witness actually admit it.

Cross-examination works because the questioner has a pre-identified goal in mind, such as challenging the witness's ability to observe an event. Good cross-examiners put the witness in a box without leaving him room to wiggle out. This can be done by asking general questions about a topic and then asking progressively more specific questions that lead the jury to the desired conclusion. Poor cross-examiners often ask questions for the sake of asking questions without a clear plan or goal in mind. As a result, they often have the witness repeat what they have just testified to, reinforcing the witness's testimony in the minds of the jury.

The difficulty with cross-examination is that the cross-examiner does not know for sure what answers will come out of the witness's mouth. Thus, attorneys will usually not ask questions on cross-examination that they do not know the answers to. For instance, asking why a witness did something is usually not a good idea since it is impossible to predict what the witness's motivations were.

Practical Example

Here is an example of basic cross-examination technique. Assume that a witness testifies that he observed the defendant police officer punch and kick a suspect after an altercation at a bar. The cross-examiner's job is to discredit the reliability of the witness's perceptions.

Defense Attorney: *You testified that you were at dinner with a date at the time of the altercation, correct?*

Witness: *Yes.*

Defense Attorney: *You were on you first date that night, correct?*

Witness: *Yes.*

Defense Attorney: *You were trying to impress your date that evening, correct?*

Witness: *I guess you can say that.*

Defense Attorney: *So you were paying attention to your date rather than the crowd in the restaurant, is that fair to say?*

Witness: *We were engaged in conversation, yes.*

Defense Attorney: *I see you're wearing glasses. Are you near- or far-sighted?*

Witness: *I'm near-sighted.*

Defense Attorney: *So you need your glasses to see things far away, correct?*

Witness: *Yes.*

Defense Attorney: *You weren't wearing your glasses that evening, were you?*

Witness: *No.*

Defense Attorney: *You were paying more attention to your date than the commotion in the bar, right?*

Witness: *That's true.*

Although the witness never says she did not see the confrontation in the bar, the jury is left with the impression that she did not get a good look at the fight.

CHAPTER SUMMARY

Impeachment is the process by which each side attacks the credibility of the other side's witnesses. Anyone can impeach a witness, including the party who calls him. There are several methods of impeachment. A witness can be impeached by showing his biases or motives to lie; getting the witness to contradict his testimony; showing that the witness had some incapacity to either perceive or recall the event he is testifying about; attacking his character for truthfulness through reputation or prior acts; attacking his character by questioning the witness about prior convictions; and questioning the witness about prior inconsistent statements. Depending on the type of impeachment used, extrinsic or outside evidence may be presented to complete the impeachment.

Witnesses can be impeached using their prior convictions. Most felony convictions can be used for this purpose as long as they are less than 10 years old. Misdemeanor convictions can also be used for impeachment, but only if they involve false statements or dishonesty.

Most impeachment occurs through the use of cross-examination. This is the method for questioning the opposing party's witnesses. Cross-examination is conducted using leading questions. It is designed to get the witness to admit or make concessions to a series of questions. The goal is to form an impression in the minds of the jury that the witness is lying or has not testified completely and accurately.

KEY TERMS

- Credibility
- Cross-examination
- Extrinsic evidence
- Impeachment
- Impeachment by bias or motive

- Impeachment by contradiction
- Impeachment by conviction
- Impeachment by incapacity
- Impeachment by prior conduct

- Impeachment by prior inconsistent statements
- Juvenile adjudications
- Leading questions

REVIEW QUESTIONS

1. What is meant by the phrase "the credibility of a witness"? What is the importance of credibility to a witness's testimony?

2. What is meant by the term impeachment? Who can impeach a witness?

3. Name the six types of impeachment.

4. Name three ways in which a witness can be biased.

5. What is impeachment by contradiction? Give one example.

6. Can a witness be impeached with prior bad conduct for which he has not been convicted? Explain and give an example.

7. Can a witness be impeached with a felony conviction? What about a felony that is 15 years old?

8. Under what circumstances can a witness be impeached with a misdemeanor conviction?

9. What is cross-examination? What types of questions are used during cross-examination?

10. What are leading questions? When can they be asked of a witness?

APPLICATION PROBLEMS

1. George is on trial for murdering Susan. Elaine is called to testify for the prosecution. She testifies that she saw George and Susan in a heated argument the morning of the murder. The defense attorney tries to impeach Elaine with the fact that she is Susan's best friend. What type of impeachment is this?

2. Flanders is on trial for fraud. He testifies in his own defense that he was just trying to help the church. The prosecutor wants to impeach Flanders with a felony conviction for possession

of stolen property that is five years old. Can he be impeached with this conviction? Explain. Now the prosecutor wants to impeach him with a misdemeanor conviction for giving a false name to a police officer seven years ago. Can he be impeached with this conviction? Explain.

3. Joey is on trial for sexual assault. Chandler testifies as a character witness in his defense. The prosecutor asks him whether he is familiar with Joey's reputation for truthfulness in the community. Chandler says yes and that he believes it to be a good one. The prosecutor then asks whether Chandler is familiar with an incident that occurred four years ago where Joey was accused of fondling Monica, a misdemeanor charge. Can the prosecutor impeach Chandler with this incident? Explain.

4. Fraser is on trial for drug possession. His dad testifies that Fraser hadn't used drugs in the past three years and had been clean for that period. The prosecutor tries to impeach the dad's testimony by asking if the dad remembers making a statement to the cops the night of Fraser's arrest to the effect that the cops needed "to get that deadbeat hophead out of my house."

The dad replies that he was just angry that night. What type of impeachment is this an example of?

5. Michael is a famous athlete. He is busted for contributing to the delinquency of a minor. Michael's sister testifies in his defense. She states she believes Michael is a great person who wouldn't do such a thing. The prosecutor asks her if she is familiar with an incident that occurred two years ago where Michael was allegedly seen at a party smoking marijuana. The defense objects to this question. Should the prosecutor be able to impeach the sister's testimony in this manner? Explain.

Notes

1. Cross-examination of a medical examiner, *Things People Said: Courtroom Quotations*, http://www.rinkworks.com/said/counrtroom.shtml.
2. F.R.E. 607.
3. Behler v. Hanlon, 199 F.R.D. 553, 556 (D. Mary. 2001).
4. F.R.E. 610.
5. Jack B. Weinstein & Margaret A. Berger, *Weinstein's Federal Evidence*, § 607.04.
6. Wikipedia entry, *Scottsboro Boys*, citing James Goodman, *Stories of Scottsboro* at 128.
7. Behler, supra at 558.
8. Doug Linder, *The Trials of Alger Hiss: A Commentary* (2003), available at http://www.law.umkc.edu/faculty/projects/ftrials/hiss/hissaccount.html.
9. F.R.E. 608(a).
10. Behler, 199 F.R.D. at 559.
11. Black's Law Dictionary, at 597 (8th ed. 2004).
12. F.R.E. 609(b).
13. State v. Bryant, 633 S.E.2d 152 (S.C. 2006).
14. Id. at 155.
15. *See e.g.*, Colo. Rev. Stat. § 13-90-101.
16. United States v. Estrada, 430 F.3d 606 (2d Cir. 2005).
17. Estrada, 430 F.3d at 617.
18. Id. at 618.
19. Id.
20. Bryant, 633 S.E.2d at 156.
21. People v. Segovia, 196 P.3d 1126, 1131 (Colo. 2008).
22. *See* United States v. Dunson, 142 F.3d 1213 (10th Cir. 1998); Rhodes v. State, 634 S.W.2d 107 (Ark. 1982).
23. Segovia, 196 P.3d at 1132.
24. United States v. Estrada, 430 F.3d 606 (2d Cir. 2005).
25. F.R.E. 609(d).
26. United States v. Morrow, 2005 WL 1017827 (D.D.C. 2005) (unpublished decision).
27. People v. Poindexter, 361 N.W.2d 346 (Mich. App. 1985).
28. *See* Pallett v. State, 381 N.E.2d 452 (Ind. 1978).
29. People v. Gray, 646 N.E.2d 444 (N.Y. App. 1995).
30. In Re Manzy W., 930 P.2d 1255 (Cal. 1997).
31. Behler, 199 F.R.D. at 560.
32. F.R.E. 613(a).
33. Behler, 199 F.R.D. at 560.
34. http://www.law.umkc.edu/faculty/projects/ftrials/Simpson/mckintest.html; http://web.mit.edu/dryfoo/Info/fuhrman.html.

CHAPTER 12

Character Evidence

"Character is like a tree and reputation like its shadow. The shadow is what we think of it; the tree is the real thing."[1]—*Abe Lincoln*

Chapter Topics

Objectives

After completing this chapter, students will be able to:

- Understand the definition of character evidence and the rules regarding its exclusion and admission

- Understand how character evidence is introduced and proven at trial

- Understand the difference between a defendant's own good character and the victim's character and the roles they play in trial

- Understand the exclusion of evidence of the victim's character under a rape shield law and distinguish between the various types of shield laws

- Understand when and why prior bad acts can be admitted in a case

- Understand why evidence of prior bad acts is considered to be more relevant and likely to be more admissible in sexual assault and domestic violence cases

Introduction

Evidence of a person's character can play an important role in criminal cases. As you saw in the previous chapter on impeachment, a witness can be impeached with his prior actions that reflect on his credibility. The key to using those prior acts for impeachment is whether they reflect on the witness's capacity to tell the truth. When it comes to the presentation of evidence against the defendant directly to prove his guilt or innocence, however, the rules regarding the use of character evidence are different.

It may come as a surprise that the prior criminal acts of defendants are generally inadmissible to prove that a defendant is guilty of the current charge. But the issue comes down to fairness. Most of us would not want our innocence or guilt to rest on what we did in the past. Prior acts of misconduct, particularly those unrelated to the charged offense, are largely irrelevant to proving a defendant's guilt. Thus, the general rule is that the prosecution may not admit evidence of a defendant's prior bad character to prove that he or she committed the current criminal offense.

By way of example, evidence that a defendant has been previously convicted of theft and burglary is inadmissible to prove that he committed the burglary he is currently charged with. Likewise, the defendant's three prior DUI convictions are inadmissible to show that he drove drunk in the current case. The prior convictions would still be potentially usable to impeach the defendant's credibility, however.

Of course, like everything in law, there are exceptions to the rule. If the defendant first introduces evidence of his good character, the prosecutor can rebut that evidence by introducing evidence that contradicts that angelic image of the defendant. Similarly, if the defendant attempts to attack the character of the victim (usually by introducing evidence that the victim was the initial aggressor), then the prosecution can rebut that evidence by showing the victim's peaceful character or attacking the defendant's character. For example, a murder defendant may want to show that he feared the victim due to his reputation for being a hit man and therefore acted in self-defense when he killed him. The prosecutor could then introduce evidence that the victim was a peaceful person or that the defendant was also a violent person.

Thirty to forty years ago, it was also common practice for defense attorneys to attack the character of rape victims. The goal was to convince the jury that the woman consented to sex based on her prior promiscuous behavior. All states have since enacted rape shield laws that bar the admission of the prior sexual conduct of the victim, except in limited circumstances.

Finally, the prosecution can introduce evidence of the prior acts of the defendant where they are used to prove something other than the fact the defendant has a tendency to commit crime. Where the prior acts are used to prove independent purposes such as proof of identity, modus operandi, and motive, judges are more likely to admit the character evidence since it is limited to proof of that other purpose. For crimes involving sexual assault, however, some states and the federal courts have eliminated the ban on character evidence altogether. In those cases, the prosecution can admit the defendant's prior acts of sexual misconduct without proving a separate, independent purpose for their admission. The reasoning behind such laws is that prior offenses are considered to be more relevant and necessary to proving sexual assault since such crimes are often hard to prove and sexual predators often repeat their crimes.

I. CHARACTER EVIDENCE IS GENERALLY EXCLUDED: RULE 404(a)

Character evidence
evidence that is submitted for the purpose of proving that a person acted in a particular way on a particular occasion based on the character or disposition of that person

Character evidence is evidence that is submitted for the purpose of proving that a person acted in a particular way on a particular occasion based on the character or disposition of that person. The basic premise behind its use is to create the inference that a person acted according to some trait on this occasion because the person has committed specific acts consistent with that trait in the past or has developed a reputation for having that trait. Although our court system favors the admission of all relevant evidence, some evidence is considered too prejudicial or inflammatory to admit. Character evidence falls squarely within this category.

There are two major justifications for the exclusion of character evidence. First, the prior acts of the defendant may be irrelevant to the issue of the defendant's guilt. For instance, the question of whether the defendant is a bad driver or a recreational drug user is not relevant to the issue of whether he burglarized a house six months ago. The other concern is that character evidence may be too relevant and persuasive. There is a real possibility that if a jury hears that a defendant has previously committed a similar type of crime, it will convict him of the current offense, based not on proof that the defendant actually committed that crime but on "generally being a bad person."[2] Thus, while judging a person's character from his prior acts might prove to be accurate over a period of time, it is not very useful in helping judge how a person acted on one particular occasion.[3]

In 1948, Justice Jackson of the Supreme Court addressed these dangers of admitting character evidence:

> Courts that follow the common-law tradition almost unanimously have come to disallow resort by the prosecution to any kind of evidence of a defendant's evil character to establish a probability of his guilt.... The inquiry is not rejected because character evidence is irrelevant; on the contrary, it is said to weigh too much with the jury and to so over persuade them as to prejudice one with a bad general record and deny him a fair opportunity to defend against a particular charge. The overriding policy of excluding such evidence, despite its admitted probative value, is the practical experience that its disallowance tends to prevent confusion of issues, unfair surprise and undue prejudice.[4]

Rule 404(a)
a rule of evidence that provides that evidence of a person's prior misconduct cannot be introduced to show that he acted similarly in the present case

Due to these concerns, **Rule 404(a)** provides that "evidence of a person's character or a trait of character is not admissible for the purpose of proving action in conformity therewith on a particular occasion."[5] This rule prevents the prosecution from introducing evidence that the defendant has previously committed crimes or other bad acts to show that he must have done the same thing in the current case.

II. THE EXCEPTIONS UNDER WHICH CHARACTER EVIDENCE IS ADMISSIBLE

Rule 404. Character Evidence Not Admissible to Prove Conduct; Exceptions; Other Crimes

(a) Character evidence generally.—Evidence of a person's character or a trait of character is not admissible for the purpose of proving action in conformity therewith on a particular occasion, except:

(1) Character of accused.—In a criminal case, evidence of a pertinent trait of character offered by an accused, or by the prosecution to rebut the same, or if evidence of a trait of character of the alleged victim of the crime is offered by an accused and admitted under Rule 404(a)(2), evidence of the same trait of character of the accused offered by the prosecution;

(2) Character of alleged victim.—In a criminal case, and subject to the limitations imposed by Rule 412, evidence of a pertinent trait of character of the alleged victim of the crime offered by an accused, or by the prosecution to rebut the same, or evidence of a character trait of peacefulness of the alleged victim offered by the prosecution in a homicide case to rebut evidence that the alleged victim was the first aggressor;

(3) Character of witness.—Evidence of the character of a witness, as provided in Rules 607, 608, and 609.

Character evidence is not always inadmissible, however. There are four exceptions to the rule barring the use of character evidence:

- The defendant can introduce evidence of his own good character (such as showing that he is a nonviolent person or is a trustworthy individual). Once the defendant does so, the prosecution can introduce evidence of his bad character to rebut such evidence;
- The defendant may introduce evidence of the character of the alleged victim (such as to show that the victim was an aggressive, violent person);
- The prosecutor can introduce the prior bad acts of the defendant for a limited purpose (to prove some other fact, independent of the inference that he is a bad person); and
- A party may impeach a witness by examining his character for truthfulness.

This chapter will discuss the first three exceptions; impeachment of witnesses was covered in the previous chapter.

Before discussing the specific exceptions for introduction of character evidence, it is important to note that the form in which it can be admitted is often limited. A character trait can be established either by proving specific acts consistent with that trait or by testimony in the form of **reputation or opinion evidence**. Evidence of specific acts is the strongest form of proof, while reputation evidence is the weakest form. Testimony about a person's reputation is a summary of a character trait based on what actions or words a person has taken over a period of time. It is also based largely on hearsay or rumor and can often lack the personal knowledge of the person giving the opinion as to someone's reputation. Reputation or opinion evidence is also given in vague generalities, such as a person has a reputation for being truthful, honest, or peaceful. Such terms can cover a wide variety of behavior and are subject to varying interpretations. As one commentator noted, "both reputation and opinion testimony sweep with a broad, conclusory brush that significantly limits their actual value."[6]

Rule 405 controls what form of character evidence is usable in given situations. Despite the fact that reputation and opinion evidence is generally weaker than testimony about specific instances of conduct, character witnesses can usually only testify as to the defendant's reputation in the community for that character trait or in the form of an opinion.[7] Testimony regarding specific instances of conduct is only permitted on cross-examination, or where the "character or a trait of character of a person is an essential element of a charge, claim, or defense."[8] The use of specific instances of conduct is limited because it has the greater ability to arouse prejudice, confuse, surprise, or waste time.[9] Unfortunately, the jury can get an incomplete picture of a person's character where evidence is limited to reputation or opinion since it does not get to hear what events or acts led to the creation of that reputation or opinion.[10]

A. The Defendant's Own Good Character: Rule 404(a)(1)

The first exception to the general bar against character evidence permits the defendant to introduce evidence of his own **good character**. Rule 404(a)(1) states that character evidence can be admitted if it is "evidence of a pertinent trait of character offered by an accused, or by the prosecution to rebut the same."[11] For instance, the defendant can offer evidence of his good character to show that he is not the type of person that would commit such a crime. The introduction of good character evidence is a double-edged sword, however. The prosecution cannot introduce evidence of the defendant's bad character first. Once the defendant presents evidence of his good character, it opens the door for the prosecution to offer contrary evidence to rebut it.

The defendant can introduce evidence of his good character in two ways: (1) he can have a third party (known as a character witness) testify

Reputation or opinion evidence
a summary of a character trait based on what actions or words a person has taken over a period of time

Good character
evidence of a defendant's reputation for good deeds offered to show that he could not have committed the crime charged

about his reputation in the community as to some pertinent character trait; or (2) he can testify in his own defense and introduce evidence of that trait himself. Where the defendant introduces his good character, the prosecution can ask about any prior instances of conduct that contradict his alleged good character.[12] For example, a Pennsylvania court explained that "a witness may be required to answer questions tending to show that he has committed, been charged with, or been convicted of any offense, if he has presented evidence tending to prove his own good character or reputation."[13] There, the prosecutor was permitted to question the defendant about his armed robbery conviction since the defendant had testified he was a peaceful person and had never shot anyone.[14] In another case, an Ohio court ruled that where the defendant introduced evidence of his good character, including his attendance at church, the prosecution was properly allowed to introduce evidence of his juvenile record on cross-examination.[15]

Practical Example

Assume the defendant is being tried for assaulting a police officer. The defendant has previously been convicted of assault, drug possession, and DUI. Unless the defendant gets on the witness stand to testify, the prosecution cannot introduce this evidence. Now assume the defendant introduces evidence that he is a peaceful person. He calls his mother, who testifies that he would never hurt a fly and is a good person. The prosecutor can now introduce evidence of the defendant's prior bad character in two ways: he can cross-examine the mother about her son's prior assault conviction and can call character witnesses to testify that the defendant has a reputation for being a violent person.

B. Character of the Victim: Rules 404(a)(1) and (2)

First aggressor
the person who uses physical force first in a fight or other confrontation. The defendant is permitted to claim that he was entitled to use self-defense if the victim was the first aggressor

The second use of character evidence is to attack the character of the victim. Rule 404(a)(2) provides that the defendant may introduce a pertinent trait of character of the alleged victim of the crime or to prove that the victim was the **first aggressor** in a homicide case. Conversely, the rule permits the prosecution to do the same to rebut those allegations. In addition, Rule 404(a)(1) allows the prosecutor to introduce evidence of a character trait of the accused to rebut evidence of that same character trait of the victim offered by an accused. While this rule prevents the jury from receiving a one-sided picture of the participant's character in a homicide, it leaves the defendant something of a Hobson's choice—either introduce evidence of the victim's bad character and risk the prosecution admitting evidence of your bad character, or do not attack the victim's character and risk the jury blaming you (perhaps unfairly) for the assault or murder.

1. Self-Defense

Self-defense

an affirmative defense to assault or murder. A defendant can claim self-defense if he used a reasonable amount of force to defend himself and was not the first aggressor

Attacking the character of the victim is particularly relevant where the defendant claims self-defense in assault or murder cases. Recall from Chapter 8 that **self-defense** is an affirmative defense. A person is allowed to use reasonable force to defend himself as long as he is not the first aggressor and the amount of force used is proportional to the amount of force used by the initial aggressor.[16] In some states, the defendant cannot claim self-defense if he had an opportunity to retreat at the time of the confrontation.[17] Self-defense can be proven by several different types of evidence, including eyewitness testimony as to who threw the first punch, the presence of physical evidence like defensive wounds, and character evidence relating to the victim and defendant. Character evidence may be particularly important to proving self-defense where eyewitness testimony and forensic evidence are lacking. In such a situation, the defendant has to support his self-defense claim by alleging that the victim has a reputation for being a violent person and that he feared the victim due to that reputation.

Not all states use the same approach to admission of character evidence about the victim, however. Some states like Wyoming allow the defendant to prove the victim's character for aggressive or violent behavior through specific acts of misconduct, not just opinion or reputation evidence.[18] In 2005, the Massachusetts Supreme Court determined that evidence of specific acts of violence was the best method for determining who was the first aggressor in assault and homicide cases, rejecting the admission of reputation or opinion evidence for such a purpose.[19] The court also required that the defendant and prosecution provide pretrial notice of their intent to use such specific instances of misconduct so that the court could determine their admissibility.[20]

Other states have not been so liberal. Connecticut, for example, restricts proof of the victim's prior acts to the victim's convictions for violence offenses. Still others restrict use of specific instances of the victim's prior violent conduct to homicide cases.[21] Several federal courts have held that admission of specific instances of conduct is not allowed under the rules since self-defense may be proven whether or not the victim was a violent person.[22] According to the Ninth Circuit, the relevant question for whether specific instances of conduct are admissible "is would proof, or allure of proof, of the character trait by itself actually satisfy an element of the charge, claim, or defense?"[23] The court concluded that a person could successfully claim that he acted in self-defense, even against an avowed pacifist, in the absence of such evidence.[24]

Practical Example

Assume the defendant is charged with assaulting a bar patron. Evidence is presented that the defendant punched the victim three times. The defendant could introduce evidence that the patron swung at him first in a drunken rage and that he was merely defending himself. The inference for the jury is clear in such cases: the defendant would not have acted violently but for the victim's initial act of aggression. Once again, the prosecutor is allowed to rebut this evidence. For example, the prosecutor can introduce evidence of the peacefulness of the victim if the defendant alleges that the victim had been the first aggressor in a homicide case. The prosecutor can call witnesses to establish that the victim had a peaceful reputation in the community or can cross-examine the defendant's witnesses about prior instances of the victim's peaceful behavior. In some states, both the prosecution and defense can also introduce evidence of the victim's or defendant's prior aggressive or violent behavior.

See Table 12.1 for a breakdown of acceptable uses of character evidence by the defense and prosecution.

TABLE 12.1   USES OF CHARACTER EVIDENCE BY THE DEFENSE AND PROSECUTION

Rule	Defendant	Prosecution Response
• F.R.E. 404(a)(1) & 405 Character evidence generally	• Introduce evidence of defendant's good character for some trait (either through reputation or opinion)	• Rebut with evidence of defendant's character for the same trait (either through reputation or opinion) or cross-examine as to specific instances
• 404(a)(1) & 405 Defendant's character for peacefulness	• Introduce evidence of defendant's character for peacefulness (either through reputation or opinion)	• Rebut with evidence of defendant's character for violence (either through reputation or opinion) or cross-examine as to specific instances
• 404(a)(2) & 405 Victim's character for violence in order to claim self-defense	• Introduce evidence of victim's character for violence (either through reputation or opinion)	• Rebut with evidence of victim's character for peacefulness or with evidence of defendant's character for violence (either through reputation or opinion)
• 404(a)(2) & 405 Victim was first aggressor in a homicide case	• Introduce evidence that victim was the initial aggressor (through reputation or opinion)	• Rebut with evidence of victim's peaceful character (through reputation or opinion)

2. Rape Shield Laws

Although the defendant is permitted to introduce character evidence of the victim in some circumstances, legislatures have limited such attacks in rape cases. Prior to the 1970s, character evidence was routinely used in rape cases to attack the credibility of the rape victim, often bordering on character assassination. Defense attorneys would attempt to show that the alleged victim had been sexually promiscuous prior to the alleged rape to prove that she had consented to the sex—in effect, implying that she had asked for it. At the very least, such attacks were intended to destroy the victim's credibility.[25] In fact, in many cases, the prosecution had to prove the victim's chastity.[26] While the victim's prior sexual history was not a defense to the rape charge, once the jury heard that the victim was not a chaste woman, it often acquitted the defendant.

Widespread criticism of these tactics began to emerge in the 1970s. For example, the Utah Supreme Court noted that evidence of the victim's prior sexual conduct is often not relevant to any issue in the case, including consent.[27] The court also found that even where it may have some relevance, such evidence has an "unusual propensity" to unfairly prejudice or inflame the jury.[28] As a result of such criticism, courts and legislatures began to restrict admission of evidence of the sexual history of the victim. Michigan passed the first rape shield law in 1974, and by the early 1980s, most states had followed suit. Currently, all states have a rape shield law.

Rape shield law
a law which prevents the defense from introducing the prior sexual conduct of the victim into evidence unless it satisfies a couple of limited exceptions

A **rape shield law** prevents the defense from introducing the prior sexual behavior or conduct of the rape victim except under limited circumstances. The two exceptions that are generally permitted are: (1) to show that the source of the semen or physical injury was from someone other than the defendant; or (2) to show that the victim consented to the sexual encounter with the defendant. The purpose of rape shield laws is to protect the victim from harassment and intimidation. Like most character evidence, evidence of the victim's prior sexual history may be minimally relevant to show that the victim consented or to impeach her credibility. However, by passing rape shield laws, legislatures have determined that the minimal relevance of such evidence is outweighed by its inflammatory nature and that fairness requires its exclusion.[29]

a. Types of Rape Shields

Constitutional catchall
a form of rape shield law that bars evidence of a victim's prior sexual conduct except where it meets narrowly defined exceptions or where it would impair the rights of the defendant to exclude the evidence

Although all 50 states have adopted rape shield laws, there are four basic types of such laws:

- The **constitutional catchall** or federal approach, which in addition to the above exceptions permits a judge to admit evidence if the constitutional right to cross-examine or confront the witness will be infringed;

Legislated exception
a form of rape shield law that bars evidence of a rape victim's prior sexual conduct unless it meets a couple of narrowly defined exceptions

Judicial discretion
a form of rape shield law that grants judges wide discretion in determining whether to admit evidence of the victim's prior sexual conduct

Evidentiary purpose
a form of rape shield law that permits evidence of the victim's sexual history to be used for impeachment

- The **legislated exception** or Michigan approach, which bars all evidence of a victim's sexual history subject to a couple of narrow exceptions;
- The **judicial discretion** or Texas approach, which grants judges broad discretion to admit or bar evidence of a victim's sexual history; and
- The **evidentiary purpose** or California approach, which generally bars evidence of a victim's sexual history but permits its use to impeach the credibility of a witness in limited circumstances.[30]

i. Constitutional Catchall

Federal Rule of Evidence 412 is an example of the first type of rape shield statute. It excludes evidence that any alleged victim engaged in other sexual behavior and evidence offered to prove any alleged victim's sexual predisposition.[31] The rule creates three exceptions to this general prohibition. Evidence of recent sexual activity can be admitted where the evidence is offered to show someone other than the accused was the source of the semen or injury suffered by the victim.[32] The defense can also admit evidence of prior sexual behavior between the victim and the accused to prove consent.[33] Finally, a catchall provision is included that allows the judge to admit evidence of prior sexual conduct if the constitutional rights of the defendant would be violated if the evidence was not admitted. [34]

ii. Legislated Exception

The second approach, first adopted by the state of Michigan, is the most popular type of rape shield law, with about half the states having adopted it.[35] Like the federal approach, character evidence about the rape victim is generally prohibited, subject to some specific exceptions. The defendant can admit evidence of recent acts of consensual sex with the defendant or recent sexual activity with other men to show the source of the semen or injury could have come from someone other than the defendant. A hearing must be conducted by the court to determine whether such evidence is admissible for either of these limited purposes. However, unlike the federal approach, there is no catchall provision allowing for the introduction of such evidence where constitutional concerns require it.

iii. Judicial Discretion

In contrast, the judicial discretion or Texas approach leaves the decision of whether to admit character evidence about the victims' prior sexual history entirely up to the judge. Under this type of law, evidence of the victim's prior sexual conduct with the defendant or other persons may be admissible if the judge determines that the probative value of the evidence outweighs its prejudicial effect.[36] The defense must file a motion with the court prior to trial, alleging that evidence concerning the victim's character is relevant and the court must conduct a hearing on the matter. If the defense fails to follow this procedure and references the victim's prior sexual conduct during trial, the defense can be held in contempt of court.[37]

iv. Evidentiary Purpose

Finally, the evidentiary purpose or California approach is a mixture of the above approaches. A handful of states use this type of rape shield law. It divides the prior sexual history of the victim into two categories: (1) evidence that is used to prove consent; and (2) evidence that is offered to attack the credibility of the victim.[38] In California and Delaware, evidence of the victim's prior sexual conduct, such as the way the victim was dressed at the time of the alleged assault, is inadmissible to prove consent unless the court determines its admissibility is in the "interests of justice."[39] This means the defense cannot use evidence of the victim's prior sexual conduct with other people to prove that she consented to sex in the current case but can use the victim's prior sexual conduct with the accused for such purposes. Conversely, the same evidence may be admissible to attack the credibility of the accuser if the court determines it is relevant.[40] California courts have usually limited such credibility attacks to situations where the victim has a prior history of prostitution or of making false accusations of rape, however.[41] Although the California Rape Shield law does not explicitly contain an exception to prove that another person was the source of semen or injury, the California Supreme Court recently held that the law does not "bar evidence of the complaining witness's prior sexual conduct when offered to explain injuries the prosecution alleges were the result of the defendant's conduct."[42]

b. Evidence of Prior Sexual Conduct With the Same Victim

Most rape shield laws permit the admission of prior sexual conduct between the victim and the defendant. Such evidence is considered relevant to proving whether the defendant believed the victim consented to sex based on their prior relationship. In one New Jersey case, the victim accused the defendant, a police officer, of raping her. The officer claimed the sex was consensual. The officer had wanted to introduce evidence of the victim's sexually provocative behavior toward him to help prove his consent defense. According to several witnesses, the victim had frequently engaged in sexual banter with the defendant and made sexual overtures toward him prior to the alleged rape.[43] The judge excluded most of this evidence under the state's rape shield law, admitting only a couple of isolated incidents. The New Jersey Supreme Court overturned the trial's court's ruling, holding that how the defendant's prior relationship with the victim impacted his state of mind at the time of the incident was "critical to the ultimate determination of the jury."[44] It noted that the judge's ruling gave the jury only a fragmented view of the couple's prior relationship and prevented them from hearing testimony from unbiased witnesses concerning the couple's prior actions.

Practical Example

Assume the defendant is being tried for rape. He alleges the sex was consensual and that the couple was engaged in role playing. He wants to introduce evidence that he and the victim had sex on three prior occasions and that the victim had consented to role playing on those prior occasions. The evidence of the victim's prior sexual conduct with the defendant is likely going to be admissible unless there is something extremely prejudicial about the prior acts. It is relevant to the defendant's claim of consent.

c. Evidence of Sexual Conduct With Third Parties

Generally, evidence that the victim has been sexually promiscuous with other men is not very probative of whether she was raped or assaulted in the current case. This is precisely the type of evidence that rape shield laws are designed to exclude. Some courts have made an exception, however, for sexual conduct that is made in public view. In one notable case, in an opinion authored by Supreme Court Justice David Souter, then a justice on the New Hampshire Supreme Court, the court reasoned that "evidence of public displays of general interest in sexual activity can be taken to indicate the contemporaneous receptiveness to sexual advances that cannot be inferred from evidence of private behavior with chosen sex partners."[45] The court concluded that "the jury could have taken the evidence of the complainant's openly sexually provocative behavior toward a group of men as evidence of her probable attitude toward an individual within the group."[46]

Most courts do not share Justice Souter's viewpoint. For example, in a Michigan case, the court ruled that the victim's display of sexually provocative behavior toward a group of men at a bar, including revealing her breasts, was not relevant to the issue of consent.[47] The court commented that "we fail to see how a woman's consensual sexual conduct with another in public indicates to third parties that the woman would engage in similar behavior with them."[48] The feeling is that admission of this type of evidence is highly prejudicial because it implies the victim is promiscuous and, therefore, that she is to blame for inviting the rape.

One interesting question that has recently surfaced is whether evidence concerning the victim's sexual history from social networking sites such as MySpace or Facebook is admissible. Usually, such evidence would not be admissible unless it related to recent sexual activity or fabrication. However, a North Carolina court held that a 13-year-old's comments on her MySpace page that she was not a virgin were admissible to impeach her testimony that she was a virgin at the time of the alleged assault by her father.[49] The evidence of prior sexual activity has more probative value in this instance because it shows that someone other than the father may have caused the victim's injuries.

Practical Example

Assume Wally is charged with sexual assault on a woman he met at a hotel bar. He claims the sex was consensual. The woman flies back home the next day. She schedules a rape exam on the day after arriving back home. Evidence of vaginal tearing is found during the exam. Wally wants to introduce proof that the woman had sex the day after with her boyfriend once she flew back home. The court will likely admit this evidence since it is relevant to the issue of whether the tearing came from sex with the boyfriend or sex with Wally.

Now assume that the same defendant in the above example wants to introduce evidence that the victim had routinely picked up men in hotel bars and had sex with them on prior occasions. The court will now likely exclude the evidence because the victim's conduct with other men is not relevant to whether she consented to having sex with the defendant on this particular occasion.

---

d. Prior False Allegations of Sexual Abuse

Evidence that relates to the victim's credibility is often still admissible under rape shield laws. For example, most courts have permitted prior false allegations of sexual abuse to be used for impeachment.[50] This makes sense since prior false allegations of rape should not be considered an aspect of the victim's prior sexual conduct. If the victim had made prior false allegations, such evidence is generally relevant to impeach the victim's credibility as to whether she is telling the truth this time around. However, some courts have refused to admit this type of evidence. For example, famed defense attorney and Harvard Law Professor Alan Dershowitz unsuccessfully argued that the 1991 rape conviction of boxer Mike Tyson should be overturned on such grounds. He argued that the trial court's denial of evidence relating to the victim's previous false allegations of rape under the state's rape shield statute violated the constitutional rights of the defendant. The Supreme Court refused to hear the appeal, and Tyson's conviction stood.[51] In any event, in order to determine the admissibility of such evidence, the court must conduct a hearing to determine whether the allegations of prior false reports are true and whether they are admissible to impeach the victim.[52]

Practical Example

Assume the defendant, a teacher, is accused of raping one of his students, a 14-year-old girl. He wants to introduce evidence that the girl had filed a false allegation of sexual assault against one of her middle-school teachers two years ago. The court will likely admit this evidence since it is relevant to impeaching the victim's credibility for truthfulness.

---

e. Prior History of Sexual Abuse

A related issue that can come up is whether the victim's prior history of being sexually abused is relevant. A defendant charged with sexually assaulting a child may attempt to introduce evidence that the child victim had previously been the victim of sexual abuse to show that the child has an alternate source for the sexual knowledge necessary to have made the complaint. In other words, young children are presumed to be ignorant of certain sexual terms and behavior; the fact that they do have such age-inappropriate knowledge is taken as evidence that they have been abused. Defendants will thus try and prove that this knowledge came from an incident other than the one they've been charged with. Most courts have held that evidence of prior sexual abuse is covered by the rape shield law and is therefore not admissible.[53] A few states have concluded that evidence of past abuse is not covered under the rape shield law, however, and is admissible.[54]

EVIDENCE IN ACTION

Leaks in the Kobe Bryant Rape Case Spur Changes to Rape Shield Laws

Despite the seeming strength of many rape shield laws, many states have moved to strengthen them after the defense team for Los Angeles Lakers star Kobe Bryant pushed the spirit of the rape shield law to its limit in his rape case in Colorado in 2003. Bryant was charged with sexually assaulting a 19-year-old hotel worker in July 2003. He allegedly met the woman while touring the hotel he was staying at while awaiting surgery on his knee the following day. While originally denying that he had had sex with the alleged victim, Bryant admitted to having consensual sex with her after investigators pointed out during his interrogation that a rape kit had been taken that included semen samples.[55]

Colorado's rape shield law generally prohibits evidence of the victim's sexual history but provides three exceptions. It permits the introduction of evidence of the victim's prior or subsequent sexual conduct with the defendant, evidence of specific incidents of sexual activity that would show that the source of semen or injury is someone other than the defendant, and evidence of any similar evidence of sexual intercourse that is offered for the purpose of showing that the act or acts charged were not committed by the defendant. This last exception in particular is what Bryant's attorneys exploited. It allows the judge broad discretion to admit the evidence of a woman's sexual history if it is deemed "relevant to a material issue in the case."[56]

Bryant's defense lawyers first moved to have Colorado's rape shield law declared unconstitutional. After that attack proved unsuccessful, his team filed several pretrial motions to admit evidence of the victim's prior sexual history. It sought to obtain the victim's medical records, alleging that her two prior suicide attempts indicated a pattern of creating drama in her life to seek attention. As part of this strategy, his attorneys pressed to have the victim's mother testify about her daughter's medical history. His attorneys also moved to admit evidence of her sexual history in the 72-hour window surrounding the alleged attack. They alleged that the evidence was relevant, among other things, to:

- Show a factual similarity between the prior acts and her encounter with Kobe Bryant
- Show a common plan or scheme with regard to whether she consented to sex
- Attack her credibility with regard to statements the victim made which were inconsistent with the physical evidence[57]

Of particular concern was that semen of two other men was found on a pair of panties submitted for examination as part of the rape kit taken after the alleged assault. Bryant's attorneys argued that this evidence was admissible to show that the source of her injuries was someone other than Bryant.

Up to this point, Bryant's legal strategy was quite legitimate. Such evidence would have been admissible under almost any formulation of a rape shield law, including Colorado's. The evidence was relevant both to show that the source of the semen or injury was someone other than Bryant and to impeach the victim's credibility.[58]

Problems arose when Bryant's defense team began to wage an all-out assault on the victim's character. Bryant's lead attorney, Pamela Mackey, mentioned the victim's name on six different occasions during a pretrial hearing that was open to the public despite the judge's admonitions to not do so. She also asked a detective on cross-examination during the hearing whether the victim's injuries were also consistent "with the person who'd had sex with three different men in three days."[59] Newspapers took the cue from Mackey's question, running headlines for weeks about the victim's alleged promiscuity.

The biggest damage to the victim's privacy, however, was not caused by the attorneys' questions but resulted from the tabloid news coverage of the case and the negligence of court personnel. Defenders of Bryant created product lines such as tee shirts and mugs showing the victim's photo with labels such as "lying bitch" and "whore alert."[60] Tabloids featured photos of the victim partying while newspapers across the country detailed her failed *American Idol* audition, suicide attempts, and breakup with a former boyfriend.[61] The accuser also received hundreds of daily e-mails regarding the case, including death threats.[62]

Figure 12.1 Kobe Bryant appears in court with his attorneys on May 11, 2004 to enter a not guilty plea to sexual assault charges in an Eagle, Colorado courtroom. The charges against Bryant were eventually dismissed.
© Ed Andrieski/Pool/Reuters/Corbis

Perhaps the biggest blow to the accuser came when court personnel mistakenly uploaded court documents containing her name and information about her background to the state court Web site on three separate occasions. To make matters worse, in June 2004, a court clerk mistakenly e-mailed to seven news organizations transcripts of a closed-door hearing that detailed that the accuser had had sex with another man shortly after her alleged assault. This type of information is normally protected from disclosure in sexual assault cases until its admissibility is ruled upon by the court.[63]

The damage to the victim's psyche was done. On September 1, 2004, the criminal charges against Kobe Bryant were dismissed, due in large part to the victim's decision to not testify.[64] She did, however, file a civil lawsuit against Bryant, which the parties settled in 2005 for an undisclosed amount.[65]

Because of the publicity surrounding the case and the ease with which the victim's identity was revealed, the Bryant case spurred states to change their rape shield laws to afford greater protection of victims' identities. For example, Colorado passed a law that allows the victims greater leeway to use a pseudonym in place of the real name in court documents and legal proceedings. The California legislature passed a law that closes court hearings and seals court records that discuss an accuser's sexual history until a judge considers it to be admissible evidence.[66]

f. Criticisms of Rape Shield Laws

Rape shield laws have been criticized as both being too protective of the victim's rights and not being protective enough. On one side, critics allege such laws violate the defendant's right to confront witnesses since they restrict the right to fully examine a victim about matters relating to prior sexual conduct or reputation.[67] As one commentator noted, "rape shield statutes significantly restrict the opportunity to defend, as their intent is to control the flow of information a defendant can introduce to influence a jury."[68] Courts have consistently upheld the constitutionality of rape shield laws against defense challenges, however, on the ground that the probative value of evidence of prior sexual conduct is usually low in comparison to the state's interest in protecting the rape victim from humiliating and harassing questioning.[69]

When that balance shifts in favor of the defendant such that the evidence is relevant and necessary to a fair determination of the issues, courts have held that rape shield laws must yield to the defendant's interests. For example, the Massachusetts Supreme Court held that the defendant should have been allowed to cross-examine the victim about the fact she had been found naked having sex in an automobile as a prostitute on two prior occasions. The court found that the evidence was relevant to the question of whether her testimony was biased by her desire to avoid another arrest for prostitution.[70]

On the other side of the fence, some scholars have pushed for more widespread changes to rape shield laws. Hopeful that such laws would have led to the fair and equitable prosecution of rape cases, women's groups have reported that gender bias continues to be a problem for women in courtrooms. Only minimal improvements in the number of rape cases reported and successfully prosecuted were noted after the implementation of rape shield laws in many places.[71] And in some cases, rape shield laws failed to prevent the introduction of the very type of evidence they were designed to exclude.

Professor Michelle Anderson, one of the leading commentators on rape shield laws, has called for reforms to rape shield laws to ensure their intended purpose is being met:

> Federal and state rape statutes are so riddled with holes that they often function more like sieves than shields.... The Bryant case signals that it is time to reform rape shield laws to provide victims with real protection at trial. [72]

Professor Anderson believes that rape shield laws should be tightened to permit evidence of the victim's sexual activity only where it is necessary to prove one of three narrow exceptions:

- Evidence of an alternate source for the semen, pregnancy, disease, or injury that the complainant suffered;

- Evidence of negotiations between the complainant and the defendant to convey consent in a specific way or to engage in a specific sexual act at issue;
- Evidence of the complainant's bias or mode to fabricate the charge of rape.[73]

But even had a more restrictive shield law like the one Professor Anderson proposes been in place during the Kobe Bryant case, the outcome likely would have been similar. Evidence of the victim's sexual history in the three days prior to the alleged rape would still have been admissible to show that there may have been an alternate source for the semen or injury.

AUTHOR'S NOTE

The real complaint of Professor Anderson and others seems to be that inadequate protections were put in place to ensure that the victim's identity was not released. A better approach would be to do what Colorado and California did in the wake of the Bryant case—strengthen laws limiting the disclosure of the victim's name and mandating closed-door pretrial hearings. Shield laws can only exclude evidence of a victim's sexual history up to a point; evidence of a victim's prior sexual history cannot be entirely excluded because such a rule would violate the defendant's right to present a defense and confront the witnesses against him.

Practical Example

Wayne is charged with sexually assaulting Sue at a fraternity party. Sue is an exotic dancer hired to perform at the party. Wayne wants to introduce evidence that she was dancing provocatively with several other fraternity brothers earlier in the evening to prove she consented to having sex with him later that night. He argues that the court's exclusion of that evidence would violate his right to present a defense. The court would likely exclude the evidence on the ground that it was not relevant and therefore would not violate his constitutional right to confrontation.

Now assume that Wayne wants to introduce evidence that Sue had been placed on probation for prostitution. As part of her probation, she was required to stop exotic dancing. The evidence is not admissible under the two primary exemptions to rape shield laws but is admissible under a catchall provision since it is relevant to impeaching the victim as to her bias or motive to fabricate the rape story.

III. USE OF CHARACTER EVIDENCE TO PROVE AN INDEPENDENT PURPOSE: RULE 404(b)

Rule 404. Character Evidence Not Admissible to Prove Conduct; Exceptions; Other Crimes

(b) Other Crimes, Wrongs, or Acts.—Evidence of other crimes, wrongs, or acts is not admissible to prove the character of a person in order to show action in conformity therewith. It may, however, be admissible for other purposes, such as proof of motive, opportunity, intent, preparation, plan, knowledge, identity, or absence of mistake or accident, provided that upon request by the accused, the prosecution in a criminal case shall provide reasonable notice in advance of trial, or during trial if the court excuses pretrial notice on good cause shown, of the general nature of any such evidence it intends to introduce at trial.

Rule 404(b)

evidence rule that permits the prosecution to admit the prior acts of the defendant to show some purpose other than that he has a propensity to commit crime, such as motive, intent, or identity

Rule 404(b) contains the third exception to the bar on character evidence. It permits the prosecution to introduce the prior acts of the defendant in its case-in-chief to prove some issue independent of the inference that the defendant committed the charged crime because he has a tendency to commit crime generally. Unlike character evidence introduced under 404(a), the prosecution can prove the specific facts of the underlying acts rather than simply introducing the defendant's reputation for that trait. Before introducing such evidence, the prosecution must provide notice to the defendant that he intends to use certain prior acts to prove his guilt at trial. The court must then conduct a pretrial hearing to determine the admissibility of the prior acts so the jury is not improperly influenced by speculative or prejudicial evidence.

Courts have required the trial court to carefully evaluate several factors before admitting prior acts evidence. Typically, these include:

- Whether the defendant committed the prior act;
- Whether the evidence is relevant to the case;
- Whether the prosecution can articulate one of the purposes listed in Rule 404(b); and
- Whether the prejudicial effect of the evidence substantially outweighs its probative value.[74]

If the prior acts satisfy the above tests and are admitted under 404(b), the jury has to be instructed that it can consider the evidence for only those limited purposes selected by the court. The hope is that the impact of the prior act evidence will be lessened and juries will not consider the evidence for improper purposes. Many states also instruct the jury that if it concludes that the defendant committed the prior acts, that fact is, in and of itself, not enough to prove the defendant guilty of the crime charged.[75]

A. Whether the Defendant Committed the Prior Act

Prior acts

the previous incidents of misconduct of the defendant that are relevant to the proving the current offense

The first step in the process is to determine whether the defendant committed the **prior acts**. To do so, a pretrial hearing is held. The prosecution can prove the defendant's commission of the prior act either through an offer of proof (an affidavit from a police officer or alleged victim describing the prior act) or by calling witnesses to testify about the prior incident. The prosecution's burden of proof is lower than it is at trial. Most states and the federal courts require the prosecution to prove the defendant committed the prior act by a preponderance of the evidence, although a number of states require a higher standard—clear and convincing proof.[76]

Obviously, if the defendant was convicted of or pled guilty to the prior act, it is presumed that he committed it. The prosecution is not limited to introducing prior convictions under Rule 404(b), however. It can also introduce evidence of prior acts that the defendant was never charged with, or even in some cases, those that he was acquitted of. States are split on whether prior charges of which the defendant was acquitted can be introduced as prior acts under Rule 404(b). Most states permit the introduction of prior charges that resulted in acquittal, weighing the acquittal as one factor in the balancing of the evidence's probative value.[77]

For example, a Colorado appellate court held that the admission of the defendant's prior sexual assault charge was proper even though he had been acquitted of that charge.[78] The court noted that since an acquittal does not prove a defendant's innocence but merely establishes the prosecution's failure to prove the charges beyond a reasonable doubt, the prior charge could still be admissible.[79] A few states, however, have found that it is fundamentally unfair to admit evidence of crimes for which the defendant has been acquitted.[80] This is particularly true in states that use the clear and convincing standard for admission of prior acts since an acquittal makes it all but impossible to prove the defendant committed the prior act.[81] A few other states bar the admission of acquittals because the probative value of the evidence is significantly outweighed by its prejudicial effect.[82]

Practical Example

Assume Billy Bob is on trial for murder. He claims self-defense. The prosecutor wants to introduce evidence that Billy Bob was charged with manslaughter three years ago in a different case. Billy Bob moves to exclude the evidence on the ground he was acquitted of the charge. The evidence is certainly relevant because it would help rebut Billy Bob's claim of self-defense. The admissibility of the prior charge would depend on what state Billy Bob is tried in. If the state permits prior acts that resulted in acquittals to be admitted, then the evidence may come in. However, if the state bars such evidence, then it will automatically be excluded.

B. Relevance of the Prior Acts

The second factor that the prosecution has to establish is that the prior acts evidence is relevant to the case. Like all evidence, prior acts must be material to the crime charged and have probative value. If the prior acts do not have a connection to the charged crime, then they are irrelevant and thus inadmissible. For example, assume the prosecution offers evidence that the defendant had previously been arrested for marijuana possession. The relevance of the prior marijuana arrest will depend on what type of crime the defendant is being charged with. If the defendant is charged with tax evasion, the evidence is clearly not relevant to the charges. On the other hand, if the defendant is charged with felony drug possession, the evidence may be material to show that the defendant did not mistakenly possess drugs.

Likewise, the probative value of prior acts evidence depends on considerations of probability. Prior acts have a high probative value if they make it much more likely that the defendant had the necessary intent or motive to commit a crime than in the absence of such evidence. For example, if evidence were introduced that the defendant had committed several prior rapes, it would have a high probative value since the jury would have to believe it was merely a coincidence that the defendant had been falsely accused of rape in the current case.[83] Prior acts also tend to have higher probative value if the prosecution can show multiple incidences that occurred in a similar fashion or pattern to the charged conduct. The Supreme Court noted that "individual pieces of evidence, insufficient in themselves to prove a point, may in accumulation prove it. The sum of an evidentiary presentation may well be greater than its constituent's parts."[84]

C. Independent Purpose

The next step in proving the admissibility of prior acts evidence is determining whether the evidence is being offered for some purpose other than showing the defendant has a propensity to commit criminal acts. In other words, the prosecutor must do more than show the defendant committed the crime simply because he is a bad guy. To do so, the prosecutor has to allege that the prior acts relate to one of the **independent purposes** outlined in Rule 404(b) or to some other legitimate issue in the case. The purposes outlined in the rule do not have to be used exclusively, however.[85] The key for the court is figuring out where the line defining "bad character" ends and where the one defining those other purposes begins.[86]

To prove an independent purpose, the prosecution must show some "logical nexus" or connection between the prior incident and a material issue in the current case.[87] For example, a Colorado court held that the mere fact a person has experience or training in how to use weapons does

Independent purposes
a requirement that the prosecution prove that it intends to offer the prior acts of the defendant for some reason other than to show he has a propensity to commit crime. Several independent purposes are outlined in Rule 404(b), including motive, identity, and lack of mistake

not make it more likely that he intended to use such a weapon to injure or kill a person on a particular occasion.[88] While there is no requirement that the prior incidents and the current offense be substantially similar to one another,[89] the probative value of the prior acts evidence is increased the more similar it is to the charged offense.[90] The Colorado Supreme Court explained the distinction this way:

> Although there obviously were some differences in the circumstances surrounding each offense, it is not essential that the means of committing the other crimes replicate in all respects the manner in which the crime charged was committed. Rather, what is of critical significance is that the evidence of other crimes and the crime charged, considered in its totality, manifest significantly distinctive features to make it more likely than it would be without the other crime evidence that the person who committed the other crimes also committed the offense charged.[91]

While a lengthy lapse of time between the prior act and the commission of the charged crime can reduce the probative value of the evidence, the mere fact that a long period of time has elapsed does not make the evidence inadmissible.[92] Instead, courts will weigh the similarity of the prior acts against the length of time that has elapsed.[93] Prior acts that are very similar to the charged conduct will often be admitted, even if they are quite old, and acts that are not very similar but are recent in time may be excluded. Thus, Courts have admitted such evidence even where the prior acts occurred 15 or 20 years prior to the charged offense.[94]

Practical Example

Assume that Gabriella is being tried for shoplifting. She has a prior conviction for drug possession that the prosecutor wants to introduce under 404(b) to show she had motive to steal. She is still on probation for the drug conviction and is having trouble paying the rent and her court costs. Under the circumstances, the prior act may be relevant to prove motive since it shows Gabriella was having financial troubles and had a motive to steal.

Now assume Carlos is on trial for statutory rape of a 16-year-old girl. He claims he did not rape the girl. He was previously convicted of sexual assault on a minor 14 years ago. The facts of the two cases are similar. Although the prior act occurred a number of years ago, it still has high probative value since the acts are similar to one another.

1. Identity

One independent purpose that is often asserted by prosecutors is to prove the identity of the perpetrator. To prove identity, the prosecution must show either that the defendant engaged in a common scheme or

Modus operandi (or method of operation)
a distinct pattern or method characteristic of an individual criminal habitually followed by that offender. The prosecution must show that the similarities between the prior acts and the charged conduct are so similar as to uniquely identify the perpetrator of the crimes

plan to commit the offenses or that the acts followed the same modus operandi. **Modus operandi**, or method of operation, is a distinct pattern or method characteristic of an individual criminal habitually followed by that offender.[95] Proving modus operandi requires the prosecution to show that the similarities between the charged offense and the prior conduct are "so strong and so clearly unique that it is highly probable that the perpetrator of both is the same person."[96] For example, an Arkansas court ruled that evidence of the defendant's prior rape of an E-Z Mart clerk was properly admitted in his trial for a subsequent rape and murder of a store clerk 5 years later. Both incidents were committed shortly after midnight at an E-Z Mart after the defendant had purchased several items from the store earlier in the day. The defendant had also physically struggled with his victims in each attack. Thus, the court concluded that the evidence was relevant to the issues of intent and modus operandi.[97]

Common scheme or plan
an independent purpose for which prior act evidence may be admitted to prove. In many states, the prosecution must show that the prior acts are related in time, character, and place to establish some plan which encompassed both the prior acts and the current charged offense

The prosecution can also prove the identity of the perpetrator by showing that the defendant engaged in a **common scheme or plan** in committing the offenses. Some courts have liberally interpreted the definition of common scheme or plan. For example, the Colorado Supreme Court upheld the admission of the fact that the defendant had strangled two other women he had had an intimate relationship with in his prosecution for murdering his girlfriend. The court found the evidence was relevant to his identity as the murderer since, in each case, the partially nude or nude victim was found strangled with a blanket covering most of the body.[98] Other courts have strictly interpreted this exception to allow admission of prior acts only where they are "so related in character, time and place of commission as to establish some plan which embraced both the prior and subsequent criminal activity and the charged crime."[99] Under this view, prior acts should not be admitted to prove a common plan or scheme where the defendant committed them "wholly independent of the one for which he is then on trial."[100]

Practical Example

Assume that Peter is charged with molesting two young boys at a drive-in theater. He picked up the kids near their school and drove them to the drive-in, where he molested them. Previously, he was convicted of molesting another boy 10 years ago. In that incident, Peter was accused of picking up a child at an arcade and bringing him back to his house, where he molested the boy. The prosecutor moves to admit the evidence as relevant to Peter's common plan or scheme or as evidence of his modus operandi. The evidence will be admitted in those states that interpret common plan or scheme broadly. It will be excluded in those states that require the acts to be related to one another as an ongoing criminal enterprise. In any state, the court will reject the evidence as proof of modus operandi since the incidents do not involve a unique signature.

2. Intent and Motive

Intent or motive
an independent purpose for which prior act evidence may be admitted under Rule 404(b). Intent is the necessary mental state required to commit a given crime, while motive is the reason the perpetrator committed the crime

Another purpose that is often used by prosecutors to admit prior acts evidence is proof of **intent or motive**. Intent is required mental state necessary to prove someone committed a given crime. Motive is reason the perpetrator may have had for committing the crime. Determining whether to admit prior acts to prove motive and intent is perhaps the toughest decision for courts to make in this area since the distinction between admissible evidence of motive and inadmissible evidence of character or propensity is often "subtle."[101] Due to the fact that there is often little or no direct evidence of a person's intent or motive, some courts have given wide latitude to prosecutors in admitting prior acts evidence for this purpose.

A New Jersey court explained that proof of motive or intent often requires proof of prior acts because:

> [o]therwise there would often be no means to reach and disclose the secret design or purpose of the act charged in which the very gist of the offense may consist.... All evidentiary circumstances which are relevant to or tend to shed light on the motive or intent of the defendant or which tend fairly to explain his actions are admissible in evidence against him although they may have occurred previous to the commission of the offense.[102]

The court held that the prosecution could use the defendant's white supremacist drawings and writings to help explain the defendant's seemingly random attack on an elderly black man, reasoning that the material "is compelling, powerful evidence of a motive which helps explain an otherwise inexplicable act of random violence."[103] In a similar situation, a Michigan court instructed why such evidence is relevant:

> [I]f... all the defendant's prior victims were African-American and [the] defendant had previously expressed his hatred toward blacks, then the evidence of the defendant's prior assaults would be admissible to prove the defendant's motive for his conduct. By establishing that the defendant harbors a strong animus against people of the victim's race, the other-acts evidence goes beyond establishing a propensity toward violence and tends to show why the defendant perpetrated a seemingly random and inexplicable attack.[104]

Practical Example

June is charged with murder of her male boss. The prosecution wants to introduce evidence that she had posted entries on her blog on several prior occasions that expressed a frustration with male-dominated society. She made reference to the fact that women who killed men were heroes. The court will likely admit such evidence since it helps prove her motive for killing her boss.

3. Absence of Mistake

Absence of mistake or accident
an independent purpose for which prior acts may be admitted under Rule 404(b). The prior acts are introduced to show that since the defendant has committed similar acts in the past, he could not have mistakenly done so in this instance

Another common reason for the admission of prior acts is to prove **absence of mistake or accident**. Prior acts evidence is used to defeat a defense that the charged act was a mistake, an accident, or consensual. The defendant's commission of prior related incidents makes it considerably more likely that he possessed the necessary criminal intent in committing the current offense. For instance, an Ohio court admitted evidence of prior instances of domestic violence committed by the defendant to disprove his claim that the current charged incident of domestic violence was an accident. The court found the prior acts evidence was relevant since it showed intent and knowledge on the part of the defendant to injure the victim.[105]

Practical Example

Mike and Wendy have been dating for three years. Mike is charged with pushing Wendy and choking her. Mike claims the incident was a misunderstanding and that he accidentally pushed Wendy. The prosecution wants to introduce evidence that Wendy has filed two prior reports of domestic violence against Mike to rebut his defense of mistake. The judge will likely admit the evidence since it is relevant to the issue of intent.

D. Balancing the Probative Value Against the Prejudicial Effect

Prejudicial effect
evidence is prejudicial if the jury will pay undue attention to it or it distracts the jury from more proper questions because it is inflammatory

If the court finds that the evidence is relevant and offered for some independent purpose, then the court must conduct a balancing test to determine if the probative value is substantially outweighed by its **prejudicial effect**. Evidence is prejudicial if the jury will pay undue attention to it or it distracts the jury from more proper questions because it is inflammatory.[106] All prior act evidence is to some degree prejudicial. Therefore, the balance usually weighs in favor of the defendant where the evidence adds little to the question of the defendant's guilt. Conversely, if the evidence is highly probative, then it is unlikely that it will be excluded as prejudicial. For example, the admission of a defendant's armed confrontation with an apartment manager (where he never drew his weapon) is prejudicial because the prior incident is not very probative of whether the defendant had the intent to threaten the victim with a firearm in the current case (where he did draw his weapon). In contrast, such prior evidence would be relevant to a current charge where the defendant had pulled a weapon in a similar fashion on several other individuals in the past.[107]

Another factor that courts weigh is the severity of the prior conduct in comparison with the charged offense.[108] For instance, a California court admitted evidence that the defendant had previously chased a woman around a living room with a knife in the defendant's trial for murder of his girlfriend. The court found that the evidence was not prejudicial or inflammatory in relation to the charged crime since the defendant was charged with killing his pregnant girlfriend and burying her on a hiking trail.[109]

Practical Example

Michael is charged with animal cruelty for kicking his dog. The prosecution wants to introduce evidence that he had previously operated a dog-fighting operation where he was accused of brutally killing several animals. The court is likely to exclude this prior acts evidence as prejudicial since it is so much more severe in nature than the charged offense.

Evidence of Death of Second Husband Inadmissible in Black Widow Murder Trial

In 2009 and 2010, Raynella Dossett-Leath was tried for the murder of her second husband, David Leath, in Knoxville, Tennessee. He was found shot to death in his bed on March 13, 2003. Originally, investigators thought Leath may have killed himself and ruled the death a suicide. Other evidence pointed to murder, however, such as the fact that two of three shots fired missed their mark and an autopsy revealed Leath had three prescription drugs in his system, none of which he had a prescription for, at the time of his death. Since Dossett-Leath was a registered nurse, investigators concluded she would have had the necessary knowledge to stage the scene as a suicide.[110] It took investigators three years to charge Raynella with his murder, and another three years to bring the case to trial.[111]

Dossett-Leath was dubbed the black widow because her first husband, Ed Dossett, had also died under suspicious circumstances in 1992. His death was also originally ruled an accident. Bound to a wheelchair and suffering from cancer, Dossett was trampled to death by cattle on the family's 165-acre farm. Dossett-Leath stated that she had helped her husband out to the pasture to see and feed the cattle. When she returned a few minutes later, she found him lying in the gateway of the fence, trampled. An autopsy revealed multiple internal injuries consistent with being trampled but also showed that he had twice the recommended level of morphine in his system.[112]

In 2009, investigators reopened the case and charged Dossett-Leath with Ed's murder, believing Dossett had instead died of an overdose of morphine. That case was set for trial in January 2011. Special prosecutors decided to file a *nolle prosequi* in December 2010, however, effectively

Continued on following page

Evidence in Action continued

ending that case.[113] The trail of character issues surrounding Dossett-Leath didn't end there. In 1995, Dossett Leath was charged with attempted murder of Steve Walker. The disagreement stemmed from an argument over her first husband's illegitimate child. She was accused of firing several shots at Walker inside her barn. The case was ultimately pled out prior to trial and the charges were dismissed.[114]

In Leath's murder trial, the prosecution had moved to admit evidence of Dossett's murder under Rule 404(b) to show that Dossett-Leath had motive and had formed a common plan or pattern of conduct. The prosecution filed three separate petitions to exhume Dossett's body so a second autopsy could be performed. The first alleged that an autopsy was necessary to prove the allegations that Dossett-Leath had engaged in a common plan or scheme to murder her husbands for money. The second alleged that the autopsy was necessary to prove the charge of murder in Dossett's death. The prosecution renewed that motion after a grand jury returned an indictment against Dossett-Leath for murdering her first husband. The judge denied all three motions, finding that a second autopsy would not reveal any additional evidence since the presence of morphine in Dossett's body was already known.[115]

The judge also denied the prosecution's motion to admit evidence of Dossett's death under Rule 404(b) in the trial involving Leath's death. Because Tennessee law requires the prosecutor to prove by clear and convincing evidence that the defendant committed the prior acts, the judge found the prosecution's proof lacking. He noted that "there is no proof that William E. Dossett was the victim of a homicide at all, let alone that defendant committed that homicide."[116] Furthermore, the judge noted that the prosecution had not sufficiently shown that the evidence was relevant for some independent purpose under the rule. Identity was not an issue in the case since there was no claim that some third party was responsible for Leath's death; the defendant claimed he committed suicide. Nor was there evidence that Dossett's death was part of a common plan or scheme. Since Dossett-Leath's husbands had died in different manners, the court concluded that the evidence was insufficient to show that the murders revealed a distinctive design or were similar enough to constitute signature crimes.[117] Although noting that they were some similarities in the deaths, the judge stated that "when you look at the differences… there is no way in the world" that an exhumation was warranted.[118] The judge concluded that "there simply are no facts at issue that would support or justify the introduction of the facts surrounding [Dossett's] death."[119] He warned both parties that mentioning the prior death of Dossett would result in a mistrial.

Despite losing the battle to admit evidence of Dossett's murder, the prosecution eventually won the case. The medical examiner testified that suicide was impossible in the case since the fatal shot was fired from 12 to 14 inches from Leath's head and that the drugs in his system would have incapacitated him.[120] Although the evidence pointed to Dossett-Leath's guilt, the first trial ended in a hung jury in March of 2009.[121] Dossett-Leath was retried in January of 2010. This time, the jury convicted her of first-degree murder. She is currently serving a life sentence.

E. Admission of Prior Acts in Sexual Assault and Domestic Violence Cases

The admission of prior acts evidence can play a particularly important role in sexual assault and domestic violence cases. Proving intent and/ or defeating the defense of consent can be difficult if the evidence is just limited to the facts of the charged offense. The cases often come down to swearing matches between the victim and the defendant. In domestic violence cases, the victim may be a reluctant witness or choose not to testify at all. Child sex assault cases can be even harder to prove since the jury may not give much credibility to a young witness. The introduction of prior acts of sexual misconduct or domestic violence can help tip the balance in favor of the prosecution by corroborating victims' allegations.[122] Some would argue that balance has been tipped too much in favor of the prosecution.

Courts have traditionally taken two views with respect to the admission of prior acts evidence in sexual assault and domestic violence cases. One group has applied the same set of criteria to the admission of prior acts of sexual misconduct as it does to other prior acts evidence, admitting such acts only in limited circumstances, usually only where a clear pattern or signature has been proven. A growing number of states have relaxed the rules in sexual assault cases and routinely admit prior acts evidence so long as there is the "thinnest pretext" that the evidence satisfies some independent purpose under Rule 404(b).[123] These courts have openly recognized that they are "more liberal" with respect to the admission of prior acts evidence in sexual assault cases than other types of cases.[124] The federal rules and a handful of states have gone a step further, adopting a third approach that authorizes the admission of prior acts of sexual misconduct for all purposes, not just those laid out in Rule 404(b).

1. Lustful Disposition Exception

Lustful disposition exception

an exception to the general rule barring character evidence that permits the prosecution to admit prior acts evidence in sexual assault cases. Such evidence is relevant to prove the defendant's intent or motive to commit the crime was to satisfy his lustful desire

Some courts have recognized the so-called **"lustful disposition" exception,** which holds that evidence of prior misconduct is admissible to show the defendant's motive for the attack was to satisfy his lustful desire.[125] About 20 states recognize some form of this exception.[126] Courts have justified the use of this exception on the grounds that the recidivism rate among sexual offenders is high and that the prior acts evidence helps corroborate the testimony of victims, particularly young children.

This expansive interpretation of Rule 404(b) has not been without criticism, however. Critics argue that the lustful disposition exception really is better characterized as a complete abandonment of the rule against admission of character evidence in sexual assault cases.[127] One court likened the lustful disposition exception to "forcing a square peg into a round hole."[128] As a result of such criticism, some states have abandoned the exception altogether. For example, the Indiana Supreme Court concluded that the justifications for the exception were outweighed by the "mischief created by the open-ended application of the rule."[129] The court pointed out that high recidivism rates alone cannot justify treating sexual offenders differently than other types of criminals:

> We do not allow the State to introduce previous drug convictions in its case-in-chief in a prosecution for selling illegal drugs, however, even though it can hardly be disputed that such evidence would be highly probative. This exclusionary

rule renders inadmissible character evidence offered solely to show the accuser's propensity to commit the crime with which he is charged. The rationale behind this general rule, sometimes termed "the propensity rule," is that the prejudicial effect of such evidence outweighs any probative value. If a high rate of recidivism cannot justify a departure from the propensity rule for drug defendants, logic dictates it does not provide justification for departure in sex offense cases.[130]

2. Heightened Relevance Laws

Heightened relevance laws

laws which grant increased relevance to prior acts of sexual misconduct or domestic violence to prove one or more of the factors outlined in Rule 404(b)

Some states use a slightly different approach and have adopted **heightened relevance laws** that emphasize the relevance of and need for prior act evidence in cases involving sexual assault or domestic violence. For example, Colorado law states that there is a "greater need and propriety" for prior act evidence in sexual assault cases and that the probative value of such evidence will "outweigh any danger of unfair prejudice, even when incidents are remote from one another in time."[131] The statute also lists an expansive number of purposes for which such evidence may be admitted, including refuting defenses such as consent or recent fabrication; showing a common plan or scheme, regardless of whether the charged offense has a close nexus as part of a unified transaction to the other act; and showing preparation, including grooming of a victim.[132] Colorado has a similar law for the admission of prior acts in domestic violence cases.[133] Because the prosecution still has to prove some independent purpose for the admission of the evidence, such laws are designed to emphasize the relevance of similar acts evidence in cases involving sexual assault and domestic violence, not to entirely eliminate the necessity of an analysis under Rule 404(b).[134]

Practical Example

Mike is charged with molesting his granddaughter. He allegedly fondled her and penetrated her digitally. Twenty years ago, social services was called to investigate a complaint that Mike had done a similar thing to his daughter. The elder sister also stated he had done something similar to her in the past. No charges were filed in that incident after the older sister changed her story. The prosecution now wants to admit the facts of the prior allegation. If the state has a heightened relevance law, the prior incident will likely be admissible even though it occurred 20 years earlier. It is similar in nature to the charged offense and shows a pattern of conduct.

EVIDENCE IN ACTION

Prior Acts of Sexual Misconduct Excluded in William Kennedy Smith Rape Trial

In 1991, a woman accused William Kennedy-Smith, the nephew of Senator Ted Kennedy, of raping her in the backyard of the Kennedy compound in Palm Beach County, Florida, where the family was vacationing over Easter weekend. Smith had met the 30-year-old woman earlier that night at a local nightclub. The alleged victim drove back to the house with Smith.[135] The two walked along the beach and briefly kissed. At that point, the two versions of events diverged. The victim stated Kennedy-Smith allegedly jumped into the ocean with his clothes off and then attacked her on the beach. Although the victim stated she yelled "no" and tried to fight off Smith, she claimed he raped her. Kennedy-Smith contended the sex was consensual.[136] Smith was charged with sexual battery and his trial took place in December of 1991. The case attracted nationwide attention and was aired by the fledgling Court TV network.

Prosecutors had sought to admit the testimony of three women to prove Smith's distinctive manner or signature in committing the assault. Although none of the women had reported the incidents to police, the prosecutors offered the transcripts of the depositions the women had given to Kennedy-Smith's attorneys about the incidents. One woman alleged that Smith raped her after she had gotten drunk at a party in 1988. The woman stated that Mr. Smith offered her a ride home, but ended up taking her to his home, not hers. She stated he refused to let her use his couch, and that when she got into his bed and tried to sleep, he made advances and forced himself upon her. She stated, "He was not going to take no for an answer. I was afraid he was going to hit me or something, I really was." A second woman stated that while she was dating Mr. Smith's cousin, Matthew Kennedy, Smith lunged at her, pushed her

Figure 12.2 William Kennedy Smith listens to evidence on November 21, 1991, during his rape trial in Palm Beach, Florida. © *Lannis Waters/Sygma/Corbis*

on a bed, and pinned her underneath him. He began fondling her before stopping. A third woman stated that in 1988, Mr. Smith threw her over a couch and onto the floor of his Georgetown apartment where he began kissing her "wildly."[137]

The prosecution had argued that the stories contained several similarities to the alleged Palm Beach incident. All the women were attractive brunettes whom Mr. Smith had met while they were unattended in social situations. They also claimed that he lured all of them into his "lair," just like the situation in Florida. Defense attorneys, however, argued that the situations were not similar. The earlier episodes had occurred indoors, not on a lawn in Palm Beach. Also, his attorneys pointed out that the incidents differed in the ways in which the

Continued on following page

Evidence in Action continued

victims were attacked and to what extent Smith had carried them out.[138] Under Florida law at the time, evidence of a defendant's prior bad acts was admissible only if it showed a highly particularized pattern of conduct on the defendant's part. The judge may have sealed the prosecution's fate when she prevented the three women from testifying that Kennedy-Smith had sexually assaulted them.

The ruling excluding Smith's prior acts of sexual misconduct was balanced to some degree by the judge's exclusion of the victim's prior sexual history and character. Defense attorneys had sought to introduce evidence that the victim had undergone three abortions in the past, had borne one child out of wedlock, and had previously used cocaine. The judge excluded all of that evidence under Florida's rape shield law.[139]

In December 1991, a jury acquitted Smith on all charges. It took only 77 minutes to reach a not guilty verdict. Trial observers reported that Smith's testimony in his own defense was the most compelling factor in his favor. In closing, Smith's attorney, Roy Black, referred to the victim's encounter with Smith as "right out of a romance novel."[140]

The publicity surrounding the Smith trial and his acquittal helped push efforts to strengthen laws around the country regarding admission of prior act evidence in sexual assault cases. The Federal Rules of Evidence were amended in 1994 to permit the admission of prior acts of sexual misconduct in sexual assault cases, regardless of their purpose.[141] These new rules are discussed in the next section.

3. Admission of Evidence of Prior Acts in Sexual Assault Cases in Federal Court: Rules 413 and 414

Rule 413. Evidence of Similar Crimes in Sexual Assault Cases

(a) In a criminal case in which the defendant is accused of an offense of sexual assault, evidence of the defendant's commission of another offense or offenses of sexual assault is admissible, and may be considered for its bearing on any matter to which it is relevant.

Rule 414. Evidence of Similar Crimes in Child Molestation Cases

(a) In a criminal case in which the defendant is accused of an offense of child molestation, evidence of the defendant's commission of another offense or offenses of child molestation is admissible, and may be considered for its bearing on any matter to which it is relevant.

Rulings barring the admission of other acts evidence in cases like the Smith trial led some states and Congress to go one step further, allowing for the direct admission of prior acts of sexual misconduct for any purpose, not just those laid out in Rule 404(b). As part of the Violent Crime Control and Law Enforcement Act of 1994, Congress added two new rules to the Rules of Evidence that permitted the government to introduce

Rule 413

rule of evidence that provides prior instances of sexual misconduct are admissible for any matter that they are relevant in sexual assault cases, including to prove that the defendant has a propensity to commit acts of sexual misconduct

Rule 414

rule of evidence that provides prior acts of sexual misconduct with children are admissible for any matter that they are relevant in child sexual molestation cases

evidence of prior sex offenses in sexual assault prosecutions in federal court. **Rule 413** provides that prior instances of sexual misconduct are admissible for any matter that they are relevant in sexual assault cases and **Rule 414** makes a similar provision for child molestation cases.[142]

What makes the use of prior acts evidence in sexual assault cases so different from all other types of crimes? The answer, at least according to Congress, is twofold. First, sexual assault cases are often "he said/she said" types of cases with little corroborating evidence. As such, the credibility of the victim is subject to easy attack. Second, since consent is often used as a defense in sexual assault cases, but not in other violent crimes, Congress believed that the jury should hear such evidence in evaluating the issue of consent.[143] Thus, Congress intended to create a broad exception to Rule 404 in sexual assault cases, allowing evidence of prior sexual misconduct to be used to show the defendant's propensity to commit sexual offenses, not just one of the enumerated exceptions outlined in Rule 404(b).[144] Several states followed suit, including Alaska, Arizona, California, Illinois, and Texas.[145]

These Rules work much like Rule 404(b). First, the Rules require the prosecutor provide notice to the defendant of his intent to use evidence of prior sexual misconduct. A hearing must be held prior to trial to determine the admissibility of the alleged prior misconduct. The prosecution must show that the defendant committed an act or perpetrated conduct that would constitute a criminal sexual offense.[146] The prior acts evidence must also satisfy the Rule 403 balancing test.[147] The courts will consider (1) how clearly has the prior act been proved; (2) how probative is the prior evidence of the material fact it is admitted to prove; (3) how disputed is that material fact; and (4) whether the government can introduce less prejudicial evidence to prove the same fact.[148]

The passage of Rules 413 and Rule 414 was quite controversial. Many scholars and members of the federal Judicial Conference opposed adoption of the rules, fearing that defendants in sexual assault cases would be convicted on their past transgressions, rather than on the evidence supporting the current offense.[149] Several federal courts have held that Rules 413 and 414 do not violate due process, however.[150] These rulings were largely based on the fact that the trial judge can still exclude such evidence if it is too prejudicial.[151] Similarly, the California Supreme Court upheld California's version of Rule 413 against a constitutional challenge.[152] It also pointed to the fact that the trial court must engage in a balancing of interests before deciding to admit the evidence. The court must weigh factors such as the nature of the prior act, its relevance, its remoteness, and the likelihood that it will be misleading to the jury before admitting such evidence.[153]

Some courts have not been so receptive to passage of these types of laws, however. The Supreme Court of Iowa recently held that Iowa's version of Rule 414 can only be applied to past incidents that involved the same victim as the current offense.[154] The court held that the rule does not apply where the prior incidents involve a different victim (Iowa's version of Rule 404(b) has to be used instead in that instance).[155] The court concluded that the admission of propensity evidence involving different victims is fundamentally unfair:

> A focus on the criminal or aberrant disposition of the defendant with regard to various victims is exactly the sort of prejudice which the general rule seeks to avoid. By creating an exception of this kind, we would seriously erode the impact of the general rule, proscribing evidence of prior criminal conduct, in the context of sex crimes. The resultant unfairness to those accused of sex crimes is self-evident.[156]

The Missouri Supreme Court struck down Missouri's version of Rule 413, holding that the unlimited admission of prior act evidence violated due process.[157]

Practical Example

Assume that Suzy Mae Wiggins is charged with sexually assaulting her 14-year-old pupil. Two years ago, she was convicted of contributing to the delinquency of a minor by serving her 17-year-old neighbor alcohol in her hot tub while both were nude. Would the evidence of her prior conviction be admissible to prove the current sexual assault charge? The answer depends on which rule is being applied. Under Rule 404(b), the prosecution has to allege some independent purpose for its admission. Unless the state recognizes the lustful disposition exception, it is unlikely that the court will admit the prior incident since it is not similar to the current offense and is not relevant to identity. However, under Rule 414, the evidence is now admissible. It does not matter that the prosecution cannot establish one of the independent purposes under Rule 404(b).

CHAPTER SUMMARY

The general rule is that character evidence is inadmissible to show that a witness acted in conformity with a prior incident or character trait on a particular occasion. For example, the prosecutor could not introduce evidence that the defendant was convicted of cocaine possession in 2002 to prove that he possessed cocaine in 2010. The fear is that character evidence will improperly sway the jury to base their decision on factors other than the evidence presented of the defendant's guilt.

There are four exceptions to the general rule, however. First, the defendant can introduce

evidence of his own good character that can then be rebutted by the prosecution. Second, the defendant can also introduce evidence attacking the victim's character, usually by showing that he had an aggressive or violent character. This is often done in homicide cases or other incidents where the defendant is claiming self-defense. Again, the prosecution is allowed to present rebuttal evidence by showing either that the victim actually had a peaceful character or that the defendant has had a violent history as well. Typically, both the prosecution and defense can present evidence of character in these instances only in the form of a person's reputation or opinion. The use of specific instances of misconduct is usually limited to cross-examination.

One notable exception to the defendant's ability to attack the character of the victim is a rape shield law. These laws are designed to protect the victim from embarrassment by preventing her sexual history from being paraded in front of the jury. These laws commonly contain exceptions, however, that permit the defendant to introduce evidence of the victim's sexual conduct to show that the source of the semen or injury is from another individual or that the victim's prior conduct with the defendant is relevant to the issue of consent.

The third exception to the general rule permits the prosecution to introduce evidence of the defendant's prior bad acts for some purpose other than to show the defendant has a propensity to commit crime. In order to introduce prior acts of misconduct, the prosecution has to show that the defendant probably committed the prior act and that the evidence is relevant to prove some independent purpose such as intent, motive, or identity. In sexual assault cases, some jurisdictions have given the prosecution greater leeway to admit prior acts. In those courts, the prosecution can admit evidence of the defendant's prior sexual misconduct even if that evidence does not satisfy one of Rule 404(b)'s independent purposes. The court can still exclude prior acts evidence on the ground that its prejudicial effect is too high. Under the federal rules, the prosecution may admit evidence of prior acts of sexual misconduct for any purpose.

KEY TERMS

- Absence of mistake or accident
- Character evidence
- Common scheme or plan
- Constitutional catchall
- Evidentiary purpose
- First aggressor
- Good character
- Heightened relevance laws

- Independent purposes
- Intent or motive
- Judicial discretion
- Legislated exception
- Lustful disposition exception
- Modus operandi
- Prejudicial effect
- Prior acts
- Rape shield laws

- Reputation or opinion evidence
- Rule 404(a)
- Rule 404(b)
- Rule 413
- Rule 414
- Self-defense

REVIEW QUESTIONS

1. What is character evidence? How is its admission generally viewed by courts? Do you think character evidence should be excluded, or should the jury be allowed to hear all relevant evidence?

2. Name the four exceptions for when character evidence is allowed to be admitted.

3. In what form can the defendant and prosecution present character evidence as it relates to the defendant's character or the victim's character?

4. Why are specific instances of misconduct not allowed to be introduced as character evidence for the most part? Do you agree

with this position, or do you think it gives juries an incomplete picture of the character of witnesses and the defendant? Explain.

5. When is a defendant allowed to attack the character of a victim? Give one example.

6. What is a rape shield law? What type of evidence is a design to exclude?

7. Name the four types of rape shield laws and discuss the differences between them.

8. Give two examples of evidence that would be admissible under any form of a rape shield law.

9. What is rule 404(b)? Give two examples of independent purposes that can justify the admission of character evidence.

10. What four things must the prosecution prove in order to admit prior acts of the defendant under rule 404(b)?

11. What types of factors does the court have to weigh in balancing the prejudicial effect of the evidence versus its probative value?

12. Explain the two contrasting views of courts as they relate to the admission of prior bad acts evidence in sexual assault cases. Which of the two views do you think is the better approach?

13. What is the lustful disposition exception? Why have some courts recently gotten rid of it?

14. What is the importance of Rule 413? Why did Congress exempt evidence in sexual assault cases from the restrictions of Rule 404(b)?

15. Why have some courts overturned part or all of rules that permit the direct introduction of acts of prior sexual misconduct even to prove propensity?

APPLICATION PROBLEMS

1. Al is a minister. He is charged with soliciting a male prostitute. He wants to introduce evidence that he is a minister and has an excellent reputation in the community. He also wants to introduce evidence that he went on a mission to Africa and helped save thousands of lives. Will Al be able to introduce either of these pieces of evidence? Explain. Now assume the prosecution wants to rebut this evidence with the fact that Al is hated by the parishioners of his last church because he defrauded them out of $40,000. Can the prosecutor cross-examine Al's witnesses about this incident?

2. Fred and Barney get into a scuffle. Fred threatens to kill Barney. Barney is afraid of Fred because he saw Fred beat up someone at a bowling alley last year. Barney then pulls a knife and threatens Fred. Fred tries to grab the knife but is instead stabbed in the arm. He loses a lot of blood but lives. Barney is charged with assault with a deadly weapon. He wants to introduce evidence that Fred is a violent person and in particular the incident that he witnessed last year at the bowling alley. Will the judge admit either item of evidence? Explain.

3. Clark travels cross-country to take his family to an amusement park. When he arrives, he discovers the park is closed. He punches the mascot out in front of the park. A security guard is then called to the scene. The guard tells Clark that the park is closed and he should go home. Clark refuses. The guard then says he will put Clark back in his car himself if he does not leave. Clark says, "Make me." The guard then tries to stuff Clark into his minivan. Clark then punches the guard. Clark is charged with assault.

He claims self-defense. He wants to introduce evidence that the guard was convicted of assault and also sued for excessive force and false imprisonment when he worked at Wal-Mart. The prosecutor wants to introduce evidence that Clark was the initial aggressor and that he was previously convicted for assaulting a bouncer at a nightclub. What evidence will the judge allow in? Explain.

4. Julie alleges that Quagmire sexually assaulted her after the couple met at a nightclub and he invited her back to his place. She had bruising and tearing detected during her rape kit exam. Quagmire wants to introduce several pieces of evidence. First, he wants the court to admit evidence that Julie had been dancing provocatively on the bar top with several men at the bar before she went home with him. Second, he wants to introduce evidence of the fact that she had sex with Joe the night before and suffered her injuries then. Third, he wants to introduce evidence that Julie had previously made a rape allegation against her ex-boyfriend and charges were ultimately dropped. What evidence will the judge admit? Assume the state follows the Michigan style of rape shield law.

5. Assume the prosecutor now wants to admit evidence of Quagmire's past sexual misconduct in the above example. Quagmire was convicted of contributing to the delinquency of a minor two years ago. He was also accused of sexually assaulting a woman whom he met at a work party four years ago. Will the court admit the evidence if the state recognizes the lustful disposition exception? What if courts in the state have traditionally strict limitations on the admission of acts of prior sexual misconduct?

6. Stewie plots to kill his mother, Lois. He purchases several weapons and lures his mother to his apartment, where he shoots her and then disposes of her body. The police arrest him for the murder. The prosecution wants to introduce evidence that Stewie plotted to kill his mother on several prior occasions when he was a child. He never successfully completed the attempts and was never charged with a crime. He tried to run her over with a car, smash her over the head with a heavy object, and stab her. What other purpose or purposes is this evidence relevant to prove under Rule 404(b)? Do you think the judge will admit the evidence or exclude it as too prejudicial? Explain.

7. Barry and Sammy are indicted for possession of steroids in violation of the controlled substances act. They are accused of buying steroids from a Canadian doctor. Three years ago, both were connected to an investigation of another steroid dealer. Although both were suspected of purchasing steroids from the lab in question, charges were never brought as a result of that investigation. The prosecution wants to introduce evidence from the prior investigation. Which of the three exceptions to Rule 404(a) makes the most sense for the prosecutor to use? Is the evidence relevant and is it admissible for some other purpose? Explain.

Notes

1. Josephson Institute of Ethics, available at http://josephsoninstitute.org/quotes/character.html.
2. United States v. Myers, 51 M.J. 570, 580 (U.S. Navy-Marine C. App. 1999), *quoting* Michelson v. United States, 335 U.S. 469, 475-76 (1948).
3. Christopher W. Behan, *When Turnabout Is Fair Play: Character Evidence and Self-Defense in Homicide and Assault Cases*, 86 Ore. L. Rev. 733, 745 (2007).
4. Michelson, 335 U.S. at 475-76.
5. F.R.E. 404(a).
6. Behan, *supra* note 3, at 755.
7. F.R.E. 405(a).
8. F.R.E. 405.
9. F.R.E. 405 advisory comm. note.
10. Behan, *supra* note 3, at 753.
11. F.R.E. 404(a)(1).
12. Commonwealth v. Hernandez, 862 A.2d 647 (Pa. Super. 2004).
13. Id. at 650.
14. Id.
15. State v. Hale, 256 N.E.2d 239 (Ohio. App. 1969).

16. State v. Jenewicz, 940 A.2d 269, 274-75 (N.J. 2008).
17. Behan, *supra* note 3, at 740.
18. *See* Wyo. R. Evid. 404(a)(1).
19. Commonwealth v. Adjutant, 824 N.E.2d 1 (Mass. 2005).
20. Id. at 14.
21. *See* Behan, *supra* note 3, at 771 n. 145, *citing* Andrew G. Scott, Note: *Exclusive Admissibility of Specific Act Evidence in Initial-Aggressor Self-Defense Cases: Ensuring Equity Within the Adjutant Framework*, 40 Suffolk U.L. Rev. 237, 244-50 (2006).
22. *See e.g.*, United States v. Jackson, 549 F.3d 963, 976 (5th Cir. 2008).
23. United States v. Keiser, 7 F.3d 847, 856 (9th Cir. 1995).
24. Id. at 857.
25. Cassia C. Spohn, *The Impact of Rape Law Reform on the Processing of Simple and Aggravated Rape Case*, 86 J.C.L. & Crim. 861 (1996).
26. Josh Maggard, Note: *Courting Disaster: Re-Evaluating Rape Shields in Light of People v. Bryant*, 66 Ohio State L.J. 1341, 1347-48 (2005).
27. State v. Johns, 615 P.2d 1260, 1264 (Utah 1980).
28. State v. Dibello, 780 P.2d 1221, 1229 (Utah 1989).
29. Maggard, *supra* note 26, at 1358.
30. State v. Herndon, 426 N.W.2d 347 (Wis. App. 1988); Richard I. Haddad, Note: *Shield or Sieve? People v. Bryant and the Rape Shield Law in High-Profile Cases*, 39 Colum. J. L. & Soc. Probs. 185, 190, (2006).
31. F.R.E. 412(a).
32. F.R.E. 412(b)(1).
33. F.R.E. 412(b)(2)(A).
34. F.R.E. 412(b)(1)(C).
35. For a good discussion of the various forms of rape shield laws, including the Michigan approach, *see* State v. Herndon, 426 N.W.2d 347 (Wis. App. 1988), *overturned on other grounds*, State v. Pullizano, 456 N.W.2d 325 (Wis. 1990).
36. *See e.g.*, Ark. Code Ann. § 16-42-101.
37. Ark. Code Ann. Sec. 16-42-101(d).
38. John McDonough, *Consent v. Credibility: The Complications of Evidentiary Purpose Rape Shield Statutes*, 5 L. & Soc. J. at UCSB 11 (2006).
39. Cal. Evid. Code 1103(c)(2).
40. McDonough, *supra* note 38, at 13.
41. *See* People v. Calleros, 2004 WL 2386745 (Cal. App. 4th Dist. 2004) (unpublished decision).
42. People v Fontana, 232 P.3d 1187, 1195 (Cal. 2010).
43. State v. Garron, 827 A.2d 243, 247 (N.J. 2003).
44. Garron, 827 A.2d at 259.
45. State v. Colbath, 540 A.2d 1212, 1216 (N.H. 1988).
46. Id. at 1217.
47. People v. Wilhelm, 476 N.W.2d at 753 (Mich. App. 1991).
48. Id. at 759.
49. Bita Ashtari & Jan Thompson, *Rape Shield Laws and Social Networking Websites: Is There any Privacy Left to Protect?* 2 F.C.D.J. 72, 93, available at http://www.cwsl.edu/content/trial_advocacy/Microsoft%20Word%20-%20Ashtari%20and%20Thompson%20final%20edit.pdf, *citing* In re K.W., 666 S.E.2d 490, 492-93 (N.C. App. 2008).
50. State v. Bray, 813 A.2d 571 (N.J. App. Div. 2003).
51. *Rape Shield Laws: Can They Be Fair?* http://law.jrank.org/pages/9643/Rape-Rape-Shield-Laws-Can-They-Be-Fair.html.
52. Bray, 813 A.2d at 578.
53. *See* People v. Parks, 766 N.W.2d 650, 655 (Mich. 2009).
54. *See* Raines v. State, 383 S.E.2d 738 (1989).
55. Kobe Bryant Police Interview Transcript, *The Smoking Gun* (September 2, 2004), available at http://www.thesmokinggun.com/archive/0924041kobea1.html.
56. Colo. Rev. Stat. sec. 18-3-407(2)(e).
57. People v. Bryant, 04SA83, Government's Petition of Relief Pursuant to C.A.R. 21 (March 9, 2004).
58. Richard I. Haddad, Shield or Sieve? *People v. Bryant* and the Rape Shield Law in High-Profile Cases, 39 Colum. J. L. & Soc. Problems 185, 194-95 (2005).
59. Id. at 202.
60. Id. at 186.
61. Id.
62. Id. at 187.
63. Id. at 203-04.
64. *Rape Case Against Bryant Dismissed*, NBCSports.com (September 2, 2004), available at http://nbcsports.msnbccom/id/5861379/print/1/displaymode/1098.
65. Charles Montaldo, *The Kobe Bryant Case*, About.com, available at http://crime.about.com/od/current/a/kobe_2.htm.
66. Alex Sundby, *Bryant Case Spurs States to Fortify Rape Shield Laws*, Stateline.org (October 18, 2004), available at www.stateline.org/live/iew:Page.action?siteNodeId=136&langaugeId=1&contentId.
67. *See, e.g.*, J. Alexander Tanford & Anthony J. Bocchino, *Rape Victim Shield Laws and the Sixth Amendment*, 128 U. PA. L. REV. 544, 589 (1980).
68. Maggard, *supra* note 26, at 1356.
69. *See, e.g.*, People v. Harris, 43 P.3d 221, 227 (Colo. 2002) (noting that the Sixth Amendment right to confrontation only allows the defendant to introduce relevant and admissible evidence).
70. Commonwealth v. Joyce, 415 N.E.2d 181 (Mass. 1981).
71. Cassia C. Spohn, *The Impact of Rape Reform*, *supra* note 25, at 862-63.
72. Michelle J. Anderson, *Toughen Rape Shield Laws*, Chicago Trib. (September 3, 2004), at C21.
73. Michelle Anderson, *From Chastity Requirement to Sexuality License: Sexual Consent and a New Rape Shield Law*, 70 Geo. Wash. L. Rev. 51 (2002).
74. United States v. Stout, 509 F.3d 796, 799 (6th Cir. 2007).
75. *See e.g.*, Cal. J.I.C. 2.50.02.
76. *See* Huddleston v. United States, 485 U.S. 681 (1988).
77. Christopher Bello, *Admissibility of Evidence as to Other Offenses as Affected by Defendants Acquittal of That Offense*, 25 A.L.R. 934 (1983).
78. People v. Wallen, 996 P.2d 182 (Colo. App. 1999).
79. Id. at 184, *citing* Dowling v. United States, 493 U.S. 342 (1990).
80. *See e.g.*, State v. Perkins, 349 So. 2d 161 (Fla. 1977).
81. *See* State v. Holman, 611 S.W.2d 411 (Tenn. 1981).
82. State v. Little, 350 P.2d 756 (Az. 1960).
83. David J. Karp, *Evidence of Propensity and Probability in Sex Offense Cases and Other Cases*, 70 Chi.-Kent L. Rev. 15 (1994).
84. Huddleston, 485 U.S. at 690-91.
85. State v. Cox, 781 N.W.2d 757 (Iowa 2010).
86. Nicholia v. State, 34 P.3d 344 (Alaska App. 2001).
87. People v. Garner, 806 P.2d 366, 374 (Colo. 1994).
88. Kaufman v. People 202 P.3d 543 (Colo. 2009).
89. People v. Spoto, 795 P.2d 1314 (Colo. 1990).
90. People v. Falsetta, 986 P.2d 182, 190 (Cal. 2000).

91. Garner, 806 P.2d at 375.
92. State v. Jacobson, 930 A.2d 628, 638 (Conn. 2007).
93. People v. Donoho, 788 N.E.2d 707, 722 (Ill. 2003).
94. *See* People v. Davis, 631 N.E.2d 392 (Ill. App. 1994).
95. Youngblood v. Sullivan, 628 P.2d 400, 402 (Or. App. 1981).
96. Lannan v. State, 600 N.E.2d 1340, (Ind. 1992).
97. Sasser v. State, 902 S.W.2d 773 (Ark. 1995).
98. Garner, 806 P.2d at 374.
99. Lannan, 600 N.E.2d at 1339.
100. State v. Wright, 191 N.W.2d 638, 641 (Iowa 1971).
101. People v. Hoffman, 570 N.W.2d 146 (1997).
102. State v. Crumb, 649 A.2d 879, 882 (1994).
103. Id.
104. Hoffman, 570 N.W.2d at 149.
105. Vinson v. Beightler, 2009 WL 3837045 (N.D. Ohio 2009) (unpublished decision).
106. Stout, 509 F.3d at 800.
107. Yusem v. People, 210 P.3d 458 (Colo. 2009).
108. People v. Ewoldt, 7 Cal. 4th 380, 405 (1994).
109. People v. Gaeta, 2009 WL 4912723 (Cal App. 2d Dist. 2009) (unpublished decision).
110. Yvette Martinez, *Medical Examiner Says Leath's Death Was Homicide*, WBIR.com, available at www.wbir.com/print. aspx?storyid=80001.
111. *Guilty: Jury Finds Raynella Dossett-Leath Guilty in Murder of Husband*, WBIR.com, available at http://www.wbir.com/news/local/story.aspx?storyid=111718&catid=2.
112. Matt Lakin, *Judge to Mull Exhuming Dossett's Body*, Knownews.com (December 14, 2007), available at http://knoxnews.com/news/2007/dec/14/judge-mull-exhuming-dossetts-body/?print=1.
113. Jim Balloch, *Raynella Dossett Leath Charges to Be Dropped*, Knoxnews.com, December 15, 2010, available at http://www.knoxnews.com/news/2010/dec/15/dossett-charges-to-be-dropped/.
114. Erica Estep, *Widow Charged With Husband's Murder Three Years Later* (November 30, 2006), available at wate.com/Global/story.asp?s=5751986.
115. In re Disinterment of William Edward Dossett deceased July 9, 1992 in Knox County, Tennessee, Order of Judge Richard R. Baumgartner (February 19, 2008) (Case No. 88215 Knox County Crim. Ct.).
116. Id at 4-5.
117. Id. at 7-8.
118. Jim Balloch, *Judge: Facts Not Similar Enough to Warrant Exhumation*, February 15, 2008, available at http://knoxnews.com/news/2008/feb/15/judge-wont-order-das-body-exhumed/?print=1.
119. Jim Balloch, *Dossett Case Can't Be Used in Reduced Trial*, February 20, 2008, available at http://www.knoxnews.com/news/2008/feb/20/doessett-case-cant-be-used-widows-trial/?print=1.
120. Jim Balloch, *Expert Testifies That Leath Suicide Impossible: Drugs in System Left Leath "Incapacitated," Medical Examiner Says*, March 5, 2009, available at http://knoxnews.com/news/2009/mar/05/expert-testifies-suicide-impossible/?printi=1.
121. Hana Kim, *Mistrial Declared for Raynella Leath in 2nd Husband's Shooting* (March 12, 2009),WATE.com, available at http://wate.com/Global/story.asp?s=9993092&clienttype=printable.
122. Karp, *supra* note 83, at 21.
123. Sara Sun Beale, *Prior Similar Acts in Prosecutions for Rape, and Child Sex Abuse*, 4 Crim. L. Forum 307, 309 (1993).
124. *See* State v. Jacobson, 930 A.2d 628, 637 (Conn. 2007).
125. State v. Schlack, 111 N.W.2d 289, 291 (Iowa 1961).
126. United States v. Castillo, 140 F.3d 874, 881 10th Cir. 1998).
127. *See* 1 McCormick on Evidence sec. 190, at 803-04 (Strong 1992).
128. Lannan, 600 N.E.2d at 1334, *quoting* State v. Lachterman, 812 S.W.2d 759, 768 (Mo. App. 1991).
129. Id. at 1338.
130. Id. at 1337 (citations omitted).
131. Colo. Rev. Stat. 16-10-301(1).
132. Colo. Rev. Stat. 16-10-301(3).
133. Colo. Rev. Stat. 18-6-801.5(1).
134. People v. Martinez, 36 P.3d 154 (Colo. App. 2001).
135. Mary Jordan, "Jury Finds Smith not Guilty of Rape," *Washington Post*, A-1, December 12, 1991.
136. Rachel Bell, *William Kennedy Smith*, The Crime Library on TruTV, available at http://www.trutv.com/library/crime/notorious_murders/celebrity/william_k_smith/4.html
137. David Margolick, *Why Jury in Smith Case Never Heard From Three Other Women*, December 13, 1991, New York Times, available at http://www.nytimes.com/1991/12/13/ne`ws/why-jury-in-smit-case-never-heard-from-3-other-women.
138. Id.
139. David Margolick, *Credibility Seen as Crux of Celebrated Rape Trial*, New York Times (December 1, 1991), available at http://www.nytimes.com/1991/12/01/us/credibility-seen-as-Crux-of-celebrated-rape-trial.
140. Jordan, *supra* note 134, at 4.
141. Thomas A. Vogele, *Hyperbole and the Laws of Evidence: Why Chicken Little is Generally Wrong*, at 7 n. 17 (2006), available at http://works.bepress.com/cgi/viewcontent.cgi?article=1000&context=thomas_vogele.
142. F.R.E. 413 and 414.
143. Robert F. Thompson, III, *Character Evidence and Sex Crimes in the Federal Courts: Recent Developments*, 21 U. Ark. Little Rock L. Rev. 241, 243 (1999).
144. United States v. Guidry, 456 F.3d 493, 503 (5th Cir. 2006).
145. People v. Donoho, 788 N.E.2d 707 (Ill. 2003).
146. United States v. Guidry, 456 F.3d 493 (5th Cir. 2006).
147. Guidry, 456 F.3d at 503.
148. United States v. Emjady, 134 F.3d 1427, 1433 (10th Cir. 1998).
149. Thompson, *supra* note 142, at 243.
150. United States v. Castillo, 1409 F.3d 874 (10th Cir. 1998).
151. Id. at 883.
152. People v. Falsetta, 986 P.2d 182, 189 (Cal. 2000).
153. Id. at 189-90.
154. *See* State v. Cox, 781 N.W.2d at 768 (reviewing § 701.111 of the Iowa Code).
155. Id.
156. Id. at 767, *quoting* State v. Cott, 283 N.W.2d 324, 327 (Iowa 1979).
157. State v. Ellison, 239 S.W.2d 603, 607-08 (Mo. 2007).

Hearsay Evidence

Judge: Mr. Hutz, we've been in here for four hours. Do you have any evidence at all?

Lionel Hutz: Well, your Honor. We've plenty of hearsay and conjecture. Those are *kinds* of evidence.[1]

Chapter Topics

Objectives

After reading this chapter, students will be able to:

- Define hearsay and recognize the two exemptions

- Distinguish between the various exceptions to the hearsay rule

- Understand the difference between exceptions that depend on the unavailability of the witness and those that do not

- Understand the meaning of testimonial hearsay and the situations that it applies to

- Identify the circumstances that the forfeiture by wrongdoing doctrine applies to

Introduction

Imagine being convicted of a crime you did not commit because someone made an accusation against you and then did not have to appear in court to testify. The jury would simply hear about the accusation second hand from another person, probably a police officer or other witness. The details of the accusation would be put on record as fact. You could not cross-examine the person and the jury could not assess the credibility of that witness because he or she was not present at trial. The person who made the statement originally could have been mistaken or even lied in making the statement, but there would be no way for the jury to tell.

If this situation seems unfair, then you understand the fundamental objection against hearsay evidence—it is inherently unreliable because there is no way to verify the accuracy of the person originally making the statements. Also, since the statement is made out of court, there is no opportunity to observe the witness's demeanor or hold him to an oath when making the statement. The hearsay rule was created to prohibit such testimony from being offered at trial. The premise of the hearsay rule is that testimony that is based on first-hand knowledge is more reliable than that which is based on second- or third-hand knowledge. As one commentator noted, "the objective of the hearsay rule is Truth; it is about keeping out evidence that categorically is so unreliable that it does not help us find the truth."[2]

Hearsay is an out-of-court statement that is offered to prove the truth of its contents. Statements that are based on second- or third-hand information are considered hearsay and are often inadmissible. Anyone who has played the telephone game has seen this problem firsthand. When playing the telephone game, a statement or phrase is whispered to the first person in a room. That person then has to whisper the same statement to the next person. It is repeated around the room until it has been whispered to everyone in the room. Invariably, the original statement has changed significantly when it is repeated back by the last person in the room. This is the danger of relying on hearsay testimony in the courtroom. The original statement may have been altered or parts of it omitted as it was communicated from one person to another.

Of course, just as quickly as the rule developed, courts began riddling the rule with exceptions. Some types of statements are not considered to be hearsay at all, such as prior statements of a witness made at a previous hearing or trial. Other types of statements are considered to be so reliable that they are admitted despite the fact that they are hearsay. You will learn that there are 28 different exemptions and exceptions to the hearsay rule, and you will explore many of these in greater detail in this chapter.

Determining whether a statement is hearsay or falls under one of the exceptions does not end the inquiry, however. Even though some hearsay statements ordinarily would have been admissible, the court may still exclude them because they violate the defendant's right to confront the witnesses against him. As you shall learn in this chapter, the prosecutor may not introduce hearsay statements that are testimonial in nature, except in limited circumstances. Testimonial statements are those made to law enforcement officers where their primary purpose is to investigate past criminal conduct or statements made to others in anticipation that they would be used later at trial. Thus, even if a statement qualifies under a hearsay exception, it may be inadmissible under the Confrontation Clause.

I. ORIGINS OF THE HEARSAY RULE

The origins of the hearsay rule can be traced back to the trial of Sir Walter Raleigh in England in 1603. Raleigh was a noted nobleman and explorer who was tried for treason against King James I. He was convicted of treason based largely on the testimony of his alleged accomplice, Lord Cobham, who testified that he had overheard someone else say that Raleigh stated he would slit the King's throat. Raleigh argued that Cobham had lied to save himself.[3] Although he was convicted, Raleigh's skillful defense of himself against the charges led King James to commute his death sentence and instead imprison him in the Tower of London. Perhaps the flimsy basis of Raleigh's conviction was recognized by King James, who later freed Raleigh to perform another expedition to Venezuela in search of the treasure of El Dorado. Raleigh may have wished he had stayed in prison, however, for he was beheaded in 1618 for alleged war crimes against the Spanish during that failed expedition.

Anger and outrage over the verdict in Raleigh's case is credited in part with laying the foundation for the modern hearsay rule that largely excludes such secondhand evidence. The reliability of hearsay evidence like that used in Raleigh's trial is obviously suspect. There is no way to verify the accuracy of the original witness's statement since that person does not appear in court and is not subject to cross-examination.

II. MODERN RULE

A. Definition of Hearsay

Rule 801. Definitions

The following definitions apply under this article:

(a) Statement.—A "statement" is an oral or written assertion or nonverbal conduct of a person, if it is intended by the person as an assertion.

(b) Declarant.—A "declarant" is a person who makes a statement.

(c) Hearsay. —"Hearsay" is a statement, other than one made by the declarant while testifying at the trial or hearing, offered in evidence to prove the truth of the matter asserted.

Rule 802. Hearsay Rule

Hearsay is not admissible except as provided by these rules or by other rules prescribed by the Supreme Court pursuant to statutory authority or by act of Congress.

Hearsay
a statement made by an out-of-court declarant that is offered to "prove the truth of the matter asserted"

Rule 802 codifies the hearsay rule. It provides that hearsay evidence is not generally admissible unless its admission is specifically authorized under the rules or an act of Congress.[4] **Hearsay** is a statement made by an out-of-court declarant that is offered to "prove the truth of the matter asserted."[5] The classic example of hearsay is a witness who testifies to what someone else said. The statement could be an observation of some event or a comment about a third person, such as that the person does drugs or slept with the neighbor's husband. Hearsay can also come in double or triple form. The reliability of double or triple hearsay is even less than single hearsay because there are more links in the chain that could fail. Rule 801 exempts two circumstances from the definition of hearsay that will be discussed in the next section.

Declarant
a person who makes a statement

A **declarant** is simply someone who makes a statement. Although this usually means the person testifying to the statement in court is different than the person who originally made it, hearsay even covers out-of-court statements made by the witness testifying. A statement is either an "oral or written assertion" or nonverbal conduct intended by the person as an assertion. A live person must make the statement in order for it to be hearsay. Information automatically generated by a computer, electronic time and date stamps, and a radar gun's readout are not hearsay.[6] An **assertion** is a person's words, writing, or conduct made with the intent of expressing a fact or an opinion.[7] In other words, the assertion is simply what was said or written by the out-of-court declarant. It is the "text" of the out-of-court statement.[8]

Assertion
the words, writings, or conduct of a person made with the intent of expressing a fact or opinion

In order to determine if the statement is being offered for the truth of the matter asserted, the original assertion should match the purpose for which it is being offered in court. For example, assume the witness, Steve, is testifying to a statement of a third party, Sarah, that the light was red in the truck's direction of travel at the time of the accident. The original assertion was that the light was red. The purpose for the statement being offered is to prove that the defendant's light was red at the time of the accident. Since the two are the same, the statement is hearsay. Conversely, if the two do not match (the statement is relevant to prove some issue regardless of whether it is true or not), then the statement is not hearsay. The impeachment of a witness using a prior inconsistent statement is an example of nonhearsay. The out-of-court statement is being used to prove the inconsistency of the witness, not prove which statement is correct.

In summary, for testimony to qualify as hearsay, it must have the following elements:

- The witness repeats an oral or written statement or describes conduct intended as an assertion made at a time and place by some person other than now in the courtroom;

- The statement is offered as evidence of the truth of whatever the statement asserts; and
- The statement is not exempted under Rule 801(d).[9]

Let's look at some additional examples to help explain the various elements of the definition of hearsay.

Practical Example

Assume the defendant, Scott, is on trial for murdering his wife. The prosecutor wants to introduce testimony from the man's neighbor, James. James will testify that his wife, Jeanie, told him that she overheard the couple arguing two weeks ago and that she heard the woman scream. Is the testimony hearsay? Yes. The statement was originally made by Jeanie, an out-of-court declarant. The statement is being offered to prove its contents— the fact that Jeanie saw the defendant arguing with his wife and heard her scream. As a result, the prosecution will have to show that the statement falls within one of the hearsay exceptions discussed below or it will be inadmissible.

Practical Example

Assume the same as the previous example. Now assume that the prosecutor wants to introduce testimony from James about an argument he observed occurring in Scott's front yard. James will testify that he saw Scott arguing with another man. He saw the man nod his head "yes" in response to Scott asking him a question about whether he hit his wife. Even though this conduct is not an actual statement, the nodding of the head was intended as an assertion. Therefore, it would be considered hearsay. Again, the prosecutor would have to show the statement falls under a hearsay exception (or is exempted under Rule 801(d)) in order for it to be admissible.

B. Exemptions from the Hearsay Rule

Exemption
an exclusion from the definition of hearsay. Prior testimony of witnesses and admissions of the defendant are the two exemptions from hearsay

Not all hearsay is created equal. Courts admit many forms of hearsay where the circumstances surrounding the making of the statement make it more reliable or trustworthy than other forms of hearsay. These types of statements may be admissible under an exception to the hearsay rule outlined in Rules 803 and 804. Rule 801 exempts two types of out-of-court statements from the definition of hearsay altogether: prior testimony of the witness and admissions of a party-opponent (the defendant). If a statement is covered under an **exemption**, it means that the court does not consider it to be hearsay at all and it is admitted as long as it is relevant and not overly prejudicial.

1. Prior Testimony: Rule 801(d)(1)

Rule 801. Definitions

(d) Statements which are not hearsay.

A statement is not hearsay if—

(1) **Prior statement by witness**. The declarant testifies at the trial or hearing and is subject to cross-examination concerning the statement, and the statement is (A) inconsistent with the declarant's testimony, and was given under oath subject to the penalty of perjury at a trial, hearing, or other proceeding, or in a deposition, or (B) consistent with the declarant's testimony and is offered to rebut an express or implied charge against the declarant of recent fabrication or improper influence or motive, or (C) one of identification of a person made after perceiving the person.

Prior testimony exemption
an exemption from the definition of hearsay. Statements made by a witness while testifying in a prior trial or hearing are not considered hearsay if the other party had an opportunity to cross-examine the witness and the statement is inconsistent with the witness's trial testimony, is used to rebut a charge of recent fabrication, or is a statement of identification

The first exemption to the hearsay rule applies to the **prior testimony** of witnesses. The testimony of the witness at a prior trial or hearing is not considered to be hearsay if the witness was subject to cross-examination at the prior hearing and the testimony is inconsistent with the witness's current trial testimony or is being offered to rebut a charge of recent fabrication. The witness can be cross-examined about the prior statement, but if the witness denies making it, then a transcript of the witness's prior testimony can be admitted into evidence. This exemption does not apply to all prior testimony, however. If the testimony occurred in a setting where the opportunity for cross-examination was not available, such as testimony before a grand jury, the exemption is inapplicable. If the statement does not meet the requirements of the Rule 801 exemption, then it may only be used for impeachment purposes.[10]

Practical Example

Linda is a witness to a shooting. She is scheduled to testify at trial. She testifies at the preliminary hearing. She is cross-examined by the defense attorney. Two weeks before trial, she is shot and killed in what is believed to be a gang-related shooting in retaliation for her testimony. Is her preliminary hearing testimony considered to be nonhearsay? No. Since it is not being offered to rebut her prior inconsistent statement or a charge of recent fabrication, her prior testimony is still hearsay. However, it will likely be admissible under an exception under Rule 804 for unavailable witnesses.

2. Admissions of the Defendant: Rule 801(d)(2)

Rule 801. Definitions

(d) Statements which are not hearsay.

A statement is not hearsay if—

(2) **Admission by party-opponent**. The statement is offered against a party and is (A) the party's own statement, in either an individual or a representative capacity or (B) a statement of which the party has manifested an adoption or belief in its truth, or (C) a statement by a person authorized by the party to make a statement concerning the subject, or (D) a statement by the party's agent or servant concerning a matter within the scope of the agency or employment, made during the existence of the relationship, or (E) a statement by a coconspirator of a party during the course and in furtherance of the conspiracy.

The second type of hearsay exemption is the admission of a party opponent (in criminal trials this would be the defendant or accused) offered against that party. An **admission** is simply a statement made by the party it is offered against; it does not have to be an incriminating statement in order to fall under the exemption.

Admission

an exemption from the definition of hearsay. In criminal trials, this exemption would apply to any statements of the defendant

> **AUTHOR'S NOTE**
>
> In the proposed revisions to the Rules of Evidence, Rule 801(d) no longer refers to "admissions" of party opponents but now describes them as "statements" of a party opponent. The comment to the proposed rule indicates that this change is intended to eliminate confusion between Rule 801(d) and Rule 804(b)(3). Under the latter rule, admissions of witnesses must be made against their penal or pecuniary interest in order to qualify as an exception.[11]

Admissions of a party opponent are admissible as nonhearsay on the theory that the person is present in court to explain his or her own statement offered into evidence.[12] Thus, to offer a statement under this exemption, the offering party must show that (1) the statement was made by a party to the litigation; and (2) that the statement is being offered against that party.[13] For example, the statements of a truck driver who was charged with raping a woman in his truck could not be offered against his employer as proof that it negligently hired the driver since the employer was not the party who made the statement.[14]

There are several types of statements that are considered to be admissions of a party under Rule 801, including the defendant's own statement, a statement by a person authorized to make a statement on the defendant's behalf (i.e., a press agent), or a statement made by an agent or other party authorized to act on behalf of the defendant (i.e., an attorney). A statement made by a co-conspirator during the course and furtherance of a conspiracy is also considered to be nonhearsay under this exemption.[15] In order to satisfy the requirements of this last exemption, the prosecution must show that (1) a conspiracy existed; (2) the defendant and the declarant were part of the conspiracy; and (3) the declaration was made during the course and furtherance of the conspiracy.[16] Thus, in the absence of a conspiracy, one co-defendant's hearsay statements cannot be offered against another co-defendant.[17]

Practical Example

Assume the defendant, Homer, is on trial for robbery. The prosecutor wants to introduce testimony from the defendant's friend, Carl, that Homer told him he got all these cool iPods from people he had stuck up. Can the prosecutor admit the testimony of the friend? Yes. It is nonhearsay because Homer's statement is being offered against him to prove his guilt.

C. Hearsay Exceptions

Like all things in law, there are no bright lines or absolutes with regard to the hearsay rule. In fact, one could say that there are more instances where the hearsay rule does not apply than where it does. Having covered the basic definitions and requirements of the hearsay rule in the last section, this section covers the multitude of exceptions to the rule. Unlike exemptions, these types of statements are still considered to be hearsay, but they are admitted under some **exception** due to their enhanced degree of trustworthiness.

The exceptions are divided into two types: those that require the unavailability of the witness and those that do not. A person is unavailable to testify if he cannot appear due to circumstances out of his control (injury or death) or asserts a right or privilege preventing him from testifying. For example, a witness who asserts the privilege against self-incrimination or marital privilege would make him unavailable as a witness. In contrast, a person is available to testify if he is capable of testifying but voluntarily chooses not to do so. A person is also considered an available witness if a party could have called that person as a witness but simply decided not to do so. For example, a person is an available witness if he is subpoenaed to testify but decides not to show up so he can play golf instead.

Exception
a deviation from the hearsay rule that permits the admission of a hearsay statement due to its enhanced reliability. Exceptions are divided into two types: those that depend on the unavailability of the declarant and those that do not

1. Availability of the Declarant Immaterial

The first set of exceptions to the hearsay rule applies regardless of whether the declarant is available to testify in court. Rule 803 contains 23 separate exceptions. A discussion of some of the more commonly used exceptions follows. See Table 13.1 for a complete listing of all the hearsay exceptions under Rule 803.

a. Present Sense Impression: Rule 803(1)

Present sense impression
a statement made contemporaneously with an event that describes or explains the event

A **present sense impression** is a statement "describing or explaining an event or condition made while the declarant was perceiving the event or condition, or immediately thereafter."[18] It's simply a statement that describes an event just after it occurs. In order to be admissible under this exception, the statement must describe or explain the event, the declarant must perceive the event he is describing, and the description must be made contemporaneously with the event.[19] The timing of the statement in relation to the event is the key consideration under this exception. A small lapse of time between the event and statement is usually acceptable. A statement made after a significant lapse of time is not considered to be a present sense impression, however, since the delay can allow the speaker time to fabricate the statement. The greater the amount of time that elapses between the

TABLE 13.1   HEARSAY EXCEPTIONS: AVAILABILITY OF THE DECLARANT IS IMMATERIAL

(1) Present sense impression	(14) Records of documents affecting an interest in property
(2) Excited utterance	(15) Statements in documents affecting an interest in property
(3) Then existing mental, emotional, or physical condition	(16) Statements in ancient documents
(4) Statements for purposes of medical diagnosis or treatment	(17) Market reports, commercial publications
(5) Recorded recollection	(18) Learned treaties
(6) Records of regularly conducted activity	(19) Reputation concerning personal or family history
(7) Absence of regularly conducted activity	(20) Reputation concerning boundaries or general history
(8) Public records and reports	(21) Reputation as to character
(9) Records of vital statistics	(22) Judgment of previous conviction
(10) Absence of public record or entry	(23) Judgment as to personal family or general history or boundaries
(11) Records of religious organizations	
(12) Marriage, baptismal, and similar certificates	
(13) Family records	

event and statement, the less trustworthy the statement is presumed to be and the less likely it is to be admissible. Thus, a caller's description of an event to a 911 operator just a minute or two after the event was held to be a present sense impression.[20] Conversely, a statement made by a confidential informant 50 minutes after a controlled drug buy was not.[21]

Practical Example

Assume that a couple observes an automobile accident. The wife turns to the husband and says, "Wow. That white car was sure in a hurry. I can't believe he ran the red light." The husband could testify to the wife's statement since it was made just after the accident. Now assume that the wife told the husband a half hour later that she now remembers that the light was yellow for the white car because other traffic was entering the intersection with the white car as well. The court would not consider this statement to be a present sense impression since too long a period had elapsed between the accident and the statement. Thus, the wife would have to testify to her own statement or the court would have to consider it under the excited utterance exception discussed below.

b. Excited Utterance: Rule 803(2)

Excited utterance
a statement made under the excitement or stress of a startling event

An **excited utterance** is a "statement relating to a startling event or condition made while the declarant was under the stress of the excitement caused by the event or condition."[22] The rationale behind the excited utterance exception is that the statement is believed to be more reliable because the excitement of the event limits the witness's ability to fabricate a statement. For a statement to qualify as an excited utterance, the party offering the statement must establish (1) the occurrence of a startling event; (2) that the declarant made the statement while under the stress of excitement caused by the event; and (3) that the declarant's statement relates to the startling event.[23] Unlike present sense impressions, the mere lapse of time between the event and the statement does not prevent it from being considered as an excited utterance. The court will look at a range of factors to determine if the statement is made while under the influence of the startling event, including the time elapsed, the characteristics of the event, the subject matter of the statement, whether the statement was made in response to questioning, the declarant's age, and his motive to lie.[24]

For example, a New York federal court held that a statement taken from the victim approximately 40 minutes after having been shot was an excited utterance even though he had used heroin between the time of the event and his statement. It found that at the time the witness gave his statement to police, he was still experiencing the stress caused by having witnessed the murder and being shot himself. The court also noted that at the time the statement was taken from the witness, he was still bleeding from his wounds and was being treated by a doctor in an emergency room.[25]

Practical Example

Assume that a witness has been the victim of a robbery. Two hours after being robbed, the man sees a television story about a suspect arrested in connection with another robbery. The victim turns to his wife and says, "Oh my god. That's the man that robbed me today." The statement would be considered an excited utterance even though it was made two hours after the event. The key consideration is that the viewing of the robbery suspect on TV brought back the stress of the earlier events. Therefore, his wife would be able to testify about his statement even if he does not do so himself in court. Thus, unlike a present sense impression, the statement does not have to be made contemporaneously with the event in order for it to be admissible.

c. State of Mind: Rule 803(3)

State of mind
an exception to the hearsay rule that covers statements pertaining to the declarant's existing state of mind. The statement must mirror the declarant's state of mind at the time he made the statement, not describe a past memory or belief

A statement is admissible under the **state of mind** exception to the hearsay rule if it is "a statement of the declarant's then existing state of mind, emotion, sensation, or physical condition (such as intent, plan, motive, design, mental feeling, pain, or bodily health), but not including a statement of memory or belief to prove the fact remembered or believed."[26] In order to be admissible under this exception, the statement should not describe a past memory or belief about another's conduct. Instead, the admission must mirror the state of the mind of the declarant at the time he experienced the past event. The state of mind exception, therefore, is simply a specialized subset of the present sense impression exception.[27] Like other hearsay exceptions, such statements are reliable because the declarant does not have an opportunity to reflect or fabricate the statement before making it.[28]

This exception covers emotions felt by the declarant at the time he made the statement, such as joy, fear, suspicion, or mistrust. It also covers statements of the declarant's intention to do something or go somewhere in the future.[29] While a statement reflecting the person's state of mind is admissible under this exception, the reasons or facts behind it are not. Thus, a statement that the victim feared the defendant is admissible, but the fact that the defendant had threatened to cut off child support if she didn't do what he said is not.

Practical Example

A defendant is on trial for murdering his wife. The prosecution wants to introduce evidence that the wife had told her neighbor that the husband had abused her on several prior occasions and that she feared for her life because the husband was acting particularly unstable lately. The statement that the wife feared for her life would be admissible but the details about the prior abuse would not be admissible under this exception.

d. Medical Diagnosis or Treatment: Rule 803(4)

i. General Requirements

Medical diagnosis or treatment
a hearsay exception that permits the admission of hearsay statements made to medical personnel for the purpose of seeking a medical diagnosis

Hearsay statements made to medical personnel for the purposes of **medical diagnosis or treatment** are admissible under Rule 803(4). The justification for the exception is that patients are assumed to be truthful when explaining the cause or source of their injuries to a doctor so as to obtain an accurate diagnosis of their illness or injury. Statements made for purposes of medical diagnosis are thus presumed to be reliable and trustworthy. Conversely, statements made to a physician strictly for the purpose of trial preparation, such as during a physical or mental examination paid for by the opposing party, are not covered by the exception.

AUTHOR'S NOTE

The assumption that statements made to physicians are reliable is a questionable one, however. Many patients may be too embarrassed to disclose the true cause of their injuries even though a more accurate treatment or diagnosis may result. For example, a woman may tell a doctor that she fell down the stairs when questioned about her facial injuries, despite the fact that she was physically assaulted by her husband. As a result, the basis for the medical diagnosis exception has been criticized.

The party offering such statements under this exception must prove that the statements were made for the purpose of medical diagnosis or treatment and that the statements were pertinent to that diagnosis or treatment.[30] Many courts require that the offering party also show that the patient was motivated by a desire to receive medical diagnosis or treatment and thus made the statements with the understanding that they would lead to medical diagnosis or treatment. Some courts have relaxed this requirement, as long as it would be reasonable for the physician to rely on the statement to make a diagnosis or treatment.[31]

For example, the North Carolina Supreme Court held that statements made by a four-year-old sexual assault victim to a nontreating clinical psychologist two weeks after her initial exam were not admissible under the medical diagnosis exception since there was no evidence that the child was informed of the importance of telling the truth or what the purpose of the doctor's questions was.[32] The court also found that the statements were not reasonably pertinent to a medical diagnosis since they were obtained through a series of suggestive and leading questions surrounding the victim's abuse.

Practical Example

Assume a six-year-old boy's grandmother brings the boy into the hospital shortly after he is physically assaulted by his stepfather. A doctor asks the boy what happened. The boy tells the doctor that his stepfather beat him with a wooden board and held his head under water in the bathtub for a minute. These statements would be admissible under the medical diagnosis exception since the intent of the boy and the doctor is to obtain statements to assist with the medical diagnosis. On the other hand, if the grandmother brought the boy in to see a social worker, who was accompanied by a doctor, two weeks later to explain what had happened, the statements would probably not be considered under this exception. The court would likely find that the primary intent of the interview was to investigate the criminal nature of the child abuse matter rather than to seek medical treatment.

ii. Medical Records

Parties often seek to admit medical records under the medical diagnosis exception. Medical records contain double hearsay, however. This means both the patient's statement contained in the record and the record itself are considered to be hearsay. Thus, each aspect of the record has to qualify under separate hearsay exceptions in order for it to be admitted without the testimony of the person who prepared it. This usually means that the offering party must also show that the medical record qualifies under the business record exception discussed in the next section.

e. Business Records: Rule 803(6)

Business record
a record that is kept in the ordinary course of business, such as an accident report. It is admissible as long as the person making the record had personal knowledge of the events and made the record shortly after the event

Ordinary business records such as safety inspection reports or accident reports can be admitted as long as they are kept in the course of "regularly conducted business activity."[33] A **business record** can be admitted if the party offering it establishes that (1) the person making the record had personal knowledge of the events to record accurate statements; (2) the person making the record recorded the statements contemporaneously with the actions that were the subject of the report; (3) the writer made the record in the regular course of business activity; and (4) such records were regularly kept by the business.[34] Entries in business records are presumed to be reliable because they are created on a day-to-day basis and in a routine fashion.[35]

The exception does not apply when the person making the record does not act in the regular course of business when doing so. For example, a manager may create a record after the fact or alter a record to help head off legal liability. Since such a record is not kept in the ordinary course of business but is instead created for litigation purposes, it does not qualify under the business records exception. Another example of records that are inadmissible under this exception is information provided on hotel registration cards since guests are under no duty to accurately provide that information.[36]

When admitting a business record under this exception, the offering party does not have to call the person who made the record as a witness. Instead, the party may call the records custodian for that business to testify to the necessary foundational requirements. The Federal rules and many state statutes also provide that the offering party may provide a certification from the records custodian in lieu of his testimony. Such a declaration must certify that the record (A) was made at or near the time of the occurrence of the matters set forth by a person with knowledge of those matters; (B) was kept in the course of the regularly conducted activity; and (C) was made by the regularly conducted activity as a regular practice.[37]

Practical Example

Suppose a woman is injured at a hardware store. A door display fell on her when she was pushed into it by a customer who got into a disagreement with her. A witness to the incident was questioned by the store manager. The manager records her statement in his report. The witness cannot be found for trial. The manager is required to write a report any time there is an accident or injury in the store. Can the prosecutor introduce the witness's statement contained in the manager's report as a business record? Since the manager is required to keep the record routinely and made his entries about the interview with the witness contemporaneously to the event, the record is admissible as long as the foundational requirements can be established. This can be done either through testimony or certification from the records custodian.

f. Public Records: Rule 803(8)

Public records

records or official reports kept by a governmental agency. They are admissible as long as a member of the agency offering the record has certified that the record is a true and accurate copy of that agency's record

Public records and reports of public officials or agencies, detailing the activities of the office or agency or matters observed by public officials pursuant to their legal duty to report, are admissible as an exception to the hearsay rule.[38] Most public records and government reports are admissible under this exception. Public records are admissible as a long as a member of the agency certifies that the record is a true and accurate copy of that agency's record. No testimony from an agency official is required to admit the record.

Notably, police reports are excluded from this exception. Rule 803(8)(B) provides that matters observed by police officers and other law enforcement personnel that are recorded in a report are not covered by the public records exception.[39] Unlike other public records, police reports are not as inherently reliable since they often contain hearsay statements of witnesses. They may even contain double hearsay. Therefore, in order for hearsay statements contained in police reports to be admissible, those statements must satisfy another exception to the rule, such as present sense impression or excited utterance. While police reports are generally not admissible to prove the defendant's guilt, the defendant may offer police records to support his defense under the business records exception.[40] Statements contained in police reports that are the product of the officer's own observations and knowledge are generally admissible for this purpose.

Practical Example

In a prosecution for willfully violating the Clean Water Act, the prosecutor wants to introduce EPA records that show that the agency sent the defendant three noncompliance letters prior to the alleged illegal dumping charge. The records were prepared by an EPA official pursuant to his authority under the Clean Water Act and regulations created by the EPA. The records are hearsay but are admissible under the public records exception as long as an official certifies the letters as accurate copies of agency records. An official from the EPA does not have to testify as to their creation or accuracy.

---

2. Unavailability of the Declarant

Rule 804. Hearsay Exceptions; Declarant Unavailable

(a) Definition of unavailability.

"Unavailability as a witness" includes situations in which the declarant—

(1) is exempted by ruling of the court on the ground of privilege from testifying concerning the subject matter of the declarant's statement; or

(2) persists in refusing to testify concerning the subject matter of the declarant's statement despite an order of the court to do so; or

(3) testifies to a lack of memory of the subject matter of the declarant's statement; or

(4) is unable to be present or to testify at the hearing because of death or then existing physical or mental illness or infirmity; or

(5) is absent from the hearing and the proponent of a statement has been unable to procure the declarant's attendance (or in the case of a hearsay exception under subdivision (b)(2), (3), or (4), the declarant's attendance or testimony) by process or other reasonable means.

> A declarant is not unavailable as a witness if exemption, refusal, claim of lack of memory, inability, or absence is due to the procurement or wrongdoing of the proponent of a statement for the purpose of preventing the witness from attending or testifying.

Unavailability
a requirement for the applicability of some hearsay exceptions. A witness is unavailable where he is unable to appear in court due to no fault of his own or the party wishing to call him

Some exceptions to the hearsay rule do not apply unless the declarant is unavailable to testify. A witness is unavailable where he is unable to appear in court due to no fault of his own or the party wishing to call him. **Unavailability** requires something more than the witness's absence from the courtroom, however. If the party offering the hearsay statement could have reasonably gotten the witness to court through the use of a subpoena or otherwise, but chose not to do so, then the witness will not be considered to be unavailable. This means that the party offering the hearsay statement must show that the witness will not or cannot testify due to some legal or physical inability to testify. Further, the witness's unavailability cannot be caused by the party seeking to introduce the statement.

The party seeking to introduce the hearsay statement has the burden of proving that the declarant is unavailable. That party must use reasonable, good faith efforts to get the witness into court but does not have to use any and all available methods.[41] For example, a witness who refuses to testify can still be found unavailable, even if the prosecution did not offer the witness immunity. As long as the prosecution used reasonable methods to compel the witness's attendance at trial, such as a subpoena, the court will find that the offering party has met its burden. In contrast, courts have held that the government failed to meet its burden due to the failure of law enforcement officers to obtain the identity of the declarant, making his attendance at trial impossible.[42] Common situations where the witness will be found unavailable include the death of the witness since making the statement, the witness is protected by a privilege from testifying (such as the privilege against self-incrimination), or the witness has refused to respond to a subpoena.

If the witness refuses to answer questions by asserting his Fifth Amendment rights, he may be, but is not necessarily, unavailable. In other words, the court cannot take it for granted that the witness's refusal to testify is genuinely due to a fear that his statements will result in his prosecution. The court must therefore question the witness and determine whether the witness faces a "real danger" of prosecution.[43]

Practical Example

Assume that the prosecution wishes to call a domestic violence victim as a witness. The victim is subpoenaed to testify but does not show up to trial. The prosecutor believes that the defendant has intimidated the witness, preventing her from attending trial. Is the witness unavailable? No. Unless the prosecution can prove that the defendant actively interfered with the witness and prevented her from testifying, the witness will not be considered unavailable.

a. Former Testimony: Rule 804(b)(1)

Prior testimony exception

a hearsay exception that permits the admission of prior testimony of a witness as long as the declarant is unavailable, and there was an opportunity to cross-examine the statements in a prior proceeding

The **prior testimony** of a witness may be admissible if that witness is unavailable to testify and the party against whom the testimony is offered had an opportunity and "similar motive" to cross-examine the witness in the prior proceeding. This rule is somewhat similar to the hearsay exemption under Rule 801 for prior testimony. It applies to a broader range of statements, however, since Rule 801 limits the prior testimony exclusion to just three types. Any type of prior testimony is admissible under Rule 804 as long as the opportunity for cross-examination existed. To determine whether prior testimony is admissible under Rule 804, the court will consider the type of proceeding during which the testimony was given, the trial strategy of the parties during the first hearing or trial, the potential penalties at stake during the prior proceeding, and the number of issues and parties involved.[44]

Statements contained in grand jury testimony are not generally admissible as an exception to the hearsay rule. By design, the defendant and his attorney are excluded from the grand jury room and thus cannot examine the witnesses. Even if the statements contained in the grand jury testimony are against the witness's interest, and thus potentially admissible under 804(b)(3), their admission would likely violate the Confrontation Clause.

Several years ago, Judge Easterbrook of the Seventh Circuit Court of Appeals eloquently noted the objections to admitting grand jury testimony:

> Trial by affidavit was the bugbear that led to the confrontation clause; trial by grand jury testimony is not far removed. Grand jury testimony, like an affidavit, is one-sided, and ex-parte narration over which the prosecutor has ample control. To avoid the introduction of unilateral narrations, rule 804(b)(1) provides that prior testimony is admissible only if the party against whom the evidence is offered had both opportunity to examine the declarant and motive to do so. That the testimony has indicia of trustworthiness cannot be controlling; many affidavits appear to be trustworthy. A defendant's entitlement to confront the witnesses against him is not limited to confronting apparently untrustworthy witnesses. Confrontation is viable in large measure because it may establish that what seems to be accurate is misleading or deceitful or rests on an inadequate foundation. Conditions on the use of rule 804(b)(1) ensure that the defendant retains the right of confrontation in circumstances that lie at the core of the constitutional guarantee. Temptation to get "around this limitation by moving to rule 804(b)(5) [now Rule 807] and slighting its introductory language should be resisted."[45]

b. Dying Declaration: Rule 804(b)(2)

Rule 804(b)(2) provides that statements regarding the cause or circumstances of the declarant's impeding death are admissible in a homicide trial or civil case as long as the declarant believed his death was imminent. Even if part of the witness's statement qualifies as a **dying declaration**, courts will exclude self-serving portions of the statement if they do not relate to the cause or circumstances of the person's death.[46] In order to qualify as a dying declaration, the declarant must have been "conscious of impending death and under the belief that there is no chance of recovery."[47] The classic example of a dying declaration is a person near death who makes statements about the cause of the injuries, such as the identity of the person who stabbed him. In contrast, courts have typically held that statements contained in suicide notes are not dying declarations since the "aspect of control" in an intentional death diminishes the spontaneity intended by the exception and suicide notes often do not pertain to the cause or circumstances of one's death.[48]

The declarant need not actually die for the statement to be admissible. The key is that the declarant believes his death is imminent. The assumption behind this exception is that dying people are unlikely to lie. Nevertheless, this exception has been criticized for admitting one of the more unreliable forms of hearsay.[49] As a result, 12 states no longer recognize it as an exception to the hearsay rule.[50]

Dying declaration
a hearsay exception that applies to statements made by a person who believes his death is imminent and that relate to the cause or circumstances of his injuries

Practical Example

Johnny Four Eyes is shot by Tony the Lip outside a local restaurant. He staggers into the bar of the restaurant and collapses. Before he loses consciousness, he states that Tony did this to him and not to let him get away with it. Assuming the bartender is willing to testify, can the prosecutor admit Johnny's statement through the bartender? Yes. Johnny is obviously unavailable for trial and the statement concerned the cause of his death, so it would qualify as a dying declaration.

c. Statement Against Penal or Pecuniary Interest: Rule 804(b)(3)

The third exception that applies to the hearsay statements of an unavailable declarant is one for **statements against interest**. Think of this exception as being similar to the exemption for admissions of the defendant. Like the prior testimony exception from 804(b)(1), this exception applies to all witnesses, not just the defendant. A statement against interest is admissible if the witness is unavailable and, at the time the statement was made, it was "so far contrary to the declarant's pecuniary or proprietary interest, or so far tended to subject the declarant

Statement against interest
a hearsay exception that permits the admission of hearsay statements made by an unavailable declarant that are adverse to the declarant's penal or monetary interest

to civil or criminal liability" that a reasonable person would not have made the statement unless he believed it to be true.[51] A statement goes against someone's penal (criminal) or pecuniary (monetary) interest when it "threatens the loss of employment, or reduces the chances for future employment, or entails possible civil or criminal liability."[52] Just like an admission on the part of the defendant, such statements are trustworthy because it is presumed no one would make a statement damaging to one's self-interest unless it is true.[53]

Practical Example

Shauna is on trial for theft. The prosecutor wants to use a statement made by Shauna's friend, Sara, that the two of them had conspired to steal money from her mother. Sara made this statement in front of her younger sister. Sara cannot be located prior to trial and therefore is not present to testify. The prosecutor wants to call Sara's sister to testify to the statement. The sister can testify to the hearsay statement because Sara cannot be found and the statement was made against her penal interest since she admitted to a crime.

3.   Residual Exception: Rule 807

Rule 807. Residual Exception

A statement not specifically covered by Rule 803 or 804 but having equivalent circumstantial guarantees of trustworthiness, is not excluded by the hearsay rule, if the court determines that (A) the statement is offered as evidence of a material fact; (B) the statement is more probative on the point for which it is offered than any other evidence which the proponent can procure through reasonable efforts; and (C) the general purposes of these rules and the interests of justice will best be served by admission of the statement into evidence.

Residual exception
a hearsay exception that allows the admission of hearsay even if does not fit within one of the enumerated exceptions as long as it has "equivalent guarantees" of trustworthiness

The Rules of Evidence also contain a catchall exception that allows for the admission of otherwise reliable hearsay that does not fall under one of the other enumerated exceptions. The so-called **residual exception** allows for the admission of hearsay that contains "equivalent guarantees of trustworthiness" as the other listed exceptions.[54] The rule was created in recognition of the fact that judicial flexibility to deal with situations not covered by the rules was still necessary since not all desirable or necessary exceptions to the hearsay rule have been cataloged.[55] The residual exception should be a last resort; it is intended to be used in only "truly exceptional" cases.[56] If another exception covers the admissibility of evidence, then the more specific exception should be used. However, the residual exception is useful in two cases: (1) where the evidence or situation is new or novel and the rules have not yet addressed that particular situation; or (2) where the evidence is useful and reliable but falls just short of qualifying under one of the listed exceptions.[57]

In order to be admissible under this exception, the party offering the statement must show that the statement is relevant, it is more probative than any other evidence on that point, and that "interests of justice" will be served by its admission.[58] Courts will consider a number of factors to determine whether a statement has the necessary trustworthiness, including the unavailability of the declarant, the circumstantial guarantees of trustworthiness surrounding the statement, whether the statement relates to a material fact, whether the statement is the most probative evidence on the point, whether the interests of justice are served by admission of the statements, and whether the opposing party has been given reasonable notice of the statement.[59]

The analysis of the admissibility of evidence should not end when it fails to qualify under one of the listed exceptions, but it should also be evaluated under the residual exception. For example, the Sixth Circuit admitted purchase orders and ledger sheets of a business even though the evidence did not qualify under the business record exception.[60]

Practical Example

Ted is charged with defrauding investors. He wants to admit a document that he claims he sent all investors advising them of the risks of the investment. The court rejects it as a business record since there is no evidence it was kept in the regular course of the defendant's business. The defendant then wants to introduce it under the residual exception. The court should reject this argument as well since there is no evidence that the document has equivalent guarantees of trustworthiness as other hearsay exceptions. The document appears to have simply been created as a self-serving document to help bolster the defendant's case.

D. Impeachment of a Missing Declarant: Rule 806

Rule 806. Attacking and Supporting Credibility of Declarant

When a hearsay statement, or a statement defined in Rule 801(d)(2)(C), (D), or (E), has been admitted into evidence, the credibility of the declarant may be attacked, and if attacked may be supported, by any evidence which would be admissible for those purposes if the declarant had testified as a witness. Evidence of the statement or conduct by the declarant at any time, inconsistent with the declarant's hearsay statement, is not subject to any requirement that the declarant may have been afforded an opportunity to deny or

explain. If the party against whom the hearsay statement has been admitted calls the declarant as a witness, the party is entitled to examine the declarant on the statement as if under cross-examination.

If hearsay evidence is admitted under one of the above exceptions, Rule 806 permits the other party to attack the credibility of the missing declarant "by any evidence which would be admissible for those purposes if declarant had testified as a witness."[61] In other words, the other party could impeach his statements just as if he were on the witness stand using one of the methods of impeachment discussed in Chapter 11. For example, even though the person making the statement did not testify, a federal district court permitted the defendant to impeach the credibility of the hearsay declarant by introducing evidence of his felony conviction for possession of a weapon, the fact he snorted heroin before making the statement, and his inability to identify the defendant from a photo array.[62]

E. *Res Gestae*

Res gestae

Latin term meaning "things done." Hearsay statements that are res gestae are admissible because they help explain the surrounding circumstances or commission of crime

Res gestae (race jest-eye) is a Latin term that means "things done." It is a doctrine that has been used to admit evidence of acts or statements that are not proof themselves of the charged crime but are so closely related to it that they help explain the circumstances or context of the crime. Res gestae is both an exception to the hearsay rule and an exception to Rule 404(a). In order to be admissible, however, the prosecution must still establish that the prejudicial effect of the res gestae evidence does not substantially outweigh its probative value.[63]

The Supreme Court has held that the term res gestae is synonymous with evidence of the surrounding circumstances of the crime, while other courts have characterized it as allowing for the admission of evidence that is "inextricably intertwined" with proof of the charged offense.[64] Since it is part of the criminal episode, res gestae evidence is admitted to give the jury a better understanding of the events surrounding the crime charged.

Res gestae consists of facts, circumstances, and statements that are connected to the main crime and includes evidence that is closely related in time and character to the main crime.[65] Courts have also noted that in order to be considered res gestae, such acts or statements must be "so spontaneous and contemporaneous with the main fact as to exclude the idea of deliberation or fabrication."[66] In order for a hearsay statement to be admissible as res gestae, the declaration (1) must be spontaneous, (2) must be contemporaneous with the act, and (3) must explain or in some way characterize the criminal act. The key is whether the person made the statement "under the spur of the event."[67] Thus, res gestae includes the words and acts of the participants as the crime is being carried out but not their words and acts when narrating the events after the fact.[68]

Courts have distinguished res gestae evidence from other act evidence considered under Rule 404(b). Res gestae is considered to be intrinsic to the charged conduct because it is not separate and distinct from the charged offense. Conversely, other acts evidence reviewed under Rule 404(b) involves conduct that is "wholly independent" from the offense charged.[69] What this means, practically speaking, is that the prosecution does not have to prove one of the listed independent purposes under Rule 404(b) to admit res gestae but only has to show that the evidence is relevant because it helps prove the context or circumstances of the current charge. For example, the Tenth Circuit ruled that a conversation between two co-defendants regarding potential targets five days prior to the charged bank robbery was admissible under the res gestae doctrine.[70] The court held that other act evidence was intrinsic to the crime charged because it was a "necessary preliminary" to the crime charged.[71] Conversely, the South Carolina Supreme Court held that admission of numerous prior thefts from the defendant's ex-wife as res gestae evidence was error in defendant's trial for the murder of his father-in-law. The court held that the connection between the incidents was too remote and attenuated to justify admitting the prior incidents as res gestae.[72]

Practical Example

Assume that the defendant is charged with sale of drugs. The prosecution wants to introduce evidence that the defendant was arrested and incarcerated five years ago for possession of drugs. He also wants to introduce evidence that the defendant spoke to Jose one week before the drug bust and told him he needed a quick fix and asked about getting him some dope. Because the defendant's arrest for drug possession five years ago has no connection to the present drug charge and is remote in time from it, it does not qualify as res gestae. The prosecution would have to show that the evidence helps to show motive, identity, or one of the other purposes under Rule 404(b). However, the statement to Jose helps explain the context of the drug sale and should be treated as res gestae as it helps explain the context and the motive for the drug sale.

III. TESTIMONIAL HEARSAY UNDER THE CONFRONTATION CLAUSE

The Sixth Amendment to the Constitution provides in part that "in all criminal prosecutions, the accused shall enjoy the right...to be confronted with the witnesses against him."[73] The Confrontation Clause is based on two policies—a preference for face-to-face confrontation at trial and the right of cross-examination of witnesses. The fear of the Founding Fathers was that the government could manipulate either what is said by the witness or how it is recorded.[74] The concern with some hearsay statements is that in addition to being potentially unreliable they may also violate the Confrontation Clause due to the absence of the declarant from the courtroom. Thus, **testimonial hearsay** statements, those statements that are made for the purpose of establishing some opinion or fact or developing testimony, are subject not only to the requirements of the hearsay rule but the Confrontation Clause as well.

Prior to 2004, the Supreme Court had liberally interpreted the wording of the Confrontation Clause, holding in *Ohio v. Roberts* that the admission of an out-of-court witness's statement did not violate the confrontation clause as long as it had "adequate indicia of reliability." In other words, a hearsay statement could be admitted against the defendant as long as it fell within one of the firmly rooted hearsay exceptions or bore "particularized guarantees of trustworthiness."[75] Starting in 2004, the Supreme Court decided a series of decisions that overruled *Roberts* and restricted the circumstances under which out-of-court statements could be admitted against a defendant. Their effect was to bar the admission of testimonial hearsay statements that had previously been admissible under various exceptions to the hearsay rule.[76]

Testimonial hearsay
hearsay statements that are made for the purpose of establishing some opinion or fact

A. *Crawford v. Washington*

In *Crawford v. Washington*, the Court was asked to rule on the admissibility of out-of-court statements made to the police that implicated the defendant in a stabbing. The statements had been made by the wife of the defendant during the investigation, but spousal privilege prevented her from testifying. The prosecutor introduced the statements under an exception to the hearsay rule. The Court examined the terms of the Confrontation Clause and concluded that the admission of testimonial hearsay statements violated the Confrontation Clause, absent a showing that the witness was unavailable for trial and that the defendant had had a prior opportunity to cross-examine that witness.[77]

The Court defined the term "witness," as it was used in the Clause, to mean those who "bear testimony."[78] Testimony was defined as a "solemn declaration or affirmation made for the purpose of establishing or proving some fact."[79] Thus, the Court held that the Confrontation Clause's restrictions applied only to "testimonial" statements made by a witness; the admissibility of all other forms of hearsay is still covered by the hearsay rule. The Court imposed a more stringent test to review the reliability of testimonial evidence to protect the defendant against the "evils" that the Framers feared such evidence could pose.[80]

While it did not spell out all situations that could be testimonial in nature, the Court found that the term applied, at a minimum, to three situations: (1) prior un–cross-examined testimony of a witness at a hearing or trial; (2) out-of-court statements that are contained in "formalized testimonial materials," such as affidavits or depositions; and (3) statements made pursuant to police interrogation or under similar circumstances that would lead an objective witness reasonably to believe that the statement would be available for use at a later trial.[81]

B. *Davis v. Washington*

Two years later, the Court clarified the definition of the term "testimonial" as it applied to statements made in response to police questioning in *Davis v. Washington*. Two cases involving domestic violence were consolidated— in one, the prosecution had offered statements made to a 911 operator; in the other, the prosecution had offered statements made by the victim in response to police questioning as to the circumstances of the domestic assault. Although both cases involved questioning by government officials, the Court distinguished the two on the ground that one sought information to assist with an ongoing emergency while the other sought information to investigate a past crime. The Court looked at the **primary purpose of the interrogation** to determine whether the statements were testimonial. It held that statements are nontestimonial when "made in the course of police interrogation under circumstances objectively indicating that the primary purpose of the interrogation is to enable police assistance to meet an ongoing emergency" but are testimonial "when the circumstances objectively indicate that there is no such ongoing emergency, and that the primary purpose of the interrogation is to establish or prove past events potentially relevant to later criminal prosecution."[82]

> **Primary purpose of the interrogation**
>
> test for determining whether statements made pursuant to police questioning are testimonial in nature. Where the primary purpose of the interrogation is to prove or establish the commission of a crime, the statements are testimonial. Where the primary purpose is to seek police assistance with an ongoing emergency, statements made to the police are nontestimonial

In determining whether statements made to law enforcement officers are testimonial, the *Davis* Court set out a number of factors for trial courts to examine.[83] Justice Alan Page of the Minnesota Supreme Court summarized these factors as follows: (1) when the statement was made (for example, whether the statement was made contemporaneous with or after the incident); (2) what the statement describes (for example, whether the statement describes the current emergency or past events); (3) if describing the current emergency, whether the declarant's statement is necessary to resolve the current emergency; and (4) the circumstances giving rise to the statement (such as by whom the statement was initiated and the level of its formality).[84] A totality of the circumstances test is used to determine whether statements made to government officials are testimonial.[85] Because of the dual nature of many police investigations, the *Davis* Court noted that an examination that begins as nontestimonial could turn into one where testimonial statements are given. As a result, it urged courts to redact or exclude those portions of statements that are testimonial from those that are not.[86] For example, the Sixth Circuit held that statements made by a victim to officers who arrived on scene shortly after a 911 call and found the victim hysterical and exclaiming that the suspect had pulled a gun on her were nontestimonial. The court concluded that "no reasonable officer could arrive at a scene while the victim was still 'screaming' and 'crying' about a recent threat to her life by a an individual who had a gun and who was likely still in the vicinity without perceiving that an emergency still existed."[87]

A question that has come up since *Davis* was decided is whether the objective witness test (circumstances that would lead an objective witness reasonably to believe that the statements would later be used in a prosecution) announced in *Crawford* was still valid. Most courts have interpreted the two decisions as complementing one another. For example, the Connecticut Supreme Court explained that the primary purpose test from *Davis* "provides a practical way to resolve what *Crawford* had identified as the crucial issue in determining whether out-of-court statements are testimonial, namely, whether the circumstances would lead an objective witness reasonably to believe that the statements would later be used in a prosecution."[88] Thus, in order to determine whether a statement is testimonial, it concluded courts should examine "both the primary purpose of the person making the statement and the primary purpose of the person asking the questions."[89]

C. *Michigan v. Bryant*

The Supreme Court further clarified (perhaps muddied is a better description) the distinction between the response to ongoing emergencies and investigation of past conduct in *Michigan v. Bryant*.[90] There, Detroit police officers responded to a dispatch call of a man having been shot, and found the victim at a gas station, lying outside his car, near death. The victim had been shot through the back door of the defendant's home and had driven to the gas station to call for help. Upon arrival, five different officers questioned the victim about the circumstances of the shooting, including the identity of the person who had shot him. The victim died shortly thereafter.

The Court ruled that the statements were nontestimonial. It held that the analysis of the primary purpose of the police interrogation is an objective one—meaning that the relevant inquiry is not the "subjective or actual purpose of the individuals involved in a particular encounter, but rather the purpose that reasonable participants would have had, as ascertained from the individuals' statements and actions and the circumstances in which the encounter occurred."[91] The Court also highlighted the importance of the level of formality of the encounter between police and a witness in determining the testimonial nature of statements.

The Court also instructed that the existence of an ongoing emergency should be assessed from the perspective of the parties to the interrogation at the time of the incident, without the benefit of hindsight. In other words, the focus should be on the information the parties had at their disposal at the time of the encounter and whether that information would have led a reasonable person to conclude that an emergency was ongoing, regardless of whether that belief was later proven to be incorrect.[92] The Court cautioned that the term "emergency" should not be construed too narrowly as lasting "only for the time between when the assailant pulls the trigger and the bullet hits the victim."[93] Instead, the existence and duration of an emergency depend on the type and scope of the danger posed to the victim, the public, and the police.

In order to determine the primary purpose of the interrogation, the Court created a new multi-factor test, including:

- The type of weapon involved
- Whether the threat posed to the police and the victim is ongoing
- The victim's medical state
- The level of formality of the encounter between the witness and the police
- The identity of the interrogator and the content of his questions
- The existence of an emergency or the parties' perception that one exists
- The circumstances of the interrogation[94]

The Court concluded that the primary purpose of the interrogation in *Bryant* was to meet an ongoing emergency and held the victim's statements were nontestimonial. First, at the time of questioning, the police were uncertain of whether the threat was limited to the victim since they did not know why, where, or when the shooting had occurred.[95] The types of questions asked by police were thus of the type necessary to assess the situation. The Court also found it significant that the interrogation was much less formal than the station-house interview found to be testimonial in *Crawford*, noting that it occurred out in the open, prior to the arrival of emergency medical services.[96]

AUTHOR'S NOTE

This new balancing test may make the determination of whether statements are testimonial more difficult. As Justice Thomas pointed out in his concurrence, this test will create uncertainty for police officers and judges alike. Time will tell whether lower courts will, in fact, struggle in applying it.

D. Statements to Persons Who Are Not Law Enforcement Officials

One question left unanswered by *Davis* is whether statements made to nongovernmental persons can be testimonial.[97] Some courts felt that the Supreme Court drew a "clear distinction" between statements made to police officers and statements made to lay persons.[98] Those courts have concluded that statements made to law enforcement should be presumed to be testimonial, whereas statements made to nongovernmental actors should be presumed to be nontestimonial.[99] The Arkansas Supreme Court summarized the test as follows: "Where a statement is made to a government official, it is presumptively testimonial, but the statement can be shown to be nontestimonial where the purpose of the statement is to obtain assistance in an emergency. Where a statement is made to a nonofficial, it is presumptively nontestimonial, but can be shown to be testimonial if the primary purpose of the statement is to create evidence for use in court."[100]

AUTHOR'S NOTE

This analysis unnecessarily injects the issue of presumptions where it does not belong. Although such presumptions will likely prove to be accurate most of the time, a better approach is to determine to whom the statements were made and then analyze them under the appropriate test from either *Davis* or *Crawford*. Under this approach, the court should first determine whether the statements were made to law enforcement officials or other government officials acting on behalf of law enforcement. If the court determines that the statements were not made to law enforcement, it should then assess the statements in light of the other factors laid out in *Crawford*—namely, whether the statements were contained in formalized testimonial materials or made under circumstances that a witness would reasonably foresee would be used in the investigation or prosecution of a crime. To determine whether something is reasonably foreseeable, the court should examine a number of factors, including the person's age, the circumstances surrounding the making of the statement, and whether the witness was aware that the defendant faced the possibility of criminal punishment at the time he made the statement.[101]

---

1. Statements Made to Lay Persons

Courts that have addressed the issue of statements made to non–law enforcement officials have typically found that such statements are nontestimonial. For example, the Montana Supreme Court held that a domestic violence victim's statements to a neighbor about her husband's assault of her were not testimonial.[102] The court characterized the conversation between the victim and her neighbor primarily as a cry for help. Similarly, the Colorado Supreme Court found that a victim's statements about her abuse to a neighbor were also nontestimonial. According to the court, the key consideration was that the victim had no objective basis to believe her statements would be used to prosecute her husband at the time she made them.[103]

Statements made by children about the nature of their abuse to parents or other family members have also been held to be nontestimonial. The general rule is that where the questions asked of children are designed to determine the nature of the child's injury, not implicate the criminal suspect, such statements have been held to be nontestimonial.[104] For example, in a Colorado case, the court found that the statements made by a seven-year-old victim to his father about the details of his sexual abuse were nontestimonial. The court noted the child was speaking informally about the incident with an interest in seeking "comfort and help."[105] The court also found that the boy's father was not questioning the boy "with a view toward developing testimony."[106] Similarly, the Arkansas Supreme Court held that statements made by a child to her mother about her abuse were nontestimonial. The court found that the child sought out her mother to "seek relief from the pain she was experiencing, not report her father's actions."[107]

Practical Example

A woman is physically abused by her husband. She is choked to unconsciousness. When she comes to, she runs over to her neighbor. The neighbor asks her what happened. She tells the neighbor that she had an argument with her husband and that he choked her. Is this statement testimonial? The statement is not testimonial since the neighbor was simply trying to aid her friend, not investigate or prosecute the husband for domestic violence.

2. Forensic Interviews of Child Sex Assault Victims

Children who are the victims of sexual assault are routinely interviewed by social workers and/or forensic interview specialists about the details of their abuse. Questions have frequently arisen in court about whether statements made by child victims during such interviews are testimonial and, if they are, under what circumstances they can be admitted. The general rule is that statements made by children during forensic interviews are testimonial.

To determine whether statements produced during forensic child interviews are testimonial, courts have looked at factors such as the location of the interview, the involvement of law enforcement in the interview, and whether the child is asked to recount specific details of past abuse. For example, the Idaho Supreme Court concluded that a forensic interview was testimonial because the interviewer was acting in conjunction with the police, put the video and other physical evidence into the police evidence locker, and asked questions about the details of the abuse but did not ask any questions regarding the child's medical condition.[108]

On the other hand, the Connecticut Supreme Court held that a forensic interview conducted at a sex abuse clinic was nontestimonial because the primary purpose of the interview was to provide medical care and treatment to the child, not investigate the suspect. There, the interviewer worked in close conjunction with a medical professional who relied upon the interviewer's mental health evaluation of the child to assist with diagnosing and treating the child's injuries. The court found that this interview lacked the significant involvement of law enforcement in the interview process that was present in prior cases.[109]

Forensic interviews of children are often videotaped, so the question of whether that videotape is admissible can also arise. Prior to *Crawford* and *Davis* being decided, many states had passed laws that permitted the videotaped interview of children in sexual assault cases to be admitted at trial if the state could prove that live testimony would traumatize the child.[110] After these decisions, however, it is clear that the admission of videotaped statements would violate the defendant's right to confrontation.[111] The videotapes are admissible only if the child testifies at trial and the statements are found to be sufficiently reliable.[112] In other words, the interview must have been conducted in a way that did not suggest answers to the child, such as by using leading questions.

A related issue that comes up in child sexual abuse cases is whether the child witness can testify via closed circuit television, out of the presence of the defendant. In *Maryland v. Craig*, the United States Supreme Court upheld the use of closed-circuit television since the confrontation clause does not guarantee the defendant an absolute right to a face-to-face meeting with the witnesses against him at trial.[113] The Court found the state's interest in protecting child witnesses from the trauma of testifying in a child abuse case is sufficiently important to justify the use of such a special procedure. Moreover, it noted that face-to-face confrontation in this case could have caused such significant emotional distress to the child that such an arrangement would disserve the truth-seeking goal of the Clause.[114]

Practical Example

Deanne, a child who claims to have been sexually assaulted, is questioned by a child advocate working for the department of social services. The advocate questions Deanne about the abuse and who committed it. At the end of the interview, the advocate gives Deanne's mother a referral for psychological counseling. The advocate's report will be given to the counselor but will also be turned over to the police along with a copy of a video from the interview. Are the statements of Deanne testimonial? The statements are testimonial since the primary purpose of the interview was not to aid the child's recovery but to prosecute the perpetrator of the abuse.

3. Statements Made to a Doctor for Medical Diagnosis

Another question that courts must consider is whether hearsay statements made to a physician about a criminal incident are testimonial. Courts have usually held that such statements are nontestimonial because the declarant is making them to assist the doctor diagnose his injuries and does not expect that they will be used as evidence at a subsequent trial.[115] The Colorado Supreme Court, for example, found that statements made by a child sex assault victim to a physician about his bruising and swelling were nontestimonial because the statements were made to help the doctor assess whether the child had been sexually assaulted.[116] Similarly, the Washington Court of Appeals held that statements made by a child sex assault victim the morning after the assault to a physician were nontestimonial because the doctor was not acting as a representative of the government and there was no evidence the statements were made with the intent to preserve them for trial.[117]

A small number of courts have held that statements made to a physician concerning the identity of the perpetrator are testimonial because they are not a necessary component of medical diagnosis or treatment. An Illinois court held that statements of a child victim to a physician about the identity of her abuser, six months after the abuse had occurred, were testimonial since the statements were not relevant to her diagnosis and treatment. [118]

Other courts have rejected this analysis, however. For example, the California Supreme Court held that statements concerning the identity of the perpetrator made by a domestic violence victim to the treating physician in the emergency room were nontestimonial.[119] The court concluded that the primary purpose of the surgeon's questioning of the witness was not to establish or prove past facts for possible prosecutorial use but rather was to help the surgeon deal with the medical situation. It likened the situation to the 911 operator's questioning of the victim in Davis.[120] The Washington Court of Appeals went one step further, holding that questions about the perpetrator's identity are nontestimonial because the "identity of the abuser is pertinent and necessary to the victim's treatment."[121] Similarly, the Arkansas Supreme Court noted that a doctor "must be able to identify and treat not only physical injury, but also emotional and psychological problems that typically accompany sexual abuse by a family member due to the nature of child sexual abuse."[122]

Practical Example

Assume Sam is shot by his wife. He is rushed to the hospital by ambulance. When he arrives at the emergency room, the attending physician asks him about how he was wounded. Sam tells the doctor that his wife shot him after the couple argued. Is the statement testimonial? The answer to this question depends on what state it occurs in. Most states would rule the statement to be nontestimonial since its purpose was to diagnose the victim's injuries. In some states, however, Sam's statement implicating his wife in the shooting would be considered to be testimonial since it serves to identify the perpetrator.

4. Forensic Lab Reports and Other Certificates of Analysis

In 2009, the Supreme Court again looked at the issue of testimonial hearsay in *Melendez-Diaz v. Massachusetts.*[123] In that case, it ruled that laboratory reports confirming the identity or concentration of an unknown substance were testimonial under the Confrontation Clause. Before this ruling, it had been longstanding practice in many states to simply submit an affidavit or certificate of analysis from the chemist or other laboratory technician in lieu of in-court testimony. The Court struck down this practice, ruling that lab reports are testimonial if they are "functionally identical" to in-court testimony by replacing what a witness would do on direct examination.[124] The Court held such reports were not the equivalent of mere business records because they were created for the sole purpose of providing evidence against a defendant in a criminal prosecution.[125]

The Court noted that its ruling was not likely to overwhelm crime laboratories since many defendants are unlikely to request the in-court appearance of analysts whose testimony will simply highlight their guilt. It also noted that many states have already addressed this problem by enacting notice and demand statutes. Under this type of statute, the prosecution must provide notice of its intent to use a forensic analyst's report at trial, and if the defendant objects, he must demand the appearance of the analyst at trial within a fixed period of time. The Court explicitly approved the use of this type of statute in *Melendez-Diaz.*[126] See Table 13.2 for an example of a notice and demand statute.

TABLE 13.2 COLORADO'S NOTICE AND DEMAND STATUTE

Colo. Rev. Stat. 16-3-309(5) provides in part:

Any report or copy thereof ... of the criminalistics laboratory shall be received in evidence in any court... in the same manner and with the same force and effect as if the employee or technician of the criminalistics laboratory who accomplished the requested analysis, comparison, or identification had testified in person. Any party may request that such employee or technician testify in person at a criminal trial on behalf of the state before a jury or to the court, by notifying the witness and other party at least 10 days before the date of such criminal trial.[127]

Not all reports prepared by or on behalf of the police are testimonial, however. The Montana Supreme Court ruled that the weekly field certification reports prepared by the police to show that the Breathalyzer machine was operating properly are nontestimonial.[128] The court noted that such reports were not prepared as substantive evidence (unlike the Breathalyzer test result itself) but were merely foundational evidence for the admission of Breathalyzer results. Similarly, the proof of service of a driver's license suspension prepared by the Department of Revenue is not testimonial and is therefore admissible as an exception to the hearsay rule. Since this type of document is created for the ordinary business or administrative purpose of notifying the driver that his privilege to drive has been suspended or revoked, courts have held them to be nontestimonial.[129]

Practical Example

Officer Smith arrests Juan on suspicion of methamphetamine possession. The evidence seized from Juan is sent to the local crime lab for analysis. The chemist tests the evidence, determines it to be meth, and writes a report. The chemist is scheduled to testify at Juan's trial but is called out of town. Can the prosecutor submit an affidavit attesting to the accuracy of the report in lieu of the chemist's testimony? No. The report is testimonial and the report does not qualify under the limited exception for testimonial hearsay. While the chemist is unavailable for trial, his testimony was not subject to cross-examination prior to trial.

E. Workflow for Testimonial Hearsay

Based on the above cases and situations, a simple analytical framework can be developed to help determine whether a statement is testimonial or nontestimonial hearsay and whether it is admissible. You should first ask to whom the statement is being made. If it is made to law enforcement, the key question is whether the statement is being made to investigate a past crime (testimonial) or to assist with an ongoing emergency (nontestimonial). If the statement is made to a person who is not in law enforcement, then you should ask whether the statement was recorded in a formalized manner or is made under circumstances where a person would reasonably conclude it will be preserved for later use at trial. See Figure 13.1 on page 407 for a workflow for testimonial hearsay.

In summary, if the statement is testimonial but the witness is not available or was not subject to cross-examination previously, then the statement is inadmissible. If the statement is not testimonial, then the statement must still meet one of the hearsay exceptions discussed above in order for it to be admissible.

See Table 13.3 on page 408 for examples of testimonial and nontestimonial statements.

Figure 13.1
Analytical Workflow for
Testimonial Hearsay

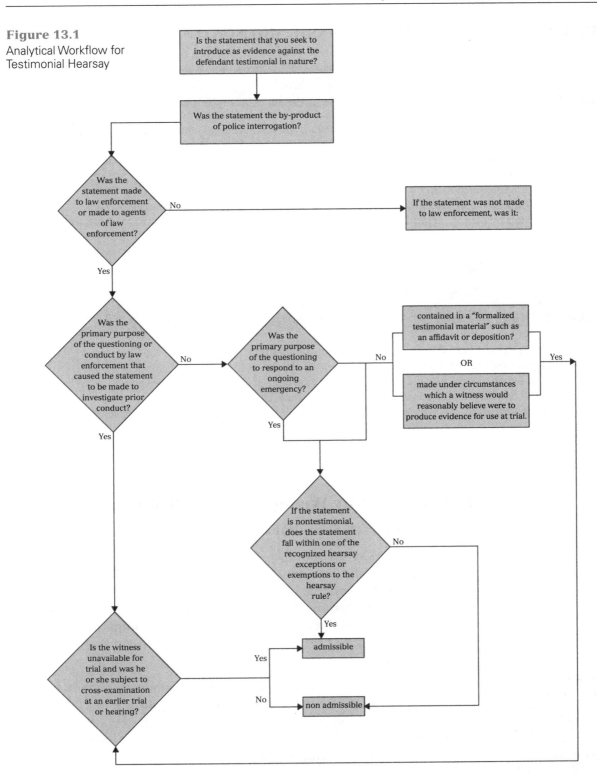

TABLE 13.3   EXAMPLES OF TESTIMONIAL AND NONTESTIMONIAL STATEMENTS

Testimonial Statements

○ Hearsay statements made by a witness or victim to police in response to questioning about the specific facts of the incident
○ Hearsay statements made by a witness or victim to agents of the police such as social workers or other investigators in response to specific questions about the incident
○ Hearsay statements made by a witness at a prior hearing or trial
○ Hearsay statements of a witness contained in an affidavit or deposition
○ Hearsay statements of a codefendant contained in a confession that implicate the defendant in the current case
○ Analytical reports prepared by government agents stating facts that are primarily used to prove the guilt of the defendant

Nontestimonial

○ Statements made to neighbors or friends about the incident
○ Statements made to a 911 operator describing the nature of the emergency
○ Statements made to police describing the nature or circumstances of the emergency
○ Statements made to a physician for purpose of medical diagnosis
○ Reports generated by government personnel intended to be used for mainly administrative purposes

F. Forfeiture by Wrongdoing: Rule 804(b)(6)

Rule 804. Hearsay Exceptions; Declarant Unavailable

(b) Hearsay exceptions.

The following are not excluded by the hearsay rule if the declarant is unavailable as a witness:

(6) Forfeiture by wrongdoing. A statement offered against a party that has engaged or acquiesced in wrongdoing that was intended to, and did, procure the unavailability of the declarant as a witness.

Forfeiture by wrongdoing
a rule of evidence that prevents a person from claiming the protections of the Confrontation Clause when he has caused the absence of the witness with the intent of preventing that person from testifying

Thirteen states and the federal courts recognize an exception to the Confrontation Clause called **forfeiture by wrongdoing**. Rule 804(b)(6) prevents the defendant from benefiting from the protections of the Confrontation Clause if he procures the "unavailability of the declarant as a witness."[130] The defendant must do more than commit a criminal act that results in a witness's unavailability to testify, however.[131] The defendant must cause the witness to be absent and do so with the express intent of preventing the person from testifying. Examples of conduct covered under the doctrine include intimidating, bribing, or killing a witness scheduled to testify against the defendant.

In *Giles v. California*, the Supreme Court held that the forfeiture by wrongdoing doctrine does not apply to situations where the defendant simply causes the death of a witness but lacks the necessary intent to deprive the court of her testimony.[132] There, the defendant shot his ex-girlfriend and claimed the shooting was in self-defense. The prosecution sought to admit statements the victim had made to police three weeks prior to her murder about an incident of domestic violence that the defendant had committed against her. The prosecution conceded that the statements were testimonial but argued that they should come in under the forfeiture by wrongdoing exception.[133] The Court rejected the prosecution's argument, ruling that where the defendant has caused a person's absence from court but had not done so to prevent him from testifying (as in the typical murder case), the exception does not apply.[134] The Court noted, however, that where acts of domestic violence are intended to dissuade a victim from reporting the abuse or seeking outside help, the evidence may support a finding that the crime is covered under the forfeiture by wrongdoing doctrine.[135]

The Court held that in order to prove forfeiture by wrongdoing, the prosecution must show by a preponderance of the evidence that (1) the witness is unavailable for trial; (2) the defendant was involved in or responsible for procuring the unavailability of the witness; and (3) the defendant acted with the intent to deprive the criminal justice system of evidence.[136] Criminal conduct, however, is not required to establish forfeiture; the defendant must merely be responsible for making the witness unavailable.[137] For example, a defendant could satisfy this requirement by convincing his wife to not testify against him in a domestic violence case.

Practical Example

Assume the defendant is involved in a sexual assault. He then stabs the victim. The victim survives long enough to describe her attacker to police and the facts of the assault. She then dies. At trial, the prosecution wants to introduce her statements made to the police officer. Assume the statements are held to be testimonial (and not admissible as a dying declaration) and not admissible under Crawford. *Are they admissible under the forfeiture by wrongdoing doctrine? No. There is not enough evidence that the defendant intended to kill his victim to keep her from testifying.*

Now assume the defendant had previously been convicted of sexual assault based largely on the eyewitness testimony of the victim. His good friend will testify that the defendant told him he had to kill the victim to shut her up so the same thing did not happen to him again. In this case, there is enough evidence to prove the forfeiture and the victim's testimonial statements will be admitted.

Prosecutors Move to Introduce Hearsay Statements in Drew Peterson Murder Trial

Drew Peterson, a former police sergeant, was tried in 2010 in Illinois for killing his third wife, Kathleen Savio. Although the couple divorced in 2002, Savio was found drowned in her bathtub two years later by Peterson. Peterson said he went over to check on her after she did not return his calls. Although Savio had a gash to her head, her death was originally ruled an accident and no evidence was collected from the scene. However, after Peterson's fourth wife, Stacy Peterson, disappeared in 2007, Savio's remains were ordered exhumed, and her death was ruled a homicide. Peterson was then charged in her death.

One of the issues in the case was whether hearsay evidence should be admitted under Illinois's version of the forfeiture by wrongdoing statute. The law provides that testimonial hearsay can be admitted in first-degree murder cases if prosecutors can show the defendant killed the victim to prevent him or her from testifying.[138] Under the statute, the judge must hold a pretrial hearing to determine whether the statements are trustworthy in order to be admissible. The statute was dubbed "Drew's Law" since it was passed mainly in response to the facts of Peterson's case.[139]

First, the Court upheld the statute against a challenge that the statute violated the Confrontation Clause. The court then held an extensive hearing on whether hearsay statements made by Savio and Stacy Peterson should be admitted into evidence. Sixty-eight witnesses were called to testify. The prosecution's theory of the case was that Peterson killed Savio to prevent her from testifying in a pending divorce action against him. Savio's sister, Susan Doman, testified that Savio had told her, "Drew is going to kill me and it's going to look

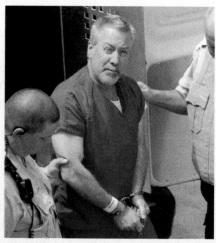

Figure 13.2   Former Bolingbrook, Illinois police sergeant Drew Peterson arrives in court on July 7, 2010 for his arraignment on charges of first-degree murder in the 2004 death of his former wife, Kathleen Savio. *© 2010 AP Photo/M. Spencer Green*

like an accident…. He can make me disappear." Stacy Peterson's minister, Neil Schori, testified that Stacy said Drew had told her he had murdered his third wife and had been told to lie about his whereabouts the night of the murder. The judge ruled, however, that Schori could not testify to Drew's statement that he had murdered Savio since it violated husband/wife privilege. Other witnesses testified that Drew had broken into Savio's home in 2002, held a knife to her throat, and threatened to kill her.[140]

The defense questioned the reliability of many of the statements, alleging that the witnesses broke their silence on national TV rather than to authorities. Defense attorney Steve Greenberg commented that the witnesses "put Kato Kaelin to shame." He noted that "not a single person said a word to anybody [prior to the hearing]. Who could keep that kind of secret? And everybody kept it. Everybody."[141]

On May 18, 2010, the judge agreed with the prosecution that Peterson had intended to cause the unavailability of his wives and likely did kill them but found that several of the statements were not trustworthy. In a sealed ruling, he excluded 8 of the 13 statements. The prosecution has filed an interlocutory appeal of that ruling, and Peterson's trial has been delayed until that appeal is resolved.[142]

AUTHOR'S NOTE

The media and defense made more of an issue of the use of Drew's Law than it needed to. Many of the statements prosecutors sought to admit were nontestimonial in nature since they were made by the alleged victims to friends or family. As a result, they were not subject to the Confrontation Clause and application of the forfeiture statute was unnecessary to admit the statements. The real issue was whether the statements were trustworthy enough to admit under more traditional exceptions.

CHAPTER SUMMARY

Hearsay is an out-of-court statement made by someone other than the person attempting to testify to it in court offered to prove the contents of the statement. Hearsay statements can be verbal, written, or conduct intended as an assertion. Hearsay is not admissible unless it falls within one of several exceptions outlined by the Rules of Evidence.

Some types of hearsay statements are exempted from the definition of hearsay because they are considered to be inherently reliable. These include the prior testimony of witnesses where it is inconsistent with the witness's testimony or served to identify the perpetrator in an earlier court proceeding such as a preliminary hearing. The testimony must have been subject to cross-examination. The other exclusion involves admissions of the defendant.

Many types of hearsay are admissible as an exception to the hearsay rule. Most of them do not depend on the availability of the declarant to testify. Such exceptions include present sense impressions, excited utterances, statements made for medical diagnosis, and business records. Some exceptions require that the declarant be unavailable to testify. A declarant is unavailable where he cannot testify through no fault of his own, such as injury or death. Prior testimony of witnesses can be admitted under this exception as well as statements made under a belief of one's own impending death.

The Confrontation Clause prevents certain types of hearsay from being admitted, even if it satisfies one of the above exceptions, unless the declarant is unavailable and the statement was subject to cross-examination. Only statements that are testimonial in nature are covered by the Clause. Testimonial statements are those that a person should reasonably expect to be preserved for use at trial. Testimonial statements include those made to law enforcements officers during investigation of a criminal matter, sworn in an affidavit or other formal document, or that a person would reasonably expect to be used at trial. Statements made to law enforcement are testimonial if the primary purpose of the police interrogation was to investigate a prior crime as opposed to assist with an ongoing emergency. Statements made to friends, neighbors, and physicians are usually nontestimonial. The defendant can forfeit his rights under the Confrontation Clause by intentionally preventing a witness from testifying. If it is proven that the defendant intentionally prevented a witness from testifying, then that witness's statements can be admitted as long as the statements satisfy one of the hearsay exceptions.

KEY TERMS

- Admission
- Assertion
- Business record
- Declarant
- Dying declaration
- Excited utterance
- Exception
- Exemption

- Forfeiture by wrongdoing
- Hearsay
- Medical Diagnosis or treatment
- Present sense impression
- Primary purpose of the interrogation
- Prior testimony exception

- Prior testimony exemption
- Public records
- Res gestae
- Residual exception
- State of mind
- Statement against interest
- Testimonial hearsay
- Unavailability

REVIEW QUESTIONS

1. What is hearsay? What is the general rule regarding its admissibility?

2. What is a declarant?

3. An out-of-court statement is hearsay only when it is offered for what purpose?

4. What are two types of statements that are exempted from the hearsay rule under Rule 801?

5. What is a present sense impression? What must the party offering a statement under this exception show in order for it to be admissible?

6. What is an excited utterance? How is it different from a present sense impression?

7. What is the key factor for the court in determining whether a hearsay statement made to a doctor qualifies under the medical diagnosis and treatment exception?

8. What is a business record? What are the requirements for admitting one under the business record exception?

9. Are police reports admissible under the public record exception? Explain why this is the case.

10. Give two examples where a witness is unavailable for trial. Name two circumstances where hearsay can be admitted if the witness is unavailable for trial.

11. Is grand jury testimony admissible under the former testimony exception listed in Rule 804(b)(1)? Explain.

12. Name two things that must be shown in order for a dying declaration to be admitted.

13. What kinds of statements are admissible under the residual exception?

14. What is the Confrontation Clause? What types of statements does it apply to?

15. Name two kinds of testimonial statements.

16. What two things must be shown in order for testimonial statements to be admissible?

17. Are reports of laboratory analysts admissible under the business records exception, or are they testimonial? Explain.

18. What is the doctrine of forfeiture by wrongdoing? What is it designed to prevent?

APPLICATION PROBLEMS

1. A couple witnesses an auto accident. The couple gives a statement to the officer, and then half an hour later, the wife states, "You know, now that I think about it, the motorcyclist never swerved to avoid the accident. He seemed to drive right into the pile." Can the husband testify to the wife's statement at trial under the present sense impression exception? Explain.

2. A girl is kidnapped. She is returned to her parents two weeks later. Four days pass, and when she sees a dog like the kidnapper had, she says, "That's a puppy just like the bad man had. His dog was white and fluffy, too. Mommy, mommy, is that the bad man's house?" Can the mother testify to the child's statement under the excited utterance exception? Explain.

3. A man is at the doctor's office seeking treatment for a broken leg. He tells the doctor he got the injury "during a fight at the Grizzly Coyote bar when some guy insulted my wife." Can the doctor testify to the man's statement at trial under the statements made for medical diagnosis exception? Explain.

4. A man is run over by a car. The paramedic that attends to him asks him how the accident happened. The man, knowing he is in bad shape, says, "I was minding my own business when a Hummer came out of nowhere and came across the median." He dies 15 minutes later. Can the paramedic testify to his statement under the dying declaration exception? Explain.

5. The prosecution wants to introduce a copy of an officer's report of his investigation into a traffic fatality. In the report, the officer has statements from witnesses and his calculations about how the accident was caused. Will the judge admit the report into evidence? Explain.

6. The prosecution tries to impeach a witness with the fact that he was convicted of a felony for sexual assault six years ago. The witness denies the conviction. The prosecution then attempts to introduce a certified copy of the witness' drug conviction. Should the trial judge admit it? Explain.

7. The defendant, Paul, is on trial for destruction of city property. The defendant brags to his buddy in the bar shortly after the alleged incident occurred, "Hey, I just cut the head off some parking meters." His buddy is called to testify to the statement. Is the statement hearsay? Explain.

8. John is on trial for theft of a car. At the preliminary hearing, the complaining witness, Ed, testifies that John did not have permission to take the car. Ed is sent to Iraq with his military unit before the trial. He cannot testify. Is his prior preliminary hearing testimony admissible? Explain.

9. Sarah is a public official. She finds a look-a-like double, Tina. Sarah is supposed to make a speech before the public safety conference but she does not want to do it. Instead, she hires Tina to appear for her. Tina makes a statement at the conference (at the behest of Sarah) that she doesn't think illegal poachers should be prosecuted. An investigation of Sarah is launched weeks later when a man is not prosecuted for killing three elk out of season. The prosecutor wants to admit Tina's statement from the conference. Sarah claims it is hearsay because Tina made the statement. Is she correct? Explain.

11. Sally overhears Gwynn talking on the phone. Gwynn says that she can't go Thursday night because she is going to get a lot of meth that night. Sally tells her best friend Wanda about what she heard Gwynn say. Gwynn is later arrested for drug dealing. Sally is called to testify at Gwynn's trial. Before the trial, Sally is run over by a bus and dies. Can Wanda testify about Gwynn's statement? Explain.

12. Martin is accused of beating up his wife, Julie. Julie made a 911 call and stated her husband had hit her in the face and threatened to kill her. She also made several statements to officers when they responded to the 911 call. First, when she opened the door, she stated, "Oh, thank goodness you're here. I am afraid my husband is going to kill me." The husband is not in the house. She then writes out a written statement about the incident. Julie fails to show up for trial. Can the prosecutor introduce a transcript of the 911 call, can he introduce the statements Julie made to the police when they first arrived at the house, and can he introduce a copy of her written statement? Explain.

13. Jackson is five. He is sexually molested by a coach who runs the youth soccer league. Jackson reports to his mother that "his soccer coach touched him in bad places." Jackson is then interviewed by a social worker. She is a trained child forensic interviewer. She asks Jackson several questions about the incident, such as where he was touched, how often, and what location it occurred at. The interview is videotaped. She refers Jackson to psychological counseling but also turns her report over to the police. The coach is arrested. At trial, Jackson is not deemed competent to testify. Can the prosecutor have the mother testify to Jackson's statement he made to her about the abuse? Can the forensic interviewer testify about the statement, or can the video of her interview be admitted? Explain.

14. Sid is on trial for possession with intent to distribute. The cops searched his house and recovered eight baggies of white powder. The baggies are sent to the crime lab and tested. Jim tests the baggies and determines their contents to be cocaine, weighing 80 grams total. Jim is called away to a conference in Hawaii and can't testify at trial. Can the prosecutor submit his lab report in place of Jim's testimony? Explain.

15. Sunflower Sparkle Venus is a hippie. She grows her vegetables and lives almost self-sufficiently. She also grows her own marijuana. She has an affidavit from a doctor that the marijuana is for medical use. Sunflower suffers from severe anxiety. The local cops then raid her house. She waves the affidavit at them in protest. The cops don't listen and confiscate her marijuana. At trial, Sunflower can't find the doctor to come testify. She wants to introduce his affidavit that the marijuana was for medical use. Is the affidavit admissible? Explain.

16. Scott is accused of killing his wife. She died on March 18. She was set to testify against him on May 1 in a domestic violence case. Other than the timing of the murder, there is no other evidence that Scott murdered her with the intent to keep her from testifying. The prosecution now wants to introduce the statements his wife made to police involving the domestic incident as excited utterances. Are these statements admissible under the forfeiture by wrongdoing doctrine? Explain.

Notes

1. *The Simpsons*, "The Day the Violence Died," Season 7, Fox (1996).
2. C. Michael Fenner, *The Hearsay Rule*, at 5 (2009).
3. Crawford v. Washington, 541 U.S. 36, 51 (2004).
4. F.R.E. 802.
5. F.R.E. 801.
6. Fenner, *supra* note 2, at 15.
7. *Black's Law Dictionary*, at 124 (8th ed. 2004).
8. Fenner, *supra* note 2, at 16-17.
9. Id. at 13-14.
10. United States v. Disantis, 565 F.3d 354 (7th Cir. 2009).
11. *See* Federal Rules Of Evidence—2011 Pending Amendment to Restyle The Federal Rules of Evidence, available at http://federalevidence.com/downloads/blog/2010/Current-Amendments/EV_Rules_801-1103.pdf.
12. Canter v. Wilt, 188 F. Supp. 2d 773 (E.D. Mich. 2002).
13. Canter, 188 F. Supp. 2d at 782.
14. Stalbosky v. Belew, 205 F.3d 890, 894 (6th Cir. 2000).
15. F.R.E. 801(d).
16. United States v. McCarroll, 1996 WL 99442 (N.D. Ill. 1996).
17. United States v. Sauza-Martinez, 217 F.3d 754, 760 (9th Cir. 2000).
18. F.R.E. 803(1).
19. United States v. Campbell, 782 F. Supp. 1258, 1260 (N.D. Ill. 1991).
20. *See* United States v. Shoup, 476 F.3d 38, 42 (1st Cir. 2007).
21. United States v. Green, 556 F. 3d 151 (3d. Cir. 2009).
22. F.R.E. 803(2).
23. United States v. Moore, 791 F.2d 566, 570 (7th Cir. 1986).
24. United States v. Delvi, 275 F. Supp. 2d 412, 414-415 (S.D. N.Y. 2003).
25. Id. at 415.
26. FRE 803(3).
27. Fenner, *supra* note 2, at 163.
28. United States v. Lentz, 282 F. Supp. 2d 399 (E.D. Va. 2002).
29. Fenner, *supra* note 2, at 166-67.
30. State v. Hinnant, 523 S.E.2d 663, 667 (N.C. 2000).
31. United States v. Joe, 8 F. 3d 1488, 1494 (10th Cir. 1993).
32. Hinnant, 523 S.E.2d at 671.
33. F.R.E. 803(6).
34. United States v. Pelullo, 964 F.2d 193, 200 (3d Cir. 1992).
35. McCormick on Evidence, section 286, 5th ed.
36. United States v. McIntyre, 997 F.2d 687, 698-99 (10th Cir. 1993).
37. F.R.E. 902(11).
38. F.R.E. 803(8).
39. F.R.E. 803(8)(B).
40. United States v. Carneglia 256 F.R.D. 384 (E.D. N.Y. 2009).
41. United States Reed, 227 F.3d 763, 767 (7th Cir. 2000).
42. United States v. Wrenn, 170 F. Supp. 2d 604 (E.D. Va. 2001).
43. In re Crabtree, 90 B.R. 871 (E.D. Bankr. 1988), *quoting* In re Morganroth, 718 F.2d 161, 167 (6th Cir. 1983).
44. Reed, 227 F.3d at 768.
45. United States v. Dent, 984 F.2d 1453, 1466 (7th Cir. 1993) (Easterbrook, J., concurring).
46. United States v. Gallagher, 57 Fed. Appx. 622, 628 (6th Cir. 2003).
47. United States v. Peppers, 302 F.3d 120, 137-38 (3d Cir. 2002).
48. United State v. Angleton, 269 F. Supp. 2d 878, 884-85 (S.D. Tex. 2003).
49. F.R.E. 802, advisory committee note.
50. *See, e.g.,* Colo. R. Evid. 804(2).
51. United States v. Hsia, 87 F. Supp. 2d 10, 14 (D.D.C. 2000), *quoting* F.R.E. 804(b)(3).
52. Id.
53. Id.
54. F.R.E. 807.
55. F.R.E. 807, advisory committee note.
56. United States v. Walker, 410 F.3d 754 (5th Cir. 2005).
57. Fenner, *supra* note 2, at 338.
58. Id.
59. Lentz, 282 F. Supp. 2d at 425, *citing* United States v. Shaw, 69 F. 3d 1249, 1253 (4th Cir. 1995).
60. United States v. Laster, 258 F.3d 525 (6th Cir 2001).
61. F.R.E. 806.
62. Delvi, 275 F. Supp. 2d at 417.
63. People v. Quintana, 882 P.2d 1366, 1374 (Colo. 1994).
64. United States v. Weeks, 716 F.2d 830, 832 (11th Cir. 1983).
65. Quintana, 882 P.2d at 1373.
66. State v. Snowden, 345 So. 2d 856 (Fla. App. 1st Dist. 1977).
67. Jones v. Commonwealth, 396 S.E.2d 844, 850 (Va. App. 1990).
68. Id.
69. Quintana, 882 P.2d at 1372.
70. United States v. Lambert, 95 F.2d 1006 (10th Cir. 1993).
71. Id.
72. State v. King, 514 S.E.2d 578, 583 (S.C. 1999).
73. U.S. Const. Amend. VI.
74. State v. Mizenko, 127 P.3d 458 (Mont. 2006).
75. Crawford, 541 U.S. at 66.
76. State v. Newell, 710 N.W.2d 6, 24 (Iowa 2006).
77. Crawford, 541 U.S. at 68.
78. Id. at 51.
79. Id.
80. Mizenko, 127 P.3d at 461.
81. Crawford, 541 U.S. at 68.
82. Davis v. Washington, 126 S.Ct. 2266, 2273-74 (2006).
83. Id. at 2276-78.
84. State v. Krasky, 736 N.W.2d 636, 647 (Minn. 2007) (Page, J., dissenting).

85. *See* State v. Justus, 205 S.W.3d 872 (Mo. 2006); State v. Henderson, 160 P.3d 776 (Kan. 2007).
86. Davis, 126 S.Ct. at 2277.
87. United States v. Arnold, 486 F.3d 177, 190 (6th Cir. 2007).
88. State v. Arroyo, 935 A.2d 975, 995-96 (Conn. 2007).
89. Seely v. State, 282 S.W.3d 778, 787 (Ark. 2008).
90. 131 S.Ct. 1143 (2011).
91. Bryant, 131 S.Ct. at 1156.
92. Id. at 1157 n. 8.
93. Id. at 1164.
94. Id. at 1158-62.
95. Id. at 1164.
96. Id. at 1160.
97. Davis, 126 S.Ct. at 2274 n.2.
98. Seely, 282 S.W.3d at 786.
99. Id; Mizenko, 127 P.3d at 465.
100. Seely, 282 S.W.3d at 787.
101. People v. Vigil, 127 P.3d 916, 925 (Colo. 2006).
102. Mizenko, 127 P.3d at 465.
103. Compan v. People, 121 P.3d 876 (Colo. 2005).
104. *See* State v. Ladner, 644 S.E.2d 684, 689-90 (S.C. 2007).
105. Vigil, 127 P.3d at 929.
106. Id.
107. Seely, 282 S.W.3d at 788.
108. State v. Hooper, 176 P.3d 911, 917 (Idaho 2007).
109. Arroyo, 935 A.2d at 996.
110. *See e.g.,* Colo. Rev. Stat. 13-25-129.
111. People v. Moreno, 60 P.3d 242, 246 (Colo. 2007).
112. People v. Argomaniz-Ramirez, 102 P.3D 1015, 1017 (Colo. 2004).
113. 497 U.S. 836, 857 (1990).
114. Id.
115. State v. Moses 119 P.3d 906 (Wash. App. 2005).
116. Vigil, 127 P.3d at 927.
117. State v. Fisher, 108 P.3d 1262, 1269 (Wash. App. 2005).
118. In re T.T., 815 N.E.2d 789, 804 (Ill. App. 2004).
119. People v. Cage, 155 P.3d 205 (Cal. 2007).
120. Clark v. State, 199 P.3d 1203, 1211-12 (Ak. App. 2009), *quoting* Cage, 155 P.3d at 218.
121. Moses, 119 P.3d at 911.
122. Seely, 282 S.W.3d at 789.
123. 129 S.Ct. 2527 (2009).
124. Id. at 2532.
125. Id. at 2539.
126. Id. at 2541.
127. Colo. Rev. Stat. 16-3-309(5).
128. State v. Carter, 114 P.3d 1001 (Mont. 2005).
129. See People v. Espinoza, 195 P.3d 1122, 1126 (Colo. App. 2008).
130. F.R.E. 804(b)(6).
131. People v. Moreno, 160 P.3d 242, 245 (Colo. 2007).
132. 128 S.Ct. 2678 (2008).
133. Giles, 128 S.Ct. at 2681-82.
134. Id. at 2685.
135. Id. at 2693.
136. People v. Vasquez, 173 P.3d 1099, 1101 (Colo. 2007).
137. Vasquez, 173 P.3d at 1101.
138. 725 ILCS 5/115-10.6.
139. Martin Bashir, *Will Drew Peterson Be Condemned From the Grave?* ABC News, February 22, 2010, available at http://abcnews.com/print?id=9908667.
140. Stacy St. Clair and Erika Slife, *Controversy Surrounds Drew Peterson Hearsay Hearings,* Chicago Tribune, February 2010, available at http://www.chicagotribune.com/news/local/ct-met-drew-pterson-hearsay-hearing-expe20100209,0,518581.story.
141. Id.
142. Steve Schmadeke, *Drew Peterson Case: Further Details of Sealed Ruling Come to Light,* Chicago Tribune, July 20, 2010, available at http://articles.chicagotribune.com/2010-07-20/news/ct-met-0721-peterson-ruling-20100720_1_drew-peterson-case-kathleen-savio-third-and-fourth-wives.

CHAPTER 14

Authentication of Evidence and the Best Evidence Rule

"The need for digital evidence is not confined to obvious cybercrime events such as hacking, fraud and denial of service attacks....It's also required when transactions are disputed, in employee disputes, and almost all forms of non-cyber crime, including murder, forgery, industrial espionage and terrorism."—Peter Sommer

Chapter Topics

Objectives

After reading this chapter, students will be able to:

- Understand the basic requirements for authenticating evidence

- Distinguish between the rules for authenticating various types of photographic evidence

- Learn the purpose of using demonstrative evidence and how it is different from other types of evidence

- Understand the requirements of the best evidence rule and know the circumstances of when an original writing is required

Introduction

Up to this point, this book has primarily focused on physical evidence and the testimony of witnesses. In this chapter, you will turn your attention to the use of written documents, electronically stored evidence, and photographs and other demonstrative evidence. But first, this chapter will discuss the requirements for authenticating all types of evidence, in particular as it relates to the admission of documentary evidence and demonstrative exhibits. A sufficient foundation must be laid for the admission of evidence. This usually involves calling a person to testify that the exhibit is authentic (testimony that the exhibit is what the offering party says it is) and having that witness testify that the exhibit is accurate. This chapter will cover the authentication of several types of evidence, including physical evidence, electronic evidence, and demonstrative exhibits.

This chapter will also cover the use of documentary evidence. Documentary evidence is any evidence that is a writing or other document, including those stored in electronic form. Documents can come in numerous forms, including business records, medical records, e-mails, and court records. Documents are routinely admitted in criminal trials to prove such things as the fact of a person's death, the fact of a prior conviction, or that the defendant sent harassing e-mails to the victim. Documents have to be authenticated before being admitted as well. While many types of documents are self-authenticating, a witness with knowledge of a document may have to authenticate it and verify the accuracy of its contents before it can be admitted.

This chapter will also discuss the requirement that the originals of writings be produced where possible. This is known as the best evidence rule. This rule requires that the originals of writings must be presented in court to prove their contents in most circumstances. This means that the document or photograph itself must be presented as an exhibit rather than having other evidence (i.e., a person's testimony) establish the contents of the writing. There are several exceptions to the rule, however, where copies or other secondary evidence can be admitted in place of the originals.

I. AUTHENTICATION OF EVIDENCE

Rule 901. Requirement of Authentication or Identification

General provision.—The requirement of authentication or identification as a condition precedent to admissibility is satisfied by evidence sufficient to support a finding that the matter in question is what its proponent claims.

Authentication

the process of vouching for the accuracy and authenticity of evidence. The party offering a piece of evidence must show that the evidence is what the party says it is

Rule 901 requires that the party offering a piece of evidence must authenticate it. There must be sufficient evidence that the evidence "is what its proponent claims" it to be.[1] The Rule provides a number of illustrations for how **authentication** of evidence can occur, including testimony of a witness with knowledge of the exhibit, comparison of the exhibit by an expert or the jury with specimens that have been authenticated, distinctive characteristics of the object that make it unique or identifiable, identification of the voice of the speaker by someone familiar with the person's voice, evidence that a writing was recorded or filed in a public office, and evidence that the process or system used to produce the exhibit actually produces an accurate result.[2]

The most common method of authentication is to have a witness who has personal knowledge of the evidence or exhibit testify that the evidence is what the party offering it says it is. This is not a particularly high barrier to admission. The party offering the evidence need only produce sufficient evidence such that the jury might ultimately find the evidence to be authentic.[3] For example, if the prosecutor wants to introduce a threatening letter allegedly written by the defendant, there must be enough proof to establish a foundation such that a reasonable juror could conclude that the defendant wrote the letter. If this foundation is proven and the letter is relevant, it is then up to the jury to decide whether the defendant wrote it and what weight to give the evidence.[4] A party can also authenticate evidence though a number of other methods, some of which are discussed below.

A. Physical Evidence

Physical evidence is usually authenticated by calling a witness with personal knowledge of the evidence who can identify it. Physical evidence can also be authenticated by a witness establishing that the evidence has unique characteristics that make it easily identifiable. The chain of custody also has to be established for the evidence to ensure that it has not been altered or tampered with. Preserving the chain of custody for physical evidence was discussed in detail in Chapter 2.

Practical Example

Kathy is charged with child abuse. The prosecutor wants to introduce a piece of evidence seized from her home, a bloody paddle, that helps prove the charge of abuse. In order to authenticate the paddle, the prosecutor would call the officer who collected the paddle from Kathy's home on January 18 of this year. The officer can then authenticate the paddle by testifying that it is the same one he seized from her home on January 18. Because the officer placed the paddle in a bag and marked and sealed the bag, he can identify the evidence and attest to the fact that, to the best of his knowledge, it has not been tampered with.

B. Documentary Evidence

1. Hard Copies

Document
any writing that provides information, such as a contract or e-mail. Before its admission into evidence, it must be authenticated

One form of evidence frequently admitted at trial is documentary evidence. A **document** is any writing that provides some information, such as a contract, e-mail, or death certificate. In order to admit a traditional paper copy of a document, the party offering it must authenticate the document and establish its relevancy and reliability (usually that it satisfies some exception to the hearsay rule).[5] Challenges to the authenticity of a document can come on a number of fronts. The opposing party could allege that the document (such as a will or letter) is a forgery or that a supposed business record is not one prepared or maintained by that business. Traditionally, a witness with knowledge of the document or how it was prepared and stored was required to testify in order to establish its authenticity. In recent years, however, the process has been considerably simplified for the authentication of many forms of business records and public records.

Self-authenticating documents
documents that can be offered without establishing a foundation for their authentication. Public records under seal, official publications, and newspapers are examples of self-authenticating records

Rule 902 provides that certain types of documents are self-authenticating and an adequate foundation can be established without having a witness testify. **Self-authenticating documents** include public records under seal, certified copies of public records, official publications such as books and pamphlets issued by a public authority, newspapers and periodicals, commercial paper, and business records of regularly conducted activities accompanied by a certification.[6] In addition, business records can now be authenticated without the need for testimony by the records custodian of the business. Rule 902 provides that the party offering the business record can authenticate the record by providing a certification from the records custodian. This certification must state (1) that the record was made at or near the time of the occurrence of the matter discussed in the record by a person with knowledge; (2) that it was kept in the course of the regularly conducted activity; and (3) that the keeping of such records is a regular practice.[7] Many states have a similar provision for the admission of business records.

Practical Example

Walter is a security guard for a jewelry store. The store was burglarized at night and $150,000 worth of diamonds was taken. The prosecutor wants to introduce evidence that Walter was working the night of the heist and used his key card to unlock the store for the burglars. The prosecutor wants to submit a document from the jeweler that shows Walter's key card was used at 12:37 a.m. the night of the burglary. In order to admit the document, the prosecutor could either call the records custodian for the jewelry store or get him to sign a certification to authenticate the record.

---

2. Electronically Stored Information

Electronically stored information

any material created or stored in electronic format. E-mails, digital photographs, and word processing documents are examples of ESI

Documents are increasingly being stored in electronic form. The filing cabinet has been replaced by the hard drive. Thus, the introduction of **electronically stored information** (ESI)—data stored on a computer or other electronic storage device—is becoming increasingly prevalent in criminal cases. E-mails, text messages, and cell phone records can all play an important role in cases. Information that is stored in electronic format can present unique issues with respect to proving its accuracy and authenticity, however. The accuracy of electronic data may be reduced by incomplete data entry, programming errors, and damage to storage media.[8] As Dr. Hany Farid, the founder of digital forensics, has noted, anyone with "a digital camera, a PC, Photoshop and an hour's worth of time can make fairly compelling digital forgeries."[9] It is also hard to verify who sent e-mails and other electronic communications. Of course, similar uncertainties exist with regard to traditional written documents (a signature can be forged, etc).

When ESI was first introduced in court in the late 1980s and early 1990s, some courts were reluctant to embrace the new technology. In one rather comic example of judicial restraint, a federal court judge once referred to the Internet as "voodoo information" and held that the information on a Web page was "inherently untrustworthy."[10] Today, such a statement would seem absurd. As technology has evolved and computers and the Internet have become commonplace, courts have lessened the restrictions on establishing the foundation for such evidence. The admissibility of ESI should be evaluated on a case-by-case basis just like any other evidence. Factors that should be considered in evaluating the reliability of electronically stored evidence include the error rate in data entry and the security of the storage system.[11] One federal court held that the degree of foundational evidence required to authenticate electronically stored information depends on the quality and completeness of the data input, the complexity of the computer processing, the routines of the computer operation, and the ability to test and verify results of the computer processing.[12]

In its Guidelines for Searching and Seizing Computers, the Department of Justice cautioned that digital evidence should be carefully authenticated:

> For the time being, however, most computer evidence can still be altered electronically—in dramatic ways or in imperceptible detail—without any sign of erasure. But this does not mean that electronic evidence, having become less distinctive, has become any less admissible. It simply may require us to authenticate it in other ways.[13]

The authenticity of computer records is often established by testimony from someone with personal knowledge of how the records are maintained. This witness must provide information about how the data was created, stored, and maintained.[14] E-mails and other electronic communications can be authenticated in this manner, by expert testimony, or even as a business record.[15] Proving the contents of postings on Websites may pose additional concerns since someone other than the Website sponsor may have posted the information. Some courts have required that someone from the organization actually testify that the organization actually posted the information or comments on the Website.[16]

Practical Example

Assume that Mary is charged with fraud and embezzlement from an insurance company. The prosecutor wants to introduce evidence that several claims filed via the Internet claim system set up by the insurance company were actually fraudulently filed by Mary. He wants to introduce printouts of the claim forms as evidence of the fraud. The prosecutor would have to authenticate the claim forms like any other business record but would not have to call expert witnesses to testify that the insurance company's Internet claim system can accurately produce reports.

C. Demonstrative Evidence

Demonstrative evidence
evidence that is offered to explain or clarify other evidence. It is not substantive evidence of guilt itself

Unlike other types of evidence discussed in this text, **demonstrative evidence** is not substantive evidence of guilt. Instead, it is an explanatory aid such as a PowerPoint slide, chart, or graph. Photographs, videos, and computer-generated animations are examples of demonstrative evidence. The purpose of demonstrative exhibits is to explain or clarify other evidence. For example, if the jury just heard testimony about how the defendant embezzled funds from a retirement account, it would probably not excite or impress the jury. A demonstrative exhibit such as a graphical representation of the accounts showing how the funds were embezzled would help the jury better grasp this type of technical testimony. Like other pieces of evidence, demonstrative exhibits must be authenticated before being admitted.

1. Photographs and Video Generally

For purposes of establishing a foundation for admissibility, photographs and videos are treated the same.[17] In order to be admitted into evidence, the party offering photographs must demonstrate four things: (1) that the photos are relevant; (2) that they have been properly authenticated; (3) that the chain of custody for their collection and preservation has been adequately established; and (4) that the probative value of the photos is not substantially outweighed by their prejudicial impact.[18]

First, a photograph is relevant as long as it relates to some pertinent fact in the case. Photographs in criminal cases are almost always relevant since they may depict the crime scene, the physical evidence located at the scene, or the wounds and injuries of the victim. Second, a photograph is properly authenticated under Rule 901 as long as sufficient evidence is produced to support a finding that the photograph is "what its proponent claims."[19] A proper foundation is thus established through testimony where a party with personal knowledge of the scene it depicts is able to testify that:

> (1) The photograph is an accurate reproduction of what it purports to represent; and (2) the reproduction is of the scene at the time of the incident in question, or, in the alternative, the scene has not changed between the time of the incident in question and the time of the taking of the photograph.[20]

To authenticate a photograph, the party does not have to call the person who took the photograph. Instead, the witness must have sufficient personal knowledge of the scene or object to testify that the photograph fairly and accurately depicts the scene or object as it existed on the date in question.[21] For example, although the lead investigator may not have taken the photographs of a crime scene, he is qualified to lay the foundation for them since he observed the collection of evidence and helped process the scene.

The party offering the photograph must also establish its chain of custody by showing that it has not been altered or tampered with between the time it was taken and the time it is offered into evidence Proving the chain of custody was not much of an issue in the days when film was used to capture photographic images. The party simply had to show that the exposed film was placed into evidence, developed in the department or at an outside lab, and not altered or changed in the process. The resulting print could easily be compared to the original negative if its authenticity was challenged.

Practical Example

Sergeant Graves took several photographs of a murder scene. The prosecutor wants to introduce the photos into evidence. He calls Stan Smith, the detective who was the lead investigator on the case, to establish the foundation for the photographs. The detective testifies that the photos are a fair and accurate depiction of the scene as he remembers it on the day the body was discovered. The defense objects on the ground that Sergeant Graves should have been called to establish their foundation. Should the objection be granted? No. As long as a witness can attest from personal knowledge that the photographs are a fair and accurate depiction of the scene, the original photographer does not have to be called.

2. Digital Photographs

Digital photograph
any photograph taken in electronic form or one taken on film using traditional photographic methods that is then scanned into electronic form. Digital photographs can be broken down into three categories for determining their admissibility: (1) original, digital images that are unaltered; (2) digitally converted images (photographs produced by traditional film methods and scanned into electronic form); and (3) digitally enhanced images

With the advent of digital photography, however, courts have had to pay closer attention to the authentication of photographs. A **digital photograph** is any photograph taken in electronic form or one taken on film using traditional photographic methods that is then scanned into electronic form. One federal court noted that "digital photographs present unique authentication problems because they are a form of electronically produced evidence that may be manipulated and altered."[22] Due to the fact that editing software such as Photoshop can dramatically change the original image to the point that an entirely new image may be created, an additional foundation may have to be laid before the court will admit the photograph. At the very least, the opposing party should inquire into the process used to edit and enhance the images produced for court.

Edward Imwinkelried, a noted evidence scholar, breaks down digital photographs into three categories for determining their admissibility: (1) original, digital images that are unaltered, (2) digitally converted images (photographs produced by traditional film methods and scanned into electronic form), and (3) digitally enhanced images.[23]

AUTHOR'S NOTE

The third category, digitally enhanced images, can be further broken down by degree—images that have undergone minor enhancement and those that have undergone major enhancement (material alteration). Since small changes (such as changing the color space or subtly modifying the color or contrast of the image) have to be made to the original images in order to properly project or print them, original, unaltered images are rarely submitted in court and are usually used for comparison purposes only. However, the resulting images are virtually indistinguishable from the originals and therefore should be treated the same as the originals for purposes of admissibility.

The first three categories of images (all but those receiving major enhancements) are usually admissible under the basic foundational requirements for traditional photographs discussed above. Although the techniques for digital conversion or image improvement are technically scientific processes that could require expert testimony to properly establish a foundation, they are so commonplace that the court will simply take judicial notice of their reliability (if their reliability is challenged at all). Thus, the foundation for the admissibility of these types of digital photographs is established simply by having a witness with personal knowledge of the scene testify that the photos are a fair and accurate depiction of the scene photographed.[24]

Minimally enhanced versions of an original photograph or video are also admissible with only basic proof of authentication. The party has to simply show that the enhanced version has not materially altered the accuracy of the image. For instance, a federal district court ruled that an enhanced version of surveillance video was admissible even though a technician had enhanced the image's brightness and contrast to make for easier viewing.[25] The court explained that such enhancements did not materially alter the original footage:

> The Court finds that adjustments to brightness or contrast, or enlargement of the image, while arguably manipulation, are in fact no more manipulative than the recording process itself. The image is black and white; the world is not. In the non-digital world, a camera's lens, its aperture, shutter speed, length of exposure, film grain, and development process all affect the image. Each of these is entirely unremarkable so long as the "image" remains an accurate recording of that which occurred before the camera. If a photographic negative were magnified by lens, and an enlargement resulted, no one would question the larger picture. Similarly, in the event of the tape recording, no one would comment if the volume were increased to make the recorded conversation more easily heard again, so long as the volume-increased words were accurately recorded by the recording medium.[26]

Materially altered photograph

a photographic image or print that is produced by significantly altering the original image. A materially altered image has to be offered as the product of a scientific process, and expert testimony is necessary to authenticate it

With regard to a **materially altered photograph**, however, additional testimony is necessary to establish a proper foundation. A materially altered photograph is one that is produced by significantly altering the original image. In fact, the resulting image may be so dramatically changed or altered that not even the photographer can testify that it is a fair and accurate depiction of the scene as he saw it. As a result, the photograph will have to be offered as the by-product of a scientific process, and expert testimony will have to be offered to authenticate it. Imwinkelried recommends that the foundation be laid for altered or enhanced images by having the expert testify to the following:

(1) That he is an expert in digital photography (or more properly photography editing); (2) a description of the image enhancement technology used, including both the creation of a digital image consisting of pixels and the computer

manipulation of the pixels; (3) that both processes used are valid; (4) that there has been adequate research into the specific application of image enhancement technology used in the case; (5) that the software used was developed from such research; (6) that he followed correct procedure in using the computer software to enhance the digital file; and (7) that he recognizes the exhibit as the photograph that was produced through the enhancement process.[27]

Some courts have strictly enforced these foundational requirements. For example, the Connecticut Supreme Court rejected the admission of a digitally enhanced photograph where the prosecution failed to lay a proper foundation for its admission.[28] There, the prosecution had admitted digitally enhanced photographs showing the superimposition of the defendant's teeth over photographs of bite marks retrieved from the victim. The odontologist who testified about the photographs was not familiar with how the images were created or the reliability of the process used. The court stated that the foundational witness must, at a minimum, be able to:

> Testify, adequately and truthfully as to exactly what the jury is looking at, and the defendant has a right to cross-examine the witness concerning the evidence. Without a witness who can satisfactorily explain or analyze the data and the program, the effectiveness of cross-examination can be seriously undermined, particularly in light of the extent to which the evidence in the present case has been "created."[29]

In contrast, the admission of digital photographs produced from mammography films as a demonstrative aid was upheld by a Massachusetts court despite the fact that the contrast had been altered from the original films. The court found a sufficient foundation had been laid for the photographs since the expert witness testified that the images were a substantial likeness of the originals and had not been artificially enhanced.[30]

Because of the potential for easy alteration or manipulation of digital photographs, courts could also impose more stringent requirements on the prosecution to establish the chain of custody. To date, courts have not done so, holding that the chain of custody is established for digital files so long as the department has taken adequate precautions to prevent tampering or alteration of the original files. For example, a New Jersey court held that the mere potential for alteration does not break the chain of custody:

> [T]he fact that digital technology is a medium that can be easily altered or manipulated is not detrimental to the State's request for admission of the digital photographs, particularly where, as here, the defense failed to suggest that the photographs in question were enhanced or altered in any way, but merely cited the possibility of alteration in a hypothetical sense. Certainly, an inquiry into possible manipulation of a photograph is a matter for cross-examination or possibly

expert testimony. Here, the trial judge properly concluded that the potential for manipulation was "not a basis to not admit the digital photos into evidence."[31]

The same technology that allows a person to alter or manipulate a photo can also be used to preserve the chain of custody. Tools such as Photoshop enable the user to track any change made to an original file. Thus, the evidence custodian can print a history log, showing all changes made to a file. Other suggestions for preserving the chain of custody for digital files are provided in the Evidence in Action Box below.

EVIDENCE IN ACTION

Suggestions for Establishing a Chain of Custody for Digital Images

Establishing the chain of custody for digital images is important since digital files can be subject to easy manipulation or alteration. Erik Berg, the Forensic Services Supervisor for the Tacoma Police Department, emphasizes that it is necessary to address the following questions regarding the chain of custody of digital images:

- Who captured the image and when?
- Who had access to the image between the time it was captured and the time it was introduced in court?
- Has the original image been altered in any way since it was captured?
- Who enhanced the image and when?
- What was done to enhance the image and is it repeatable?
- Has the enhanced image been altered in any way since it was first enhanced?[32]

The chain of custody of digital files can be preserved in a number of ways. The most common method tracks the image capture and enhancement processes as well as restricts access to the original images. A detailed trail should be kept on each image from the time the image was shot to the time it was printed out for court or burned to a CD.[33] Each memory card should be assigned to a given officer and checked in at the end of each shift. An evidence technician should download the files and save the original files. Access to those original files should be restricted. Any changes that are made to the image should be limited to copies of the original image. The original file must remain intact. The original in effect serves as a control for comparison purposes if any challenge is made to the authenticity of the image. Changes or alterations that are made to a copy of the image should be documented as well. Photoshop contains a function called "History Log" that allows the user to track each change that is made to the image from the time it is opened.[34]

Other methods that can be used to maintain the chain of custody include encrypting or watermarking digital images to prevent tampering or to authenticate the source of an image. Encryption involves assigning a key code or password to a file to make it impossible to view. A watermark is an emblem embedded in the image that can be used to authenticate the image. Unfortunately, encryption and watermarking both alter the image, and it would have to be shown that the process did not materially affect the resulting image.[35]

Practical Example

Assume that the prosecution wants to admit evidence of digital photographs. The following dialogue between a prosecutor and a witness demonstrates how the proper foundation can be laid for the admission of such photographs:

DA: *Officer, I'm handing you what have been previously marked as People's Exhibits 1-10. Do you recognize what they are?*

Officer: *Yes. These are photographs of the double homicide at 123 Crook St. that occurred on October 6 of last year.*

DA: *How do you recognize them as such?*

Officer: *The back of each photograph has been marked with the date and case number as well as my initials, the officer who took them.*

DA: *Are the photos a fair and accurate representation of the scene as you found it on October 6 of last year?*

Officer: *Yes.*

DA: *What did you do with the photos once you took them?*

Officer: *The photos were taken on a department-issued digital camera. I took the memory card out of the camera and placed it into evidence that same day. Our computer technician then downloaded the files and made copies of the files.*

DA: *Have the photos been altered in any significant manner since you took them on October 6 of last year?*

Officer: *No, other than some minor color or exposure correction, they are in substantially the same condition as when I took them on October 6.*

---

3. Remote Cameras

Automated remote camera
a camera operated mechanically without a photographer. Automated remote cameras must be authenticated through testimony about the type of camera used and the fact that it was operating properly at the time it took the photos

Some cameras known as **automated remote cameras** are operated without a photographer. Bank security cameras and surveillance cameras are examples of this type of camera. If the photograph is taken from an automated remote camera or security camera, an alternate method of authentication must be used called the silent witness method. Under the silent witness method, a witness must describe the process or system that allows the camera to produce an accurate result since a person does not physically operate this type of camera. The silent witness method authenticates a photograph as a "mute or silent independent photographic witness" due to the fact that no one has personal knowledge of what the camera was seeing at the time the photo was recorded.[36] A surveillance video is properly authenticated under this method if a witness familiar with the operation of the system testifies to the type of equipment or camera used, its general reliability, the quality of the recorded product, or the general reliability of the entire system.[37]

For example, the Fifth Circuit found that a sufficient foundation was laid for the admission of photographs obtained from bank security camera footage during a bank robbery. There, a witness testified as to the manner in which the film was installed in the camera, how the camera is activated, the fact that the film was removed immediately after the robbery, and the fact that it was properly developed and contact prints were made from it.[38] In contrast, the Massachusetts Supreme Court reversed the admission of a composite of surveillance footage compiled from eight different cameras. The court noted that the person who created the compilation did not testify and there was no evidence provided as to the process used to create the blended footage nor was any evidence presented as to the manner of operation of the cameras.[39]

Practical Example

The prosecutor is trying a bank robbery case. He wants to introduce evidence of bank security camera footage that shows one of the robbers' faces. The prosecutor calls one of the detectives to testify that the security camera photo was in fact a photo of one of the defendants. He testifies that the photo is a fair and accurate depiction of the robbery and bears a close resemblance to one of the defendants. Is this sufficient to establish a foundation for the photograph? No. In addition to the police officer, the prosecutor must call a bank manager to testify that the security camera was set up to capture a certain area of the bank and was working properly at the time of the robbery and how the tape or digital file was retrieved and handed over to police.

4. Computer Graphics and Animations

The use of computerized models of crime scenes or animations that reenact the crime is becoming more popular in criminal cases. **Computer-generated animations** (CGAs) are series of drawings created by computer that produce the illusion of motion when assembled frame by frame. The resulting animated image is a graphic representation explaining or demonstrating the opinion or testimony of a witness.[40] A CGA does not create any independent conclusions or data; as a result, it is simply demonstrative evidence. A CGA is admissible as demonstrative evidence if (1) it is properly authenticated; (2) it is relevant; and (3) its probative value is not substantially outweighed by its prejudicial effect.[41]

CGAs are authenticated like other demonstrative evidence as long as it can be shown that the model or animation fairly and accurately depicts the

Computer-generated animation
a series of drawings created on a computer that produces the illusion of motion. It must be authenticated by expert testimony about how the CGA was created

scene it is supposed to represent. The witness testifying to the foundation for the computerized animation must be familiar with the process of how the animation was created and the source and accuracy of the input data used to create it. Obviously, it is unreasonable to expect that every measurement and possible position of vehicles and people will be taken, so minor flaws in the preparation of the CGA go to its weight, not its admissibility.[42]

CGAs are usually relevant if they help the jury better understand the testimony presented. For example, the Pennsylvania Supreme Court found the use of a CGA to illustrate the prosecution's theory of a homicide was relevant since it clearly and accurately depicted the prosecution's theory of the case and aided the jury in understanding the collective testimony without the use of extraneous graphics and information.[43]

Finally, the court must examine the potential prejudicial effect of a CGA. The cost of using a CGA is certainly one factor that must be considered. The cost of preparing CGAs may run between $10,000 and $20,000, which could put them out of reach of all but the wealthiest defendants. Of course, as technology advances, the cost will go down. However, just because only one party uses a CGA does not mean that the other side is overly prejudiced. Studies have shown that CGAs are not "silver bullets" that can guarantee one side success.[44] Further, the visual nature of a CGA can have a profound impact on a jury and could be prejudicial if it overly relies on drama to create emotional impact. The Pennsylvania court found the CGA used was not inflammatory or prejudicial because it did not include sounds, facial expressions, signs of wounds or injury, or effects that were unnecessary.[45] The court also noted that the use of a cautionary instruction by the trial court that educated the jury about the exact nature and role of the CGA was an effective safeguard against prejudice.[46]

Practical Example

James is accused of drunk driving and causing a fatal accident where a third car swerved and ran into oncoming traffic. He hires a consultant to create a CGA of the accident. Based on the expert's calculations and data obtained from the state patrol, the CGA is created. It shows James could not have caused the accident. The defense attorney calls the technician who created the CGA. He testifies that the model is an accurate depiction of the scene based on the calculations provided. He also testifies to which program was used to create the animation. The expert admits he used some different calculations than those used by the state patrol. Has the foundation been sufficiently established? Yes. Any issues with respect to the accuracy of the input data goes to the weight, not the admissibility of the CGA.

II. BEST EVIDENCE RULE

Rule 1002. Requirement of Original

To prove the content of a writing, recording, or photograph, the original writing, recording, or photograph is required, except as otherwise provided in these rules or by act of Congress.

A. Requirement That the Original Writing Be Produced

Best evidence rule
a rule of evidence that requires that the original of a writing be produced instead of secondary evidence of its contents unless otherwise allowed by rule or statute

Rules 1001–1008 codify a common law doctrine known as the "**best evidence rule**." In essence, the rule requires that the original of a document or writing be produced instead of secondary evidence (oral testimony, drafts, etc.) of its contents unless otherwise provided by rule or statute.[47] The rule was developed in the eighteenth century when copying documents by hand was the only way to reproduce originals and pretrial discovery procedures were nonexistent.[48] As a result, the only way to verify the accuracy of the contents of a document was to produce the original of the document itself in court. Many commentators have suggested, therefore, that the rule should more properly be known as the original document or original writing rule.[49]

Primary evidence
the best or highest quality evidence, such as the original of a document

Secondary evidence
all other evidence that falls short of this mark, such as oral testimony or a duplicate of the document. It is admissible to prove the contents of a writing where the original is lost or destroyed, is in possession of the other party and is not obtainable through subpoena, is not closely related to the main issue, or is otherwise unavailable

The best evidence rule divides evidence into two levels based on the quality of the evidence—primary and secondary. **Primary evidence** is the best or highest quality of evidence, such as the original of a document. **Secondary evidence** is all other evidence that falls short of this mark, such as a duplicate of the original or testimony about its contents. Under the best evidence rule, if the party offering a writing could neither produce the original document nor provide a satisfactory reason for its nonproduction, then secondary evidence could not be offered to prove the contents of the document.[50]

This distinction says nothing about the strength of the evidence, however. Both primary and secondary evidence can provide excellent proof of the contents of a writing, assuming they are authenticate and reliable. While the best evidence rule historically required the actual original of the writing to be produced in court, today copies or duplicates are equally admissible in place of the original in most circumstances. Given this fact, perhaps the rule should simply now be called the primary evidence rule.

The main purpose of the best evidence rule is to ensure that the contents of a writing are accurately presented in court. The Ninth Circuit summarized the concerns of the best evidence rule as follows:

> When the contents of a writing are at issue, oral testimony as to the terms of the writing is subject to a greater risk of error than oral testimony as to events or other situations. The human memory is not often capable of reciting the precise terms of

a writing, and when the terms are in dispute only the writing itself, or a true copy, provides reliable evidence. To summarize then, we observe that the importance of the precise terms of writings in the world of legal relations, the fallibility of the human memory as reliable evidence of the terms, and the hazards of inaccurate or incomplete duplication are the concerns addressed by the best evidence rule.[51]

The best evidence rule applies "when a witness seeks to testify about the contents of a writing, recording or photograph without producing the physical item itself—particularly when the witness was not privy to the events those contents describe."[52] The rule only applies where the document is offered to prove the contents of the writing or recording, however.[53] It does not apply where the contents of the writing are merely tangential to the fact trying to be proved. For example, a North Carolina court found that the prosecution did not have to produce the original of a life insurance policy where it was offered to show the defendant's knowledge that the policy existed, not its contents or terms.[54] Similarly, a Georgia court held that the best evidence rule was not violated where the prosecution did not admit the card from which an officer had read the defendant a warning of his implied consent rights in a DUI case. The court found that the contents of the card—the actual wording of the implied consent warning—was not at issue in the case. Instead, the issue was whether the defendant had been adequately informed of his implied consent rights. The court found that the prosecution had substantially complied with this requirement through the testimony of the officer.[55] In contrast, the Ninth Circuit held that the best evidence rule applied to the readout of a GPS showing the path of travel of a boat. Since the agent had observed a "graphical representation of data" that the GPS had compiled about the path of defendant's boat, the court concluded that the agent's testimony concerned the "content" of the GPS.[56]

The rule also does not apply to situations where a party seeks to prove some fact that exists independent of a writing. In such a case, an event or fact may be proved by non-documentary evidence even though a written record of the event was made.[57] For example, payment for an item may be proved through testimony about the payment even though a written record—the receipt for its purchase—was created but not produced. However, the best evidence rule would apply if the only proof of payment was the receipt itself.

Original
the writing or recording itself. The best evidence rule applies to original writings, recordings, photographs, and electronically stored data

For purposes of the best evidence rule, an **original** of a writing or recording is the writing or recording itself. More than just written documents are covered by the best evidence rule, however. While the rule originally applied only to writings, it has been broadened to encompass photographs, recordings, and electronically stored data as technology has advanced.[58] This expanded definition of writing was developed in recognition of the fact that "evidentiary rules concerning the admissibility of originals should be fashioned with a breadth sufficient to encompass modern techniques for storing and retrieving data."[59] Today, the rule covers anything that is put down by "handwriting, typewriting, printing, photostatting, photographing, magnetic impulse, mechanical or electronic recording, or other form of data compilation."[60] An original of a photograph includes the negative or any print made from it.[61] An original of electronically stored data is a "printout or other output readable by sight."[62] This includes the readable display on the monitor of the writing or data, the hard drive, or a printout of the information as long as it accurately reflects the data.[63] Thus, the party does not have to produce in court the hard drive or other device that the data is stored on.[64] For example, an Indiana court held that the content of an Internet chat room conversation between the defendant and an undercover cop that was pasted into a word processing program was an original for purposes of the rule.[65] Similarly, a Virginia court held that a bit-for-bit copy of a hard drive should be considered an original for purposes of the best evidence rule since the forensic copy is an exact duplicate of the original.[66]

Given the number of exceptions, one commentator stated, "the Best Evidence Rule had been treated by the judiciary and legislature as an unpleasant fact which must be avoided through constantly increasing and broadening the number of 'loopholes.'"[67] Table 14.1 provides a summary of evidence that the best evidence rule does not exclude.

TABLE 14.1   SUMMARY OF EVIDENCE NOT EXCLUDED BY BEST EVIDENCE RULE

- Printed representations of computer information and computer programs
- Printed representations of images stored on video or digital media
- Secondary evidence of writings that have been lost or destroyed without fraudulent intent of the party offering the evidence
- Secondary evidence of unavailable writings
- Secondary evidence of writings an opponent has but fails to produce as requested
- Secondary evidence of writings that are collateral to issues in case
- Secondary evidence of writings in the custody of a public entity
- Secondary evidence of writings recorded in public records
- Secondary evidence of voluminous writings
- Official records or certified copies of records in official custody
- Photographic copies made as business records
- Photographic copies of records that have been lost or destroyed
- Duplicates of originals where there is no genuine issue as to the authenticity of the original
- Testimony or deposition of the party against whom the exhibit is offered or that party's admission[68]

Practical Example

Jamie is charged with murder. Her defense is that she had an alibi for the murder. She wants to introduce evidence that her boss e-mailed her a work assignment and that she was doing that at the time of the murder. She testifies about the e-mail but does not produce it. Should she have introduced the actual e-mail? Yes. The e-mail is a writing and the original should have been produced.

B. Exceptions to the Best Evidence Rule

1. Admission of Copies or Duplicates

Rule 1003. Admissibility of Duplicate

A duplicate is admissible to the same extent as an original unless (1) a genuine question is raised as to the authenticity of the original or (2) in the circumstances it would be unfair to admit the duplicate in lieu of the original.

Duplicate

a carbon copy, photocopy, microfilm, or offset print made from an original

Rule 1001 defines a **duplicate** as "a counterpart produced by the same impression as the original, or from the same matrix, or by means of photography, including enlargements and miniatures, or by mechanical or electronic re-recording, or by chemical reproduction, or by other equivalent techniques which accurately reproduces the original."[69] Thus, four types of duplicates are recognized by the rule: same impression (carbon paper), same matrix (offset printing), photography (microfilm), and chemical process (photocopying). Handwritten copies are not recognized as duplicates.[70]

Many decades ago, copies were not admissible in place of the original unless the party could account for the nonproduction of the original. For example, in 1814, a Connecticut court rejected the admission of a certified copy of a deed filed with the town clerk in place of the original deed where the landowner could not account for the original's nonproduction.[71] With the invention of the photocopier in 1937, this attitude changed dramatically, however. Mechanical duplicates began to be considered to be much more trustworthy than handwritten copies. As a result, the rule has been relaxed considerably, and copies are admissible under most circumstances.[72] Today, duplicates are more often admitted than originals.[73]

The modern best evidence rule creates two exceptions to the admission of duplicates. Duplicates are not admissible in place of an original if there are questions about the authenticity of the original or the admission of the copy would be unfair.[74] Where there is a question about the authenticity of the duplicate, the original must still be produced because, as Judge Weinstein points out, there may be noticeable differences between the original and a duplicate:

> The original [of a document] may contain, and the copy may lack, such features as handwriting impressions, type of paper, and the like as may afford the opponent valuable means of objecting to admissibility. For example, the original may be a pasted-together version that gives an entirely different impression than a smooth photocopy.[75]

Despite this concern, courts today rarely reject duplicates where there may be genuine questions as to the authenticity of the duplicate.[76] Instead, courts prefer to admit the copy and let the jury sort the issue out.[77] One scholar found that courts routinely reject claims of authenticity even where the opposing party has pointed out inconsistencies between the duplicate and the original.[78] The few courts that have rejected duplicates have done so where the other party admitted to altering either the duplicate or the original from which it was made.[79] For example, one federal court excluded copies of letters where there were genuine concerns about the copies having been forged.[80] In essence, these courts have held that the party opposing the admission of a duplicate raises a genuine issue of authenticity only where the evidence would require the jury to find that the original is not authentic.

An interesting dilemma was raised in the 1982 movie *The Verdict*. There, a key piece of evidence in a medical malpractice trial was a patient admission form. On the form admitted into evidence, it stated that the patient last ate nine hours ago. During rebuttal, it is revealed that the doctor altered the original form and changed the initial entry from a "1" to a "9." The nurse who initially created the form kept a copy as evidence, which she produced on the stand while testifying. The trial judge, however, refused to admit the copy, since the alleged "original" was already in evidence. He also struck from the record the nurse's testimony regarding the alteration of the original. The judge erred in his ruling. Where a party seeks to introduce a duplicate as evidence that the original was altered, the duplicate is admissible, regardless of whether there are questions about the authenticity of the original. This is so because the duplicate was made before the original was altered and is the best available evidence to resolve the discrepancy.[81]

The second exception to the admission of duplicates applies where prejudice or unfairness could result if the copy is admitted. Prejudice may be shown if only part of the original is reproduced in making the duplicate and important or critical parts of the original are missing but needed by the opposing party for cross-examination.[82] There must be more than a mere allegation that the proponent's action is responsible for the loss of the original to show prejudice, however.[83]

Practical Example

Juan is on trial for cocaine possession and distribution. The prosecutor wants to introduce evidence of a customer list that was found during a search of Juan's house performed by the DEA. The original of the list is kept by the DEA, so the local prosecutor introduces a copy into evidence. Is the copy admissible? Yes. There is no question as to the authenticity of the original.

---

2. Admissibility of Secondary Evidence

Rule 1004. Admissibility of Other Evidence of the Contents

The original is not required, and other evidence of the contents of a writing, recording, or photograph is admissible if—

(1) Originals lost or destroyed.—All originals are lost or have been destroyed, unless the proponent lost or destroyed them in bad faith; or

(2) Original not obtainable.—No original can be obtained by any available judicial process or procedure; or

(3) Original in possession of opponent.—At a time when an original was under the control of the party against whom offered, that party was put on notice, by the pleadings or otherwise, that the contents would be a subject of proof at the hearing, and that party does not produce the original at the hearing;

(4) Collateral matters—The writing, recording, or photograph is not closely related to a controlling issue.

Secondary evidence of the contents of the original can be admitted if the original is lost or destroyed, is in the possession of the other party and is not obtainable through subpoena or other means, is not closely related to the main issue, or is otherwise unavailable.[84] Secondary evidence is any proof of the contents of the writing other than the original or duplicate writing, including testimony by the author of the document or someone who has read it, earlier drafts of the document, or an outline used to prepare it.[85] There are no degrees or categories of secondary evidence.[86] There is no requirement, for example, that a party produce a duplicate rather than oral testimony on the ground that one is "better evidence" than another.[87] Once a party has met the requirements for admission of secondary evidence, he can admit whatever type of evidence he wishes.

Under the first exception, Rule 1004 permits the use of secondary evidence if the original is lost or destroyed. The party wishing to use secondary evidence has the burden of proving the loss or destruction of the document and that its loss or destruction was not done in bad faith.[88]

This is not a difficult hurdle for the proponent to overcome. Inadvertent or negligent destruction of originals is not enough to warrant exclusion of secondary evidence.[89] Unless someone witnessed the loss or destruction of the document, such proof is usually provided through circumstantial evidence that "an appropriate search for the document was made without locating it."[90] Thus, the party wishing to admit secondary evidence under this exception must show that he has made a "diligent but unsuccessful" effort to locate the missing original.[91]

A party must also make similar efforts to obtain an original through the discovery process in order to justify admission of secondary evidence under the second exception—that the original cannot be obtained through judicial process.[92] For example, a federal court held that the plaintiff had met her burden where the original medical records were unobtainable by available judicial process since the records were in Italy and not easily located.[93] In contrast, another federal court held that the plaintiff failed to conduct a diligent search for an allegedly discriminatory e-mail since she did not serve any discovery requests for the e-mail or inquire into whether it still existed.[94] Courts have also refused to admit secondary evidence where the requesting party tried to obtain the original through discovery but failed to enforce those requests.[95]

The third exception requires the proponent to show that the original is in the possession of the opposing party, the proponent requested the document in discovery, and that request was denied. For example, in a prosecution for a minor knowingly driving a vehicle containing alcohol, the prosecution requested the defendant's license to prove his age. The defendant refused. As a result, the court permitted the prosecution to call the ranger who arrested the defendant to testify as to his age.[96]

If the court finds that one of the exceptions under Rule 1004 has been proven, the party may offer secondary evidence to prove the contents of the lost or unobtainable original. The party must then lay a sufficient foundation for the secondary evidence. The party has to show that the original writing existed, was executed properly, and was genuine. For example, oral testimony of the contents of the original is admissible only where there is evidence that the witness is able to recount or recite with substantial accuracy all of the contents of the original.[97]

If this foundation is laid, it is then up to the opposing party to attack the sufficiency of the secondary evidence. If the offering party can show more than "mere speculation" exists as to the contents of the original writing, the attack goes to the weight, not the admissibility of the evidence.[98] For example, a South Carolina appellate court concluded that it was error for the trial judge to exclude secondary evidence of the contents of a letter where no evidence was provided that the original was destroyed in bad faith.[99]

Practical Example

Hans is charged with stealing a rare first edition of **Harry Potter**. *Hans' defense is that the owner of the book had intended to give him the book as a gift. A contract was drafted to that effect. Hans never received a copy. There were two witnesses to the contract. The owner of the book later reneged on the contract and refused to turn over the book. Hans took the book, thinking it was his to take. At trial, Hans' attorney wants to introduce testimony of one of the witnesses to the contract's existence. He cannot produce the original since the owner of the book allegedly destroyed it. The judge will likely admit testimony about the contents of the contract since a foundation for the secondary evidence has been established.*

3. Public Records

Rule 1005 provides that a copy of a public record may be submitted in place of the original as long as the copy is certified by the public agency. If a copy cannot be reasonably obtained, then secondary evidence can be provided of the record's contents.[100] This exception may take on less significance because many government agencies such as the FDA and EPA now permit electronic recordkeeping, reducing the risk that paper records will be lost or destroyed.

4. Summaries

Federal Rule 1006 permits charts or summaries of writings to be entered into evidence when the original is too voluminous or inconvenient for the jury to examine in court.[101] Under this exception, however, the originals or duplicates from which the summary or chart were prepared must be made available to the other party for inspection, In effect, Rule 1006 is not an exception to the rule that the proponent must produce an original or duplicate; it simply eases the burden on a party who has already complied with that requirement from having to produce such large documents in court.[102]

Practical Example

Assume the prosecution has compiled an extensive Internet history on the defendant's viewing of child pornography online. The originals are thousands of pages, detailing the Web page usage of the defendant. If the prosecutor discovers the original documents to the defense prior to trial or makes them available for inspection, he can present a summary or chart of the evidence at trial that simplifies it for the jury.

California Simplifies Best Evidence Rule

Many commentators have criticized the need for the best evidence rule. In light of technological developments that have made it simpler to copy documents and made the process more accurate along with broad pretrial discovery, some commentators feel that "the rationale for the rule no longer withstands scrutiny."[103]

One state has taken an aggressive approach to modernizing the best evidence rule. California tasked its Law Revision Committee to examine the continuing need and vitality of the best evidence rule. In 1996, the Commission concluded that the rule was confusing and no longer needed:

> The Best Evidence Rule is an anachronism. In yesterday's world of manual copying and limited pretrial discovery, it served as a safeguard against misleading use of secondary evidence. Under contemporary circumstances, in which high quality photocopies are standard and litigants have broad opportunities for pretrial inspection of original documents, the Best Evidence Rule is no longer necessary to protect against unreliable secondary evidence.[104]

Because the rule's benefits outweigh its costs, the Commission recommended that the rule be repealed and a simpler form of the rule be adopted in its place.

The Commission found that the two primary justifications for the best evidence rule—that it prevents fraud and guards against misinterpretation of writings—are no longer valid. Mandating the admission of an original does not protect against fraud since an unscrupulous party could manufacture evidence and submit it as an original or hide the original and fabricate secondary evidence.[105] The best evidence rule is also unnecessary where the honesty of the party introducing the document is not in question. In such a situation, the rule could actually exclude legitimately relevant evidence. One commentator pointed out the significant costs of this rule:

> While the rule ostensibly protects against fraud and inaccuracy, it has been blindly applied as a technical hurdle that must be overcome if documentary evidence is to be admitted, despite the fact that fraud or inaccuracy are but minute possibilities in the particular case....Thus, exclusion may be required under the rule even though the party opposing the document has had adequate opportunity to scrutinize the original writing....[106]

The Commission also noted that the rule may be costly in a more basic way—the parties may have to waste time tracking down original documents when secondary evidence would be easier to obtain and submit. It found that a simplified rule that emphasized substance over form would help eliminate unnecessary disputes and occasional injustice.[107]

The Commission also found that the rule is no longer needed to minimize the misinterpretation of writings. The theory went that the intent of the drafter of the document would be easier to determine from an original than by examining a copy. However, since the parties are now able to examine originals through the discovery process, there is no need to require the admission of the original in court.[108] The Commission noted that "it is now so routine that litigants are almost always quite familiar with the critical documents by the time of trial." [109]

Although noting that discovery in criminal cases had been greatly expanded since the adoption of the best evidence rule, the Commission stated that an exception needed to be made for criminal cases where discovery is not as broad as it is in civil cases.

Thus, if a party wanted to introduce secondary evidence of a document's contents in a criminal case, it would have to make the original available if it was still in its possession.[110]

In 1996, the California Law Revision Committee recommended that the state abandon the best evidence rule and in its place adopt a simplified form of the rule that would generally allow for the admission of secondary evidence to prove the contents of a writing. Under the new rule, the content of a writing could be proved by either admission of an original document or by secondary evidence.[111] Secondary evidence would still be excluded if a genuine dispute existed about the authenticity of the original or admission of such

evidence would be unfair. Oral testimony would also be inadmissible to prove content, except in circumstances where it is currently permitted under the best evidence rule.[112]

California adopted the recommendations of the Commission in 1999. It repealed the best evidence rule and instead adopted the simpler Secondary Evidence Rule.[113] The new rule allows for the contents of an original writing to be proven through the admission of the original or by secondary evidence in most circumstances. Copies and other secondary evidence are admissible in place of the original as long as there is no dispute as to their genuineness or their admission would be unfair.[114]

CHAPTER SUMMARY

Before they can be admitted, physical evidence, documentary evidence, and demonstrative exhibits need to be authenticated. A party authenticates evidence by proving the evidence is what that party says it is. This can be done in a number of ways, most commonly through testimony by someone with personal knowledge of the evidence. Many records are also considered to be self-authenticating under the rules. Business records can now be admitted through a certification by the records custodian that the record is kept in the regular course of business and was made at or near the time of the event.

There are special considerations for authenticating documents stored in electronic format such as e-mails or Web page content. The proponent of the evidence may also have to establish how the digital files were created and stored and attest that the storage and retrieval system is reliable. Since digital files are easily modified, there is some real concern that digital documents may be altered more easily

than hard-copy originals. However, most courts have admitted electronic documents unless there has been a showing of actual alteration.

Photographs are authenticated by having a witness attest that the photograph is a fair and accurate depiction of the scene it shows. This can be done by anyone with personal knowledge of the scene at the time the photograph was taken. Despite concerns that digital images could be easily modified or altered, they are usually authenticated in a similar manner. If the images have been substantially altered or modified, then testimony about the process used to modify or alter the original should be given as well.

The best evidence rule applies to the admission of the contents of all writings. The rule requires that the original or a reliable copy be produced if it can be obtained. Secondary evidence such as testimony about the contents can be admitted only where the party cannot reasonably obtain the original.

KEY TERMS

- Authentication
- Automated remote camera
- Best evidence rule
- Computer-generated animations
- Demonstrative evidence

- Digital photographs
- Document
- Duplicate
- Electronically stored information
- Materially altered photos

- Original
- Primary evidence
- Secondary evidence
- Self-authenticating documents

REVIEW QUESTIONS

1. What does it mean to authenticate an exhibit? Why is authentication necessary?

2. Name three ways in which an exhibit can be authenticated.

3. Why are some records self-authenticating? Name three types of self-authenticating records.

4. How are photographs authenticated? Does the person who took the photographs have to authenticate them? Explain.

5. Are digital photographs authenticated differently? Why not?

6. Name three suggestions for ensuring that the chain of custody is maintained for digital photographs.

7. What is a computer-generated animation? What must be shown in order for one to be admissible?

8. What is the best evidence rule? Why was it originally created, and do those justifications for its creation still exist today? Explain.

9. What is an original under the best evidence rule? What is a writing? What types of new technologies are covered under the best evidence rule?

10. Are copies admissible under the best evidence rule? When are they not admissible?

11. What is secondary evidence? Give two examples of secondary evidence. When is it usable to prove the contents of a writing?

12. When is oral testimony allowed to prove the contents of a writing? What must be shown to admit oral testimony about a writing?

APPLICATION PROBLEMS

1. Lois is on trial for murder. The victim was having an affair with her husband. The prosecutor wants to introduce evidence that Lois sent e-mails to the victim threatening her that if she doesn't leave her husband alone, she will kill her. How must the prosecutor authenticate the e-mails?

2. Jim is accused of sexual assault. The victim was attacked along a wooded path. She suffered severe bruises and scrapes on her back during the attack. The prosecutor wants to admit digital photographs of the location of the attack and the wounds to the victim's body. What foundation does the prosecutor have to lay to authenticate

the photos before they can be admitted? Would this foundation be different if the photos were taken on film?

3. Bruce is accused of embezzling from the local children's museum where he works. The prosecutor wants to introduce several business records and computer printouts from the museum's payroll and accounting software system. What foundation does the prosecutor have to lay to authenticate the exhibits?

4. Axel is being tried for fraud. Axel allegedly agreed to a contract to fix a woman's roof, charged her $5,000, and merely pretended to fix the roof. The prosecutor claims that the contract Axel signed is evidence of the fraud. The victim

no longer has a copy of the contract. The district attorney wants to introduce the woman's testimony as proof of the contract. Can he do so under the best evidence rule? Explain.

5. Bill is accused of murdering his wife. He took out a life insurance policy on his wife in the amount of $500,000 two months prior to her death. The prosecution claims he made it look like an accident. The prosecutor asked for a copy of the policy in discovery but the defendant refused to provide it. The prosecutor therefore wants to call an insurance agent for the company to testify to the policy and the amount. Should the trial judge allow the oral testimony about the policy? Explain.

Notes

1. F.R.E. 901(a).
2. F.R.E. 901(b).
3. Lorraine v. Markel American Ins. Co., 241 F.R.D. 534 (D. Md. 2007).
4. Deborah R. Eltgroth, Note: *Best Evidence and the Wayback Machine*, 78 Fordham L. Rev. 181, 187 (2009).
5. Steven E. Bizar, *The Foundations of Foundations: Admission of Documentary Exhibits Into Evidence at Trial,* Upon Further Review, December 5, 2008, available at http://uponfurtherreview.philadelphiabar.org/page/Article?articleID=847acebe-8a27-4064-9161-3fbbf12e69ae.
6. F.R.E. 902.
7. F.R.E. 902(11).
8. Lorraine, 241 F.R.D. at 544.
9. Colin Miller, *Even Better Than the Real Thing: How Courts Have Been Anything But Liberal in Finding Genuine Questions Raised as to the Authenticity of Originals Under Rule 1003*, 68 Md. Law Rev. 160, 207, *quoting* Claudia Dreifus, *A Conversation with Hany Farid: Proving That Seeing Shouldn't Always Be Believing*, N.Y. Times, October 2, 2007 at F2.
10. St. Clair v. Johnny's Oyster & Shrimp, Inc., 76 F. Supp. 2d 773, 774-75 (S.D. Tex. 1999).
11. Lorraine, 241 F.R.D. at 544.
12. Id.
13. Miller, *supra* note 9, at 208, *quoting* Department of Justice Computer Crime and Intellectual Property Section, Federal Guidelines for Searching and Seizing Computers 119 (July 1994), available at http://epic.org/security/computer_search_guidelines.txt.
14. Lorraine, 241 F.R.D. at 546.
15. Id. at 554.
16. *See* United States v. Jackson, 208 F.3d 633, 638 (7th Cir. 2000).
17. Washington v. State, 961 A.2d 1110 (Md. 2008).
18. Renzi v. Paredes, 890 N.E.2d 806, 817 (Mass. 2008); State v. Dawara, 2006 WL 3782964, slip op. at 5 (N.J. App. 2006) (unpublished decision).
19. F.R.E. 901.
20. Dawara, 2006 WL 3782964, slip op. at 5.
21. Renzi, 890 N.E.2d at 817.
22. Lorraine, 241 F.R.D. at 559.
23. Edward J. Imwinkelried, *Can this Photo Be Trusted?* Trial at 49 (October 2005).
24. Lorraine, 241 F.R.D. at 560.
25. United States v. Seifert, 351 F. Supp. 2d 926 (D. Minn. 2005).
26. Id. at 928.
27. Imwinkelried, *supra* note 23, at 54.
28. State v. Swinton, 847 A.2d 921, 950-52 (Conn. 2004).
29. Swinton, 847 A.2d at 951-52.
30. Renzi, 890 N.E.2d at 817.
31. Dawara, 2006 WL 3782964, slip op. at 6.
32. Erik C. Berg, Legal Ramifications of Digital Imaging in Law Enforcement, October 2000.
33. George Reis, *Admissibility in Court*, Evidence Technology Magazine at 23 (September-October 2004).
34. Id. at 22.
35. Id.
36. Washington, 961 A.2d at 1115.
37. Id. at 1116.
38. Taylor v. United States, 530 F.2d 639, 640 (5th Cir. 1976).
39. Washington, 961 A.2d at 1117.
40. Commonwealth v. Serge, 898 A.2d 1170 (Pa. 2006).
41. Id. at 1179.
42. Id. at 1181.
43. Id. at 1182.
44. R. Bennett, Jr., J. Leibman, & R. Fetter, *Seeing Is Believing; or Is It? An Empirical Study of Computer Simulations as Evidence*, 34 Wake Forest L. Rev. 257, 285 (1999).

45. Serge, 898 A.2d at 1183.
46. Id. at 1186.
47. F.R.E. 1002.
48. California Law Revision Commission, *Best Evidence Rule*, at 373 (November 1996), available at http://www.clrc.ca.gov/pub/Printed-Reports/REC-BestEvidenceRule.pdf.
49. Seiler v. Lucasfilm, 797 F.2d 1504 (9th Cir. 1986).
50. Miller, *supra* note 9, at 165-66.
51. Seiler, 797 F.2d at 1507.
52. United States v. Bennett, 363 F.3d 947, 953 (9th Cir. 2004).
53. Boroughf v. Bank of America, 159 S.W.3d 498, 503 (Mo. App. 2005).
54. State v. Clark, 377 S.E.2d 54, 60 (N.C. 1989).
55. State v. Hortman, 365 S.E.2d 887, 889 (Ga. App. 1988).
56. Bennett, 363 F.3d at 953.
57. F.R.E. 1002, advisory committee comm.
58. Bennett, 363 F.3d at 1507.
59. Schozer v. William Penn Life Ins. Co., 644 N.E.2d 1353, 1356 (N.Y. 1994).
60. F.R.E. 1001(1).
61. F.R.E. 1001(3).
62. Id.
63. Lorraine, 241 F.R.D. at 577-78.
64. Miller, *supra* note 9, at 171.
65. Laughner v. State, 769 N.E.2d 1147, 1159 (Ind. App. 2002).
66. Midkiff v. Commonwealth, 678 S.E.2d 287 (Vir. App. 2009).
67. California Law Revision Comm., *supra* note 49 at 375, *quoting* Taylor, *The Case for Secondary Evidence*, Case & Comment 46, 48 (January-February 1976).
68. California Law Revision Comm., *supra* at 375-76.
69. F.R.E. 1001(4).
70. Miller, *supra* note 9, at 171.
71. Cunningham v. Tracy, 1 Conn. 252 (Conn. 1814).
72. F.R.E. 1003.
73. Lorraine, 241 F.R.D. at 576.
74. F.R.E. 1003.
75. Carroll v. Leboeuf, Lamb, Greene, & Macrae, 614 F. Supp. 2d 481 (S.D. N.Y. 2009), *quoting* 6 Joseph M. McLaughlin, *Weinstein's Federal Evidence* § 103.03[4].
76. Miller, *supra* note 9, at 172-73.
77. John Beaudette, Inc. v. Sentry Insurance, 94 F. Supp. 2d 77, 138 (D. Mass. 1999).
78. Miller, *supra* note 9, at 187.
79. *See, e.g.*, S.E.C. v. Hughes Capital Corp., 124 F.3d 449, 456 (3d Cir. 1997) (duplicate checks stubs were not admissible where proponent admitted to altering original stubs before photocopying them).
80. Carroll, 614 F. Supp. 2d at 485.
81. Miller, *supra* note 9 at 212, *citing* Christopher B. Mueller & Laird C. Kirkpatrick, *Evidence* sec. 10.8 (1995).
82. *See* F.R.E. 1003, Advisory Committee's Note.
83. United States v. Moore, 710 F.2d 157 (4th Cir. 1983).
84. F.R.E. 1004.
85. Lorraine, 241 F.R.D. at 576.
86. Miller, *supra* note 9, at 175.
87. Id.
88. Boroughf, 159 S.W.3d at 503.
89. United States v. Codrington, 2009 WL 1766001 (E.D. N.Y. 2009) (unpublished decision).
90. 2 McCormick on Evidence § 237 (6th ed. 2006).
91. Medina v. Multaler, Inc., 2007 WL 5124009, slip op. at 3 (C.D. Cal. 2007) (unpublished decision).
92. Id., *citing* United States ex rel. Magid v. Wilderman, 2004 WL 1987219 (E.D. Pa. 2004) (unpublished decision).
93. Allegra v. Bowen, 670 F. Supp., 465 (E.D. N.Y. 1987).
94. Medina, 2007 WL 5124009, slip op. at 5.
95. *See* Cartier v. Jackson, 59 F.3d 1046 (10th Cir. 1995).
96. United States v. Cuesta, 2007 WL 2729853 at 20 (E.D. Cal. 2007) (unpublished decision).
97. Schozer v. William Penn Life Ins. Co., 644 N.E.2d 1353 (N.Y. 1994).
98. In re Oakley, 397 B.R. 36 (S.D. Ohio Bankr. 2008).
99. State v. Halcomb, 676 S.E.2d 149 (S.C. App. 2009).
100. F.R.E. 1005.
101. F.R.E. 1006.
102. Miller, *supra* note 9, at 179.
103. California Law Rev. Comm., *supra* note 49 at 373.
104. Id. at 389.
105. Id. at 379.
106. Kenneth Broun, *Authentication and Contents of Writings*, 1969 Law & Soc. Order 611-12.
107. California Law Rev. Comm., *supra* note 49 at 388.
108. Id. at 381.
109. Id. at 382.
110. Id. at 384.
111. Cal. Evid. Code § 1520-21.
112. California Law Rev. Comm., *supra* note 49 at 377.
113. *See* Cal. Evid. Code §§ 1520-1523.
114. Cal. Evid. Code § 1521.

Federal Rules of Evidence

Effective July 1, 1975, as amended to December 1, 2009

ARTICLE I. **GENERAL PROVISIONS**

Rule 101. Scope

These rules govern proceedings in the courts of the United States and before the United States bankruptcy judges and United States magistrate judges, to the extent and with the exceptions stated in rule 1101. (As amended Mar. 2, 1987, eff. Oct. 1, 1987; Apr. 25, 1988, eff. Nov. 1, 1988; Apr. 22, 1993, eff. Dec. 1, 1993.)

Rule 102. Purpose and Construction

These rules shall be construed to secure fairness in administration, elimination of unjustifiable expense and delay, and promotion of growth and development of the law of evidence to the end that the truth may be ascertained and proceedings justly determined.

Rule 103. Rulings on Evidence

(a) Effect of erroneous ruling.—Error may not be predicated upon a ruling which admits or excludes evidence unless a substantial right of the party is affected, and

> **(1) Objection.**—In case the ruling is one admitting evidence, a timely objection or motion to strike appears of record, stating the specific ground of objection, if the specific ground was not apparent from the context; or

(2) Offer of proof.—In case the ruling is one excluding evidence, the substance of the evidence was made known to the court by offer or was apparent from the context within which questions were asked.

Once the court makes a definitive ruling on the record admitting or excluding evidence, either at or before trial, a party need not renew an objection or offer of proof to preserve a claim of error for appeal.

(b) Record of offer and ruling.—The court may add any other or further statement which shows the character of the evidence, the form in which it was offered, the objection made, and the ruling thereon. It may direct the making of an offer in question and answer form.

(c) Hearing of jury.—In jury cases, proceedings shall be conducted, to the extent practicable, so as to prevent inadmissible evidence from being suggested to the jury by any means, such as making statements or offers of proof or asking questions in the hearing of the jury.

(d) Plain error.—Nothing in this rule precludes taking notice of plain errors affecting substantial rights although they were not brought to the attention of the court.

(As amended Apr. 17, 2000, eff. Dec. 1, 2000.)

Rule 104. Preliminary Questions

(a) Questions of admissibility generally.—Preliminary questions concerning the qualification of a person to be a witness, the existence of a privilege, or the admissibility of evidence shall be determined by the court, subject to the provisions of subdivision (b). In making its determination it is not bound by the rules of evidence except those with respect to privileges.

(b) Relevancy conditioned on fact.—When the relevancy of evidence depends upon the fulfillment of a condition of fact, the court shall admit it upon, or subject to, the introduction of evidence sufficient to support a finding of the fulfillment of the condition.

(c) Hearing of jury.—Hearings on the admissibility of confessions shall in all cases be conducted out of the hearing of the jury. Hearings on other preliminary matters shall be so conducted when the interests of justice require, or when an accused is a witness and so requests.

(d) Testimony by accused.—The accused does not, by testifying upon a preliminary matter, become subject to cross-examination as to other issues in the case.

(e) Weight and credibility.—This rule does not limit the right of a party to introduce before the jury evidence relevant to weight or credibility.
(As amended Mar. 2, 1987, eff. Oct. 1, 1987.)

Rule 105. Limited Admissibility

When evidence which is admissible as to one party or for one purpose but not admissible as to another party or for another purpose is admitted, the court, upon request, shall restrict the evidence to its proper scope and instruct the jury accordingly.

Rule 106. Remainder of or Related Writings or Recorded Statements

When a writing or recorded statement or part thereof is introduced by a party, an adverse party may require the introduction at that time of any other part or any other writing or recorded statement which ought in fairness to be considered contemporaneously with it.
(As amended Mar. 2, 1987, eff. Oct. 1, 1987.)

ARTICLE II.   JUDICIAL NOTICE

Rule 201. Judicial Notice of Adjudicative Facts

(a) Scope of rule.—This rule governs only judicial notice of adjudicative facts.

(b) Kinds of facts.—A judicially noticed fact must be one not subject to reasonable dispute in that it is either (1) generally known within the territorial jurisdiction of the trial court or (2) capable of accurate and ready determination by resort to sources whose accuracy cannot reasonably be questioned.

(c) When discretionary.—A court may take judicial notice, whether requested or not.

(d) When mandatory.—A court shall take judicial notice if requested by a party and supplied with the necessary information.

(e) Opportunity to be heard.—A party is entitled upon timely request to an opportunity to be heard as to the propriety of taking judicial notice and the tenor of the matter noticed. In the absence of prior notification, the request may be made after judicial notice has been taken.

(f) Time of taking notice.—Judicial notice may be taken at any stage of the proceeding.

(g) Instructing jury.—In a civil action or proceeding, the court shall instruct the jury to accept as conclusive any fact judicially noticed. In a criminal case, the court shall instruct the jury that it may, but is not required to, accept as conclusive any fact judicially noticed.

ARTICLE III. PRESUMPTIONS IN CIVIL ACTIONS AND PROCEEDINGS

Rule 301. Presumptions in General in Civil Actions and Proceedings

In all civil actions and proceedings not otherwise provided for by Act of Congress or by these rules, a presumption imposes on the party against whom it is directed the burden of going forward with evidence to rebut or meet the presumption, but does not shift to such party the burden of proof in the sense of the risk of nonpersuasion, which remains throughout the trial upon the party on whom it was originally cast.

Rule 302. Applicability of State Law in Civil Actions and Proceedings

In civil actions and proceedings, the effect of a presumption respecting a fact which is an element of a claim or defense as to which State law supplies the rule of decision is determined in accordance with State law.

ARTICLE IV. RELEVANCY AND ITS LIMITS

Rule 401. Definition of "Relevant Evidence"

"Relevant evidence" means evidence having any tendency to make the existence of any fact that is of consequence to the determination of the action more probable or less probable than it would be without the evidence.

Rule 402. Relevant Evidence Generally Admissible; Irrelevant Evidence Inadmissible

All relevant evidence is admissible, except as otherwise provided by the Constitution of the United States, by Act of Congress, by these rules, or by other rules prescribed by the Supreme Court pursuant to statutory authority. Evidence which is not relevant is not admissible.

Rule 403. Exclusion of Relevant Evidence on Grounds of Prejudice, Confusion, or Waste of Time

Although relevant, evidence may be excluded if its probative value is substantially outweighed by the danger of unfair prejudice, confusion of the issues, or misleading the jury, or by considerations of undue delay, waste of time, or needless presentation of cumulative evidence.

Rule 404. Character Evidence Not Admissible to Prove Conduct; Exceptions; Other Crimes

(a) Character evidence generally.—Evidence of a person's character or a trait of character is not admissible for the purpose of proving action in conformity therewith on a particular occasion, except:

> **(1) Character of accused.**—In a criminal case, evidence of a pertinent trait of character offered by an accused, or by the prosecution to rebut the same, or if evidence of a trait of character of the alleged victim of the crime is offered by an accused and admitted under Rule 404(a)(2), evidence of the same trait of character of the accused offered by the prosecution;

> **(2) Character of alleged victim.**—In a criminal case, and subject to the limitations imposed by Rule 412, evidence of a pertinent trait of character of the alleged victim of the crime offered by an accused, or by the prosecution to rebut the same, or evidence of a character trait of peacefulness of the alleged victim offered by the prosecution in a homicide case to rebut evidence that the alleged victim was the first aggressor;

> **(3) Character of witness.**—Evidence of the character of a witness, as provided in Rules 607, 608, and 609.

(b) Other crimes, wrongs, or acts.—Evidence of other crimes, wrongs, or acts is not admissible to prove the character of a person in order to show action in conformity therewith. It may, however, be admissible for other purposes, such as proof of motive, opportunity, intent, preparation, plan, knowledge, identity, or absence of mistake or accident, provided that upon request by the accused, the prosecution in a criminal case shall provide reasonable notice in advance of trial, or during trial if the court excuses pretrial notice on good cause shown, of the general nature of any such evidence it intends to introduce at trial.

(As amended Mar. 2, 1987, eff. Oct. 1, 1987; Apr. 30, 1991, eff. Dec. 1, 1991; Apr. 17, 2000, eff. Dec. 1, 2000; Apr. 12, 2006, eff. Dec. 1, 2006.)

Rule 405. Methods of Proving Character

(a) Reputation or opinion.—In all cases in which evidence of character or a trait of character of a person is admissible, proof may be made by testimony as to reputation or by testimony in the form of an opinion. On cross-examination, inquiry is allowable into relevant specific instances of conduct.

(b) Specific instances of conduct.—In cases in which character or a trait of character of a person is an essential element of a charge, claim, or defense, proof may also be made of specific instances of that person's conduct.
(As amended Mar. 2, 1987, eff. Oct. 1, 1987.)

Rule 406. Habit; Routine Practice

Evidence of the habit of a person or of the routine practice of an organization, whether corroborated or not and regardless of the presence of eyewitnesses, is relevant to prove that the conduct of the person or organization on a particular occasion was in conformity with the habit or routine practice.

Rule 407. Subsequent Remedial Measures

When, after an injury or harm allegedly caused by an event, measures are taken that, if taken previously, would have made the injury or harm less likely to occur, evidence of the subsequent measures is not admissible to prove negligence, culpable conduct, a defect in a product, a defect in a product's design, or a need for a warning or instruction. This rule does not require the exclusion of evidence of subsequent measures when offered for another purpose, such as proving ownership, control, or feasibility of precautionary measures, if controverted, or impeachment.
(As amended Apr. 11, 1997, eff. Dec. 1, 1997.)

Rule 408. Compromise and Offers to Compromise

(a) Prohibited uses.—Evidence of the following is not admissible on behalf of any party, when offered to prove liability for, invalidity of, or amount of a claim that was disputed as to validity or amount, or to impeach through a prior inconsistent statement or contradiction:

(1) furnishing or offering or promising to furnish—or accepting or offering or promising to accept—a valuable consideration in compromising or attempting to compromise the claim; and

(2) conduct or statements made in compromise negotiations regarding the claim, except when offered in a criminal case and the negotiations related to a claim by a public office or agency in the exercise of regulatory, investigative, or enforcement authority.

(b) Permitted uses.—This rule does not require exclusion if the evidence is offered for purposes not prohibited by subdivision (a). Examples of permissible purposes include proving a witness's bias or prejudice; negating a contention of undue delay; and proving an effort to obstruct a criminal investigation or prosecution.
(As amended Apr. 12, 2006, eff. Dec. 1, 2006.)

Rule 409. Payment of Medical and Similar Expenses

Evidence of furnishing or offering or promising to pay medical, hospital, or similar expenses occasioned by an injury is not admissible to prove liability for the injury.

Rule 410. Inadmissibility of Pleas, Plea Discussions, and Related Statements

Except as otherwise provided in this rule, evidence of the following is not, in any civil or criminal proceeding, admissible against the defendant who made the plea or was a participant in the plea discussions:

(1) a plea of guilty which was later withdrawn;

(2) a plea of nolo contendere;

(3) any statement made in the course of any proceedings under Rule 11 of the Federal Rules of Criminal Procedure or comparable state procedure regarding either of the foregoing pleas; or

(4) any statement made in the course of plea discussions with an attorney for the prosecuting authority which do not result in a plea of guilty or which result in a plea of guilty later withdrawn.

However, such a statement is admissible (i) in any proceeding wherein another statement made in the course of the same plea or plea discussions has been introduced and the statement ought in fairness be considered

contemporaneously with it, or (ii) in a criminal proceeding for perjury or false statement if the statement was made by the defendant under oath, on the record and in the presence of counsel.
(As amended Dec. 12, 1975; Apr. 30, 1979, eff. Dec. 1, 1980.)

Rule 411. Liability Insurance

Evidence that a person was or was not insured against liability is not admissible upon the issue whether the person acted negligently or otherwise wrongfully. This rule does not require the exclusion of evidence of insurance against liability when offered for another purpose, such as proof of agency, ownership, or control, or bias or prejudice of a witness.
(As amended Mar. 2, 1987, eff. Oct. 1, 1987.)

Rule 412. Sex Offense Cases; Relevance of Alleged Victim's Past Sexual Behavior or Alleged Sexual Predisposition

(a) **Evidence Generally Inadmissible.**—The following evidence is not admissible in any civil or criminal proceeding involving alleged sexual misconduct except as provided in subdivisions (b) and (c):

(1) Evidence offered to prove that any alleged victim engaged in other sexual behavior.

(2) Evidence offered to prove any alleged victim's sexual predisposition.

(b) **Exceptions.**

(1) In a criminal case, the following evidence is admissible, if otherwise admissible under these rules:

(A) evidence of specific instances of sexual behavior by the alleged victim offered to prove that a person other than the accused was the source of semen, injury or other physical evidence;

(B) evidence of specific instances of sexual behavior by the alleged victim with respect to the person accused of the sexual misconduct offered by the accused to prove consent or by the prosecution; and

(C) evidence the exclusion of which would violate the constitutional rights of the defendant.

(2) In a civil case, evidence offered to prove the sexual behavior or sexual predisposition of any alleged victim is admissible if it is otherwise admissible under these rules and its probative value substantially outweighs the danger of harm to any victim and of unfair prejudice to any party. Evidence of an alleged victim's reputation is admissible only if it has been placed in controversy by the alleged victim.

(c) Procedure To Determine Admissibility.

(1) A party intending to offer evidence under subdivision (b) must—

(A) file a written motion at least 14 days before trial specifically describing the evidence and stating the purpose for which it is offered unless the court, for good cause requires a different time for filing or permits filing during trial; and

(B) serve the motion on all parties and notify the alleged victim or, when appropriate, the alleged victim's guardian or representative.

(2) Before admitting evidence under this rule the court must conduct a hearing in camera and afford the victim and parties a right to attend and be heard. The motion, related papers, and the record of the hearing must be sealed and remain under seal unless the court orders otherwise.

(As added Oct. 28, 1978, eff. Nov. 28, 1978; amended Nov. 18, 1988; Apr. 29, 1994, eff. Dec. 1, 1994; Sept. 13, 1994, eff. Dec. 1, 1994.)

Rule 413. Evidence of Similar Crimes in Sexual Assault Cases

(a) In a criminal case in which the defendant is accused of an offense of sexual assault, evidence of the defendant's commission of another offense or offenses of sexual assault is admissible, and may be considered for its bearing on any matter to which it is relevant.

(b) In a case in which the Government intends to offer evidence under this rule, the attorney for the Government shall disclose the evidence to the defendant, including statements of witnesses or a summary of the substance of any testimony that is expected to be offered, at least fifteen days before the scheduled date of trial or at such later time as the court may allow for good cause.

(c) This rule shall not be construed to limit the admission or consideration of evidence under any other rule.

(d) For purposes of this rule and Rule 415, "offense of sexual assault" means a crime under Federal law or the law of a State (as defined in section 513 of title 18, United States Code) that involved—

(1) any conduct proscribed by chapter 109A of title 18, United States Code;

(2) contact, without consent, between any part of the defendant's body or an object and the genitals or anus of another person;

(3) contact, without consent, between the genitals or anus of the defendant and any part of another person's body;

(4) deriving sexual pleasure or gratification from the infliction of death, bodily injury, or physical pain on another person; or

(5) an attempt or conspiracy to engage in conduct described in paragraphs (1)–(4).
(Added Sept. 13, 1994, eff. July 9, 1995.)

Rule 414. Evidence of Similar Crimes in Child Molestation Cases

(a) In a criminal case in which the defendant is accused of an offense of child molestation, evidence of the defendant's commission of another offense or offenses of child molestation is admissible, and may be considered for its bearing on any matter to which it is relevant.

(b) In a case in which the Government intends to offer evidence under this rule, the attorney for the Government shall disclose the evidence to the defendant, including statements of witnesses or a summary of the substance of any testimony that is expected to be offered, at least fifteen days before the scheduled date of trial or at such later time as the court may allow for good cause.

(c) This rule shall not be construed to limit the admission or consideration of evidence under any other rule.

(d) For purposes of this rule and Rule 415, "child" means a person below the age of fourteen, and "offense of child molestation" means a crime under Federal law or the law of a State (as defined in section 513 of title 18, United States Code) that involved—

(1) any conduct proscribed by chapter 109A of title 18, United States Code, that was committed in relation to a child;

(2) any conduct proscribed by chapter 110 of title 18, United States Code;

(3) contact between any part of the defendant's body or an object and the genitals or anus of a child;

(4) contact between the genitals or anus of the defendant and any part of the body of a child;

(5) deriving sexual pleasure or gratification from the infliction of death, bodily injury, or physical pain on a child; or

(6) an attempt or conspiracy to engage in conduct described in paragraphs (1)–(5).
(Added Sept. 13, 1994, eff. July 9, 1995.)

Rule 415. Evidence of Similar Acts in Civil Cases Concerning Sexual Assault or Child Molestation

(a) In a civil case in which a claim for damages or other relief is predicated on a party's alleged commission of conduct constituting an offense of sexual assault or child molestation, evidence of that party's commission of another offense or offenses of sexual assault or child molestation is admissible and may be considered as provided in Rule 413 and Rule 414 of these rules.

(b) A party who intends to offer evidence under this Rule shall disclose the evidence to the party against whom it will be offered, including statements of witnesses or a summary of the substance of any testimony that is expected to be offered, at least fifteen days before the scheduled date of trial or at such later time as the court may allow for good cause.

(c) This rule shall not be construed to limit the admission or consideration of evidence under any other rule.
(Added Sept. 13, 1994, eff. July 9, 1995.)

ARTICLE V.   PRIVILEGES

Rule 501. General Rule

Except as otherwise required by the Constitution of the United States or provided by Act of Congress or in rules prescribed by the Supreme Court pursuant to statutory authority, the privilege of a witness, person, government, State, or political subdivision thereof shall be governed by the principles of the common law as they may be interpreted by the courts of the United States in the light of reason and experience. However, in civil actions and proceedings, with respect to an element of a claim or defense as to which State law supplies the rule of decision, the privilege of a witness, person, government, State, or political subdivision thereof shall be determined in accordance with State law.

Rule 502. Attorney-Client Privilege and Work Product; Limitations on Waiver

The following provisions apply, in the circumstances set out, to disclosure of a communication or information covered by the attorney-client privilege or work-product protection.

(a) Disclosure made in a Federal proceeding or to a Federal office or agency; scope of a waiver.—When the disclosure is made in a Federal proceeding or to a Federal office or agency and waives the attorney-client privilege or work-product protection, the waiver extends to an undisclosed communication or information in a Federal or State proceeding only if:

(1) the waiver is intentional;

(2) the disclosed and undisclosed communications or information concern the same subject matter; and

(3) they ought in fairness to be considered together.

(b) Inadvertent disclosure.—When made in a Federal proceeding or to a Federal office or agency, the disclosure does not operate as a waiver in a Federal or State proceeding if:

(1) the disclosure is inadvertent;

(2) the holder of the privilege or protection took reasonable steps to prevent disclosure; and

(3) the holder promptly took reasonable steps to rectify the error, including (if applicable) following Federal Rule of Civil Procedure 26(b)(5)(B).

(c) Disclosure made in a State proceeding.—When the disclosure is made in a State proceeding and is not the subject of a State court order concerning waiver, the disclosure does not operate as a waiver in a Federal proceeding if the disclosure:

(1) would not be a waiver under this rule if it had been made in a Federal proceeding; or

(2) is not a waiver under the law of the State where the disclosure occurred.

(d) Controlling effect of a court order.—A Federal court may order that the privilege or protection is not waived by disclosure connected with the litigation pending before the court—in which event the disclosure is also not a waiver in any other Federal or State proceeding.

(e) Controlling effect of a party agreement.—An agreement on the effect of disclosure in a Federal proceeding is binding only on the parties to the agreement, unless it is incorporated into a court order.

(f) Controlling effect of this rule.—Notwithstanding Rules 101 and 1101, this rule applies to State proceedings and to Federal court-annexed and Federal court-mandated arbitration proceedings, in the circumstances set out in the rule. And notwithstanding Rule 501, this rule applies even if State law provides the rule of decision.

(g) Definitions.—In this rule:

(1) "attorney-client privilege" means the protection that applicable law provides for confidential attorney-client communications; and

(2) "work-product protection" means the protection that applicable law provides for tangible material (or its intangible equivalent) prepared in anticipation of litigation or for trial.
(As added Sept. 19, 2008.)

ARTICLE VI.   WITNESSES

Rule 601. General Rule of Competency

Every person is competent to be a witness except as otherwise provided in these rules. However, in civil actions and proceedings, with respect to an element of a claim or defense as to which State law supplies the rule of decision, the competency of a witness shall be determined in accordance with State law.

Rule 602. Lack of Personal Knowledge

A witness may not testify to a matter unless evidence is introduced sufficient to support a finding that the witness has personal knowledge of the matter. Evidence to prove personal knowledge may, but need not, consist of the witness' own testimony. This rule is subject to the provisions of rule 703, relating to opinion testimony by expert witnesses.

   (As amended Mar. 2, 1987, eff. Oct. 1, 1987; Apr. 25, 1988, eff. Nov. 1, 1988.)

Rule 603. Oath or Affirmation

Before testifying, every witness shall be required to declare that the witness will testify truthfully, by oath or affirmation administered in a form calculated to awaken the witness' conscience and impress the witness' mind with the duty to do so.

   (As amended Mar. 2, 1987, eff. Oct. 1, 1987.)

Rule 604. Interpreters

An interpreter is subject to the provisions of these rules relating to qualification as an expert and the administration of an oath or affirmation to make a true translation.

   (As amended Mar. 2, 1987, eff. Oct. 1, 1987.)

Rule 605. Competency of Judge as Witness

The judge presiding at the trial may not testify in that trial as a witness. No objection need be made in order to preserve the point.

Rule 606. Competency of Juror as Witness

(a) At the trial.—A member of the jury may not testify as a witness before that jury in the trial of the case in which the juror is sitting. If the juror is called so to testify, the opposing party shall be afforded an opportunity to object out of the presence of the jury.

(b) Inquiry into validity of verdict or indictment.—Upon an inquiry into the validity of a verdict or indictment, a juror may not testify as to any matter or statement occurring during the course of the jury's deliberations or to the effect of anything upon that or any other juror's mind or emotions as influencing the juror to assent to or dissent from the verdict or indictment or concerning the juror's mental processes in connection therewith. But a juror may testify about (1) whether extraneous prejudicial information was improperly brought to the jury's attention, (2) whether any outside influence was improperly brought to bear upon any juror, or (3) whether there was a mistake in entering the verdict onto the verdict form. A juror's affidavit or evidence of any statement by the juror may not be received on a matter about which the juror would be precluded from testifying.

(As amended Dec. 12, 1975; Mar. 2, 1987, eff. Oct. 1, 1987; Apr. 12, 2006, eff. Dec. 1, 2006.)

Rule 607. Who May Impeach

The credibility of a witness may be attacked by any party, including the party calling the witness.

(As amended Mar. 2, 1987, eff. Oct. 1, 1987.)

Rule 608. Evidence of Character and Conduct of Witness

(a) Opinion and reputation evidence of character.—The credibility of a witness may be attacked or supported by evidence in the form of opinion or reputation, but subject to these limitations: (1) the evidence may refer only to character for truthfulness or untruthfulness, and (2) evidence of truthful character is admissible only after the character of the witness for truthfulness has been attacked by opinion or reputation evidence or otherwise.

(b) Specific instances of conduct.—Specific instances of the conduct of a witness, for the purpose of attacking or supporting the witness' character for truthfulness, other than conviction of crime as provided in rule 609, may not be proved by extrinsic evidence. They may, however, in the discretion of the court, if probative of truthfulness or untruthfulness, be inquired into on cross-examination of the witness (1) concerning the witness' character for truthfulness or untruthfulness, or (2) concerning the character for truthfulness or untruthfulness of another witness as to which character the witness being cross-examined has testified.

The giving of testimony, whether by an accused or by any other witness, does not operate as a waiver of the accused's or the witness' privilege against self-incrimination when examined with respect to matters that relate only to character for truthfulness.

(As amended Mar. 2, 1987, eff. Oct. 1, 1987; Apr. 25, 1988, eff. Nov. 1, 1988; Mar. 27, 2003, eff. Dec. 1, 2003.)

Rule 609. Impeachment by Evidence of Conviction of Crime

(a) General rule.—For the purpose of attacking the character for truthfulness of a witness,

> (1) evidence that a witness other than an accused has been convicted of a crime shall be admitted, subject to Rule 403, if the crime was punishable by death or imprisonment in excess of one year under the law under which the witness was convicted, and evidence that an accused has been convicted of such a crime shall be admitted if the court determines that the probative value of admitting this evidence outweighs its prejudicial effect to the accused; and

> (2) evidence that any witness has been convicted of a crime shall be admitted regardless of the punishment, if it readily can be determined that establishing the elements of the crime required proof or admission of an act of dishonesty or false statement by the witness.

(b) Time limit.—Evidence of a conviction under this rule is not admissible if a period of more than ten years has elapsed since the date of the conviction or of the release of the witness from the confinement imposed for that conviction, whichever is the later date, unless the court determines, in the interests of justice, that the probative value of the conviction supported by specific facts and circumstances substantially outweighs its prejudicial effect. However, evidence of a conviction more than 10 years old as calculated herein, is not admissible unless the proponent gives to the adverse party sufficient advance written notice of intent to use such evidence to provide the adverse party with a fair opportunity to contest the use of such evidence.

(c) Effect of pardon, annulment, or certificate of rehabilitation.— Evidence of a conviction is not admissible under this rule if (1) the conviction has been the subject of a pardon, annulment, certificate of rehabilitation, or other equivalent procedure based on a finding of the rehabilitation of the person convicted, and that person has not been convicted of a subsequent crime that was punishable by death or imprisonment in excess of one year, or (2) the conviction has been the subject of a pardon, annulment, or other equivalent procedure based on a finding of innocence.

(d) Juvenile adjudications.—Evidence of juvenile adjudications is generally not admissible under this rule. The court may, however, in a criminal case allow evidence of a juvenile adjudication of a witness other than the accused if conviction of the offense would be admissible to attack the credibility of an adult and the court is satisfied that admission in evidence is necessary for a fair determination of the issue of guilt or innocence.

(e) Pendency of appeal.—The pendency of an appeal therefrom does not render evidence of a conviction inadmissible. Evidence of the pendency of an appeal is admissible.

    (As amended Mar. 2, 1987, eff. Oct. 1, 1987; Jan. 26, 1990, eff. Dec. 1, 1990; Apr. 12, 2006, eff. Dec. 1, 2006.)

Rule 610. Religious Beliefs or Opinions

Evidence of the beliefs or opinions of a witness on matters of religion is not admissible for the purpose of showing that by reason of their nature the witness' credibility is impaired or enhanced.

    (As amended Mar. 2, 1987, eff. Oct. 1, 1987.)

Rule 611. Mode and Order of Interrogation and Presentation

(a) Control by court.—The court shall exercise reasonable control over the mode and order of interrogating witnesses and presenting evidence so as to (1) make the interrogation and presentation effective for the ascertainment of the truth, (2) avoid needless consumption of time, and (3) protect witnesses from harassment or undue embarrassment.

(b) Scope of cross-examination.—Cross-examination should be limited to the subject matter of the direct examination and matters affecting the credibility of the witness. The court may, in the exercise of discretion, permit inquiry into additional matters as if on direct examination.

(c) Leading questions.—Leading questions should not be used on the direct examination of a witness except as may be necessary to develop the witness' testimony. Ordinarily leading questions should be permitted on cross-examination. When a party calls a hostile witness, an adverse party, or a witness identified with an adverse party, interrogation may be by leading questions.

    (As amended Mar. 2, 1987, eff. Oct. 1, 1987.)

Rule 612. Writing Used To Refresh Memory

Except as otherwise provided in criminal proceedings by section 3500 of title 18, United States Code, if a witness uses a writing to refresh memory for the purpose of testifying, either—

    (1) while testifying, or

    (2) before testifying, if the court in its discretion determines it is necessary in the interests of justice, an adverse party is entitled to have

the writing produced at the hearing, to inspect it, to cross-examine the witness thereon, and to introduce in evidence those portions which relate to the testimony of the witness. If it is claimed that the writing contains matters not related to the subject matter of the testimony the court shall examine the writing in camera, excise any portions not so related, and order delivery of the remainder to the party entitled thereto. Any portion withheld over objections shall be preserved and made available to the appellate court in the event of an appeal. If a writing is not produced or delivered pursuant to order under this rule, the court shall make any order justice requires, except that in criminal cases when the prosecution elects not to comply, the order shall be one striking the testimony or, if the court in its discretion determines that the interests of justice so require, declaring a mistrial.

(As amended Mar. 2, 1987, eff. Oct. 1, 1987.)

Rule 613. Prior Statements of Witnesses

(a) Examining witness concerning prior statement.—In examining a witness concerning a prior statement made by the witness, whether written or not, the statement need not be shown nor its contents disclosed to the witness at that time, but on request the same shall be shown or disclosed to opposing counsel.

(b) Extrinsic evidence of prior inconsistent statement of witness.—Extrinsic evidence of a prior inconsistent statement by a witness is not admissible unless the witness is afforded an opportunity to explain or deny the same and the opposite party is afforded an opportunity to interrogate the witness thereon, or the interests of justice otherwise require. This provision does not apply to admissions of a party-opponent as defined in rule 801(d)(2).

(As amended Mar. 2, 1987, eff. Oct. 1, 1987; Apr. 25, 1988, eff. Nov. 1, 1988.)

Rule 614. Calling and Interrogation of Witnesses by Court

(a) Calling by court.—The court may, on its own motion or at the suggestion of a party, call witnesses, and all parties are entitled to cross-examine witnesses thus called.

(b) Interrogation by court.—The court may interrogate witnesses, whether called by itself or by a party.

(c) Objections.—Objections to the calling of witnesses by the court or to interrogation by it may be made at the time or at the next available opportunity when the jury is not present.

Rule 615. Exclusion of Witnesses

At the request of a party the court shall order witnesses excluded so that they cannot hear the testimony of other witnesses, and it may make the order of its own motion. This rule does not authorize exclusion of (1) a party who is a natural person, or (2) an officer or employee of a party which is not a natural person designated as its representative by its attorney, or (3) a person whose presence is shown by a party to be essential to the presentation of the party's cause, or (4) a person authorized by statute to be present.

    (As amended Mar. 2, 1987, eff. Oct. 1, 1987; Apr. 25, 1988, eff. Nov. 1, 1988; Nov. 18, 1988; Apr. 24, 1998, eff. Dec. 1, 1998.)

ARTICLE VII. OPINIONS AND EXPERT TESTIMONY

Rule 701. Opinion Testimony by Lay Witnesses

If the witness is not testifying as an expert, the witness' testimony in the form of opinions or inferences is limited to those opinions or inferences which are (a) rationally based on the perception of the witness, and (b) helpful to a clear understanding of the witness' testimony or the determination of a fact in issue, and (c) not based on scientific, technical, or other specialized knowledge within the scope of Rule 702.

    (As amended Mar. 2, 1987, eff. Oct. 1, 1987; Apr. 17, 2000, eff. Dec. 1, 2000.)

Rule 702. Testimony by Experts

If scientific, technical, or other specialized knowledge will assist the trier of fact to understand the evidence or to determine a fact in issue, a witness qualified as an expert by knowledge, skill, experience, training, or education, may testify thereto in the form of an opinion or otherwise, if (1) the testimony is based upon sufficient facts or data, (2) the testimony is the product of reliable principles and methods, and (3) the witness has applied the principles and methods reliably to the facts of the case.

    (As amended Apr. 17, 2000, eff. Dec. 1, 2000.)

Rule 703. Bases of Opinion Testimony by Experts

The facts or data in the particular case upon which an expert bases an opinion or inference may be those perceived by or made known to the expert at or before the hearing. If of a type reasonably relied upon by experts in the particular field in forming opinions or inferences upon the subject, the facts or data need not be admissible in evidence in order for the opinion or inference to be admitted. Facts or data that are otherwise inadmissible shall not be disclosed to the jury by the proponent of the opinion or inference unless the court determines that their probative value in assisting the jury to evaluate the expert's opinion substantially outweighs their prejudicial effect.

(As amended Mar. 2, 1987, eff. Oct. 1, 1987; Apr. 17, 2000, eff. Dec. 1, 2000.)

Rule 704. Opinion on Ultimate Issue

(a) Except as provided in subdivision (b), testimony in the form of an opinion or inference otherwise admissible is not objectionable because it embraces an ultimate issue to be decided by the trier of fact.

(b) No expert witness testifying with respect to the mental state or condition of a defendant in a criminal case may state an opinion or inference as to whether the defendant did or did not have the mental state or condition constituting an element of the crime charged or of a defense thereto. Such ultimate issues are matters for the trier of fact alone.

(As amended Oct. 12, 1984.)

Rule 705. Disclosure of Facts or Data Underlying Expert Opinion

The expert may testify in terms of opinion or inference and give reasons therefor without first testifying to the underlying facts or data, unless the court requires otherwise. The expert may in any event be required to disclose the underlying facts or data on cross-examination.

(As amended Mar. 2, 1987, eff. Oct. 1, 1987; Apr. 22, 1993, eff. Dec. 1, 1993.)

Rule 706. Court Appointed Experts

(a) **Appointment.**—The court may on its own motion or on the motion of any party enter an order to show cause why expert witnesses should not be appointed, and may request the parties to submit nominations. The court may appoint any expert witnesses agreed upon by the parties, and may appoint expert witnesses of its own selection. An expert witness shall not be appointed by the court unless the witness consents to act. A witness so appointed shall be informed of the witness' duties by the court in writing, a copy of which shall be filed with the clerk, or at a conference in which the parties shall have opportunity to participate. A witness so appointed shall advise the parties of the witness' findings, if any; the witness' deposition may be taken by any party; and the witness may be called to testify by the court or any party. The witness shall be subject to cross-examination by each party, including a party calling the witness.

(b) Compensation.—Expert witnesses so appointed are entitled to reasonable compensation in whatever sum the court may allow. The compensation thus fixed is payable from funds which may be provided by law in criminal cases and civil actions and proceedings involving just compensation under the fifth amendment. In other civil actions and proceedings the compensation shall be paid by the parties in such proportion and at such time as the court directs, and thereafter charged in like manner as other costs.

(c) Disclosure of appointment.—In the exercise of its discretion, the court may authorize disclosure to the jury of the fact that the court appointed the expert witness.

(d) Parties' experts of own selection.—Nothing in this rule limits the parties in calling expert witnesses of their own selection.
(As amended Mar. 2, 1987, eff. Oct. 1, 1987.)

ARTICLE VIII.   HEARSAY

Rule 801. Definitions

The following definitions apply under this article:

(a) Statement.—A "statement" is (1) an oral or written assertion or (2) nonverbal conduct of a person, if it is intended by the person as an assertion.

(b) Declarant.—A "declarant" is a person who makes a statement.

(c) Hearsay.—"Hearsay" is a statement, other than one made by the declarant while testifying at the trial or hearing, offered in evidence to prove the truth of the matter asserted.

(d) Statements which are not hearsay.—A statement is not hearsay if—

(1) Prior statement by witness.—The declarant testifies at the trial or hearing and is subject to cross-examination concerning the statement, and the statement is (A) inconsistent with the declarant's testimony, and was given under oath subject to the penalty of perjury at a trial, hearing, or other proceeding, or in a deposition, or (B) consistent with the declarant's testimony and is offered to rebut an express or implied charge against the declarant of recent fabrication or improper influence or motive, or (C) one of identification of a person made after perceiving the person; or

(2) Admission by party-opponent.—The statement is offered against a party and is (A) the party's own statement, in either an individual or a representative capacity or (B) a statement of which the party has manifested an adoption or belief in its truth, or (C) a statement by a person authorized by the party to make a statement concerning the subject, or (D) a statement by the party's agent or servant concerning a matter within the scope of the agency or employment, made during the existence of the relationship, or (E) a statement by a coconspirator of a party during the course and in furtherance of the conspiracy. The contents of the statement shall be considered but are not alone sufficient to establish the declarant's authority under subdivision (C), the agency or employment relationship and scope thereof under subdivision (D), or the existence of the conspiracy and the participation therein of the declarant and the party against whom the statement is offered under subdivision (E).

(As amended Oct. 16, 1975, eff. Oct. 31, 1975; Mar. 2, 1987, eff. Oct. 1, 1987; Apr. 11, 1997, eff. Dec. 1, 1997.)

Rule 802. Hearsay Rule

Hearsay is not admissible except as provided by these rules or by other rules prescribed by the Supreme Court pursuant to statutory authority or by Act of Congress.

Rule 803. Hearsay Exceptions; Availability of Declarant Immaterial

The following are not excluded by the hearsay rule, even though the declarant is available as a witness:

(1) Present sense impression.—A statement describing or explaining an event or condition made while the declarant was perceiving the event or condition, or immediately thereafter.

(2) Excited utterance.—A statement relating to a startling event or condition made while the declarant was under the stress of excitement caused by the event or condition.

(3) Then existing mental, emotional, or physical condition.—A statement of the declarant's then existing state of mind, emotion, sensation, or physical condition (such as intent, plan, motive, design, mental feeling, pain, and bodily health), but not including a statement of memory or belief to prove the fact remembered or believed unless it relates to the execution, revocation, identification, or terms of declarant's will.

(4) Statements for purposes of medical diagnosis or treatment.— Statements made for purposes of medical diagnosis or treatment and describing medical history, or past or present symptoms, pain, or sensations, or the inception or general character of the cause or external source thereof insofar as reasonably pertinent to diagnosis or treatment.

(5) Recorded recollection.—A memorandum or record concerning a matter about which a witness once had knowledge but now has insufficient recollection to enable the witness to testify fully and accurately, shown to have been made or adopted by the witness when the matter was fresh in the witness' memory and to reflect that knowledge correctly. If admitted, the memorandum or record may be read into evidence but may not itself be received as an exhibit unless offered by an adverse party.

(6) Records of regularly conducted activity.—A memorandum, report, record, or data compilation, in any form, of acts, events, conditions, opinions, or diagnoses, made at or near the time by, or from information transmitted by, a person with knowledge, if kept in the course of a regularly conducted business activity, and if it was the regular practice of that business activity to make the memorandum, report, record or data compilation, all as shown by the testimony of the custodian or other qualified witness, or by certification that complies with Rule 902(11), Rule 902(12), or a statute permitting certification, unless the source of information or the method or circumstances of preparation indicate lack of trustworthiness. The term "business" as used in this paragraph includes business, institution, association, profession, occupation, and calling of every kind, whether or not conducted for profit.

(7) Absence of entry in records kept in accordance with the provisions of paragraph (6).—Evidence that a matter is not included in the memoranda reports, records, or data compilations, in any form, kept in accordance with the provisions of paragraph (6), to prove the nonoccurrence or nonexistence of the matter, if the matter was of a kind of which a memorandum, report, record, or data compilation was regularly made and preserved, unless the sources of information or other circumstances indicate lack of trustworthiness.

(8) Public records and reports.—Records, reports, statements, or data compilations, in any form, of public offices or agencies, setting forth (A) the activities of the office or agency, or (B) matters observed pursuant to duty imposed by law as to which matters there was a duty to report, excluding, however, in criminal cases matters observed by police officers and other law enforcement personnel, or (C) in civil actions and proceedings and against the Government in criminal cases, factual findings resulting from an investigation made pursuant to authority granted by law, unless the sources of information or other circumstances indicate lack of trustworthiness.

(9) Records of vital statistics.—Records or data compilations, in any form, of births, fetal deaths, deaths, or marriages, if the report thereof was made to a public office pursuant to requirements of law.

(10) Absence of public record or entry.—To prove the absence of a record, report, statement, or data compilation, in any form, or the nonoccurrence or nonexistence of a matter of which a record, report, statement, or data compilation, in any form, was regularly made and preserved by a public office or agency, evidence in the form of a certification in accordance with rule 902, or testimony, that diligent search failed to disclose the record, report, statement, or data compilation, or entry.

(11) Records of religious organizations.—Statements of births, marriages, divorces, deaths, legitimacy, ancestry, relationship by blood or marriage, or other similar facts of personal or family history, contained in a regularly kept record of a religious organization.

(12) Marriage, baptismal, and similar certificates.—Statements of fact contained in a certificate that the maker performed a marriage or other ceremony or administered a sacrament, made by a clergyman, public official, or other person authorized by the rules or practices of a religious organization or by law to perform the act certified, and purporting to have been issued at the time of the act or within a reasonable time thereafter.

(13) Family records.—Statements of fact concerning personal or family history contained in family Bibles, genealogies, charts, engravings on rings, inscriptions on family portraits, engravings on urns, crypts, or tombstones, or the like.

(14) Records of documents affecting an interest in property.—The record of a document purporting to establish or affect an interest in property, as proof of the content of the original recorded document and its execution and delivery by each person by whom it purports to have been executed, if the record is a record of a public office and an applicable statute authorizes the recording of documents of that kind in that office.

(15) Statements in documents affecting an interest in property.—A statement contained in a document purporting to establish or affect an interest in property if the matter stated was relevant to the purpose of the document, unless dealings with the property since the document was made have been inconsistent with the truth of the statement or the purport of the document.

(16) Statements in ancient documents.—Statements in a document in existence twenty years or more the authenticity of which is established.

(17) Market reports, commercial publications.—Market quotations, tabulations, lists, directories, or other published compilations, generally used and relied upon by the public or by persons in particular occupations.

(18) Learned treatises.—To the extent called to the attention of an expert witness upon cross-examination or relied upon by the expert witness in direct examination, statements contained in published treatises, periodicals, or pamphlets on a subject of history, medicine, or other science or art, established as a reliable authority by the testimony or admission of the witness or by other expert testimony or by judicial notice. If admitted, the statements may be read into evidence but may not be received as exhibits.

(19) Reputation concerning personal or family history.—Reputation among members of a person's family by blood, adoption, or marriage, or among a person's associates, or in the community, concerning a person's birth, adoption, marriage, divorce, death, legitimacy, relationship by blood, adoption, or marriage, ancestry, or other similar fact of personal or family history.

(20) Reputation concerning boundaries or general history.— Reputation in a community, arising before the controversy, as to boundaries of or customs affecting lands in the community, and reputation as to events of general history important to the community or State or nation in which located.

(21) Reputation as to character.—Reputation of a person's character among associates or in the community.

(22) Judgment of previous conviction.—Evidence of a final judgment, entered after a trial or upon a plea of guilty (but not upon a plea of nolo contendere), adjudging a person guilty of a crime punishable by death or imprisonment in excess of one year, to prove any fact essential to sustain the judgment, but not including, when offered by the Government in a criminal prosecution for purposes other than impeachment, judgments against persons other than the accused. The pendency of an appeal may be shown but does not affect admissibility.

(23) Judgment as to personal, family, or general history, or boundaries.—Judgments as proof of matters of personal, family or general history, or boundaries, essential to the judgment, if the same would be provable by evidence of reputation.

(24) [Other exceptions.] [Transferred to Rule 807]
    (As amended Dec. 12, 1975; Mar. 2, 1987, eff. Oct. 1, 1987; Apr. 11, 1997, eff. Dec. 1, 1997; Apr. 17, 2000, eff. Dec. 1, 2000.)

Rule 804. Hearsay Exceptions; Declarant Unavailable

(a) Definition of unavailability.—"Unavailability as a witness" includes situations in which the declarant—

(1) is exempted by ruling of the court on the ground of privilege from testifying concerning the subject matter of the declarant's statement; or

(2) persists in refusing to testify concerning the subject matter of the declarant's statement despite an order of the court to do so; or

(3) testifies to a lack of memory of the subject matter of the declarant's statement; or

(4) is unable to be present or to testify at the hearing because of death or then existing physical or mental illness or infirmity; or

(5) is absent from the hearing and the proponent of a statement has been unable to procure the declarant's attendance (or in the case of a hearsay exception under subdivision (b)(2), (3), or (4), the declarant's attendance or testimony) by process or other reasonable means. A declarant is not unavailable as a witness if exemption, refusal, claim of lack of memory, inability, or absence is due to the procurement or wrongdoing of the proponent of a statement for the purpose of preventing the witness from attending or testifying.

(b) Hearsay exceptions.—The following are not excluded by the hearsay rule if the declarant is unavailable as a witness:

(1) Former testimony.—Testimony given as a witness at another hearing of the same or a different proceeding, or in a deposition taken in compliance with law in the course of the same or another proceeding, if the party against whom the testimony is now offered, or, in a civil action or proceeding, a predecessor in interest, had an opportunity and similar motive to develop the testimony by direct, cross, or redirect examination.

(2) Statement under belief of impending death.—In a prosecution for homicide or in a civil action or proceeding, a statement made by a declarant while believing that the declarant's death was imminent, concerning the cause or circumstances of what the declarant believed to be impending death.

(3) Statement against interest.—A statement which was at the time of its making so far contrary to the declarant's pecuniary or proprietary interest, or so far tended to subject the declarant to civil or criminal liability, or to render invalid a claim by the declarant against another, that a reasonable person in the declarant's position would not have made the statement unless believing it to be true. A statement tending to expose the declarant to criminal liability and offered to exculpate the accused is not admissible unless corroborating circumstances clearly indicate the trustworthiness of the statement.

(4) Statement of personal or family history.—(A) A statement concerning the declarant's own birth, adoption, marriage, divorce, legitimacy, relationship by blood, adoption, or marriage, ancestry, or other similar fact of personal or family history, even though declarant had no means of acquiring personal knowledge of the matter stated; or (B) a statement concerning the foregoing matters, and death also, of another person, if the declarant was related to the other by blood, adoption, or marriage or was so intimately associated with the other's family as to be likely to have accurate information concerning the matter declared.

(5) [Other exceptions.] [Transferred to Rule 807]

(6) Forfeiture by wrongdoing.—A statement offered against a party that has engaged or acquiesced in wrongdoing that was intended to, and did, procure the unavailability of the declarant as a witness.

(As amended Dec. 12, 1975; Mar. 2, 1987, eff. Oct. 1, 1987; Nov. 18, 1988; Apr. 11, 1997, eff. Dec. 1, 1997.)

Rule 805. Hearsay Within Hearsay

Hearsay included within hearsay is not excluded under the hearsay rule if each part of the combined statements conforms with an exception to the hearsay rule provided in these rules.

Rule 806. Attacking and Supporting Credibility of Declarant

When a hearsay statement, or a statement defined in Rule 801(d)(2) (C), (D), or (E), has been admitted in evidence, the credibility of the declarant may be attacked, and if attacked may be supported, by any evidence which would be admissible for those purposes if declarant had testified as a witness. Evidence of a statement or conduct by the declarant at any time, inconsistent with the declarant's hearsay statement, is not subject to any requirement that the declarant may have been afforded an opportunity to deny or explain. If the party against whom a hearsay statement has been admitted calls the declarant as a witness, the party is entitled to examine the declarant on the statement as if under cross-examination.

 (As amended Mar. 2, 1987, eff. Oct. 1, 1987; Apr. 11, 1997, eff. Dec. 1, 1997.)

Rule 807. Residual Exception

A statement not specifically covered by Rule 803 or 804 but having equivalent circumstantial guarantees of trustworthiness, is not excluded by the hearsay rule, if the court determines that (A) the statement is offered as evidence of a material fact; (B) the statement is more probative on the point for which it is offered than any other evidence which the proponent can procure through reasonable efforts; and (C) the general purposes of these rules and the interests of justice will best be served by admission of the statement into evidence. However, a statement may not be admitted under this exception unless the proponent of it makes known to the adverse party sufficiently in advance of the trial or hearing to provide the adverse party with a fair opportunity to prepare to meet it, the proponent's intention to offer the statement and the particulars of it, including the name and address of the declarant.

 (Added Apr. 11, 1997, eff. Dec. 1, 1997.)

ARTICLE IX.   AUTHENTICATION AND IDENTIFICATION

Rule 901. Requirement of Authentication or Identification

(a) General provision.—The requirement of authentication or identification as a condition precedent to admissibility is satisfied by evidence sufficient to support a finding that the matter in question is what its proponent claims.

(b) Illustrations.—By way of illustration only, and not by way of limitation, the following are examples of authentication or identification conforming with the requirements of this rule:

(1) Testimony of witness with knowledge.—Testimony that a matter is what it is claimed to be.

(2) Nonexpert opinion on handwriting.—Nonexpert opinion as to the genuineness of handwriting, based upon familiarity not acquired for purposes of the litigation.

(3) Comparison by trier or expert witness.—Comparison by the trier of fact or by expert witnesses with specimens which have been authenticated.

(4) Distinctive characteristics and the like.—Appearance, contents, substance, internal patterns, or other distinctive characteristics, taken in conjunction with circumstances.

(5) Voice identification.—Identification of a voice, whether heard firsthand or through mechanical or electronic transmission or recording, by opinion based upon hearing the voice at any time under circumstances connecting it with the alleged speaker.

(6) Telephone conversations.—Telephone conversations, by evidence that a call was made to the number assigned at the time by the telephone company to a particular person or business, if (A) in the case of a person, circumstances, including self-identification, show the person answering to be the one called, or (B) in the case of a business, the call was made to a place of business and the conversation related to business reasonably transacted over the telephone.

(7) Public records or reports.—Evidence that a writing authorized by law to be recorded or filed and in fact recorded or filed in a public office, or a purported public record, report, statement, or data compilation, in any form, is from the public office where items of this nature are kept.

(8) Ancient documents or data compilation.—Evidence that a document or data compilation, in any form, (A) is in such condition as to create no suspicion concerning its authenticity, (B) was in a place where it, if authentic, would likely be, and (C) has been in existence 20 years or more at the time it is offered.

(9) Process or system.—Evidence describing a process or system used to produce a result and showing that the process or system produces an accurate result.

(10) Methods provided by statute or rule.—Any method of authentication or identification provided by Act of Congress or by other rules prescribed by the Supreme Court pursuant to statutory authority.

Rule 902. Self-authentication

Extrinsic evidence of authenticity as a condition precedent to admissibility is not required with respect to the following:

(1) Domestic public documents under seal.—A document bearing a seal purporting to be that of the United States, or of any State, district, Commonwealth, territory, or insular possession thereof, or the Panama Canal Zone, or the Trust Territory of the Pacific Islands, or of a political subdivision, department, officer, or agency thereof, and a signature purporting to be an attestation or execution.

(2) Domestic public documents not under seal.—A document purporting to bear the signature in the official capacity of an officer or employee of any entity included in paragraph (1) hereof, having no seal, if a public officer having a seal and having official duties in the district or political subdivision of the officer or employee certifies under seal that the signer has the official capacity and that the signature is genuine.

(3) Foreign public documents.—A document purporting to be executed or attested in an official capacity by a person authorized by the laws of a foreign country to make the execution or attestation, and accompanied by a final certification as to the genuineness of the signature and official position (A) of the executing or attesting person, or (B) of any foreign official whose certificate of genuineness of signature and official position relates to the execution or attestation or is in a chain of certificates of genuineness of signature and official position relating to the execution or attestation. A final certification may be made by a secretary of an embassy or legation, consul general, consul, vice consul, or consular agent of the United States, or a diplomatic or consular official of the foreign country assigned or accredited to the United States. If reasonable opportunity has been given to all parties to investigate the authenticity and accuracy of official documents, the court may, for good cause shown, order that they be treated as presumptively authentic without final certification or permit them to be evidenced by an attested summary with or without final certification.

(4) Certified copies of public records.—A copy of an official record or report or entry therein, or of a document authorized by law to be recorded or filed and actually recorded or filed in a public office, including data compilations in any form, certified as correct by the custodian or other person authorized to make the certification, by certificate complying with paragraph (1), (2), or (3) of this rule or complying with any Act of Congress or rule prescribed by the Supreme Court pursuant to statutory authority.

(5) Official publications.—Books, pamphlets, or other publications purporting to be issued by public authority.

(6) Newspapers and periodicals.—Printed materials purporting to be newspapers or periodicals.

(7) Trade inscriptions and the like.—Inscriptions, signs, tags, or labels purporting to have been affixed in the course of business and indicating ownership, control, or origin.

(8) Acknowledged documents.—Documents accompanied by a certificate of acknowledgment executed in the manner provided by law by a notary public or other officer authorized by law to take acknowledgments.

(9) Commercial paper and related documents.—Commercial paper, signatures thereon, and documents relating thereto to the extent provided by general commercial law.

(10) Presumptions under Acts of Congress.—Any signature, document, or other matter declared by Act of Congress to be presumptively or prima facie genuine or authentic.

(11) Certified domestic records of regularly conducted activity.— The original or a duplicate of a domestic record of regularly conducted activity that would be admissible under Rule 803(6) if accompanied by a written declaration of its custodian or other qualified person, in a manner complying with any Act of Congress or rule prescribed by the Supreme Court pursuant to statutory authority, certifying that the record—

(A) was made at or near the time of the occurrence of the matters set forth by, or from information transmitted by, a person with knowledge of those matters;

(B) was kept in the course of the regularly conducted activity; and

(C) was made by the regularly conducted activity as a regular practice. A party intending to offer a record into evidence under this paragraph must provide written notice of that intention to all adverse parties, and must make the record and declaration available for inspection sufficiently in advance of their offer into evidence to provide an adverse party with a fair opportunity to challenge them.

(12) Certified foreign records of regularly conducted activity.—In a civil case, the original or a duplicate of a foreign record of regularly conducted activity that would be admissible under Rule 803(6) if accompanied by a written declaration by its custodian or other qualified person certifying that the record—

(A) was made at or near the time of the occurrence of the matters set forth by, or from information transmitted by, a person with knowledge of those matters;

(B) was kept in the course of the regularly conducted activity; and

(C) was made by the regularly conducted activity as a regular practice. The declaration must be signed in a manner that, if falsely made, would subject the maker to criminal penalty under the laws of the country where the declaration is signed. A party intending to offer a record into evidence under this paragraph must provide written notice of that intention to all adverse parties, and must make the record and declaration available for inspection sufficiently in advance of their offer into evidence to provide an adverse party with a fair opportunity to challenge them.

(As amended Mar. 2, 1987, eff. Oct. 1, 1987; Apr. 25, 1988, eff. Nov. 1, 1988; Apr. 17, 2000, eff. Dec. 1, 2000.)

Rule 903. Subscribing Witness' Testimony Unnecessary

The testimony of a subscribing witness is not necessary to authenticate a writing unless required by the laws of the jurisdiction whose laws govern the validity of the writing.

ARTICLE X.   **CONTENTS OF WRITINGS, RECORDINGS, AND PHOTOGRAPHS**

Rule 1001. Definitions

For purposes of this article the following definitions are applicable:

(1) Writings and recordings.—"Writings" and "recordings" consist of letters, words, or numbers, or their equivalent, set down by handwriting, typewriting, printing, photostating, photographing, magnetic impulse, mechanical or electronic recording, or other form of data compilation.

(2) Photographs.—"Photographs" include still photographs, X-ray films, video tapes, and motion pictures.

(3) Original.—An "original" of a writing or recording is the writing or recording itself or any counterpart intended to have the same effect by a person executing or issuing it. An "original" of a photograph includes the negative or any print therefrom. If data are stored in a computer or similar device, any printout or other output readable by sight, shown to reflect the data accurately, is an "original".

(4) Duplicate.—A "duplicate" is a counterpart produced by the same impression as the original, or from the same matrix, or by means of photography, including enlargements and miniatures, or by mechanical or electronic re-recording, or by chemical reproduction, or by other equivalent techniques which accurately reproduces the original.

Rule 1002. Requirement of Original

To prove the content of a writing, recording, or photograph, the original writing, recording, or photograph is required, except as otherwise provided in these rules or by Act of Congress.

Rule 1003. Admissibility of Duplicates

A duplicate is admissible to the same extent as an original unless

(1) a genuine question is raised as to the authenticity of the original or

(2) in the circumstances it would be unfair to admit the duplicate in lieu of the original.

Rule 1004. Admissibility of Other Evidence of Contents

The original is not required, and other evidence of the contents of a writing, recording, or photograph is admissible if—

(1) Originals lost or destroyed.—All originals are lost or have been destroyed, unless the proponent lost or destroyed them in bad faith; or

(2) Original not obtainable.—No original can be obtained by any available judicial process or procedure; or

(3) Original in possession of opponent.—At a time when an original was under the control of the party against whom offered, that party was put on notice, by the pleadings or otherwise, that the contents would be a subject of proof at the hearing, and that party does not produce the original at the hearing; or

(4) Collateral matters.—The writing, recording, or photograph is not closely related to a controlling issue.
(As amended Mar. 2, 1987, eff. Oct. 1, 1987.)

Rule 1005. Public Records

The contents of an official record, or of a document authorized to be recorded or filed and actually recorded or filed, including data compilations in any form, if otherwise admissible, may be proved by copy, certified as correct in accordance with rule 902 or testified to be correct by a witness who has compared it with the original. If a copy which complies with the foregoing cannot be obtained by the exercise of reasonable diligence, then other evidence of the contents may be given.

Rule 1006. Summaries

The contents of voluminous writings, recordings, or photographs which cannot conveniently be examined in court may be presented in the form of a chart, summary, or calculation. The originals, or duplicates, shall be made available for examination or copying, or both, by other parties at reasonable time and place. The court may order that they be produced in court.

Rule 1007. Testimony or Written Admission of Party

Contents of writings, recordings, or photographs may be proved by the testimony or deposition of the party against whom offered or by that party's written admission, without accounting for the nonproduction of the original.

(As amended Mar. 2, 1987, eff. Oct. 1, 1987.)

Rule 1008. Functions of Court and Jury

When the admissibility of other evidence of contents of writings, recordings, or photographs under these rules depends upon the fulfillment of a condition of fact, the question whether the condition has been fulfilled is ordinarily for the court to determine in accordance with the provisions of rule 104. However, when an issue is raised (a) whether the asserted writing ever existed, or (b) whether another writing, recording, or photograph produced at the trial is the original, or (c) whether other evidence of contents correctly reflects the contents, the issue is for the trier of fact to determine as in the case of other issues of fact.

ARTICLE XI. MISCELLANEOUS RULES

Rule 1101. Applicability of Rules

(a) Courts and judges.—These rules apply to the United States district courts, the District Court of Guam, the District Court of the Virgin Islands, the District Court for the Northern Mariana Islands, the United States courts of appeals, the United States Claims Court, 1 and to United States bankruptcy judges and United States magistrate judges, in the actions, cases, and proceedings and to the extent hereinafter set forth. The terms "judge" and "court" in these rules include United States bankruptcy judges and United States magistrate judges.

(b) Proceedings generally.—These rules apply generally to civil actions and proceedings, including admiralty and maritime cases, to criminal cases and proceedings, to contempt proceedings except those in which the court may act summarily, and to proceedings and cases under title 11, United States Code.

(c) Rule of privilege.—The rule with respect to privileges applies at all stages of all actions, cases, and proceedings.

(d) Rules inapplicable.—The rules (other than with respect to privileges) do not apply in the following situations:

(1) Preliminary questions of fact.—The determination of questions of fact preliminary to admissibility of evidence when the issue is to be determined by the court under rule 104.

(2) Grand jury.—Proceedings before grand juries.

(3) Miscellaneous proceedings.—Proceedings for extradition or rendition; preliminary examinations in criminal cases; sentencing, or granting or revoking probation; issuance of warrants for arrest, criminal summonses, and search warrants; and proceedings with respect to release on bail or otherwise.

(e) Rules applicable in part.—In the following proceedings these rules apply to the extent that matters of evidence are not provided for in the statutes which govern procedure therein or in other rules prescribed by the Supreme Court pursuant to statutory authority: the trial of misdemeanors and other petty offenses before United States magistrate judges; review of agency actions when the facts are subject to trial de novo under section 706(2)(F) of title 5, United States Code; review of orders of the Secretary of Agriculture under section 2 of the Act entitled "An Act to authorize association of producers of agricultural products" approved February 18, 1922 (7 U.S.C. 292), and under sections 6 and 7(c) of the Perishable Agricultural Commodities Act, 1930 (7 U.S.C. 499f, 499g(c)); naturalization and revocation of naturalization under sections 310–318 of the Immigration and Nationality Act (8 U.S.C. 1421–1429); prize proceedings in admiralty under sections 7651–7681 of title 10, United States Code; review of orders of the Secretary of the Interior under section 2 of the Act entitled "An Act authorizing associations of producers of aquatic products" approved June 25, 1934 (15 U.S.C. 522); review of orders of petroleum control boards under section 5 of the Act entitled "An Act to regulate interstate and foreign commerce in petroleum and its products by prohibiting the shipment in such commerce of petroleum and its products produced in violation of State law, and for other purposes", approved February 22, 1935 (15 U.S.C. 715d); actions for fines, penalties, or forfeitures under part V of title IV of the Tariff Act of 1930 (19 U.S.C. 1581–1624), or under the Anti-Smuggling Act (19 U.S.C. 1701–1711); criminal libel for condemnation, exclusion of imports, or other proceedings under the Federal Food, Drug, and Cosmetic Act (21 U.S.C. 301–392); disputes between seamen under sections 4079, 4080, and 4081 of the Revised Statutes (22 U.S.C. 256–258); habeas corpus under sections 2241–2254 of title 28, United States Code; motions to vacate, set aside or correct sentence under section 2255 of title 28, United States Code; actions for penalties for refusal to transport destitute seamen under section 4578 of the Revised Statutes (46 U.S.C. 679); 2 actions against the United States under the Act entitled "An Act authorizing suits against the United States in admiralty for damage caused by and salvage service rendered to public vessels belonging to the United States, and for other purposes", approved March 3, 1925 (46 U.S.C. 781–790), as implemented by section 7730 of title 10, United States Code.

(As amended Dec. 12, 1975; Nov. 6, 1978, eff. Oct. 1, 1979; Apr. 2, 1982, eff. Oct. 1, 1982; Mar. 2, 1987, eff. Oct. 1, 1987; Apr. 25, 1988, eff. Nov. 1, 1988; Nov. 18, 1988; Apr. 22, 1993, eff. Dec. 1, 1993.)

Rule 1102. Amendments

Amendments to the Federal Rules of Evidence may be made as provided in section 2072 of title 28 of the United States Code.
(As amended Apr. 30, 1991, eff. Dec. 1, 1991.)

Rule 1103. Title

These rules may be known and cited as the Federal Rules of Evidence

Table of Cases

Glossary

Absence of mistake or accident: an independent purpose listed under Rule 404(b) that allows for the introduction of character evidence where it is relevant to proving that the defendant's criminal conduct was not an accident or mistake.

Admissible: quality of evidence that permits it to be entered into trial record and considered by the fact finder at a trial. It includes any evidence that can be lawfully admitted in court to prove the guilt or innocence of the defendant.

Admissible evidence: anything that can be lawfully admitted in court to prove the guilt or innocence of the defendant.

Admission: a statement made by a suspect that connects him to the offense.

Admission of a party opponent: an exemption to the hearsay rule. It is a statement made by the party it is offered against; it does not have to be an incriminating statement in order to fall under the exemption.

Affirmative defense: a defense that seeks to justify, excuse, or mitigate the commission of an offense. Insanity and self-defense are examples of affirmative defenses.

Alibi witness: a witness who provides testimony about a defendant's alibi.

Alternate light source: a light that uses wavelengths other than white light, such as ultraviolet or infrared, to detect the presence of trace evidence.

Appellant: the party who files the appeal.

Appellee: the party who responds to an appeal.

Arraignment: the initial step in the court process in which the defendant is advised of the charges against him and asked to enter a plea.

Assertion: the words, writings, or conduct of a person made with the intent of expressing a fact or opinion.

Attenuation: an exception to the exclusionary rule that provides that discovery of evidence that is so far removed or attenuated from an earlier illegal seizure of evidence is admissible.

Attorney/client privilege: a privilege that protects the disclosure of confidential information to an attorney for the purpose of seeking legal advice.

Authentication: a party offering a piece of evidence must authenticate it, usually by showing that the evidence is what the party says it is.

Automated remote camera: an automatically operated camera such as a security camera that does not use a photographer. The silent witness method must be used to authenticate photographs taken by a remote camera. Under the silent witness method, a witness must describe the process or system that allows the camera to produce an accurate result since a person does not physically operate this type of camera.

Bad faith destruction of evidence: duty on the part of the prosecution to not destroy potentially exculpatory evidence in bad faith. It violates due process only where such evidence is destroyed in bad faith.

Bail: the posting of some security in exchange for one's freedom pending trial.

Baseline: an arbitrary straight line placed in a scene that allows for the measuring of distances from an object to the line and along the line.

Best evidence rule: a rule requiring that the original of a document or writing be produced instead of admitting secondary evidence (oral testimony, drafts, etc.) of its contents unless otherwise provided by rule or statute.

Beyond a reasonable doubt: a level of proof required to convict a criminal defendant. It is proof beyond which a reasonable person would not hesitate in a matter of importance to make a decision. It is not a speculative doubt or proof beyond all doubt.

Biggers factors: factors that the Supreme Court laid out in *Neil v. Biggers* to assess the reliability of an otherwise suggestive identification. The factors include the opportunity to observe the suspect, the time elapsed between the identification and the crime, the accuracy of the witness's description, the degree of attention of the witness, and the level of certainty of the witness in the identification.

Booking exception: an exception to the *Miranda* rule that allows detention officers to ask basic identifying information of the suspect when booking him into jail without giving him a *Miranda* advisement.

Brady rule: a Supreme Court ruling that due process is violated where the prosecution fails to disclose exculpatory evidence which can result in either suppression of the evidence or dismissal of the charges.

Bruton Rule: a Supreme Court rule that bars the admission of a co-defendant's confession that implicates the defendant, absent the ability to cross-examine that co-defendant, where both parties are tried together.

Burden of persuasion: a party's duty to convince the fact-finder of the strength of evidence in favor of that party.

Burden of production: the party's duty to produce some evidence of a fact's existence such that the jury can decide the issue rather than the court.

Burden of proof: the duty of one party to prove a disputed charge or assertion.

Business record: a hearsay exception that permits the introduction of records that are kept in the ordinary course of business and where the person making the record had personal knowledge of the events and the record was made shortly after the event.

Case-in-chief: the amount of evidence presented by a party between the time the first witness is called and the party rests.

Chain of custody: the maintenance of control over an item of evidence such that it can be documented that the evidence has not been altered or tampered with since its collection, or if its condition has changed, an adequate explanation can be given for the change. Each person who handles an item of evidence after its collection is a link in the chain.

Character evidence: evidence that is submitted for the purpose of proving that a person acted in a particular way on a particular occasion based on the character or disposition of that person.

Character witness: a witness testifying to some character trait of the defendant or another witness.

Circuit court of appeals: a federal appellate court that hears appeals from the various district courts in its circuit or region.

Circumstantial evidence: evidence that allows proof of one fact by drawing inferences or conclusions from the proof of another set of facts.

Clear and convincing evidence: a level of proof requiring more than a preponderance of the evidence but less than proof beyond a reasonable doubt.

Clergy/communicant privilege: a privilege that applies to confidential communications made to ordained priests and ministers for the purpose of seeking religious salvation.

Coerced compliant confession: a false confession made to achieve some gain such as the ending of torture.

Coerced internalized confession: a false confession made by a suspect who comes to believe he actually committed the crime.

Coercion: interrogation techniques or other conduct of law enforcement, including physical violence and psychological pressure, that are calculated to break the suspect's will.

Common law: a series of judicial rulings or precedents that build upon one another to help the judge decide a ruling in the current case.

Common scheme or plan: an independent purpose listed under Rule 404(b) that allows for the introduction of character evidence.

Competency: a quality of evidence that makes it admissible. Evidence is competent if it is not subject to some statutory or other restriction on its admissibility.

Competency of a child: children are presumed to be competent to testify in many states only if they are older than a certain age, usually 10 or 12. The judge must determine the competency of a child witness under that age.

Competent: prerequisite for a witness's testimony. A person is competent to testify as a witness if he has personal knowledge of the events he is testifying to, is capable of understanding the oath to testify truthfully, and is capable of testifying coherently.

Computer-generated animations: drawings created by computer that produce the illusion of motion when assembled frame by frame. The resulting animated image is a graphic representation explaining or demonstrating the opinion or testimony of a witness.

Conclusive presumption: a presumption that requires a jury to reach a given inference or conclusion once a certain set of facts is proven. Its use in a criminal case violates due process.

Confession: the admission of guilt by a suspect to all the necessary elements of a crime.

Constitutional catchall: a type of rape shield law that provides for an exception to the usual ban on the introduction of a rape victim's sexual conduct if it would intrude on a defendant's constitutional rights.

Coroner: an elected official who is charged with the investigation of suspicious and unattended deaths. He may or may not be qualified to conduct autopsies.

***Corpus delicti* rule:** a Latin term meaning body or elements of the crime. It is used by many states as a way of corroborating confessions. The prosecution must prove that some harm or injury occurred that was caused by criminal activity before admitting a confession into evidence.

Credibility: the believability of a person's testimony as determined from his ability to perceive events and provide unbiased testimony.

Crime scene investigators: law enforcement personnel who process the crime scene for evidence, including photographing and searching the scene, identifying evidence, and collecting evidence.

Crime scene photographs: photographs taken of anything in a crime scene. They may show scene layout or particular pieces of evidence found at a scene.

Critical stage: a segment of the criminal justice process in which significant adverse consequences can result, or where there is a reasonable likelihood of prejudice to the defendant from the absence of counsel. The right to counsel applies to all critical stages.

Cross-examination: the process of challenging the credibility of a witness's testimony. Either party may cross-examine a witness, including the party calling the witness.

CSI effect: a phenomenon based on the TV show *CSI* where jurors have been requiring more forensic evidence to prove cases.

Custody: a requirement under *Miranda* that before a person need be advised of his rights, he must be placed under formal arrest or his freedom limited in a significant manner and he does not feel free to leave.

Daubert test: a test for evaluating the reliability of expert testimony based on a scientific theory or technique. The reliability must be evaluated using various factors, not just whether the technique is generally accepted.

Daubert hearing: a pretrial hearing to assess the qualifications of an expert witness and whether that expert used reliable methodology in reaching his conclusions.

Declarant: a person who makes a statement.

Defense: an allegation made by the defendant as to the existence of a set of circumstances or conditions that relieve him of responsibility for the criminal offense.

Defense attorney: an attorney representing the defendant in a criminal case. Attorneys can be retained by the defendant or appointed at government expense for defendants who cannot afford a privately retained attorney.

Demonstrative evidence: evidence that is offered to explain or clarify other evidence. It is not substantive evidence of guilt itself.

Dependent corroboration: corroboration of a confession using the details of the crime purposefully withheld from the public.

Digital photographs: photographs that are created electronically instead of being developed on film or scanned into electronic form from film. They are divided into three categories for determining their admissibility: (1) original, digital images that are unaltered, (2) digitally converted images (photographs produced by traditional film methods and scanned into electronic form), and (3) digitally enhanced images.

Direct evidence: evidence that does not require any assumptions or inferences to prove the existence of facts. It comes directly from the witness's personal observations and knowledge.

Direct examination: the process of questioning one's own witness. Direct questions cannot imply the answer in the question.

Discovery: the process through which each side discloses the relevant statements and other evidence it intends to produce at trial to prove its case.

DNA profiling: a scientific process that compares the DNA profile found at the crime scene to a potential suspect's.

Document: any writing that provides information, such as a contract or e-mail. Before its admission into evidence, it must be authenticated.

Double-blind sequential lineup: a lineup or photo array where the witness is shown photos or individuals one at a time and the person conducting the lineup does not known the identity of the suspect.

Due process: a legal doctrine that equates to fundamental fairness; something essential to a fair trial.

Duplicate: a counterpart produced by the same impression as the original, or from the same matrix, or by means of photography, including enlargements and miniatures, or by mechanical or electronic re-recording, or by chemical reproduction, or by other equivalent techniques that accurately reproduce the original. This includes carbon copies, photocopies, microfilms, and offset reprints made from originals.

Dust fingerprints: impressions left in dust.

Dying declaration: a hearsay exception that applies to statements made by a person who believed his death was imminent and that relates to the cause or circumstances of his injuries. It is applicable only if the declarant is unavailable.

Electronically stored information: any material created or stored in electronic format. It includes information created or stored on a computer, such as e-mail, scanned documents, and metadata.

Enhanced interrogation techniques: interrogation techniques used by military interrogators to extract information from terrorist suspects at the Guantanamo Bay detention facility. Some of the techniques used included facial slaps, wall standing (forcing a suspect to lean against a wall using only his fingers for support), sleep deprivation, and waterboarding (the suspect is strapped to an inclined board while water is poured over a cloth that is placed over the suspect's face).

Estimator variables: environmental variables that affect the accuracy of an identification, such as the quality of lighting or opportunity to observe a suspect.

Evidence: anything that can be used to prove or disprove a fact in a case. It can also refer to the collective mass of items admitted during the trial.

Evidentiary purpose: a type of rape shield law that provides for exceptions to the usual ban on the introduction of a rape victim's sexual conduct based on impeachment or other evidentiary issues.

Exception: a deviation from the hearsay rule that permits the admission of a hearsay statement due to its enhanced reliability. Exceptions are divided into two types: those that depend on the availability of the declarant and those that do not.

Excited utterance: a hearsay exception for statements made under the excitement or stress of a startling event.

Exclusionary rule: a judge-made rule barring illegally seized physical evidence and statements from being admitted as evidence in a defendant's trial. It is designed to deter the police from violating suspects' constitutional rights.

Exculpatory evidence: evidence that is favorable to the accused (i.e., it tends to show his innocence) and is material to either guilt or punishment.

Exemption: an exclusion from the definition of hearsay covering prior testimony of witnesses and admissions of the defendant. If a statement qualifies under an exemption, the court does not consider it to be hearsay and it will be admitted as long as it is relevant and not overly prejudicial.

Exhibit: any item of physical, tangible evidence such as a piece of paper or document that is admitted during a court trial or hearing to prove a fact.

Expert disclosures: discovery requirement that both sides disclose the qualifications and a summary of testimony of any expert witness that they intend to call at trial.

Expert witness: a witness who can testify as to his or her opinions about the evidence based on his or her specialized training and experience.

Express waiver: a waiver of a privilege through an express authorization or agreement to do so.

Extrinsic evidence: evidence independent of the testimony of the witness being impeached.

Eyewitness: a witness who has personal knowledge about the case or incident in question.

False confession: a confession given by a suspect that is not true.

Federal courts: courts that can hear disputes involving federal laws or civil disputes between citizens of different states.

Federal Rules of Evidence: a set of standardized rules that guide evidence practice in all federal courts. They were approved for use in 1975.

Fifth Amendment right to counsel: requirement of the *Miranda* decision that a suspect must be advised of his right to an attorney before being questioned while in custody.

Fifth Amendment right to remain silent: a provision in the Fifth Amendment that provides that no person "shall be compelled in any criminal case to be a witness against himself." It is a requirement of the *Miranda* decision that a suspect must be advised of his right to remain silent before being questioned while in custody.

Fillers: people who look like the suspect and are placed in an identification procedure such as a lineup.

Firearms identification: the process of comparing microscopic striae from two different bullets or breech faces. Firearms evidence collected from a crime scene is compared with a test-fired round from a weapon.

First aggressor: the person who uses physical violence first in a confrontation. It is an allegation made by a criminal defendant when claiming self-defense that the victim was the initial aggressor.

For-cause challenge: a challenge made to a prospective juror alleging that the juror should be excused for some bias or other reason that prevents the person from serving as a fair and impartial juror.

Forfeiture by wrongdoing: a rule that prevents the defendant from benefiting from the protections of the Confrontation Clause if he causes the unavailability of the declarant with the intent of preventing that person from testifying as a witness.

Formal diagram: a scaled drawing of the crime scene created using either an architect's rule or CAD software. It shows the precise relationship of items to one another in the crime scene.

Foundation: the evidence or testimony that establishes the admissibility of some other piece of evidence.

Fourth Amendment: an amendment to the Constitution that provides that no warrant shall issue without probable cause and that searches must be reasonable.

Friction ridge identification: the process of identifying consistent features between two friction ridge impressions such as those made by fingerprints and palm prints.

Fruit of the poisonous tree: a rule requiring that all evidence derived from an illegal search or seizure be excluded from evidence as well as the original, illegally seized evidence.

Frye test: rule for evaluation of expert testimony. Such testimony will be admitted if the expert used a scientific technique that is generally accepted in the scientific community.

Gatekeeper: the role of the trial judge to screen out expert testimony that does not meet minimum standards of relevancy and/or reliability.

Giglio material: material the prosecution must turn over that can impeach the credibility of one of the witnesses; it is part of its duty to produce exculpatory material.

Good character: proof that a person is a good person and could not have done the type of action claimed. The defendant can introduce evidence of his good character in a criminal case. Once he does so, however, the prosecution can introduce evidence of his bad character.

Good faith exception: an exception to the exclusionary rule that provides that where an officer reasonably relies in good faith on a search warrant, the evidence will be admissible even if the warrant is later declared invalid.

Grand jury: a group of citizens empanelled to determine if there is probable cause to charge a suspect with a crime.

Grid search: a search pattern that subdivides the search area into small, square units like a piece of graph paper.

Handwriting analysis: a comparison of a suspect's handwriting to a questioned document in a case.

Hearsay: a statement made by an out-of-court declarant that is offered to prove the truth of the matter asserted.

Heightened relevance laws: a law that liberally interprets Rule 404(b) in sexual assault prosecutions. Several states follow this interpretation of the rule.

Identity of a confidential informant: the name of a confidential informant can be withheld until the identity is relevant and helpful to the defense.

Immunity: a protection given to a witness in exchange for giving up his right to remain silent.

Impeachment: the process of challenging a witness's credibility, such as by pointing out inconsistencies in his story or attacking his character.

Impeachment by bias or motive: a form of impeachment that attacks the credibility of the witness by showing that he has some reason to lie due to some relationship to a party.

Impeachment by character: a method of impeachment that involves demonstrating that the witness has a poor character for truthfulness. This is usually demonstrated through reputation or opinion evidence by calling a second witness to testify to the first's character.

Impeachment by contradiction: a form of impeachment that attacks the witness's credibility by getting the witness to admit to flaws or errors in his testimony or by calling a separate witness to do the same.

Impeachment by conviction: a form of impeachment that involves questioning a witness about his prior felony convictions or any misdemeanor that relates to dishonesty or false statements.

Impeachment by incapacity: a form of impeachment that involves questioning a witness about his or her ability to accurately perceive events, such as whether the witness could have gotten a good look at the suspect.

Impeachment by prior conduct: a form of impeachment that involves asking the witness about prior instances of misconduct that relate to untruthfulness but that did not result in a conviction.

Impeachment by prior inconsistent statement: a form of impeachment that compares a statement made during a witness's testimony with one made by the witness at an earlier date. If the witness admits making the earlier statement, the impeachment is complete. If the witness denies it, then the other party can introduce evidence of the earlier statement.

Impermissibly suggestive: an identification procedure that improperly indicates to the witness who the police have identified as the suspect.

Implied waiver: a waiver of a privilege through conduct that is inconsistent with keeping the communication confidential.

Independent corroboration: corroboration of a confession with details of the crime provided by the suspect.

Independent purpose: an exception to the normal rule banning the introduction of character evidence against a criminal defendant. The evidence must have some purpose other than to prove the defendant had a propensity to commit criminal acts.

Independent source: an exception to the exclusionary rule that provides that evidence that is lawfully discovered through a source independent from the illegal seizure is admissible.

Indictment: a charging document issued by the grand jury. It contains a list of the charges and a plain statement of the facts supporting the charges.

Inevitable discovery: an exception to the exclusionary rule that provides evidence that is illegally seized but would have been inevitably discovered through lawful means is admissible.

Information: a charging document prepared by the prosecutor that eliminates the need for a grand jury. About half the states use informations, but the Constitution requires federal courts to use grand juries.

Intent or motive: an independent purpose listed under Rule 404(b) that allows for the introduction of character evidence where it is relevant to proving the defendant's intent or motive to commit the charged offense.

Interlocutory appeal: an appeal filed before the case has become final that is filed by the prosecutor to challenge a ruling that excludes all or substantially all of the evidence.

Interrogation: an accusatory process designed to get a suspect to confess. For purposes of *Miranda*, an interrogation is questions or conduct that is designed to elicit an incriminating response from a suspect.

Interview: a nonconfrontational process designed to gain information from a witness or suspect.

Interview notes: notes taken during an interview by a law enforcement officer. Such notes have to be turned over in discovery whenever the substance of the notes has not been replicated in a written report.

Investigation witness: a witness who testifies about some aspect of the investigation of the defendant's guilt or innocence. Such witnesses are usually law enforcement officers or private investigators.

Irresistible impulse test: a version of the insanity defense that requires the defendant to prove that he lacked the substantial capacity to appreciate the wrongfulness of his acts or conform his conduct to law.

Jencks Act: a federal statute requiring the prosecution in a federal case to produce the pretrial statements of any witness after the witness is called to testify in court.

Judicial discretion: a type of rape shield law that provides for judicial determination of any exceptions to the usual ban on the introduction of a rape victim's sexual conduct.

Judicial notice: a process where the judge finds proof of a given fact without the parties presenting evidence of that fact. Judges can take judicial notice of readily verifiable facts such as weather conditions and facts contained in authoritative sources such as almanacs.

Jury instructions: instructions read to the jury at the conclusion of a trial. They contain the law the jury must follow in deciding the guilt or innocence of the defendant.

Juvenile adjudication: a conviction sustained while a person is under the age of 18 in juvenile court. It is usable to impeach a witness only if there is showing that the witness cannot be impeached with other evidence and it is probative of dishonesty.

Lands and grooves: rises and depressions cut into the metal of gun barrels during the manufacturing process.

Latent fingerprint: a fingerprint that is not easily visible without the aid of development.

Lay witness: a witness who offers testimony based on his own personal observations or perceptions of an event and who needs no specialized training or experience to offer such testimony. A lay witness can offer an opinion that is based on his perception of an event and that may help the jury understand the event he is testifying about.

Leading questions: questions asked of witnesses that imply the answer in the question. The use of leading questions is reserved for the cross-examination of witnesses.

Legislated exception: a type of rape shield law that provides for limited exceptions to the usual ban on the introduction of a rape victim's sexual conduct.

Lineup: an in-person identification procedure where a witness is asked to identify a suspect from five or six people of similar physical characteristics.

Lustful disposition exception: an exception to the normal ban on the admission of character evidence. It permits the prosecution to admit prior acts evidence of sexual misconduct in sexual assault cases to prove the defendant's intent or motive to commit the crime was to satisfy his lustful desire.

M'Naghten Rule: a requirement that the defendant prove insanity either by showing that he failed to understand the nature of his actions or that he could not distinguish the difference between right and wrong.

Mandatory presumption: a presumption that requires the jury to reach a certain conclusion after proof of certain facts.

Marital communication privilege: a form of marital privilege that protects only the confidential communications that occurred between the spouses during the marriage but does not prevent the other spouse from testifying about matters he or she observed during the marriage.

Massiah doctrine: a Supreme Court doctrine that requires the police to refrain from questioning a suspect outside the presence of his attorney once he has been charged with a crime.

Materiality: the logical connection of evidence to a matter of importance in the case.

Materially altered photograph: a photographic image or print that is produced by significantly altering the original image. A materially altered image has to be offered as the product of a scientific process, and expert testimony is necessary to authenticate it.

Medical diagnosis or treatment: a hearsay exception that permits the admission of hearsay statements made to medical personnel for the purpose of seeking medical treatment or diagnosis.

Medical examiner: a medical doctor who is a trained forensic pathologist and is responsible for investigation of suspicious or unattended deaths.

Memory variables: a witness's ability to recognize and recall faces that affect the accuracy of an identification.

Mezzanatto agreement: an agreement signed by the defendant prior to plea negotiations that waives the protections of Rule 410.

Miranda rights: a set of rights that a suspect must be advised of before he can be interrogated while in custody. Those rights are as follows: you have the right to remain silent. Anything you say can and will be used against you in a court of law. You have the right to an attorney, and if you cannot afford one, one will be appointed for you.

Modus operandi: a Latin term meaning method of operation. It is an independent purpose listed under Rule 404(b) that allows for the introduction of character evidence to prove the defendant committed a series of criminal acts following a distinct pattern or method characteristic of that offender. Such evidence is offered to prove identity.

Motion: a written or oral request asking the court to issue a particular ruling or order. Motions are commonly filed by parties to admit or exclude evidence.

Motion to compel discovery: a motion filed by a party seeking a court order to force compliance with a discovery request.

Motion to suppress: a request filed by the defendant, alleging that certain evidence was illegally seized or obtained.

National Academy of Sciences report on forensic science: a 2009 government report that emphasized the need for consistent standards in forensic science and the need for more rigorous scientific testing of the foundation for many disciplines in forensic science.

Negating defense: a defense that attempts to negate or modify one or more elements of the offense. An alibi and consent are examples of negating defenses.

Nolo contendere: a plea of no contest.

Notice of alibi: a notice of an alibi defense provided to the prosecution containing the basis of a defendant's alibi along with the names and addresses of all alibi witnesses.

Oath or affirmation: an expression of a person's willingness to testify truthfully without calling into question their religious beliefs.

Objection: a statement opposing some action or question in court. The judge may either sustain or overrule the objection.

Opening statement: a summary of the evidence expected to be presented at trial given by the attorneys for each side at the start of trial.

Original: the writing, recording, photograph, or computer data itself as opposed to a copy of it.

Parallel or lane search: a search pattern conducted by dividing the search area into long lanes like a swimming pool.

Parent/child privilege: a privilege that protects the disclosure of confidential communications made between a parent and child. Only five states recognize a parent/child privilege.

Peremptory challenge: a challenge made by one of the parties against a potential juror for no particular reason. A person's race or sex cannot be a basis for the challenge, however.

Permissive inference: a presumption that allows, but does not require, the jury to reach a certain conclusion after proof of certain facts.

Personal knowledge: a requirement that a witness must have personal knowledge of the matters he is testifying to, which means that his testimony must be based on events perceived through one of the five senses.

Personal recognizance bond: a type of bond that allows a defendant to be released in exchange for his promise to appear.

Petition for certiorari: a Latin term meaning "to be more fully informed." It is a petition filed with the Supreme Court to determine whether the Court will accept review of the case.

Photo array: a series of photographs shown to a witness that are of persons similar in appearance to the described suspect.

Physician/patient privilege: a privilege that covers confidential statements made to a physician that are necessary for the patient's diagnosis or treatment and covers medical records as well as the statements made between the physician and the patient. Forty states, but not the federal courts, recognize it.

Plastic fingerprint: a fingerprint impression made in a malleable substance like soap or grease.

Plea agreement: an agreement entered into between the defendant and the prosecution that usually involves the defendant agreeing to plead guilty to a reduced charge or number of charges in exchange for a lesser sentence.

Polygraph: a test designed to detect deception in a subject by measuring various changes in physiological responses to questioning.

Polymerase chain reaction: a method of DNA amplification used commonly in preparation of forensic DNA profiles.

Potentially exculpatory evidence: evidence whose exculpatory value is not clearly evident on its face.

Precedent: prior cases that form the basis for determining the same or similar issue in future cases.

Prejudicial effect: evidence is prejudicial if the jury will pay undue attention to it or it distracts the jury from more proper questions because it is inflammatory.

Prejudicial evidence: evidence that has a tendency to sway a jury to decide an issue on some improper basis such as bias, sympathy, or hatred.

Preliminary hearing: a pretrial hearing held to determine whether there is probable cause for the charges.

Preponderance of the evidence: a level of proof requiring a showing that the majority of evidence favors a ruling in one party's favor. It is used for civil trials and to determine the outcome of hearings in criminal cases, such as suppression motions.

Present sense impression: a hearsay exception for statements made contemporaneously with an event that describe or explain the event.

Presumption: proof of one set of circumstances that would allow the jury to infer a given conclusion.

Presumption of innocence: a presumption that states that the defendant is innocent until proven guilty.

Pretrial lineup: a procedure conducted at a police station where the witness is shown several individuals and asked if he or she recognizes anyone as the suspect.

Prima facie case: a Latin term meaning on the face of it. The prosecution establishes a prima facie case if it presents a sufficient amount of evidence to convict the defendant as to each and every element of the offense.

Primary evidence: the best or highest quality of evidence, such as an original writing.

Primary purpose of the interrogation: test for determining whether statements made pursuant to police questioning are testimonial in nature. Where the primary purpose of the interrogation is to prove or establish the commission of a crime, the statements are testimonial. Where the primary purpose is to seek police assistance with an ongoing emergency, statements made to the police are nontestimonial.

Prior testimony exception: a hearsay exception that permits the admission of prior testimony of a witness as long as the declarant is unavailable, and there was an opportunity to cross-examine the statements in a prior proceeding.

Prior testimony exemption: an exemption from the definition of hearsay. Statements made by a witness while testifying in a prior trial or hearing are not considered hearsay if the other party had an opportunity to cross-examine the witness and the statement is inconsistent with the witness's trial testimony, is used to rebut a charge of recent fabrication, or is a statement of identification.

Privilege: a legal right that prevents a witness from being compelled to disclose confidential information.

Privilege against self-incrimination: a Fifth Amendment right allowing a witness to choose not to testify or otherwise provide information to the police on the ground that it would tend to incriminate him.

Prior acts: prior conduct of defendant that can be used to prove some independent purpose under Rule 404(b). Such acts can be charged or uncharged.

Probable cause: a level of proof showing that a crime has probably been committed, that a suspect committed a crime, or that evidence of a crime will be found in the place to be searched. It is used to obtain search warrants, arrest suspects, and indict suspects.

Probative value: the ability of evidence to prove or disprove the existence of that fact.

Prosecutor: an attorney representing the government in a criminal prosecution. At the state level, the prosecutor is often known as a district attorney or state's attorney. At the federal level, the prosecutor is known as a United States attorney.

Psychotherapist/patient privilege: a privilege that protects confidential communications made between licensed psychologists and psychiatrists and, in some states, even protects statements made to counselors and social workers.

Public records: records kept by public agencies that are admissible as a hearsay exception as long as the party offering the record proves that an agency official has certified that the record is a true and accurate copy of that agency's record.

Public safety exception: an exception to the *Miranda* rule that allows officers to question a suspect, without advising him of his rights, about the presence of a weapon or other item that presents an immediate danger to officer safety or public safety.

Rape shield law: a statute that prevents the defense from introducing the prior sexual conduct of the victim into evidence unless it satisfies one or more limited exceptions.

Rational corroboration: corroboration of a confession by making logical sense of the motivations and accounts of the crime provided by the suspect.

Reasonable hypothesis of innocence: a rule that requires the prosecution to prove not only that circumstantial evidence establishes the guilt of the accused but that it also is inconsistent with a theory of innocence. It is applied in some states where circumstantial evidence is the only proof of guilt.

Reasonable suspicion: a level of proof less than probable cause requiring a showing that criminal activity is occurring or has taken place.

Rebuttable presumption: a presumption that once proven allows the other party an opportunity to produce facts that refute the permitted presumption.

Rebuttal: the opportunity of the prosecution to present any evidence that counters evidence put on by the defense.

Rebuttal witness: a witness who is called to rebut some testimony or evidence presented by the defense.

Rectangular coordinates: a method of measurement conducted by measuring the distance of an object to two points at right angles to one another.

Redaction: the editing of the transcript of a confession by the removal of any reference to the defendant's name or to his existence.

Reid Technique: a nine-step interrogation process that is designed to establish a rapport with the suspect and then break down his resistance to confessing his guilt.

Relevance: evidence is relevant when it has "any tendency to make the existence of any fact that is of consequence to the determination of the action more probable or less probable than it would be without the evidence." It is composed of the materiality and probative value of the evidence.

Reliability: the degree of accuracy or authenticity of evidence.

Reporter/source privilege: a privilege that protects a journalist from having to reveal the identity of his source. If the state does not have such a privilege, the reporter could be found in contempt of court and face jail time for failing to reveal his source.

Reputation or opinion evidence: a form of evidence limited to testimony about a person's reputation in the community for having some character trait or the witness's opinion of that person's character. The introduction of character evidence is often limited to reputation or opinion evidence.

***Res gestae*:** Latin term meaning things done. It is a hearsay exception that allows the admission of hearsay statements that help explain the surrounding circumstances or commission of a crime.

Residual exception: a hearsay exception that allows the admission of hearsay even if doesn't fit within one of the enumerated exceptions as long as it has "equivalent guarantees" of trustworthiness to other exceptions.

Rough sketch: a hand-drawn representation of the crime scene as the investigator saw it during his initial examination of the scene. It is usually not drawn to scale.

Rule 16: a rule of the Federal Rules of Criminal Procedure requiring the prosecution and defense to share certain information prior to trial during the discovery process, including statements the defendant made to law enforcement, expert witness reports, and any documents or other objects the prosecution intends to use at trial.

Rule 404(a): a rule of evidence that provides that evidence of a person's prior misconduct cannot be introduced to show that he acted similarly or consistent with his past character in the present case.

Rule 404(b): a rule of evidence permitting the prosecution to admit the prior acts of the defendant to show some purpose (other than the fact that he has a propensity to commit crime), such as motive, intent, or identity.

Rule 413: federal rule of evidence that eliminates the restrictions on the admission of character evidence under Rule 404(a) for past acts of sexual misconduct in sexual assault cases.

Rule 414: a federal rule of evidence that eliminates the restrictions on the admission of character evidence for past acts of sexual misconduct in child molestation cases.

Scene assessment: a preliminary evaluation of the crime scene conducted prior to searching the scene that includes establishing a perimeter, identifying responsibilities for personnel, and conducting a scene walk through.

Search warrant: a judicial authorization to search a given premises for contraband or evidence of a crime. It must be supported by probable cause and specify the place to be searched and the items to be seized.

Searching in stages: a search method that relies on searching a scene in progressively more invasive stages. During the first stage, no objects in the scene are moved. In the second stage, doors and drawers are opened. In the last stage, contents of drawers are emptied and carpet may be ripped up.

Secondary evidence: all evidence that falls short of being primary evidence, such as a duplicate of the original or testimony about its contents. Secondary evidence of the contents of the original can be admitted if the original is lost or destroyed, is in the possession of the other party and is not obtainable through subpoena or other means, is not closely related to the main issue, or is otherwise unavailable.

Second sample: a second sample of some item of physical evidence that is preserved for independent testing by the defense. Most states do not require that the police preserve second samples unless requested by the defendant.

Self-authenticating documents: some documents, such as business records and public records, are self-authenticating, which means that the party offering them can establish a foundation without calling a witness to authenticate them.

Self-defense: a defense based on the claim that reasonable force was necessary to defend one's person or others from the imminent threat of harm from physical force. A defendant can claim self-defense if he used a reasonable amount of force to defend himself, was not the first aggressor, and, in some states, did not have an opportunity for retreat.

Show-up: a one-on-one identification made at the crime scene or other location by the witness.

Sixth Amendment right to counsel: an amendment to the Constitution that provides, in part, that a suspect has a right to counsel that applies to any critical stage of the criminal justice process.

Special agents: federal law enforcement officers who investigate violations of federal crimes.

Spiral search: a search pattern that involves walking around the crime scene in increasingly bigger or smaller circles.

Spousal privilege: a privilege that protects against the disclosure of confidential communications that occur during the marriage.

Standing: the authorization to challenge a ruling or assert some right in court. It requires that the defendant argue that his own rights were violated by the police's unlawful conduct, not those of some third party.

Stare decisis: Latin term that means to stand by things decided. Future courts will often try to follow previous court rulings on similar issues in deciding current cases.

State courts: courts at the state level that hear all types of disputes involving issues of state or local law. In criminal cases, state courts are usually divided into those that handle misdemeanors and those that handle felonies.

State of mind: a hearsay exception that permits the admission of hearsay statements that describe the declarant's emotional state at the time he made the statement or his intention to do something in the future.

Statement against interest: a hearsay exception that permits the admission of hearsay statements adverse to someone's penal or monetary interest. It is applicable only if the declarant is unavailable.

Stipulation: an agreement as to the existence of a given fact and/or its admissibility. A stipulation relieves the burden of proof of a party to prove that fact's existence.

Striations: unique, microscopic marks and scratches on the metal of the gun barrel that are imparted to the bullet during firing.

Subpoena: a legal document issued to a witness compelling him to appear in a court hearing or legal proceeding.

Systemic variables: variables that affect the accuracy of eyewitness identification that are introduced by the police during a lineup or photo array.

Testimonial hearsay: hearsay statements that are made formally for the purpose of establishing some opinion or fact. They are inadmissible unless the declarant is unavailable to testify and they were made with the opportunity for cross-examination by the opposing party.

Testimonial privilege: a form of marital privilege that prevents one spouse from testifying without the consent of the other.

Three-stage search method: a method of searching a crime scene where only openly visible evidence is collected in the first stage, minimally intrusive methods such as opening windows and drawers are used in the second stage, and aggressive methods such as emptying drawers or searching files is reserved for the final stage.

Transactional immunity: a form of immunity that protects against prosecution for any crime disclosed in the immunized statements of a witness.

Trial: the determination of the parties' legal issues by a fact finder based on a hearing of the evidence. Trials are used to determine the guilt or innocence of a defendant in a criminal case. A trial can be held either to a judge or to a jury.

Triangulation: a measurement method that involves taking measurements from an object to two fixed points, such as trees or lampposts.

Trustworthiness rule: a replacement for the corpus delicti rule that requires the prosecution to corroborate the essential details of a confession before its admission.

Two-step interrogation: an interrogation process where officers first obtain un-Mirandized statements from a suspect in custody, subsequently advise him of his Miranda rights, and then complete the interrogation.

Unavailability: a witness is unavailable to testify if some circumstance prevents him from appearing in court or testifying due to the invoking of a privilege.

United States district courts: the trial courts for the federal court system.

United States Supreme Court: the court of last resort in the federal system. It hears appeals from the circuit courts or from state high courts on constitutional issues.

Use immunity: a form of immunity that protects against use of the immunized statements to convict the witness.

Victim advocate privilege: a privilege that covers confidential communications made to rape crisis or domestic violence abuse counselors. The victim advocate or counselor privilege covers confidential communications made only to private counselors. It does not cover statements made to victim advocates working for law enforcement agencies.

Visible fingerprint: fingerprint that is visible due to being made while ridged surfaces such as fingertips were stained with a colored substance such as blood.

Voir dire: the process of questioning jurors to determine their biases or conflicts prior to being seated on a jury.

Voluntariness: a requirement that a suspect willingly waive his rights before talking to police and, once he has done so, provide a statement of his own free will. Voluntariness is determined by examining whether the confession was "the product of an essentially free and unconstrained choice by its maker," whether it was "the product of a rational intellect and a free will," and whether at any time the defendant's will was "overborne."

Voluntary confession: a false confession made to gain notoriety.

Waiver: a relinquishment of a right or privilege.

Witness: a person who provides testimony in a trial or hearing.

Work product: notes and documents created by attorneys in preparation for litigation, including memoranda and letters discussing trial strategy. Work product is protected from disclosure during the discovery process unless a compelling need can be shown for its disclosure.

Zone search: a search pattern that subdivides the area to be searched into separate zones or quadrants.

Index